SCOUTS OUT

SCOUTS OUT

A History of German Armored Reconnaissance Units in World War II

Robert Edwards
with contributions from
Michael H. Pruett and Michael Olive

STACKPOLE BOOKS
Guilford, Connecticut
Blue Ridge Summit, Pennsylvania

STACKPOLE BOOKS
An imprint of Globe Pequot, the trade division of
The Rowman & Littlefield Publishing Group, Inc.
4501 Forbes Blvd., Ste. 200
Lanham, MD 20706
www.rowman.com

Distributed by NATIONAL BOOK NETWORK

Copyright © 2013 by Robert Edwards

All rights reserved. No part of this book may be reproduced in any form or by any electronic or mechanical means, including information storage and retrieval systems, without written permission from the publisher, except by a reviewer who may quote passages in a review.

British Library Cataloguing in Publication Information available

Library of Congress Cataloging-in-Publication Available

ISBN: 978-0-8117-1311-5 (cloth : alk. paper)
ISBN: 978-0-8117-7089-7 (paper : alk. paper)
ISBN: 978-0-8117-5327-2 (electronic)

Library of Congress Control Number: 2013031997

∞™ The paper used in this publication meets the minimum requirements of American National Standard for Information Sciences—Permanence of Paper for Printed Library Materials, ANSI/NISO Z39.48-1992.

Contents

Foreword

As its title states, this book attempts to provide an overview of all aspects of German armored reconnaissance forces during the World War II era. It is hoped that the book will be a handy reference guide for the subject matter and, further, serve as impetus for further research into the topic.

My interest in things military started as a boy. Living in close proximity to both Gettysburg and other Civil War battlefields as well as the Aberdeen Proving Grounds for much of my youth provided ample fuel to fire my imagination. Over time, my interest became more focused on armor. In researching the history of maneuver warfare, I became increasingly fascinated with the *Panzertruppe* and the role it played in decisively shaping operations in the European theater of World War II. As a newly commissioned armor officer attending the basic course at Fort Knox in 1977, I was further exposed to armored cavalry theory and doctrine and was intrigued by the role played by the scout platoon within the armored battalion of the time and its function as the "eyes and ears" of the commander.

Once stationed overseas in Erlangen—home of the prewar *Panzer-Regiment 25* and the wartime *Panther* school and just down the road from the storied *Panzer-Regiment 35* in Bamberg—with the 1-35 Armor Battalion, I soon learned that the premier job of a lieutenant in an armored battalion was that of scout platoon leader, a position I soon aspired to and eventually obtained. In a subsequent overseas assignment to Wildflecken, our battalion worked closely with the 11th Armored Cavalry Regiment since we were also stationed close to the border in the "Fulda Gap," serving as "speed bumps" for the Warsaw Pact assault that never came. I was always impressed by the regiment's *élan* and *esprit de corps* and the impressive and professional way it conducted its business. I encountered the regiment again while serving full-time with the Nevada Army National Guard as its Mobilization and Readiness Officer in the mid-1990s. The state's armored battalion, the 221st Cavalry, served as a "Roundout" to the 11th ACR, and I spent several enjoyable, if hot, trips to the National Training Center to see the Nevada soldiers working with their modern-day cavalry counterparts.

As luck would have it, I also had several encounters with modern German Army armored reconnaissance forces while serving on active duty in Germany. The first time was in 1978, while serving as a liaison officer to German umpire forces during a REFORGER exercise. Standing on the side of the road at the entrance to a small German town one afternoon during the maneuver phase of the exercise, I was talking to my jeep driver and facing away from the road when I heard a sudden whooshing noise and blast of air behind me coming from the road. When I turned around, I saw the tail end of a *Spähpanzer 2 "Luchs"* as it moved into the town at high speed. For such a large vehicle, it was virtually silent. The second time was in the mid-1980s during a maneuver exercise being conducted near the Baumholder Training Area. The "red" forces had a German *Panzeraufklärungskompanie* attached to them, and my tank company engaged a patrol that was probing our lines during the defensive phase of the exercise. What impressed me most about the encounter was the rapid response of the *Spähpanzer 2* when the vehicle commander realized he was about to run into an M60A3 in a reverse-slope position. Within what seemed to be a fraction of a second, the rear driver took the vehicle out of harm's way by moving rapidly in reverse.

Much has happened over the intervening years. Together with Michael Pruett, I published two monographs on uniforms related to the *Panzertruppe*, and I was eventually fortunate enough, after retiring from a full-time position with the National Guard, to pursue more fully my interest in all things World War II, first as a partner in J. J. Fedorowicz Publishing in Canada and now as a freelance translator and consultant on military history topics. All the while, I have actively collected militaria relating to the *Panzertruppe*, with an emphasis of late on reconnaissance forces. Correspondingly, the desire within me grew to eventually write a book, together with my friends Mike Pruett and Mike Olive, that addressed my personal interest in this topic.

I truly hope you enjoy our efforts. We would welcome any comments you might have and can be reached through the publisher. Any errata and addenda to the book will also be published at my site: www.battlebornbooks.com. A largely complete series of organizational charts for reconnaissance elements is also available on the site, at www.battlebornbooks.com/?page_id=491.

Robert Edwards
Summer 2013

Technical Notes

Since the authors rely on a number of German-language sources in which technical, professional, and military terminology and soldier slang are used, it might be prudent to outline our approach to translating and naming German units and ranks.

In general, German unit and formation titles will be given their full designation upon first introduction, with no effort made to produce a German-English hybrid, as is often the case in English-language texts that make extensive reference to German formations, equipment, and ranks. Thus, the German 4th Armored Reconnaissance Battalion will initially be rendered as *Panzer-Aufklärungs-Abteilung 4*. If extensive reference is made to it, then an abbreviated form may be introduced, such as *Pz.Aufkl.Abt. 4*. In all instances, the abbreviations will follow German practice. To assist in "deciphering" these, extensive use will be made of endnotes. Ordinal numbers are rendered by the use of a period in German; thus, the 1st Armor Division is *1. Panzer-Division*. Subordinate units within formations are indicated by Arabic numerals in the case of company-size formations and Roman numerals for battalions. Generally, division and higher commands are indicated by ordinal numbers. Brigades are usually indicated by ordinal numerals when an organic part of a higher command, while separate brigades are indicated by the numerical designator following the unit designator. Of course, there were exceptions to this rule of thumb; regiments, battalions, and separate companies generally had the numerical designator following the unit designator.

The term *Abteilung* will generally be translated as "battalion" when it refers to a combat formation and as "detachment" when it refers to an element of the training base. For instance, *Panzer-Ersatz- und Ausbildungs-Abteilung 4* would be the 4th Replacement and Training Detachment, even though it is a battalion-size element.

Generally, when the word "formation" is used, it refers to a battalion or higher element. The term "unit" is reserved for company-size elements and smaller. Although the term *Schwadron* is literally translated as "squadron," this is actually a troop or company in U.S. usage. When the original German is unclear or a mixture of formations and units is being described, then the term "elements" will be used.

German ranks will be used throughout the text; thus, captain will be rendered as *Hauptmann* or *Rittmeister*, depending on the type of unit or actual rank title. Ranks for SS personnel will use the prefix *SS-*, which was the official way of describing the rank, with a second lieutenant in the SS, for example, being *SS-Untersturmführer*. The prefix may be deleted, however, when translating firsthand accounts, since it was not used in colloquial German. For those who are unfamiliar with German ranks, a comparison table is provided at the back of the book.

In cases where official German documents are translated, portions may be changed slightly to facilitate meaning, e.g., abbreviations written out or text added to "shotgun passages" to make complete sentences.

CHAPTER 1

The Development of Armored Reconnaissance

SETTING THE STAGE

Ever since the dawn of mankind and the conflicts that soon followed, the leaders of armed forces have always sought information about the enemy and, if fighting in an unfamiliar area, about the terrain, climate, and other factors that could aid or impede their efforts to subdue the foe. Only a foolhardy leader would attempt to gain victory without first gathering at least rudimentary information concerning the enemy's forces, dispositions, positions, morale, and intent.

The gathering of information—which is then transformed through analysis into intelligence—may take many forms, especially in modern times with the advent of electronic intelligence-gathering methods, remote sensors, and remotely piloted vehicles (drones). In the case of field armies and ground forces, however, the function is usually performed by select forces whose primary mission is to gather information and provide it to the commander in a timely manner, thus allowing him to shape his decision-making process, no matter how simple or complex, into a coherent course of action. Information is needed at all levels of command, since what is important to the commander of a field army may be of little consequence to a company commander and vice-versa. Operational intelligence is usually gathered at the corps level and higher, tactical intelligence at the division level and below, and battlefield intelligence at the battalion level and below (the fire-and-maneuver or movement level). The ground effort to physically gather information for the intelligence effort is referred to as reconnaissance.[1]

It was not uncommon to see armored vehicles on the roadways of prewar Germany, either on exercise or simply to test road worthiness after repairs or maintenance, as seems to be the case with this *Sd.Kfz. 223 (Fu)*. JIM HALEY

THE CAVALRY TRADITION

In the European tradition, at least since the eighteenth and nineteenth centuries, reconnaissance has been the primary responsibility of certain types of horse cavalry formations, generally hussars. Cavalry was the logical choice for such missions since it was capable of covering large distances relatively rapidly and operating in terrain that was often difficult for infantry to negotiate. The patrols dispatched by hussar units tended to be relatively small, lightly armed, and led by officers. Their mission was to gather information about the enemy, not to fight him. Indeed, patrols were usually instructed not to fight the enemy, unless it was absolutely essential to accomplishing the mission. They were to see, not be seen, to hear, not be heard.

Of course, there were other types of cavalry formations, such as "battle cavalry" (cuirassiers) and mounted infantry (dragoons). It has often been argued—with some merit—that these types of cavalry were the antecedents for modern mechanized forces,[2] and during the motorization era initiated during World War I, the cavalry branch of many nations was considered the logical choice to "own" armored forces.

In the wake of World War I, the role of horse cavalry was questioned by many, since in general none of its major roles—whether as battle cavalry or operational-level reconnaissance—had been successfully executed, especially as a result of trench warfare and the widespread employment of automatic weaponry. By the end of the war, in fact, most of Germany's horse cavalry divisions had dismounted and become cavalry rifle divisions. On the other hand, armored vehicles, like the tank, were employed on both sides, with the Allies making greater use of them.

As early as 1915, the Germans had established an armored car detachment, designating it *Straßen-Panzerkraftwagenabteilung 1*. It had three purpose-built armored cars in addition to a number of modified commercial vehicles. The three armored cars were built by the firms of Daimler, Büssing, and Ehrhardt. The battalion was employed in Romania, where it performed relatively well. In the end, the firm of Ehrhardt was chosen to develop the standard German armored car, of which thirty-two were ordered (with apparently twenty being delivered). In 1917, three platoons of two armored cars each were established, with additional platoons appearing by the end of the

The Treaty of Versailles allowed Germany only very limited military assets, such as these early armored cars of the *Reichswehr*, the *gepanzerter Kraftwagen (Kfz. 3)*, initially intended solely for police duties. With a machine gun mounted, it could carry an additional six men; without the machine gun, it was designed to move twelve personnel. JIM HALEY

A civilian car, the *Adler Standard-6*, was modified with a sheet-metal superstructure in early attempts to create an armored car for the force. This vehicle, apparently outfitted with a frame antenna, crosses a watercourse on an engineer ferry while soldiers look on. JIM HALEY

war, complemented by captured Belgian and Russian vehicles.[3]

Any early progress the Germans might have made in the development of armor and supporting weapons during the Great War was brought to an abrupt halt with their defeat in the war and the relatively draconian provisions of the Treaty of Versailles that followed. Limited to a 100,000-man volunteer army with virtually no heavy weapons (let alone tanks), an overrepresentation of horse cavalry, and the elimination of a General Staff—to name but a few of the more onerous restrictions placed on the defeated nation—*Generaloberst* Hans von Seeckt struggled to mold a force with the potential to serve as an effective military in the future. Ironically, some of the restrictions placed on the German military forces might have also helped it rebuild so rapidly when Hitler came to power. Officers and noncommissioned officers were career soldiers, with a minimum of twelve-year service obligations. Correspondingly, emphasis was placed on training and developing leadership, building a solid core for subsequent expansion. The overrepresentation of cavalry—there were seven infantry divisions and three cavalry divisions allowed by the treaty—also cultivated a crop of officers amenable to doctrine that incorporated maneuver as a core principle, even to the point of forsaking their mounts for motorization. While those feelings were by no means universal, a large number of highly successful armor commanders in World War II started as cavalry officers.

RECONNAISSANCE IN THE AGE OF ARMOR: CAVALRY, ARMOR, AND INFANTRY VIE FOR THE MISSION

Oskar Munzel has characterized the development of postwar reconnaissance doctrine in Germany as follows: "Since the concept of how war would be waged was still hotly disputed [in the interwar years], the opinions concerning the employment fundamentals of both horse mounted and motorized reconnaissance, as well as the force ratios to one another, were likewise divided."[4]

With limited resources, abundant restrictions, interbranch rivalry, and disagreement on the conduct of future wars, it comes as no surprise that the German Army did not emerge from the Great War with a

This *Adler* appears to be a mock-up meant to look like an armored car. The *Reichswehr* and *Wehrmacht* had to do a great deal of improvising in the early 1930s before they started receiving purpose-built armored vehicles for their fledgling armored force. JIM HALEY

unified theory on how to employ its reconnaissance assets. During the 1920s most of the discussion concerning the role and mission of reconnaissance (particularly motorized) forces focused on which branch should exercise oversight and developmental functions. The arguments were often heated, not only in Germany, but also in other European countries and in the United States.[5] The cavalry branch saw reconnaissance forces as falling within its purview, but it continued to stress the need for horse-mounted units or mixed units comprised of both horse-ridden and vehicle-mounted elements. The proponents of armor as a separate arm saw the necessity for reconnaissance elements to come under its wing, since they were expected to work hand-in-glove with armor forces in developing situations and facilitating the exploitation of opportunities on the battlefield. Not to be outdone, the infantry branches of various nations also showed some interest in developing their own motorized reconnaissance elements, since there was a large school of thought that believed that armor needed to be tied to the infantry in its employment and not the other way around.

As is usually the case with internecine fighting like this, the combat arm that takes the first step, and takes it decisively, emerges the winner. In Germany the *Kavallerie* branch only halfheartedly advanced the concept of motorized reconnaissance, while the *Kraftfahrtruppe*, the motorized transport forces, which served as the clandestine breeding ground for the eventual *Panzertruppe*, wholeheartedly embraced the concept of any and all things mechanical. As John McGraph notes in his monograph concerning the development of modern reconnaissance:

> In contrast to what happened in the U.S. Army in the same period, the German cavalry leadership's devotion to the cavalry in the main battle led to the cavalry's ready surrender of the operational-level reconnaissance mission to the motorized troops branch, the predecessor of the armored forces. Despite later attempts to shift this role back to the cavalry, the motorized troops retained the mission. The Germans became the first major army to effectively divorce operational reconnaissance from horse cavalry, at least in theory.[6]

A number of German firms produced prototypes of armored cars for the police and the military. Here we see a Krupp *Polizei-Streifenwagen* displayed at the International Automobile Show in Berlin in 1938. The police patrol vehicle had a 70-horsepower engine and appeared to have the capability of mounting a machine gun in a revolving turret. The date and location are unknown. MICHAEL H. PRUETT

In 1929 the first decisive step was taken in the development of what was to become the *Panzertruppe*. *Kraftfahrabteilung 6* in Münster was designated as a test bed for the new concepts being advanced by men like Guderian. The truck battalion was reorganized as a combined-arms battalion with three line companies: a *Kraftradschützen-Kompanie* (motorcycle infantry company); a *Kampfwagen-Nachbildungs-Kompanie* (fighting vehicle simulation company); and a *Panzerspähwagen-Nachbildungs-Kompanie* (armored car simulation company).[7] By 1930 it was decided to restructure the remaining *Kraftfahrabteilungen* in a similar fashion, with then-*Major* Guderian assuming command of *Kraftfahrabteilung 3* in Wünsdorf on 1 February 1930.[8] By 1934 all six of the truck battalions had been converted, although they all retained the original designation as *Kraftfahrabteilungen* as a deception measure.[9]

It was during this period that the initial organization for motorized/armored reconnaissance battalions was established: two armored car companies (or troops), one motorcycle infantry company (or troop), and a heavy company/troop containing engineer, antitank, and infantry gun assets at platoon levels. This was to remain the theoretical norm leading into the war, even if the practice was often quite different, generally because of a lack of adequate and suitable reconnaissance vehicles but also because of changing missions and roles for the reconnaissance forces. Although some of the first-wave infantry divisions also received a small complement of armored cars, these were few and far between. All of the organizational nuances will be discussed in the next chapter.[10]

The specific vehicles used by the armored reconnaissance forces will be covered in depth in a later chapter, but at this point it will suffice to say that the German Army entered the war and conducted combat operations with reconnaissance assets that had originally been designed solely as training vehicles and interim measures. In this sense, it was similar to the tanks used by the armored regiments, which had to fight for a not inconsiderable period with the *Panzer I* and *Panzer II* long after they had outlived their battlefield effectiveness. In the case of the reconnaissance

One of the first armored cars to see widespread service in the early reconnaissance formations of the *Reichswehr* and *Wehrmacht* was the *Machinengewehr-Kraftfahrwagen*, the *Kfz. 13*, which was based on the *Adler* passenger car. This photograph was taken during the transition from the *Reichswehr* to the *Wehrmacht* as the personnel still wear *Reichswehr*-style caps while the vehicle has *Wehrmacht* license plates. Note the three-tone, hard-edged camouflage scheme. JIM HALEY

This image shows the relatively rare initial version of the *Sd.Kfz. 247* armored command-and-control vehicle with a rear dual axle (only ten were built). It was later succeeded by a four-wheel version. The image shows the ceremonial entry of the forces into the new facilities at Krampnitz for the fledging motorized reconnaissance force in 1937. The officer saluting is *Major* Cramer, the second commander of the *Kavallerie-Lehr und Versuchs-Abteilung*. JIM HALEY

Despite the rigors of training, time is found to pose for a group photograph. The scouts in berets wear the blue HBT drill-and-work uniform authorized for armored personnel. Although commonly assumed to be a prewar item, it manufactured until late in the war, and its wear can be seen on all fronts and theaters.

forces, the vehicles were the *Kraftfahrwagen 13* and *Kraftfahrwagen 14*, which were essentially converted civilian vehicles outfitted with a machine gun (*Kfz. 13*) and a medium-range radio set (*Kfz. 14*). Even when purpose-built armored cars were introduced—such as the light *Sd.Kfz. 221, 222*, and *223* and the medium *Sd.Kfz. 231, 232, 233* and *263*—there were other issues, such as inadequate cross-country maneuverability. Later efforts in design and development were more successful, but they were too little and too late—a problem obviously not limited to the *Panzeraufklärungstruppe*. In terms of production, tanks were always the first priority for the limited industrial capacity of the Reich, with armored cars being relatively low in the pecking order for production. In fact, it was the lack of suitable fighting platforms that forced the Germans to place such emphasis on the motorcycle infantry, the *Kradschützen*, since motorcycles were in relatively plentiful supply. That worked out well along the well-developed road networks of Western Europe but soon encountered major obstacles in the vast expanse of the Soviet Union, where improved roads were a scarce commodity and the weather wreaked havoc on the motorcycles, forcing an eventual shift to wheeled vehicles and half-tracks, which were also always in short supply.

Of course, the design of armored cars was an issue that affected all of the major combatants. Coupled with the usual requirements of maneuverability, armor, and armament inherent in all armored-vehicle design was the necessity of speed and stealth. It proved to be a complicated equation that was never really solved satisfactorily. Give a scout too much firepower, and he is tempted to use it. Give him too little, and he may not survive even the smallest of opposition. The key to success for the armored reconnaissance soldier was foremost his speed. His mission was not to destroy the enemy, but to report on him so that the higher commander could devise a plan to destroy him with more suitable assets. As Munzel succinctly observes, "In summary, it can be said that the technical problems for mechanized reconnaissance are more difficult to solve than for the armor force. Scouting elements should move as quietly as possible, be faster than other vehicles, be capable of cross-country movement, and be able to defend themselves against superior enemy armored vehicles. Those demands did not allow themselves to be combined in a satisfactory manner at the time."[11]

Excerpt from the After-Action Report of an Armored Reconnaissance Battalion

CONCERNING THE EMPLOYMENT OF *PANZERSPÄHKOMPANIE (C)* IN THE PERIOD FROM 9 MARCH TO 25 APRIL 1944

1. The company[1] arrived at the division location southwest of Kriwoj-Rog on 5 March 1944. It was initially designated as a divisional reserve. The employment of armored reconnaissance sections during that period of predominantly bottomless muck was very difficult. In the course of the retrograde movements in the direction of Wossnessensk and the Bug initiated on 9 March 1944, the company was employed as part of the division's armored battle group. The *Kampfgruppe* was formed in the main by the company, because there were no operational tanks or assault guns or even *SPW's* on hand.

Operations were restricted to reconnoitering the enemy forces marching in the direction of Nikolajew on the deep right flank, to attacking enemy columns with reinforced armor reconnaissance patrols and to disrupting his lines of communication. Along with three attached *Wespen*,[2] two *Hummeln*,[3] and two 7.5cm antitank guns (the latter from the battalion's 5th Company), the company was able to achieve success and, above all, perform its reconnaissance missions well, despite the difficult terrain and the extremely muddy roads.

Because of the loss of almost all communications means (radio net centers) in not only the battalion but also the division, the coordinated employment of patrols could not be effected. The acting company commander[4] had to conduct operations based on his own assessment of the situation. On top of that was the fact that the division proper was employed in completely different sectors of the front and the *Kampfgruppe* frequently changed its attachment status [to other commands].

The commander's vehicle and the radio vehicles of reconnaissance sections not employed at the front had to be used as radio relay stations. It was determined that the radio operators for the patrols needed to have the best radio training that there is. The radio operator needs to have physical endurance and intellectual prowess so that he can stay the course through the nerve-wracking exertions that occur when he sits next to the radio all by himself for days on end.

2. Other demands were placed on the company in the fighting north of the Pruth and in the area around Jassi.

For the most part, combat missions were conducted. As a consequence of the mountainous terrain, the operations were conducted at platoon level, together with assault guns and infantry.

The enemy, coming from Balti and advancing in the direction of the Pruth, was located a few kilometers north of the Pruth bridges at Ungheni and had cut the main supply line between Kischinew and Jassi.

The terrain was very broken and parts of it were still under high snow.

The *Kampfgruppe*, consisting of five armored reconnaissance halftracks, two assault guns and a weak company of infantry, had the mission of opening the road again in order to open a path for the motorized divisions coming from the north.

---

1. The *Panzerspähkompanie (c)* in the title of the report is the armored reconnaissance company issued the *Sd.Kfz. 250/9 SPW*, equipped with a revolving gun turret similar to the one employed on the *Sd. Kfz. 222* armored car. The company was organized under *Kriegsstärkennachweisung 1162c* of 1 November 1943 and was theoretically organized with a company headquarters and headquarters section (one *Sd.Kfz. 250/5*) and four line platoons, each equipped with two *Sd.Kfz. 250/5* and four *Sd.Kfz. 250/9*. The headcount in each line platoon was eighteen, with two of the platoons authorized officers as platoon leaders. The company also had an integral maintenance section and combat and field trains. Based on the discussions of the area employed, this report was most likely written by *Panzer-Aufklärungs-Abteilung 13* of the *13. Panzer-Division*, commanded by a *Major* Schütz at the time.
2. The Wasp was a medium self-propelled artillery piece mounting a *leichte Feldhaubitze 18* (10.5cm) on a *Panzer II* chassis. They were found in the mechanized artillery battalions of armored divisions (generally two batteries of six guns each) from 1943 on.
3. The Bumble Bee was a heavy self-propelled artillery piece mounting a *schwere Feldhaubitze 18/1 L30* (15cm) on a hybrid *Panzer III/IV* chassis. There was usually one battery of six guns in an armored division's mechanized artillery regiment from about 1943 on.
4. The original German refers to him as the *Kompanieführer*. In non-military German, this could also mean company commander, but since this is part of an after-action report, it is assumed that acting company commander is meant, not the officially appointed company commander (*Kompaniechef*).

Geheim!
NACHRICHTENBLATT
DER PANZERTRUPPEN
Nr. 13
Juli 1944
HERAUSGEGEBEN VOM
GENERALINSPEKTEUR DER PANZERTRUPPEN
VORSCHRIFTENSTELLE

If it was at all possible—despite the difficult terrain and the minimal combat power—to force the enemy back into the mountains without suffering any friendly losses and, on a single day, knocking out thirteen Shermans, then it is due to the following reasons:

a) The enemy has to be tackled hard and decisively.

b) You don't always have to move on the road.

c) Identify weak spots in the defense—even while conducting the attack—and break through there.

d) Exploit the greater range of the 2cm weapons over the infantry weapons.

It was seen how the 2cm weapon is greatly feared by the Russian infantry and even antitank guns and rifles were unable to get off a round whenever they were identified and held under suppressive fire.

The prerequisite for that is crews well trained in the firefight, focused observation and rapid, independent action on the part of the vehicle commanders, as well as a seamless shift between fire and movement.

The combination of combat and reconnaissance vehicles together in the form of the half-tracked armored reconnaissance vehicle proved its worth in the fighting north of the Pruth along the Jassi–Kischinew road. Decisive in the process was the multifaceted and good training of all of the crews, some of which consisted of veteran *SPW* grenadiers and some of armored reconnaissance scouts, which combined the spirit of the attack of the former with the inventiveness and agility of the latter.

A third chapter in the employment of the company was the defensive operations north of Jassi. In a manner similar to the way things were portrayed in *Nachrichtenblatt der Panzertruppen* No. 9 of 1 March 1944, the company was used as "eyes on the enemy" in conducting battlefield observation on dominant terrain behind the main line of resistance and the deep flanks of the two neighboring divisions. The patrols submitted continual reports on the enemy situation. In many cases, the patrols established passage points for the friendly forces moving back and, on more than one occasion, they effectively supported friendly infantry in conducting immediate counterattacks after acting on their own and identifying critical situations.

It was never possible to employ the entire company together in the heavily broken and mountainous terrain, because there was too little room to maneuver. In the forelands of the Carpathians, there is little employment opportunity for a larger armored force. It is always confined to roads, paths or narrow mountain ridges.

The patrol elements of the *Panzerspähkompanie (c)* are better suited to executing reconnaissance missions in this terrain than bicycle elements due to their better cross-country capability.

COMMENTS BY THE INSPECTOR GENERAL OF THE ARMORED FORCES

Based on the after-action report of the battalion, it is clear that the *Halbketten-Spähkomanie (c)* can maneuver in difficult terrain and despite muddied routes and bring in good reconnaissance results.

The joint operations conducted with the *Wespen* and *Hummeln* mentioned in Paragraph 1 do not correspond to the employment fundamentals of self-propelled artillery. The example given is an exception and should not become the norm.

What bears particular emphasis is the successful employment of the five armored reconnaissance vehicles mentioned in Paragraph 2, which were only supported by a weak infantry company of 35 men and 2 assault guns. This example is proof that the Russians can be beaten at places where they are attacked decisively, even with meager forces.

Because of its maneuverability in difficult terrain, the *Halbketten-Spähkomanie (c)* is better suited for conducting combat and reconnaissance missions than a bicycle reconnaissance company. Whenever conducting combat missions (reconnaissance-in-force or the disruption of supply routes), it is advantageous for the armored reconnaissance section to be reinforced by assault guns as a means of protection from enemy tanks.

SCHOOLHOUSE AND DOCTRINAL DEVELOPMENT

Training

More pressing, at first, for the theoreticians was the development of doctrine and tactics for the reconnaissance forces that would complement the doctrine and tactics emerging for the *Panzertruppe*. Then there needed to be a training base for passing on that information, and that necessitated the creation of training institutions for armored reconnaissance personnel.

The initial schoolhouse for the *Panzertruppe* was the *Kraftfahrkampftruppenschule Wünsdorf*, located near Berlin.[12] Established in 1936, it had responsibility for training tankers, antitank gunners, motorized reconnaissance personnel, and motorcycle infantry. It was also responsible for issues involving motorization.[13] The schoolhouse also supervised the recently established armor gunnery school at Putlos on the North Sea (*Schießlehrgang Putlos*). In 1937 the schoolhouse was split in two, with the *Panzertruppenschule Wünsdorf* retaining responsibility for armor training and doctrine, as well as motorization issues, and the *Kavallerieschule Döberitz* (jointly "owned" by the *Panzertruppe* and the *Kavallerie*, with a role also played by the *Infanterie*) taking the lead on cavalry, motorized infantry, and motorized reconnaissance topics.[14] As will be seen in the following discussion of the training base and the school formations, it can prove difficult even for someone steeped in the inner workings of the German training and military school system to keep track.

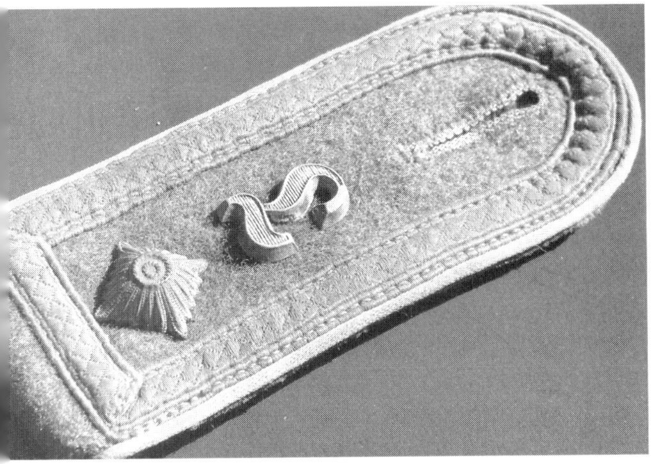

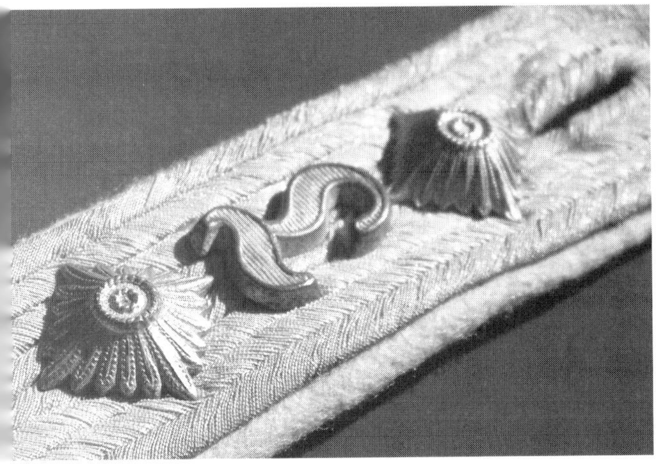

A shoulder strap for an *Oberwachtmeister* and a shoulder board for a *Rittmeister*, both of whom were assigned to one of the training establishments for cavalry and armored reconnaissance personnel, as indicated by the Gothic L, which stands for *Lehr* (instructional or training). These are piped in the golden-yellow branch-of-service color (*goldgelbe Waffenfarbe*) of the cavalry. CHRISTOPHER VARRICHIO

In 1938 the schoolhouse at Döberitz moved to the newly constructed military facilities at rural Krampnitz, thus becoming *Kavallerieschule Krampnitz*. *Oberstleutnant* Degener was the first garrison commander, with *Major* Hans Cramer assuming command of the instructional battalion.[15] The instructional battalion, designated the *Kavallerie Lehr- und Versuchsabteilung*, served a variety of purposes. It provided demonstrations of cavalry-related topics to visiting dignitaries, it supervised the "hands on" component for training course participants, and it also tested new equipment. When first established, the battalion had the following five troops, commanders, and cadre elements:

- *(Reiter) Lehrschwadron*: *Rittmeister* von Wedel. Cadre primarily formed from the *4./Reiter-Regiment 4*.
- *(Panzerspäh) Lehrschwadron*: *Rittmeister Freiherr* von Bromberg. Cadre primarily formed from the *2./Kraftfahr-Versuchsabteilung*.
- *(Kradschützen) Lehrschwadron*: *Rittmeister* Häublein. Cadre primarily formed from the *3./Kraftfahr-Versuchsabteilung*.
- *4. (schwere) Lehrschwadron*: *Rittmeister Freiherr* von Ohlen. Cadre came from troop levies from all military districts.
- *Stabsschwadron*: *Rittmeister* Pannicke. Cadre formed from mounted elements from the *1.*

Scouts along a line of *Sd.Kfz. 221's*, along with other vehicles, await orders to move out on a dreary day. This image was probably taken around 1935 or 1936, as indicated by the lack of a national insignia on the berets, as well as the "eagle" with the narrow wingspan on the officer trooping the line. Of interest is the prominent display of signal flags since these vehicle did not carry radios. The machine guns have muzzle covers to protect them from the elements; a rudimentary attempt at camouflage has been applied.

Kavallerie-Brigade and motorized elements from *Aufklärungs-Abteilung (mot) 7*.[16]

When the schoolhouse moved to Krampnitz in 1938, an armored car gunnery instruction platoon, the *Panzerspäh-Schieß-Lehrzug*, was also formed, under *Leutnant* Winter.

In keeping with the training philosophy of the German Army, cadre personnel at the various branch schoolhouses and the instructional battalions were expected to get "muddy boots" in order to keep current and not become too "academic" during their tenure. The troopers at Krampnitz were no exception, with elements participating in the occupations of both Austria and the *Sudetenland*.[17]

They later went on to fight with distinction in the campaigns in Poland and the West. After the campaign in the West, it continued to perform schoolhouse duties, returning to Krampnitz in August 1940. In 1941 the battalion was attached to the *1. Kavallerie-Division* for additional combat experience. In November of the same year, the battalion returned to Krampnitz, only to return to the Eastern Front in early 1942, after being redesignated as the *Kradschützen-Lehr-Bataillon*. Augmented by two motorcycle infantry companies, it participated in the summer offensive as part of the *11. Panzer-Division*. Prior to moving out, the battalion had to give up its armored car troop, the *1. Panzer-Späh-Lehr-Schwadron*, to the *10. Infanterie-Division (mot.)*. It returned to Krampnitz in October 1942 and was redesignated as the *Panzer-Aufklärungs-Lehr-Abteilung* (once again) on 1 April 1943, after having sent its horse-mounted and bicycle reconnaissance elements to the infantry school in Bromberg.

Later that year, the battalion was tasked to provide cadre and personnel for the formation of the *Panzergrenadier-Lehr-Regiment*, as well as the remainder being reassigned from the school in September 1943 to reconstitute the reconnaissance battalion of the reforming *21. Panzer-Division* in France, with its 4th Company having been already reassigned to that division's *Panzergrenadier-Lehr-Regiment 902*. The

Despite the rigorous training pace of the prewar years, as with all militaries, there was time for drill and ceremonies and pomp and circumstance. This image shows a change-of-command ceremony for a soldier later assigned to *Aufklärungs-Abteilung (mot) 37* (*7. Panzer-Division*). The date given is 1938, which most likely makes this *II./Aufklärungs-Regiment 7* (*2. leichte Division*). A pristine *Sd.Kfz. 232 (Fu) (8-Rad)* is on prominent display behind the color guard.

A musical group on a unique bandstand consisting of two *Sd.Kfz. 231 (8-Rad)* heavy armored cars. The image is attributed to *Aufklärungs-Abteilung (mot) 4* (*1. Panzer-Division*) and was probably taken during an Armed Forces Day presentation to the general public. JIM HALEY

A unit photo of one of the troops of *Aufklärungs-Abteilung (mot) 6*. Depending on the date when the image was taken, the battalion could have been *I./Aufklärungs-Regiment 6* (*1. leichte Division*).

schoolhouse at Krampnitz then started the difficult task of rebuilding its armored reconnaissance instructional battalion, an effort made more difficult by the reassignment of the *Panzergrenadier-Lehr-Regiment* to the newly forming *Panzer-Lehr-Division* in France. *Major* von Fallois was assigned as commander of the battalion, and he used elements of two armored reconnaissance battalions that had been effectively destroyed in North Africa—*Panzer-Aufklärungs-Abteilungen 3* and *33*—as part of the reconstitution.[18] Those efforts were also assisted by the return of the *1. Panzer-Späh-Lehr-Schwadron*, which had returned from its attachment to the *10. Panzergrenadier-Division*, where it had served with *Kradschützen-Bataillon 40*.[19]

The schoolhouse was again tasked to produce a combat formation, with *Bataillon Krampnitz* being formed and dispatched to the Eastern Front on 27 July 1944. It had the standard organization of the time, with three mechanized infantry companies, an armored car company (the 4th), and a heavy company. It was attached to *Fallschirm-Panzer-Division "Hermann Göring"* in the area west of Warsaw, where it was shattered in hard fighting and its commander, *Major* von Nagel, killed while leading from the front in his *SPW*. The battalion was then reorganized and redesignated as *Kampfschule Krampnitz*.

By August 1941, the schoolhouse had been renamed *Schule für schnelle Truppen Krampnitz*, albeit retaining the same responsibilities as before. By December 1942, the term *Schützen* (motorized infantry) was replaced by *Panzergrenadiere* (armored infantry) in all designations. In July 1943, when the *schnelle Truppen* were redesignated as the *Panzertruppen*, the school was redesignated as *Panzertruppenschule II Krampnitz*, retaining responsibility for the training of *Panzeraufklärer* and *Panzergrenadiere*. Portions of the school, specifically the *Lehrgruppe I* and *Aufklärungs-Lehr-Abteilung*,[20] were reassigned to the new *Aufklärungs- und Kavallerie-Schule Bromberg*, retaining responsibility for training horse-mounted and bicycle-equipped reconnaissance elements. At the same time, *Lehrstab 3*, which was responsible for the training of motorized infantry personnel, and the motorized rifle companies of the former *Grenadier-Lehr-Bataillon (mot.)* were transferred from the *Infanterieschule Döberitz*. The school in Krampnitz was to be renamed one more time. In

Given the attention being paid to their uniforms, these scouts appear to be getting ready for a parade or ceremony of some sort. These soldiers are attributed to one of the troops of *Aufklärungs-Abteilung (mot) 6.* The lead armored car is an *Sd.Kfz. 221* armed with a single machine gun in a manually traversing turret. It is followed by several *Sd.Kfz. 223's*, essentially the radio version of the same vehicle, identifiable by its typical prewar and early-war frame antenna.

Scouts were expected to perform their duties in all types of weather—not especially comfortable in winter in an open vehicle with no heater. While infantry soldiers were subjected to the same conditions, they frequently had the latitude to move about to stay warm, whereas armored personnel often spent hours in stationary positions. The lead vehicle seen here is the *Kfz. 13.* JIM HALEY

The two crewmembers of an *Sd.Kfz. 221* take a breather during an exercise. These scouts are assigned to *Aufklärungs-Abteilung (mot) 5* (*2. Panzer-Division*) as indicated by the A/5 on their shoulder straps. The scout on the viewer's left is an NCO candidate, as indicated by the strip of silver-colored ribbon (*Tresse*) wrapped around his shoulder strap. JIM HALEY

July 1944 the Roman numeral *II* was dropped from its official title.

Because of the increasingly untenable situation on the home front and the drastic combing out of the training base to establish additional formations, the school was moved to Bergen in January 1945, where it was consolidated with the armor schoolhouse, which had also moved there, and renamed *Panzertruppenschule Bergen*. About the time of the move at Krampnitz, a section was detached from the school in order to form a training cadre at Luschtieniz near the Milowitz Training Area in Czechoslovakia. It was designated as the *Panzeraufklärungslehrgänge für die Ausbilder des Ersatzheeres* (Armored Reconnaissance Training Courses for Trainers of the Replacement Army). Instruction ceased there at the beginning of 1945, with the personnel then sent to the *Heeres-Unteroffizier-Schule Sondershausen*, an army noncommissioned officer academy.

The NCO academy at Sondershausen was not the first such institution that had been devoted to training the future leaders of the reconnaissance force; *HUS Putlos* had that distinction. Within the instructional detachment, its 4th and 5th companies were dedicated to the training of reconnaissance and motorcycle infantry NCO candidates. After the first training cycle, the school was split up and another one established at Sternberg (1 September 1941). It also eventually had five training companies, with the last two being for reconnaissance and motorcycle infantry personnel, the same as at Putlos. Eventually, the training focus shifted, and by June 1943, all of the instruction was devoted solely to training armored reconnaissance candidates. The school started moving to Sondershausen, a displacement that started in December 1943 but did not end until March 1945. Eventually, that schoolhouse had three companies devoted to NCO candidates and one company for officer-candidates. Apparently, the school also had an armored car company as part of its training establishment, but it is not known how or if it was committed to combat operations at the end of the war.[21]

In addition to the officer training eventually offered at Sondershausen, there as a schoolhouse dedicated entirely to the training of officer-candidates for the armored reconnaissance force. The *Panzer-Aufklärungs-Ausbildungsabteilung für Offizier-Bewerber Insterburg/Meiningen* proved to be the smallest of the officer-candidate schools within the *Panzertruppe*, although it eventually had the equivalent of three companies (*Inspektionen*). The school was initially established at Insterburg (in December 1943) and then eventually moved to Meiningen (being closed there in March 1945).[22]

Experiences of an Armored Reconnaissance Battalion (Free Organization) in the East

THE EXPERIENCES STEM FROM THE FIGHTING WITHDRAWAL DURING THE PERIOD FROM 13 JULY TO 12 AUGUST 1944

After initially being employed piecemeal with different corps, the battalion was employed in its entirety within the framework of the defensive fighting and retrograde operations of a corps on 25 July 1944.

The missions of the battalion were primarily as follows:

a) Defend for a specified period;

b) Conduct deception operations and safeguard the withdrawal movements of friendly infantry;

c) Act as the Immediate Counterattack Force.

The battalion was fully capable of conducting these three missions based on its new organization (Free Organization).*

The missions it was given could be executed in every case. In four weeks of uninterrupted operations, during which tolerable losses were sustained, approximately 1,500 casualties were inflicted. In addition, four assault guns and seventeen antitank guns were eliminated.

The following lessons learned were collected:

WITH REGARD TO A) DEFEND FOR A SPECIFIED PERIOD

In most cases, the battalion had large infantry forces with heavy weapons but without appreciable armored forces in front of it.

Battalion Mission

Hold a sector as part of a hastily established main line of defense that only had to be held for a certain period in order to enable friendly infantry forces to pull back undisturbed.

Execution

The *SPW* companies moved mounted up to the defensive sector in such a manner that they could not be identified until someone was right next to them.

Small patches of woods, shallow reverse slope areas and grain fields with high growth were suitable for accomplishing that.

Critical to success was thorough camouflage, complete quiet, and lack of movement.

The enemy, pursuing in massed formations, was allowed to approach to within close range.

Fire was opened by all weapons on radio command and, following that, the forces advanced rapidly into the completely disoriented enemy. The enemy was quickly overrun, and the battalion returned just as rapidly to a previously reconnoitered alternate position.

In almost all cases, the effect was to cause the enemy not to repeat his attack efforts in the battalion sector.

It turned out to be beneficial in those types of operations not to have either the wheeled vehicles or the C Company (half-tracked armored reconnaissance company) established in the main line of resistance from the outset.

Since it was generally not possible to send motorized patrols forward due to the friendly demolition of bridges, laying of mines and establishment of abatis, the wheeled reconnaissance sections and a few tracked reconnaissance sections were set up as stand-

* The *freie Gliederung* concept was introduced in 1944 as a means of further streamlining organizations within *Panzer* and *Panzergrenadier-Divisionen* and "freeing" line company commanders from the burdens of worrying about logistical support (logistical functions were consolidated into a supply company at the battalion level). The armored reconnaissance battalion of 1944 packed a considerable punch, if organized in accordance with authorization documents. The battalion had the following heavy weapons and vehicles: battalion headquarters with headquarters company (armored) with sixteen armored cars and ten medium *SPW's*; one *Panzerspähkompanie (c)* with twenty-five light *SPW's* (sixteen *Sd.Kfz. 250/9's*); one *leichte Panzeraufklärungskompanie (gp)* with twenty-six light *SPW's*, two light *SPW's* with two medium mortars, and two light *SPW's* with *7.5cm KwK 37's*; one *Panzeraufklärungskompanie (gp)* with twenty-three medium *SPW's* with two 7.5cm *KwK 37's*, seven 2cm *Flak*, four heavy machine guns, and two mortars; one *schwere Panzeraufklärungskompanie (gp)* with headquarters section (two medium *SPW's*), one *schwerer Kanonenzug* (eight medium *SPW's* with six 7.5cm *KwK 37's*), one *schwerer Granatwerferzug* (seven medium *SPW's* with four heavy mortars), and one *Pionierzug (gp)* with seven medium *SPW's*; and *Versorgungskompanie (mot)*.

ing patrols on dominant pieces of terrain in both of the neighboring sectors behind the main line of resistance. The mission of those patrols was to constantly inform the battalion concerning the situation in the neighboring sectors.

This measure also turned out to be especially fortuitous, since there were repeated breakthroughs in the neighboring sectors, which would have led to the envelopment and bypassing of the battalion, if immediate countermeasures had not be initiated. The most effective countermeasure turned out to be an immediate counterattack into the flanks of the enemy forces breaking through. Those jabs to the flank were conducted with both the C Company (most of which was being held as the battalion reserve) or one of the *SPW* companies. The latter option proved more effective.

An *SPW* company was quickly and stealthily dispatched from a defensive position and the sector that was left uncovered was then monitored by a half-tracked armored reconnaissance platoon.

WITH REGARD TO B) CONDUCT DECEPTION OPERATIONS AND SAFE GUARD THE WITHDRAWAL MOVEMENTS OF FRIENDLY INFANTRY

The employment of the *SPW* company in a blocking position took place as described in Point A) above behind the section of the main line of resistance that was to be given up and in the vicinity of the former hot spot.

Important in that instance was the dispersed deployment [of the company] in order to avoid casualties through enemy artillery fires. The primary reason for the success [of the operation] once again was the occupation of the position completely unnoticed by the enemy.

The enemy situation frequently required the establishment of two or more blocking positions along a frontage of eight to ten kilometers.

In the process, it proved beneficial to form blocking sections of platoon strength that were reinforced by individual mortars and 2cm cannon. The areas between the positions were monitored by roving patrols from the C Company.

Whenever dominant terrain was found in those open areas, it was found to be better to position standing patrols since they were then able to prevent the enemy from prematurely locating the positions of the battalion.

The cannon platoon, as well as any assault guns or tanks, were held in reserve so as to be able to employ them at the focal point of the enemy's greatest pressure during the course of the fighting.

The open flanks of the battalion were screened by patrols from the C Company, since the enemy almost always attempted to pull back whenever he collided into a position with *SPW's* and then bypass as far as possible.

Whenever there were good road conditions, wheeled patrols were also especially suitable for those types of missions due to their speed.

Whenever those patrols discovered enemy groups attempting to bypass, they immediately engaged them. They always attacked from several different sides. The enemy proved especially sensitive to that method of conducting operations, with the result that the employment of larger forces was not necessary in most cases.

Individual *SPW's* of the engineer platoon were sent to bridges that were necessary for the subsequent march back of the battalion. They had the mission of preventing the premature demolition of the bridges. That precautionary measure paid for itself many times over, since the employment of the battalion in a deception mission happened in an overly hasty manner many times during crisis situations and the demolition parties of the forces moving back were not properly oriented.

WITH REGARD TO C) ACT AS THE IMMEDIATE COUNTERATTACK FORCE

The battalion was employed as the immediate reaction force of a corps, whose sector extended approximately forty-five kilometers, for fourteen days.

The following points had to be adhered to throughout the execution of this mission:

1. The battalion had to take up quarters widely dispersed and well camouflaged and employ weak, local security, even behind the main line of resistance, so as to avoid the bulk of the enemy's artillery fires and the main blows of aerial attacks.

2. Immediate and thorough route reconnaissance of the entire corps sector by all available reconnaissance sections.

While conducting the route reconnaissance, the following is to be taken into consideration:

a) The trace of the main line of resistance.

b) The command posts, down to battalion level.

c) Positions of friendly artillery and armor-defeating weaponry.

d) Enemy situation in the individual sectors.

e) Areas that can be observed by the enemy.

f) Road and bridge conditions behind the friendly main line of resistance.

g) Sectors of terrain that cannot be negotiated by vehicles.

The results of that reconnaissance need to be reviewed each day, since small things frequently change in both the friendly and enemy situation that could later be of importance for the employment of the battalion.

3. Personal contact is established by the Battalion Commander with all of the divisions and regiments in order to discuss possible conditions for employment.

4. Establish dependable communications means.

5. Discussions with the artillery for the purpose of support later on.

6. Constant monitoring of the main line of resistance along the entire front by a few standing patrols, which constantly provide information on the situation. By doing that, the battalion is capable of conducting actions on its own in crisis situations when communications means are lost.

7. If two enemy penetrations occur at the same time that are not too far apart, then there is a greater chance of success of cleaning up one penetration after the other with the entire battalion together than to employ a reinforced company in each of the areas of penetration.

8. Those types of immediate counterattacks need to be conducted rapidly and with a sense of urgency, since it is usually only possible to successfully cross through heavy enemy artillery, mortar and antitank-gun fires through speed. Every hesitation or even stopping leads to painful losses and complete write-offs.

9. For the same reasons, the mounted battalion may not remain stationary for any length of time after reaching the attack objective.

It must be stressed that the infantry is to follow closely behind the attack of the *SPW's* so as to be able to occupy the retaken position immediately.

In many cases, the infantry remained mounted on the *SPW's* until the onset of aimed enemy defensive fires and then followed the attack rapidly on foot (similar to the way infantry operates with assault guns).

On the other hand, if the infantry waits until the *SPW* attack has reached its objective, then it runs into heavy enemy denial fires and suffers considerable casualties.

10. Due to the number of heavy enemy weapons and the intense antitank-gun defense, it is absolutely necessary that at least one forward observer accompanies the attack to the forwardmost lines.

Flawless radio communications must be established.

In all three of the situations described, the joint efforts with the assault guns and tanks worked well.

On the other hand, an attached towed 7.5cm antitank gun platoon proved unsuitable for all of the missions.

COMMENTS BY THE INSPECTOR GENERAL OF THE ARMORED FORCES

In the after-action report above, the examples cited in "B) Conduct Deception Operations and Safe Guard the Withdrawal Movements of Friendly Infantry" can be considered the proper employment of an armored reconnaissance battalion. If the armored reconnaissance battalion is employed in its entirety, then its organization, cross-country mobility, firepower, radio equipment and armored vehicles are especially well suited for executing this mission. By skillful employment of armored surveillance, the battalion is in position to control large sectors and even hold up the advance of the enemy by means of armored reconnaissance sections.

When considering the lessons learned in A) Defend for a Specified Period, the mounted defensive operations of the battalion should be stressed. This type of employment is new. The advantages can be seen from the report and consist of the fact that the battalion both continues to be capable of movement and unified command through radio remains possible.

A prerequisite for this type of employment is rolling, vegetated terrain that offers the opportunity for the armored vehicles to be positioned off to the side and be well camouflaged. In flat, open terrain that offers little cover and concealment for vehicles, this type of operation is not possible because of the enemy's armor-defeating weapons.

Employment as a counterattack reserve is not the mission of an armored reconnaissance battalion. If any other types of forces are available to serve as the counterattack reserve, then the armored reconnaissance battalion is not to be used and is to be held back for proper missions.

When executing separate missions, the battalion is to be habitually reinforced with antitank forces or assault guns. Although it is equipped with numerous lightly armored vehicles, it does not have any appreciable antitank capability at its disposal.

A rest halt along a country road for *Aufklärungs-Abteilung (mot) 5.* The *Sd.Kfz. 231 (6-Rad)* is an early variant and is followed by an *Sd.Kfz. 221* and *Kfz. 13.* Of interest is the unique prewar unit identification symbol painted on the right front fender of the *Sd.Kfz. 231 (6-Rad).* JIM HALEY

Theory, Tactics, and Doctrine

German theory prior to the war held that reconnaissance assets should be neither seen nor heard. Their job was to operate stealthily, avoiding physical enemy contact but always maintaining visual contact. As necessary, they would also scout terrain and man-made features to determine their military value, particularly in terms of movement and maneuverability. It was in opposition to the diehard theorists of heavy cavalry, who saw their arm as an instrument of shock and firepower, coupled with speed and maneuverability: It was the perfect storm in determining an enemy's weak spot and exploiting it. The German operations manual, *Heeresdienstvorschrift 300/1* (17 October 1933), described the reconnaissance effort this way:

> Motorized reconnaissance battalions are in the position of being able to gather information quickly and at great distance. . . . High demands are placed on everyone from the leader of the forces employed in the ground reconnaissance down to the individual patrol. The personality of the [patrol] leader is of decisive importance for success. Cunning, nimbleness, understanding of the mission, decisive movement . . . resourcefulness in the field, including the nighttime, unflappability, rapid and independent action are called for. All leaders are responsible for ensuring that contact gained with the enemy is not lost, either by day or by night . . .[23]

For the proponents of the armored force and mechanization, "The reconnaissance formations could only fulfill their missions if they were *completely* motorized, had cross-country capability, and possessed sufficient combat power. . . . It was intended for the formations [battalions] to be able to penetrate an enemy screen with their own forces."[24]

One of the first training manuals for the motorized reconnaissance battalion was produced by the cavalry branch in 1939. *Heeresdienstvorschrift (HdV) 299/10* covered both the motorized reconnaissance battalion and the partially motorized counterpart (which still had horse-mounted elements). Its opening paragraph reinforces the concerns of *HdV 300/1*: "Reconnaissance is intended to create a picture of the enemy as quickly, as completely and as reliably as possible. Its results form the most important basis for the measures taken by command and for the exploitation of the effects of weaponry."

The first section of the manual is dedicated to general remarks concerning reconnaissance, discussing it at the operational, tactical, and combat levels. Operational reconnaissance is generally considered to come under the purview of the air force, augmented by "the signals reconnaissance conducted by special means, the interrogation of prisoners, the evaluation of captured documents, statements made by the local populace, etc."

From there, the manual narrows its focus to tactical reconnaissance, which can generally be considered the responsibility of the field armies, especially the corps and the divisions, the latter of which generally held the means for conducting it with their organic reconnaissance assets.

> Tactical reconnaissance provides the support needed for command and control and employment of the forces in the field. It is primarily concerned with the detailed determination of the enemy's concentrations, his approach routes, his organization, his deployment and the extent of his forces in both depth and width.
>
> The closer one gets to the enemy, the more the need for tactical reconnaissance to focus on details. Combat reconnaissance is to be initiated, at the latest, with enemy contact. It creates the prerequisites for the conduct of the fight. All branches are involved in it.

Note that as contact is made, combat reconnaissance is initiated, which is a responsibility of all forces on the ground, regardless of their combat arm. Indeed, as will be seen later in the manual, once contact is made, the mission of the divisional reconnaissance battalion is no longer gaining information from the enemy but denying him from obtaining his own information, generally by conducting flank, rearguard, and security missions.

The manual specifies why the ground reconnaissance effort is also of decisive importance:

> A deep view of what is going on in the enemy's sector is not generally available through ground reconnaissance. Aerial reconnaissance generally often only provides the direction in which it is to be conducted. In contrast, however, *it is only ground reconnaissance that can generally determine without doubt whether certain terrain is clear of the enemy* [emphasis added]. It is only through prisoners, enemy dead and other means that conclusions can be drawn concerning the enemy's organization for combat; that contact can be maintained with the enemy; and details obtained concerning his actions, his strength and disposition and, occasionally, his combat worthiness. In addition, contamination of the terrain can be determined in a timely manner. Furthermore, it can also provide information when aerial reconnaissance is not possible or is only very difficult as a result of weather conditions or at night.
>
> The forces mainly responsible for ground tactical reconnaissance are motorized reconnaissance battalions, horse-mounted reconnaissance battalions of the cavalry and the reconnaissance battalions of infantry divisions.

While the motorized reconnaissance battalions are given credit for greater speed and distance, they were considered to be limited in the amount of detail that could be acquired due to that same speed. To that end, horse- and bicycle-mounted elements were considered to have greater mobility, albeit at the cost of speed. Of course, it must be remembered that these observations were made based on the existing organizational structures of the time and the equipment issued. The German Army still did not field any armored cars that provided the cross-country capabilities that would cancel out that apparent lack of "mobility" on the part of motorized assets. Once better generations of vehicles were introduced, it was generally the horse- and bicycle-mounted elements that were considered to lack the mobility for anything other than what is considered combat reconnaissance.

As with all armies, great emphasis was placed on the quality of the soldiers who filled the ranks of reconnaissance elements. While all combat arms proudly claim that certain skill sets are required for

As is typical of all soldiers, exceptions to the more mundane aspects of the day-to-day routine were often captured on film. Scouts pose in uniform while taking some type of maritime excursion.

The daughter of a soldier is given a martial background for a posed photograph. It is not known why the white silhouettes of the armored cars are painted on the superstructure of the *Sd.Kfz. 232 (Fu)* vehicles.

Among the earliest motorized assets of the *Leibstandarte* and the *SS-Verfügungstruppe* were reconnaissance sections. Many of the early soldiers were detached to army schools for advanced and professional training. In this image, we see scouts training on an *Sd.Kfz. 222*, one of the more readily identifiable German armored cars of the Second World War. This appears to be a relatively early image as the scouts wear what appear to be modified army *Panzer* uniforms, which was done in the years prior to the start of the war, when the SS started fielding its own armored vehicle uniforms. The caps are also modified *Allgemeine SS* black caps, worn prior to the introduction of an overseas cap specifically for *SS-Verfügungstruppen* and the *Leibstandarte* in 1938.

their personnel, it is a peculiarity of reconnaissance forces that they often feel their enlisted personnel were a "cut above" those of the other branches, being capable of performing what were usually officer-level responsibilities (e.g., reports preparation and submission, interpretations of enemy intent, the classification rating of bridges, roads and other man-made infrastructure, and so on). Emphasis was always placed on independent thinking and action: "High demands are placed on the leaders of the forces employed in the service of ground reconnaissance—all the way down to the patrol leader. The leadership qualities of the leader are the determinant of success. Cunning, skill, understanding of the mission, decisive movement and riding in all types of terrain, offensive spirit, resourcefulness in the field, to include at night, unflappability, rapid and independent actions must be expected."[25]

In discussing movement, the manual states that the march performance of a motorized reconnaissance battalion

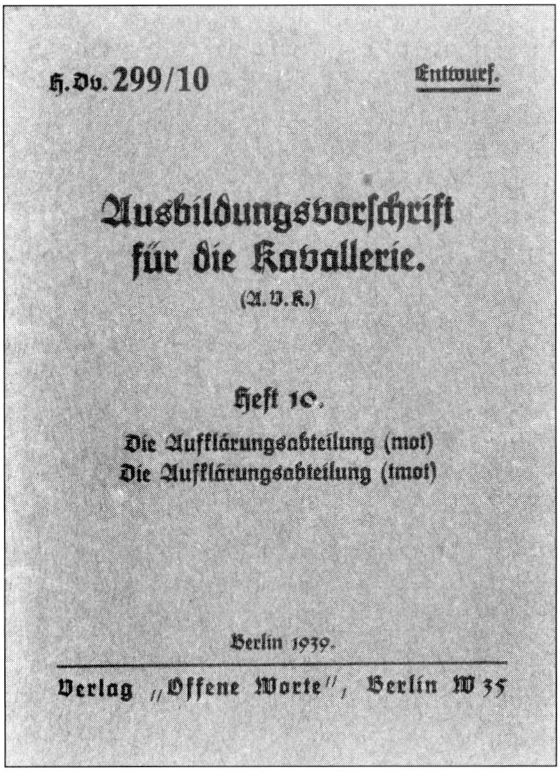

H.Dv. 299/10 Entwurf.

Ausbildungsvorschrift für die Kavallerie.

(A.V.K.)

Heft 10.

Die Aufklärungsabteilung (mot)

Die Aufklärungsabteilung (tmot)

Berlin 1939.

Verlag „Offene Worte", Berlin W 35

Heeresdienstvorschift 299/10 (draft) of 1939 for the motorized and partially motorized reconnaissance battalion. MICHAEL H. PRUETT

> is primarily dependent on the enemy situation and the terrain. Whenever there is a lack of resistance, favorable terrain conditions and a ready source of fuel, a march performance of between 200 and 250 kilometers can be achieved by armored reconnaissance patrols and reconnaissance battalions. Average march speeds—as long as the enemy does not appear—can be considered to be:
>
> —approximately 30 kilometers an hour for motorized reconnaissance battalions and
>
> —approximately 40 kilometers [an hour] for armored reconnaissance patrols.
>
> Speed decreases considerably whenever it is night or there is fog.
>
> An armored reconnaissance troop can generally reconnoiter along a width of 25 kilometers.

Because there were still partially motorized reconnaissance battalions in the wartime mobilization of infantry divisions, which theoretically included a section of armored cars in the heavy troop of the battalion, the manual also discusses its march performance:

> The march performance of a partly motorized reconnaissance battalion is primarily dependent on the enemy situation and the terrain. Whenever there is a lack of resistance and the terrain is favorable, approximately 75 kilometers can be covered by horse-mounted and bicycle patrols, approximately 200 kilometers for armored car patrols and from 50 to 60 kilometers can be covered by the reconnaissance battalion proper. If the upper hand in the reconnaissance area has to be forced through combat, then those figures are no longer valid.

As can be seen, there is a great disparity among the capabilities of the different elements of the infantry division's reconnaissance battalion. The figures given above were for optimal conditions. Under average conditions, the march rates were considerably reduced, ranging from 8 kilometers an hour for horse-mounted patrols to 40 kilometers an hour for armored car patrols.

While leadership for a motorized reconnaissance battalion could be considered a challenge, the differing rates of speed and logistical requirements for the disparate elements of an infantry division's partially motorized battalion practically made it a nightmare.

Section 3 of the manual gets into the meat and potatoes of reconnaissance operations. In keeping with general German tactical doctrine of the time, offensive operations were the key to success, even in conditions where the enemy force was superior in size and defensive operations were being conducted:

> Even in cases of enemy superiority, the reconnaissance battalion can obtain success by exploiting its maneuverability. This frequently allows limited-objective attacks against the wings, flanks and rear of the enemy with the element of surprise, the frequent repetition of attacks at different locations, the rapid concentration of forces to eliminate dispersed weaker enemy forces and the employment of elements as a mobile reserve or the launching of immediate counterattacks during the defense.

Like the armored force, the armored reconnaissance force also captured the imagination of the public at large. After the fall of France in 1940, booklets such as this one—*Panzerspähtruppüberfällig* ("Armored Reconnaissance Patrol Overdue")—were produced for the youth market.

In general, direct combat was to be avoided, unless it was to eliminate the enemy's reconnaissance patrols or the effort expended did not jeopardize the over-all requirements of the reconnaissance mission. In cases where the reconnaissance battalion was moving against an enemy occupying a piece of terrain, envelopment was the preferred method of attack or movement. In such cases, the manual stressed that armored cars were especially well suited for deep flanking movements. Whenever an attack had to be conducted against enemy forces occupying a line, in order to break through to gain freedom of maneuver to continue the reconnaissance effort, the forces were to be concentrated against a specific weak point. In such instances, they were to be reinforced with additional forces. As a practical matter, this reinforcement—whether through engineer, artillery, armored forces, or a combination of all three—was soon habitual in actual combat zones.

When the battalion was forced to defend, it was to attempt to find a fighting position where it could force the enemy to attack along a narrow front. In addition, the "flanks of the reconnaissance battalion have to be secure through the terrain or other forces. It is generally recommended that a mobile reserve is formed. The reserve can be committed in defending against an enemy envelopment, in interdicting an enemy force that has penetrated into the main battle area or in tossing back an enemy force in an immediate counterattack."

The deliberate defense was the least preferred type of combat operation of the battalion. On the other hand, economy-of-force missions, in which the battalion had to guard, screen, or delay against an enemy force, was an easier task, since the battalion had the requisite speed to successfully disengage, as needed. As the manual states:

> The execution of a defense as a delaying action corresponds more to the nature of the reconnaissance battalion than the [deliberate] defense. It is especially important that the line of resistance is tied in to terrain that offers protection against armor. Armored cars are well suited for providing supporting fires and, in the case of weak enemy forces, to conduct immediate counterattacks. When disengaging from the enemy, they are often the last to remain in contact with the enemy.

After Germany was forced over to the strategic defensive in 1943, the use of reconnaissance assets as delaying forces and rear guards became the norm, rather than the exception. Since those actions generally required contact with the enemy, losses among the reconnaissance force, both in equipment and personnel, rose correspondingly.

Section 3 also attempts to define procedures for conducting reconnaissance. It starts by delineating the difference between armored reconnaissance patrols conducted for operational reconnaissance (corps assets reporting to a field army) and those conducted for tactical purposes (the reconnaissance battalions of armor, light and mechanized infantry divisions). Although maximums are indicated in the preceding section concerning sector width and spacing in front of the divisional sector for battalions, this section basically states that sectors "and the lead out front will be based on the situation and the mission." The commander determines the size and the composition of the patrols he is to send out to accomplish the division mission. According to paragraph 34, they "should never be stronger than necessary to conduct the mission. As a minimum, however, they have to consist of at least two vehicles (including a radio vehicle)."

The manual further defines five types of reconnaissance patrols:

- Heavy armor reconnaissance patrols (heavy armored cars)
- Light armored reconnaissance patrols (light armored cars)
- Mixed armored reconnaissance patrols (heavy and light armored cars)
- Reinforced armored reconnaissance patrols (armored reconnaissance patrols with attached motorcycle infantry, engineers or elements of the senior command)
- Motorcycle infantry patrols.

The types of patrols deployed were dependent upon the mission and the commander's assessment of the enemy situation, the terrain and the road network. Generally, if the battalion had two armored car troops, one of the troops was kept in reserve,

It was not uncommon to see armored vehicles on the roadways of prewar Germany, either on exercise or simply to test road worthiness after repairs or maintenance, as seems to be the case with this *Sd.Kfz. 223 (Fu)*.
JIM HALEY

although exceptions were granted when the reconnaissance zone was especially large or there was an extensive road network. The reason for holding back one of the armored car troops was to enable twenty-four-hour operations by allowing one troop to relieve another and to provide for contingencies. Further,

> 38. The situation and terrain determine whether the patrols will be dispatched from the assembly area of the motorized reconnaissance battalion or only after reaching a section of terrain farther to the front.
>
> The lead employed by the first wave of reconnaissance is to be measured by the distance to the enemy, the terrain and the range of the radio equipment.
>
> 39. Contact is maintained between the patrols and the leader of the motorized reconnaissance battalion by means of radio. When it is imperative to maintain radio silence so as not to betray the approach of the battalion, reports can be made by attached messenger vehicles and, if opportune, by means of the postal network. [The post offices in European countries had responsibility for telephone communications.]
>
> 40. The patrols will be assigned phase lines that have to be reported when crossed, even without enemy contact.

The general format for mission orders to patrol leaders contained the following:

- Leader, strength and organization of the patrol
- Mission
- Reconnaissance objective
- Movement route of advance
- Actions on reaching the objective (maintaining contact with the enemy, reconnaissance into the depths of the enemy or return)
- Location and time of patrol departure
- Details concerning actions (differs depending on the situation and terrain)—e.g., actions at certain terrain features or localities

The next two sections of the manual then go on to describe more mundane aspects of battalion activities that are generally common to all combat-arms battalions: Security on the march and security when resting. The next section, "March and Reporting Activities," covers a number of points that were specific to the conduct of those activities by reconnaissance forces:

> 54. The reconnaissance battalion establishes a reconnaissance reserve, reporting points and backup for its reconnaissance patrols. It moves forward by bounds. The length of the bounds is influenced by the closeness of the enemy and the nature of the terrain and its vegetation. As the distance to the enemy becomes closer, the length of the bounds is to be shortened.
>
> Terrain that is anticipated to be clear of the enemy is to be crossed rapidly, generally by marching at night.
>
> Uniform blackout measures taken by the vehicles during a night march must be established (dimmed or complete blackout).
>
> 55. The march column is to be formed by infiltration while moving. The battalion determines waypoints for the advance guard and the main body and establishes the times they are to be crossed by the lead elements.
>
> 56. The selection of the route of advance is based on the mission and the situation. Generally, a road that allows the battalion to leave it rapidly and reduces its visibility from the air is preferable to a road that goes across open terrain or crosses natural obstacles that are easily blocked (sector of terrains; bottlenecks).
>
> 57. The commander of a motorized reconnaissance battalion generally locates himself in the advance guard right behind the leader of the advance guard, since reports reach him rapidly and securely there and orders can be sent in a timely manner to the formations marching behind him.
>
> 58. Collocated with the battalion commander are generally the signals officers, the leader of the reconnaissance reserve and the commander of the heavy troop.
>
> The reconnaissance platoon generally moves with enough of its elements in the advance

GUIDELINES FOR TRAINING

The following guidelines were taken from an unidentified training manual or guide and were designed to provide instructors and leaders with ready answers to questions from subordinates or leaders from other branches who indicated incorrect notions about the capabilities and missions of armored reconnaissance forces. This type of *falsch / richtig* analysis was commonly used by the German Army in its training literature at the time and usually presented in table form like this.*

* Munzel, *Die deutschen gepanzerten Truppen*, 313–15.

Incorrect (*Falsch*)	Correct (*Richtig*)
1. Armored cars are also tanks. They can take a lot of punishment and are suitable for any type of fighting.	Armored cars are not "tanks." Their name alone demonstrates their properties. (Scouting armored vehicle) [A *Panzerspähwagen* is literally an armored "peering" vehicle; a *Panzerkampfwagen*, an armored fighting vehicle.]
2. Armored cars are cross-country capable, after all. It'll get through.	Believe the patrol leader; he knows perfectly well the limits of his vehicles. The armored car is limited in its cross-country ability. In addition, the vehicles are not immediately ready for operations again after having been used for some time.
3. "Armored cars will provide security at night."	By themselves, armored cars are not suited for pulling night security. It is only to be done in conjunction with riflemen. If the crew is too tired from operations during the day, then pull the armored car back.
4. Armored car patrol will reconnoiter at night toward . . .	Armored car patrol is not normally employed at night. Poor visibility! Engine gives away its location from afar. Forces easily fall into traps.
5. Leave a stationary patrol in place during the day when taken under fire.	Give the patrol freedom of movement! Its strength is its agility.
6. Leave distant patrols in contact with the enemy until darkness.	Either withdraw when it turns dark or leave in place as a stationary listening post. It then needs to change its position.
7. Prescribe an exact route for the patrol!	Only a patrol moving ahead of the lead elements of a battalion will have its route prescribed. Otherwise, only issue a reconnaissance mission and order a general line of march.
8. Just send the weapons vehicles ahead; leave the radio vehicle behind!	The patrol unit is always at least two vehicles. It is only by doing that that reports can be submitted rapidly and new missions given.
9. Whenever close-in reconnaissance is conducted, divide the patrol into individual vehicles.	Always use at least two vehicles for a patrol, in case one is lost. Only send individual vehicles out as far as they can be seen.
10. Require constant operational readiness!	Readiness to move out only after between twenty and thirty minutes, when the vehicles are ready to move and the new mission is clear to every member of the crew. During the winter, allow the engines to warm up first.
11. The patrol itself should determine how the friendly minefields are laid out.	Allow the patrol to see the minefield plan. In case there are difficult lanes to negotiate, provide guides, especially when returning when it is dark.

Incorrect (*Falsch*)	Correct (*Richtig*)
12. Employ the 7.5cm 8-wheeled armored car platoon or 8-wheeled vehicles by themselves while screening or reconnoitering.	Only employ those heavy vehicles in support of light armored cars.
13. Patrols sent to the flanks to establish friendly contact are pressed into the service of other officers for different missions.	Only the [battalion] commander has command over his own battalion. Do not allow patrols to be impressed into different service; if necessary, send a radio inquiry.
14. Order the patrol to establish observation points based on the map.	Allow the patrol leader to have freedom of movement. It is not until you are on the terrain that you see the best opportunities for observation.
15. Order a standing patrol to constantly remain on the radio!	Only the battalion radio is constantly on "receive." The patrol reports immediately when it see something important and is only on "receive" at specified times. Spare batteries and radio operators!
16. Urge the patrol to speed up by means of radio or messenger.	The patrol leader and the patrol leader alone is responsible for the mission and his forces. The situation cannot be judged from the rear.
17. Speed is of the essence! Move immediately from "A" through "B" to "C" and determine whether there are enemy forces there.	Thoroughly brief the patrol on the battalion's situation, the enemy situation, the mission and the location of the forward-most forces and the neighboring forces.
18. Use the patrol as the lead element when attacking a village or woods.	Use the armored cars to interdict enemy forces pulling back by means of envelopment.
19. My grenadier company cannot advance here. There are two machine guns over there along the woodline. Move forward and take them out. Or: Over there are some bunkers; probably unoccupied. You can move passed them without any problems. Or: Why are you taking so long to observe? Move with a sense of purpose. There's nothing there.	The armored car is only conditionally suited for combat. It cannot hit the dirt and, when fired upon by antitank guns, cannot make itself any smaller. Its strengths are in its great speed, its (limited) firepower, it great operating range and the distance of its radio coverage. So, you need to ask: How can you help me best in this situation?
20. Detach an armored car for the artillery observer at Point X.	Although armored cars are well suited for artillery observation, they must retain their freedom to operate.
21. Stay where you are and tow this truck out of the ditch.	An armored car is not a prime mover. Only in exceptional circumstance should it tow vehicles up to its own weight.

H. Dv. 299/11 c

Nur für den Dienstgebrauch!

Ausbildungsvorschrift

für die

Panzertruppe

(A. V. Pz.)

Heft 11 c

Richtlinien für Führung und Kampf der Panzer-Aufklärungs-Abteilung (gp)

Vom 15. 8. 44

Heeresdienstvorschift 299/11 of 1944 for the armored reconnaissance battalion. MICHAEL H. PRUETT

> guard (1st section), so that necessary contact can be maintained with the reconnaissance patrols employed, with superior headquarters, with neighboring reconnaissance formations and within the march column proper. The remainder of the signals platoon remains with the main body.

As with all reconnaissance activities, timely reporting is critical and the radio was often considered by commanders in the field to be the most powerful weapon in the battalion's arsenal. This is stressed in the following two paragraphs:

> 68. Information concerning the enemy is only of value if it reaches the commander in a timely manner. If information concerning the enemy is lacking, the reporting of the location of the reconnaissance patrol or the motorized reconnaissance battalion can be of importance to the superior headquarters.
>
> 69. Initial contact with the enemy is always to be reported, unless other orders have been issued. If possible, the strength and combat arm is to be indicated. It is especially important to report enemy movement and the direction of movement early to the superior commander.

Reconnaissance was an ongoing requirement, since the terrain and the enemy situation could change rapidly, especially in fluid situations, such as movements to contact. To that end, single patrols might not always capture the information needed by the higher commander:

> Frequently, the first employment of reconnaissance patrols will not suffice in sufficiently clarifying the enemy situation in the reconnaissance area or satisfying the missions assigned by superior headquarters. Intensifying reconnaissance efforts in the direction the enemy has been determined will often be necessary based on the initial reports. By means of increasingly focused individual missions that are given to subsequent reconnaissance patrols, which increasingly concentrate on details, the effort must be made to complete the picture of the enemy. When the enemy situation changes, it may be necessary to send out additional reconnaissance efforts.
>
> The commander of the reconnaissance battalion must be prepared at all times for enemy countermeasures in the reconnaissance area of operations. If reports from individual reconnaissance patrols are not received and it is believed that they may have been lost after contact with the enemy, then the dispatching of new reconnaissance patrols will be necessary.

While the above manual seems to be relatively detailed and comprehensive, one only need to review its 1944 counterpart, *HdV 299-11c*, dated 15 August 1944, to see how five years of war had both finely tuned the practical aspects of the manual as well as expanded the scope of the missions and capabilities of an armored reconnaissance battalion. The "Guidelines for Command and Control and Combat Employment of the Armored Reconnaissance Battalion (Armored)" wastes no time in diving directly into the subject matter (emphasis in the original):

I. Nature and Missions

1. The **Armored Reconnaissance Battalion (Armored)** is the eyes of an armored division. Its **particular nature** lies in the ability to switch between **reconnaissance** and **fighting**. It is **fast, maneuverable** and **capable of crossing all types of terrain**.

Based on its being equipped with numerous armored vehicles and automatic weapons and possessing a wide operating radius, the battalion is also capable of conducting reconnaissance through force.

2. The **main mission** of the battalion is the **conduct of tactical reconnaissance** for the division, so that, in supplementing aerial reconnaissance, the prerequisites for its employment can be created. In addition, the battalion is suitable for the execution of **combat missions**.

Those are:

(1.) Employment as an advance guard.

(2.) Advances into the rear and flanks of the enemy.

(3.) Pursuit.

(4.) Screening of gaps along the flanks, in the rear and to the front.

(5.) Screening of withdrawal movements.

(6.) Advancing into enemy air-landed and parachute formations; destroying, sealing off or monitoring them.

(7.) Masking of friendly movements.

3. Those responsible for reconnaissance are the armored scout sections. Combat power and support are provided by the armored reconnaissance companies and the heavy company.

4. Reconnaissance is only successful when the battalion is **employed in a timely manner**, in order to get the necessary head start (time—3–4 hours; space—up to 100 kilometers).

5. To conduct its reconnaissance, the battalion is assigned a movement zone (reconnaissance zone). Unless there are special reasons (advance guard), it is not to be limited to a **single** route. The width of the reconnaissance sector can be up to 60 kilometers; in the case of open flanks, even more.

6. When given separate **combat missions**, the battalion is to be reinforced with **mobile antitank elements** (self-propelled antitank guns, tank destroyers, assault guns), **engineers**, and **artillery**.

7. Combat with tanks or strong enemy defensive forces is to be avoided, so as to be able to advance at another location. The **weak armor** of the armored cars and the *SPW's* **prohibits their use as tanks**.

8. **The battalion fights mounted**. That is the only way that that armor, maneuverability, and strong firepower can be fully exploited.

9. Every type of reconnaissance is to also be simultaneously used to scout roads and terrain and report to the division in a timely manner.

10. Advancing and fighting across the breadth of the sector is a hallmark of its organization. Pressed together in a small area, it cannot be completely effective.

11. **Every splitting up of the force** by assignment of dual missions calls the success of the operation into question.

12. **Short-term** missions, which can be performed through movement, correspond to the organization and equipment of the battalion. Any combat operations lasting a longer time bring about increased attrition and, as a result, reduced capabilities.

What stands out when comparing the two texts is the addition of fighting as part of its capabilities, inasmuch as its "particular nature lies in the ability to switch between reconnaissance and fighting." While pre-war theory acknowledged that the reconnaissance battalion might have to fight on occasion, the thinking had evolved in the course of battlefield experience into giving the battalion a combat mission as well. Its main mission is still the conduct of tactical reconnaissance, but the battalion is also "suitable for the execution of combat missions." To that end, seven combat missions are listed for which the battalion is suitable.

Two *Sd.Kfz. 223 (Fu)* vehicles lined up on a road. They belong to *Aufklärungs-Abteilung (mot) 5*, which is easily determined by the unique battalion symbol painted on the front left fender. JIM HALEY

Below: Scouts stand in front of their *Sd.Kfz. 232 (Fu) (6-Rad)* vehicles, lined up in a motor pool. This image was probably taken around 1935 since the national insignia ("eagle") is not present on either the *Panzer* jackets or the berets. The turrets have had form-fitted tarpaulins placed over them to protect the vehicle interior from the elements. It was also common German practice to christen vehicles in accordance to a unit- or battalion-dictated formula. In this case, the name of choice was apparently that of famous German generals, as indicated by "Gneisenau" on the middle vehicle (names on the other two vehicles cannot be deciphered). JIM HALEY

This evolution in thinking was based on the changed tactical and operational scenarios the German Army faced with the onset of the campaign in the East and the ultimate surrender of the strategic offense to the strategic defense. Early in the fighting against the Soviet Union, the forces were in frequent contact with one another, obviating the need for tactical reconnaissance (combat reconnaissance talking its place). With front-line elements capable of conducting their own battlefield reconnaissance, reconnaissance battalions increasingly began to be used for flank and rear guard and screening missions. When local battlefield success allowed a penetration of substance, the reconnaissance battalions were called into action in a more traditional role, but they were often a part of *ad hoc* combat formations—*Kampfgruppen* (battle groups)—since their own organic assets were often insufficient in dealing adequately with the oftentimes superior Soviet armored or antitank elements encountered. Even after organizations were changed, e.g., the *Kradschützen* abandoning their motorcycles for half-tracks to provide more combat power, the numbers of personnel or equipment were frequently insufficient to make up the difference. The manual specifically directs that when "given separate combat missions, the battalion is to be reinforced with mobile antitank elements (self-propelled antitank guns, tank destroyers, assault guns), engineers, and artillery."

The leadership within the armored reconnaissance battalion is once again stressed. As in the pre-war publication, the leaders of the units had to be "bold" and "agile." The concept of *Auftragstaktik* (mission-type orders) is emphasized since

> 14. The battalion needs to be informed about the **intent** of the division so as to be able to act **independently** in the event of signals disruptions.
>
> Unity of effort is a requirement as well as a massing of available heavy weapons:
>
> 18. Keeping forces together for **unified, simultaneous** employment is essential.

Further:

> 22. By using the **mortar** and **cannon platoons**, the commander is in the position to decisively influence the fight by means of establishing a main effort for fires. The **unified** employment of the platoons is a prerequisite.The attachment of individual sections to the armored reconnaissance companies is only justifiable when operations are being conducted on a broad front, in broken-up terrain or separate employment.

As always in discussing command and control, the German concept was to have leadership far forward, even the battalion commander, whose forces were frequently spread out across a wide front. The commander was to place himself in the "hot spot" of the fight. In addition, the commander was to have the following with him: commander of the heavy company; commanders of the attached weapons; battle staff; and at least two reserve patrol sections. The battle staff consisted of adjutant; liaison officer; signals officer; battalion surgeon; messengers and orders bearers; as well as communications centers needed for command & control and reconnaissance traffic.

As was common with formations below division and brigade level, written orders were to be the exception, rather than the norm. They were to be "[r]apid, unmistakable and short." It was felt that verbal orders made the strongest impression. As was common in the German Army, the orders were to be paraphrased back to the issuer by the recipient to ensure they were properly understood. Once in combat, command and control were to be exercised by voice radio. Based on what had become practical experience in the Soviet Union, vehicles used for messenger purposes were to travel in pairs.

In the third major section of the manual, tactical reconnaissance and reporting is covered. Once again, the fact that information about the enemy can often only be gained by fighting is highlighted:

> **Complete clarity** concerning the enemy will often only be brought about by **fighting**, especially through bold and aggressive operations directed against him.

Patrols were to initially follow the "main roads," with the first wave of reconnaissance establishing contact with the enemy. The commander would dispatch more patrols, as necessary, particularly to add density to the reconnaissance effort or whenever initially dispatched patrols had not reported for some time. Given the mix of wheeled, half-track, and occasionally even fully tracked vehicles within the later-war reconnaissance battalions, the roles of each type of vehicle were specifically defined:

> Armored cars **(wheeled)** are to be used when there are good road and terrain conditions, which allow them to exploit their speed for **long-range objectives; half-track; and fully tracked vehicles** are to be used on poor road and terrain condition, especially to add **density to the reconnaissance**. To conduct combat reconnaissance in terrain where the wheeled patrols are limited exclusively to improved roads, the employment of mixed patrols, consisting of both wheeled and halftrack/fully tracked vehicles, is imperative.

Situations are discussed in which the commander needs to reinforce his patrols. These include reconnaissance against extended obstacles and barriers, waterways, the occupation of important sectors or terrain, situations where enemy outposts or other reconnaissance elements are expected, the execution of demolition missions and reconnaissance through partisan-held terrain or under conditions of limited visibility (night, fog, woods, mountains, and so on). As can be seen by the scenarios listed, augmentation by combat engineers was anticipated as a frequent necessity.

In keeping with the idea that the radio was one of the more important weapons of the reconnaissance soldier, there is extensive coverage of what is to be reported (as standard operating procedures) and when:

> The **Battalion Commander** evaluates the reports of the patrols and follows up in the case of discrepancies. He will render a **summary report** to the **division**:
>
> (1.) After important sectors have been reached.
>
> (2.) By time intervals (every 1 to 2 hours).
>
> Important reports will be forwarded immediately. **It is better to report frequently and succinctly rather than infrequently and long.** In the case of a fundamental change in the situation or if important documents are captured, an officer will be sent to inform the division.

The content of reports to higher entities is also spelled out:

> Reports to the division contain:
>
> (1.) **Estimate of the enemy situation**: Location; actions and direction of movement; type; strength; deployment (gaps); organization; appearance of tanks and antitank guns; chemical obstacles.
>
> (2.) **Terrain data**: Evaluation of the roads, bridges, fords, terrain difficulties and information concerning barriers, terrain enhancement and obstacles.
>
> (3.) **Friendly situation**: Location; intended measures; casualties.

Route reconnaissance was considered to be a part of every mission and all significant aspects of trafficability and terrain were to be reported immediately as well.

After discussing march organization and discipline, topics that apply to almost all combat formations, the manual goes on to discuss "Deployment for Combat." The guidance states that there were "no templates for deployment" and that it was "determined by the terrain, the enemy situation and the intended method" of engagement. When the situation was uncertain, the units were to be deployed along a narrow and deep front, thus allowing the commander the latitude to maneuver as needed once contact was made by the lead element. If the enemy situation was known (e.g., continuous front lines) or the terrain dictated, then the battalion was to deploy across a wide frontage.

In keeping with the emphasis of the battalion's ability to fight, offensive operations are covered in Chapter 6 of the manual. It starts with general instructions for conducting those types of operations:

Training: "Sweat Spares Blood"

It's an old German military adage that *Schweiß spart Blut* ("sweat spares blood"), which means that a rigorous training program ensures that battle-inexperienced troops have a better chance of survival in their baptisms of fire. The German Army also practiced that adage, and its training programs were probably second-to-none in the prewar years. It was superior German training, coupled with flexible leadership and well-defined doctrine, that allowed the Germans to compensate for inferior numbers and occasionally inferior equipment. As the war lengthened and expanded in scope, the Germans were unable to sustain the rigorous training pace of the peacetime army. In addition, the continued attrition of the leadership ranks, particularly at the junior level, virtually assured a continuous decline in quality that also contributed in part to the inevitable downfall.

Those factors also weighed heavily on the reconnaissance force, but because it and the other mechanized and armored forces shared a certain *élan*, they were called upon to be the backstop for the less mobile elements of the army and were often able to achieve far more than their mere numbers would indicate.

The training for the force could be geared toward the individual soldier, the crew, the section, the platoon, and higher levels of command and also toward other service branches, but the end effect was directly related to the quality of the instruction and the instructors. The Germans insisted on after-action reports, thorough discussions of what transpired, and a debriefing of the entire unit or formation. In this image, a reconnaissance officer talks to some of his soldiers at the Bruck Training Area in modern-day eastern Austria in 1943.

In order to be effective, the training also had to be practical. Here an armored scout is tested by two noncommissioned officers next to a heavy armored car. Judging by the decorations on the front NCO, it must be later in the war, since he has both a Wound Badge and an Iron Cross, First Class. Although frontline units were reluctant to let personnel go, there was a huge demand for combat-experienced leaders on the home front in order to provide the best training possible, and it was not uncommon to see leaders detached for such duties for periods of time.

The ability to properly camouflage vehicles became increasingly important as the war continued and the Western Allies and the Soviet Union first gained air dominance, followed by air supremacy, especially on the Western Front. It was doubly important for the armored scout, since his mission was to see and hear and not to be seen or heard. While relatively easy to hide positions for individuals, the task for armored vehicles, particularly heavy armored cars with relatively high silhouettes such as this one, was exponentially more difficult. During the wintertime, when deciduous trees lost their foliage, the task was made even harder.

Voice radio communications was another area in which all armored scouts and other reconnaissance personnel had to be conversant. While other types of formations could rely on specially trained school personnel to maintain continuous communications, the very nature of reconnaissance—operating alone in front of friendly forces or performing economy-of-force missions—demanded that all soldiers know how to observe and to prepare and submit reports. Voice communication was the norm and could also be used when reporting to higher headquarters in exigent circumstances. For long-range communications, the Germans preferred Morse, for which specially trained personnel manned the radio cars. Here soldiers practice encryption and decryption using the famous Enigma encoder, which the Allies eventually broke, to overrated advantage. Generally, the Enigma coding device remained an effective means of submitting secure messages throughout the war.

While the ability to move tactically on the battlefield was paramount, it was also imperative to train soldiers in road marching so that march discipline could be maintained. Proper dispersal and weapons orientation assured protection of the force, while intervals and maintenance of speed allowed planners to ensure a smoother traffic flow in the congested rear area. As motorcycle-sidecar combinations move past, soldiers from a reconnaissance unit take a break from their road march along one of the recently constructed German freeways, the *Autobahn*.

A column of light armored cars, *Sd.Kfz. 221's*, move out along a dirt road during a prewar exercise. Note the maintenance of exact intervals between the vehicles. JIM HALEY

A motorcyclist awaits orders to move out. The *Sd.Kfz. 232 Fu (6-Rad)* behind him has oriented its guns over the right side of the vehicle. JIM HALEY

Below: While combat was downplayed in prewar training for reconnaissance forces, gunnery was still conducted to prepare crews for just such an eventuality. This image and the top image on the following page were taken in 1943 at the Bruck Training Area and show *Sd.Kfz. 232 (8-Rad)* armored cars preparing to fire and conducting night firing. While there were no night-sighting devices fielded at the time, gunnery training also included nighttime exercises to familiarize soldiers with the difficulties of firing in darkness. On moonlit nights, targets could sometimes be made out with the naked eye or binoculars, but usually assistance was needed to acquire and engage targets with any sort of accuracy—aerial flares, lights or fires purposely emplaced down range, or range cards and sketch maps.

Recovery operations were also part and parcel of the training of all armored vehicle crewmen. Here the recovery operation takes on a benign character as scouts and even civilians attempt to get a stuck truck from an unidentified reconnaissance battalion (see fenders) out of a ditch. During actual operations in a combat zone, the ability to quickly recover stuck, combat-damaged, or mechanically broken vehicles was of utmost importance. In addition to the sheer mechanics of retrieving the vehicle with another relatively lightweight vehicle, the effort was made more difficult by the prospect of being discovered by the enemy or by attempting the entire operation while receiving fire.

Driver training also consumed a great deal of unit time during training cycles, since many draftees reaching the training base before the war had never driven a vehicle before. The ranks were usually combed to see who had some sort of vehicle experience; those individuals were generally selected first for driver training on the tactical vehicles. In addition to learning how to drive, they also had to learn how to drive cross-country and move tactically. This was made all the more difficult by the fact that almost all German armored car designs—indeed, almost all German armored vehicles—were often underpowered and overengineered. Given the confusion in a combat situation, it is easy to see why so many vehicles got stuck, as relayed in countless firsthand reports. These two images show a cutaway *schwerer Panzerspähwagen Fu Sd. Kfz. 232 (6-Rad)* that was used for driver training. It appears that a second steering wheel has been added to the vehicle to enable the driving instructor to compensate for any novice mistakes. JIM HALEY

Since most long-distance movement by armored and mechanized infantry divisions was conducted by rail to avoid unnecessary wear and tear on vehicles and equipment, it was imperative that rail-loading procedures flowed seamlessly. This unit, believed to be from *Aufklärungs-Abteilung 6 (mot)*, which was initially part of *1. leichte Division* before ultimately being assigned to *6. Panzer-Division*, finishes tying down vehicles for the trip.

Once individual training was completed, the next step was to train the members of the crews in their functions and responsibilities. Before proceeding to training areas, exercises or demonstrations were often conducted at suitable areas within the garrisons. Here an *Sd.Kfz. 232* takes advantage of manmade smoke and orients its weaponry.

Hans=Wolfgang von Fabeck
Hauptmann und Adjutant der 4. Panzer=Division

Schulübungen für die Gefechtsausbildung im Aufklärungsdienst

(Die Besatzung des Einzelfahrzeugs im Rahmen des Spähtrupps)

1939/40
14 Aufgaben mit den entsprechenden Lageskizzen

Verlag „Offene Worte"
Berlin W 35

Jeder Nachdruck verboten

Exercises were outlined in training pamphlets and books such as this one, titled *Schulübungen für die Gefechtsausbildung im Aufklärungsdienst.* Once crews were given theoretical instruction and conducted a number of dry runs, they participated in exercises in the field under tactical and combat conditions. These included crossing bodies of water and negotiating obstacles.

Below: In addition to being able to report observations concerning the enemy to higher headquarters, the armored scout obviously had to know where he was at all times. Map reading was an essential skill and required constant practice. This *Unteroffizier* from *Aufklärungs-Abteilung 5* of *2. Panzer-Division* studies a map while members of his section provide security from their *Sd.Kfz. 13* light armored cars. JIM HALEY

The first three images of field training are attributed to *Aufklärungs-Abteilung 6 (mot)*, while the last one is from *Aufklärungs-Abteilung 1 (mot)*, serving briefly with *1. Kavallerie-Brigade*, before becoming a separate reconnaissance battalion and later being assigned to *3. Panzer-Division*. FIRST IMAGE COURTESY JIM HALEY

WH-72685

89. **Mounted attack exploiting speed** promises the greatest success. **The attack conducted against the flanks and rear while simultaneously fixing forces to the front is the preferred method of fighting.** Only difficult terrain and obstacles should force temporary dismounting.

90. The mission of tactical reconnaissance it to determine the weaknesses of the enemy. Combat power and firepower are to be employed against those weaknesses. A surprise and rapid initiation of the attack, together with a sudden start to the fires of all weapons, is the goal.

The next subsection discusses the attack from a movement to contact, which is described as one of the "battalion's core competencies" and is recommended against an enemy, who "is not completely ready to defend." That type of operation required

Rapid and accurate estimate of the situation,
Bold and wholehearted **decisiveness**,
Courageous and powerful aggressiveness.

Deliberate (planned) attacks, pursuit operations and the deliberate (planned) defense are then discussed. Since the guidelines presented apply to virtually all combat arms, they will not be discussed here. These are followed by a discussion of "Disengaging and Withdrawals," a role for which the battalion seemed well suited, given its mix of heavy weapons, speed and maneuverability:

Whenever disengaging under combat, the battalion is in the position to disengage from the enemy and withdraw rapidly by using **its cross-country mobility and its armor protection**.

It is therefore suited to assume the role of rearguard for the division in screening withdrawal movements across a broad front.

Since this economy-of-force mission was increasingly entrusted to the divisional reconnaissance battalions in the later-war years, the doctrinal details of its execution are quoted at length here:

131. The battalion pulls back **by bounds from sector to sector**. A **passage point** is to be established in each sector. Strong **rearguards**, reinforced by antiarmor forces and heavy weapons, are to be left in contact with the enemy. They are to be employed in such a fashion that they can overwatch the sector as powerful patrol detachments or in a strongpoint fashion.The **main body of the battalion** holds the passage point.

132. The **withdrawal of the rearguards** only takes place on battalion **order**.

133. Withdrawal is possible both during the day and at night. Only extensive visibility and air superiority on the part of the enemy necessitates a withdrawal at night. Especially important is an **early extraction** of the elements not needed for fighting and **reconnaissance** and **marking** of the routes for the numerous vehicles.

134. The fighting will be conducted in a mobile fashion. The enemy is to be held up by constant advances into his flanks and rear. The employment of deception makes it difficult to determine friendly strength.

135. Artillery supports [the operation] either from firing positions in the battalion's passage point position or through the mobile employment of self-propelled batteries. Generous commitment of forward observers enables a responsive artillery and deceives the enemy.

136. Active reconnaissance in the flanks and the timely employment of forces—preferably, antiarmor weapons and engineers—are necessary to prevent a leapfrogging pursuit by fast enemy forces.

Aerial reconnaissance supports the fight by monitoring enemy movements.

137. Emplacement of obstacles slows down the enemy pursuit. The engineer platoon is capable of being employed to disrupt railway and communications facilities and the road network, both with and without demolitions. Smaller-scale disruptions are directed by the Battalion Commander. The division is responsible for directing larger-scale obstacles. The emplacement [of the obstacles] is to be assured

Another early image of the *Sd.Kfz. 232 (Fu) (6 Rad)* from the same unit seen in the previous image. As before, the soldiers do not wear national insignia. The prewar three-tone, hard-edged camouflage scheme is nicely displayed. JIM HALEY

through coordination with an engineer liaison officer or by the attachment of engineers.

138. In the case of river sectors that need to be crossed, **several crossing points** need to remain open depending on the width of the area of operations of the battalion. The blocking or the demolition of those points is only to be done by the rearguards. Maintaining only one crossing point forces the shifting of the withdrawal movement in the case it is lost by enemy air, partisans or advances.

139. **Contact** must be maintained with the friendly forces on the flanks and with the forces in the newly established main line of resistance of the division. Radio and messengers must be used exclusively to maintain **signals contact**.

140. Only **mechanically sound vehicles** are to be employed in this type of fighting. Maintenance and recovery assets are to be kept close at hand during the operations in the event of losses.

141. Increased importance must be placed on the evacuation and care of wounded. It is of decisive importance for the morale of the fighting forces.

When reading unit accounts of rearguard and delaying actions being conducted by divisions, one is generally surprised when the divisional reconnaissance assets are not used in this role.

The rest of the manual is taken up with guidance for special types of operations—forced crossings of waterways, operations under limited visibility, fighting in built-up areas, operations against partisans, operations against air-landed forces, fighting in woods, marshland, mountainous terrain and deserts, winter combat, and so on—that, by and large, are also generally applicable to all combat-arms formations.

Of course, the concrete advice and doctrinal guidance provided in the late-war manual was not created in a vacuum. Time permitting, extensive after-action reports were required at all levels of command. These formed an immense body of literature that was often disseminated to other troop formations whenever higher-level commanders found particularly well-written and/or informative reports. The Inspector General of the *Panzertruppe* also collected these reports and either distilled "lessons learned" through circulars or as part of its periodic publication, *Nachrichtenblatt der Panzertruppen* (Information Bulletin for the Armored Forces).[26] Several excerpts concerning actions of reconnaissance formations that were published there are posted in this chapter as sidebars. Naturally, that represents just a small fraction of publications, both official and privately published, which offered tips, tactics, and procedures for the reconnaissance force. As early as 1940, a training primer was published that offered fourteen exercises for combat training in reconnaissance for crews of armored cars. The *Schulübungen für die Gefechtsausbildung im Aufklärungsdienst*, written by then-*Hauptmann* Hans-Wolfgang von Fabeck, himself a reconnaissance officer, no doubt made use of recent experience in Poland, even though the exercises are couched in generic terms.

In the end, the proponents of a strictly intelligence-gathering role for the reconnaissance forces had to give way to a more flexible response that often saw the necessity for fighting for that information, even if only for a short period. This was generally acknowledged even in the early days of armored reconnaissance, even if the force structure did not necessarily reflect that. It was not that the Germans did not want more and heavier weaponry and vehicles capable of transporting scouts and deflecting the blows of an enemy force. Instead, it was more a question of "too much, too soon" in terms of rapidly expanding a force which the industrial base was ill prepared to support.

As Munzel states well, if somewhat harshly, in summarizing the German experience in fielding motorized reconnaissance forces:

> Ground reconnaissance by all forces had become more difficult as a result of the defensive firepower of modern weapons and the ability to maneuver. Timely recognition of the enemy's intent was more important than ever, however, since a motorized opponent was in a position of being able to regroup quickly or even being flown in.
>
> In general, tactical reconnaissance was no longer possible without a fight. Due to the increasing number of armor-defeating weapons, close-in reconnaissance by even mechanized forces became more and more difficult. It was only when the fronts were fluid or torn open through combat action that ground reconnaissance was still able to obtain information that was of more importance than at just at a local level. It was then that armored scouting sections were able to move into the enemy's area of operations, observe from a hidden position and report important enemy movements. If there was a continuous front, however, then reconnaissance efforts had to be limited almost entirely to infantry patrols, which could generally only determine details about the [enemy's] front lines. It was only through the combat actions of armored groups or infantry assault detachments supported by tanks and artillery that more detailed results were obtained.
>
> If combat-capable reconnaissance assets are missing, armored vehicles from the force must be temporarily used for *tactical reconnaissance*, especially during advances or during a mobile defense. This emergency measure did not work well, however. Speed and range were not sufficient enough to get to the enemy quickly, go around him and then gain a deeper insight. In addition, the sound of the tracks betrayed the location of the tank prematurely. The range of the radio equipment was frequently not long enough. The tank patrols then had to have a radio vehicle attached to them. In addition, they had to bring along extra fuel, either on their own vehicles or on another vehicle. In the generally broken and difficult terrain in the east, they often also needed support from engineers or grenadiers. That made command and control difficult and limited mobility con-

Personnel of an unidentified reconnaissance element prepare to move out from their garrison. Three different types of armored cars can be seen, as well as staff cars, trucks, and motorcycles.

Left: The vehicle commander of this *Sd.Kfz. 14 (Fu)* awaits orders to move out during a rest and maintenance halt along the road. JIM HALEY

siderably. Those types of patrols were also unable to cling to the enemy.

The 8-wheeled armored cars of the armored reconnaissance battalions were much better suited for such missions. Whenever possible, a few of those types of armored cars were attached to *Kampfgruppen*, which had been given relatively independent missions. Frequently, officer patrols in *Kübelwagen* or captured jeeps as well as squads from the route reconnaissance and engineer platoons of the battalions had to help out. That measure often led to casualties that bore no relationship to the results obtained.

The execution of close-in and battlefield reconnaissance was a particular weakness of the German forces. Since they were usually overextended and numerically very weak, they took pains to keep their forces together. The fear of being captured and the expected inhumane treatment in the east was also very large. In addition, the enemy understood how to camouflage himself very well, to set up ambushes and to keep his heavy weapons silent for a long time. Deserters and the eavesdropping on enemy radio traffic usually brought the best information. An attack usually required complete clarity concerning the strength and dispositions of the enemy.[27]

This opinion is shared somewhat by McGraph, albeit in discussing the reconnaissance forces of all the major combatants:

> After the war started and the combatants gained experience, much prewar theory, particularly that related to the sharp division between reconnaissance missions and combat actions, evaporated in the face of battlefield reality. Most telling, light reconnaissance forces often could not survive to effectively use their speed and nimbleness. As the war progressed, organizations adjusted, and most armies became heavier, either in design, by fielding heavier equipment, or through habitual augmentation.[28]

A favorite image for amateur soldier photographers, this one was taken from the driver's seat of an *Sd.Kfz. 13* and shows an alert scout taking aim with his MG 13. He wears an overcoat to help shield him from the cold in the open fighting compartment. JIM HALEY

One of the more mundane but absolutely essential duties of armored soldiers was the constant maintenance of his vehicle. In these images, soldiers of the *Reichswehr-Wehrmacht* transition period tend to *Sd.Kfz. 231* (both 6- and 8-wheel versions) and *Sd.Kfz 232 (Fu) (6-Rad)* vehicles. As was typical in a garrison environment, weapons were not generally mounted on the vehicles but stored in arms rooms. JIM HALEY

PERSONAL PHOTO ALBUM FROM AUFKLÄRUNGS-ABTEILUNG 2 (MOT)

With the prewar years being the formative ones for the newly established *schnelle Truppen*, it is no wonder that many unit soldiers liked to take pictures of their units, equipment, training, and comrades for loved ones back home. Empty photo albums with unit designations stamped on the covers and usually a history of the branch of service were sold at canteens on posts throughout Germany. These were then filled with images taken by the soldiers or with photos and postcards available at the canteens. Of course, basic civilian-style photo albums were also used, which makes it difficult to identify the owner's unit.

In some cases, it is possible to establish the original owners based on entries made. In most cases, however, unless the photo album comes directly from a family, the albums remain anonymous. Despite that, the units or formations can usually be identified, either through markings on vehicles or insignia worn by personnel. Since most prewar German vehicles displayed the tactical symbol of their formation, the element can be established as long as it is readily identifiable in an image. The same holds true in the case of uniforms, since prewar regulations called for distinctive ciphers and numerals to be placed on shoulder boards (officers) and straps (enlisted personnel) that frequently also allow for a rapid identification of the formation as long as the basic type of unit is known.

The photo album here comes from a scout assigned to *Aufklärungs-Abteilung 2 (mot)* of the *2. Infanterie-Division (mot)*. The division, which eventually became the *12. Panzer-Division*, was formed in 1935 as a regular infantry division. On 10 November 1938, the reconnaissance battalion was added to its rolls, initially with a motorcycle infantry troop (1st Troop) and an armored car troop (2nd Troop). The first two wartime commanders of the battalion were *Major/Oberstleutnant* Walter (1 September 1939 to August 1940—it is assumed that Walter assumed command prior to the outbreak and remained after) and *Major* Wolf (August 1940 to 1 October 1940). The majority of these images were probably taken around the time of the battalion's integration into the *2. Infanterie-Division (mot)*.

The cover of the canteen-purchased photo album for the battalion.

Below: Sample page from the text that usually accompanied such albums. This one includes a stock image of one of the first armored cars to be delivered to the armored reconnaissance forces, the *Sd.Kfz. 13*, which mounted a manually traversed 7.92mm machine gun in the center of the superstructure, which was manned by the vehicle commander. Although basically obsolete upon introduction, some of these vehicles saw active frontline service through the end of the campaign in Poland. Of interest here is the vehicle's *Reichswehr* license plate, which dates the image around the time of Hitler's accession to power in 1933.

h stark sein, das heißt, Panzerkräfte in ausreichendem Maße
ß sich häufig mit der Abwehr begnügen, um dann im Schwer-
fe in größter Stärke einsetzen zu können.
e Notwendigkeit der Panzerabwehr und ihrer Sonderwaffen zu
nzerwaffe ist die Panzerabwehrtruppe aus einem neu-
n eigenen Heer ergänzen beide einander in taktischer und
rt und Schild; als Feinde sind sie geeignet, das alte Sprich-
n Schwert das andere in der Scheide hält", also entweder
ein zu sichern oder im Kampf den Gegner zu lähmen, das
tzen.

motorisierte Aufklärung

ng wie für den Einsatz aller Waffengattungen ist ferner eine vorzügliche Aufklärung. Es ist selbstverständlich, daß sie im Zeitalter der Technik motorisiert ist. Mehr als die anderen Einheiten der Kraftfahrkampftruppe werden die Aufklärungsabteilungen von der Schnelligkeit ihres Motors Gebrauch machen können und müssen, um überraschend in den Feind vorzustoßen und seine Absichten aufzudecken. Kühn und verwegen muß die Truppe geführt werden; noch kühner und noch verwegener muß der einzelne Spähtrupp handeln, der der Erste am Feind ist — ganz auf seine verantwortungsvolle Aufgabe eingestellt, die ihn zum Auge und Ohr des oberen Truppenführers werden läßt ...!
Sein Gerät ist der leichte und der schwere Panzerspähwagen, die in Züge und Kompanien zusammengefaßt sind.

Die motorisierten Schützen

Den Reigen der Kraftfahrkampftruppe beschließen die motorisierten Schützen, die in Verbänden bis zu Regimentsstärke im Zusammenwirken mit den anderen Teilen nicht unwesentlich

Photo Schröter, Osnabrück

Leichter Panzerspähwagen im Gelände

7

Opposite page: Images such as these—available in garrison canteens as post cards—often complemented the personal photography in a soldier's photo album. The cartoon drawing is actually quite telling in representing the various roles and skills of the scouts. The vehicle commander is seen observing but also carrying the traditional lance of the German cavalry. The dismounted armored car crewman carries a variety of weapons, from handheld to antitank rifles and a machine gun, demonstrating the need for proficiency in each. He also carries aiming stakes, representative of indirect-fire weapons, such as the artillery, for which he was expected to be able to call for fire. The pouch behind him is probably a report satchel, since the scout was expected to submit a variety of reports concerning the enemy forces observed. Finally, he also carries a pair of large shears, representative of the combat-engineer skills needed to breach obstacles. In short, the armored scout was a jack-of-all-trades who needed a variety of skill sets to accomplish his missions.

The album's owner was not camera shy. The scout is usually seen wearing the armored vehicle special-purpose uniform, designed to be worn while performing duties on the vehicle. Based on popular ski clothing of the time, the black uniform was intended to hide the grease and oil stains from servicing an armored vehicle. The uniform proved so popular that it was frequently worn as a walking-out uniform as well, although regulations forbade that. The uniform jacket seen here, commonly referred to as a "wrap" because of the overlapping front panels, is the first version, which was introduced in 1935 and replaced by a second version around 1937. As was common with prewar uniforms, a soldier's unit of assignment could be determined from a combination of branch colors (*Waffenfarben*) and a combination of numerical designators and/or ciphers. The chain-stitched A/2 on the shoulder straps identifies this soldier as being assigned to *Aufklärungs-Abteilung 2 (mot)*. The one field-gray uniform is the parade-dress uniform, the *Waffenrock*. Since he is wearing an officer-grade silver wire embroidered national insignia, which was permissible for enlisted soldiers as long as they paid for it themselves, he was probably a career soldier.

The line of armored cars consists of the *Sd.Kfz. 231 (6-Rad)* and the radio version, the *Sd.Kfz. 232 (6 Rad)*, based on a commercial truck chassis of the time. These were introduced in the early 1930s and gradually started being replaced by 8-wheeled versions of the same designation in 1937. Due to the chronic shortage of purpose-built armored cars, these early 6-wheeled versions were employed in all major theaters until the middle of the war.

The entrance to the *Panzer-Kaserne* (Armor Barracks) in Stettin, home of *Aufklärungs-Abteilung 2 (mot)* as well a host of other motorized formations. One of the battalion's soldiers is standing guard at the front gate, the subject of much interest for local schoolboys.

Men of the battalion, most likely the 2nd Troop, form up in front of their barracks in the black *Panzer* uniform. A number of the soldiers wear the marksmanship lanyard, the *Schützenschnur.*

The battalion forms up for some sort of ceremony—perhaps a change of command—near the motor pools. A delegation of higher-ranking officers and dignitaries stands off to the left, while two *Sd.Kfz. 231 (8-Rad)* armored cars flank the elements in the background.

A group of radio armored cars put on some sort of display for a group of military and civilian onlookers. In the foreground is the *leichter Panzerspähwagen Fu Sd. Kfz. 223* while the *schwerer Panzerspähwagen Fu 232 (6-Rad)* is in the back.

The photo album owner poses on an early *schwerer Panzerspähwagen Fu Sd.Kfz. 232 (6-Rad)* with a comrade. As was typical in most armored reconnaissance battalions, the individual armored cars carried names significant in German military history. In this case, it is named after the Siege of Kolberg in 1807, a failed effort on the part of Napoleon to take the last remaining Prussian stronghold in Pomerania.

Members of the battalion view a Czech armored car, the Skoda PA III/OA vz. 27. This vehicle was taken after the occupation of Czechoslovakia in October 1938.

Heavy and light armored cars of the battalion are lined up in a motor pool. They have had protective form-fitted tarpaulins placed over the turrets and open superstructures of the vehicles. Of interest is the tarpaulins, which have also been painted in the distinctive prewar three-tone camouflage pattern.

At first glance, these images would seem to show the motorcycle Infantry troop of the battalion, but given the lack of weaponry and the large number of motorcycles without sidecars, it may well be the battalion's motorcycle messenger section.

The owner of the album can be seen above left. Perhaps he later transferred to the messenger section?

In prewar exercises, chemical warfare training was frequently stressed, given the experiences of the Great War. Motorcyclists were expected to be able to drive for extended periods while wearing the cumbersome gas mask. This particular soldier rides what appears to be a civilian model of unknown type pressed into military service.

Scouts of the battalion take a break after some sort of training activity, probably a road march, based on the dusty faces and the presence of driving goggles. The radio armored cars either did not mount their weapons or they have already been removed for post operations maintenance, as suggested by the tools and equipment on the front slope of the lefthand vehicle, which would be a logical place for cleaning weapons.

The scouts wear the padded crash helmet and beret combination as well as what appear to be coveralls. This photograph was probably taken around 1935 or 1936, when the national "eagle" was not yet uniformly worn above the cockade on the berets.

This *schwerer Panzerspähwagen Fu Sd.Kfz. 232 (8-Rad)* was named after the Siege of Stralsund of 1628, which resulted in the first defeat of the Catholic League and the entry of Sweden into the Thirty Years' War.

One of the last images from the album is this *leichter Panzerspähwagen Sd.Kfz. 222*, seen probably around the time of the campaign in Poland. Following the fighting there in September 1939, the white identification crosses were generally removed from combat vehicles since they provided the enemy with a good aiming point.

CHAPTER 2

Organization

OVERVIEW

No matter the size of the military element, its basic organization, personnel authorizations, and equipment are dictated by some sort of organizational document in all modern armies. In Germany, the directorate at the Army High Command with overall responsibility for establishing, maintaining, issuing, updating, rescinding, and overseeing the implementation of these documents was the *Organizations-Abteilung*. It issued the *Kriegsstärkenachweisungen*[1]—literally, the "Wartime Strength Authorizations"—which were the equivalent of the Tables of Organization and Equipment used in the U.S. Army. While each of the service branches of the German Army provided input and staff officers to the *Organizations-Abteilung*, the directorate had the job of standardizing the formats and maintaining the historical records for all the ground forces.[2]

While it is relatively easy to simplify what constituted the combat power of a fighting formation, the authorization document was the product of intense staff work, since it had to determine not only the number of weapons and weapons systems in a unit[3] or larger formation—a daunting task in itself when weapons and systems were updated, retired or replaced, and introduced constantly—but the personnel, command-and-control, and support requirements as well. In the case of personnel, not only the numbers but also the ranks and specialties of the individuals needed to be determined. Of course, they also needed some sort of administrative apparatus to support them in matters such as records maintenance, payroll issues, continuing professional education, leaves and passes, and so on. For command-and-

An *Sd.Kfz. 222* rolls along a road in terrain that appears reminiscent of Tunisia, thus placing this late in the campaign, most likely in 1943. The crew has covered the muzzle of the 2cm cannon in an effort to prevent dust from entering the barrel and clogging the mechanism.

control purposes, the commander needed a staff, communications, and vehicular support (above and beyond the commander's requirement for his own combat vehicle or equipment). Depending on how logistics was viewed, the bulk of the day-to-day requirements were handled within the unit or somewhere else within the parent formation. This included not only the obvious requirements of "beans and bullets," but also the ability to maintain and repair equipment, receive and issue supplies, refuel, and feed the force.

As a result, organizational documents are in constant flux, with efforts made to improve them undertaken constantly, either pushed down from higher commands or received as recommendations from the field. As with most large bureaucratic entities, the actual adherence to the *KStN's* varied in practice, either through design, chance or benign neglect on the part of commanders in the field. This especially applies to the armored reconnaissance formations, as with much of the armored force, since the *KStN's* in the early years often varied from formation to formation, a situation that occurred as a result of continually evolving doctrinal development, coupled with chronic shortages of the equipment that was theoretically needed.[4]

SQUARING THE CIRCLE: THEORY MEETS REALITY

On 15 March 1935, Hitler declared he was no longer bound by the restrictions the Treaty of Versailles placed on his nation's military. He was not only throwing off the shackles of the restrictive treaty in terms of what types of organizations and equipment the 100,000-man force was allowed to have, but he was also flaunting it with his proposals for an expanded military that initially called for two cavalry divisions, three armored divisions, two cavalry brigades, three armored brigades, and ten sets of corps troops, which included six motorized reconnaissance battalions.[5]

Four years later, Hitler's vision had been largely realized, and the peacetime army consisted of thirty-nine infantry divisions (1st through 36th, 44th through 46th), five armored divisions (1st through 5th), two separate armored brigades (4th and 6th), three mountain divisions (1st through 3rd), and four light divisions (1st through 4th). All of these major formations had a wartime reconnaissance asset, and some were authorized an armored reconnaissance element.[6]

Upon mobilization, this peacetime force was to be increased by an additional fifty-one infantry divisions, for a total of eighty-six infantry and four motorized infantry divisions. To create these new divisions, the term *Welle* was used, which is usually translated as "wave" although "iteration" might be more instructive. By the end of the war, some thirty-five *Wellen* had been introduced, each represented by a distinct *KStN* and most with relatively significant organizational differences.[7] The "waves" were initially required in order to address some of the unique needs created by the war—e.g., occupation and security duties for which frontline combat forces could not be spared.[8] Most of the subsequent *Wellen* did not foresee any armored reconnaissance asset being part of the divisional force. Whether that was by design (the infantry divisions were not expected to perform much in the way of reconnaissance other than battlefield reconnaissance, which fell within the skill set of all of the divisional combat forces) or because of a lack of resources remains an open question.

Within the divisions "owned" by the cavalry—i.e., the four light divisions and, initially, the fast troops (the armored and motorized infantry divisions)—there was also a great deal of non-standardization, with no two armored or light divisions being exactly alike. The issues of non-standardization were exacerbated by the onset of hostilities. The great success of the armored forces in Poland in 1939 and the Low Countries in 1940 greatly impressed Hitler, who ordered a doubling of the armored force. As has already been mentioned, the German armaments industry could not keep pace with the theoretical increase in numbers of weapons systems. The doubling of the force was accomplished by bureaucratic sleight of hand: each of the armored divisions lost one of its *Panzer-Regimenter*, and the *leichte Divisionen* of the cavalry were reorganized into *Panzer-Divisionen*. While the increased production of the heavier and more modern *Panzer III's* and *Panzer IV's* was supposed to offset the loss of combat power, those benefits were never really seen. The armored reconnaissance battalions of the armored divisions

Gültigkeitslisten: List of Approved Publications

As organizations constantly changed and evolved, so did the *KStN's* governing them. To avoid confusion, periodic lists were published that specified which organization documents were in effect and which had been rescinded. Several late-war *Gültigkeitslisten* are preserved in the U.S. National Archives.*

The ones shown here are from 15 July 1944 and demonstrate the difficulty of remaining current with force-structure documents. As is obvious from the handwritten entries, new documents were added and old documents were rescinded faster than the ability of the *Organizations-Abteilung* to publish changes. The first column details the applicable *KStN*, while the second column lists the title of the *KStN* in an abbreviated format. The next two columns list the date of the authorized organization documents, and the final column is reserved for notes, which almost always reference the *Allgemeine Heeresmitteilungen* (General Army Announcements), where changes for the force were dictated.

The *Gültigkeitsliste* dated 20 January 1945 appears to have been an interim document, since it was typed. As opposed to the previously seen listing, this document provides the date not only of the current *KStN*, but also of the one it superseded and the preliminary document that had been issued by the *Generalinspekteur der Panzertruppe*. This probably represented an attempt to clean up the printed lists, which were becoming overcrowded with handwritten entries.

The final list shows applicable documents for training and replacement elements, which were likewise governed by a series of *KStN's*.

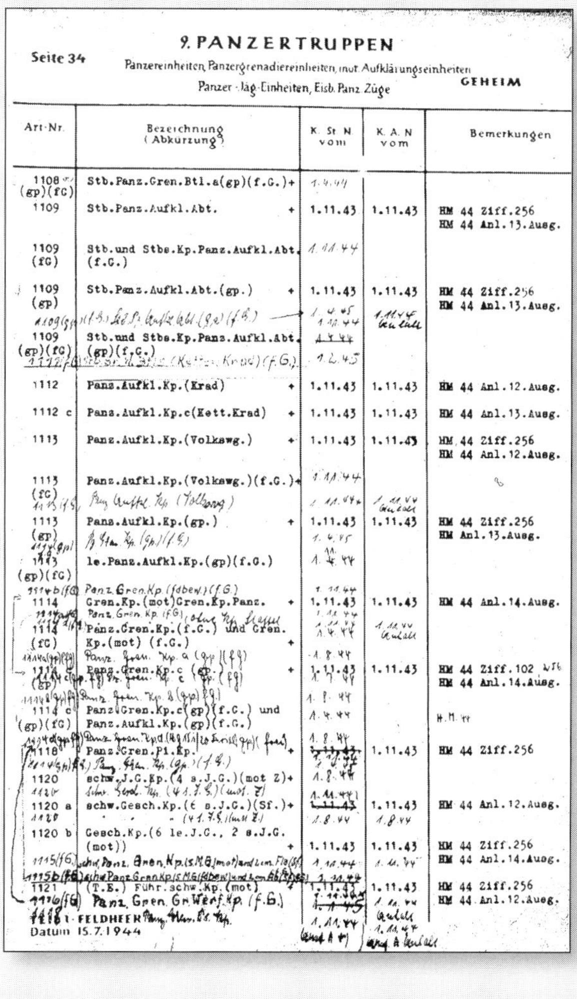

Seite 34

9. PANZERTRUPPEN

Panzereinheiten, Panzergrenadiereinheiten, mot. Aufklärungseinheiten

Panzer-Jäg-Einheiten, Eisb. Panz. Züge

GEHEIM

Art-Nr.	Bezeichnung (Abkürzung)	K. St. N vom	K. A. N vom	Bemerkungen
1108 (gp)(fG)	Stb.Panz.Gren.Btl.a(gp)(f.G.)+	1.4.44		
1109	Stb.Panz.Aufkl.Abt. +	1.11.43	1.11.43	HM 44 Ziff.256 HM 44 Anl.13.Ausg.
1109 (fG)	Stb.und Stbs.Kp.Panz.Aufkl.Abt. (f.G.)	1.11.44		
1109 (gp)	Stb.Panz.Aufkl.Abt.(gp.) +	1.11.43	1.11.43	HM 44 Ziff.256 HM 44 Anl.13.Ausg.
1109 (gp)(fG)	Stb.und Stbs.Kp.Panz.Aufkl.Abt. (gp)(f.G.)	1.4.44		
1112	Panz.Aufkl.Kp.(Krad) +	1.11.43	1.11.43	HM 44 Anl.12.Ausg.
1112 c	Panz.Aufkl.Kp.c(Kett.Krad) +	1.11.43	1.11.43	HM 44 Anl.13.Ausg.
1113	Panz.Aufkl.Kp.(Volkswg.) +	1.11.43	1.11.43	HM 44 Ziff.256 HM 44 Anl.12.Ausg.
1113 (fC)	Panz.Aufkl.Kp.(Volkswg.)(f.G.)+	1.11.44		
1113 (gp)	Panz.Aufkl.Kp.(gp.) +	1.11.43	1.11.43	HM 44 Ziff.256 HM Anl.13.Ausg.
1113 (gp)(fG)	le.Panz.Aufkl.Kp.(gp)(f.G.)	1.4.44		
1114	Gren.Kp.(mot)Gren.Kp.Panz. +	1.11.43	1.11.43	HM 44 Anl.14.Ausg.
1114 (fC)	Panz.Gren.Kp.(f.G.) und Gren. Kp.(mot) (f.G.) +	1.4.44		
1114 c (gp)	Panz.Gren.Kp.c (gp.) +	1.11.43	1.11.43	HM 44 Ziff.102 HM 44 Anl.14.Ausg.
1114 c (gp)(fG)	Panz.Gren.Kp.c(gp)(f.C.) und Panz.Aufkl.Kp.(gp)(f.G.)	1.4.44		
1118	Panz.Gren.Pi.Kp. +	1.11.43	1.11.43	HM 44 Ziff.256
1120	schw.J.G.Kp.(4 s.J.G.)(mot Z)+			
1120 a	schw.Gesch.Kp.(6 s.J.G.)(Sf.)+	1.11.43	1.11.43	HM 44 Anl.12.Ausg.
1120 b	Gesch.Kp.(6 le.J.G., 2 s.J.G. (mot)) +	1.11.43	1.11.43	HM 44 Ziff.256 HM 44 Anl.14.Ausg.
1121	(T.E.) Führ.schw.Kp.(mot) +	1.11.43	1.11.43	HM 44 Ziff.256 HM 44 Anl.12.Ausg.

1. FELDHEER

Datum 15.7.1944

---

* The sample pages shown here are from holdings in the National Archives (*Gültigkeitslisten der Kriegsstärke- und Ausrüstungsnachweisungen*, files dated 15 Jul 44 in the National Archives Record Group 242, Publication T78, Roll 391, Sturmpanzer file: T78R391_H1_001.pdf and *Gültigkeitslisten der Kriegsstärke- und Ausrüstungsnachweisungen*, files dated 1 April 1943 in the National Archives Record Group 242, Publication T78, Roll 397. Sturmpanzer file: T78R397_H1_032.pdf).

Gültigkeitsliste dated 15 July 1944. Additional pages pertaining to armored reconnaissance elements:

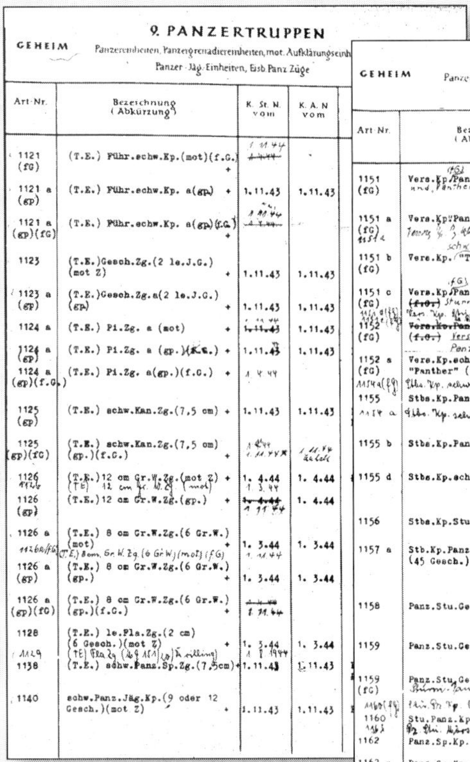

9. PANZERTRUPPEN

GEHEIM Panzereinheiten, Panzergrenadiereinheiten, mot. Aufklärungseinheiten, Panzer-Jäg.-Einheiten, Eisb.Panz.Züge

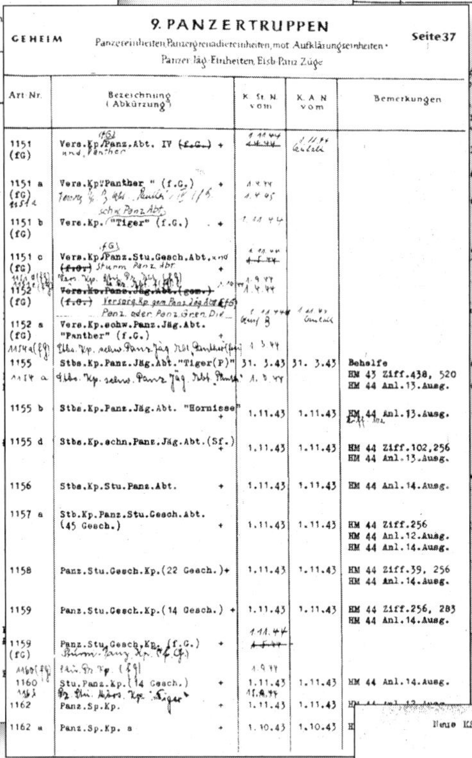

GEHEIM 9. PANZERTRUPPEN Seite 37

Panzereinheiten, Panzergrenadiereinheiten, mot. Aufklärungseinheiten, Panzer-Jäg.-Einheiten, Eisb.Panz.Züge

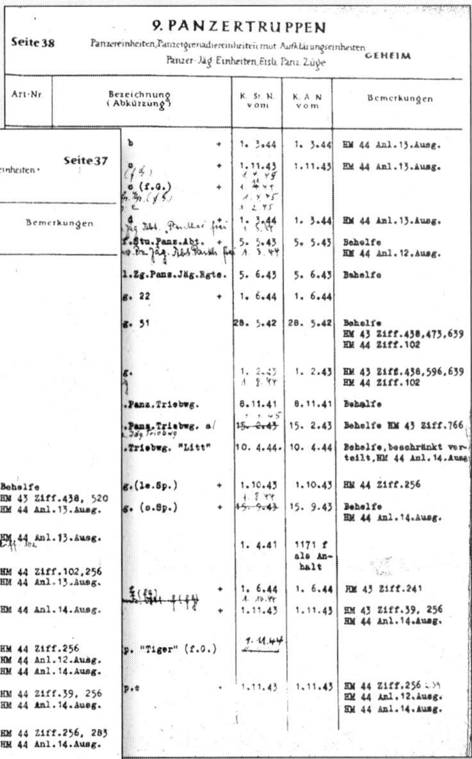

Seite 38 9. PANZERTRUPPEN GEHEIM

Panzereinheiten, Panzergrenadiereinheiten, mot. Aufklärungseinheiten, Panzer-Jäg.-Einheiten, Eisb.Panz.Züge

Gültigkeitsliste dated 20 January 1945. Typewritten version, probably intended as a work copy for a future printed edition:

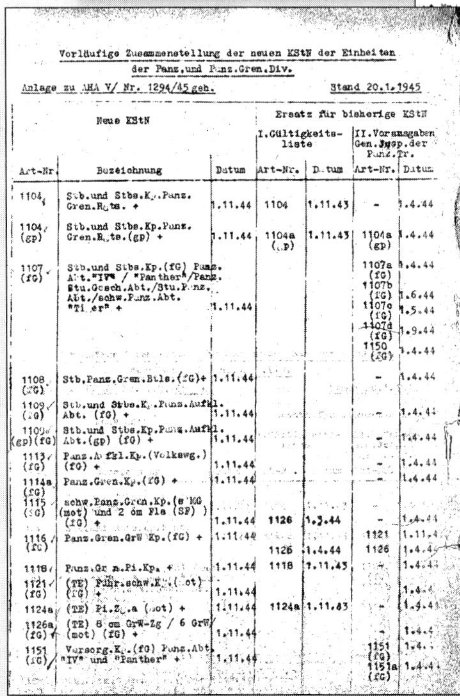

Vorläufige Zusammenstellung der neuen KStN der Einheiten der Panz.und Panz.Gren.Div.

Anlage zu AHA V/ Nr. 1294/45 geh. Stand 20.1.1945

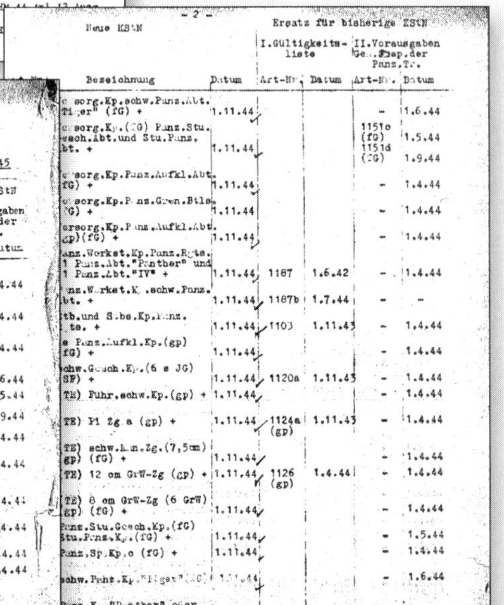

- 2 -

also lost one of their two armored car companies to help field the expanded force.[9]

The start of the campaign in the Soviet Union in 1941 continued the strain on the system and the ability of the army to field the force it needed to maintain its operational momentum. In the case of motor vehicles, the constant combat, the poor road network, and the reliance on a vast network of commercially impressed wheeled vehicles that were basically unsuited to the conditions encountered in the East led to immense shortfalls which, in turn, contributed to an inability to maintain adequate logistical support or operational reserves of substance. Similarly, the attrition to personnel manpower led to less effective units; leadership qualities and training that took years to produce in peacetime could not be replicated in the truncated training and leader development cycles necessitated by combat operations.

To cope, the *Organizations-Abteilung* wanted to make some drastic changes to the force, including large-scale reduction in the motorized assets of the line infantry divisions, reduction in the size of most formations, and deactivation of some twenty infantry divisions at the end of the first winter of fighting in the Soviet Union. Hitler initially agreed to much of this, only to subsequently announce his intention to continue the strategic offensive against the Soviet Union the following summer and refuse to disband formations for largely political and psychological reasons. Veit Scherzer sums up these continuing problems:

> His [Hitler's] stubborn position [not to disband formations] coupled with the demand to constantly activate new ones initiated the ruin of the army; sufficient replacements for the bloody losses, which primarily affected the infantry, could no longer be provided. Correspondingly, the ratio of combatants to combat support personnel shifted and became disproportional. Additional losses affected the core, inasmuch as officers and noncommissioned officers could no longer be replaced; the standards of training sank and, increasingly, the quality of the force. As a result of forced movements (retrograde operations) and the deficient mobility of the force, there were high losses in equipment and materiel. Operational possibilities faded and the leadership was hampered. The forces in the field were forced into purely defensive operations, in which it was used up along overextended fronts. In the end, that led to an increasing number of formations that lost the ability to conduct offensive operations; the lack of operational forces continuously increased. That, in turn, led commanders in chief of field-army groups and field armies in the further course of the war to request reinforcement over and over again by divisional formations that possessed full operational capabilities. By doing so, Hitler felt justified in his demands for the establishment of additional formations.[10]

Thus, 1942 saw the consolidation of the reconnaissance and antitank assets in many of the infantry divisions, with the corresponding official loss of any armored reconnaissance assets the pre-war formations might have once possessed. Motorized infantry and armor formations were similarly affected in terms of reductions in manpower and vehicular strength. In addition, in order to support the upcoming offensive in the south, many formations were transferred to augment the depleted divisions of *Heeresgruppe Süd*. This frequently led to the often bewildering force structure changes described in unit histories, changes that usually are not adequately explained, since those processes were often not transparent to the subordinate commands. By the end of the year, the motorcycle infantry and armored reconnaissance battalions of those divisions consolidated, with the reconnaissance battalion being absorbed into the division's *Kradschützen-Bataillon*.[11]

By the end of 1942, the *Organizations-Abteilung* once again attempted to streamline the force, generally by both reducing strengths and equipment authorizations. The assumption by the force structure branch was that the German military would remain on the defensive in 1943, thus allowing these changes to be effected. Once again, this proved to be a fatal error, especially since the problems were compounded by the virtually complete loss of approximately twenty divisions at Stalingrad and another six in Tunisia. Once again, Hitler ordered the reconstitution of the virtually all of the elements partially or completely destroyed; he also ordered a limited offensive for the

Tactical Symbols: Explanation of German Unit and Organizational Symbols

For those used to NATO-style map symbols, the myriad German tactical symbols used organization charts (and maps) of the World War II era can seem to be a daunting task at first. Once the basic system is understood, however, the symbols offer a form of shorthand that allows a great deal of information to be packed into a very small space. The symbols were initially established in *Heeresdienstvorschrift 272, Muster für taktische Zeichen des Heeres* ("Standards for Tactical Symbols of the Army") of 1938, but they were modified throughout the war due to the introductions of new weapons systems and organizations. Like shorthand, there were occasionally variations and modifications that were introduced by individuals that did not follow the "norm." Dr. Leo Niehorster has provided a concise overview on his web site:

The different functions and mobility additions were used to enhance the echelon's symbol to indicate a specific purpose.

Company-sized units and sub-units symbols were also modified in a similar fashion.

An interesting feature of company and sub-unit symbols is that their size and shape dimensions could be altered to fit the diagram being depicted with them. Several infantry companies, for example, were placed side-by-side, elongated upwards, (so that all weapons symbols could fit within), and only the left-hand company had the thickened edge used to indicate its size (more of this below). The variations in size and shape followed the original configuration, so that the basic symbol was still recognizable as such.

At the start of the war, these symbols were being used.

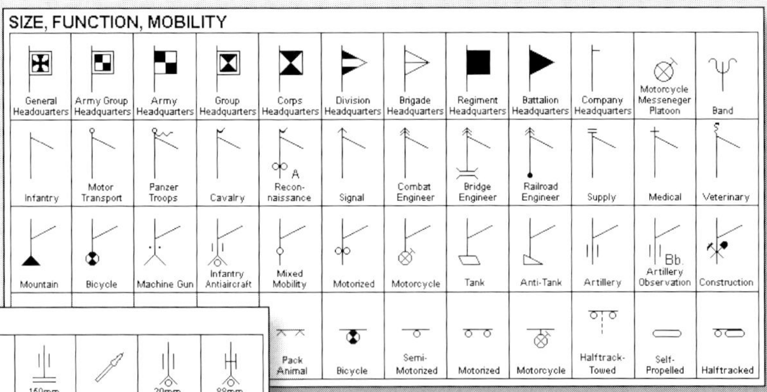

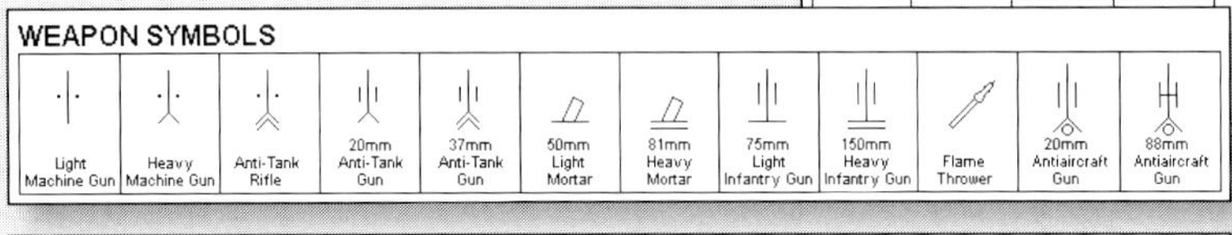

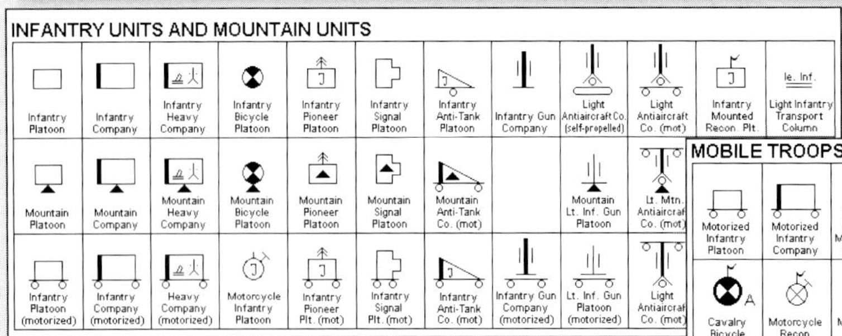

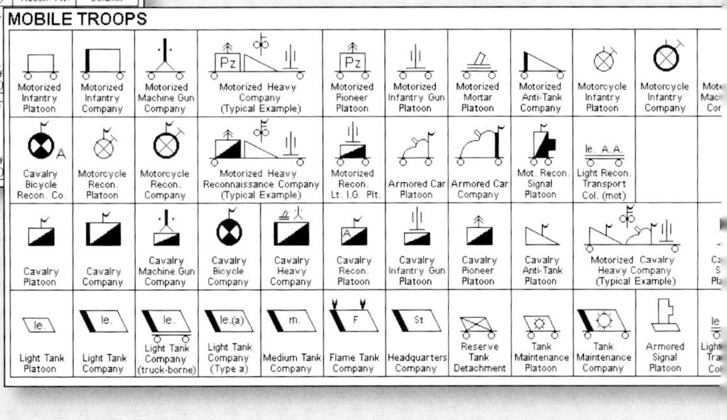

The mobility of the unit was also quickly recognizable. The two small circles ("wheels") underneath a symbols identified the unit as being motorized. . . . Elongated ovals ("tracks") applied underneath the symbol meant that the unit was selfpropelled. A wheel and a track symbol indicated a half-tracked armored vehicle.

Although the official handbook indicated that armored infantry units should have the halftrack symbol underneath them instead of the motorized symbol, this practice was not yet followed in most organizational charts at that time . . .

The lozenge symbol represented armor. All tank units used this symbol. It was shaped to reflect World War I tanks, and hence provided a good memory assist.

Company-sized units had, somewhere within their symbol, a thickened part, usually a side…

Where several columns, platoons, or detachments were gathered under a company headquarters . . . such as a heavy company . . . and each of these sub-units had its own *KStN* . . . these symbols were placed side-by-side and had a company echelon symbol placed over them.

The Germans numbered their units on organizational charts from the right . . . the first company was on the far right, and the last company was on the far left. The same applied to battalions and regiments.*

* Dr. Leo Niehorster at http://niehorster.orbat.com. The graphics and quoted text seen here come from pages http://niehorster.orbat.com/011_germany/symbols/_symbols_39.html, http://niehorster.orbat.com/011_germany/symbols/_symbols_41.html, http://niehorster.orbat.com/011_germany/symbols/_symbols_39.html and http://niehorster.orbat.com/011_germany/symbols/_symbols_vehicles.html.

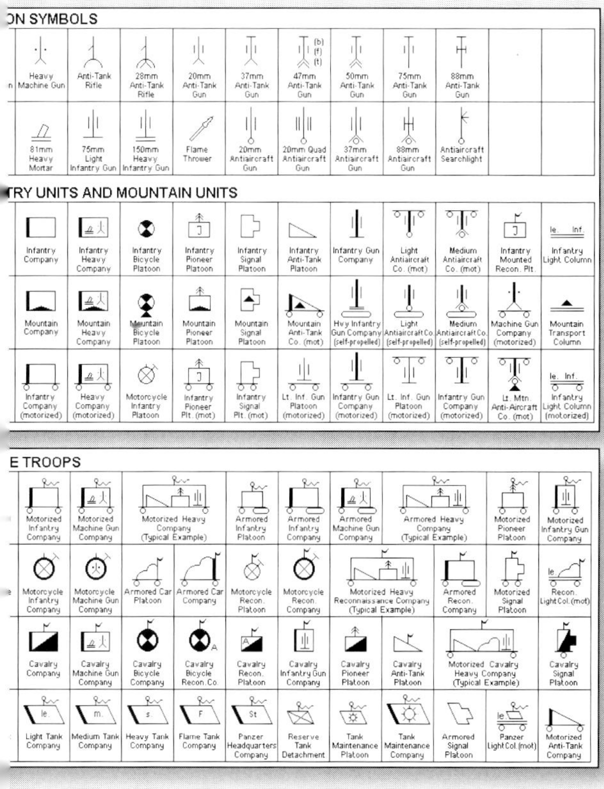

On 24 March 1941, a 176-page update to *Heeresdienstvorschrift 272* was published. The above additions and modifications were made.

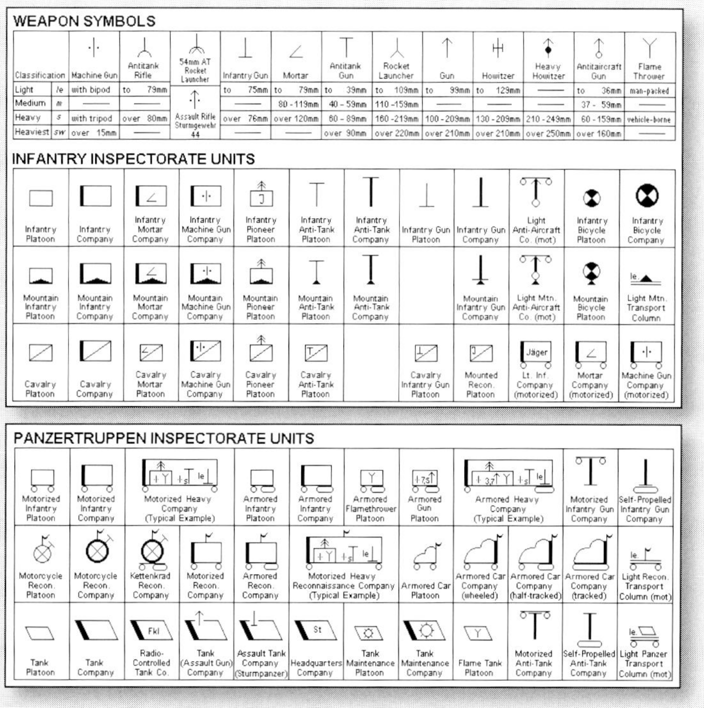

Additional symbols were introduced in 1943. Of most relevance to this study are those shown above.

East in 1943. The situation was partially alleviated by the declaration of total war on 13 January 1943, which served to free up non-essential personnel on the home front and increase the production of weapons, vehicles and equipment.

By the end of 1943, the *Organizations-Abteilung* initiated plans to standardize all the division-level combat forces within the army, thus leading to the *Infanterie-Division neuer Art* (infantry division–new type) at the end of 1943, as well as similar directives for the streamlining of the mechanized infantry and armored divisions as *Panzergrenadier-Division 43* and *Panzer-Division 43*. Within the infantry divisions, the reconnaissance elements reemerged under the designation of *Füsilier-Bataillon*, albeit without any armored reconnaissance assets authorized. The *Krad-schützen-Bataillone* were redesignated within the *Panzergrenadier-* and *Panzer-Divisionen* as *Panzer-Aufklärungs-Abteilungen*, with corresponding organizational changes, which will be discussed in detail in the following sections.

The years of 1944 and 1945 also saw the introduction of *KStN's* that were further streamlined for the combat force, which basically saw continued

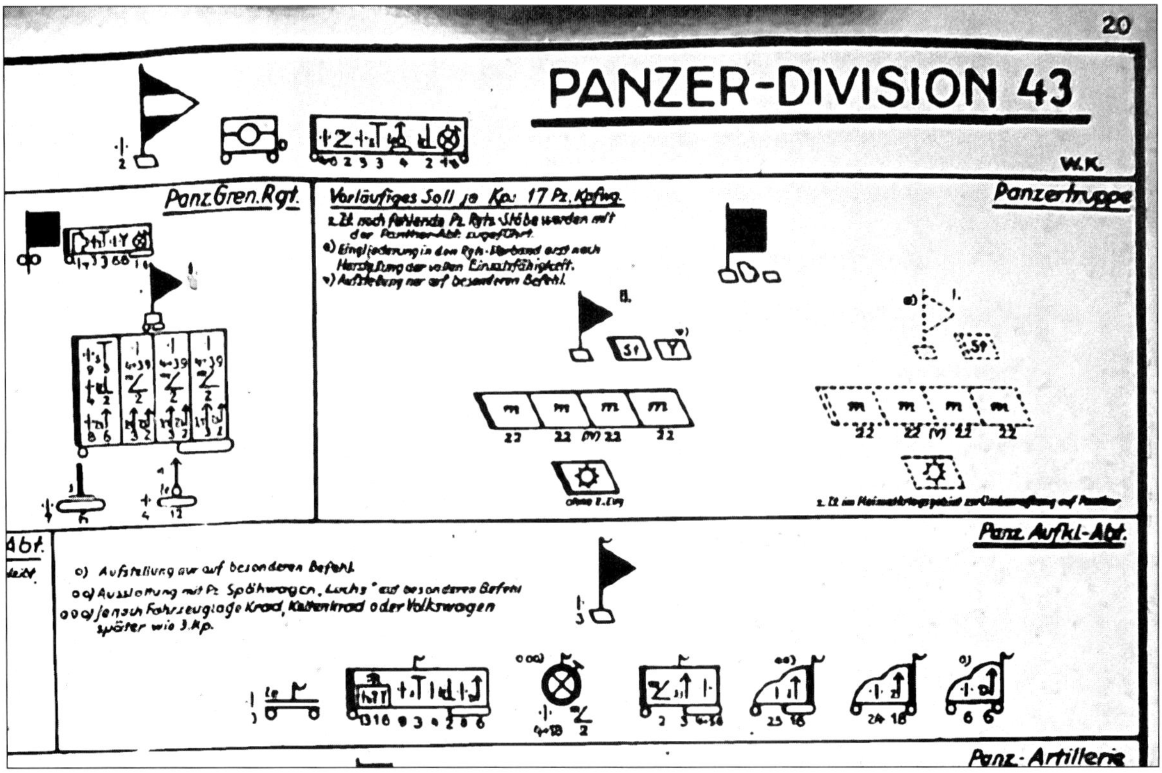

Organizational charts for the "standard" armored and mechanized divisions that were introduced in 1943. While great strides were made in standardization, many formations still did not adhere to the new models or were only able to implement them incrementally. This resulted from a number of factors, chief among them the inability of Germany's industry to produce sufficient arms and equipment for its forces, the wide variety in the fielding of equipment, and the increasingly chaotic situation at the front. This image shows *Panzer-Division 43*, which maintained an armored reconnaissance battalion of four line companies—two scout and two reconnaissance—and a heavy company.

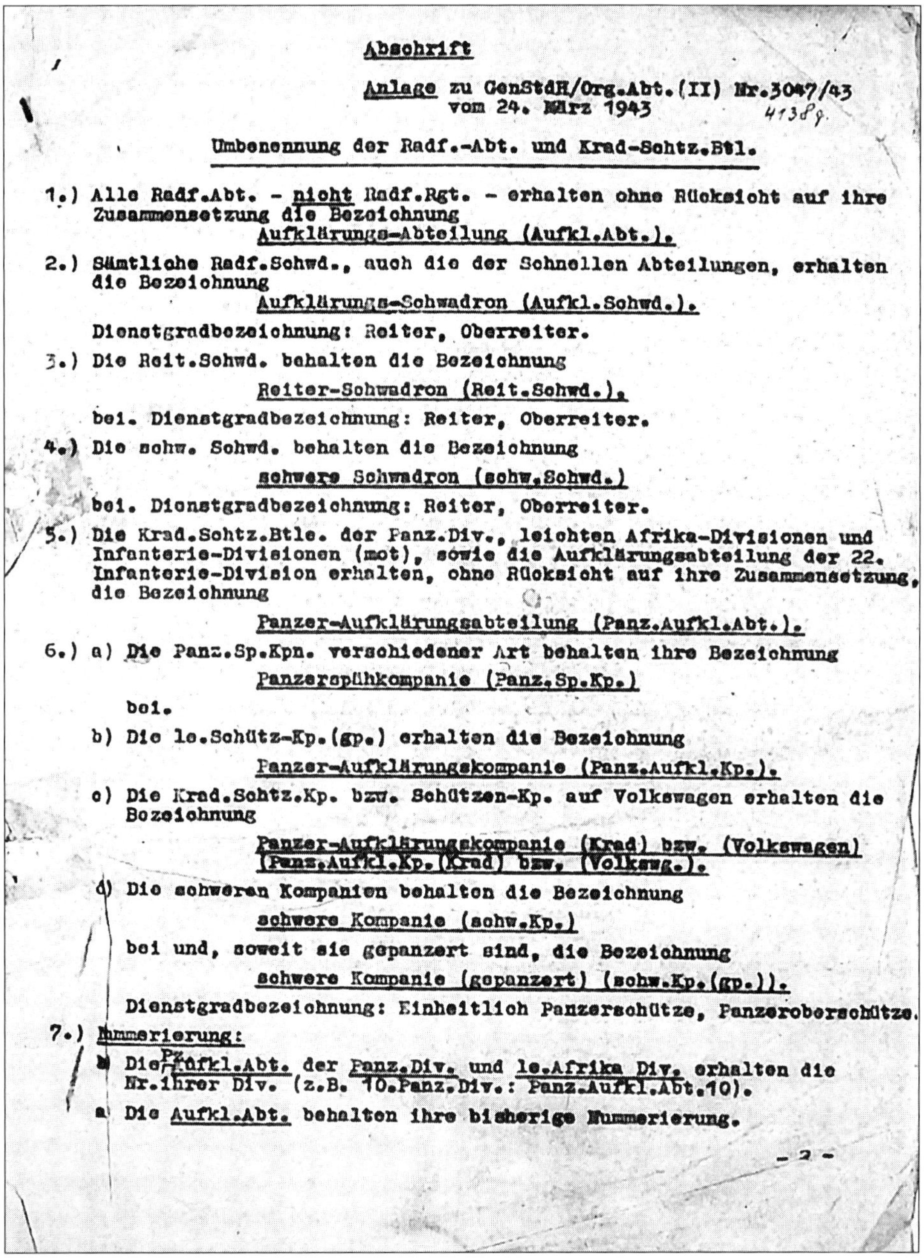

Abschrift

Anlage zu GenStdH/Org.Abt.(II) Nr.3047/43
vom 24. März 1943 41389.

Umbenennung der Radf.-Abt. und Krad-Schtz.Btl.

1.) Alle Radf.Abt. - nicht Radf.Rgt. - erhalten ohne Rücksicht auf ihre Zusammensetzung die Bezeichnung
Aufklärungs-Abteilung (Aufkl.Abt.).

2.) Sämtliche Radf.Schwd., auch die der Schnellen Abteilungen, erhalten die Bezeichnung
Aufklärungs-Schwadron (Aufkl.Schwd.).
Dienstgradbezeichnung: Reiter, Oberreiter.

3.) Die Reit.Schwd. behalten die Bezeichnung
Reiter-Schwadron (Reit.Schwd.),
bei. Dienstgradbezeichnung: Reiter, Oberreiter.

4.) Die schw. Schwd. behalten die Bezeichnung
schwere Schwadron (schw.Schwd.)
bei. Dienstgradbezeichnung: Reiter, Oberreiter.

5.) Die Krad.Schtz.Btle. der Panz.Div., leichten Afrika-Divisionen und Infanterie-Divisionen (mot), sowie die Aufklärungsabteilung der 22. Infanterie-Division erhalten, ohne Rücksicht auf ihre Zusammensetzung, die Bezeichnung
Panzer-Aufklärungsabteilung (Panz.Aufkl.Abt.).

6.) a) Die Panz.Sp.Kpn. verschiedener Art behalten ihre Bezeichnung
Panzerspähkompanie (Panz.Sp.Kp.)
bei.

b) Die le.Schütz-Kp.(gp.) erhalten die Bezeichnung
Panzer-Aufklärungskompanie (Panz.Aufkl.Kp.).

c) Die Krad.Schtz.Kp. bzw. Schützen-Kp. auf Volkswagen erhalten die Bezeichnung
Panzer-Aufklärungskompanie (Krad) bzw. (Volkswagen)
(Panz.Aufkl.Kp.(Krad) bzw. (Volkswg.).

d) Die schweren Kompanien behalten die Bezeichnung
schwere Kompanie (schw.Kp.)
bei und, soweit sie gepanzert sind, die Bezeichnung
schwere Kompanie (gepanzert) (schw.Kp.(gp.)).
Dienstgradbezeichnung: Einheitlich Panzerschütze, Panzeroberschütze.

7.) Nummerierung:

a) Die Pz. Aufkl.Abt. der Panz.Div. und le.Afrika Div. erhalten die Nr. ihrer Div. (z.B. 10.Panz.Div.: Panz.Aufkl.Abt.10).

b) Die Aufkl.Abt. behalten ihre bisherige Nummerierung.

- 2 -

Correspondence from the *Organizations-Abteilung* on 24 March 1943 dictated a wide-ranging number of changes in the way formations and units were designated in an effort to further streamline the force. The bicycle battalion and companies of the infantry divisions were uniformly redesignated as *Aufklärungs-Kompanien* or *-Abteilungen*. The horse cavalry retained the traditional designation for their company-size elements, *Schwadronen*. The *Kradschützen* battalions were universally redesignated as *Panzer-Aufklärungs-Abteilungen*. Those formations equipped with *Volkswagen* or motorcycles/*Kettenkräder* were to indicate that at the end of their official designation—e.g., *Panzer-Aufklärungs-Abteilung (Krad)*. The heavy companies continued to be referred to as *schwere Kompanien*, regardless of the type of battalion they served. In addition, the armored division reconnaissance battalions were to be assigned the number of their division, and the reconnaissance assets of the motorized infantry divisions were to have the number of their divisions, except that the number 100 would be added to it—e.g., *Panzeraufklärungs-Abteilung 129* belonged to the *29. Panzergrenadier-Division*. It was further established that the branch-of-service color (*Waffenfarbe*) for *Aufklärungs-Abteilungen* would be golden yellow (*goldgelb*), while that of the *Panzer-Aufklärungs-Abteilungen* would be rose pink (*rosa*). While this had generally been followed in the past, there were enough deviations that necessitated a formal reminder.

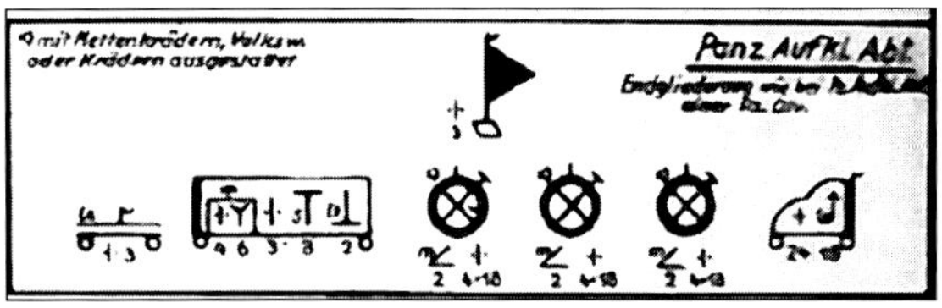

The counterpart battalion in the mechanized infantry division of *Panzergrenadier-Division 43* also had four line companies, but only one of them was composed of scouts, while the rest were reconnaissance.

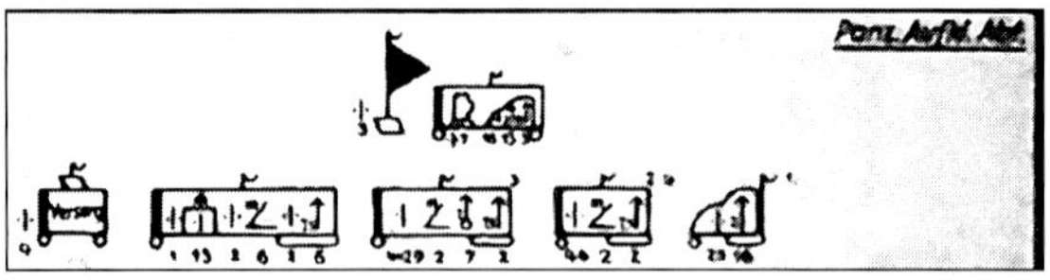

The *Panzer-Division 44* armored reconnaissance battalion, which had the equivalent of a wheeled armored scout company located in the battalion headquarters company.

reduction of the combat support assets of the divisions and their consolidation into unified trains elements. In the case of the *Panzertruppe*, this reorganization of the force was referred to as a *freie Gliederung* ("free organization"), ostensibly because it freed the combat commander from worrying about logistical issues and let him concentrate instead on combat operations. In fact, the 1945 plan saw the exact same organization for both *Panzer-* and *Panzergrenadier-Divisionen*, although it is doubtful if any major formations had the luxury of fully converting to the new system.

ARMORED RECONNAISSANCE WITHIN THE INFANTRY

Traditional Infantry Formations (*Infanterie-Verbände*)

Armored reconnaissance within the standard infantry divisions was an anomaly. In fact, prior to the call for mobilization, the infantry divisions did not have a dedicated reconnaissance asset at all. The prewar *Kavallerie-Regimenter* were tasked to provide those assets upon mobilization, with those regiments disbanding.

Once formed, the reconnaissance battalions of the first- and second-wave divisions were still a relatively

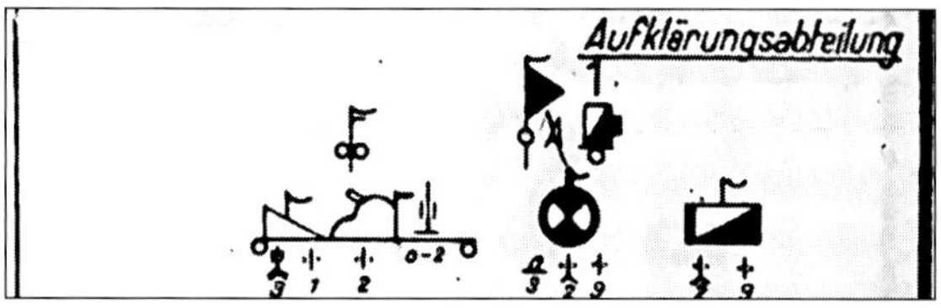

Example reconnaissance battalion of a first-wave division—in this case *Aufklärungs-Abteilung 1* of the East Prussian *1. Infanterie-Division*, seen in February 1941. Only two armored cars are present in the Heavy Troop.

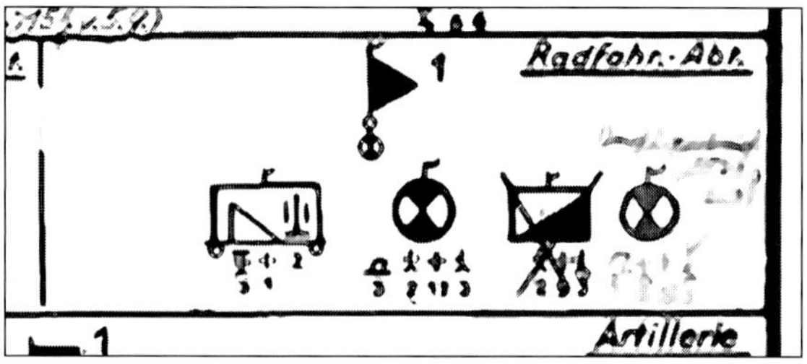

Aufklärungs-Abteilung 1 in September 1942. The armored car section has been stricken from the organizational chart.

Spartan organization. Although the battalion had an end strength of 19 officers, 2 civilian officials, 90 noncommissioned officers and 512 enlisted, there were only two armored cars within it, organized into a section within the battalion's heavy troop, along with the other support entities, the infantry gun platoon (two light infantry guns), and the antitank platoon (three 3.7cm antitank guns). The heavy troop was designed to support the mounted troop (*1. Schwadron*) and the bicycle troop (*2. Schwadron*).

With the motorized infantry divisions and the armored divisions receiving priority—they had organic reconnaissance and motorcycle infantry battalions from the onset—the "leg" infantry divisions were also largely given hand-me-downs when they did receive armored cars, obsolescent *Kfz. 13's* and *14's*.[12] By 1942, the process was begun by which the reconnaissance battalions of the first-wave divisions were redesignated and reorganized as *Radfahr-Abteilungen* (bicycle battalions). All armored car sections were eliminated, although some divisions received a motorcycle infantry platoon to augment the bicycle elements and some battalions maintained their armored cars for a considerable period into the war.[13] By the end of 1943, the bicycle battalions were again redesignated and reorganized as reconnaissance

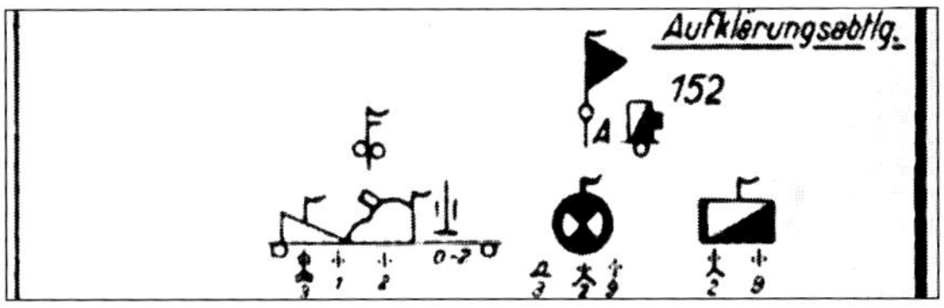

Aufklärungs-Abteilung 152 was part of the *52. Infanterie-Division* (November 1940). Most divisional troops in second-wave divisions had their divisional number plus one hundred. The reconnaissance battalion is organized exactly the same as in the *1. Infanterie-Division.*

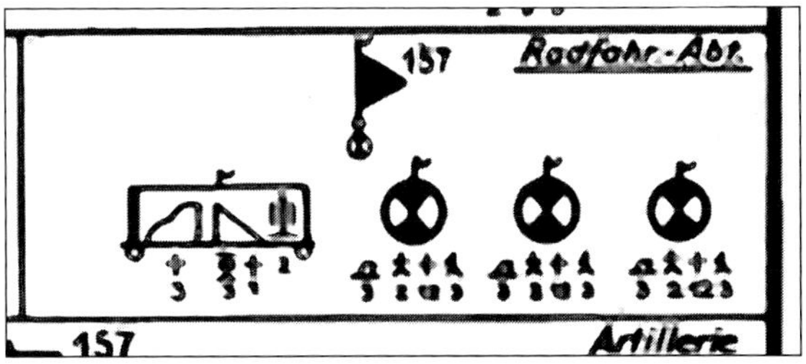

In September 1942, the division still had an armored car section on its books, even though its reconnaissance battalion was officially a *Radfahr-Abteilung.*

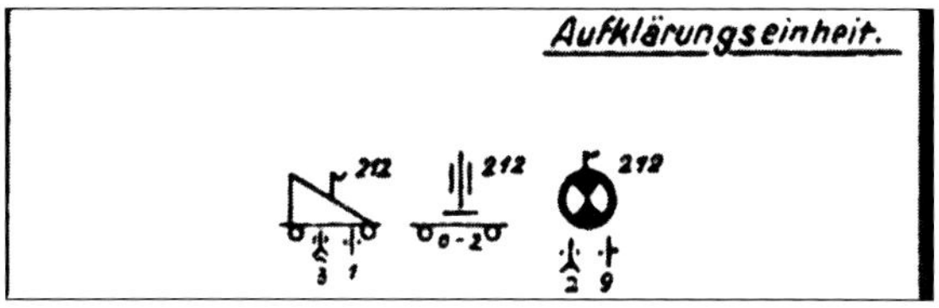

The *212. Infanterie-Division*, a division of the third wave, did not have any armored reconnaissance assets (November 1940).

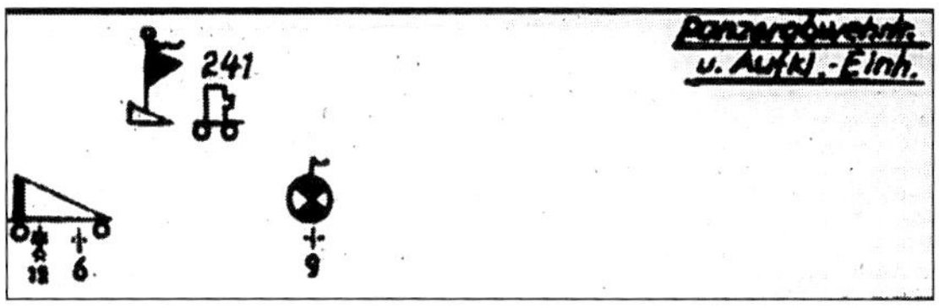

Because of the reduction in the availability of reconnaissance personnel and equipment, as well as the perceived notion that foot infantry divisions had little need for anything other than battlefield reconnaissance, the divisional reconnaissance assets were often consolidated with the divisional antitank battalion, with the gunners taking precedence in the redesignation of the resulting element. This is reflected in the organizational chart from a division of the seventh wave, the *161. Infanterie-Division* (January 1940). In other divisions, these combined assets were sometimes designated as *schnelle Abteilungen* ("fast battalions"), since they represented virtually all of the mobile assets of the division.

battalions. These changes were generally also applied to divisions of the second wave as well; however, when the antitank battalions and reconnaissance battalions were consolidated in 1942, they were redesignated as *schnelle Abteilungen* in some of the divisions (56, 61, 78, 86, and 87) since they represented practically all of the motorized frontline force of those divisions. Those divisions that did not convert to a *schnelle Abteilung* redesignated their reconnaissance assets as *Radfahr-Abteilungen.*[14]

The third wave of divisions, generally numbered in the 200 series, was constituted in September 1939 and made use of little, if any, active-duty personnel. Approximately 46 percent came from the *Landwehr* (militia).[15] Starting with this wave, the infantry division no longer had any armored reconnaissance assets as a rule.[16] With the constitution of fourth-wave divisions, also in September 1939, the infantry divisions were no longer authorized any armored car platoons. Fifth- through eighth-wave divisions (September 1939–February 1940) had bicycle troops or battalions.

The ninth wave, activated in February–March 1940, consisted of four positional, eight militia, and two reserve divisions. While the positional forces and the reserve divisions had no organic reconnaissance elements, the militia division had a theoretical authorization of two light armored cars within each reinforced bicycle troop, although it is unlikely that these were ever fielded before the formations were deactivated.

In anticipation of the campaign against the Soviet Union, Hitler ordered the army increased to 180 divisions. This occurred in four iterations, starting with the eleventh wave (October 1940). While most of these divisions had reconnaissance assets—either battalion or troop—none was authorized armored vehicles. The fifteenth wave (started May 1941) produced fifteen divisions, but none had any reconnaissance assets.[17] Between the sixteenth and seventeenth waves was the Spanish "Blue" Division (*250. Infanterie-Division [span.]*), but its reconnaissance assets consisted of bicycle troops. Most of the infantry divisions and brigades formed in 1942 that were part of a "wave" had the combined reconnaissance and antitank battalion, the so-called *schnelle Abteilung*, but the reconnaissance portion generally consisted of a bicycle troop or troops. The security, coastal security, and immobile divisions[18] generally had no reconnaissance assets. In September 1942, two Croatian divisions were formed with German cadre for leadership. Apparently, *Radfahr-Abteilung 369* of the *369. Legionärs-Division (kroat.)* had an armored car platoon authorized, although it is not known whether it was ever formed.[19] In the summer of 1943, several more divisions were formed with a majority of non-German personnel. The *373. Infanterie-Division (kroat.)* initially had no armored vehicles in its reconnaissance battalion (*Aufklärungs-Abteilung 373*), but it later formed two armored car companies from captured Italian stocks. A Turkmen division was also formed, the *162. Infanterie-Division (Turk.)*, and its reconnaissance battalion (*Aufklärungs-Abteilung 236*) likewise did not have any armored vehicles initially. When it converted to an *Infanterie-Division 44*, it also added an armored car platoon, again consisting of captured Italian stocks.

As can be see from the simplified outline provided above, the vast array of differing divisional types made force-structure management a nightmare. Correspondingly, the *Organizations-Abteilung* introduced the "new-style" infantry division—*Infanterie-Division neuer Art*—in late 1943, with the aim of streamlining the organization of the infantry force. As part of this process, the infantry divisions were to have their reconnaissance assets redesignated and reorganized as *Füsilier-Bataillone*. The fusilier battalions had a headquarters, three line companies, and a heavy company, but no armored cars or other mechanized assets were envisioned. This type of division was replaced in 1944 with the *Infanterie-Division 44*, which further streamlined the forces and reduced overall headcount by another 800 personnel. The *Füsilier-Bataillone* remained largely untouched by that reorganization. Subsequent "waves" of divisions followed these models.

Through the twenty-fifth wave, there were no discernible armored reconnaissance elements within any of the divisions formed. In February 1944, an infantry division was formed out of Replacement Army assets in the General Government of Poland (*Infanterie-Division "Generalgouvernement"*), which was later absorbed into the *72. Infanterie-Division*. For a short

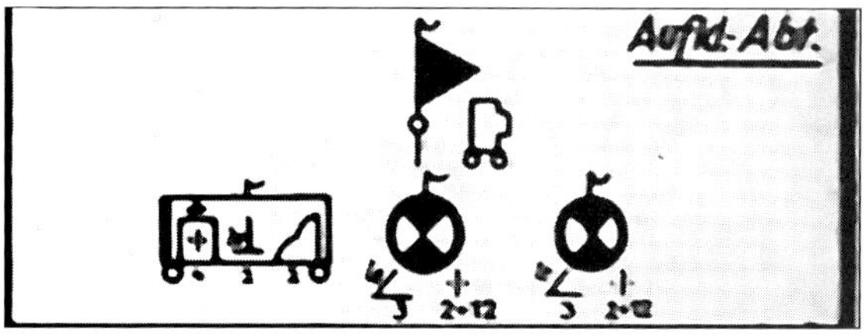

Aufklärungs-Abteilung 373 of the *373. Infanterie-Division (kroat.)* in September 1943. It was later to form two armored cars out of captured Italian vehicle stocks.

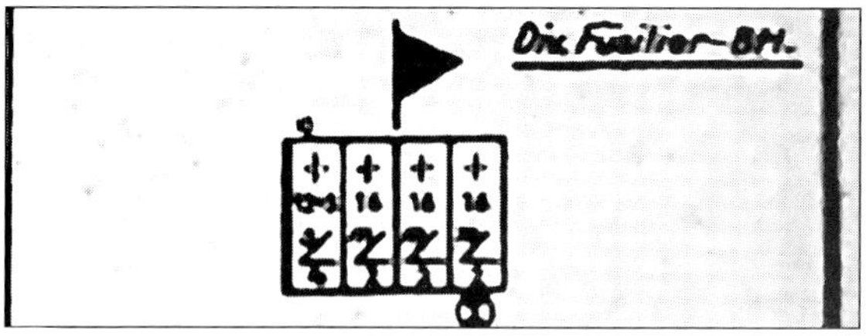

The "new type" infantry division had no place for motorized reconnaissance assets, let alone armored ones.

time, it had a reconnaissance battalion composed of personnel and equipment from the armor school at Rembertow. As such, it had a unique organization: A battalion headquarters, two machine-gun companies, a heavy company, a tank company, a self-propelled antitank gun company, an armored car platoon with three four-wheeled armored cars, and an armored car platoon with one eight-wheeled and two four-wheeled armored cars. Upon consolidation with the *72. Infanterie-Division*, however, *Aufklärungs-Abteilung Rembertow* reverted back to Replacement Army control.

In the twenty-seventh wave of July 1944, five immobile divisions were formed. Of those, the reconnaissance battalion of the *232. Infanterie-Division (bo)*, became an exception, inasmuch as it received an armored car platoon consisting of Italian vehicles.

In the late summer of 1944, under the twenty-ninth wave, seventeen so-called *Sperr-Divisionen* (blocking divisions) were formed, later redesignated as *Grenadier-Divisionen* and ultimately as *Volksgrenadier-Divisionen*. These divisions were formed with a *Füsilier-Kompanie*, but their sole means of transport was the bicycle. The *Volksgrenadier-Divisionen* were also unique in that the *Waffen-SS* had oversight authority over them. From the late summer of 1944 on, as the situation became increasingly desperate and militarily untenable, the force

Kriegsstärkenachweisungen: Tables of Organization & Equipment

Kriegsstärkenachweisungen were the building blocks of any unit or formation. In general, these were company in size or smaller. In instances of headquarters or heavy companies, the *KStN* generally only listed the headquarters and headquarters staff, with the building blocks of the unit, the separate platoons and sections, referred to in German as *Teileinheiten*, covered by their own *KStN's*. The *KStN's* that governed the reconnaissance force were generally in the 1100 series. There was a similar set of documents that governed the issue of specific equipment for these elements as well. It was referred to as the *Kriegsausrüstungsnachweisung*, or *KAN* for short. For the purposes of this study, only the *KStN's* will be examined.

Sample *KStN's* are shown in this series of images. The documents were labeled *"Nur für den Dienstgebrauch,"* which is roughly equivalent to the "For Official Use Only" label applied to sensitive documents in the U.S. military. The lefthand column provides a running line number for ready reference, e.g., when requests for changes were being made. The second column, the *Stellengruppe*, indicates the pay grade authorized for each line requiring personnel, with *K* being officers, *Z* senior NCO's, *G* junior NCO's, and *M* enlisted personnel. The next column provides the *KStN* title and description, with the subparagraphs usually entered in the following sequence for combat elements: Command (Command Group and Headquarters), Combat Elements, and Trains. The next

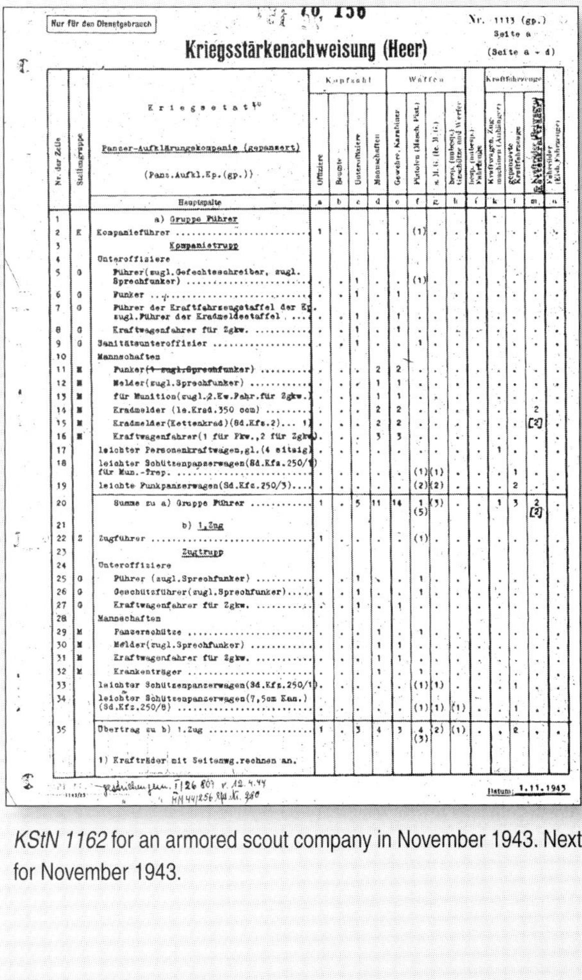

Nur für den Dienstgebrauch — 76, 156 — Nr. 1113 (gp.) Seite a (Seite a – d)

Kriegsstärkenachweisung (Heer)

Kriegsetat 40 — Panzer-Aufklärungskompanie (gepanzert) (Panz.Aufkl.Kp.(gp.))

Nr. der Zeile	Stellengruppe	Hauptspalte	a Offiziere	b Beamte	c Unteroffiziere	d Mannschaften	e Gewehre, Karabiner	f Pistolen (Masch. Pist.)	g s.M.G. (le. M.G.)	h besp. (unbesp.) Geschütze und Werfer	i besp. (unbesp.) Fahrzeuge	k Kraftwagen, Zugmaschinen (Anhänger)	l gepanzerte Kraftfahrzeuge	m Krafträder (Beiwagen) (Kettenkrad)	n Fahrräder (Kleinkrafträder)
1		a) Gruppe Führer													
2	K	Kompanieführer	1					(1)							
3		Kompanietrupp													
4		Unteroffiziere													
5	G	Führer (zugl. Gefechtsschreiber, zugl. Sprechfunker)			1			(1)							
6	G	Funker			1		1								
7	G	Führer der Kraftfahrzeugstaffel der Kp. zugl. Führer der Kradmeldestaffel			1		1								
8	G	Kraftwagenfahrer für Zgkw.			1		1								
9	G	Sanitätsunteroffizier			1			1							
10		Mannschaften													
11	M	Funker (~~1 zugl. Sprechfunker~~)				2	2								
12	M	Melder (zugl. Sprechfunker)				1	1								
13	M	für Munition (zugl. 2 Kw.Fahr. für Zgkw.)				1	1								
14	M	Kradmelder (le.Krad.350 ccm)				2	2							2	
15	M	Kradmelder (Kettenkrad) (Sd.Kfz.2) ... 1)				2	2							[2]	
16	M	Kraftwagenfahrer (1 für Pkw., 2 für Zgkw.)				3	3								
17		leichter Personenkraftwagen, gl. (4 sitzig)										1			
18		leichter Schützenpanzerwagen (Sd.Kfz.250/1) für Mun.-Trsp.						(1)	(1)				1		
19		leichte Funkpanzerwagen (Sd.Kfz.250/3)						(2)	(2)				2		
20		Summe zu a) Gruppe Führer	1		5	11	14	1 (5)	(3)			1	3	2 [2]	
21		b) 1. Zug													
22	Z	Zugführer	1					(1)							
23		Zugtrupp													
24		Unteroffiziere													
25	G	Führer (zugl. Sprechfunker)			1			1							
26	G	Geschützführer (zugl. Sprechfunker)			1			1							
27	G	Kraftwagenfahrer für Zgkw.			1		1								
28		Mannschaften													
29	M	Panzerschütze				1		1							
30	M	Melder (zugl. Sprechfunker)				1	1								
31	M	Kraftwagenfahrer für Zgkw.				1	1								
32	M	Krankenträger				1		1							
33		leichter Schützenpanzerwagen (Sd.Kfz.250/1)						(1)	(1)				1		
34		leichter Schützenpanzerwagen (7,5cm Kan.) (Sd.Kfz.250/8)						(1)	(1)	(1)			1		
35		Übertrag zu b) 1. Zug	1		3	4	3	4 (3)	(2)	(1)			2		

1) Krafträder mit Seitenwg. rechnen an.

Datum: 1.11.1943

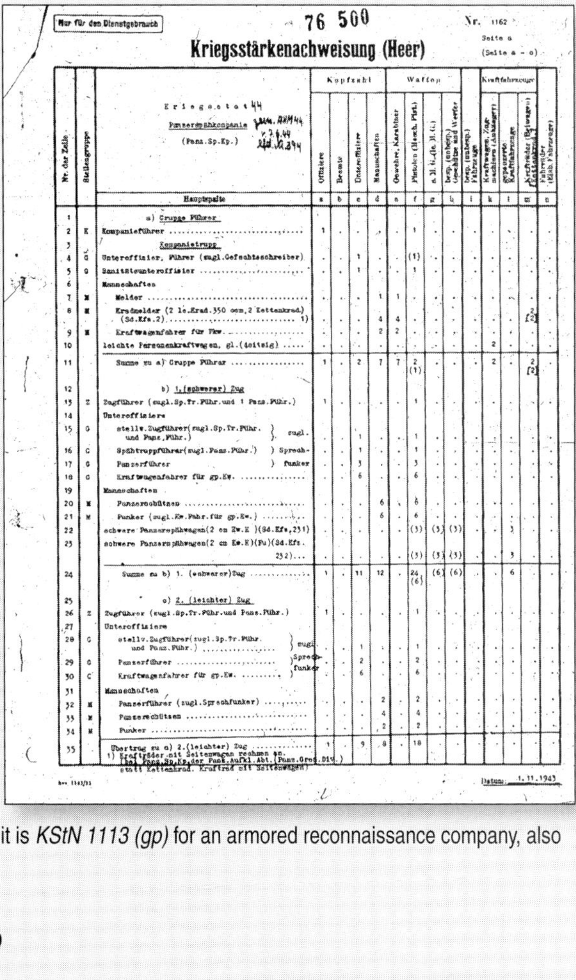

Nur für den Dienstgebrauch — 76 500 — Nr. 1162 Seite a (Seite a – c)

Kriegsstärkenachweisung (Heer)

Kriegsetat 44 — Panzerspähkompanie (Panz.Sp.Kp.)

Nr. der Zeile	Stellengruppe	Hauptspalte	a Offiziere	b Beamte	c Unteroffiziere	d Mannschaften	e Gewehre, Karabiner	f Pistolen (Masch. Pist.)	g s.M.G. (le. M.G.)	h besp. (unbesp.) Geschütze und Werfer	i besp. (unbesp.) Fahrzeuge	k Kraftwagen, Zugmaschinen (Anhänger)	l gepanzerte Kraftfahrzeuge	m Krafträder (Beiwagen) (Kettenkrad)	n Fahrräder (Kleinkrafträder)
1		a) Gruppe Führer													
2	K	Kompanieführer	1					1							
3		Kompanietrupp													
4	G	Unteroffizier, Führer (zugl. Gefechtsschreiber)			1			(1)							
5	G	Sanitätsunteroffizier			1			1							
6		Mannschaften													
7	M	Melder				1	1								
8	M	Kradmelder (2 le.Krad.350 ccm, 2 Kettenkrad) (Sd.Kfz.2) ... 1)				4	4							2 [2]	
9	M	Kraftwagenfahrer für Pkw.				2	2								
10		leichte Personenkraftwagen, gl. (4sitzig)										2			
11		Summe zu a) Gruppe Führer	1		2	7	7	2 (1)				2		2 [2]	
12		b) 1. (schwerer) Zug													
13	Z	Zugführer (zugl. Sp.Tr.Führ. und 1 Pans.Führ.)	1					1							
14		Unteroffiziere													
15	G	stellv. Zugführer (zugl. Sp.Tr.Führ. und Pans.Führ.) } zugl.			1			1							
16	G	Spähtruppführer (zugl. Pans.Führ.)) Sprech-			1			1							
17	G	Panzerführer) funker			3			3							
18	G	Kraftwagenfahrer für gp.Kw.			6			6							
19		Mannschaften													
20	M	Panzerschützen				6		6							
21	M	Funker (zugl. Kw.Fahr. für gp.Kw.)				6		6							
22		schwere Panzerspähwagen (2 cm Kw.K) (Sd.Kfz.231)						(3)	(3)	(3)			3		
23		schwere Panzerspähwagen (2 cm Kw.K) (Fu) (Sd.Kfz. 232)						(3)	(3)	(3)			3		
24		Summe zu b) 1. (schwerer) Zug	1		11	12		24 (6)	(6)	(6)			6		
25		c) 2. (leichter) Zug													
26	Z	Zugführer (zugl. Sp.Tr.Führ. und Pans.Führ.)	1					1							
27		Unteroffiziere													
28	G	stellv. Zugführer (zugl. Sp.Tr.Führ. und Pans.Führ.) } zugl.			1			1							
29	G	Panzerführer) Sprechfunker			2			2							
30	G	Kraftwagenfahrer für gp.Kw.)			6			6							
31		Mannschaften													
32	M	Panzerführer (zugl. Sprechfunker)				2		2							
33	M	Panzerschützen				4		4							
34	M	Funker				2		2							
35		Übertrag zu c) 2. (leichter) Zug	1		9	8		18							

1) Krafträder mit Seitenwagen rechnen an. (bei Panz.Sp.Kp. der Panz.Aufkl.Abt. (Panz.Gren.Div.) statt Kettenkrad. Kraftrad mit Seitenwagen)

Datum: 1.11.1943

KStN 1162 for an armored scout company in November 1943. Next to it is *KStN 1113 (gp)* for an armored reconnaissance company, also for November 1943.

series of columns indicated the authorized number of personnel (*Kopfzahl*), weapons (*Waffen*) and vehicles (*Kraftfahrzeuge*). In the case of larger weapons systems and vehicles, the actual type was frequently listed in descriptions as well. In cases where personnel had an additional duty, e.g., assistant driver of a vehicle, these were annotated in the description column. Whenever certain types of vehicles could be substituted for what was authorized, these were usually indicated in the description column as a note at the end of the document. The documents seen here are from the National Archives and represent work copies used by the *Organizations-Abteilung*.

The basic format of the *KStN* was the same for all units. These are theoretical constructs, which did not always correspond to reality, even in ideal situations (e.g., after being activated initially or reconstituted in accordance with a new *KStN*, since not all vehicles, personnel, or equipment might have been available). Once organized in table format, it becomes easier to see the progression the various *KStN's* took over the course of the war. Several sample tables in graphical format are presented here. For those interested in seeing most of the *KStN's* that applied to the reconnaissance force, they may be seen at the authors' web site at this landing page: http://battlebornbooks.com/?page_id=491.

Der Generalinspekteur der Panzertruppen
Nur für den Dienstgebrauch

Vorausgabe, nach Erscheinen des Neudrucks vernichten.
Kriegsstärkenachweisung (Heer)

76 523
Nr. 1162 f (f.G.)
Blatt a
(Blatt a - d)

Nr. der Zeile	Stellengruppe	Gemischte Panzerspähkompanie (f.G.) (gem. Panz.Sp.Kp. (f.G.))	Kopfzahl: Offiziere	Beamte	Unteroffiziere	Mannschaften	Waffen: Gewehre, Karabiner	Pistolen (Masch.Pist.)	s.M.G. (le. M.G.)	besp. (unbesp.) Geschütze und Werfer	Fahrzeuge: besp. (unbesp.) Fahrzeuge [Wasserfahrzeuge]	Krad (Krad mit Seitenwagen) [Kettenkrad]	Personenkraftwg. (Lastkraftwagen) [Gleiskett.Lkw.]	Zugkw. (Vollkett. Schlepper) [Radschlepper]	gp. Vollkett. Kfz. (gp. Halbkett. Kfz) [gp. Räder-Kfz.]	Fahrräder (Anhänger) [Eisenbahnfahrz.]
		Hauptspalte	a	b	c	d	e	f	g	h	i	k	l	m	n	o
1		a) Gruppe Führer														
2																
2–3	K	Kompanieführer, Kommandant (zugl. Sprechfunker)	1					(1)								
4	O	Hauptfeldwebel			1			1								
5	O	Waffenunteroffizier (Wffm.)			1			1								
6–7	G	Kompanietruppführer (zugl. Richtschütze und Sprechfunker)			1			(1)								
8	G	Kraftwagenfahrer für gp. Kw.			1											
9	G	Sanitätsunteroffizier			1			1								
10	G	Funker (zugl. 2. Kw.Fahrer für gp.Kw.)			1			1								
11–12	M	Kradmelder (1 Krad mit Seitenwagen, 2 le. Krad 350 ccm)				3	3					2 (1)				
13	M	Kraftwagenfahrer für Pkw.				2	2									
14–15		leichte Personenkraftwagen, gl. (4-sitzig)											2			
16–17		schwerer Panzerspähwagen, (2 cm) (Sd.Kfz. 234/1)						(1)	(1)	(1)					[1]	
18	-	Summe zu a) Gruppe Führer	1		6	5	5	4 (3)	(1)	(1)		2 (1)	2		[1]	

Datum: 1. 4. 45

KStN 1162f (fG) for a mixed armored scout company. This draft document (*Vorausgabe*) was produced on 1 April 1945.

Headquarters and Headquarters Company of an Armored Reconnaissance Battalion (Free Organization)

KStN	Type of Unit	German	Date
1 1 0 9 (fG)	Headquarters and Headquarters Company of an Armored Reconnaissance Battalion (Free Organization)	*Stab and Stabskompanie einer Panzer-Aufklärungs-Abteilung (freie Gliederung)*	1 Nov 1944

a) Command Group

Light Motorcycle

Kettenkrad

Light Utility Vehicle, Cross-Country (4 Seat)

Heavy Cross-Country Armored Utility Vehicle (*Sd. Kfz. 247*)

Total Command Group: 4x Officers, 3x NCO's, 9x Enlisted Personnel; 8x Rifles, 4x Pistols, 4x Submachine Guns; 3x Motorcycles, 1x *Kettenkrad*, 2x Light Utility Vehicles, 1x Heavy Armored Cross-Country Utility Vehicle

b) Headquarters Company (Type A with 3 Light Armored Scout Platoons)

a) Command Section

Light Motorcycle (125 ccm)

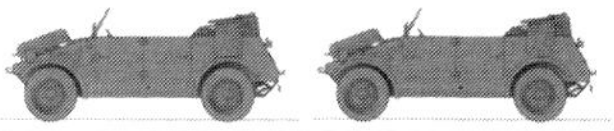

Light Utility Vehicle, Cross-Country (4 Seat)

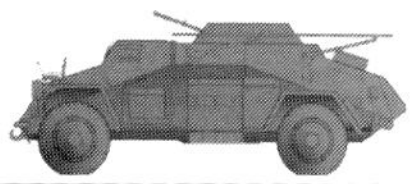

Light Armored Car (Radio) (*Sd.Kfz. 223 [Fu]*)

Total Command Group: 1x Officers, 5x NCO's, 5x Enlisted Personnel; 4x Rifles, 5x Pistols, 2x Submachine Guns, 1x Light MG; 2x Motorcycles, 2x Light Utility Vehicles, 1x Light Armored Car (Radio)

b) 1st Platoon (Signals)

Light Utility Vehicle, Cross-Country (4 Seat)

1st Medium Field Wire Section 12 (Motorized)

Truck, 2t, Open Cargo Area, Cross-Country

2nd Medium Field Wire Section 12 (Motorized), same as the 1st Section

Truck, 2t, Open Cargo Area, Cross-Country

1st and 2nd Backpack Radio Section g Medium Wave (Motorized)

Truck, 2t, Open Cargo Area, Cross-Country

1st Light Radio Section 80 Medium Wave (Motorized)

Truck, 2t, Open Cargo Area, Cross-Country

2nd Light Radio Section 80 Medium Wave (Motorized), same as 1st LightRadio Section

Truck, 2t, Open Cargo Area, Cross-Country

3rd Light Radio Section 80 Medium Wave (Motorized), same as 1st Light Radio Section

Truck, 2t, Open Cargo Area, Cross-Country

Light Air-Ground Radio Section 20 Short Wave (Motorized **)

Total Signals Platoon: 1x Officers, 8x NCO's, 26x Enlisted Personnel; 34x Rifles, 1x Submachine Gun; 1x Light Utility Vehicle, 6x Trucks

Notes: * Sd.Kfz. 260 counts in lieu of truck; ** Loaded with 1st Light Radio Section 80 Medium Wave (Motorized)

c) 2nd Platoon (Light Armored Car)

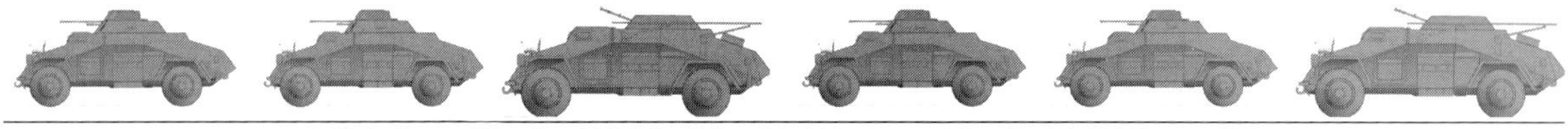

4x Light Armored Car (2cm) (*Sd.Kfz. 222*) and 2x Light Armored Car (Radio) (*Sd.Kfz. 223 [Fu]*)

Total 2nd Platoon: 1x Officers, 5x NCO's, 12x Enlisted Personnel; 11x Pistols, 7x Submachine Guns, 6x Light MG's, 4x Main Guns; 6x Light Armored Cars

d) 3rd Platoon (Light Armored Car), same as 2nd Platoon (Except NCO Platoon Leader)

4x Light Armored Car (2cm) (*Sd.Kfz. 222*) and 2x Light Armored Car (Radio) (*Sd.Kfz. 223 [Fu]*)

Total 3rd Platoon: 6x NCO's, 12x Enlisted Personnel; 11x Pistols, 7x Submachine Guns, 6x Light MG's, 4x Main Guns; 6x Light Armored Cars

e) 4th Platoon (Light Armored Car), same as 2nd Platoon (Except NCO Platoon Leader)

4x Light Armored Car (2cm) (*Sd.Kfz. 222*) and 2x Light Armored Car (Radio) (*Sd.Kfz. 223 [Fu]*)

Total 4th Platoon: 6x NCO's, 12x Enlisted Personnel; 11x Pistols, 7x Submachine Guns, 6x Light MG's, 4x Main Guns; 6x Light Armored Cars

Total Type A Headquarters Company: 7x Officers, 33x NCO's, 76x Enlisted Personnel; 46x Rifles, 42x Pistols, 28x Submachine Guns, 19x Light MG's, 12x Main Guns; 5x Motorcycles, 1 Kettenkrad, 5x Utility Vehicles, 6x Trucks, 20x Armored Cars

Notes: Drivers on armored vehicles are directed to use the vehicular small arms as their personal weapons. Sidecar motorcycles and Light Utility Vehicles count in lieu of *Kettenkräder*.

b) Headquarters Company (Type B with 2 Heavy Armored Scout Platoons)
a) Command Section

Light Motorcycles (125 ccm)

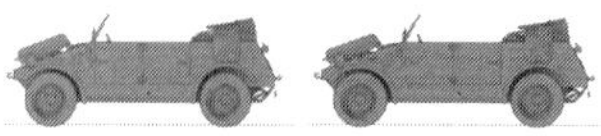

Light Utility Vehicle, Cross-Country (4 Seat)

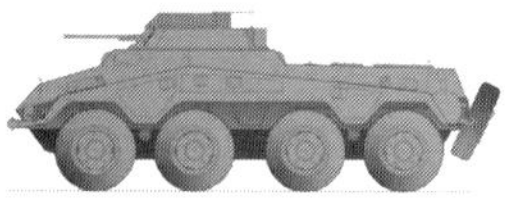

Heavy Armored Car (*Sd.Kfz. 234/1*)

Total Command Group: 1x Officers, 5x NCO's, 5x Enlisted Personnel; 4x Rifles, 5x Pistols, 2x Submachine Guns, 1x Light MG, 1x Main Gun; 2x Motorcycles, 2x Light Utility Vehicles, 1x Heavy Armored Car

b) 1st Platoon (Signals) (No change from Type A Headquarters Company)

Total Signals Platoon: 1x Officers, 8x NCO's, 26x Enlisted Personnel; 34x Rifles, 1x Submachine Gun; 1x Light Utility Vehicle, 6x Trucks

c) 2nd Platoon (Heavy Armored Car)
1st Armored Scout Section

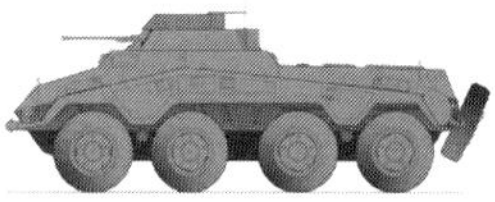

Heavy Armored Car (2cm) (*Sd.Kfz. 234/1*)

Heavy Armored Car (7.5cm) (*Sd.Kfz. 234/3*)

2nd Armored Scout Section (Same as 1st Section except Platoon Leader is NCO)

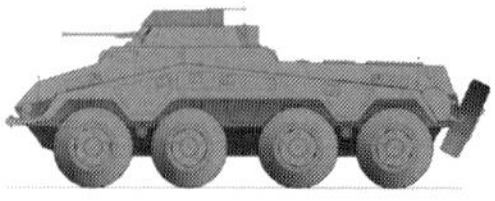

Heavy Armored Car (2cm) (*Sd.Kfz. 234/1*)

Heavy Armored Car (7.5cm) (*Sd.Kfz. 234/3*)

3rd Armored Scout Section (Same as 1st Section except Platoon Leader is NCO)

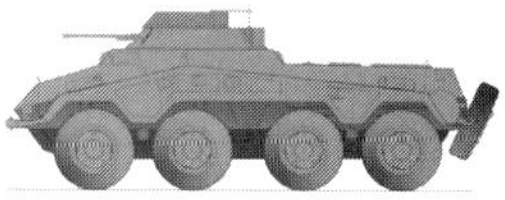

Heavy Armored Car (2cm) (*Sd.Kfz. 234/1*)

Heavy Armored Car (7.5cm) (*Sd.Kfz. 234/3*)

4th Armored Scout Section (Same as 1st Section except Platoon Leader is NCO)

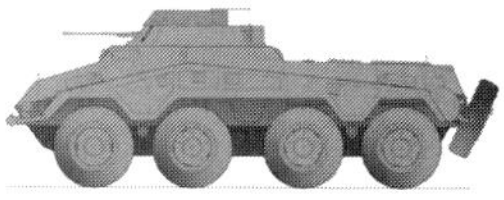

Heavy Armored Car (2cm) (*Sd.Kfz. 234/1*)

Heavy Armored Car (7.5cm) (*Sd.Kfz. 234/3*)

Total 2nd Platoon: 1x Officers, 11x NCO's, 20x Enlisted Personnel; 20x Pistols, 12x Submachine Guns, 8x Light MG's, 8x Main Guns; 8x Heavy Armored Cars

c) 3rd Platoon (Heavy Armored Car)
5th Armored Scout Section

Heavy Armored Car (2cm) (*Sd.Kfz. 234/1*)

Heavy Armored Car (7.5cm) (*Sd.Kfz. 234/3*)

6th Armored Scout Section (Same as 5th Section)

Heavy Armored Car (2cm) (*Sd.Kfz. 234/1*)

Heavy Armored Car (7.5cm) (*Sd.Kfz. 234/3*)

7th Armored Scout Section (Same as 5th Section)

Heavy Armored Car (2cm) (*Sd.Kfz. 234/1*)

Heavy Armored Car (7.5cm) (*Sd.Kfz. 234/3*)

Total 3rd Platoon: 9x NCO's, 15x Enlisted Personnel; 15x Pistols, 9x Submachine Guns, 6x Light MG's, 6x Main Guns; 6x Heavy Armored Cars

ARMORED SCOUTS

1162 Armored Scout Company or Armored Scout Troop *Panzerspäh-Kompanie bzw. Panzerspäh-Schwadron* 1 Oct 1938

Notes: Draft issued: 1 October 1936. Officially published: 1 October 1938 (shown below). Updated 1 February 1941. *Panzerspäh-Schwadron* deleted from title. Updated again on 1 November 1941 and 1 November 1943.

a) Command Group Company Headquarters Section

6x Sidecar Motorcycles,
3x Light Motorcycles,
3x Medium Motorcycles

Medium Cross-Country Vehicle (*Kfz. 11*), 1x Submachine Gun

Heavy Cross-Country Armored (*Sd.Kfz. 247*), 1x Submachine Gun

Total Command Group: 1x Officer, 2x NCO's, 15x Enlisted Personnel; 15x Rifles, 2x Submachine Guns, 3x Pistols; 1x Wheeled Vehicle, 1x Armored Wheeled Vehicle, 3x Medium Motorcycles, 3x Light Motorcycles, 6x Sidecar Motorcycles

b) Signals Section

Medium Armored Radio Section b (mot)

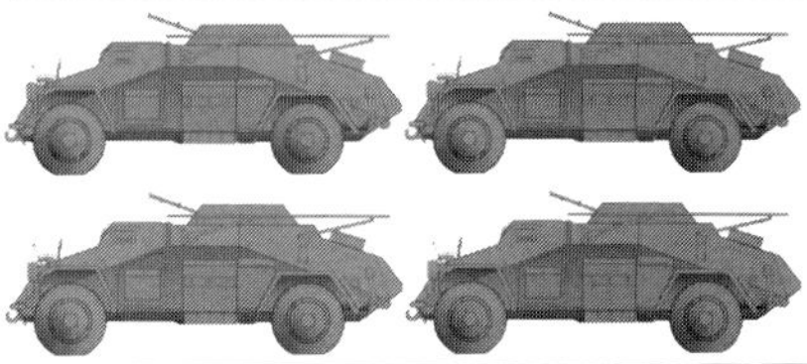

4x Light Armored Car (Radio) (*Sd. Kfz. 223) [Fu]*), 1x Light MG, 1x Submachine Gun

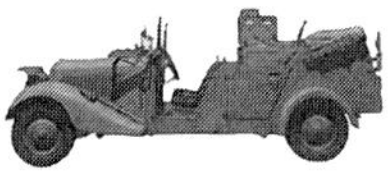

Radio Vehicle (*Kfz. 15*) Light MG, 1x Submachine Gun

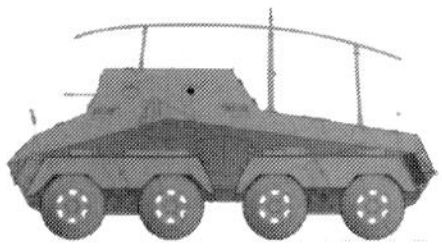

Armored Radio Car (*Sd.Kfz. 263*), 1x

Total Signals Section: 5x NCO's, 15x Enlisted Personnel; 20x Pistols, 5x Submachine Gun, 5x Light MG's; 1x Vehicle, 5x Armored Vehicles

c) 1st (Heavy) Platoon

1st Section

1x Heavy Armored Car (*Sd.Kfz. 231*), 1x 2cm Main Gun,1x Light MG, 1x Submachine Gun and 1x Heavy Armored Car (Radio) (*Sd.Kfz. 232 [Fu]*), 1x 2cm Main Gun,1x Light MG, 1x Submachine Gun

2nd Section

1x Heavy Armored Car (*Sd.Kfz. 231*), 1x 2cm Main Gun,1x Light MG, 1x Submachine Gun and 1x Heavy Armored Car (Radio) (*Sd.Kfz. 232 [Fu]*), 1x 2cm Main Gun,1x Light MG, 1x Submachine Gun

3rd Section

1x Heavy Armored Car (*Sd.Kfz. 231*), 1x 2cm Main Gun,1x Light MG, 1x Submachine Gun and 1x Heavy Armored Car (Radio) (*Sd.Kfz. 232 [Fu]*), 1x 2cm Main Gun,1x Light MG, 1x Submachine Gun

Total 1st (Heavy) Platoon: 2x Officers, 3x NCO's, 19x Enlisted Personnel; 24x Pistols, 6x Submachine Guns, 6x Light MG's; 6x Armored Vehicles

d) 2nd (Light) Platoon

1st Section

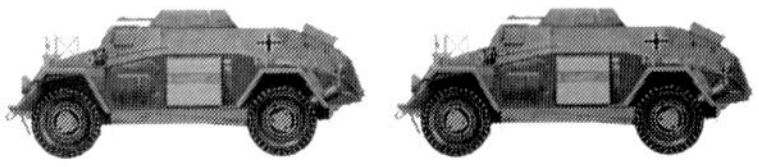

2x Light Armored Car (MG) (*Sd.Kfz. 221*), 2x Light MG, 2x Submachine Gun

2nd Section

2x Light Armored Car (MG) (*Sd.Kfz. 221*), 2x Light MG, 2x Submachine Gun

3rd Section

2x Light Armored Car (MG) (*Sd.Kfz. 221*), 2x Light MG, 2x Submachine Gun

Total 2nd (Light) Platoon: 1x Officer, 2x NCO's, 9x Enlisted Personnel; 12x Pistols, 6x Light MG's, 6x Submachine Guns; 6x Armored Vehicles

e) 3rd (Light) Platoon

1st Section

1x Light Armored Car (MG) (*Sd.Kfz. 221*), 1x Light MG, 1x Submachine Gun and 4x Light Armored Car (2cm Main Gun) (*Sd.Kfz. 222*)

2nd Section

1x Light Armored Car (MG) (*Sd.Kfz. 221*), 1x Light MG, 1x Submachine Gun and 4x Light Armored Car (2cm Main Gun) (*Sd.Kfz. 222*)

3rd Section

1x Light Armored Car (MG) (*Sd.Kfz. 221*), 1x Light MG, 1x Submachine Gun and 4x Light Armored Car (2cm Main Gun) (*Sd.Kfz. 222*)

4th Section

1x Light Armored Car (MG) (*Sd.Kfz. 221*), 1x Light MG, 1x Submachine Gun and 4x Light Armored Car (2cm Main Gun) (*Sd.Kfz. 222*)

Total 3rd (Light) Platoon: 1x Officer, 3x NCO's, 16x Enlisted Personnel; 20x Pistols, 8x Light MG's, 8x Submachine Guns; 8x Armored Vehicles

f) Combat Trains1st (Heavy) Platoon

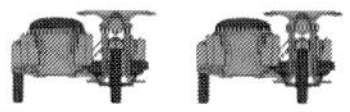

2x Sidecar Motorcycles

1x Medium, Cross-Country, Utility Vehicle with Equipment Storage Box (*Kfz. 15*)

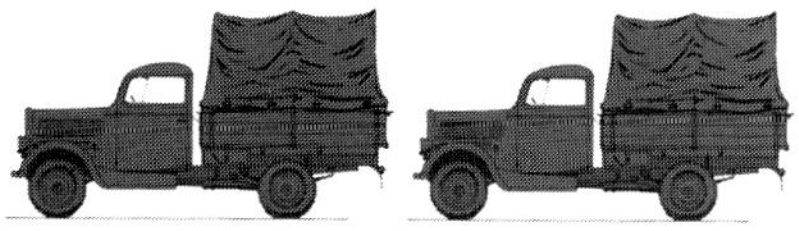

2x Light Cross-Country Trucks, Canvas Top, for Ammunition

1x Light Cross-Country Truck, Canvas Top, for Large Field Mess Stove

1x Light Cross-Country Truck, Canvas Top, for Vehicular and Engineer Equipment

1x Light Cross-Country Truck, Canvas Top, for Petroleum, Oil & Lubricants and Equipment

1x Light Cross-Country Truck, Canvas Top, for Petroleum, Oil & Lubricants

1x Light Cross-Country Truck, Canvas Top, for the Transport of Personnel

Total Combat Trains: 6x NCO's, 24x Enlisted Personnel; 25x Rifles, 5x Pistols; 8x Wheeled Vehicles, 2x Sidecar Motorcycles

Summary

	Officers	NCO's	Enlisted Personnel	Rifles	Pistols	Submachine Guns	Light MG's	Wheeled Vehicles	Armored Vehicles	Motorcycles	Sidecar Motorcycles
Command Group	1	2	15	15	3	2		1	1	6	6
Signals Section		5	15		20	5	5	1	5		
1st Platoon	2	3	19		24	6	6		6		
2nd Platoon	1	2	9		12	6	6		6		
3rd Platoon	1	3	16		20	8	8		8		
Combat Trains		6	24	25	5			8			2
Baggage Trains			4	4				1			
Totals	**5**	**21**	**102**	**44**	**84**	**27**	**25**	**11**	**26**	**6**	**8**

KStN	Type of Unit	German	Date
1162c	Armored Scout Company "c"	*Panzerspäh-Kompanie c*	1 Nov 1943

Note: This is the first scout company to use half-tracked vehicles.

a) Command Group
Company Headquarters Section

2 Light Motorcycles 350ccm, 2x *Kettenkräder*

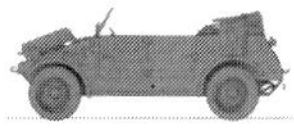

1x Light Utility Vehicle, Cross-Country, (4 seat)

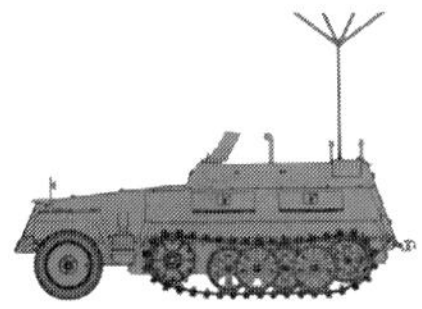

1x Light Armored Observation Half-track (*Sd.Kfz. 250/5*), 1x Submachine Gun, 1x Light MG

Totals: 1x Officer, 4x NCO's, 5x Enlisted Personnel; 6x Rifles, 3x Pistols, 2x Submachine Guns, 1x Light MG; 1x Wheeled Vehicle, 1x Armored Vehicle, 2x Motorcycles, 2x *Kettenkräder*

b) 1st Platoon
1st Section

1x Light Armored Observation Half-track (*Sd.Kfz. 250/5*), 1x Submachine Gun, 1x Light MG and 2x Light Armored Personnel Carrier (2cm) (*Sd.Kfz. 250/9*), 2x Submachine Guns, 2x Light MG, 2x 2cm Main Guns

2nd Section

1x Light Armored Observation Half-track (*Sd.Kfz. 250/5*), 1x Submachine Gun, 1x Light MG and 2x Light Armored Personnel Carrier (2cm) (*Sd.Kfz. 250/9*), 2x Submachine Guns, 2x Light MG, 2x 2cm Main Guns

Totals: 1x Officer, 11x NCO's, 6x Enlisted Personnel; 18x Pistols, 6x Submachine Guns, 6x Light MG's, 4x 2cm Main Guns; 6x Armored Half-track Vehicles

c) 2nd Platoon
1st Section

1x Light Armored Observation Half-track (*Sd.Kfz. 250/5*), 1x Submachine Gun, 1x Light MG and 2x Light Armored Personnel Carrier (2cm) (*Sd.Kfz. 250/9*), 2x Submachine Guns, 2x Light MG, 2x 2cm Main Guns

2nd Section

1x Light Armored Observation Half-track (*Sd.Kfz. 250/5*), 1x Submachine Gun, 1x Light MG and 2x Light Armored Personnel Carrier (2cm) (*Sd.Kfz. 250/9*), 2x Submachine Guns, 2x Light MG, 2x 2cm Main Guns

Totals: 1x Officer, 11x NCO's, 6x Enlisted Personnel; 18x Pistols, 6x Submachine Guns, 6x Light MG's, 4x 2cm Main Guns; 6x Armored Half-track Vehicles

d) 3rd Platoon

1st Section

1x Light Armored Observation Half-track (*Sd.Kfz. 250/5*), 1x Submachine Gun, 1x Light MG and 2x Light Armored Personnel Carrier (2cm) (*Sd.Kfz. 250/9*), 2x Submachine Guns, 2x Light MG, 2x 2cm Main Guns

2nd Section

1x Light Armored Observation Half-track (*Sd.Kfz. 250/5*), 1x Submachine Gun, 1x Light MG and 2x Light Armored Personnel Carrier (2cm) (*Sd.Kfz. 250/9*), 2x Submachine Guns, 2x Light MG, 2x 2cm Main Guns

Totals: 12x NCO's, 6x Enlisted Personnel; 18x Pistols, 6x Submachine Guns, 6x Light MG's, 4x 2cm Main Guns; 6x Armored Half-track Vehicles

e) 4th Platoon

1st Section

1x Light Armored Observation Half-track (*Sd.Kfz. 250/5*), 1x Submachine Gun, 1x Light MG and 2x Light Armored Personnel Carrier (2cm) (*Sd.Kfz. 250/9*), 2x Submachine Guns, 2x Light MG, 2x 2cm Main Guns

2nd Section

1x Light Armored Observation Half-track (*Sd.Kfz. 250/5*), 1x Submachine Gun, 1x Light MG and 2x Light Armored Personnel Carrier (2cm) (*Sd.Kfz. 250/9*), 2x Submachine Guns, 2x Light MG, 2x 2cm Main Guns

Totals: 12x NCO's, 6x Enlisted Personnel; 18x Pistols, 6x Submachine Guns, 6x Light MG's, 4x 2cm Main Guns; 6x Armored Half-track Vehicles

f) Vehicle Maintenance Section

1x Truck 2t, Canvas Top, Cross-Country, (Set up for Vehicle Maintenance Section)

1x Truck 3t, Canvas Top, Cross-Country, for Replacement Parts

1x Truck 3t, Canvas Top, Cross-Country, for Workshop Equipment, with Basic Issue for Vehicle Maintenance Section

1x Light Prime Mover 3t (*Sd.Kfz. 11*)

Totals: 4x NCO's, 9x Enlisted Personnel; 12x Rifles 1x Pistol; 4x Wheeled Vehicles

g) Combat Trains

1x Light Utility Vehicle, Cross-Country, (4 seat)	1x Truck 3t, Canvas Top, Cross-Country, for Ammunition and Equipment	1x Truck 3t, Canvas Top, Cross-Country, for Petroleum, Oil & Lubricants	1x Truck 3t, Canvas Top, Cross-Country, for Small Field Mess Stove

Totals: 4x NCO's, 8x Enlisted Personnel; 10x Rifles, 1x Pistol, 1x Submachine Gun; 4x Wheeled Vehicles

Summary

	Officers	NCO's	Enlisted Personnel	Rifles	Pistols (Submachine Guns)	Light MG's	Main Guns	Vehicles	Armored Vehicles	Motorcycles (Sidecars [*Kettenkräder*]
Command Section	1	4	5	6	3 (2)	1		1	1	2 [2]
1st Platoon	1	11	6		18 (6)	6	4		6	
2nd Platoon	1	11	6		18 (6)	6	4		6	
3rd Platoon		12	6		18 (6)	6	4		6	
4th Platoon		12	6		18 (6)	6	4		6	
Vehicle Maint. Section		4	9	12				4		
Combat Trains		4	8	10	1 (1)			4		
Baggage Trains		1	3	4				1		
Totals	**3**	**59**	**49**	**32**	**77 (27)**	**25**	**12**	**10**	**25**	**2 [2]**

structure of the German Army seemed to mirror that of the overall situation. Decimated and effectively destroyed divisions were reconstituted, reorganized, and redesignated, while units from the Replacement Army were impressed to form *ad hoc* organizations and garrisons in the pathway of the Western Allies and the Soviet Union (*Alarm-Divisionen*).

At the start of 1945, *Infanterie-Division 45* was introduced, which was to be applied to virtually all infantry divisions, with the exception of the *1. Infanterie-Division*, the divisions composed of foreign personnel, and those divisions assigned occupation duty in Norway. It is unlikely that it was ever implemented.

Assault Divisions

There were two *Sturm-Divisionen* on the rolls of the German Army in 1943: the previously discussed *78. Sturm-Division* and *Sturm-Division "Rhodos."* The latter was employed in the Aegean to protect German assets and shipping lanes. Part of the division was an armored reconnaissance battalion, *Panzer-Aufklärungs-Abteilung 999*, which had an armored car company with at least eighteen armored cars, an antitank platoon equipped with six 7.5cm armored cars, a VW-equipped armored reconnaissance company, a heavy company, and an antitank company. This unique arrangement was probably due more to happenstance than design, since the division was the beneficiary of equipment intended for Africa that could no longer be ferried over.

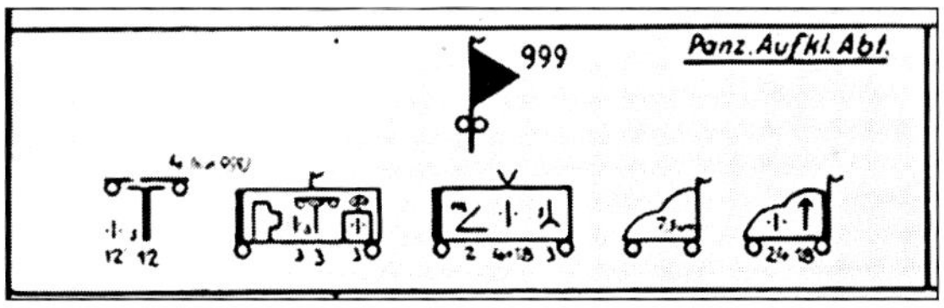

Panzer-Aufklärungs-Abteilung 999 of *Sturm-Division Rhodos.*

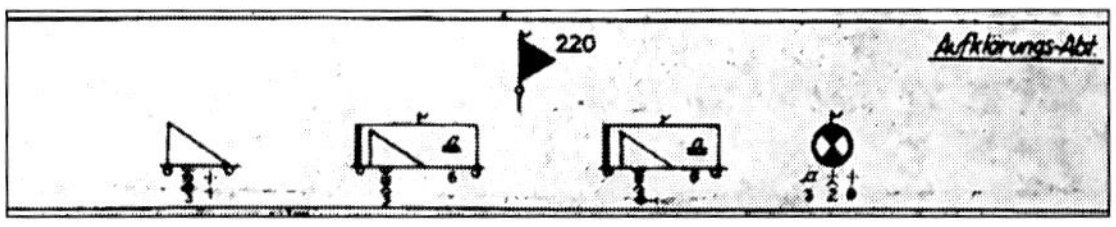

Festungs-Division Kreta had a reconnaissance battalion, but its assets were more like those of the combined antitank and reconnaissance battalions found in most infantry divisions of the time.

Militia and Border Security Divisions (*Landwehr- und Infanterie-Divisionen aus Grenzwachtkommandos*)

These formations had no reconnaissance assets.

Fortification Divisions and Brigades and Fortresses (*Festungs-Divisionen und -Brigaden aud Festungen*)

These formations generally had no discernible reconnaissance assets, although *Festungs-Division "Kreta"* did have a reconnaissance battalion, albeit with no armored assets.

Security Divisions and Brigades (*Sicherungs-Divisionen und -Brigaden*)

Nine security divisions were established in 1941 to protect the rear areas and guard important facilities. As the divisions were not intended for frontline employment, none of the original nine divisions had any reconnaissance assets. This changed slightly at the end of September 1942, when three of the divisions were authorized a tank company (using captured vehicles). One of those divisions, the *444. Sicherungs-Division* was also authorized a *Panzerspäh-Zug*, but it is unknown whether the armored car platoon was ever fielded.

In the West, the *325. Sicherungs-Division* was formed in August 1942, using assets from the guard regiments in Paris and militia entities. Apparently, one of its regiments, *Sicherungs-Regiment 190*, was authorized a *Panzerspäh-Kompanie* of eighteen 2cm armored cars, presumably coming from captured French stocks. It is unknown whether the regiment's

Security divisions were not usually authorized armored assets. When they were, they were generally fielded with obsolete and/or captured stocks of equipment. They were allocated for show-of-force purposes, not reconnaissance. At left is the 14th Company of *Sicherungs-Regiment 190*, as authorized in September 1943. At right is the mixed armor company of the *444. Sicherungs-Division* in September 1942.

14th Company was ever fielded as the division itself was lost in Paris after the invasion of Normandy in 1944.[20] Finally, a *Sicherungs-Brigades-Stab 74* was established in the West in the spring of 1944. Part of the brigade troops consisted of *Sicherungs-Aufklärungs-Abteilung 1000*, which apparently was authorized a *Panzerspäh-Kompanie*. Whether this was ever fielded is also not known. Regardless, this particular element was only short lived and was later used to provide cadre for the *189.* and *462. Infanterie-Divisionen*.

Light Infantry, Mountain Infantry, and Ski Infantry Divisions and Brigades (*Jäger-, Gebirgsjäger, und Ski-Divisionen und -Brigaden*)

While the first three mountain divisions formed as part of the first wave in August 1939 had mountain reconnaissance battalions, none of them had any armored assets. *Gebirgs-Aufklärungs-Abteilung 54* of the *1. Gebirgs-Division* did have a *Kradschützen-Schwadron*. When all three of the divisions lost their reconnaissance battalions after the campaign in the West, *Kradschützen-Schwadron 54* remained with its parent division. When the reconnaissance assets were reestablished later on, they all consisted of partially motorized bicycle battalions. The same is true of subsequent mountain divisions that were formed.

Light infantry divisions—97, 100, and 101—were established in the summer of 1942, but they also did not have any armored vehicles as part of their reconnaissance assets. In general, they had three bicycle troops and a heavy company in their reconnaissance battalions. The same held true for regular infantry divisions that were converted into light infantry divisions in May 1943.[21]

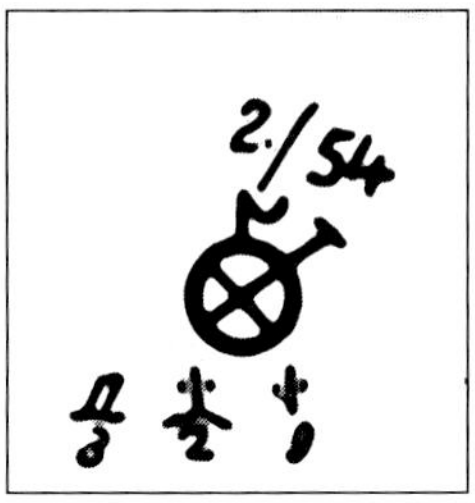

The *2./Gebirgs-Aufklärungs-Abteilung 54* was the only motorized reconnaissance among the mountain divisions. It was assigned to the *1. Gebirgs-Division* (outlined here as of February 1941). None of the mountain divisions had any armored reconnaissance assets.

Luftwaffe Field Formations (*Luftwaffen-Feld-Verbände*)

Although it is commonly assumed that the field formations that the *Luftwaffe* formed were under control of the Air Force, the divisions were absorbed into the army by November 1943 (with the exception of the *Hermann Göring* formations), albeit usually retaining their *Luftwaffe* designations. The "divisions" were originally little more than reinforced regiments with bicycle reconnaissance assets. Once reorganized into division-level entities, they received bicycle reconnaissance battalions, thus having no discernible armored assets.

ARMORED RECONNAISSANCE WITHIN THE CAVALRY

Cavalry Formations

As previously discussed, the thirteen *Kavallerie-Regimenter* of the German Army were disbanded upon mobilization in August 1939 and used to form the reconnaissance assets of the infantry divisions. The two remaining mounted formations were *Reiter-Regimenter 1* and *2*, which were used to form the *1. Kavallerie-Brigade*, the only horse-mounted major formation at the start of hostilities.

Despite its status as a "horse" unit, the cavalry brigade was motorized to some extent. Each of the regimental headquarters had a *Kavallerie-Panzerspäh-Trupp* of three armored cars. When the brigade was expanded and reorganized as a division in October 1939, it received an additional mounted regiment (*Reiter-Regiment 22*), which also had an armored car section, albeit of two vehicles. In addition, a brigade headquarters was formed with the same assets. After having fought in France, where it acquitted itself quite well, the division received yet another mounted regiment (*Reiter-Regiment 21*) and established a second brigade headquarters. *Reiter-Regiment 21* had an armored car platoon in its heavy troop, while *Reiter-Brigade 2* had a motorcycle infantry platoon in lieu of an armored car troop or platoon.

At the start of 1941, *Panzer-Aufklärungs-Lehr-Abteilung* was attached to the division for operational duty, where it served successfully on the Eastern Front until returning to Germany in October 1941.

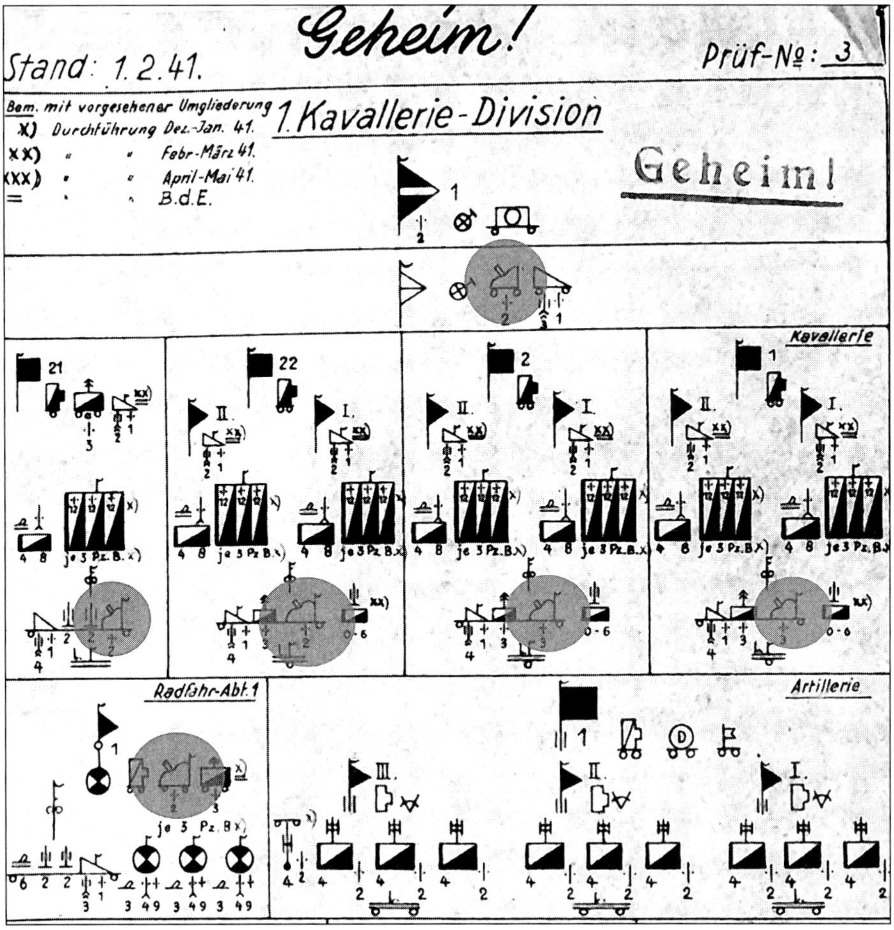

The *1. Kavallerie-Division* had a number of armored car platoons and sections scattered among its divisional regiments and troops (1 February 1941).

One month later, the division returned to Germany to be redesignated and reorganized as the *24. Panzer-Division*. The division had performed well in the East, but its losses had been extremely high, especially since it had often been employed as flank guard for armored corps, where the high operational tempo and speed of movement extracted an unusually high toll, especially on the horses.[22]

That spelled the end to horse-mounted operations on a large scale (i.e., brigade or division level) within the German Army, until Cossacks were used to form the *1. Kosaken-Division* in August 1943, the first of several horse-mounted formations that the Germans employed in the East with predominantly foreign rank-and-file. None of those formations had any identifiable armored reconnaissance assets.

The utility of larger-scale horse-mounted formations manned by German personnel was recognized in late 1943. The Soviets used horse-mounted formations throughout the war, often to great effect against German infantry divisions once breakthroughs were achieved, and orders were issued to establish two German cavalry brigades in February and March 1944. The *3. Kavallerie-Brigade* was formed from the essentially *ad hoc* formation *Heeresgruppe Mitte* had established, *Kavallerie-Regiment Mitte*. There was also a *Kavallerie-Regiment Nord*, and some thought was given to allocating it to the newly forming brigade, but the *Organizations-Abteilung* thought the resulting organization might be too unwieldy. Instead, each of the regiments was used to form a cavalry brigade.[23] The *3. Kavallerie-Brigade* formed *schwere Kavallerie-Abteilung (mot) 3*, which formed

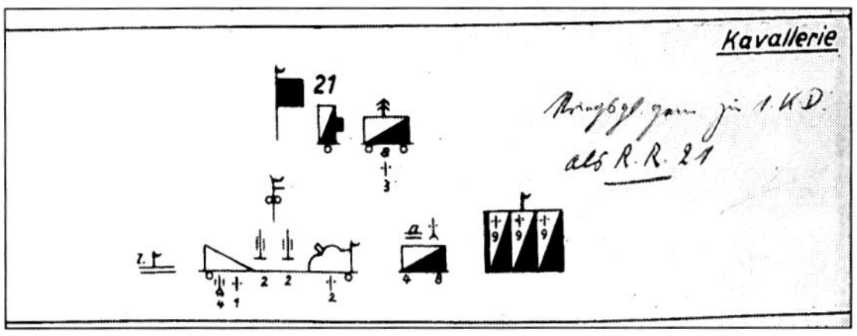

Reiter-Regiment 21 in November 1940.

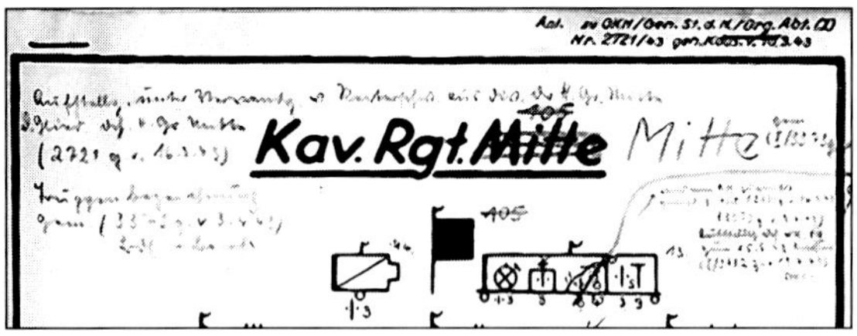

The status of *Kavallerie-Regiment Mitte* at the end of October 1942. As can be seen by the number of handwritten entries, the proposed organization of the regiment was in flux.

the core of the mechanized and armored assets of the brigades. The heavy battalion had a tank company (1st) composed of captured tanks, most likely T-34's; an *SPW* troop (2nd); a towed *Flak* troop (3rd); and a motorized combat engineer troop (4th).

The *4. Kavallerie-Brigade* was formed from the cavalry regiment of *Heeresgruppe Süd, Kavallerie-Regiment Süd*. Its organization was similar to that of its sister cavalry brigade, but it did not establish its heavy battalion until the end of 1944 and beginning of 1945.

The brigades were then ordered to stand down their heavy cavalry battalions and form armored reconnaissance battalions, but it appears this only happened with *Panzer-Aufklärungs-Abteilung (gp) 69* in the *3. Kavallerie-Brigade*. It was based on the *Panzer-Division 44* model, but without the half-tracked armored scout company (*Panzerspäh-Kompanie "C"*) or the heavy armored reconnaissance company (*schwere Panzer-Aufklärungs-Kompanie [gp]*). Some sources state that the *4. Kavallerie-Brigade* apparently kept its heavy battalion until the end of the war, but other sources list the brigade as having an armored reconnaissance battalion (*Panzer-Aufklärungs-Abteilung 70*), which had an armored car scout company, an *SPW* company, and an *SPW* armored reconnaissance company.[24] In February 1945, the cavalry brigades were redesignated as divisions, but there was no appreciable change to their organization.

Light Divisions

The light divisions, first formed in 1938 using the French *Division Légère Mécanique* as a model, were under the purview of the cavalry until being reorganized and redesignated as armored divisions after the Polish campaign in 1939. They can be considered a sort of "last hurrah" on the part of the cavalry to maintain a presence in the efforts to motorize the force. It has been said that a better term for these divisions would have been *schnelle Divisionen* or *Panzerkavallerie*.[25] Regardless of the term used, they did not live up to expectations. Although they were fast, they did not pack the punch of an armored division since they only had a single light tank battalion and the battalions of the cavalry rifle regiments, the *Kavallerie-Schützen-Regimenter*, had only a bit more end strength and the same firepower as a motorcycle infantry battalion. As to be expected in a formation fielded by the cavalry, there were large motorized reconnaissance and motorcycle infantry assets in each of the divisions, organized as a single reconnaissance regiment in three of them. The latter three divisions were almost identical in organization, at least in terms of the formations assigned to them.

Formation	Reconnaissance Asset(s)
1. leichte Division	*Kradschützen-Abteilung 6, Aufklärungs-Abteilung (mot.) 6*
2. leichte Division	*Aufklärungs-Regiment (mot.) 7*
3. leichte Division	*Aufklärungs-Regiment (mot.) 8*
4. leichte Division	*Aufklärungs-Regiment (mot.) 9*

Theoretically, the reconnaissance regiments consisted of two battalions, one of motorcycle infantry and the other of armored cars. The first battalion, the *Kradschützen-Abteilung*, was organized in a fairly standard manner with a headquarters (*KStN 1109*), three motorcycle infantry troops (*KStN 1111a*), and a motorized heavy troop (*KStN's 1121, 1122, 1123*, and *1126*).

The second battalion, the *Panzerspäh-Abteilung*, had a unique organization for the time with a headquarters (*KStN 1105*) and four armored car troops (*KStN 1191*). As only two of the light divisions were organized in strict accordance with the theoretical model, here are the differences:

1. leichte Division. Kradschützen-Abteilung 6 reported to a *Schützen-Brigade* headquarters. The bat-

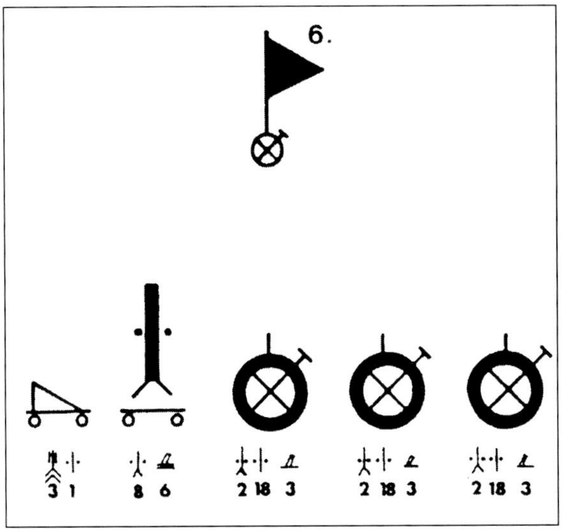

Kradschützen-Abteilung 6.

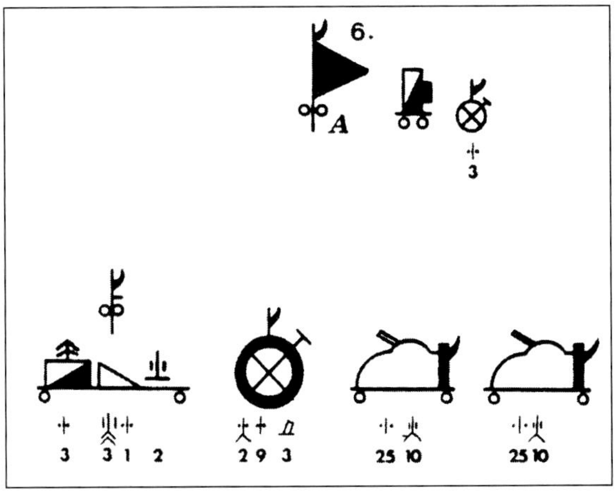

Aufklärungs-Abteilung (mot) 6.

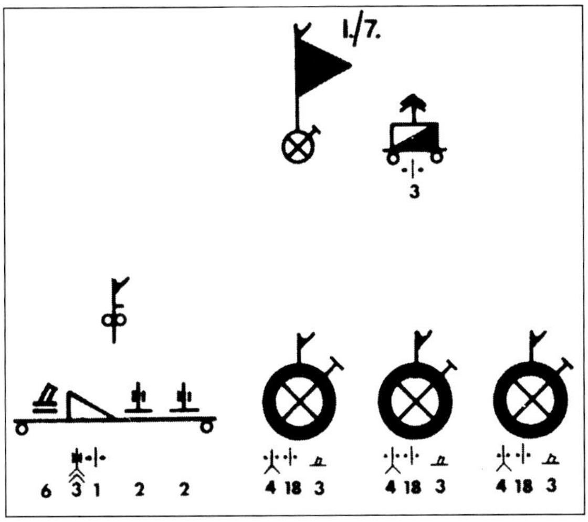

I./Aufklärungs-Regiment 7.

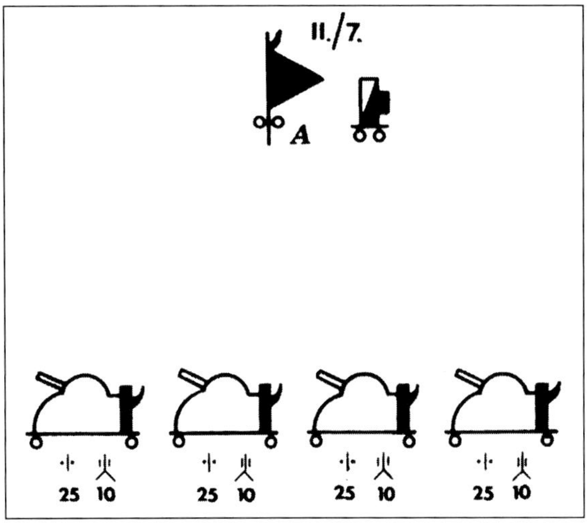

II./Aufklärungs-Regiment 7.

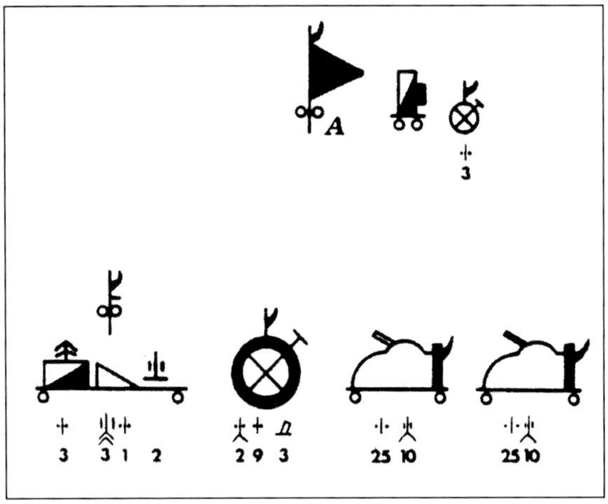

II./Aufklärungs-Regiment 8.

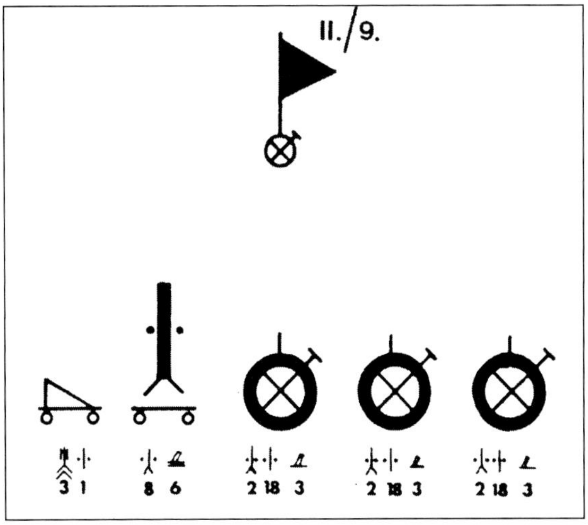

II./Kavallerie-Schützen-Regiment 9.

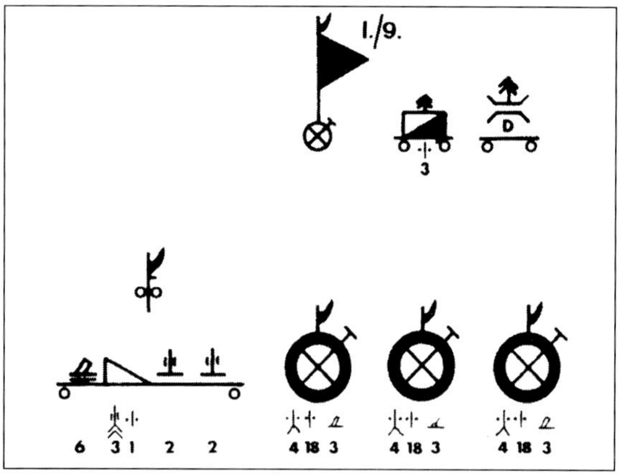

I./Aufklärungs-Regiment 9.

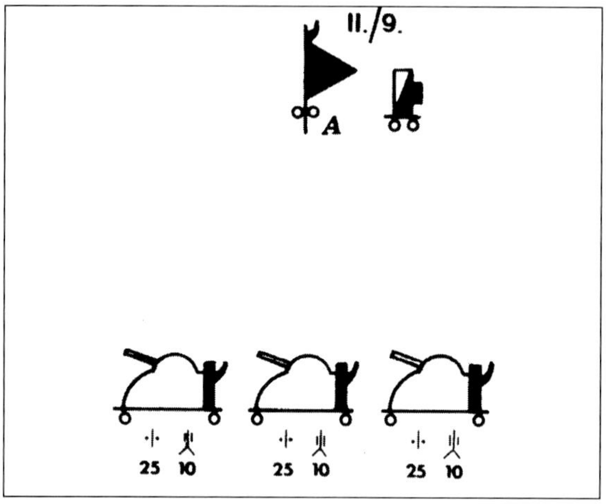

II./Aufklärungs-Regiment 9.

talion apparently did not have a heavy troop; instead, it had a *Kradschützen-Maschinengewehr-Schwadron* and a separate towed antitank platoon (three 3.7cm antitank guns). The division had only one *Kavallerie-Schützen-Regiment* (4), but it had three line battalions. The division had a separate motorized reconnaissance battalion. *Aufklärungs-Abteilung (mot.) 6* was organized like a typical armored division motorized reconnaissance of the period, with two armored car troops, one motorcycle infantry troop, and a heavy company.

2. leichte Division. Corresponds to the theoretical model above.

3. leichte Division. The *II./Kavallerie-Schützen-Regiment 9* was organized like *Kradschützen-Abteilung 6* in the *1. leichte Division*. This regiment had a total of three line battalions. The sister rifle regiment, *Kavallerie-Schützen-Regiment 8*, had only two line battalions.

Aufklärungs-Regiment 8 had two motorized reconnaissance battalions instead of a motorcycle infantry battalion and motorized reconnaissance battalion (as in the *2.* and *4. leichte Divisionen*). The reconnaissance battalions were organized like *Aufklärungs-Abteilung (mot.) 6* in the *1. leichte Division*. Further, the *I./Aufklärungs-Regiment 8* had already been detached from the light division prior to the start of the war to assist *Panzer-Division Kempf* (later *10. Panzer-Division*), eventually being assigned to the latter division.

4. leichte Division. Corresponds to the model above.

ARMORED RECONNAISSANCE WITHIN THE *SCHNELLE TRUPPEN* AND THE *PANZERTRUPPE*

Motorized Infantry and Mechanized Infantry Divisions (Infanterie-Divisionen (mot.) und Panzergrenadier-Divisionen)

The initial four motorized infantry divisions (2, 13, 20, and 29) were part of the peacetime army and originated from the first wave. They initially fell under the purview of the infantry branch, but since they were soon absorbed by the *schnelle Truppen*, they are listed here. Unlike their non-motorized infantry brethren, they had reconnaissance assets from the beginning, since their capabilities were considered to be more long range and analogous to those of the *Panzer* divisions.

Unlike the armored divisions, however, their reconnaissance battalions had only one armored car troop (as opposed to the two of the armored divisions). The reconnaissance battalions also had a motorcycle infantry troop, and each of the three motorized infantry regiments also had a motorcycle infantry platoon. Following the campaign in France in 1940, these divisions were reorganized to have a *Kradschützen-Bataillon* in addition to the reconnaissance battalion, which itself received a heavy company. As with the armored divisions, the motorcycle infantry assets often worked hand-in-glove with the reconnaissance elements, with the result that they are considered *de facto* reconnaissance assets.

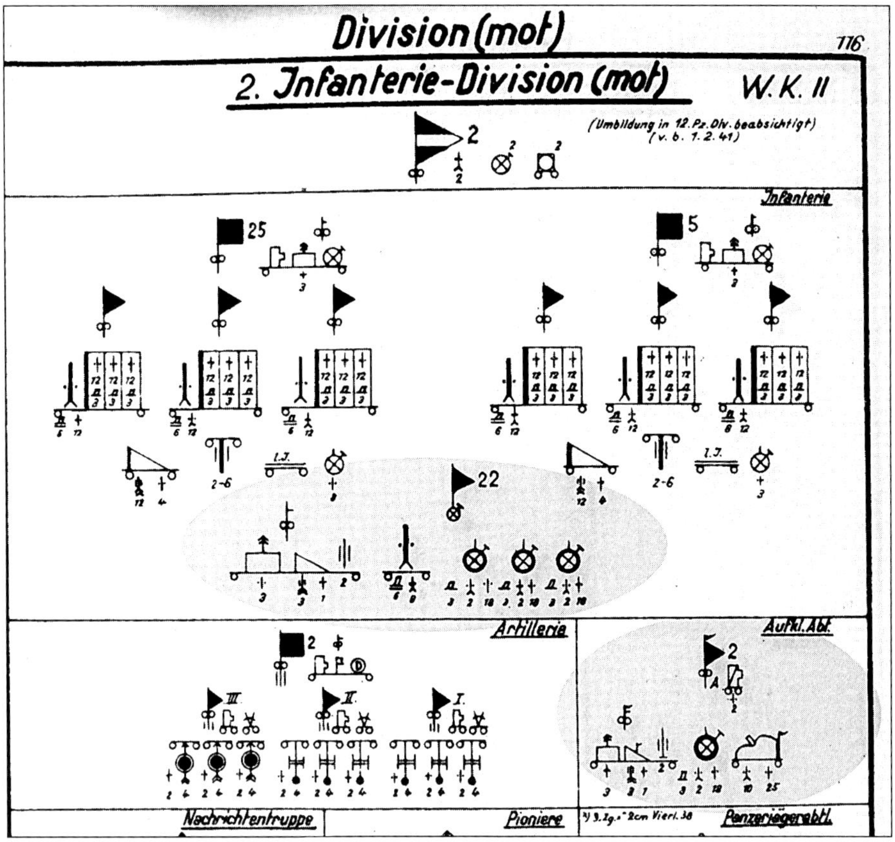

By November 1940, the *2. Infanterie-Division (mot)* had also received a motorcycle infantry battalion.

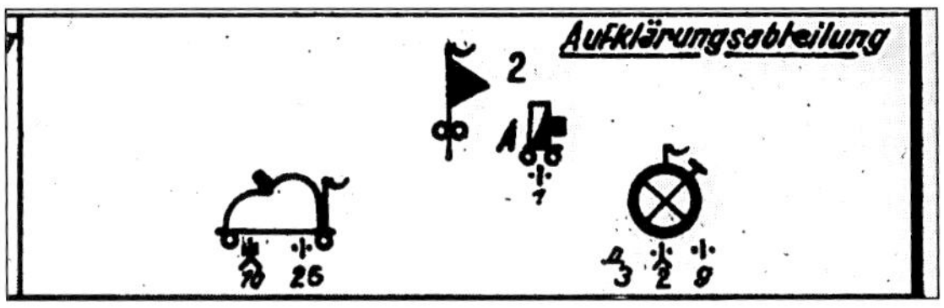

Aufklärungs-Abteilung 2 (mot) of the *2. Infanterie-Division (mot)* is illustrative of the typical organization for a motorized division's reconnaissance force in January 1940.

By the fall of 1940, seven additional infantry divisions (3, 10, 14, 18, 25, 36, and 60) were ordered to be motorized. The *16. Infanterie-Division*, which was to be reorganized as the *16. Panzer-Division*, also provided remaining cadre and equipment from the *16. Infanterie-Division (mot.)*, a numerical duplication that sometimes results in confusion when researching the two formations. Three of these divisions (3, 14, and 18) were equipped with captured French military stocks, with the result that their armored cars were probably Panhards.

On 21 April 1942, it was ordered that the motorcycle infantry and reconnaissance battalions be consolidated, with the motorcycle infantry battalions maintaining order of precedence for the designation of the formations. The "new" *Kradschützen-Bataillon* thus had three motorcycle infantry companies, an armored car company (eighteen armored cars), and a heavy company. This consolidation most likely resulted from an inability to field two complete battalions with reconnaissance assets, especially in light of the continued expansion of the field army coupled with Hitler's refusal to deactivate assets that were no longer viable. This measure was cut short when the motorcycle infantry battalions were redesignated as *Panzer-Aufklärungs-Abteilungen* in March 1943 and the motorcycle was largely replaced with a variety of wheeled and half-tracked assets, due in large part to the limited mobility of the motorcycles under the squalid conditions in the East, as well as the fact that the growing lethality of enemy weapons systems dic-

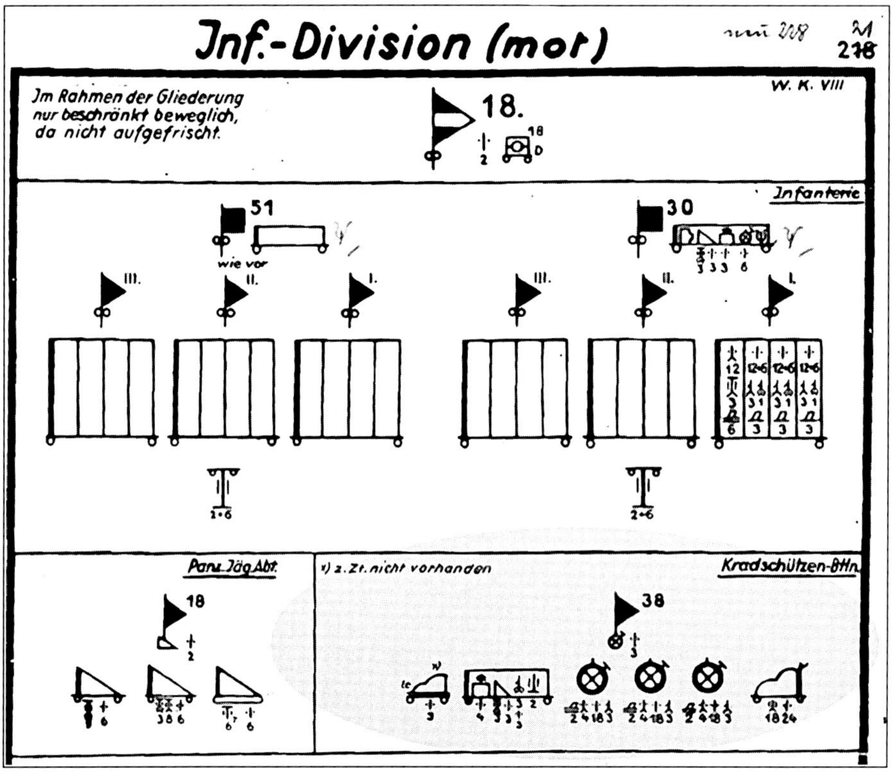

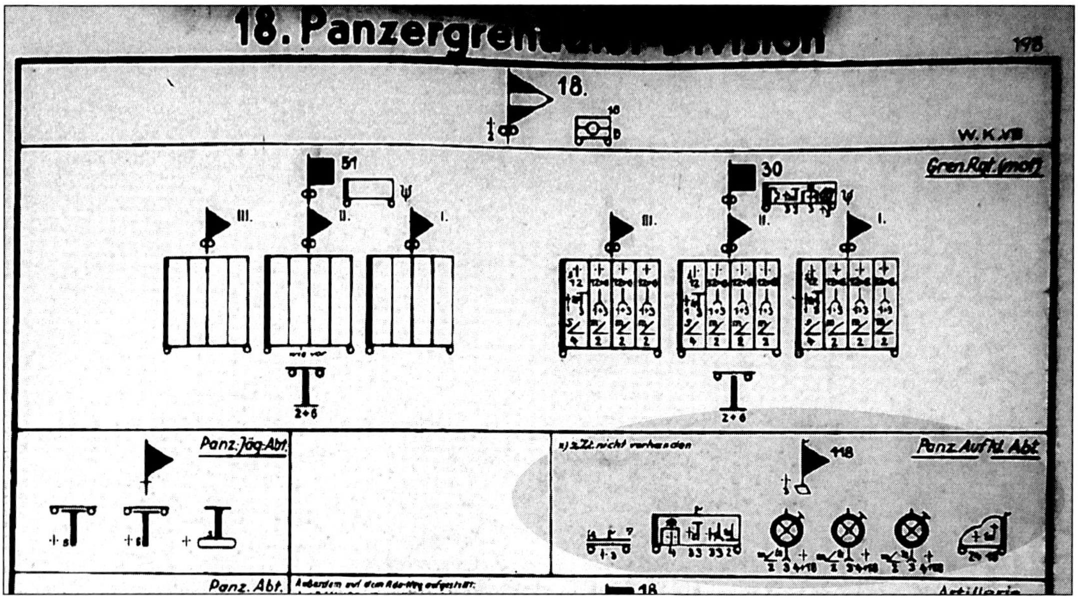

Throughout much of 1942, the armored reconnaissance force was in a state of turmoil as its battalions were consolidated with the divisional motorcycle infantry battalions. This was done primarily because of the inability of industry to keep pace with the losses being sustained as the result of continuous operations. By early 1943, however, the *Kradschützen-Bataillone* were redesignated as *Panzer-Aufklärungs-Abteilung*, signaling the demise of the motorcycle infantry as a separate force. Here the *18. Infanterie-Division (mot)* in September 1942 and again a year later, after being redesignated as the *18. Panzergrenadier-Division. Kradschützen-Bataillon 38* has become *Panzer-Aufklärungs-Abteilung 118.*

tated that these assets receive a modicum of armored protection, if possible. The former *Kradschützen-Kompanien* were redesignated as *Panzeraufklärungs-Kompanien*.

Although *Infanterie-Regiment (mot.) "Großdeutschland"* had performed successfully in combat since the start of the war, it was not until March of 1942 that it was officially expanded to a division. Prior to that, the 17th Company of its 5th Battalion was a motorcycle infantry company, augmented by an armored car platoon. Upon redesignations and reorganization as a division, it received a motorcycle infantry battalion that had an armored car company, a half-tracked motorized infantry company (equipped with *SPW's*), two wheeled motorcycle infantry companies (equipped with VW's), and a heavy company. Later that same year, two *Kriemhilde*[26] divisions were formed as motorized infantry formations (345 and 386). *Kradschützen-Bataillone 345* and *386* each had an armored car company, two motorcycle infantry companies, and an antitank company (instead of a heavy company). These two divisions were short lived, being used to reconstitute two motorized infantry divisions lost at Stalingrad (3 and 29).

As many divisions were rebuilding in early 1943 after the debacle at Stalingrad (and the one looming in Tunisia in May), the organization of the divisional reconnaissance assets also changed. Generally, the battalion headquarters had a heavy armored car platoon consisting of six vehicles equipped with the short 7.5cm main gun (*Sd.Kfz. 233*). The line units consisted of an armored car scout company (*Panzerspähkompanie*) with eighteen armored cars, a half-tracked scout company (also designated as a *Panzerspähkompanie*) with sixteen light half-tracks armed with a 2cm cannon and machine gun in a turret (*Sd.Kfz. 250/9*), two half-tracked reconnaissance companies (*Sd.Kfz. 250*) (referred to as *Panzer-Aufklärungs-Kompanien*), and a heavy company with a light infantry gun platoon, an antitank platoon, and a combat engineer platoon. At the same time that many divisions were being reconstituted, some were rebuilt as different organizations; for example, the *15. Panzer-Division* and *90. leichte Afrika-Division* were reorganized and redesignated as *Panzergrenadier-Divisionen*, while the *14.* and *36. Infanterie-Divisionen (mot.)* reverted to non-motorized infantry status.

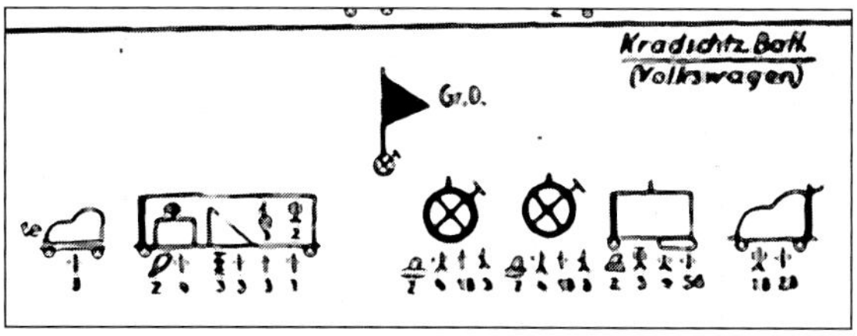

Upon redesignation and reorganization as a division, *Infanterie-Regiment (mot) "Großdeutschland"* received a *Kradschützen-Bataillon*, albeit one equipped with *Volkswagen* utility vehicles and half-tracks in lieu of motorcycles (September 1942).

By June 1943, all of the former motorized infantry divisions had been redesignated as mechanized infantry divisions, even though the name change was more symbolic than substantive.

The year 1943 also saw the continued efforts of the *Organizations-Abteilung* to further streamline and standardize the force. The result for the mechanized infantry was *Panzergrenadier-Division 43*, whose reconnaissance battalion had a battalion headquarters, an armored car company (with both medium and heavy armored cars), three light reconnaissance companies (equipped with motorcycles, VW's or *Ketterkräder*[27]), and a heavy motorized reconnaissance company, which had an infantry gun platoon, an antitank gun platoon, and a combat engineer platoon. As always, when these changes were introduced, the organization that resulted was often quite at variance from the theoretical norm.[28] On the one hand, commanders in the field were given great latitude as to when to implement the changes, based on the overall combat situation. Moreover, equipment availability and issuance continued to remain a problem. Finally, many of the battalions temporarily lost some of their subordinate units when they were sent back to the homeland or occupied territories for reorganization and, perhaps more importantly, new equipment training whenever major new items of equipment were fielded.

The streamlining effort was followed in 1944 with *Panzergrenadier-Division 44*, which applied to all mechanized infantry divisions, with the exception of *Panzergrenadier-Divisionen "Großdeutschland"* and *"Feldherrnhalle."* Its organization was similar to its *KStN* predecessor, although the armored car company was absorbed into the battalion headquarters, where the heavy gun armored car platoon was also retained (albeit with a reduction in authorizations to three guns), three light VW reconnaissance companies, and a heavy motorized reconnaissance company with a mortar platoon of six medium mortars and a combat engineer platoon.

As to be expected, the divisions formed in 1945 had a hodgepodge of assets and organization. For instance, *Panzergrenadier-Division Kurmark* had only a VW-equipped reconnaissance company designated with the same honorific. The *Führer-Grenadier-Division* had a mixed antitank gun battalion, which also had *Panzeraufklärungs-Kompanie 101* assigned to it, while the *Führer-Begleit-Division* had *Panzerspäh-Kompanie 102*. On 24 March 1945, orders were issued establishing the same *KStN* for both *Panzergrenadier-Divisionen* and *Panzer-Divisionen*, with all mechanized infantry divisions effectively being redesignated as armored divisions.[29]

Armored Divisions (*Panzer-Divisionen*)

As with the motorized infantry divisions, the armored divisions had organic reconnaissance assets assigned to their peacetime organization. These actually consisted of two battalion-level assets, the reconnaissance battalions and the motorcycle infantry battalions. Although not intended to be additional reconnaissance forces, the *Kradschützen* were quickly used in essentially that role when they habitually cross-attached forces with the reconnaissance battalion during offensive operations and pursuits. In addition, each tank regiment had a light tank platoon in its headquarters, as did each of the tank battalions, and these were often employed to act as battlefield/tactical reconnaissance. Within the divisional motorized infantry regiment, there was also a motorcycle infantry company in each battalion. Furthermore, one source places an armored car platoon of four *Sd.Kfz. 221's* and four *Sd.Kfz. 222's* in the divisional headquarters of the first three armored divisions that had been established (1, 2, and 3).[30]

As with all formations of the army, the armored divisions were in a constant state of flux organizationally because of a number of factors. The army was constantly expanding and there were never enough resources to field the force in the way it was envisioned. The armored forces in particular were subject to this dilemma, since they were also new and their theory and doctrine had not been tested on the battlefield to any significant degree before. Correspondingly, no two armored divisions were organizationally exactly the same at the start of hostilities in September 1939.

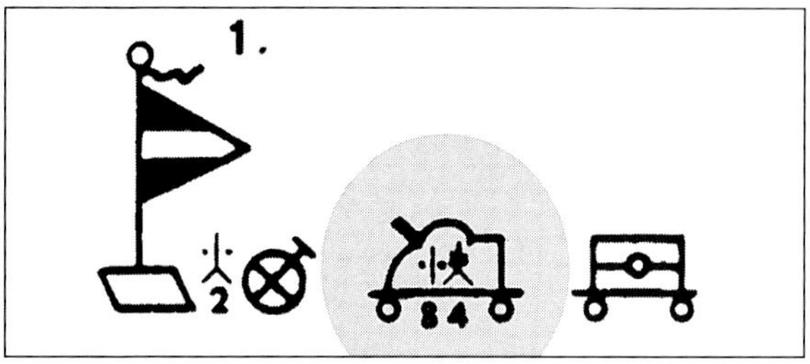

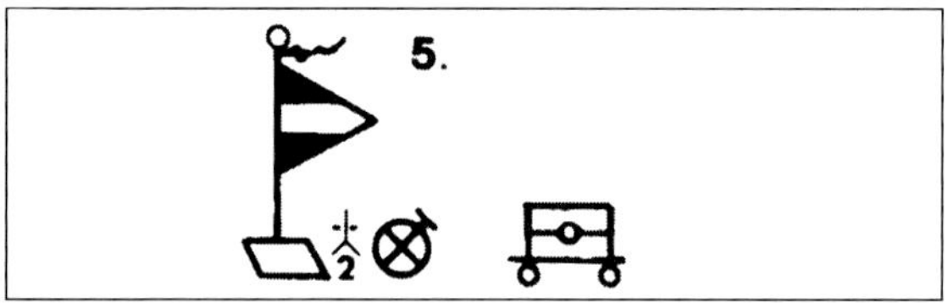

As can be seen in the graphics above, there was an armored scout platoon in the divisional headquarters of the *1. Panzer-Division*. It was also present in the *2.* and *3. Panzer-Divisionen* as well. Organized identically, with the exception of the armored car platoon, was the headquarters of the *5. Panzer-Division*. This minor variation from the norm probably only lasted through the end of the campaign in Poland.

In general terms, the *Kradschützen-Bataillon* at the start of the war was organized as follows:

- Headquarters
- Three motorcycle infantry companies (1st to 3rd), each with nine light machine guns, two heavy machine guns, and three light mortars.
- One motorcycle machine gun company (4th), with eight heavy machine guns and six medium mortars.
- One heavy company (5th) with one infantry gun platoon, two light infantry guns, one antitank gun platoon (towed) with three 3.7cm antitank guns, and one motorized combat engineer platoon

The *Aufklärungs-Abteilung (mot.)* had:

- Headquarters
- Two armored car troops (1st and 2nd), each with ten armored cars
- One motorcycle infantry troop (organized like the motorcycle infantry company above)
- One heavy troop (organized like the heavy company above)

In October 1939, the light divisions, which had come under the purview of the cavalry branch,[31] were

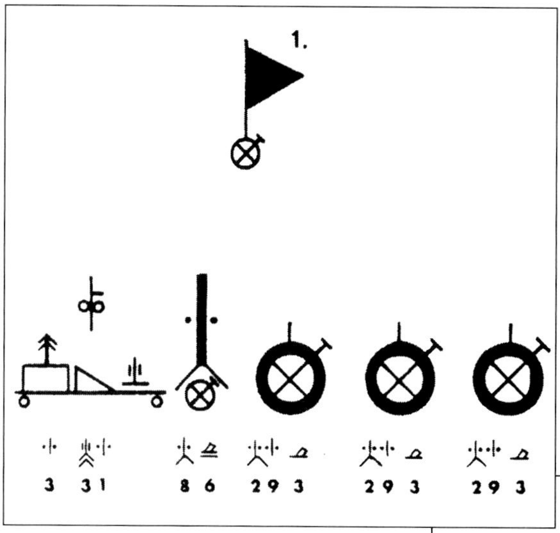

The typical prewar organization of a motorcycle infantry battalion—in this case *Kradschützen-Bataillon 1* of the *1. Panzer-Division* on the eve of the outbreak of war.

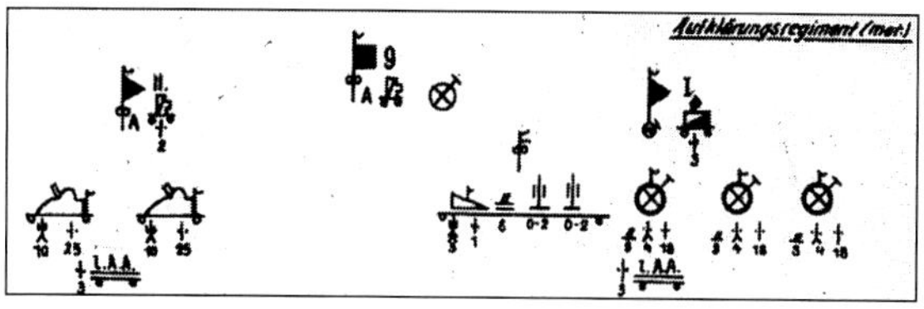

At the beginning of 1940, the *9. Panzer-Division* still had *Aufklärungs-Regiment 9 (mot)* on its rolls, which it retained through the end of the campaign in the West. The combined assets of the two battalions made it roughly equivalent in reconnaissance assets of a normal armored division.

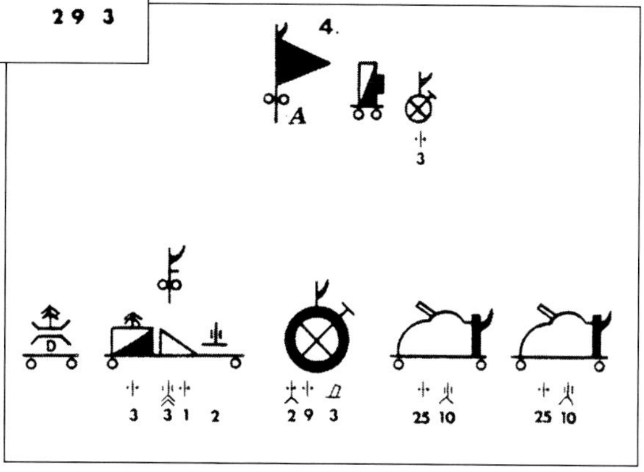

Right: The typical prewar organization of a motorized reconnaissance battalion—in this case *Aufklärungs-Abteilung 4 (mot)* of the *1. Panzer-Division* just before the campaign in Poland.

converted to armored divisions, with the *1. leichte Division* becoming the *6. Panzer-Division*; the *2. leichte*, the *7. Panzer-Division*; the *3. leichte*, the *8. Panzer-Division*; and the *4. leichte*, the *9. Panzer-Division*. The first three reorganized divisions had a "standard" armored division structure, largely formed out of the assets of the division it came from. In the case of the *9. Panzer-Division*, it retained *Aufklärungs-Regiment 9* for some time before it was also broken up to form a motorcycle infantry and a reconnaissance battalion.

The organization for combat for the campaign in the West remained essentially unchanged from the previous campaign. Several changes were undertaken in the fall of 1940, since Hitler ordered a doubling of the armored force and the only way to create that was to play organizational sleight-of-hand, as previously discussed. For the reconnaissance assets of the divisions, the biggest change was that the motorized reconnaissance battalions had to give up one of their armored car troops to the newly forming divisions.[32]

While the *Organizations-Abteilung* continued to try to standardize the *KStN's* of the divisions in 1941, there was little in the way the reconnaissance assets of the armored divisions were affected.

In the fall of 1941, three more armored divisions were activated for service on the continental mainland (22, 23, and 24), with each of them foregoing an armored reconnaissance battalion and receiving only a motorcycle infantry battalion instead. This was the new-model motorcycle infantry battalion, with an armored car company (1st), three motorcycle infantry companies (2nd to 4th), and a heavy company (5th). Apparently, the *Kradschützen-Kompanien* were organized like motorized rifle companies, although it is not clear whether they had only trucks or some *SPW's* as well.[33]

Some anomalies occurred when the force package for North Africa was being planned and assembled in late 1940 and early 1941. Since the operation was an unplanned contingency on the part of the Army, several armored formations had to be tasked to provide cadre, equipment and even entire units to form the initial forces dispatched to Libya. *Sperrverband Libyen*, as the blocking formation was known, was the nucleus of the *5. leichte Division* (no organizational connection to the previous light divisions) and then, eventually, as the *21. Panzer-Division*. Its *Panzerspäh-Kompanie* was reinforced with a total of twenty-five armored cars, and the battalion also received a reinforced reconnaissance platoon, equipped with VW's. That was the first of many deviations for the forces in Africa, many no doubt brought about by the chaotic supply situation. In the end, the *21. Panzer-Division* never had a *Kradschützen-Bataillon*, although its sister division, the *15. Panzer-Division*, did (*Kradschützen-Bataillon 15*). In both of the divisions, the motorcycles were eventually replaced by *SPW's*, since the latter proved more capable of dealing with the terrain conditions in the arid climate. The companies replaced their mortars with self-propelled antitank guns (three 7.5cm *PaK 40/3 auf Panzerkampfwagen 38(t), Ausführung H [Sd.Kfz. 138]*). The battalions also received a cannon platoon, each consisting of six *Sd.Kfz. 233's*, and the heavy companies also impressed captured British 25-pounders into their service.

In April 1942, an additional light division was activated for service in Africa, the *90. leichte Afrika-Division*. It did not receive armored reconnaissance assets until August of that year, when *Aufklärungs-Kompanie (mot.) 580* joined its parent division after completing training in Germany. When the division was redesignated as the *90. Afrika-Division*, the reconnaissance company became *Panzer-Aufklärungs-Abteilung 580*.

1942 saw the establishment of three armored and two light (Africa) divisions. The armored divisions (25, 26, and 27) all had different reconnaissance assets. Because its activation was not completed until the middle of June 1943, the *25. Panzer-Division* received an armored reconnaissance battalion (*Panzer-Aufklärungs-Abteilung 25*). The *26. Panzer-Division*, which was formed from extensive cadre levies against the *23. Infanterie-Division*, as well as assistance through levies against other armored formations, completed its activation in late 1942, thus receiving a motorcycle infantry battalion (*Kradschützen-Bataillon 26*) as its initial reconnaissance asset. The *27. Panzer-Division*, which was formed from the disbanded *22. Panzer-Division*, apparently had no organic reconnaissance assets. The *164. leichte Afrika-Division* was organized similarly to the *90. Afrika Division* and arrived in Africa in August 1942, in time to see some

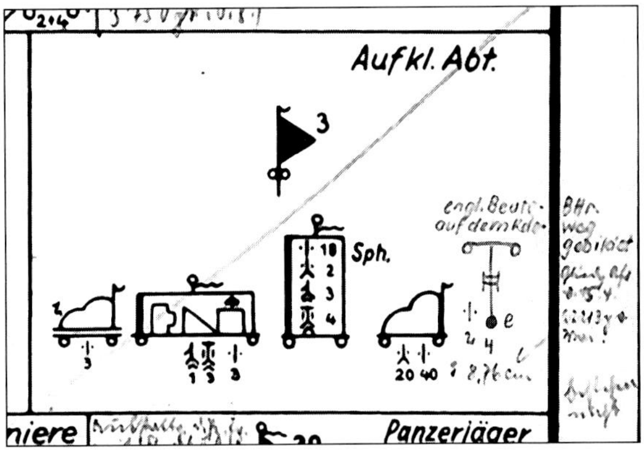

The unique organization of many divisions that fought in North Africa is reflected in this example from the *21. Panzer-Division* in May 1942, showing *Aufklärungs-Abteilung 3 (mot)*. This work reflects the addition a battery of captured English guns to the battalion's structure through direct command action (*auf dem Kommandoweg*) as opposed to a directive from the *Organizations-Abteilung*. The motorcycle infantry battalion has been replaced by an *ad hoc* motorized formation that had a number of heavy weapons.

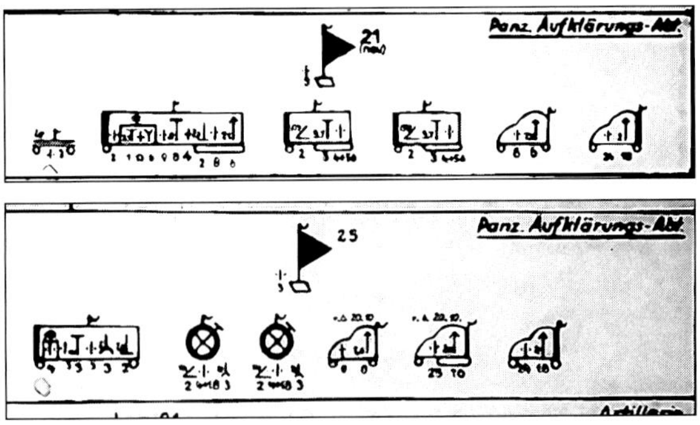

Top: Although essentially a brand-new division after having been eliminated in May in Tunisia, the *21. Panzer-Division* was reconstituted in record time. *Panzer-Aufklärungs-Abteilung 21* was particularly formidable, with a large number of mechanized assets. **Bottom:** Although it initially had a *Kradschützen-Bataillon* envisioned for it when it was being formed in 1942, the *25. Panzer-Division* had a *Panzer-Aufklärungs-Abteilung* when it finished its activation in the middle of 1943. Note that it has the traditional two armored scout companies, albeit with one of them being the new half-tracked scout unit equipped with the *Sd.Kfz. 250* family of vehicles, featuring the reconnaissance version, the *Sd.Kfz. 250/9*.

of the final fighting. *Afrika-Division 999*, on the other hand, had a more checkered existence.[34] Formed from conditionally deployable soldiers at the Heuburg Training Area in late 1942, it did not finish its activation until February of the next year. Some elements of the division made it to Tunisia only to surrender a few months later. The division's reconnaissance battalion, *Panzer-Aufklärungs-Abteilung 999*, never made it to the North African theater of war and eventually became part of *Sturm-Division Rhodos*, serving with it until May 1945.

As with the motorized divisions, 1942 saw the *Organizations-Abteilung* attempting to "norm" the armored divisions. The motorized reconnaissance battalions were consolidated with the motorcycle infantry battalions, again with the Kradschützen-Bataillone taking order of precedence with regard to the designation for the newly consolidated formations. On 24 March 1943, the formations were again redesignated as *Panzer-Aufklärungs-Abteilungen*, a convention held until the end of the war.

The newly reorganized and redesignated *Kradschützen-Bataillon* in the armored divisions had the following authorized structure:

- Headquarters
- One armored car scout company (*Panzerspäh-Kompanie*) (1st), with eighteen armored cars
- One armored reconnaissance company (*Panzeraufklärungs-Kompanie [gp]*) (2nd), equipped with *SPW's* and armed with four heavy machine guns, fifty-six light machine guns, three antitank guns, and two medium mortars
- Two motorcycle infantry companies (*Kradschützen-Kompanien*)(3rd and 4th), each with four heavy machine guns, eighteen light machine guns, two medium mortars, and three light antitank rifles
- One heavy company (5th), with one antitank rifle platoon (three heavy antitank rifles and three light machine guns), one infantry gun platoon (two towed IG's), one antitank platoon (three medium antitank guns and three light machine guns), and one engineer platoon (four light machine guns)

While a number of armored divisions had the above organization (3, 6, 7, 9 to 14, 22, 23, and 26), there were a number with an authorized deviation allowing a third *Kradschützen-Kompanie* in lieu of a *Panzeraufklärungs-Kompanie (gp)* (1, 2, 4, 5, 8, 17 to 20, and 24). As previously mentioned, the *15.* and *21. Panzer-Divisionen* in North Africa kept their motorized reconnaissance battalions.

When the armored divisions lost at Stalingrad (14, 16, and 24) were reconstituted, the motorcycle infantry battalions were reformed as armored reconnaissance battalions. For some reason, three of the divisions lost in North Africa—*10. Panzer-Division*, *164. leichte Afrika-Division*, and *999. leichte Afrika-Division*—were never reconstituted, despite Hitler's usual insistence on that. The *90. leichte Afrika-Division* and *15. Panzer-Division* were reconstituted on Sardinia and Sicily as *Panzergrenadier-Divisionen*, while the *21. Panzer-Division* was reconstituted in France with an armored reconnaissance battalion that had an armored car company, two armored reconnaissance companies (equipped with the *Sd.Kfz. 251*), and a heavy company.[35]

By the end of 1943, *Panzer-Division 43* was introduced by the *Organizations-Abteilung*.[36] In addition to numerous changes throughout the divisional organization, the armored reconnaissance battalions were to be organized as follows:

- Headquarters, with some battalions also authorized a heavy cannon platoon (*schwerer Kanonenzug*), which was authorized six armored cars with a 7.5cm main gun (Sd.Kfz. 233)
- One light wheeled armored car scout company (*leichte Panzerspäh-Kompanie [Rad]*) (1st), with eighteen armored cars
- One half-tracked armored scout company (*Panzerspäh-Kompanie "C"*) (2nd), with a total of twenty-five *Sd.Kfz. 250's*, including sixteen *Sd.Kfz. 250/9's*
- One armored reconnaissance company (*Panzeraufklärungs-Kompanie [gp]*) (3rd), equipped with the *Sd.Kfz. 250*
- One armored reconnaissance company (*Panzeraufklärungs-Kompanie (Krad)*, *(Kettenkrad)* or *(VW)*) (4th)
  - The *SPW*-equipped company had
    - Headquarters, with one *Sd.Kfz. 250/1* and two *Sd.Kfz. 250/3's*
    - Three *SPW* platoons, each with seven *Sd.Kfz. 250/1's* and one *Sd.Kfz. 250/8*

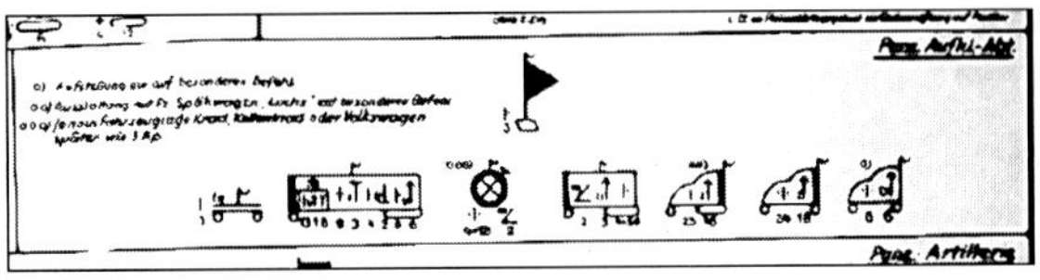

The template for an armored reconnaissance battalion of *Panzer-Division 43.* The *Organizations-Abteilung* hoped to streamline to this model of organization for all of the armored divisions. The cannon platoon on the far right is annotated to indicate that it was only to be established when ordered. The 1st Company was to continue to be wheeled armored scouts, but provisions were made for the second scout company to be outfitted with either the *Sd.Kfz. 250* series of vehicles or the fully tracked light reconnaissance armored vehicle, the *Panzer II, Ausführung L "Luchs."* The 3rd Company was the half-track-equipped reconnaissance company, while the 4th Company was to be outfitted with motorcycles, *Kettenkräder*, or *Volkswagen*, with the ultimate goal of issuing it half-tracks as well.

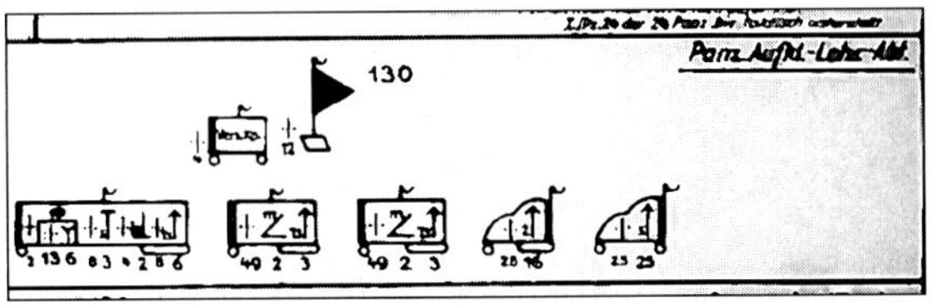

The *Panzer-Lehr-Division* was formed under the *freie Gliederung* concept—roughly "free organization"—that theoretically removed the logistical "tail" from the combat commander by concentrating all of the logistical assets of the battalion in a supply company. As a concept division, the *Panzer-Lehr* was one of the best-equipped and best-manned divisions in the army—only to take a beating in Normandy from which it never really fully recovered. The *Panzer-Aufklärungs-Lehr-Abteilung* was completely mechanized and had a company of the *Sd.Kfz. 234/2 "Puma,"* largely regarded as one of the best armored cars of World War II.

    - One mortar section with two *Sd.Kfz. 250/1's* and two *Sd.Kfz. 250/7's*
- One armored reconnaissance company (*Panzer-aufklärungs-Kompanie [Krad], [Kettenkrad], or [VW]*) (4th)
  - The motorcycle-equipped company had
    - Headquarters, with five motorcycles and two *Volkswagen*;
    - Three motorcycle platoons, each with thirteen motorcycles and two *Volkswagen*;
    - One heavy platoon, with eighteen motorcycles, two *Volkswagen*, two trucks, four heavy machine guns, and two 8cm mortars
  - The *Kettenkrad*-equipped company had
    - Headquarters, with three motorcycles, three *Kettenkräder*, and one *Sd.Kfz. 10* prime mover
    - Three *Kettenkrad* platoons, each with one motorcycle, twelve *Kettenkräder*, and two *Sd.Kfz. 10* prime movers
    - One heavy platoon, with one motorcycle, fifteen *Kettenkräder*, two *Sd.Kfz. 10* prime movers, four heavy machine guns, and two 8cm mortars
  - The *Volkswagen*-equipped company had
    - Headquarters, with three *Volkswagen*
    - Three *Volkswagen* platoons, each with fourteen *Volkswagen*
    - One heavy platoon, with fourteen *Volkswagen*, four heavy machine guns, and two 8cm mortars
- One heavy company (*schwere Aufklärungs-Kompanie* [gp]) (5th), with
    - One cannon platoon (*Kanonenzug*), with six 3.7cm antitank guns
    - One infantry gun platoon (*IG-Zug*), with two towed *IG's*
    - One heavy antitank platoon (*schwerer PaK-Zug*), with three 7.5cm antitank guns
    - One combat engineer platoon (*Pionier-Zug*), with one 2cm cannon, six flamethrowers, and thirteen light machine guns

In the case of the 4th Company, the intent was to later outfit it like the 3rd Company, i.e., with *Sd.Kfz. 251's*.

When the *Panzer-Lehr-Division* was established in January 1944, it also introduced the concept of the *freie Gliederung*, the so-called "free organization," which separated the logistics train from the combat elements, thus "freeing" the combat commander of the headache of also worrying about the everyday worries of the logistical support of his company. Under this concept, *Panzer-Aufklärungs-Lehr-Abteilung 130* was organized as follows:

- Headquarters, which also included a supply company
- One wheeled armored car scout company (*Panzerspäh-Kompanie [Rad]*) (1st), with twenty-five armored cars (the *Sd.Kfz. 234/2 Puma's*)

- One half-tracked armored scout company (*Panzerspäh-Kompanie [gp]*) (2nd), with sixteen *Sd.Kfz. 250/9's*
- Two armored reconnaissance companies (*Panzeraufklärungs-Kompanien [gp]*) (3rd and 4th), each equipped with the *Sd.Kfz. 251* and armed with forty-nine light machine guns, three 7.5cm antitank guns, and two medium mortars
- One heavy company (*schwere Aufklärungs-Kompanie [gp]*) (5th), with one infantry gun platoon (*IG-Zug*), with two towed *IG's*; one heavy antitank platoon (*schwerer PaK-Zug*), with three heavy antitank guns; and one combat engineer platoon (*Pionier-Zug*), with six flamethrowers and thirteen light machine guns

When the *116. Panzer-Division* (*"Windhund"*) was formed in March 1944, it was established along the lines intended for *Panzer-Division 44*, which was formally introduced by the *Organizations-Abteilung* in August 1944. The armored reconnaissance battalion authorized saw the dissolution of the wheeled armored car company and its incorporation into the battalion's headquarters company (*Stabskompanie*) with the same amount of assets as before (sixteen armored cars) and the retention of two reconnaissance companies but with one of them being light (the *Sd.Kfz. 250* as opposed to the *Sd.Kfz. 251*). The theoretical organization was as follows:

- Headquarters, with a headquarters company that included sixteen armored cars (2cm main gun) and ten medium *SPW's*. Its organization was headquarters and headquarters section, with one *Sd.Kfz. 234/1*; one signals platoon, with five *Sd.Kfz. 251/3's* and two *Sd.Kfz. 251/11's*; two heavy armored car platoons, each with six *Sd.Kfz. 234/1's*; one heavy gun section, with three *Sd.Kfz. 234/3's*
- One half-tracked armored scout company (*Panzerspäh-Kompanie "C"*) (1st), with a total of sixteen *Sd.Kfz. 250/9's* and an additional nine light *SPW's*, distributed as follows: Headquarters, with one *Sd.Kfz 250/5*; four line platoons, each with two *Sd.Kfz. 250/5's* and four *Sd.Kfz. 250/9's*[37]
- One light armored reconnaissance company (*leichte Panzeraufklärungs-Kompanie [gp]*) (3rd), equipped with twenty-six light *SPW's*, along with two mortar carriers and two 7.5cm antitank gun *SPW's*. This was broken down into headquarters, with two *Sd.Kfz. 250/3's*; three line platoons, each with seven *Sd.Kfz. 250/5's*; one mortar section, with one *Sd.Kfz. 250/1* and three *Sd.Kfz. 250/7's*; and one gun section, with one *Sd.Kfz. 250/1* and two *Sd.Kfz. 250/8's*
- One armored reconnaissance company (*Panzeraufklärungs-Kompanie [gp]*) (4th), equipped with twenty-three medium *SPW's*, including eleven light machine guns, two 7.5cm antitank guns, seven 2cm *Flak*, eighteen additional light machine guns (not mounted on board), four heavy machine guns, and two medium mortars. Organized as follows: headquarters, with two *Sd.Kfz. 251/3's*; three line platoons, each with three *Sd.Kfz. 251/1's* and one *Sd.Kfz. 251/17*; one heavy platoon, with three *Sd.Kfz. 251/17's*, two *Sd.Kfz. 251/2's*, and two *Sd.Kfz. 251/9's*
- One heavy armored reconnaissance company (*schwere Panzer-Aufklärungs-Kompanie [gp]*) (5th), with headquarters, with one *Sd.Kfz. 251/3* and one *Sd.Kfz. 251/11*; one light infantry gun platoon, with three *Sd.Kfz. 251/1's* and two towed light infantry guns (7.5cm); one heavy cannon platoon, with one *Sd.Kfz. 251/1*, one *Sd.Kfz. 251/3*, and six *Sd.Kfz. 251/9's*; one antitank platoon, with one *Sd.Kfz. 251/1*, four *Sd.Kfz. 251/17's*; and three towed 7.5cm antitank guns; one combat engineer platoon (*Pionier-Zug [gp]*), with seven *Sd.Kfz. 251/7's*

In March 1944, this company was further reorganized to delete the light infantry gun and antitank platoons listed above and added one heavy mortar platoon with two *Sd.Kfz. 251/1's* and six *Sd.Kfz. 251/2's*.[38] The logistical "tail" of the battalion was represented by the *Versorgungs-Kompanie (mot.)*, which had a medical section, maintenance services (weapons and vehicles), a fuel echelon, an ammunition section, and a supply section.

In all, the 1944 model of the armored reconnaissance battalion had some 945 personnel authorized, not including an additional 28 volunteer auxiliaries. In keeping with the German's traditionally relatively low numbers of officer end strength, the 24 officer positions represented less than 3 percent of the entire battalion.

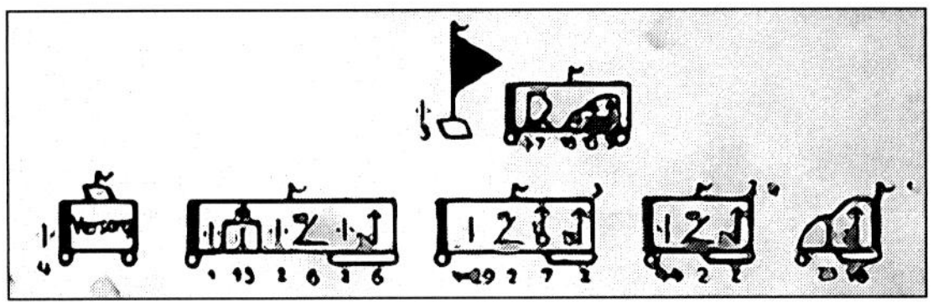

The model for *Panzer-Division 44* saw the armored car scout company consolidated with the headquarters company and formed into a platoon with seven sections. It was intended for all of the line companies of the battalion to operate from half-tracks.

In February 1945, several divisions were formed from Replacement Army assets and decimated formations. These short-lived formations—*Panzer-Divisionen Jüterbog* and *Schlesien*—had reconnaissance assets of the same name as the division, albeit only company in size. *Panzer-Division Holstein* apparently had an entire reconnaissance battalion (*Panzer-Aufklärungs-Abteilung 44*), and it was formed from the *233. Reserve-Panzer-Division* in Denmark. *Panzer-Feldausbildungs-Division Tatra* (formed in Slovakia), which became the *232. Panzer-Division*, apparently had no organic reconnaissance assets. Both *Schlesien* and *Holstein* were later consolidated with the *18. Panzergrenadier-Division* in March after having taken heavy casualties. A similar fate befell *Jüterbog*, which was incorporated into the *16. Panzer-Division* by the end of February.

There were two more major organization changes introduced by the *Organizations-Abteilung* that affected the armored force before the end of the war. Both *Panzer-Division 45* and *Kampfgruppe Panzer-Division 45* were introduced on 25 March. It was intended for all armored division-level formations to convert to *Panzer-Division 45* and, if insufficient forces were on hand, to initially convert to *Kampfgruppe Panzer-Division 45*. The reconnaissance battalions of these streamlined *KStN's* were correspondingly reduced:

- Headquarters, with one medium *SPW*, one 2cm armored car, and an armored signals platoon with two medium *SPW's*
- One mixed armored scout company (*gemischte Panzerspäh-Kompanie [gp]*) (1st), with three medium *SPW's* (*Sd.Kfz. 251/3's*), seven armored cars with the 7.5cm main gun (*Sd.Kfz. 234/4*), three medium *SPW's* with a triple-mount 2cm *Flak* (*Sd.Kfz. 251/21*), three medium *SPW's* with 7.5cm antitank gun (*Sd.Kfz. 251/22*), and eight 2cm armored cars (*Sd.Kfz. 234/1*)
- Two light wheeled armored reconnaissance companies (*leichte Aufklärungs-Kompanien [VW]*) (2nd and 3rd), each equipped with nine light machine guns, two heavy machine guns, two medium mortars, and one light machine gun (not mounted)

In keeping with the *freie Gliederung* concept, there was also a *Versorgungs-Kompanie* (mot). In cases where only a battle group could be formed, one of the light wheeled reconnaissance companies was deleted from the *KStN*. It is doubtful that any of these changes were fully implemented by any formation.

SEPARATE BRIGADES AND BRIGADE-LEVEL FORMATIONS OF THE *SCHNELLE TRUPPEN* AND *PANZERTRUPPE*

Separate brigades—generally consisting of two regiments, supporting combat-arms elements, and logistical trains capable of supporting independent operations—were not present in the prewar *schnelle Truppe*, with the exception of the *4.* and *6. Panzer-Brigaden*, which had no reconnaissance assets and were quickly dissolved to be consolidated with divisions: *Panzer-Division "Kempf"* (later *10. Panzer-Division*) in the case of the former and *2. leichte Division* in the case of the latter.

A motorized rifle brigade, the *11. Schützen-Brigade (mot.)*, was formed in December 1939, and it had an armored car platoon with seven vehicles within the brigade headquarters. Each of the subordinate rifle regiments (110 and 111) also had a motorcycle infantry company as battalion troops (11th Company) and an armored car section within the regimental headquarters. Within a year, however, this brigade would also be effectively disbanded through consolidation with the *11. Panzer-Division*.

Several tank brigades were established in France in 1941. They were equipped with captured French tanks and had no organic reconnaissance assets. In 1943, three *schnelle Brigaden* were established in France. Two of the brigades were equipped with bicycles for their reconnaissance assets, but one of the brigades, *schnelle Brigade West*, actually had an

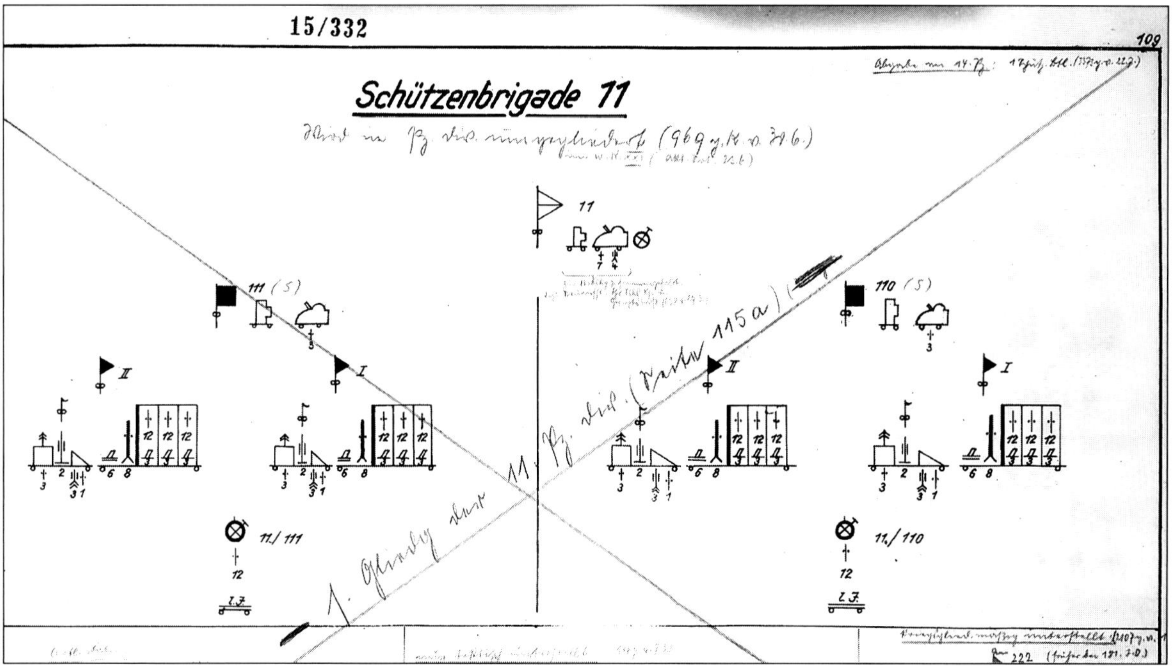

The *11. Schützen-Brigade (mot)* served as a separate brigade during its fighting in France in 1940, where it acquitted itself well. It had several armored reconnaissance elements organic to its structure before it was absorbed into the *11. Panzer-Division* and reorganized.

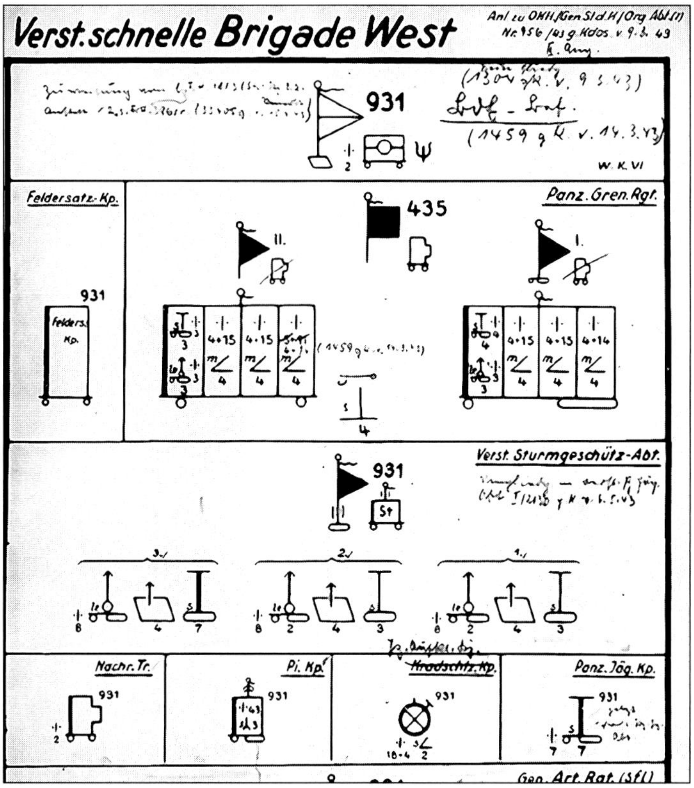

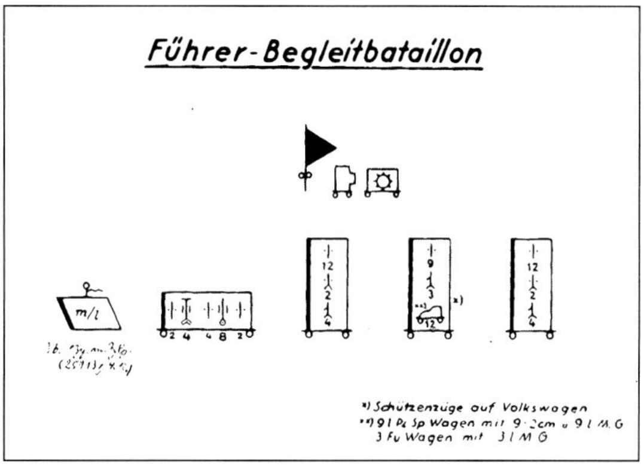

The special organization of the *Führer-Begleit-Bataillon* had a motorized company consisting of riflemen in *Volkswagen* and nine *Sd.Kfz. 222* armored cars.

Left: *Schnelle Brigade West* in September 1943 before its motorcycle infantry company was reorganized into an armored reconnaissance one. The handwritten entry from the *Organizations-Abteilung* indicates that the change was a projected one.

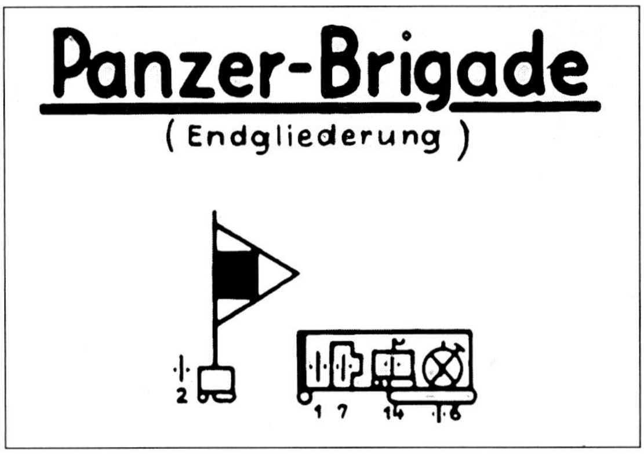

The approved template for a 1944-model separate *Panzer-Brigade* envisioned an armored reconnaissance company reporting directly to the brigade headquarters.

armored car company, *Panzer-Aufklärungs-Kompanie 941*, which was later used to form the nucleus of the armored reconnaissance battalion of the reconstituted *21. Panzer-Division* that same year.

In July 1944, the *Führer-Grenadier-Brigade*, which was later redesignated and reorganized as a division, had an armored car company, which was equipped with eighteen armored vehicles. In November of the same year, the sister formation, the *Führer-Begleit-Brigade*, was formed, and it also had an armored car company as its reconnaissance asset. Its antecedent formation, the *Führer-Begleit-Bataillon*, which had been formed to escort the Headquarters of the *Führer* in the field, had always had motorcycle and armored cars assets, although these were not for reconnaissance purposes initially. Instead, they were the only assets capable of keeping up with Hitler while he was traveling in his personal vehicle.[39]

After sustaining terrific losses to *Heeresgruppe Mitte* as a consequence of Soviet Operation Bagration, Hitler directed the formation of ten separate armored brigades—later expanded to thirteen—to act as a ready-reaction force behind the main lines of resistance to counter any Soviet or Allied breakthroughs.[40] Well-equipped and armed, but lacking substantive logistical support, the brigades were committed piecemeal and rapidly decimated. Within several months, all had been consolidated with division formations in an effort to reconstitute them. The brigades had an armored reconnaissance company that reported directly to the brigade headquarters.

Formation	Notes
Panzer-Brigade 101	Used in October 1944 to reconstitute the *20. Panzer-Division.*
Panzer-Brigade 102	Consolidated with the *7. Panzer-Division* in November 1944.
Panzer-Brigade 103	Consolidated with the *5. Panzer-Division* in November 1944. After deactivation, the headquarters of the brigade was used to command an *ad hoc* battle group, followed by the staffing of *Panzer-Division Müncheberg.*[41]
Panzer-Brigade 104	Consolidated with the *25. Panzer-Division* in November 1944.
Panzer-Brigade 105	Used in October 1944 to reconstitute the *9. Panzer-Division.*
Panzer-Brigade 106	Redesignated as *Panzer-Brigade 106 "Feldherrnhalle"* on 11 July 1944. Used in October 1944 to reconstitute the *9. Panzer-Division.*
Panzer-Brigade 107	Used in November 1944 to reconstitute the *25. Panzergrenadier-Division*
Panzer-Brigade 108	Used in November 1944 to reconstitute the *116. Panzer-Division.*
Panzer-Brigade 109	Used in October 1944 to reconstitute *Panzer-Division "Feldherrnhalle".*
Panzer-Brigade 110	Used in September 1944 to reconstitute the *13. Panzer-Division.*
Panzer-Brigade 111	Reconnaissance asset: *Panzer-Aufklärungs-Kompanie (gp) 2111.* Consolidated with the *11. Panzer-Division* in September 1944.
Panzer-Brigade 112	Reconnaissance asset: *Panzer-Aufklärungs-Kompanie (gp) 2112.* Consolidated with the *21. Panzer-Division* in September 1944.
Panzer-Brigade 113	Reconnaissance asset: *Panzer-Aufklärungs-Kompanie (gp) 2113.* Consolidated with the *15. Panzergrenadier-Division* in October 1944.

Panzer-Brigade 150 is best known as being part of *SS-Obersturmbannführer* Otto Skorzeny's failed attempt to infiltrate American lines in an effort to spread fear and confusion in the rear areas of the U.S. Army. Originally, it was to have several companies of armored reconnaissance assets outfitted with American scout cars. Most sources say that none of the plans materialized, with the exception of some *Panzer V Panther's* being modified to resemble U.S. M10 tank destroyers.[42]

Among the last-ditch efforts to defend the Reich was the formation of *Panzergrenadier-Brigade 92* in January 1945 in Hungary under the auspices of *Heeresgruppe Süd*. It initially had the *1./Panzer-Aufklärungs-Abteilung 2* of the *2. Panzer-Division* attached to it.

Also formed in January 1945 was *Panzer-Jagd-Brigade 104*, which had six antitank battalions. By the end of February 1945, it had at least three armored reconnaissance assets attached to it: *Panzer-Aufklärungs-Abteilung 115*, *Panzer-Aufklärungs-Abteilung München*, and *Panzer-Aufklärungs-Kompanie (gp) Krampnitz*. Each of the antitank battalions was supposed to have a headquarters company, two *Jagdpanzer-Kompanien* (each equipped with fourteen *Hetzer* tank destroyers), and an armored reconnaissance company (3rd) with sixteen *SPW's*. Whether some, if any, of these battalions attained theoretical strength levels or organization is unknown.

As discussed in the infantry section of this chapter, *Sturm-Division "Rhodos"* also had armored reconnaissance assets. When elements of the division were drawn off of the Isle of Rhodos in October 1943 to help form *Panzergrenadier-Division "Brandenburg,"* the remaining assets were reorganized and redesignated a brigade. One of the brigade troops was *Panzer-Aufklärungs-Abteilung "Rhodos,"* which had a unique organization consisting of an armored reconnaissance company (possibly eight 2cm armored cars or *Sd.Kfz. 250/9's*), a wheeled armored scout platoon (apparently four *Sd.Kfz. 233's*), a VW-equipped armored reconnaissance company, an antitank company (with six towed 7.5cm antitank guns), and a heavy company with a towed antitank gun platoon (three 7.5cm antitank guns), and a motorized combat engineer platoon.

One of the last *ad hoc* formations of the war was the establishment of a field command, *Panzer-Brigade Kurland*, which was also known as *Panzer-Aufklärungs-Brigade Kurland*. The reconnaissance assets of the brigade were composed of two divisional reconnaissance battalions, *Panzer-Aufklärungs-Abteilungen 12* and *14*. Together, they were referred to as *Panzer-Aufklärungs-Kampfgruppe Kurland*. Undoubtedly the last officially sanctioned formation of the *Panzertruppe* was *Panzer-Brigade XIII* (also known as *Panzer-Brigade Hobe*) in March 1945. It was formed from mobilized Replacement Army assets, most likely from Military District XIII. Theoretically, it had an armored reconnaissance battalion, *Panzer-Aufklärungs-Abteilung (mot.) XIII*.

ARMORED RECONNAISSANCE ASSETS AT VARIOUS HIGHER LEVELS OF COMMAND AND THE REPLACEMENT ARMY (*HÖHERE KOMMANDO-BEHÖRDEN UND DAS ERSATZHEER*)

Higher Levels of Command

In general, the German Army did not maintain armored ground reconnaissance assets organic to levels of command higher than the division. If a corps or higher commander wanted reconnaissance conducted, he assigned attached divisions and other assets the mission of conducting it. There were some exceptions, especially when later war armored corps were formed that had assigned corps troops.

Most instances of reconnaissance assets being found at a corps or higher organization, however, were the result of a temporary situation, whereby the higher command "held" these assets while awaiting attachment or assignment to a subordinate organization. This happened to *Aufklärungs-Abteilung (mot) 1*, pending assignment to the *3. Panzer-Division* at the end of 1940 and also within the *Deutsches Afrika Korps* while it was still the senior command in North Africa, with *Aufklärungs-Kompanie (mot.) 580* belonging to it, pending reassignment to the *90. leichte Afrika-Division*.[43] This formation was passed on to the subsequent higher headquarters, *Panzer-Armee-Afrika*, where it was listed as *gemischte Aufklärungs-Abteilung (mot) 580*. The battalion was

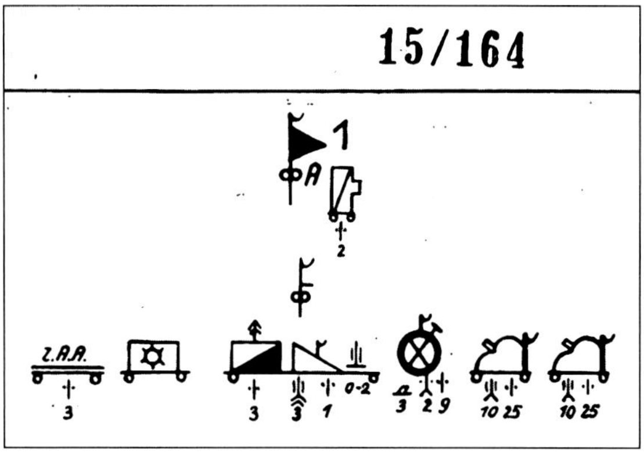

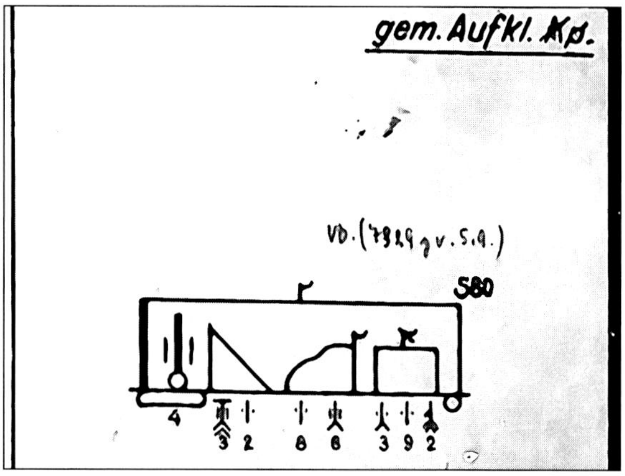

Left: *Aufklärungs-Abteilung (mot) 1* as a separate armored reconnaissance battalion before being assigned to the *3. Panzer-Division.* It was organized like a typical armored division reconnaissance battalion of the time. **Right:** *Gemischte Aufklärungs-Abteilung (mot) 580*, as assigned to the *Deutsches Afrika-Korps*, a corps-equivalent headquarters.

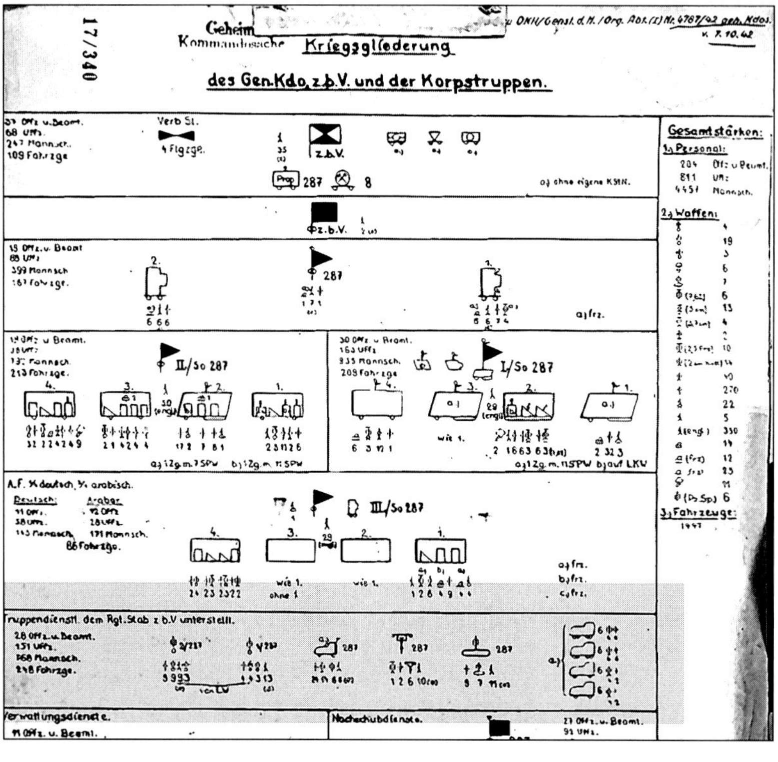

Panzer-Späh-Kompanie 287 of *Sonderverband 287* is highlighted in gray. It was authorized twenty-four armored cars representing the armor component of the formation.

eventually attached to the *90. leichte Afrika-Division* before being permanently reassigned to the *21. Panzer-Division*, where it eventually was redesignated as *Panzer-Aufklärungs-Abteilung 21* in April 1943.[44]

Some organizations were essentially "one off" elements that are considered to be field army assets. This was the case originally with *Sonderverband 287*, the core element of the *Deutsch-Arabische Legion* of *Generalleutnant* Felmy's *Sonderstab F*, which had a *Panzer-Späh-Kompanie 287* authorized. The formation, originally formed to help Arab interests, particularly those in Iraq, gradually morphed into *Panzergrenadier-Brigade 92* by the end of the war.[45] *Sonderverband 288*, a formation of roughly regimental strength, was likewise formed for potential operations in Iran, Iraq, and even India. It was eventually deployed to North Africa during the time it appeared possible that Rommel's force might capture Egypt

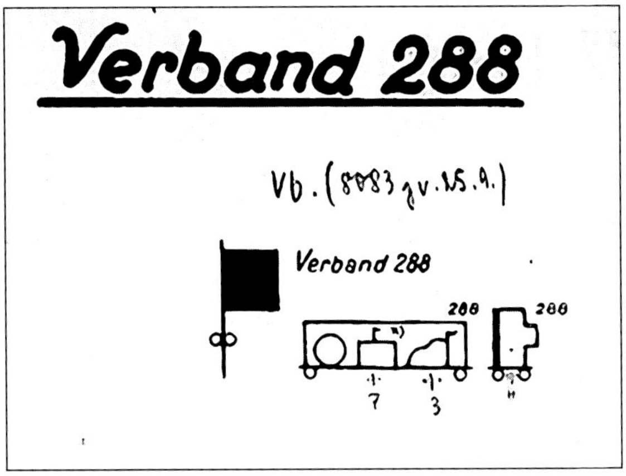

Sonderverband 288 had an armored car section and fought in North Africa.

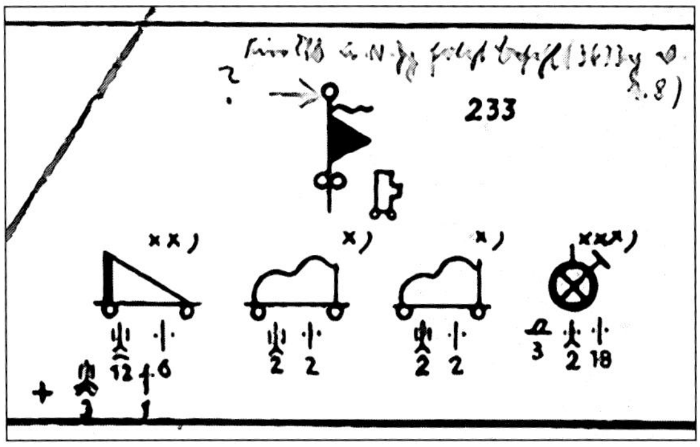

Aufklärungs-Bataillon (mot) 233 of *Infanterie-Lehr-Regiment (mot.) 900* (April 1940).

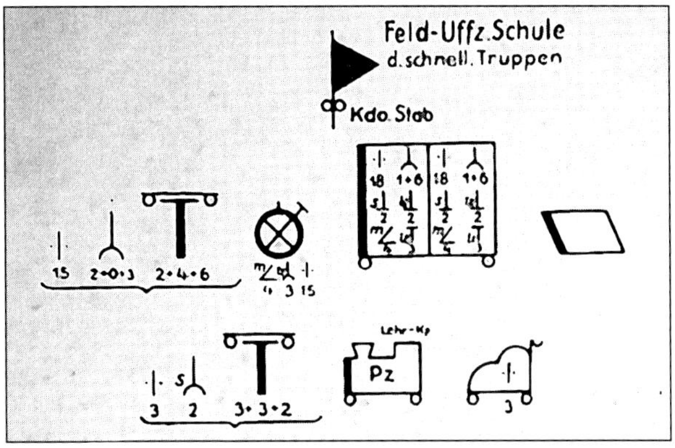

The schoolhouse at Rembertow in January 1944.

and open the way into those regions. The formation had a motorized armored reconnaissance company, also designated 288.

Infanterie-Lehr-Regiment (mot.) 900, which was not discussed in the first chapter, was also a unique formation. This regiment was also formed from "schoolhouse" assets of the infantry branch and had *Aufklärungs-Bataillon (mot) 233* as part of its regimental troops. The company had two armored car sections and a motorcycle infantry company, in addition to an antitank gun company. It was employed with that organization in the campaign in the West in 1940. By the time of Operation Barbarossa in June 1941, it had been expanded into a brigade-size entity (*Lehr-Brigade (mot) 900*), with the brigade headquarters having an armored car section and the 1st Battalion of *Lehr-Regiment 900 (mot)* having a motorcycle infantry company. It was later disbanded in 1942 so that its cadre could return to the training base at Döberitz.

When the field army started fielding some of its own training establishments in an effort to shorten the time personnel were away from their units to receive professional training, those forces were also considered to be field-army assets. Of interest to this study was the establishment of a *Feld-Unteroffiziersschule der schnellen Truppe* at the Rembertow Training Area, which had both reconnaissance and scout cadre and vehicles within its establishment.[46] There were several other field training schools established by the end of the war, but none of them ever had any substantial holdings in armored reconnaissance equipment.

Several of the security detachments in occupied territories had armored car sections assigned to them, but these obviously had little to do with the reconnaissance role of scouting and more to do with providing a show of force for the local populace. In most cases, these were obsolete armored cars or captured stocks.[47] *Radfahr-Regiment 2*, which was assigned security duties in the rear area of *Heeresgruppe Mitte*, had an armored car section within its 10th Company. Once again, the presence of these vehicles, most likely obsolete, was probably associated with convoy-protection duties or antipartisan operations. Another

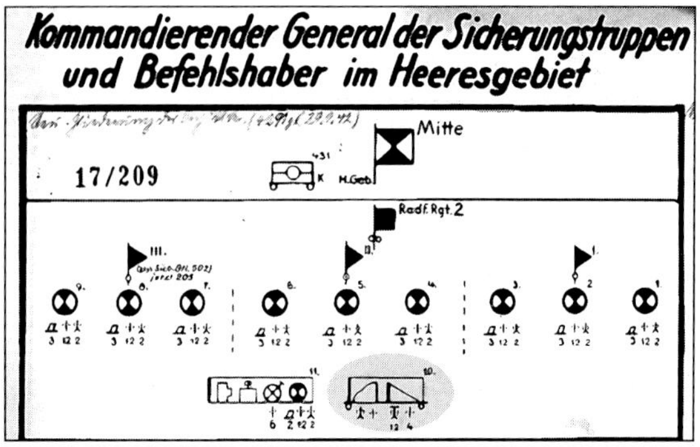

The armored car assets of *Radfahr-Regiment 2* were located in its 10th Company.

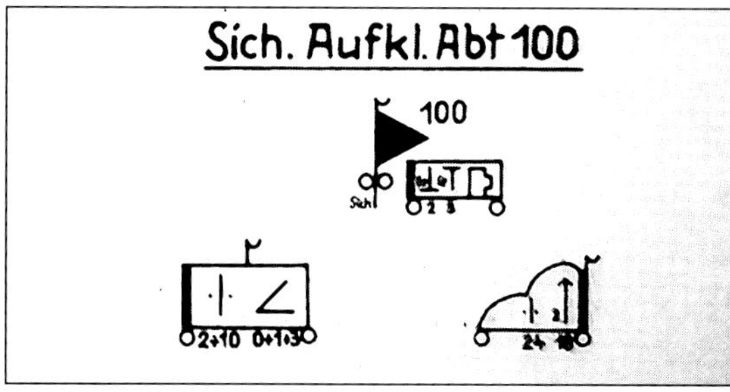

Sicherungs-Aufklärungs-Abteilung (mot.) 100 in January 1944. Like most security elements, the armored assets had little to do with reconnaissance operations and more with show-of-force and object-protection missions.

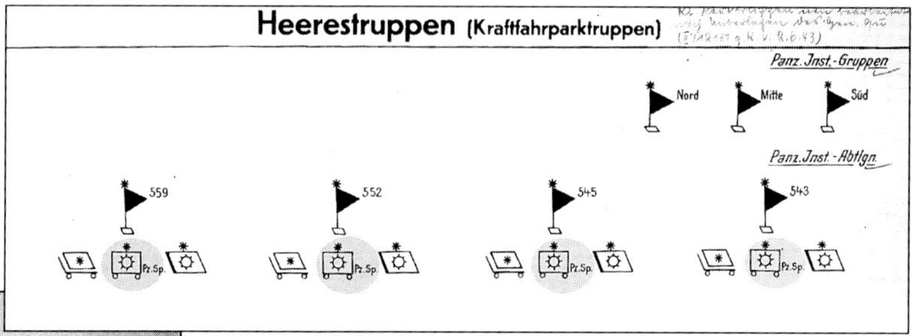

Each armored maintenance battalion had an armored car repair section.

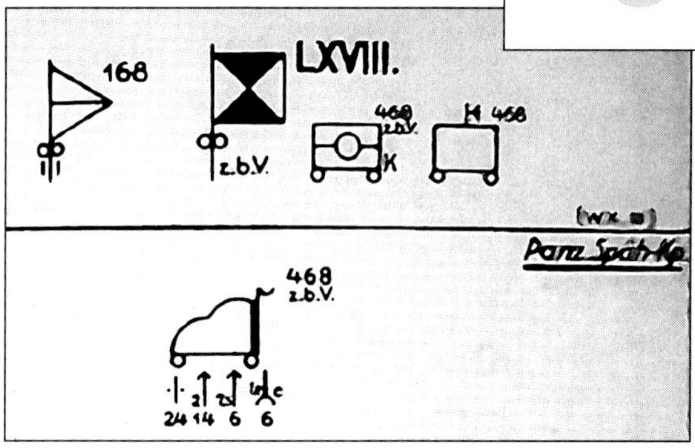

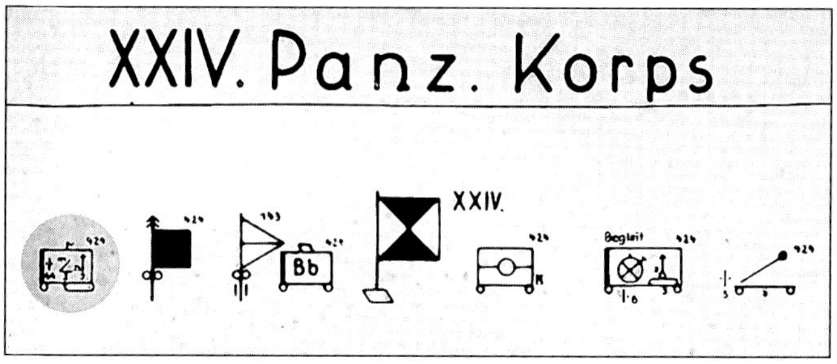

Left: In contrast to *Panzer-Korps-Aufklärungs-Kompanie 424*, *Panzer-Späh-Kompanie z.b.V. 468* of the headquarters of the *LXVIII. Armee-Korps* was strictly an armored car company. **Right:** The armored reconnaissance company organic to the headquarters of the *XXIV. Panzer-Korps.*

security organization was *Sicherungs-Aufklärungs-Abteilung (mot.) 100*, which was assigned to the military commander for France. Its strongest asset was an armored car company composed of at least twenty-four armored cars, although it is not certain whether they were from captured stocks.[48]

It should also be mentioned that the armored maintenance battalions that were field army assets—*Panzer-Instandsetzungs-Abteilungen 543, 545, 551,* and *559*—had a maintenance, overhaul, and repair section for armored cars, where a number of those vehicles would also be on hand but, of course, not permanently assigned.[49]

The *Frontnachweiser* of December 1944 lists five companies/troops as organic corps troops.[50] In addition, nine late-war elements are listed as field-army assets or are otherwise undefined.[52] (See tables at top of next page.)

Organic Corps Companies/Troops	Corps Assignment
Panzer-Korps-Aufklärungs-Kompanie "Feldherrnhalle"	Headquarters, *Panzer-Korps "Feldherrnhalle."* Established 2 February 1945.
Panzer-Korps-Aufklärungs-Kompanie 424	Headquarters, *XXIV. Panzer-Korps.* Effective 27 November 1944. Company organized in accordance with *KStN 1113 (gp)(fG)* of 1 April 1944.
Panzer-Aufklärungs-Schwadron 500	Headquarters, *Panzer-Korps "Großdeutschland."*
Panzer-Späh-Kompanie z.b.V. 468	Headquarters, *LXVIII. Armee-Korps.*[51]
Panzer-Späh-Zug 435	Headquarters, *XXXV. Armee-Korps.*

Field-Army Assets	Notes
Panzer-Aufklärungs-Abteilung "München"	Formed by Military District III (VII).
Panzer-Aufklärungs-Abteilung "Sternberg"	Formed from training cadre at the Sternberg NCO Academy.
Panzer-Aufklärungs-Abteilung "Hirschberg"	Formed by Military District IV (VIII).
Panzer-Aufklärungs-Abteilung 400	Formed by Military District VII.
Panzer-Aufklärungs-Kompanie "Döberitz" ("Schlesien")	Formed by Military District III (XIII). Later incorporated into *Panzer-Division "Schlesien."*
Panzer-Späh-Kompanie "Haberland"	Formed by Military District IV.
leichte Panzer-Aufklärungs-Kompanie "Milowitz"	Formed from training cadre at the Milowitz Training Area. Also see Replacement Army assets below.
Panzer-Aufklärungs-Zug 500	Formed in the occupied district of Poland. As the 500-series were generally corps troops, this might have been the nucleus for the reconnaissance troop formed for the *"Großdeutschland"* corps headquarters
Panzer-Späh-Kompanie "Krampnitz"	Part of *Panzer-Auffrischungs-Verband "Krampnitz,"* formed at the school at the end of March 1945. It was later absorbed into the *7. Panzer-Division.*[53]

THE REPLACEMENT ARMY

Replacement and Training Detachments

For most of the war, the Replacement Army (*Ersatzheer*) was separate from the field army (*Feldheer*). It was the training base for the field army, responsible for fielding and maintaining the various replacement and training commands. At the end of the war, the *Ersatzheer* was absorbed into the field army for obvious reasons—the home front had become the front lines, with the replacement and training detachments often having considerable combat-experienced personnel on hand, as well as a complement of vehicles suited for scouting and reconnaissance purposes.

The "schoolhouse" aspect of the training establishment was covered earlier. In addition, the detachments listed in the table below were responsible for training personnel and providing replacements for field units within their area of responsibility (defined by the military district).

These elements later moved to occupied territories to also serve as occupation forces or combat partisans. It can be assumed that each of these detachments had some armored vehicles for training purposes, although they were most likely obsolescent vehicles.

In keeping with their elite status, both *Panzergrenadier-Division "Großdeutschland"* and *"Feldherrnhalle"* maintained a training and detachment element for their armored forces. These were, respectively, *Panzertruppen-Ersatz- und Ausbildungs-Abteilung "Großdeutschland"* and *Panzertruppen-(Ersatz- und Ausbildungs-) Abteilung "Feldherrnhalle." Großdeutschland* is known to have had one troop dedicated to training armored reconnaissance

Military District	Detachment	Location
Wehrkreis III	*Aufklärungs-Ersatz-Abteilung (mot.) 3*	Potsdam
Wehrkreis IV	*Aufklärungs-Ersatz-Abteilung 10*	Dresden
Wehrkreis VII	*Ersatz-Abteilung 7 für motorisierte Aufklärungs-Einheiten*	Munich
Wehrkreis VIII	*Kradschützen-Ersatz-Bataillon 55*	Liegnitz
Wehrkreis IX	*Ersatz-Abteilung 4 für motorisierte Aufklärungs-Einheiten*	Weimar

Military District	Detachment	Location	Designation of Command
Wehrkreis I	*Kradschützen-Ersatz-Bataillon 24* (Effective December 1943: *Panzer-Aufklärungs-Ersatz- und Ausbildungs-Abteilung 24*)	Insterburg	*Kommandeur der Schnellen Truppen I*
Wehrkreis III	*Kradschützen-Ersatz-Bataillone 3* and *4* (Part of *Division-Nr. 233 (mot.)*, which became the *233. Panzergrenadier-Division* in July 1942)	Frankfurt/Oder	*Division-Nr. 233 (mot.)* (a reserve division). These elements later redesignated as *Panzer-Aufklärungs-Ersatz- und Ausbildungs-Abteilung 3* and *4*.
Wehrkreis VI	*Kradschützen-Ersatz-Bataillon 24*	Münster	*Brigadekommandeur der Schnellen Truppen VI*
Wehrkreis VII	*Kradschützen-Ersatz-Bataillon 40*	Munich	*Kommandeur der Schnellen Truppen VII*
Wehrkreis VIII	*Kradschützen-Ersatz-Bataillon 55* (Part of *Division-Nr. 178*)	Liegnitz	*Division-Nr. 178 (mot.)* (a reserve division)
Wehrkreis IX	*Kradschützen-Ersatz-Bataillone 1* and *9* (Part of *Division-Nr. 179 (mot.)*)	Weimar	*Division-Nr. 179 (mot.)* (a reserve division). These elements later redesignated as *Panzer-Aufklärungs-Ersatz- und Ausbildungs-Abteilung 1* and *9*.
Wehrkreis XVII	*Kradschützen-Ersatz- und Ausbildungs-Bataillon 2*	Vienna	*Brigadekommandeur der Schnellen Truppen XVII*

personnel; it is assumed the same applied to *Feldherrnhalle*.[54]

Other entities known to have responsibility for training and replacement detachments included the senior officer for armored forces (*Kommandeur der schnellen Truppen*, later *Panzertruppen*) within the military districts that had armored forces. Given the often confusing relationship between and among the various branches in this regard, some of the detachments/battalions listed in the table above are also shown here and elsewhere.

Reserve Divisions (*Reserve-Divisionen*)

The cadre divisions 155, 179, and 233 were incorporated into the armored force in April 1943 and eventually designated as *Reserve-Panzer-Divisionen*. *Panzer-Division Nr. 178* was likewise a reserve formation. The first three training divisions were deployed in occupied territories; the latter in Silesia. All of them were under the supervision of the senior armored force representative within each of the military districts. These divisions were never employed as such in combat; instead, they were used to reconsti-

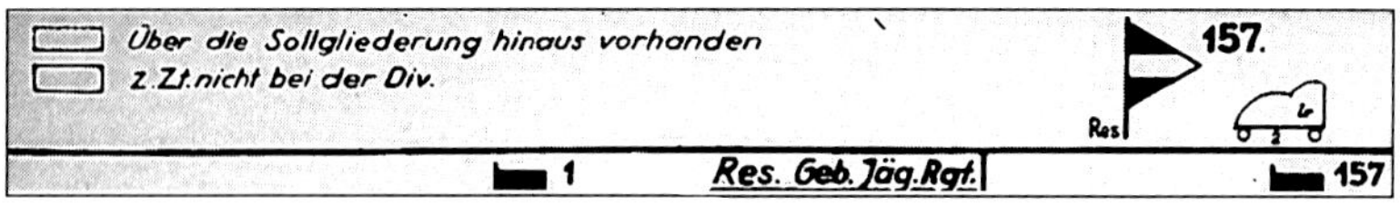

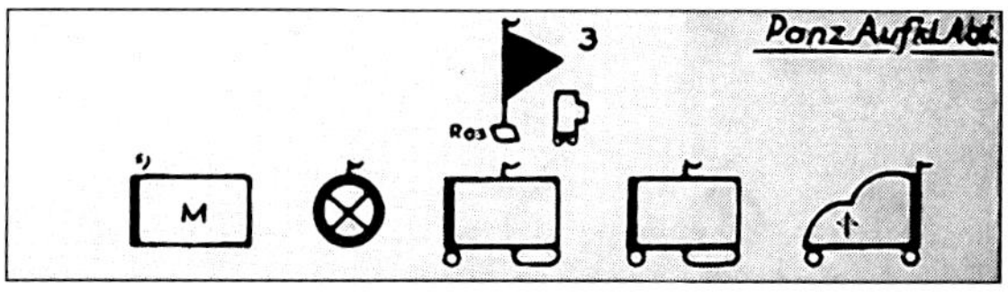

In some cases, organizations had armored cars that were not authorized, as indicated here in this organizational chart from the *157. Reserve-Division*. Although hard to tell in the image, the armored car symbol is dotted—an indicator that it is on hand but not authorized. **Right:** Although an armored reconnaissance battalion is reflected in the organizational structure of the *233. Reserve-Panzer-Division*, it had no real equipment assets and was generally a personnel holding company for trainees and replacements.

Reserve-Panzer-Division	Armored Reconnaissance Element	Location	Notes
155. Reserve-Panzer-Division	None positively located[55]	Nogent-le-Roi	Used to reconstitute the *11. Panzer-Division* in the spring of 1944
Panzer-Division-Nr. 178	*Panzer-Aufklärungs-Ersatz und Ausbildungs-Abteilung 55*	Liegnitz	Used in August 1944 to help establish *Panzer-Division Tatra.* Later reconstituted itself in February 1945 at Gleiwitz with the same reconnaissance detachment.
179. Reserve-Panzer-Division	*Reserve-Panzer-Aufklärungs-Abteilung 1*	Blois	Used to help establish the *116. Panzer-Division* (along with the decimated *16. Panzergrenadier-Division*).
233. Reserve-Panzer-Division	*Reserve-Panzer-Aufklärungs-Abteilung 3*	Horsens	Used to help reconstitute the *6., 19.,* and *25. Panzer-Divisionen.* Later reconstituted itself in December 1944 with the same reconnaissance detachment. Used in February 1945 to establish *Panzer-Division Holstein.*
273. Reserve-Panzer-Division	*Reserve-Panzer-Aufklärungs-Abteilung 7*	South of Bordeaux	

tute decimated armored divisions in 1944 and 1945. Again, there is some overlap with the entities discussed above. The armored reconnaissance elements listed above were known to exist.

Armored Training Formations

In March 1945, a last-ditch effort was made to produce more combat elements for the armored force. The armored reconnaissance elements formed consisted of the following (organization and equipment unknown):

Formation	Composition	Location	Major Command of Allocation
Panzer-Ausbildungs-Verband Böhmen	*Panzer-Aufklärungs-Ausbildungs-Abteilung 55* and *Heeres-Unteroffizierschule für Panzeraufklärer Sondershausen* [56]	Bohemia	*Heeresgruppe Mitte*
Panzer-Ausbildungs-Verband Donau	*Panzer-Aufklärungs-Lehrgang Milowitz*	Danube Region	*Heeresgruppe Süd*
Panzer-Ausbildungs-Verband Franken	*Panzer-Aufklärungs-Ausbildungs-Abteilung 9* (50 percent of detachment intended, but apparently never joined parent organization)	Franconia	*Heeresgruppe B*
Panzer-Ausbildungs-Verband Ostsee	*Panzer-Aufklärungs-Ausbildungs-Abteilung 3* [57]	Baltic	*Heeresgruppe Weichsel*
Panzer-Ausbildungs-Verband Thüringen	*Panzer-Aufklärungs-Lehr-Kompanie Bergen* and *Panzer-Aufklärungs-Schieß-Lehr-Kompanie Putlos* (apparently never joined intended parent organization)	Bergen and Putlos	*Heeresgruppe G*
Panzer-Ausbildungs-Verband Westfalen	*Panzer-Aufklärungs-Ausbildungs-Abteilung 6* and *Offiziers-Bewerber-Schule für Panzeraufklärer Meiningen* (apparently the schoolhouse never arrived nor did the 2nd Company of the reconnaissance detachment)	Meiningen	*Heeresgruppe H*

RECONNAISSANCE ELEMENTS WITHIN THE *SS-VERFÜGUNGSTRUPPE/ WAFFEN-SS*

In general, the SS used army models for organizing their forces. Initially, there is some deviance from army *KStN* numbers, but this is found at the start of the war, when the SS was initially fielding its combat troops. With the rapid expansion of the force and the requirement to cooperate with the army, it most likely became easier to adopt army models for the organizations.

The claim is often raised that the SS field formations received preferential treatment in the fielding of equipment and manpower, and the anomalies in their organizations sometime suggest that, but it must be borne in mind that the SS did not enter the war with any formations higher than a division and many of the assets available to support an Army division during combat operations were not within the SS system. Thus, the SS formations, particularly the early divisions, had extra assets built into them to overcome that deficit. While army assets could be and were used to support SS divisions, they then deprived Army divisions of some of those same assets, since the *Organizations-Abteilung* had only planned a force structure to support Army formations. As the war continued and the wartime forces of the *Waffen-SS* expanded exponentially, the line divisions took on more and more the character of their sister Army counterparts, especially within the non-Germanic formations.

The origins of the armed SS go back to the formation of the *SS-Stabswache Berlin* (SS Headquarters Guard "Berlin") on 17 March 1933, barely six weeks after Hitler's assumption of the chancellery of the Reich. The formation grew rapidly from its initial 120 volunteers and was soon redesignated as the *Leibstandarte SS Adolf Hitler* (Adolf Hitler's SS Bodyguard Standard). By 1935, the *Leibstandarte*[58] had risen to regimental strength, approximately 2,500 men, and included a number of elements that went well beyond the traditional role of a guard detachment for the head of state, to include a motorcycle infantry company, a mortar company and an armored car platoon, and it was participating in military training exercises with

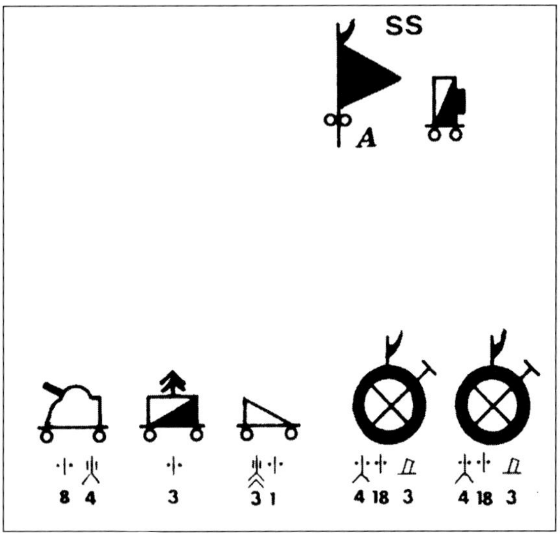

The armored reconnaissance battalion of the *SS-Verfügungstruppe*, as part of *Panzerverband Kempf* in the campaign in Poland. It is organized very similar to a typical motorized infantry division reconnaissance battalion of the time.

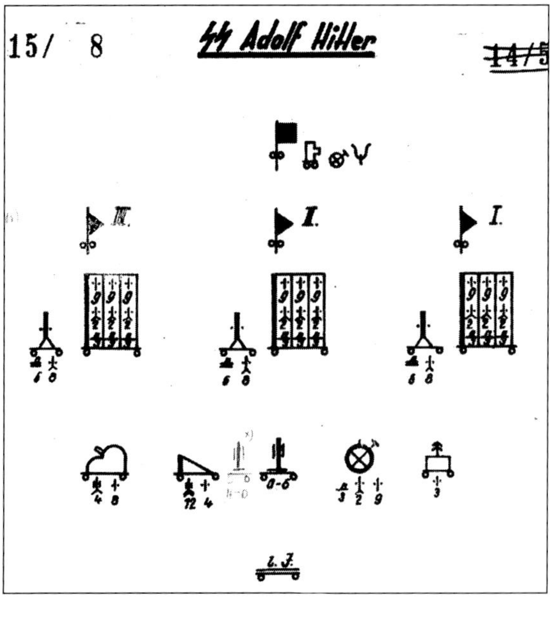

The reconnaissance assets of the *Leibstandarte* were relatively modest in January 1940, consisting of a motorcycle infantry company and an armored car platoon.

the Army and actual operations. Likewise, the initial formations of the *SS-Verfügungstruppe* (SS Unassigned Force) were also established shortly after Hitler's assumption of power, being formed in September 1934 from previously company-sized barracked forces of the SS.[59] The initial *Standarten*, as the regiments were called—*Deutschland*, *Germania*, and *Der Führer*—also possessed armored car sections, thus making the first armored elements of the SS what was later to become the nucleus of its reconnaissance battalions. In May 1938, Hitler assembled all of the *SS-VT* formations into a division, thus constituting what was to eventually become *Das Reich*, the first division of the armed SS, even though the *Leibstandarte* always retained precedence throughout its existence. Initially, the *SS-Verfügungs-Division* continued to keep armored car sections and motorcycle infantry companies within its line regiments, as well as maintaining its own reconnaissance battalion.

Somewhat later, but still well before the war, was the establishment of the *SS-Totenkopfverbände* (SS Death's Head Formations), which had the dubious distinction of being formed from concentration camp guard elements. While not part of the *SS-VT* initially, the field element eventually also evolved into a division just prior to the start of the war and became a *de facto* part of the *Waffen-SS*. Unlike the *Leibstandarte* and the *SS-Verfügungs-Division*, it had no armored car assets initially and did not receive any until shortly before the campaign against the Soviet Union.

As almost all of the Germanic *Waffen-SS* divisions, brigades and separate formations had significant armored reconnaissance assets, they will be covered in a later chapter. Those that had minimal armored reconnaissance elements will be mentioned in passing here, especially in instances where they deviated from the norm. Generally, before the divisions and brigades started to be numbered in 1944, the division and brigade troops all bore the name of the formation's honorific. After the formations also started to be numbered, the honorific was generally retained but the reconnaissance battalion also bore the number of the higher formation.

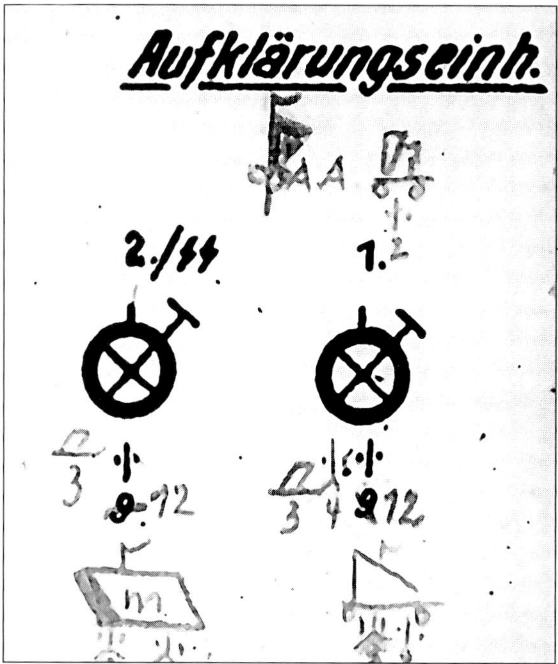

Although the *Totenkopf Division* entered the war with reconnaissance assets, they consisted only of two motorcycle infantry companies. These were later upgunned as indicated in the handwritten entries, but it took some time before the division's assets were formally organized as a battalion and eventually received armored cars (January 1940).

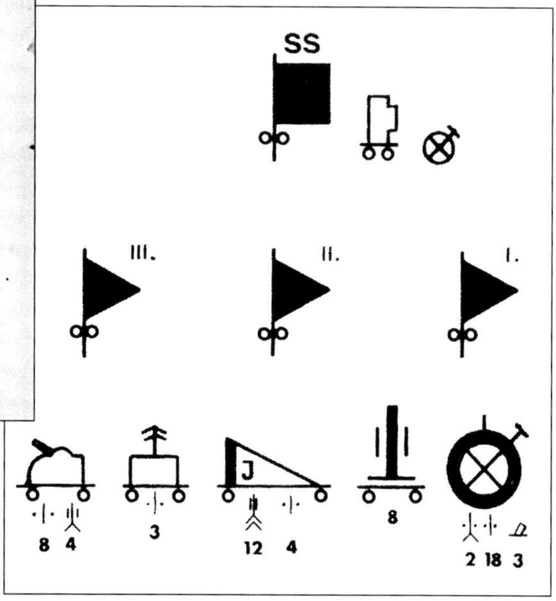

The armored reconnaissance assets of the *SS-Standarten* that fought in Poland were organized like those of the *Leibstandarte*.

SS Divisions (*SS-Divisionen*)

SS-Gebirgs-Kampfgruppe "Nord" was initially a brigade-sized element when formed in June 1941, but it had a reconnaissance battalion. Although there were no armored elements, the battalion did contain a company of motorcycle infantry and a heavy company. When the brigade expanded and reorganized into a division in September 1941, the reconnaissance battalion still contained only one *Kradschützen-Kompanie*. By the end of August 1942, the reconnaissance battalion had an additional motorcycle infantry company assigned to it. Compared to an army mountain division, it represented considerably more motorized reconnaissance assets. These were augmented by a machine-gun company in June 1943. By the middle of 1944, *SS-Aufklärungs-Abteilung (mot) 6* had changed again, deleting the machine-gun company and replacing it with a motorized reconnaissance company (wheeled), an organization that was apparently retained until the end of the war.

The *SS-Freiwilligen-Gebirgs-Division "Prinz Eugen"* initially had no motorized reconnaissance assets, although it received a light armored reconnaissance company by March 1943. This was in addition to *SS-Aufklärungs-Abteilung (mot.) 7*, which had two motorcycle infantry troops and a heavy troop, although the battalion was deactivated later that summer. Another round of reorganization followed, with the original reconnaissance battalion being reassigned to the *V. SS-Gebirgs-Korps* and redesignated as *SS-Aufklärungs-Abteilung 105* (see below). The reconstituted divisional reconnaissance battalion that was present in July 1944 was apparently a bicycle reconnaissance formation, although it also had a heavy company, which had a light armored car platoon also assigned to it (six armored cars). This apparently changed once again a month later in August 1944, when the reconnaissance battalion had an *SPW* platoon in its headquarters, two bicycle troops, one horse-mounted troop, and a heavy company, albeit now without any armored cars.

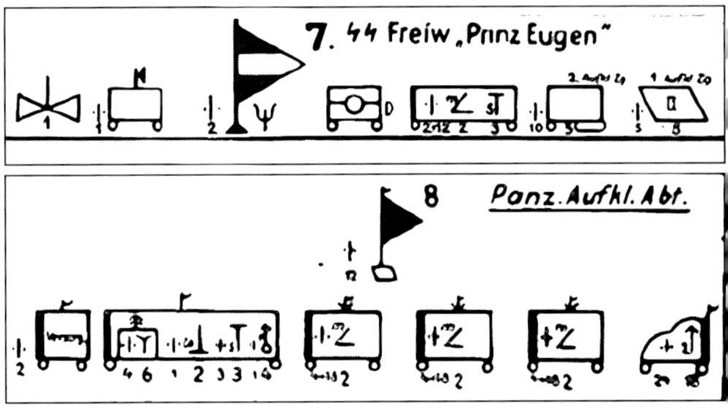

Top: The organization of *Prinz Eugen's* reconnaissance assets in April 1944. **Bottom:** The reconnaissance battalion of *Florian Geyer* in May 1944.

The premier cavalry division of the *Waffen-SS*, *Florian Geyer*, also had a unique structure, as reflected in its reconnaissance assets. In March 1941, when it was essentially a brigade equivalent, it had no formal motorized or armored reconnaissance assets as part of its line organization, but it did have an armored car platoon listed as being assigned to its replacement detachment (1st Troop). For the invasion of the Soviet Union, the brigade was split into two separate regiments, with *SS-Kavallerie-Regiment 1* listing an armored car platoon within its 1st Troop. The sister regiment, *SS-Kavallerie-Regiment 2*, apparently also had an armored car platoon, but it was listed as being attached from another source and not further identified.[60] The regiments rejoined the parent organization by the end of the year and, by February 1942, the brigade listed a bicycle reconnaissance battalion among its assets, with all mention of armored car platoons disappearing. It is only in July 1944, when the division was officially known as the *8. SS-Kavallerie-Division "Florian Geyer,"* that an armored reconnaissance battalion was listed as a divisional troop. It consisted of an armored car company, a motorized reconnaissance company and a heavy company.

When the *13. Waffen-SS-Gebirgs-Division "Handschar" (1. kroat.)* was formed out of Croatians, Muslims, ethnic Balkan Germans, and volunteers from Bosnia in France in March 1943, it had a motorized reconnaissance battalion, with two motorcycle infantry companies and one heavy company. Late in 1943, after several clashes between the ethnic groups within the division had to be forcibly quelled, the division maintained its reconnaissance battalion, but it reverted to bicycles. A horse-mounted troop was added in the late summer of 1944. In September 1944, the reconnaissance battalion was pulled from the division and ordered to become the reconnaissance battalion for the *IX. SS-Gebirgs-Korps*, where it was redesignated as *SS-Aufklärungs-Abteilung 509*.

Separate Brigades (Brigade Equivalents)

The *1. SS-Brigade "Reichsführer SS"* was initially formed in April 1941 from elements of the *Totenkopfverbände*. Its role expanded from a rear-area security force to that of a combat element. As such, it was reorganized and eventually contained *SS-Aufklärungs-Abteilung 51*, which had a motorcycle infantry company and an armored car platoon (four *Sd.Kfz. 222's* and three *Sd. Kfz. 223's*). In the latter part of 1941, after the brigade was reorganized and redesignated as the *1. SS-Infanterie-Brigade (mot)*, this element disappeared from its order of battle, only to reappear in 1943 as *SS-Kradschützen-Kompanie 51*. In 1944, the brigade was used to form the nucleus of the *18. SS-Panzergrenadier-Division "Horst Wessel."* There was also a *2. SS-Brigade "Reichsführer SS,"* initially formed for the same purposes as the first, but it apparently had no armored reconnaissance elements. When it was later expanded and redesignated to become the *SS-Freiwilligen-Brigade "Lettisch"* in February 1943, its reconnaissance asset was a bicycle battalion.

The *4. SS-Freiwilligen-Panzergrenadier-Brigade "Nederland,"* which was formed from predecessor formations composed of a number of Dutch volunteers, had a reconnaissance company (54th), when originally established on 23 October 1943. This company eventually formed the nucleus of the *SS-Division-Füsilier-Bataillon* around May 1944. The battalion had an armored car platoon (apparently with six 2cm armored cars), an antitank platoon and a light armored reconnaissance platoon (possibly company).[61]

In August 1944, *SS-Panzer-Brigade "Groß"* was formed out of elements stationed at the SS training facility in Latvia (*Seelager*). The *ad hoc* brigade apparently had an armored reconnaissance battalion of three companies of unknown composition. It was later dispatched to the west, where it was absorbed by SS field formations, ceasing to exist by April 1945.

Armored Training Formations

The SS maintained its own reconnaissance training and replacement regiment at the *Seelager* Training Area near Riga in Latvia (Courland). There were two detachments within the regiment, *SS-Panzer-Aufklärungs-Ausbildungs- und Ersatz-Abteilungen 1* and *2*. These were used to form part of the *ad hoc* formation, *SS-Panzer-Brigade "Groß"* (see above), with remaining elements apparently moved out of the camp as the Soviets drew closer and were eventually absorbed into field formations of the *Waffen-SS*.[62]

Higher Commands

As with the army, there were not any (armored) reconnaissance assets organic to a corps or higher headquarters initially. The only known exception were two of the SS mountain corps (V and IX), with *SS-Aufklärungs-Abteilung 105* within the headquarters of the *V. SS-Gebirgs-Korps* and *SS-Aufklärungs-Abteilung 109* as part of the *IX. Waffen-Gebirgs-Korps*.[63]

LUFTWAFFE (HERMANN GÖRING FORMATIONS)

The only *Luftwaffe* ground combat formation that consistently had motorized and armored reconnaissance elements was the one named after the corpulent *Reichsmarschall*, Hermann Göring. As early as 15 September 1933, *Regiment "General Göring"* had a motorcycle infantry company (13th) and a horse-mounted reconnaissance platoon, in addition to its two battalions.[64] By 1 October, the regiment had expanded to four battalions—two of *Flak*, one as a ceremonial formation, and one of parachute infantry—with the *Kradschützen-Kompanie* redesignated as the 8th Company of the 3rd Battalion of the regiment. In addition, there was also a short-lived armored car platoon, but it was inactivated on 1 November 1938.[65]

After undergoing several reorganizations, the regiment was expanded and redesignated as a brigade, with two regiments. The motorcycle infantry (10th) was located in the *III./Schützen-Regiment "Hermann Göring."* The brigade status was soon upgraded to division on 15 October 1942, with the division having its own motorized reconnaissance battalion, *Aufklärungs-Abteilung "Hermann Göring,"* consisting of headquarters with an armored car platoon; motorcycle infantry company (1st); Volkswagen reconnaissance company (2nd); armored car company (to be established by 1 April 1943) (3rd); antitank company (4th); heavy company (5th); and *Flak* company (6th).[66] The *"Hermann Göring"* reconnaissance battalion was considerably stronger than the army equivalent at the time, but its basic company building blocks were based on army organizational principles and standards.

Elements of the reconnaissance battalion (1st, 3rd, 4th and 5th Companies) were deployed to North Africa, where most of the personnel and all of the equipment were lost in May, when the Axis forces capitulated. The remaining forces of the division remained on Sicily initially and then on the Italian mainland, where the reconnaissance battalion was reconstituted and redesignated as *Panzer-Aufklärungs-Abteilung "Hermann Göring."* In subsequent reorganizations, the reconnaissance battalions all assumed an army model.

According to its organization chart dated 1 May 1944, the reconnaissance battalion consisted of battalion headquarters; armored scout company (armored car) (1st), with eighteen armored cars; armored scout company (*SPW*); armored reconnaissance company (*SPW*); armored reconnaissance company (VW); and heavy company

The division spent the first half of 1944 in Italy, before being redeployed to the Warsaw area of the Eastern Front in the middle of July. On 1 October of the same year, the division was used to provide cadre for the creation of *Fallschirm-Panzer-Korps "Hermann Göring,"* with two divisions—*Fallschirm-Panzer-Division 1* and *Fallschirm-Panzergrenadier-Division 2*, with each division authorized a reconnaissance battalion of four companies. The *Panzergrenadier-Division* had wheeled companies, while the *Panzer-Division* had *SPW* companies and heavy armored cars in its headquarters company.[67] The corps took part in the final fighting for Germany and surrendered to the Soviets in the area north of Dresden in May 1945.

Higher Commands

According to the *Frontnachweiser* of December 1944, *Fallschirm-Aufklärungs-Abteilung 14* was allocated to *Panzer-Fallschirm-Korps "Hermann Göring,"* but the exact composition of this reconnaissance battalion is unknown.[68] In addition, the two *Fallschirm-Korps* each had a reconnaissance battalion of five companies, as of 1 May 1944. *Fallschirm-Aufklärungs-Abteilung 11* was assigned to the *I. Fallschirm-Korps*, *Fallschirm-Aufklärungs-Abteilung 12* to the *II. Fallschirm-Korps*. The 1st Company of each of the battalions had armored cars. The 2nd and 3rd Companies were *SPW* armored reconnaissance companies and the 4th Company was the heavy company. The heavy company had a combat engineer platoon (*SPW*), an infantry gun platoon (two light infantry guns), a *Flak* platoon (four 2cm guns), and two anti-tank platoons (one with three 7.5cm guns and the other with six 7.5cm guns). In accordance with the *freie Gliederung* model, the 5th Company was a supply company. The tactical symbols used for the organizational chart indicate that there was a battery of assault guns organic to the armored car company as well, although no additional information is available.

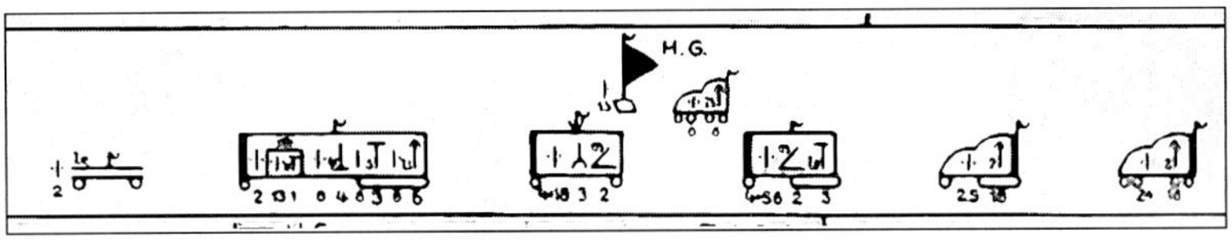

The armored reconnaissance battalion of the *Hermann Göring Division* mirrored that of its army counterparts in 1944.

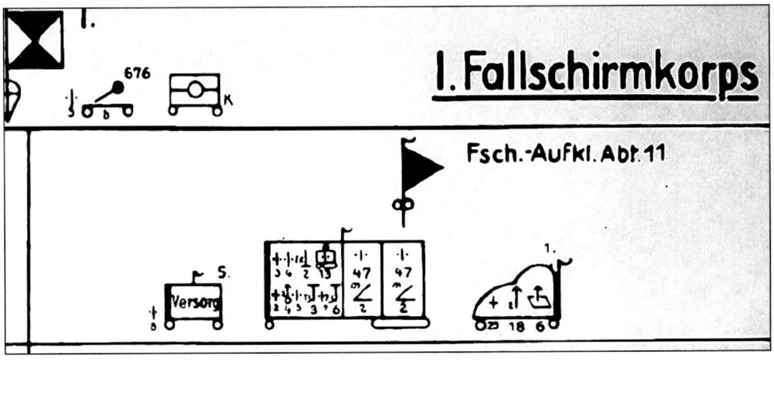

Right: *Fallschirm-Aufklärungs-Abteilung 11* of the *I. Fallschirm-Korps*. Its sister battalion in the *II. Fallschirm-Korps* was organized the same way.

Although great effort was made to glamorize the role of the motorcycle infantry, they did not have an easy time of it. They were subjected to the whims of Mother Nature just like their foot infantry brethren and their relative speed on the battlefield did little to counteract the lack of armored protection once battle was joined. While their great speed enabled them to frequently surprise and overwhelm the enemy, it also exposed them to greater danger against a prepared and determined foe, who could usually get the first shot off.

The prewar imagery of the armored forces was filled with romance, as evidenced by this mid-1930s postcard image of a column of *Kfz. 13's* moving down a rural road, accompanied by a motorcycle messenger, who must be serving as a liaison between the section and its higher headquarters. Normally, a scout section would be accompanied by a radio vehicle, but it is presumed the artist took some liberties with his subject matter.

With the onset of hostilities on 1 September 1939 in the campaign against Poland, the years of training for the fledgling armored reconnaissance force would be put to the test. In this image, we see an *Sd.Kfz. 221* crossing a waterway on an engineer bridge. The fascines on the front of the vehicle were used to assist it in self-recovery whenever the underpowered vehicle got stuck in rough terrain.

This *Sd.Kfz 232 (6-Rad)* moves through the dusty streets of a village. The solid white crosses, which presented a good aiming point for the enemy, were replaced after the campaign with more inconspicuous ones.

The crew of an *Sd.Kfz. 232 (Fu) (8-Rad)* waits along a road with the rest of a column for orders to move out. The officer in the foreground is identifiable by the cross strap attached to his belt, an arrangement that soon fell out of favor shortly after the start of the war. These images and the ones on the next three pages come from the album of a soldier who transferred from *Infanterie-Regiment 69 (mot)* of the *20. Infanterie-Division (mot)* to that division's reconnaissance battalion, *Aufklärungs-Abteilung 20 (mot)*. JIM HALEY

Right: The faces of this officer and NCO reflect the strain and stress of combat operations. Both have just been awarded the Iron Cross, Second Class (soldiers were allowed to wear the actual medal only on the day it was presented). The officer appears to have a tailor-made cap, since the *Waffenfarbe* seems unusually thick and the cap might be black (a feature that was not officially introduced until 1940).

The *1./Aufklärungs-Abteilung 20 (mot)* is lined up in preparation for a road march. The *Sd.Kfz 232 (Fu) (8-Rad)* armored cars in the front are followed by several *Sd.Kfz. 263 (Fu)* radio cars and what appear to be *Sd.Kfz. 231 (8-Rad)* and other armored cars.

The vehicle commander of this *Sd.Kfz. 231 (6-Rad)* poses for the camera. The normally spotless appearance of the vehicles in peacetime has been replaced by a layer of dust and dirt from the many miles the vehicles have covered.

The somber expressions on this officer and scout reflect the harshness of combat, as evidenced by the blown-out rear portion of the turret of the *Sd.Kfz. 221* light armored car.

The crew of this *Sd.Kfz. 232 (Fu) (8-Rad)* strikes a martial pose in the war-torn streets of a Polish town.

Below: This *Sd.Kfz. 223 (Fu)*—christened *Cäsar*—appears to have been knocked out while crossing a water obstacle, as evidenced by what appears to be seared paint, primarily around the engine compartment. The vehicle has been stripped of all usable equipment and weaponry.

Elements of an armored reconnaissance battalion move through a shattered Polish town. The battalion is most likely from one of the light or motorized infantry divisions, as evidenced by the use of the cavalry tactical sign for the formation, as seen on the left rear of the *Sd.Kfz. 231 (6-Rad).*

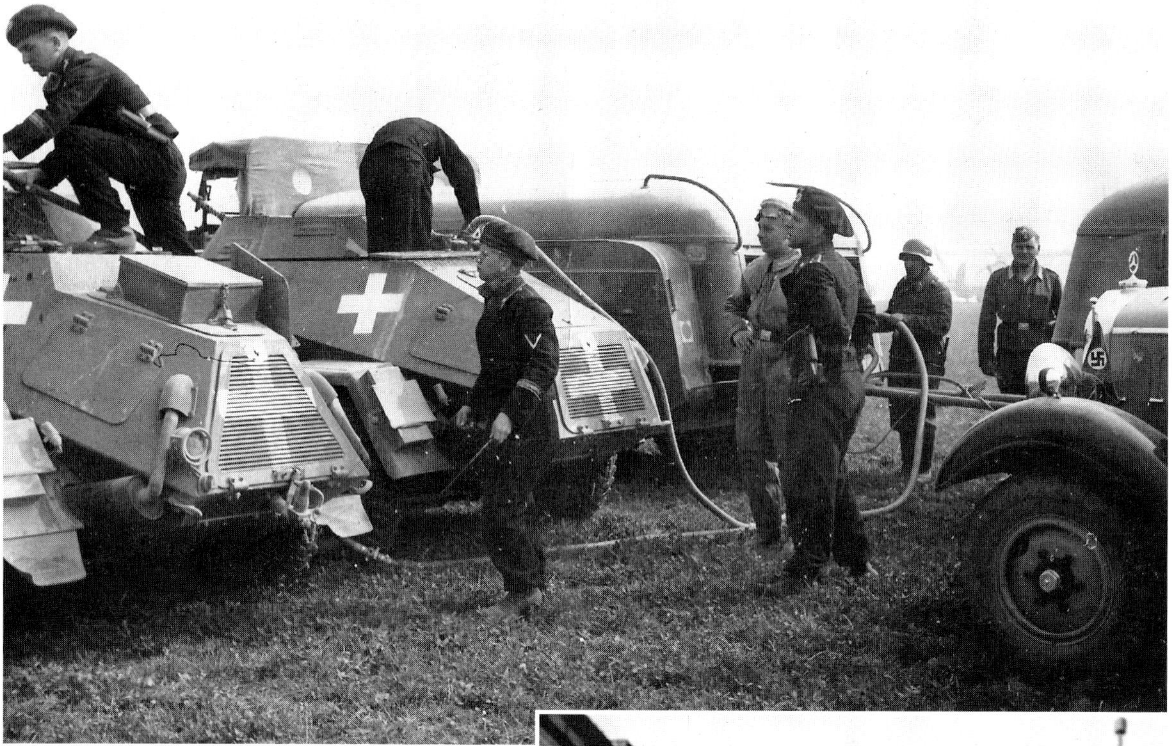

Also participating in the campaign in Poland was a detachment from the *Aufklärungs-Lehr-Abteilung (mot)*, which provided escort duties for the *Führer* when he toured the conquered country. The soldiers wear cuff titles indicating their attachment to the *Führer* Headquarters, the *Führerhauptquartier*. The wear of the cuff titles was only authorized while performing duties as part of Hitler's entourage. The armored cars consist of *Sd.Kfz. 221* and *222* vehicles. A portion of Hitler's touring car can be seen to the right of the armored cars being refueled. HENNER LINDLAR

Various armored cars of the *1./Aufklärungs-Abteilung (mot)* move down a fog-shrouded road in this atmospheric scene.

A motorcycle infantry battalion's assets assembled in its motor pool. Scenes such as this would become increasingly rare as the war progressed, since most formations never saw their home garrison again after the campaign in the East started in 1941.

These images are attributed to *Aufklärungs-Abteilung 37 (mot)* of the *7. Panzer-Division*, one of several new divisions formed after the success of the *schnelle Truppen* in Poland. While the higher commands were busy with preparations for the campaign in the West, the troops on the ground continued to train. The battalion appears to be staging for a possible movement somewhere. Of interest here is the wide variety of vehicles that can be seen, including the *Sd.Kfz. 232 (8-Rad)*, the *Sd.Kfz. 231 (6-Rad)*, and the *Sd.Kfz. 221*.

Training in the field for the motorized infantry included extensive practice with hand and arm signals, since the men on the motorcycles did not have radios. They needed to conduct battle drills without hesitation based on a signal flag from a leader positioned to the front. Training for the scouts often required traveling to larger training areas, which were the only areas were their heavier weapons could be fired. Battalion soft-skinned and tactical vehicles line up while officers appear to be headed for a briefing.

Once in the open and the Allied forces in general disarray, the reconnaissance forces were able to make good use of the generally flat countryside of northern France and the good road networks.

Right: The ground scouts were expected to operate hand-in-glove with aerial reconnaissance. This prewar image shows a Fieseler *Storch* light utility aircraft that has taxied next to an *Sd.Kfz. 232 (Fu) (6-Rad)* in an open field. If the situation was too fluid or the terrain too rough, the pilots would drop reports from their aircraft. Air-ground coordination was difficult in the best of times, since the various radios could not "talk" to one another, so the rugged "Stork" was a godsend for quick coordination in the field.

Above: An *Sd.Kfz. 247 (4-Rad)* attributed to *Aufklärungs-Abteilung 37 (mot)* halts near a staging area for tanks of the *7. Panzer-Division*. The armored utility vehicle was relatively rare, with less than 100 of the 6- and 4-wheeled versions being produced. These were usually authorized for the battalion headquarters command group.

Left: As the advance continued south in the second part of the campaign, the roads were marked by huge clouds of dust from seemingly endless columns of vehicles moving in pursuit of a beaten enemy.

Once the troops came home, there were innumerable welcoming parades in front of enthusiastic throngs.

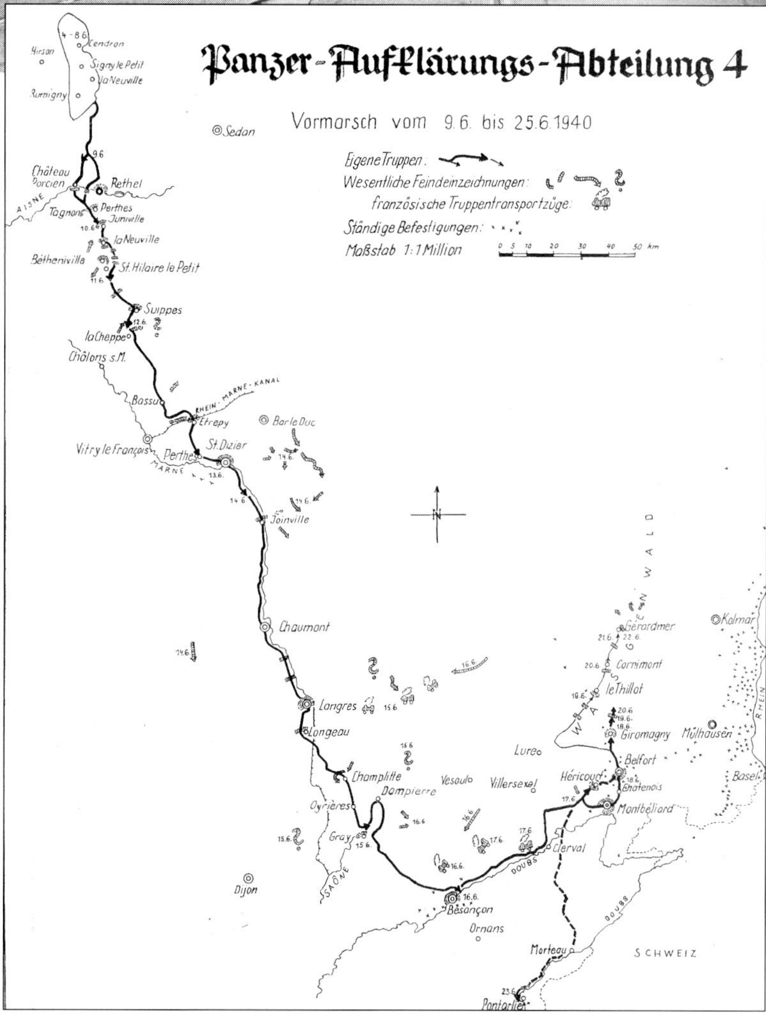

Right: As in Poland, there was a great deal of fanfare associated with the defeat of the French. Many combat formations produced unit histories or monographs, and most produced commemorative maps of the routes the campaign had taken them. In this instance, it is for *Panzer-Aufklärungs-Abteilung 4* of the *1. Panzer-Division*, tracing its combat history from 9 to 25 June during the second phase of the campaign. JIM HALEY

Obergefreiter Anton Niedermeier of *Aufklärungs-Regiment 7 (mot)* of the *2. leichte Division* paid the ultimate price on the first day of the campaign in the West, 10 May 1940. The actual regiment is not stated in the traditional death notice of the time, but an A/7 can be identified on his shoulder strap.

In getreuer Pflichterfüllung für Führer, Volk und Vaterland starb am 10. Mai 1940 den Heldentod in Holland unser einziger, innigstgeliebter Sohn und Neffe

Anton Niedermeier

Obergefreiter
in einem Panzer-Aufklärungs-Regiment
Kraftwagenführerssohn von Neumarkt-St. Veit

im Blütenalter von 22 Jahren; er liegt im Heldenfriedhof in Wyk bei Maastrich. Wer ihn kannte, weiß unsern Schmerz zu würdigen.

Eltern, trocknet Euere Tränen;
Als mich traf das kalte Erz,
War bei Euch mein letztes Sehnen,
Brich nicht, brich nicht, Mutterherz.
Gönnet mir den Tod der Helden,
Traget aufrecht Eueren Schmerz.
Konnte man Euch Edleres melden?
Brich nicht, brich nicht, Vaterherz.

„Mein Jesus Barmherzigkeit!"
Vater unser. Ave Maria.

Druck von Otto Töring, Neumarkt-St. Veit

The campaign in the Balkans and Greece in April 1941 ultimately proved to be a sideshow to the offensive launched against the Soviet Union in June of that year. The exploits of the reconnaissance elements of the SS formations are perhaps best known, both from the extensive coverage they received from SS war correspondents and photographers and from narratives by charismatic leaders such as Kurt "Panzer" Meyer. Here two *Sd.Kfz. 232 (8-Rad)* armored cars of the *Leibstandarte SS Adolf Hitler* lead a column down the road. BUNDESARCHIV

Right: An *Sd.Kfz. 232 (8-Rad)* being guided through an obstacle by a soldier from an unidentified SS element. UNSERE WAFFEN-SS POSTCARD SERIES VIA MICHAEL H. PRUETT

The next theater of operations for the Germans was North Africa, where forces started arriving in March 1941 to assist the bumbling efforts of Hitler's Italian ally, Mussolini. While initially widely successful under the charismatic command of *Generaloberst* Erwin Rommel, the German contingent was ultimately doomed by lackluster logistical support and Allied control of the sea lanes. Despite a massive influx of personnel and equipment in 1943, it was a case of "too little, too late," and the squandered formations could have been put to better use in the fighting in the East. Here a convoy crosses the Mediterranean. Close examination shows that an *Sd.Kfz. 221* has been posted on the foredeck to bolster the ship's antiaircraft defenses.

In April 1941, an additional light division was activated for service in Africa, the *90. leichte Afrika-Division*. It did not receive armored reconnaissance assets until August of that year, when *Aufklärungs-Kompanie (mot.) 580* started joining its parent division after completing training in Germany. When the division was redesignated as the *90. Afrika-Division*, the reconnaissance company became *Panzer-Aufklärungs-Abteilung 580* and was eventually reassigned to the *21. Panzer-Division*. This series of images shows the company preparing for its move to North Africa from Germany. The commanding officer, *Rittmeister* von Homeyer, talks to his subordinates in preparation for the movement to the railhead. The men wear a combination of continental uniforms and tropical headgear. The vehicles and equipment appear to be recently issued, based on their pristine appearance. Command-and-control and communications vehicles predominate, including an *Sd.Kfz. 250/3* and an *Sd.Kfz. 223 (Fu)*. ALL PHOTOGRAPHS IN THIS SERIES COURTESY OF MICHAEL H. PRUETT.

Elements of the company pass the commander on the way to the railhead.

Armored cars and half-tracks of the company leave the military facilities to head to the railhead.

This *Sd.Kfz. 250/3* appears to need some extra help in boarding the train. Once the manual labor is done, the troops receive mail and rations, draw straw for makeshift bedding and finally depart the train station, after receiving some final gifts from local civilians and family members.

17 F
WH
698570

The men get to work loading the unit vehicles onto the flat cars.

Nichtraucher
3

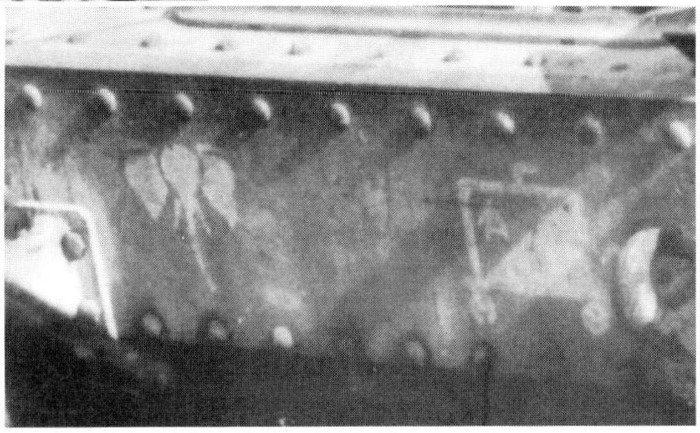

This *Marder III*, a tank destroyer built on a *Panzer 38(t)* chassis and mounting a 7.5cm Model 40 antitank gun, (Sd.Kfz. 138 für 7.5cm PaK 40/3 Ausf. H), was part of a reconnaissance battalion's inventory, based on the tactical symbol used. The close-up shows both the reconnaissance symbol and the unit insignia, which has remained unidentified. The *Marder III* was photographed at the Aberdeen Proving Grounds in Maryland, where it was shipped for testing and evaluation after capture in North Africa. MICHAEL H. PRUETT

A column of vehicles from a reconnaissance battalion rolls through a North African town. Just about all types of tactical vehicles of the period are represented: light and heavy armored cars, utility vehicles, and the still ubiquitous sidecar motorcycle.

CHAPTER 3

Armored Reconnaissance Vehicles

To a certain extent, the development of vehicles specifically designed for armored reconnaissance mirrored that of the armored forces as a whole. While the Versailles Treaty did allow Germany to possess some armored cars for internal security purposes, it forbade the development and possession of armored cars capable of conducting modern battlefield reconnaissance and scouting.

Despite those prohibitions, it was generally understood what was needed in a vehicle capable of conducting ground reconnaissance: speed, maneuverability, cross-country capability, radio communications, armored protection against small arms, extended range, and (limited) self-defense capability. Unique, perhaps, among German design features was the desire for the ability to move at the same speed in both forward and reverse, which essentially required two drivers.[1] Indeed, proposals as early as 1924 called for an all-wheel drive, an engine capable of delivering 75 horsepower, an amphibious capability, and a revolving turret with machine guns or a combination of a machine gun and a 2cm automatic cannon. Needless to say, such design concepts did not come to fruition at the time, for a variety of reasons, primarily financial.[2]

As with all armored vehicle development, the ideal combination of capabilities often proved elusive. Starting with civilian vehicles pressed into military service—the *Kfz. 13* and *14*—German industry slowly developed families of vehicles that came ever closer to the ideal. These were mostly wheeled designs, since those were the only ones initially permitted by the Allies or capable of being designed in such a way as to avoid Allied intervention. Once Hitler came into power and declared national sovereignty without sanctions, work could proceed with purpose-built

An *Sd.Kfz. 221* of *Aufklärungs-Abteilung 5 (mot)*. The unit's prewar tactical signs are painted on both fenders, and the three-tone camouflage can be identified on the cover for the spare tire. JIM HALEY

The *Adler Standard* civilian automobile was modified by the addition of thin armor and a rounded shape with a revolving turret to provide the fledgling reconnaissance forces with a training vehicle in the early 1930s. JIM HALEY

Prewar maneuvers involving an *Adler Standard* armored car (last vehicle), one of the newly introduced *Sd.Kfz. 221's*, and three Kfz. 13's. JIM HALEY

designs that ranged from light to heavy wheeled armored cars. With the onset of war, the motorcycles used by the *Kradschützen* elements eventually proved unequal to the task in the barren wastes of North Africa and the impossible road conditions of the Soviet Union. To that end, half-track designs (*Kettenkrad*), all-wheel-drive utility vehicles (*Volkswagen*), and armored personnel carriers (the *Sd.Kfz. 250* and *251* series) began to be impressed into reconnaissance and scouting service. The constant shortfall in wheeled armored cars also necessitated the use of captured stocks, such as French Panhards and Italian scout cars.

With the ever-increasing lethality of Soviet antiarmor weaponry and the gradual evolution of the campaign in the East to one of strategic defense—with less need for pure scouting capabilities and extended range—increasingly larger-caliber weaponry began to be mounted on the vehicles and incorporated into the *KStN's* of the scout and reconnaissance companies, with several varieties of armored cars fielding 5cm and 7.5cm main guns. Fully tracked vehicle designs were also explored and fielded that would allow greater cross-country mobility in comparison to the wheeled armored car fleet, which had always had issues in that regard. This resulted in the development and fielding of excellent vehicles, such as the *Luchs* and a reconnaissance version of the old stalwart, the *Panzer 38(t)*, but as with all German vehicle design, it was a matter of too little, too late: only four companies of these two vehicles were ever fielded.[3]

ARMORED CARS

Kfz. 13 (Machinengewehr-Kraftwagen 13)

Crew:	2 (commander and driver)
Armament:	1x MG 13 on a ring mount with manual traverse
Speed:	Approximately 35–44 mph
Range:	Approximately 135–199 miles
Communications equipment:	None
Production Run:	147 vehicles (by 1934)[4]
Notes:	In the early 1930s, the decision was made to use modified commercial vehicles because of the overall financial situation. Daimler was given a contract to modify the *Adler Standard 6 12 N-RW* vehicle, a commercial design, that was already being used to simulate tanks with mock-up hulls. In October 1935, a process was started to transfer these vehicles to the *Reiter-Regimenter* and *Kavallerie-Regimenter* from the *Kraftfahr-Abteilungen*. By 1938, only fifty-eight *Kfz. 13's* were left in service in standing reconnaissance battalions. Obsolete by the eve of World War II, it nevertheless saw service in the campaign in Poland.

Kfz. 14 (Funkkraftwagen 14)

Crew:	3
Armament:	None
Speed:	See *Kfz. 13*
Range:	See *Kfz. 13*
Communications equipment:	Unspecified radio set with frame antenna with voice range of around 5 miles and Morse range of 18 miles (when stationary)
Production Run:	116 (from 1932 to 1934)
Notes:	Radio version of the *Kfz. 13*.

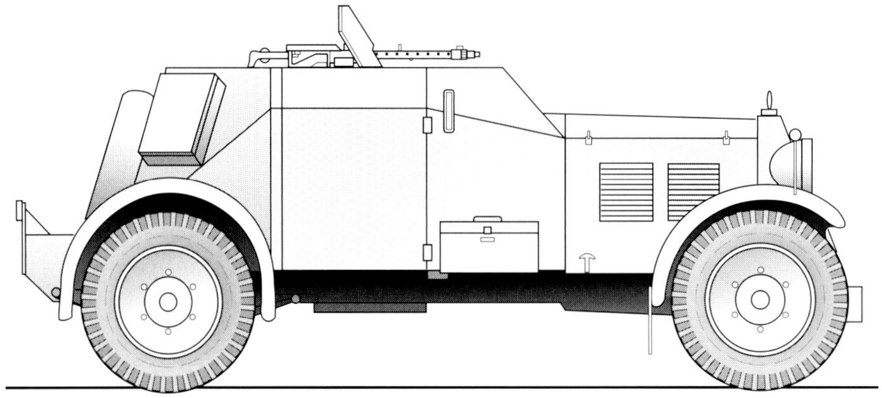

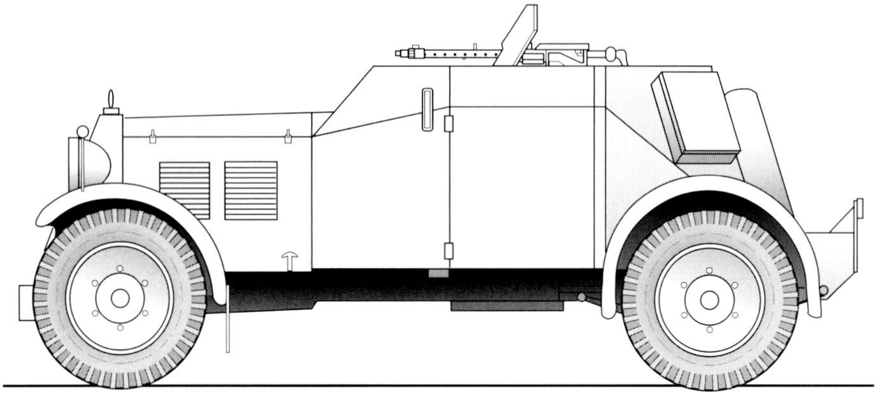

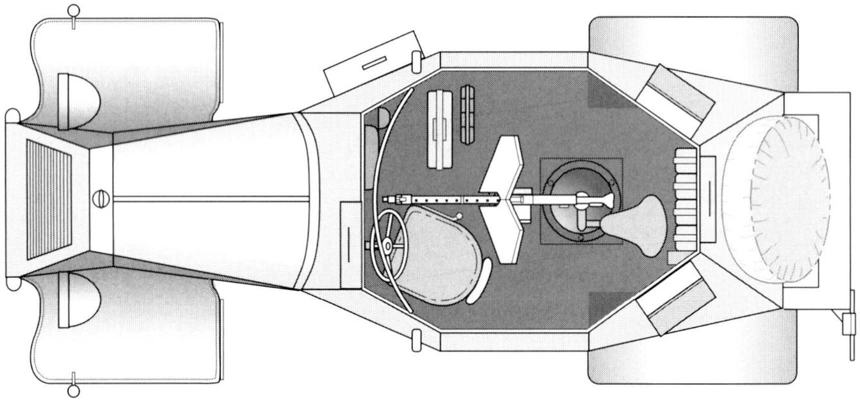

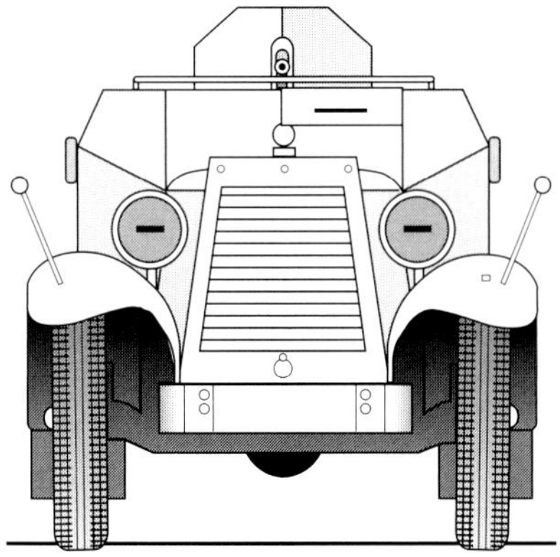

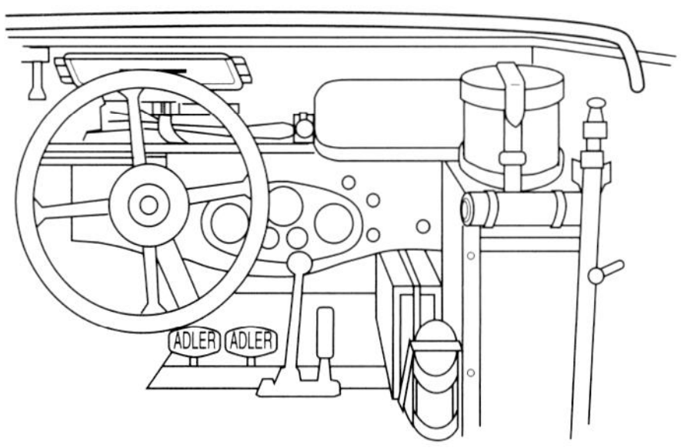

Basic dashboard & gear shift levers.

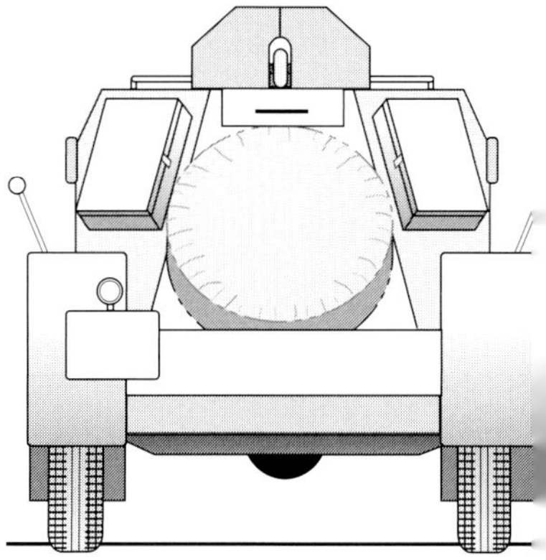

The *Kfz. 13* was used starting in the early 1930s as a training vehicle for reconnaissance forces. The modified civilian chassis had a single MG 13 on a swivel mount in the open fighting compartment. It was barely deemed combat worthy when introduced, but this vehicle and its sister armored car, the *Kfz. 14 (Fu)*, were actually still in use by 1939, and some saw action in both Poland and the West. Here the machine gun has not been mounted, and the prewar three-tone camouflage pattern can be seen. JIM HALEY

The MG 13 is mounted on this *Kfz. 13* from the *2./Aufklärungs-Abteilung 5 (mot)* of the *2. Panzer-Division.* A prewar tactical symbol readily identifies the unit the vehicle belongs to. Of interest is the painting of the vehicle's nomenclature on the left side of the superstructure. JIM HALEY

A scout poses proudly in his *Kfz. 13*. JIM HALEY

A nice close-up of a scout taking aim on his MG 13 on a *Kfz. 13*. The machine gun has had a chin guard attached to the stock to help the soldier in absorbing the recoil of the weapon. JIM HALEY

Right: The radio version of the vehicle, the *Kfz. 14*, did not have a machine gun. The frame antenna could be lowered when moving to help prevent damage to it. JIM HALEY

Scouts receive radio training on a *Kfz. 14.* They belong to *Aufklärungs-Abteilung 5 (mot)*, as readily seen by the A/5 on their shoulder straps. JIM HALEY

Sd.Kfz. 221	
Crew:	2
Armament:	Initially 1x 7.92mm MG13, followed by 1x 7.92mm MG34
Speed:	Approximately 35–50 mph
Range:	Approximately 175–199 miles
Communications equipment:	*FuG Spr a* (standard short-range radio set for communication between and among platoon or company vehicles with rod antenna and range of about half a mile).
Production Run:	339 for the army by September 1940; unspecified numbers as export version for China; separate contracts let for the SS.
Notes:	Development started in 1934. Modifications included different radio configurations and the addition of the 2.8cm *schwere Panzerbüchse 41* on some vehicles, which increased the crew to 3. The heavy antitank rifle had a muzzle velocity of 1,400 meters a second, with an ability to penetrate 39 millimeters of armor at 800 meters. This vehicle as well as the *222, 223, 260,* and *261* used the chassis of the standard *schwerer Personenkraftwagen I Horch 801* (or slightly modified versions thereof), with all axles steerable for improved cross-country performance.

Scouts take a break during prewar maneuvers. In the foreground is an *Sd.Kfz. 221*. Ahead of it is the radio version, the *Sd.Kfz. 223*. Black overseas caps were not officially introduced to the *schnelle Truppen* until 1940. JIM HALEY

A scout section is halted momentarily on the streets of a German village. The lead vehicle is an *Sd.Kfz. 221*, followed by an *Sd.Kfz. 223*. JIM HALEY

Left: A scout poses in his *Sd.Kfz. 221* that belonged to *Aufklärungs-Abteilung 7 (mot)* of the *4. Panzer-Division*. The three-toned camouflage has been sprayed on instead of hand-painted. The picture was probably taken around 1935, since the scout has no national insignia on his beret. Note the addition of the horseshoe talisman on the standard holder. JIM HALEY

These reconnaissance vehicles have quite the audience and reception as they halt in a small German village. Three different armored cars can be seen: *Sd.Kfz. 221*, *Sd.Kfz. 231 (6 Rad)*, and *Sd.Kfz. 232 (Fu) (6 Rad)*.

An *Sd.Kfz. 221* commander receives something to drink from one of the local farmers. Of interest is the wear of a reconnaissance shoulder strap by the *Unteroffizier* bent over the map, while the *Panzeraufklärer* in the turret has a "6" on his shoulder straps, indicating he was transferred into the unit from *Reiter-Regiment 6*. He wears the old field cap with visor of the *Reichswehr*, as does the soldier handing him the drink. Early on, the frugal Germans often retained old uniform items from the *Reichswehr* until new replacements were available for issue. Note that vision ports have been painted on the side of the vehicle in an effort to confuse enemy forces as to the location of the actual vision ports. JIM HALEY

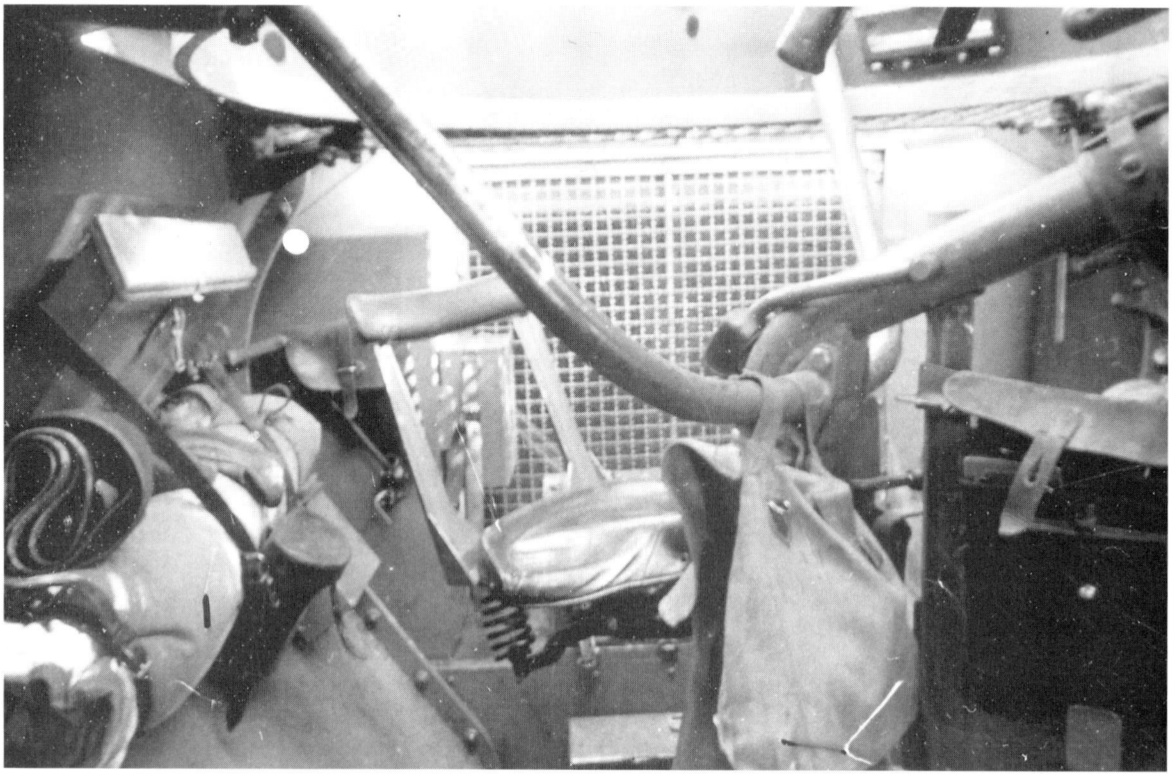

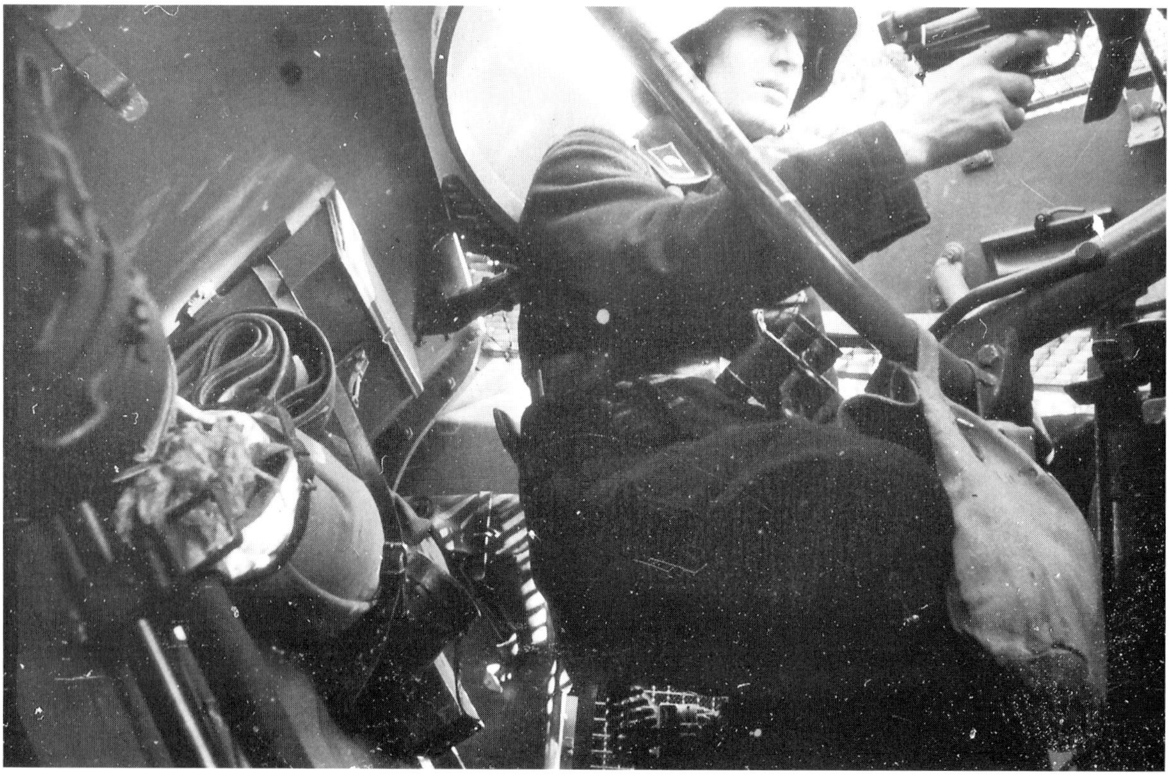

Two interior views of the *Sd.Kfz. 221*. JIM HALEY

SS scouts prepare an evening meal next to an *Sd.Kfz. 221*, probably around the period of the campaign in Poland. Of interest is the painting of a stylized armored car tactical symbol on the front fender of the motorcycle, as well as the death's head on the side of armored car. The smoking scout wears a black cap, which is probably an overseas cap from the *Allgemeine SS*, since black soft caps had not yet been introduced for the *schnelle Truppe*, even those of the SS. JIM HALEY

Left: Civilians inspect an *Sd.Kfz. 221* from *Aufklärungs-Abteilung 5 (mot)*. JIM HALEY

Two *Sd.Kfz. 221*'s from a reconnaissance battalion are passed by the first tank destroyer in the German Army, the *Panzerjäger I*, during the campaign in the West. JIM HALEY

Hurry up and wait! A scout in his *Sd.Kfz. 221* looks bored as he waits for the order to move out. His vehicle is followed by an *Sd.Kfz. 222*.

Several *Sd.Kfz. 221's* line up next to an *Sd.Kfz. 263* while preparing for a mission. The field-gray caps and large white swastikas painted on the rear decks for aerial identification are markers for the first year of the war against the Soviet Union.

Left: Scouts in a camouflaged vehicle observe in a grain field in the Soviet Union. They are from an unidentified *Kradschützen* battalion, which has been consolidated with an armored reconnaissance battalion, thus placing this image in 1942.

This *Sd.Kfz. 221* has been modified to mount a *schwere Panzerbüchse 41 (2.8cm)* in an effort to counter the armor protection found on Soviet armored vehicles.

Sd.Kfz. 222	
Crew:	3
Armament:	1x 7.92mm MG34 and 1x 2cm *KwK 30* or *38 L/55* main gun
Speed:	See *Sd.Kfz. 221*
Range:	See *Sd.Kfz. 221*
Communications equipment:	See *Sd.Kfz. 221*
Production Run:	Introduced in 1937, with production ceasing in 1944.[5] Total produced: 990.
Notes:	The 2cm main gun had a muzzle velocity of 899 meters a second, which was capable of penetrating 18 millimeteres of armor at 800 meters. The Model 30 automatic cannon had a theoretical rate of fire of 280 rounds per minute and the Model 38 a rate of fire of 480 rounds per minute. A mainstay of the early and mid-war armored reconnaissance force and one of the more immediately recognizable vehicles.

Nice profile images of the *Sd.Kfz. 222*. One is from *Aufklärungs-Abteilung 5 (mot)*, while the other is of an armored car from *1./ Aufklärungs-Abteilung 3 (mot)* with the armament displayed in the antiaircraft position.

MICHAEL H. PRUETT

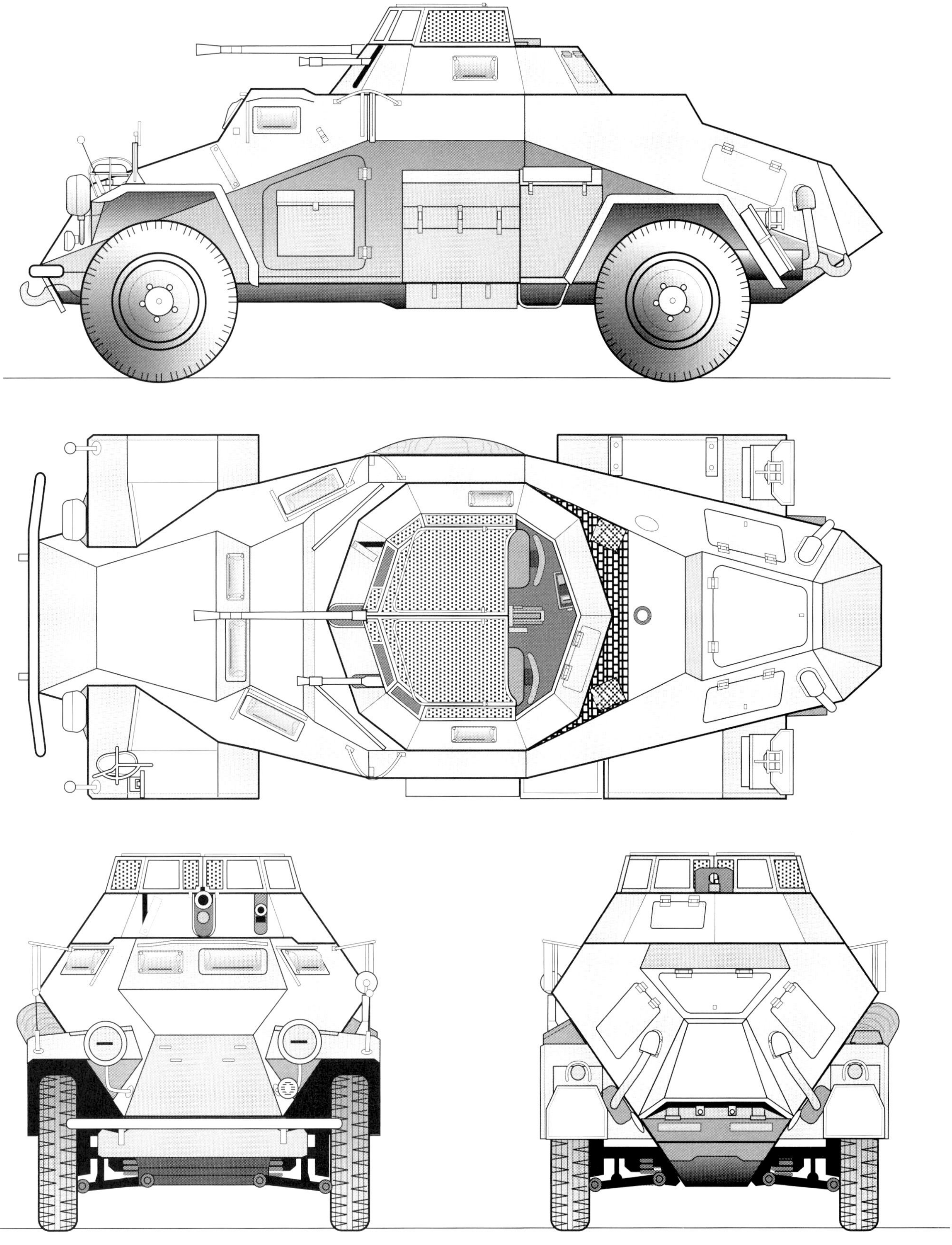

Three *Sd.Kfz. 222's* lined up in a motor pool bay. These armored cars are also from *Aufklärungs-Abteilung 7 (mot)*. JIM HALEY

This scout is in *Aufklärungs Abteilung 1 (mot)*, probably after its permanent assignment to the *3. Panzer-Division* in 1941, since the tactical symbol on the *Sd.Kfz. 222* is a stylized armored car instead of the cavalry symbol for reconnaissance.

An *Sd.Kfz. 222* from the same battalion as the bottom image on the opposite page, sometime before the war started, as evidenced by the "umpire" band on the helmet resting on the vehicle's front bumper. It has the cavalry symbol. Note the fascines on the rear deck, which were used to help the vehicle become "unstuck" whenever it bogged down or encountered especially difficult terrain.

This pristine *Sd.Kfz. 222* serves as a backdrop for some sort of military ceremony, probably a change of command.

Scouts from an unidentified reconnaissance battalion, possibly *Aufklärungs-Abteilung 5 (mot)*.

These soldiers posed atop an *Sd.Kfz. 222*. Since they are not wearing the black *Panzer* uniform, they may not be scouts.

A field funeral for a fallen comrade in an unidentified *Kradschützen-Bataillon*, thus placing the photo in the 1942 time frame after the consolidation of the motorcycle infantry and armored reconnaissance battalions. HENNER LINDLAR

A disabled or mired *Sd.Kfz. 222* from the *1./Aufklärungs-Abteilung 18 (mot)* of the *18. Infanterie-Division (mot)*. The golden "V" symbol with cross bar emblem came into use in November 1940.

Scouts in work uniforms take a break in front of a row of armored cars, starting with an *Sd.Kfz. 222*, then an *Sd.Kfz. 231 (8 Rad)*, and then three *Sd.Kfz. 232 (Fu) (8 Rad)*. Since the scouts all wear black overseas cap, the photograph was taken some time after the campaign in France in 1940. JIM HALEY

Left: SS recruits, probably from the *Leibstandarte*, undergo training on an *Sd.Kfz. 222*.

Rail-loaded *Sd.Kfz. 222's* from the same unit roll down the tracks with air guards posted.

Below: Scouts take a moment to strike a martial pose in their *Sd.Kfz. 222*, probably intended for home-front consumption. Note the fascines mounted along the front, as well as the pre-positioned tow cable, which allowed a quick recovery—an especially valuable timesaving measure under combat conditions. JIM HALEY

A close-up of the "business end" of the *Sd.Kfz. 222* seen above. JIM HALEY

Scouts from an unidentified reconnaissance unit take advantage of a warm clime to sunbathe. Judging by the architecture of the buildings, this image was probably taken somewhere in the Soviet Union. JIM HALEY

This *Sd.Kfz. 222* is positioned along a harbor, probably in France in 1940. Apparently the duty was not too hard, as evidenced by the chairs next to the vehicle. JIM HALEY

An *Sd.Kfz. 222* in an armored reconnaissance battalion, probably photographed in the Mediterranean theater of operations, as evidenced by the tropical uniforms (which were in some units in southern portions of the Soviet Union in the summer). The general officer seen in front of the scout standing at attention wears a continental uniform and has been awarded the Knight's Cross.

A scout from *Panzer-Aufklärungs-Abteilung 1* of the *3. Panzer-Division* engages in some personal hygiene during a lull in operations in the Soviet Union. Note that the barrels of both the *Sd.Kfz. 222* and the *Sd.Kfz. 221* behind it are covered to protect them from getting dirty.

The front left access hatch is open, allowing a good view into the interior of *Danzig*. An ammunition storage box can be seen behind the driver's seat, as well as a tube for the vehicular chemical protection system. Based on the fact that the M40 tropical billed field cap does not have a *soutache* in the branch-appropriate *Waffenfarbe*, which were ordered removed after 1941, this image is probably from 1942 or 1943. JIM HALEY

An *Sd.Kfz. 222* from an unidentified reconnaissance unit has taken up a well-prepared hull-down field position, complete with a living bunker, in the Soviet Union. The turret has a canvas cover to help protect those keeping watch in the fighting compartment from the elements. JIM HALEY

These scouts at a training establishment pose in front of an *Sd.Kfz. 222*. This photograph came from an album of a scout training on a variety of later-war vehicles, which will be seen later in this chapter. Even without them, the date of the image can be placed somewhere in mid-1943 or later, since the men are all wearing the black M43 field cap for armor personnel, which was not introduced for wear until then. The iconic *Sd.Kfz. 222* was produced until well into the war and was probably the most produced German armored car.

Sd.Kfz. 223	
Crew:	3 (driver, radio operator, commander)
Armament:	1x 7.92mm MG34
Speed:	See *Sd.Kfz. 221*
Range:	See *Sd.Kfz. 221*
Communications equipment:	Basic configuration with *Fu 10 SE 30* radio set, with a range of about 4 miles stationary and about 1.5 miles moving. Recognizable by large frame antenna.
Production Run:	Introduced in 1935. 567 for the army by February 1944; unspecified numbers as export version for China; separate contracts let for the SS.

These vehicles are attributed to *Aufklärungs-Abteilung 6 (mot)*, most likely belonging to the *1. leichte Division*, before it became the *6. Panzer-Division*. The frame antenna on the *Sd.Kfz. 223* is in its fully upright position.

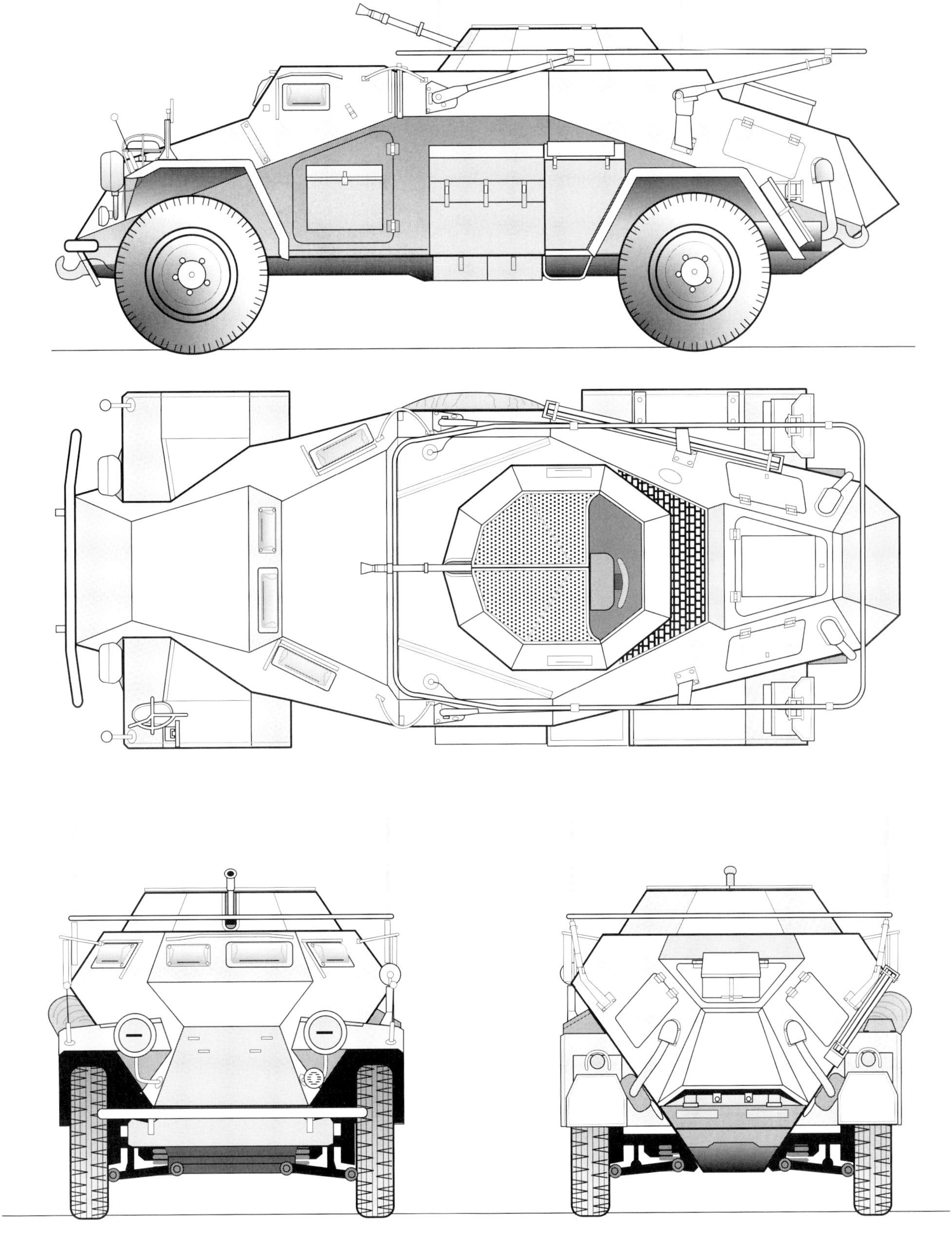

These *Sd.Kfz. 223's* were assigned to *Aufklärungs-Abteilung 5 (mot)*, and the images were taken during prewar maneuvers. JIM HALEY

This *Sd.Kfz. 223* from *Aufklärungs-Abteilung 7 (mot)* has collided with a civilian car while on maneuvers somewhere in southern Germany. JIM HALEY

Scouts of *Aufklärungs-Abteilung 3 (mot)* take a meal break next to their *Sd.Kfz. 223*. This battalion was assigned to a variety of higher headquarters before the war, ultimately being assigned to the *3. Panzer-Division* through 1941.

Right: This pristine *Sd.Kfz. 223* shows its prewar camouflage. JIM HALEY

The frame antenna and offset turret of the *Sd.Kfz. 223* are nicely displayed in this image from an unknown unit.

Scouts assigned to *Aufklärungs-Abteilung 37 (mot)* of the *7. Panzer-Division* pose with their radio vehicles in France in 1940. The top vehicle is an *Sd.Kfz. 261*, often confused with the *Sd.Kfz. 223* seen at bottom.

A communications section of a reconnaissance battalion, probably in North Africa.

An *Sd.Kfz. 223* has slid off a road and become stuck. Road and weather conditions in the Soviet Union put both man and machine to the test.

Villagers look on as German vehicles struggle to make their way through the mud roads of the town.

This *Sd.Kfz. 223* has received a number of modifications by the crew in order to increase the stowage space on the diminutive vehicle, which has become their "home."
JIM HALEY

Left: The crew members of an *Sd.Kfz. 223* from *Panzer-Aufklärungs-Abteilung 1* of the *3. Panzer-Division* take a break. The NCO in the foreground wears a proficiency badge for a master radio operator.

Sd.Kfz. 260

Crew:	4
Armament:	None
Speed:	See *Sd.Kfz. 221*
Range:	See *Sd.Kfz. 221*
Communications equipment:	Equipped with a *Fu 7 SE220u* radio set, which had a stationary range of up to 42 miles.
Production Run:	493 for both *Sd.Kfz. 260* and *261*. Production run completed by April 1943.
Notes:	Recognizable by a single mast antenna.

Sd.Kfz. 261

Crew:	2
Armament:	None
Speed:	See *Sd.Kfz. 221*
Range:	See *Sd.Kfz. 221*
Communications equipment:	Equipped with a *Fu 12 SE80* radio set, which had a stationary range of up to 75 miles (Morse) and 25 miles (voice).
Production Run:	See *Sd.Kfz. 260*
Notes:	Recognizable by a collapsible frame antenna.

An *Sd.Kfz. 260* finished in basic early and midwar dark yellow (*dunkelgelb*).

Below: A scout from an unidentified unit observes from an *Sd.Kfz. 261*.

Sd.Kfz. 231 (6 Rad)	
Crew:	4 (driver, rear driver and radio operator, gunner, and commander)
Armament:	1x 7.92mm MG13/34 and 1x 2cm KwK 30 L/55 main gun
Speed:	Approximately 37–40 MPH
Range:	Approximately 124–156 miles
Communications equipment:	See *Sd.Kfz. 221*
Production Run:	Approximately 123 *Sd.Kfz. 231* and *232* vehicles produced between 1932 and 1937. In addition, the radio version—the *Sd.Kfz. 263 (6 Rad)*—had a production run of 28 vehicles.
Notes:	Originally designated as the *Kfz. 67* and *Kfz. 67a (Fu)*. Nomenclature changed to *Sd.Kfz.* First series production armored car with front and rear drivers. High silhouette and ground pressure disadvantageous, with a ground clearance of only around 1 foot. The vehicle was designed around a commercial truck chassis (4x2).

An unidentified armored reconnaissance formation prepares to move out on a railhead. On the lead rail car is an *Sd.Kfz. 231 (6-Rad)* with a standard prewar three-tone camouflage pattern. Behind it is a *Kfz. 13*, an *Sd.Kfz. 221*, and several motorcycles.

A first sergeant of an unidentified armored reconnaissance company poses in front of an *Sd.Kfz. 231 (6-Rad)* with his men. Based on the headgear, this image was taken some time after the campaign in the West in 1940. The first sergeant can be identified by the twin rows of "piston rings" on his lower sleeves.

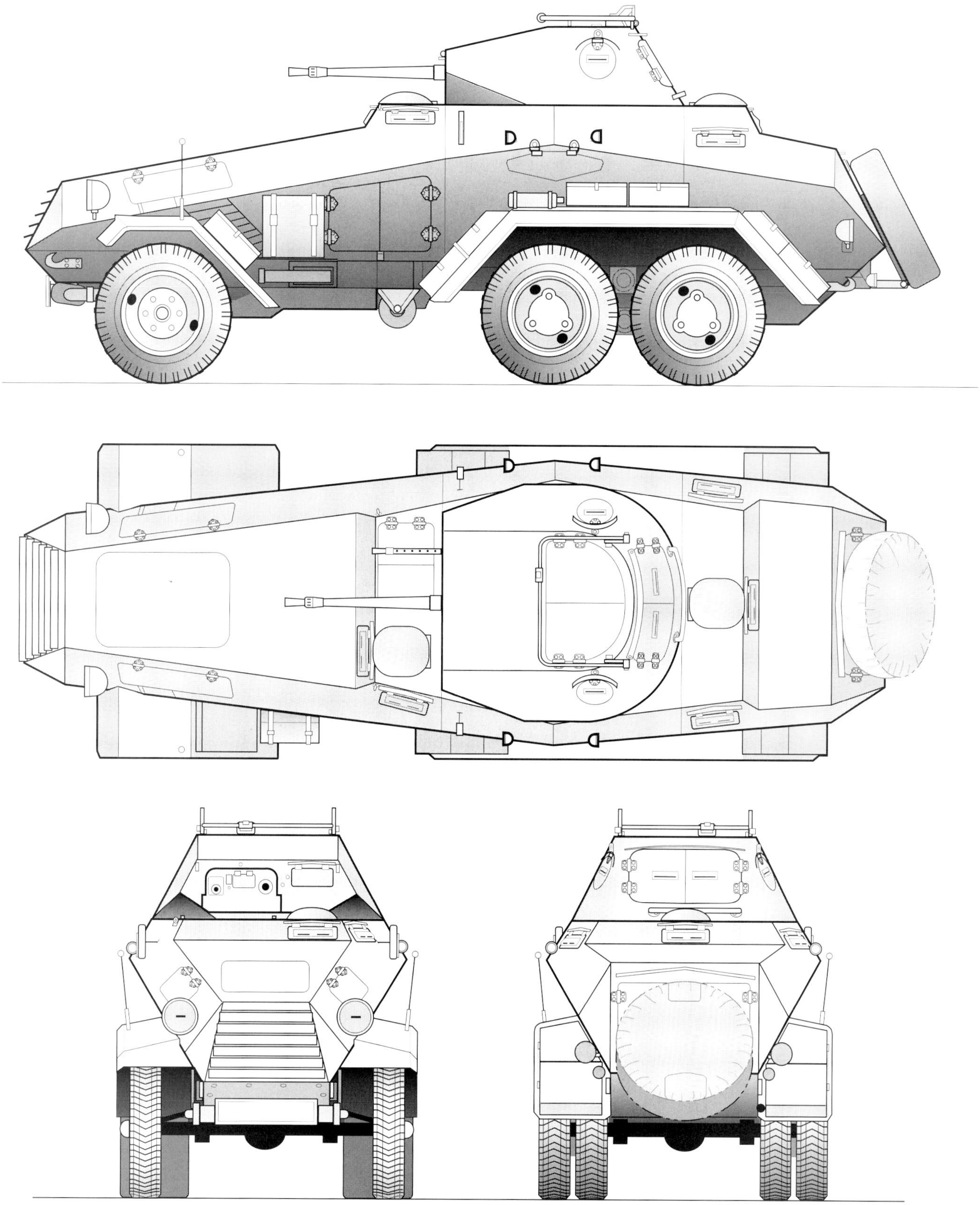

Sd.Kfz. 232 (Fu) (6 Rad)	
Crew:	4 (driver, rear driver and radio operator, gunner, and commander)
Armament:	See *Sd.Kfz. 231*
Speed:	See *Sd.Kfz. 231*
Range:	See *Sd.Kfz. 231*
Communications equipment:	One set *FuG 11 SE 100* with a Morse range of 30 miles and a voice range of 6 miles.
Production Run:	See *Sd.Kfz. 231 (6 Rad)*
Notes:	The *Sd.Kfz. 263 (Fu) (6 Rad)*—original nomenclature, *Kfz 67b (Fu)*—was outwardly very similar to the *Sd.Kfz. 232* and was produced between 1932 and 1941. It had a fixed turret and extra crewmember.

One of the earliest models of the *Sd.Kfz. 232 (Fu) (6 Rad)* produced. The frame has been folded down into the travel position. JIM HALEY

On the occasion of Hitler's birthday on 20 April 1936, a major military parade was held in Berlin. All branches of the army were represented, as this image attests.

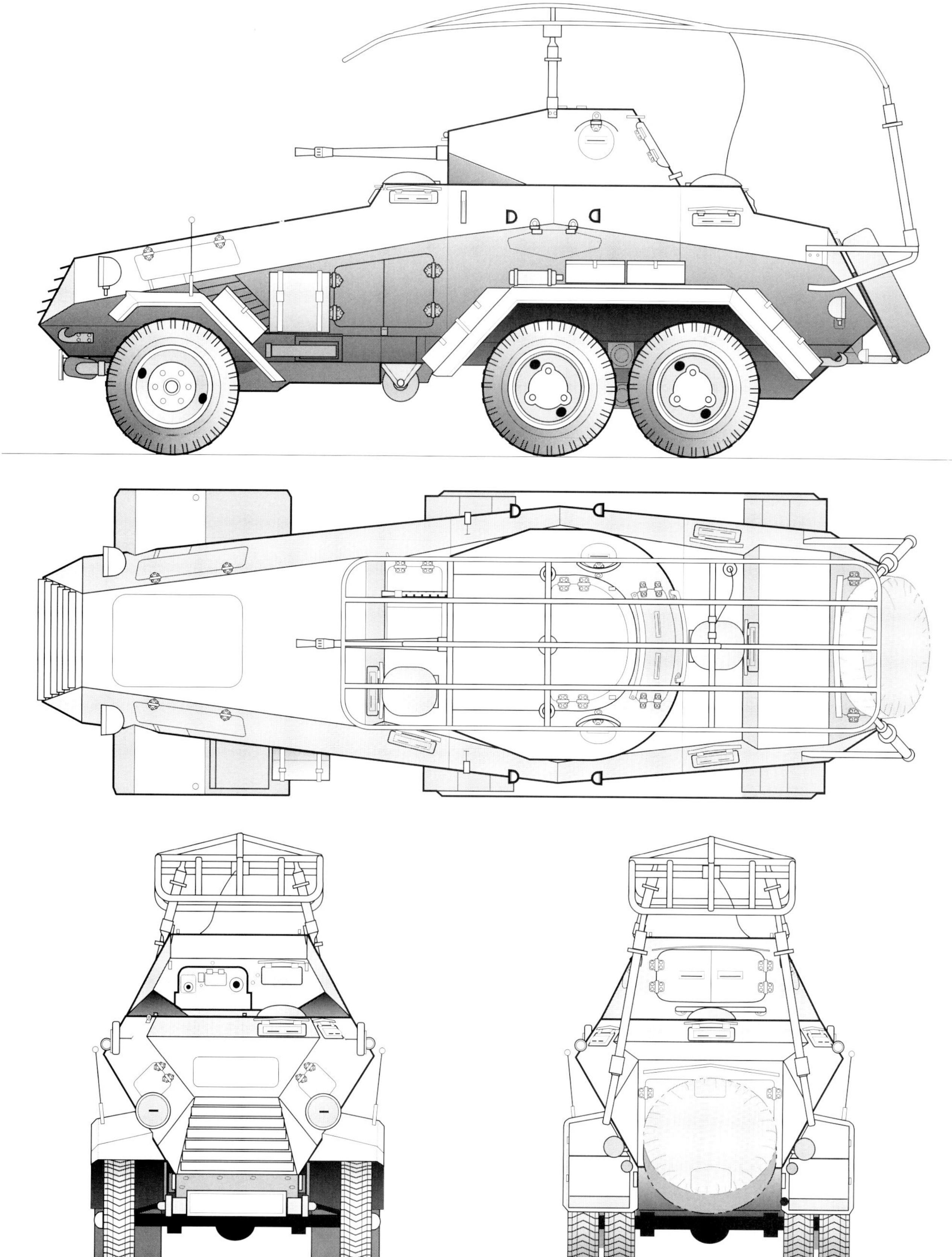

Unit training being conducted sometime in 1943, as indicated by the wear of the M43 billed field cap. Several types of armored cars can be seen, with an *Sd.Kfz. 232 (6-Rad)* in the lead, followed by two *Sd.Kfz. 231 (6-Rad)* vehicles.

The illustration of the *Sd.Kfz. 232 (Fu) (6-Rad)* seen here was featured on a collectible card that came with packs of cigarettes. The reverse of the card states that it is "only possible to maintain command communications to the rear and with neighboring formations through a large complement of radio equipment."

Salem Zigaretten

„Die deutsche Wehrmacht"

Bild Nr. **127**

Funkwagen

Nur durch eine reiche Ausstattung mit Funkgerät ist es bei Panzerverbänden möglich, die Gefechtsleitung sowie die Verbindung nach rückwärts und zum Nachbarn aufrechtzuerhalten

Unser **Sammelalbum** für 270 Bilder ist gegen Voreinsendung von RM. 1.— durch uns oder jeden Händler erhältlich.

Alle Zuschriften erbitten wir an:

CIGARETTEN-BILDERDIENST

Postfach Dresden-A. 5

An image found on postcards sold in soldier canteens of the time: an imposing view of an *Sd.Kfz. 232 (Fu) (6-Rad)*. This particular vehicle belonged to the *II./Aufklärungs-Regiment 6* of the *1. leichte Division*.

Scouts converse while conducting maintenance on their *Sd.Kfz. 232 (Fu) (6-Rad)*. The scout on the right has taken off his black *Panzer* jacket to don a work outfit. The vehicle is christened *Derfflinger*, the name of a famous Protestant cavalry general during the Thirty Years' War. JIM HALEY

Many details of the *Sd.Kfz. 232 (Fu) (6-Rad) can be seen from this vehicle from* Aufklärungs-Abteilung 5 (mot). *JIM HALEY*

This *Sd.Kfz. 232 (Fu) (Rad)* has been raised on a hoist in a motor pool bay in order to perform maintenance or repairs on the undercarriage. This vehicle is also from *Aufklärungs-Abteilung 5 (mot)* and has motorcycles of the battalion in the foreground and a Horch prime mover in the background. JIM HALEY

This *Sd.Kfz. 232 (Fu) (Rad)* from an unidentified reconnaissance unit was knocked and burned out, probably during the fighting in France.

Sd.Kfz. 231 (8 Rad)	
Crew:	4 (driver, rear driver/radio operator, gunner, and commander)
Armament:	1x 7.92mm MG34/42 and 1x 2cm *KwK 38 L/55* main gun in a manually traversed turret
Speed:	150-horsepower engine allowed a maximum road speed of approximately 53–62 mph, with a cross-country speed of approximately 19 mph.
Range:	Approximately 170–186 miles
Communications equipment:	See *Sd.Kfz. 221*
Production Run:	Approximately 90 *Sd.Kfz. 231* and *232* vehicles produced between 1936 and 1938. By the end of the production run in September 1943, a total of 607 vehicles manufactured.
Notes:	Originally designated as the *Sd.Kfz. 233* and *234*, with the nomenclature changed in September 1940. A total of about 610 *231's* and *232's* produced from late 1936 to 1943.[6] All wheels steerable.

An armored reconnaissance battalion stands ready for inspection. The scouts all stand at attention, and the commander of the lead vehicle presents arms to the officer trooping the line. The turrets of the *Sd.Kfz. 231 (8 Rad)* and *Sd.Kfz. 232 (Fu) (8 Rad)* vehicles have been traversed to the three-o'clock position.

Left: An *Sd.Kfz. 231 (8 Rad)* from an unidentified unit moves down a street lined with civilians and an honor guard of soldiers. Because of the large white "K" on the right front glacis (for *Panzergruppe Kleist*), it is most likely a victory parade somewhere in Germany after the successful conclusion of the campaign in the West.

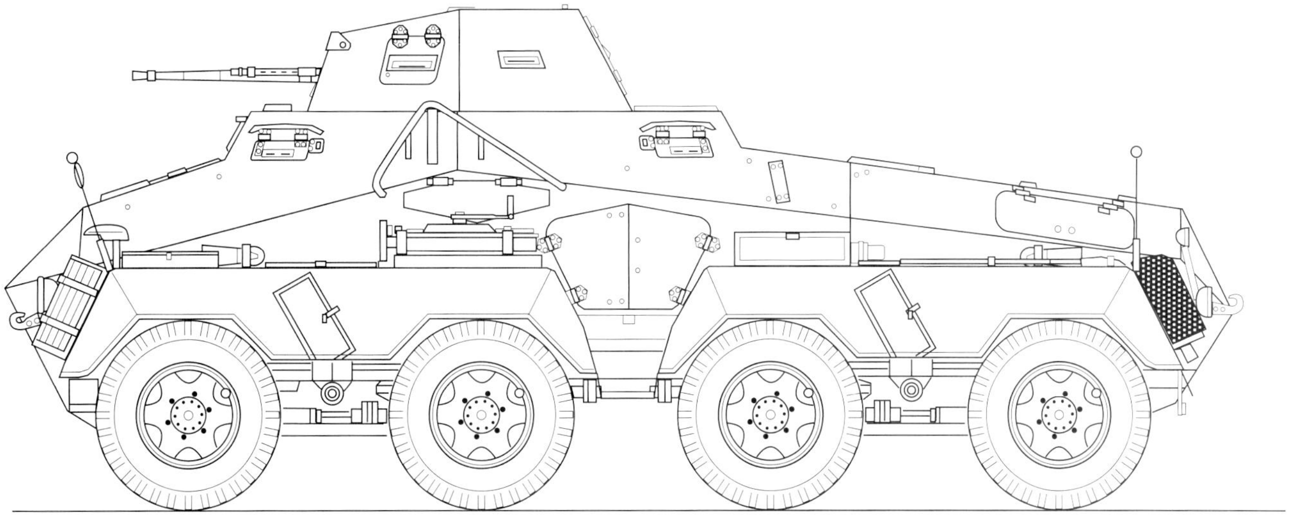

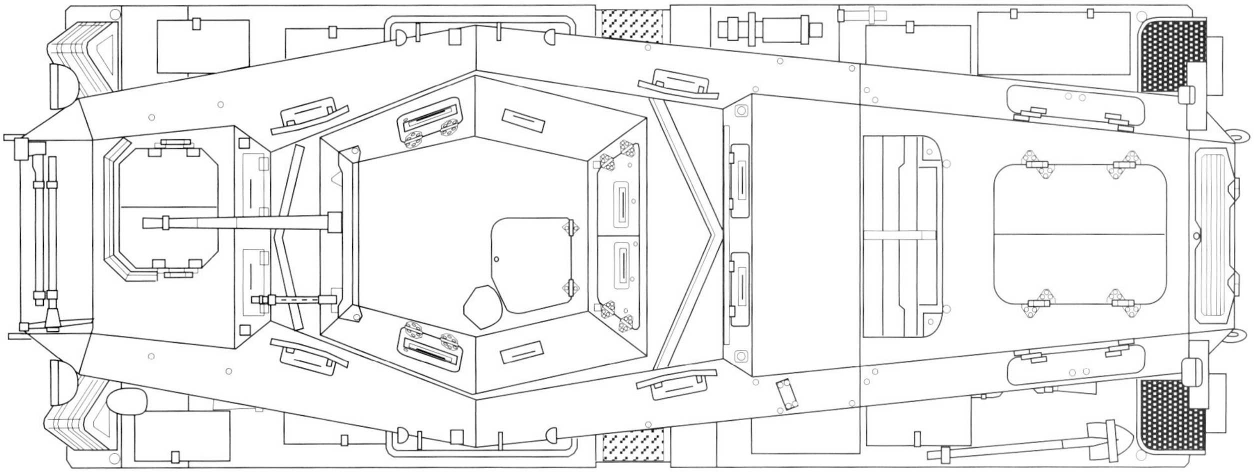

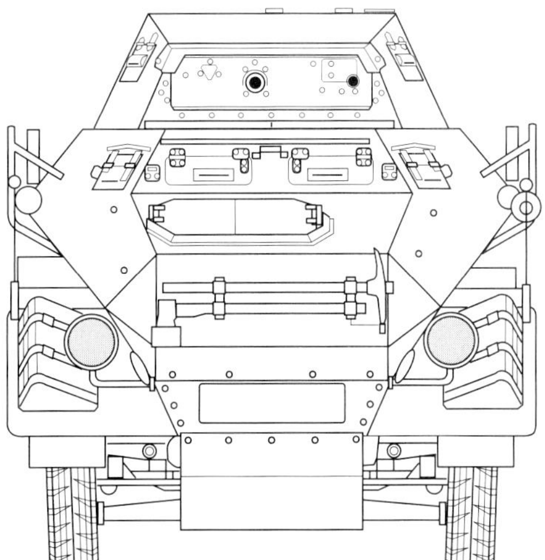

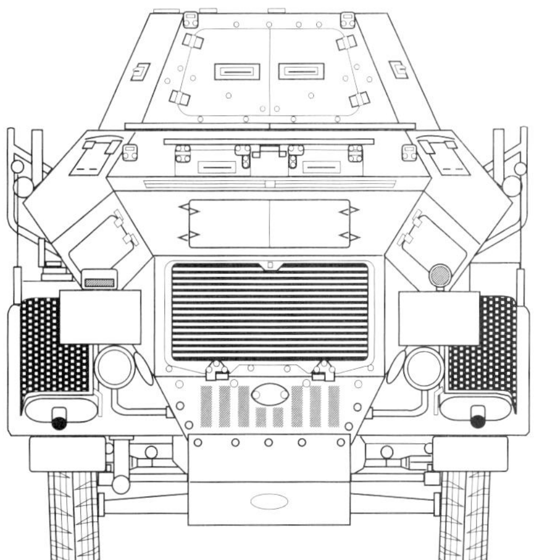

An *Sd.Kfz. 231 (8 Rad)* is positioned to the right of an artillery prime mover as it moves past, perhaps on the occasion of yet another parade.

This *Sd.Kfz. 231 (8 Rad)* appears to be bereft of all basic-issue items. The relatively short staffs with the ball tops on the front sides of the vehicle are width indicators of the vehicle as an aid for the driver. JIM HALEY

This *Sd.Kfz. 231 (8 Rad)* negotiates a sandy incline, probably at a training area. The prewar camouflage can be seen as well as a map of "Greater Germany" and *Wien* (Vienna), with a date to commemorate the "liberation" of the country and its accession into the Reich. This vehicle is attributed to *Aufklärungs-Abteilung 7 (mot).* JIM HALEY

An *Sd.Kfz. 231 (8 Rad)* moves along a snowy road, either as part of driver training or winter maneuvers. The motorcyclist behind it probably does not have quite as easy, even on an improved surface road, such as this one.

Several *Sd.Kfz. 231 (8 Rad)* vehicles from an SS element leave their garrison. The armored car commanders wear the SS version of the beret, an almost universally disliked piece of headgear, since the integral crash helmet was large and bulky and did not sit well on the head.

Left: Many units had mascots and took them into the field with them. The view inside the driver's compartment of this SS *Sd.Kfz. 231 (8 Rad)* shows the slanted steering wheel, which took some time for new drivers to get accustomed to. A stylized armored car insignia with extra wheels, denoting a heavy armored car element, can be seen on the right side of the turret. JIM HALEY

Scouts pose in front of their vehicle after it has been loaded onto a flat car in preparation for a rail movement.

Scouts pose atop their vehicle, which has received a two-tone camouflage spray pattern, which evidently was also applied to their helmets. JIM HALEY

Right: No matter the time or season, soldiers seem to like to pose with their equipment. A scout in the turret of an *Sd.Kfz. 231 (8 Rad)*, most likely somewhere in the Soviet Union. The snow provides a natural camouflage but would quickly blow off during movement, unless it happened to be frozen on the vehicle. Since there were no vehicular heaters in German combat vehicles, there was little chance it would melt off.

A crew in front of its vehicle, which has been camouflaged by means of natural foliage in this Soviet village.

These three officers take time for a photograph in front of what appears to be a freshly painted *Sd.Kfz. 231 (8 Rad)* in overall dark yellow (*dunkelgelb*).

An *Sd.Kfz. 231 (8 Rad)* takes up a concealed position behind a haystack, somewhere in the open steppes of the Soviet Union.

This *Sd.Kfz. 231 (8 Rad)* has seen some combat, as evidenced by the battle damage to the fender and the general disarray of some of the basic-issue items and fittings. This image of a vehicle from *Panzer-Aufklärungs-Abteilung 1* of the *3. Panzer-Division* was most likely taken in the Soviet Union.

These paratroopers prepare to mount up for a ride somewhere on an *Sd.Kfz. 231 (8 Rad)* from the *1./Panzer-Aufklärungs-Abteilung 115* in Italy in 1943.

Below: This *Sd.Kfz. 231 (8 Rad)* from *Panzer-Aufklärungs-Abteilung 24* of the *24. Panzer-Division* has a full complement of kit mounted on the outside. The divisional insignia is partially obscured on the front slope of the vehicle. This image was taken sometime in 1944, after the division was reconstituted (Stalingrad), fought in Italy, and was transferred to the Eastern Front. The men of the *König* ("King") wear a variety of early and late headgear and uniforms, with the vehicle commander wearing the field-gray version of the *Panzer* jacket. JIM HALEY

A crew trains on an *Sd.Kfz. 231 (8 Rad)* at an unidentified location, most likely a school environment. The vehicles are uniformly painted in the standard dark yellow of the midwar period, and the crewmembers all wear the distinctive reed-green *Panzer* uniform that was especially designed for armored reconnaissance personnel and scouts.

Sd.Kfz. 232 (Fu) (8 Rad)	
Crew:	4 (driver, rear driver/radio operator, gunner, and commander)
Armament:	See *Sd.Kfz. 231 (8 Rad)*
Speed:	See *Sd.Kfz. 231 (8 Rad)*
Range:	See *Sd.Kfz. 231 (8 Rad)*
Communications equipment:	Radio set *Fu 11 SE 100* initially and then *Fu 12 SE 80*, giving a range of around 40 miles.
Production Run:	See *Sd.Kfz. 231 (8 Rad)*

An *Sd.Kfz. 232 (8 Rad)*, most likely from *Aufklärungs-Abteilung 5 (mot)*. JIM HALEY

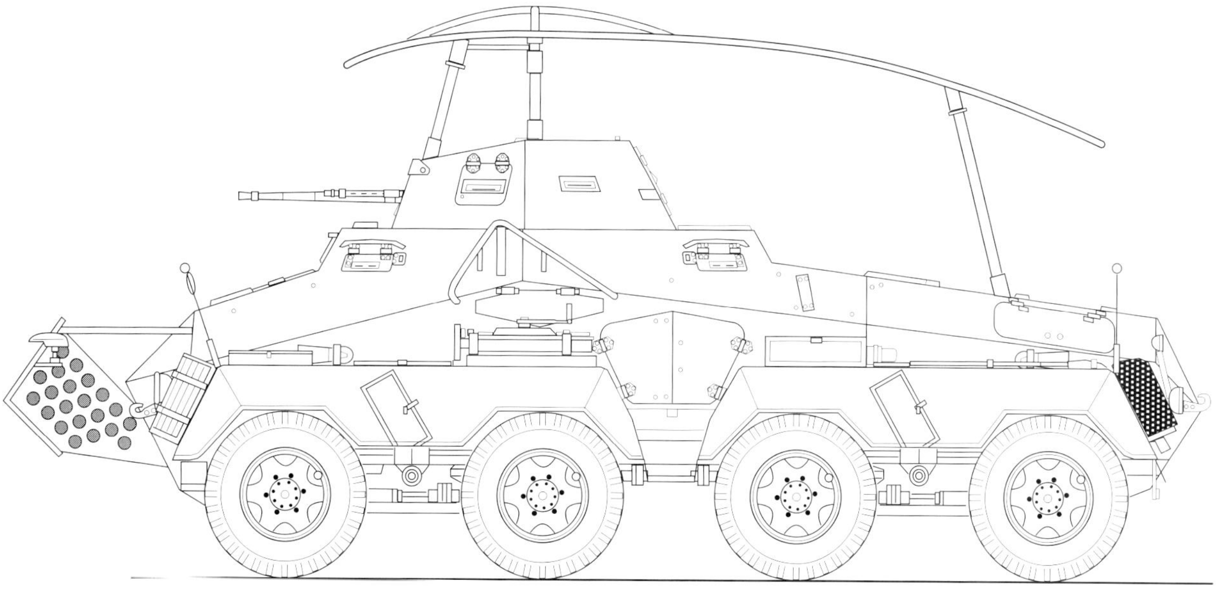

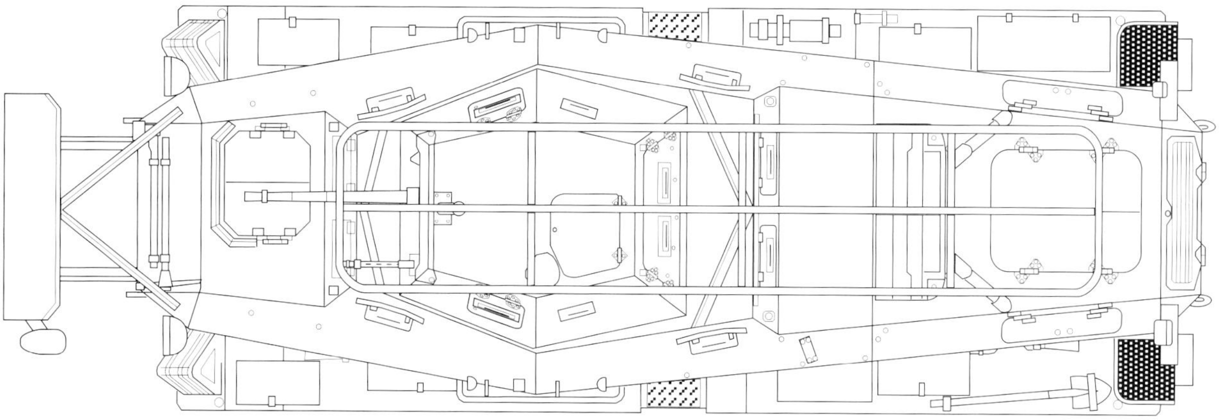

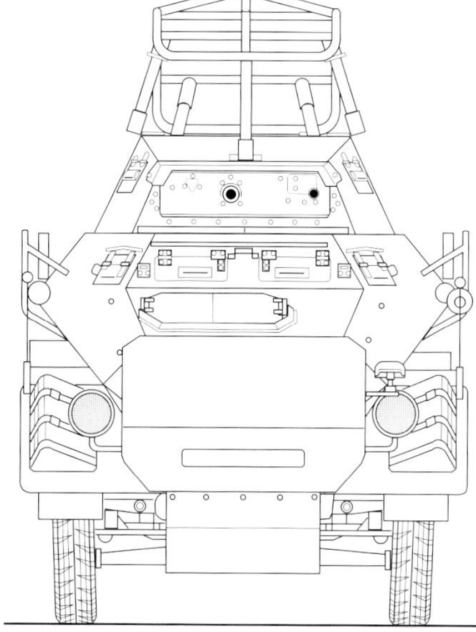

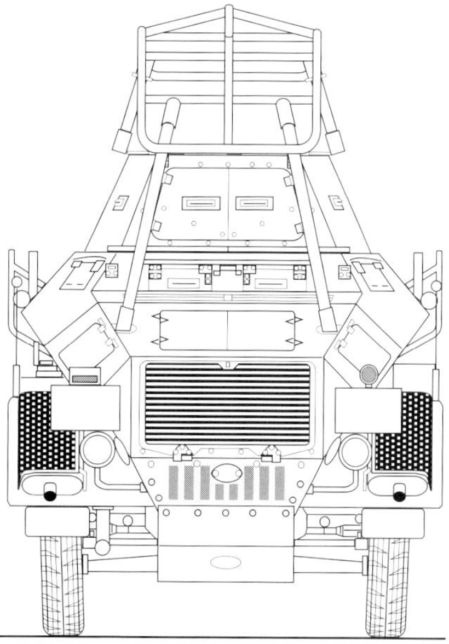

A convoy of armored cars and wheel vehicles is headed by an *Sd.Kfz. 232 (8 Rad)*. Note that the crew has already placed a prepared tow cable into position on the front of the vehicle.

A crew has finished prepping an *Sd.Kfz. 232 (8 Rad)* for rail transport. The crewmember on the side of the vehicle is wearing the blue work uniform designed for armored vehicle crews. Note that the armored car has chock blocks in front of, behind, and to the side of all of its wheels. These were nailed onto the flat car to keep the vehicle from shifting position while moving. JIM HALEY

An *Sd.Kfz. 232 (8 Rad)* has bottomed out on the banks of a shallow creek, illustrating the limitations of cross-country movement for these vehicles. JIM HALEY

The *Graz*, christened after the city in Austria, appears to be in a courtyard, possibly during maneuvers. It is from the same unit seen in the image at the top of page 189. JIM HALEY

An *Sd.Kfz. 232 (8 Rad)* from a training establishment (*Sch* = *Schule* = School) has overturned in open terrain, possibly as the result of oversteering on the part of a student driver. Details of the undercarriage can be seen to good advantage. JIM HALEY-

This *Sd.Kfz. 232 (8 Rad)* from *Panzer-Aufklärungs-Abteilung 999* is loaded on a ship in preparation for sea transport to North Africa. The canvas cover for the turret has been mounted, possibly in an effort to protect the vehicle optics and interior from the corrosive effects of salt water. JIM HALEY

Members of the reconnaissance battalion of the *Totenkopf* share a lighter moment during a maintenance halt. Although difficult to see, the iconic "skull" of the division can be seen on the glacis of the trailing vehicles.

Vehicles of a heavy section of a reconnaissance battalion take up concealed positions next to the wooden structures of a Soviet village. It appears to have most of its winter whitewash worn off, revealing its original dark-gray (*dunkelgrau*) finish, whereas the *Sd.Kfz. 232 (8 Rad)* seems to have retained most of its winter camouflage. Note the mounting of the spare tires on both of the vehicles.

Soldiers pose next to this vehicle from an unidentified formation, possibly from *Aufklärungs-Abteilung 3 (mot)*. Note the aerial recognition flag on the rear deck. A shirt or work jacket hangs from the frame antenna, which also served as a convenient "clothes line" when washing uniform articles in the field.

Sd.Kfz. 233	
Crew:	4 (driver, rear driver, gunner, and commander)
Armament:	1x 7.92mm MG42 and 1x 7.5cm *StuK 37 L/24* main gun
Speed:	See *Sd.Kfz. 231 (8 Rad)*
Range:	See *Sd.Kfz. 231 (8 Rad)*
Communications equipment:	See *Sd.Kfz. 221*
Production Run:	Production run from July 1942 to October 1943, with 129 being built.
Notes:	The main guns used were those that were excess for production of the *StuG III*. The heavy armored car was first employed in Tunisia, where eighteen were sent. The remainder of the production run was employed on the Eastern Front.

These scouts in North Africa pose with their brand-new *Sd.Kfz. 233's*. It looks as though the cannon section has just arrived in theater.
JIM HALEY

A late-model *Sd.Kfz. 233* of *Panzer-Aufklärungs-Abteilung 2* observes to the front, while other members of the unit stand by. The trident insignia was used by the *2. Panzer-Division* from 1944 until the end of the war.

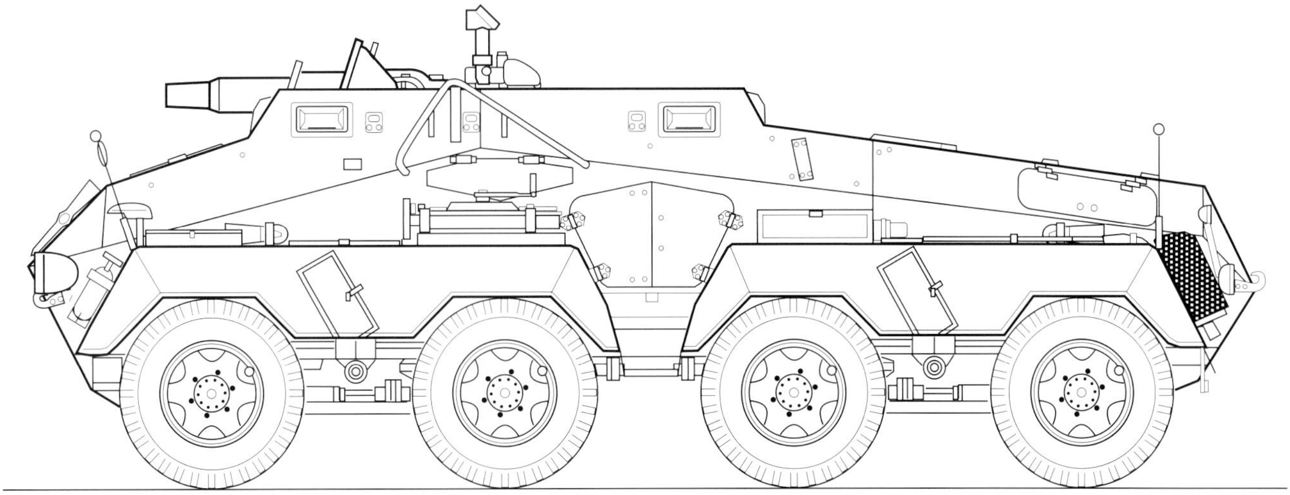

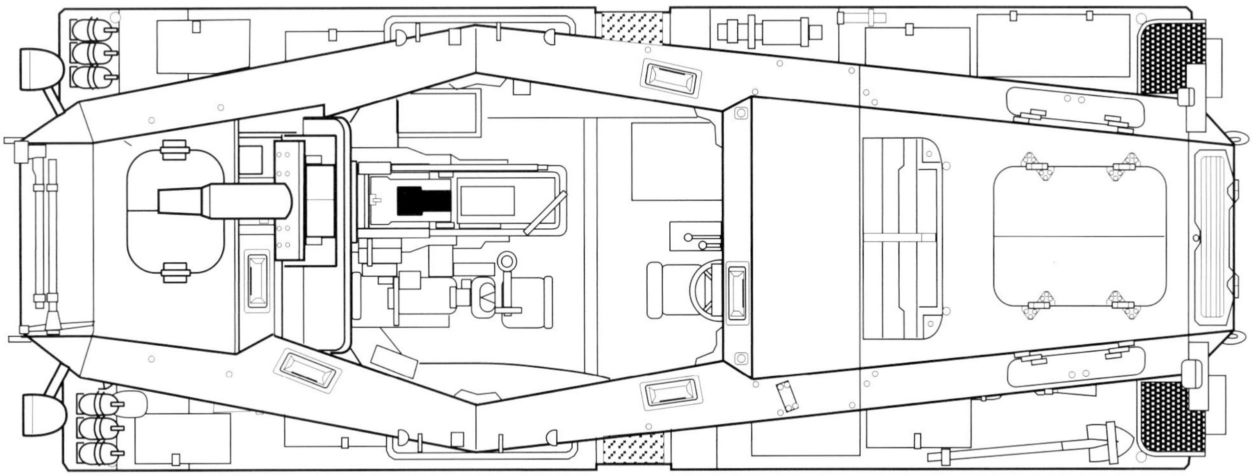

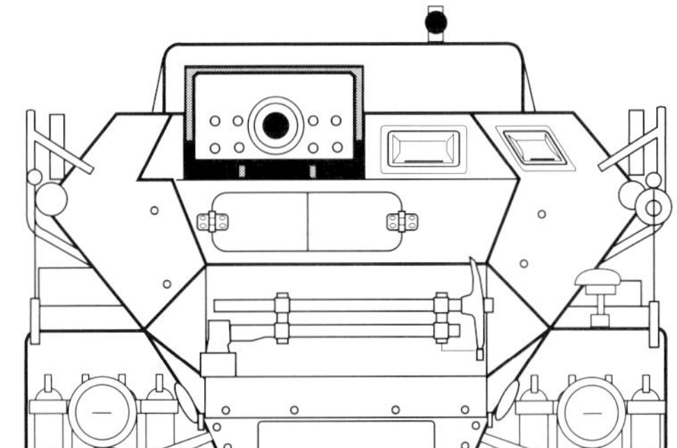

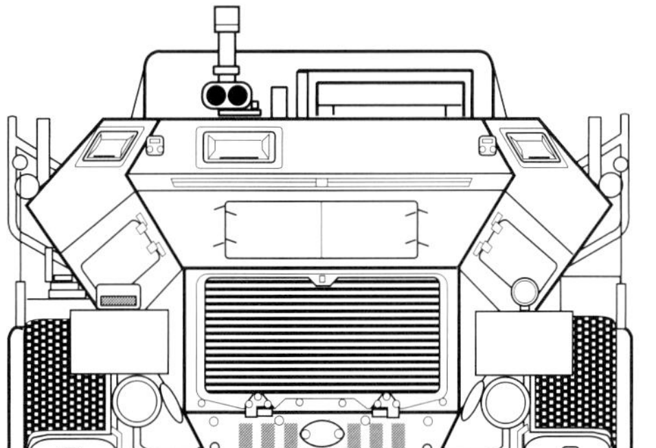

Sd.Kfz. 234/1	
Crew:	4 (driver, rear driver, gunner, and commander)
Armament:	1 x 7.92 mm MG42; 1 x 2cm *KwK 38 L55* automatic cannon
Speed:	52 mph (road), approximately 18 mph (cross-country)
Range:	372 miles
Communications equipment:	1x radio set *FuG12 SE80*, with a range of around 40 miles with a 2-meter rod antenna
Production Run:	Production run from June 1944 to January 1945, with 230 being built.
Notes:	Had a simplified turret similar to that of the *Sd.Kfz. 222*. One of the few German combat vehicles using a diesel engine (all variants). Vehicle was issued to eight armored and one mechanized infantry division, with remainder issued as replacements.

This *Sd.Kfz. 234/1* features a distinctive late-war three-tone camouflage pattern. Images of the *Sd.Kfz. 234* series of vehicles are hard to find because comparatively so few were produced and the situation at the front rarely allowed time for luxuries such as photography. JIM HALEY

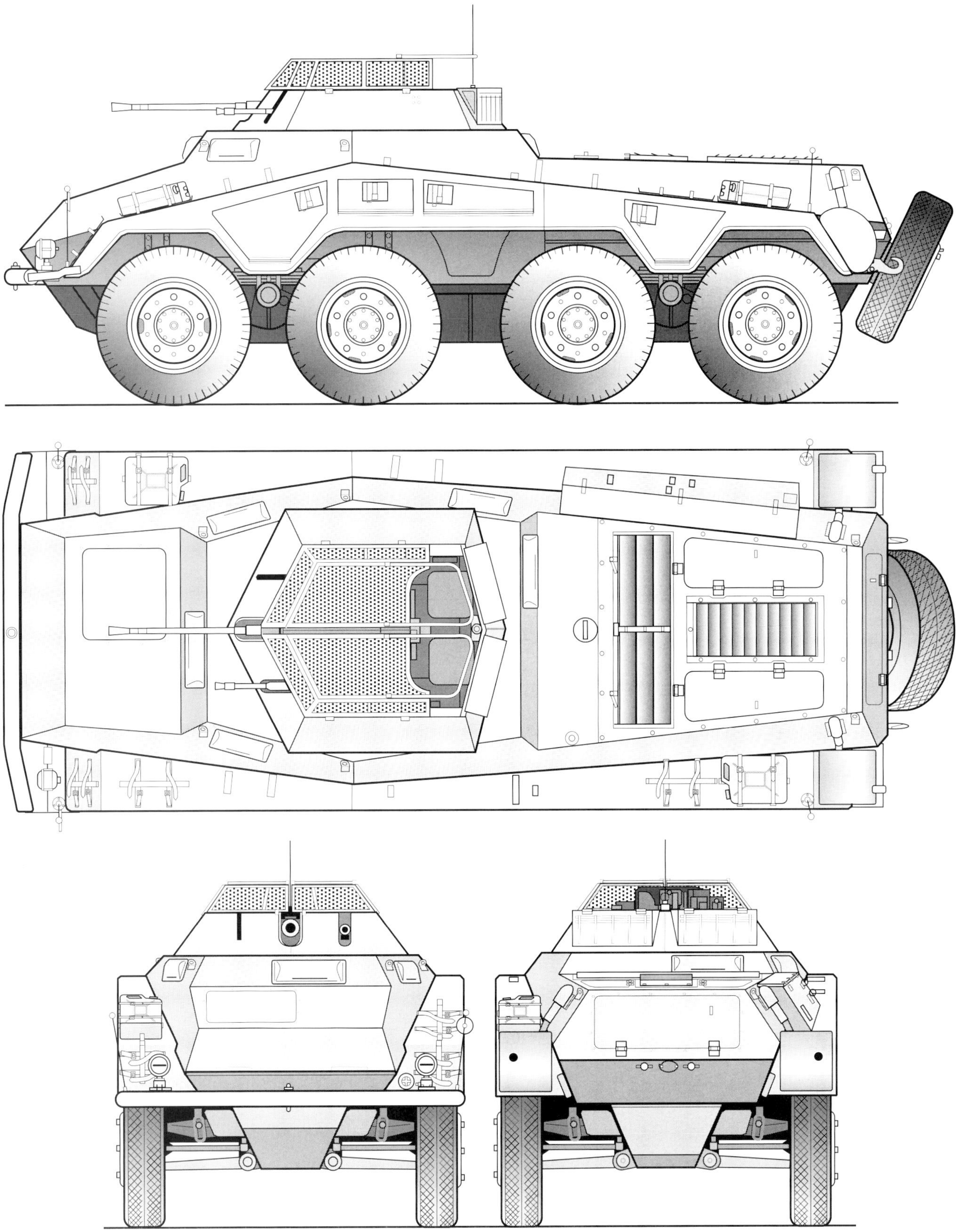

This image and subsequent ones come from the album of an unknown scout completing training late in the war on some of the most modern reconnaissance vehicles the German Army was fielding at the time. Here the scout performs maintenance on the vehicle. JIM HALEY

Here the scout poses with comrades, all of whom are wearing some type of the standard denim work outfit, with the two scouts on the viewer's right definitely wearing the dark-blue version intended for armored vehicle crewmembers. Of interest is also the fact that they all wear early war overseas caps despite what must have been the relatively late date of these photographs. JIM HALEY

A soldier poses in the turret of an *Sd.Kfz. 234/1.* JIM HALEY

A nice profile shot of a relatively rarely photographed vehicle. JIM HALEY

Sd.Kfz. 234/2	
Crew:	4 (driver, rear driver, gunner, and commander)
Armament:	1x 7.92mm MG42 and 1x 5cm *KwK 39/1 L60* main gun
Speed:	See *Sd.Kfz. 234/1*
Range:	See *Sd.Kfz. 234/1*
Communications equipment:	See *Sd.Kfz. 234/1*
Production Run:	Production run from September 1943 to September 1944, with 101 being built.[7]
Notes:	Referred to as the *Puma*. Apparently only thirteen of the twenty-five *Pumas* authorized in a company organized in accordance with *KStN 1162b* had the *FuG12 SE80*, with the remainder only having a standard platoon radio set (*FuG Spr a*).

This *Puma* from an unidentified unit has a number of fuel cans mounted on the front in an effort to extend its range.

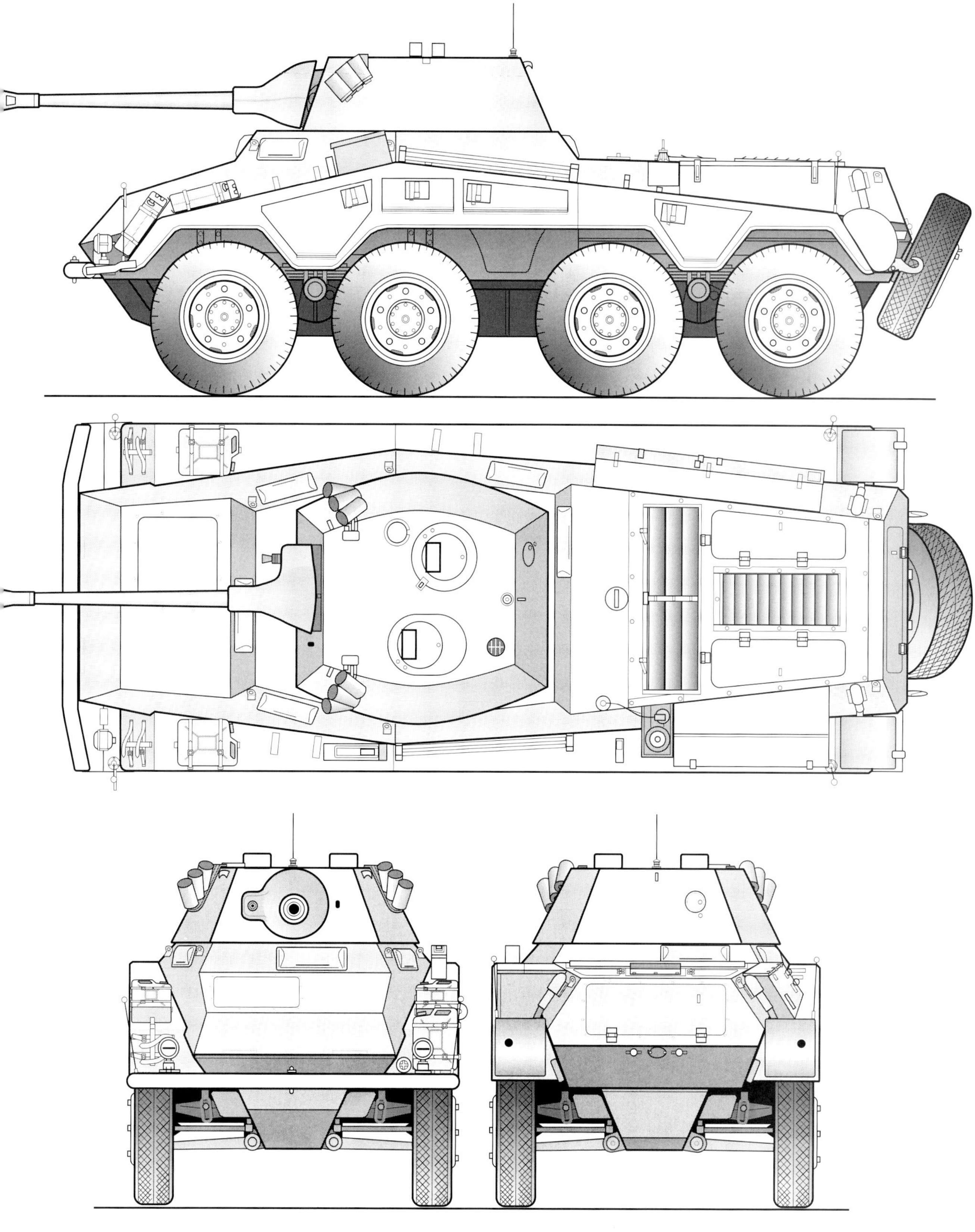

An *Sd.Kfz 234/2* and *234/3* line up along a wood line, along with what appears to be an *Sd.Kfz. 250/9*. Given the lack of any camouflage other than a base coat of dark yellow and the fact that there are few basic-issue items stowed on the exterior of the vehicles, it may be a training situation.

This film capture shows an *Sd.Kfz. 234/2* moving down a road with a considerable amount of natural foliage applied to the vehicle's surface. This heavy application of camouflage was often seen during the Normandy invasion, so the film might have been shot there.

The scout poses astride the 5cm main gun in his work coveralls. JIM HALEY

Here the scout poses for a close-up in the turret. JIM HALEY

Left: The same scout seen with the *Sd.Kfz. 234/1's* in the last set of images now appears with the *Sd.Kfz. 234/2*, commonly known as the *Puma*. The vehicle is seen here in profile. JIM HALEY

Three additional scouts strike a relaxed pose on the rear deck of the vehicle. JIM HALEY

The scout once again sits astride the main gun barrel, albeit this time in his *Panzer* uniform. JIM HALEY

Right: The scout has his picture taken in front of the vehicle. JIM HALEY

These images were provided by the family of the late *Rittmeister* Petersmann, who served as the commander of the *1. (Panzerspäh-)Kompanie* of *Panzer-Aufklärungs-Abteilung 20* and was its last commander. Unfortunately, the quality is not the best, but some interesting details can be gleaned from the collage of images, especially the water-pattern tailor-made camouflage *Panzer* jacket that Petersmann is wearing in the lower lefthand corner. MICHAEL H. PRUETT

The vehicle here has had ample natural foliage applied in an effort to help conceal its position and break up its outline.

Sd.Kfz. 234/3	
Crew:	4 (driver, rear driver, gunner, and commander)[8]
Armament:	1x 7.92mm MG42 and 1x 7.5cm *StuK 37 L/24* main gun
Speed:	See *Sd.Kfz. 234/1*
Range:	See *Sd.Kfz. 234/1*
Communications equipment:	See *Sd.Kfz. 234/1*
Production Run:	Production run from June to September 1944, with 88 being built. Production ceased in order to build only the *Sd.Kfz. 234/4*. Issued to eight armored divisions (three each), with remainder serving as replacements and also issued piecemeal.

Once again, the unidentified scout in the training unit surfaces to provide some images of rare vehicles, this time the *Sd.Kfz. 234/3*. He appears to have been at this training site for some time, as the vehicles are taken in a variety of seasons and weather conditions.

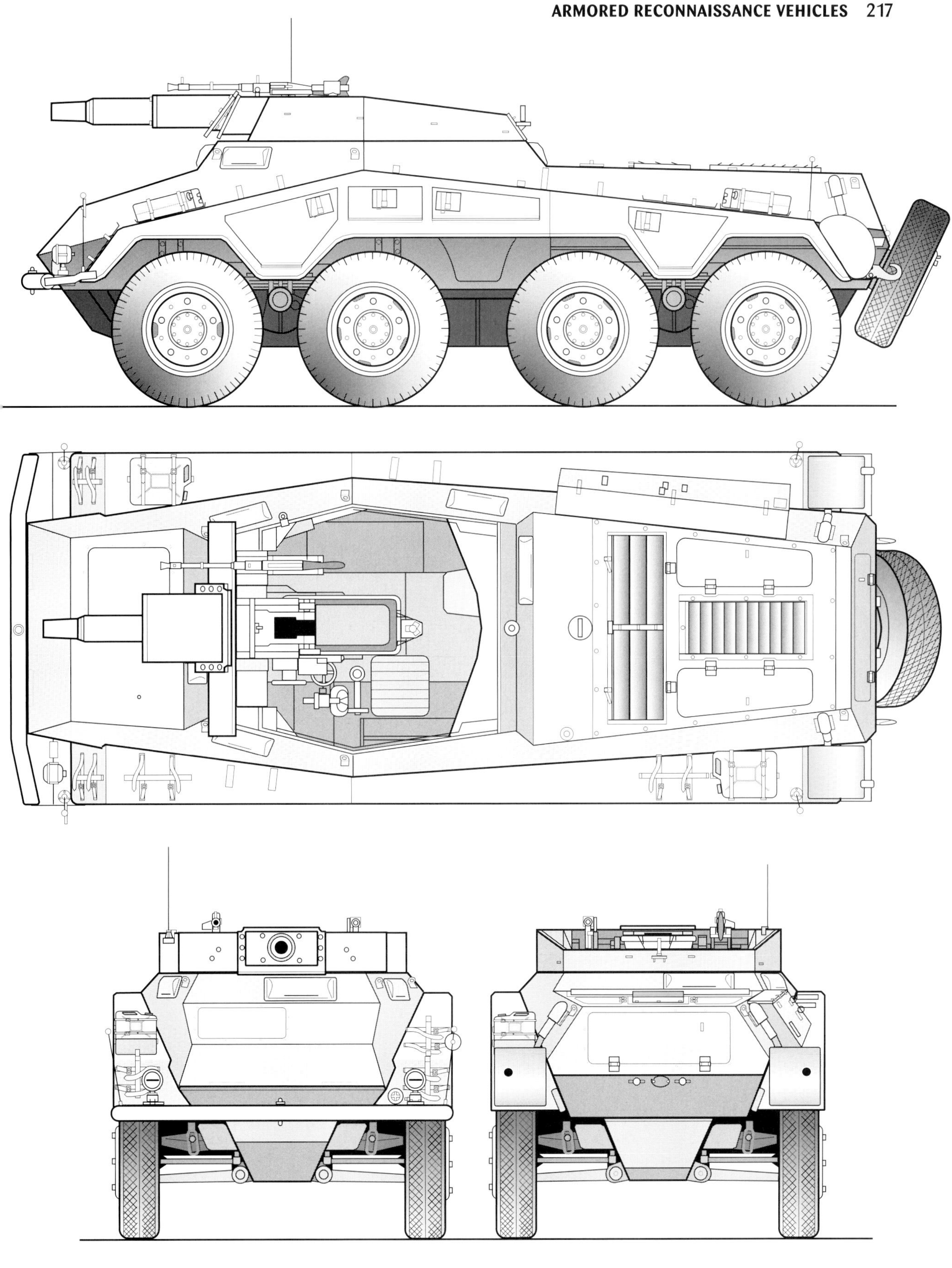

Sd.Kfz. 234/4	
Crew:	4 (driver, rear driver, gunner, and commander)
Armament:	1x 7.92mm MG42 and 1x 7.5cm *PaK 40 L/48* main gun
Speed:	See *Sd.Kfz. 234/1*
Range:	See *Sd.Kfz. 234/1*[9]
Communications equipment:	See *Sd.Kfz. 234/1*
Production Run:	Production run from December 1944 to March 1945, with 89 being built.[10]
Notes:	Issued piecemeal.

A military funeral service is being conducted for a fallen officer or highly decorated soldier somewhere in Germany in early 1945. The late-war camouflage scheme is nicely displayed. Although it cannot be ascertained even under high magnification, it almost appears as if the scout on the viewer's right in the vehicle has a sleeve badge indicating he was once a member of *Sonderverband 288*.

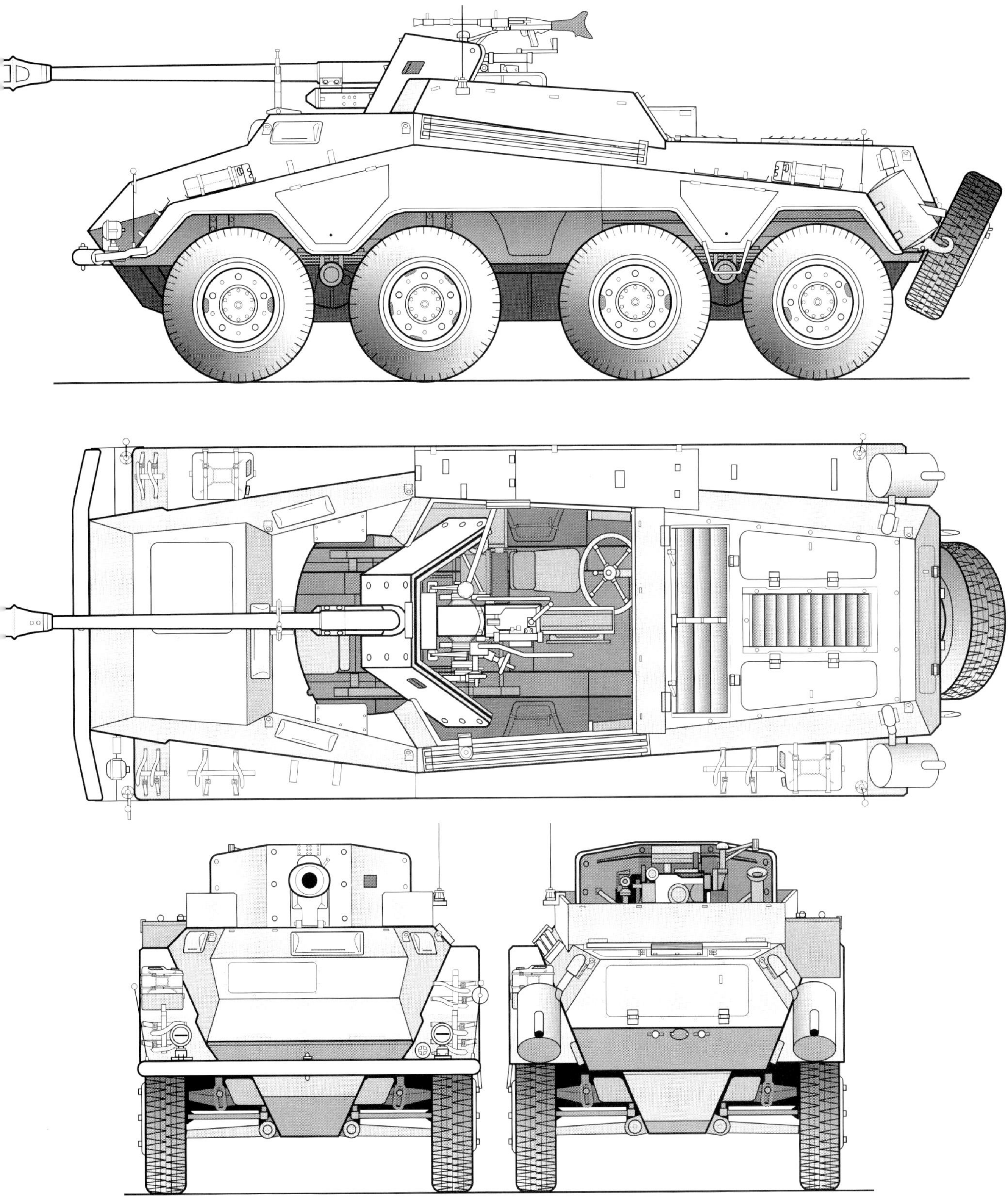

It appears the unidentified scout also trained on the last major wheeled armored vehicle to be produced. The *Sd.Kdz. 234/4*. Intended more as a tank destroyer than an armored car for scouting or reconnaissance purposes, this vehicle mounted the most lethal weapon found on a production-series wheeled vehicle. Note the late-war hard-edge camouflage scheme.

Sd.Kfz 247

Crew:	6
Armament:	Submachine gun
Speed:	Approximately 50 mph
Range:	Approximately 250 miles (road) and 170 miles (cross-country)
Communications equipment:	None (see below)
Production Run:	*Ausführung A (6-Rad)*: 10 (completed in 1938). *Ausführung B (4-Rad)*: 58 (initiated in July 1941 and completed by January 1942).
Notes:	Intended as a command-and-control vehicle, it had no radio equipment. Evidently some vehicles of the B variant were retrofitted with radio sets. Vehicles intended to be issued down to company level, but eventually eliminated from *KStN's* due to limited utility.

This *Sd.Kfz. 247 (6 Rad)* serves as a backdrop for a military ceremony, sometime after the war had started, as evidenced by the wear of a newly presented Iron Cross, Second Class, to the scout to the right of the standard bearer party. JIM HALEY

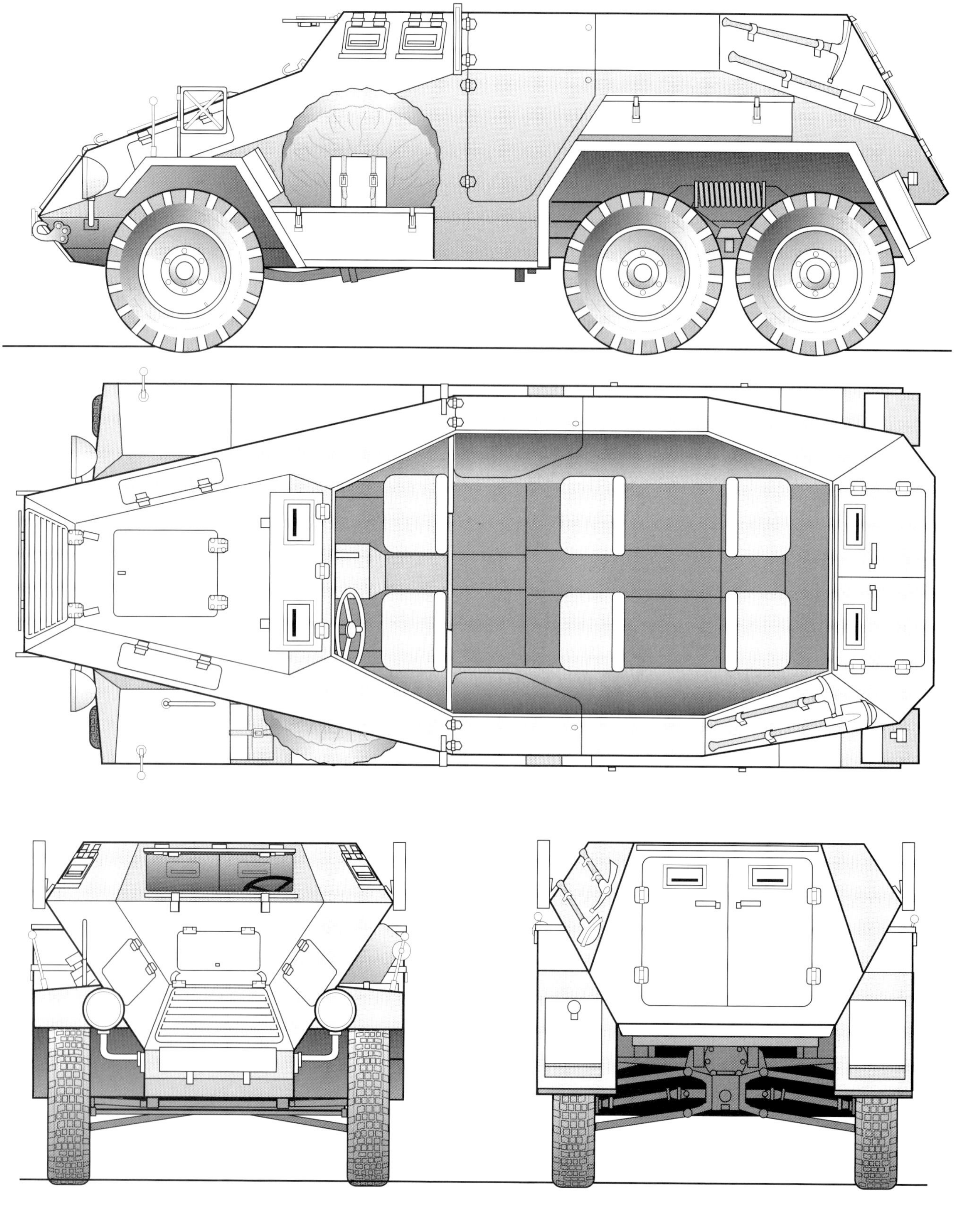

This *Sd.Kfz. 247 (4 Rad)* is most likely from *Aufklärungs-Abteilung 5 (mot)* of the *2. Panzer-Division*, based on what can be seen of the divisional insignia on the opened hatch. The officers and enlisted personnel appear to be enjoying a meal during a break in operations.

Right: This *Sd.Kfz. 263 (Fu)*—photographed before the war—was assigned to the signals platoon of *Aufklärungs-Abteilung 5 (mot)*. JIM HALEY

Elements of a heavy company of an armored reconnaissance battalion pass in review in front of their battalion commander on the occasion of a parade in an unidentified German town. The *Sd.Kfz. 247 (6 Rad)* had a production run of only ten vehicles, and only one was issued to a select number of armored reconnaissance battalions and the "schoolhouse" at Krampnitz. The 4-wheel version was produced in greater numbers, but was only seen in early to midwar formations. JIM HALEY

Sd.Kfz 263 (Fu)	
Crew:	5 (driver, rear driver, radio operators, commander)
Armament:	1x 7.92mm MG34
Speed:	150-horsepower engine allowed a maximum road speed of approximately 54 mph. Later upgraded to 180 horsepower with a maximum speed of approximately 62 mph.
Range:	Approximately 185 miles
Communications equipment:	Radio set *Fu 12 SE 80*, giving a range of around 40 miles. Outfitted with both a frame antenna and a variable height mast antenna (maximum extension: nearly 30 feet)[11]
Production Run:	240 vehicles manufactured between 1938 and April 1943.

Additional vehicles from *Aufklärungs-Abteilung 5 (mot)* prepare to conduct a road movement during wintry weather. JIM HALEY

The *Krampnitz* conducts training during an exercise. JIM HALEY

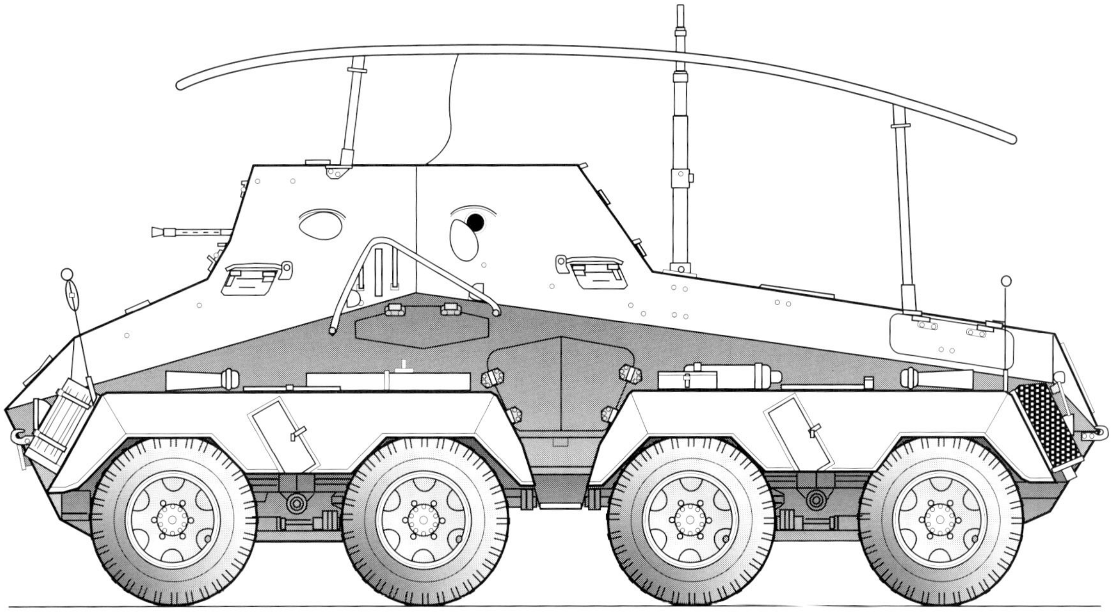

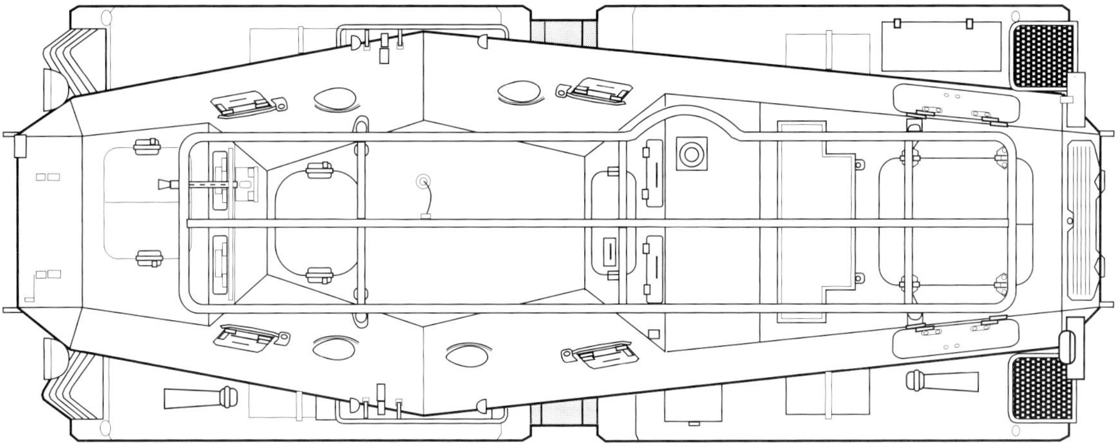

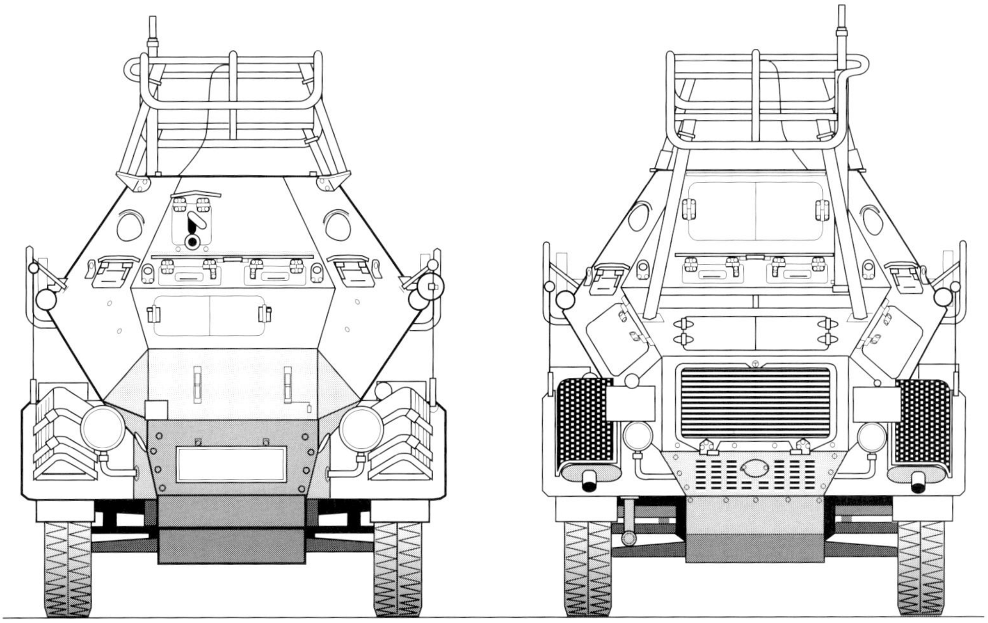

This *Sd.Kfz. 264* was knocked out somewhere in Poland in September 1939. It apparently received a direct hit from a heavy-caliber weapon, as it has completely burned out and a front access panel has been blown off. JIM HALEY

An *Sd.Kfz. 263* from *Panzergruppe Kleist* negotiates rough terrain during the campaign in the West in 1940.

An *Sd.Kfz. 263* from the *2. Panzer-Division* moving at speed through a destroyed French town in 1940. It is not known whether this radio car belonged to *Aufklärungs-Abteilung 5 (mot)*. JIM HALEY

Below: An *Sd.Kfz. 263* from an unidentified unit moves down the muddy roads of the Soviet Union.

HALF-TRACKED ARMORED SCOUT AND RECONNAISSANCE VEHICLES

Sd.Kfz. 250/1 (Light Armored Personnel Carrier)	
Crew:	6 (commander, driver, and four scouts)
Armament:	2x 7.92mm MG34/42
Speed:	Approximately 37–40 mph
Range:	Approximately 186-218 miles
Communications equipment:	FuG Spr f (Standard short-range radio set for communication between and among platoon or company vehicles with rod antenna and range of about half a mile).
Production Run:	More than 7,200 vehicles of all types produced during the production run from 1941 to 1945. Approximately 4,250 *Sd.Kfz. 250/1's* manufactured, with production not ceasing until war's end.[12]
Notes:	Vehicle based on the chassis of the light 1-ton prime mover produced by Demag, the *Sd.Kfz. 10.* Intended as a replacement for the motorcycles in the *Kradschützen* formations. Found in both armored scout and armored reconnaissance companies. In addition to variants, vehicles were also identified by design, with *alt* ("old") being the initial design with the angular superstructure and *neu* ("new") being the later production model with a streamlined superstructure (analogous to what happened with the *Sd.Kfz. 251* series). On 1 March 1945, 2,341 *Sd.Kfz. 250's* were on hand, not counting *Ausführungen 8, 9,* and *10* (accounted for separately below).[13]

An NCO test recruits on their knowledge of their equipment. In the background is an *Sd.Kfz. 250/1 (alt)*, with what appears to be an *Sd.Kfz. 247* nearby.

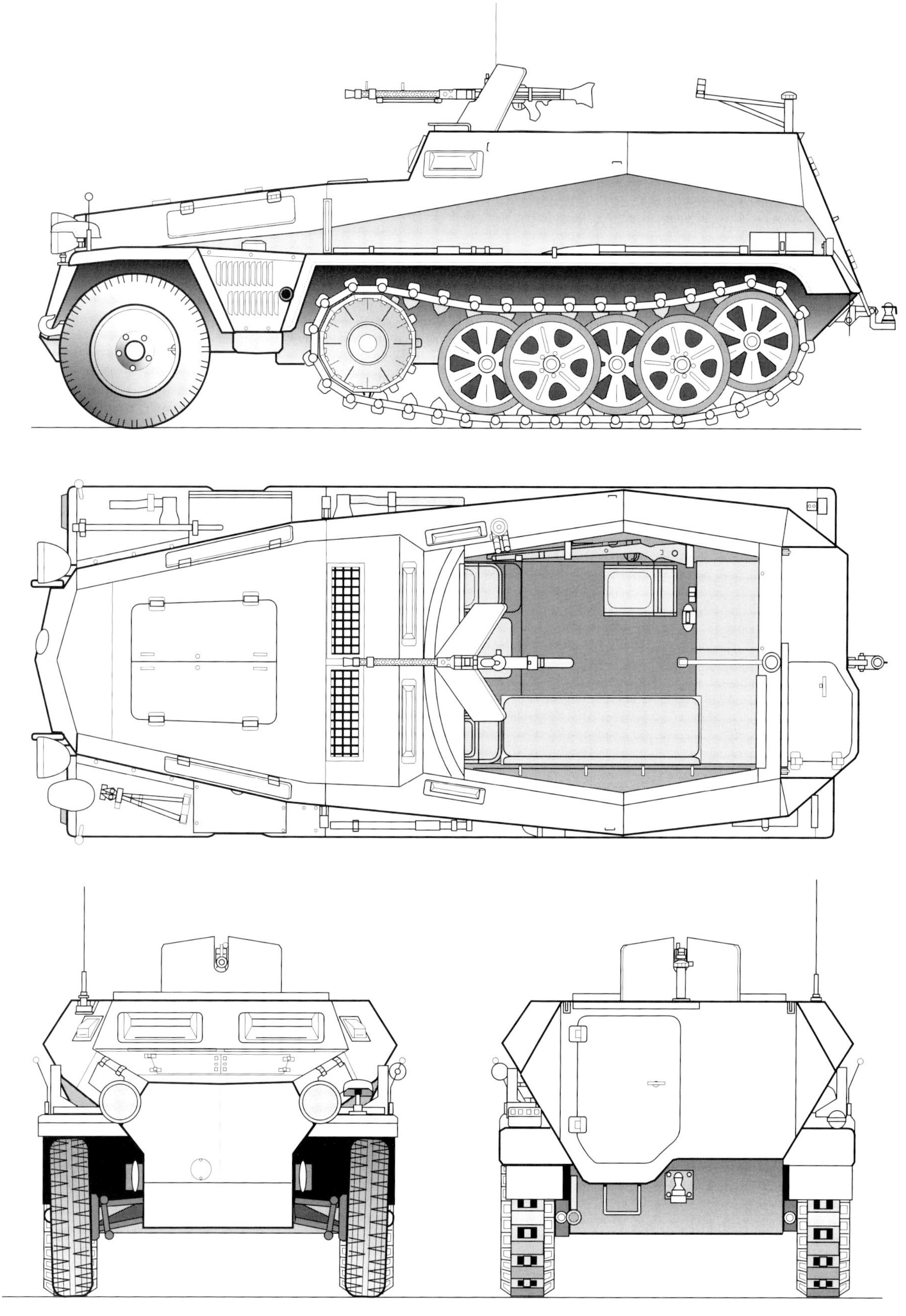

Sd.Kfz 250/3	
Crew:	4 (commander, driver, and two scouts/radio operators)
Armament:	1x 7.92mm MG34/42
Speed:	See entry for *Sd.Kfz. 250/1*
Range:	See entry for *Sd.Kfz. 250/1*
Communications equipment:	One set *FuG1* (receiver only) and one set *Fu 7 SE20* (approximately 24 miles), *8 SE30* (approximately 40 miles Morse and 6 miles voice), or *12 SE80*, with the latter giving a range of around 40 miles with a 2-meter rod antenna.[14]
Production Run:	See entry for *Sd.Kfz. 250/1*

Sd.Kfz. 250/5	
Crew:	4 (commander, driver, and two scouts/radio operators)
Armament:	1x 7.92mm MG34/42
Speed:	See entry for *Sd.Kfz. 250/1*
Range:	See entry for *Sd.Kfz. 250/1*
Communications equipment:	See *Sd.Kfz. 250/3*
Production Run:	See entry for *Sd.Kfz. 250/1*

Sd.Kfz. 250/7	
Crew:	5 (commander, driver, and mortar crew)
Armament:	1x 7.92 mm MG34/42; 1x 8cm *schwerer Granatwerfer 34*
Speed:	See entry for *Sd.Kfz. 250/1*
Range:	See entry for *Sd.Kfz. 250/1*
Communications equipment:	See entry for *Sd.Kfz. 250/1*
Production Run:	See entry for *Sd.Kfz. 250/1*
Notes:	Found in Heavy Weapons Platoons of light rifle companies (light reconnaissance companies). Two versions, with one being introduced in 1944 solely to carry mortar ammunition (66 rounds). Vehicles with mortars could carry twenty-two rounds.

"Old" and "new" versions of the *Sd.Kfz. 250* light armored personnel carrier. In the foreground is an *Sd.Kfz. 250/1 (neu)* and, in the background, an *Sd.Kfz. 250/10* or *11 (alt)*. Based on the architecture and the headgear, this image was taken sometime in late 1943 or later in the Soviet Union.

Sd.Kfz. 250/8

Crew:	3 (commander, gunner, and driver)
Armament:	1x 7.92mm MG34/42 and 1x 7.5cm *KwK 37 L24* main gun
Speed:	See entry for *Sd.Kfz. 250/1*
Range:	See entry for *Sd.Kfz. 250/1*
Communications equipment:	See entry for *Sd.Kfz. 250/1*
Production Run:	Production commenced in 1943 with eight units, followed by ten units in 1944 and fifty-one units in 1945.
Notes:	Found in Cannon Sections of Light Reconnaissance Companies. Carried twenty-two rounds of ammunition for the main gun. On 1 March 1945, there were only five vehicles of this type recorded as being on hand.

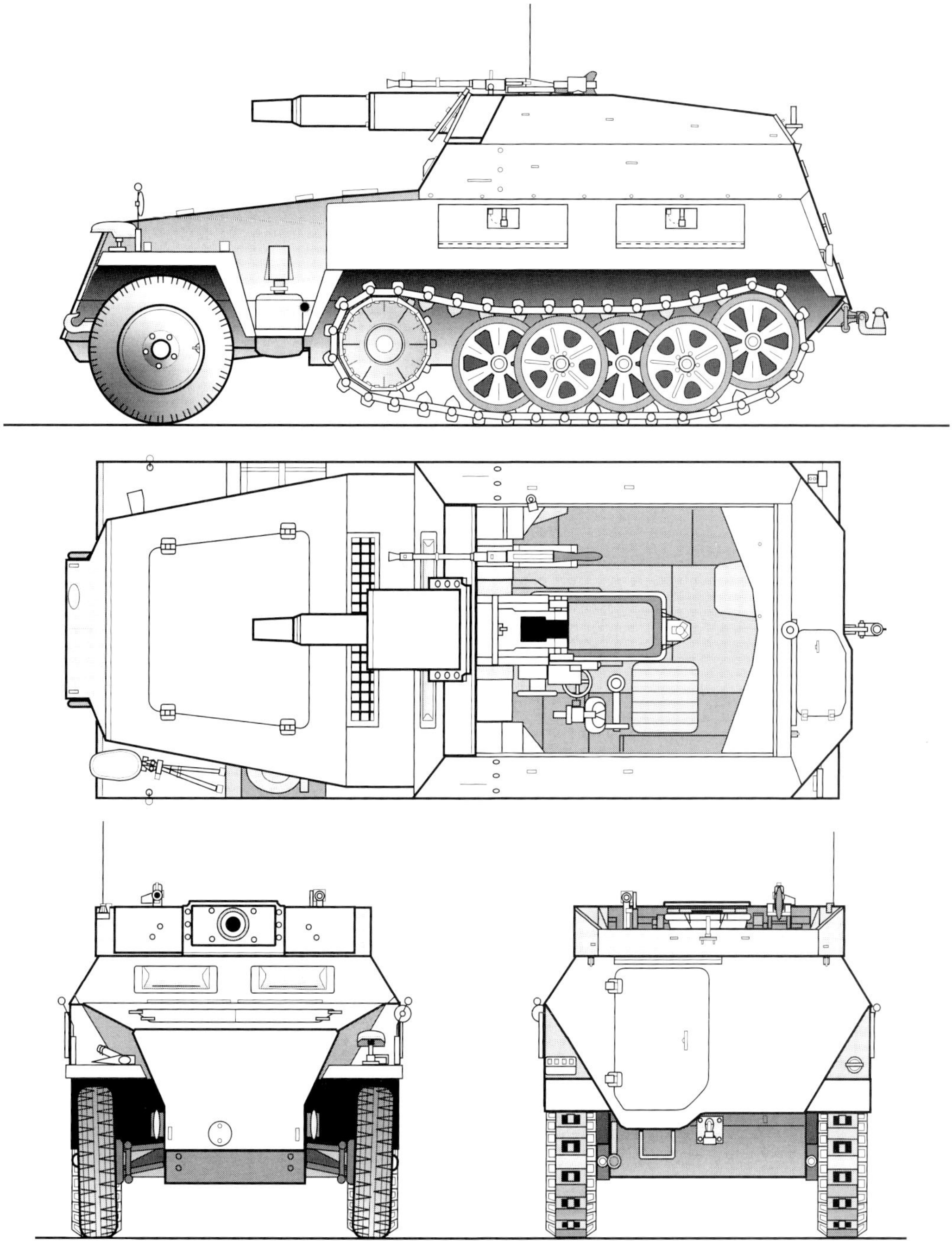

Sd.Kfz. 250/9	
Crew:	3 (commander, gunner, and driver)
Armament:	1 x 7.92 mm MG34/42; 1 x 2cm *KwK 38 L55* automatic cannon
Speed:	See entry for *Sd.Kfz. 250/1*
Range:	See entry for *Sd.Kfz. 250/1*
Communications equipment:	See *Sd.Kfz. 250/1*
Production Run:	Production run consisted of more than 700 vehicles and started in July 1942. The initial variant had the same ten-sided turret as the *Sd.Kfz. 222* (*Ausführung A*). This was changed to a similar but six-sided turret in 1943 (*Ausführung B*). 1943 saw the production of 310 units, followed by 318 units in 1944 and 154 units in 1945.
Notes:	Also referred to as the *Cäsar* vehicle. On 1 March 1945, there were 419 vehicles of this type on hand. The vehicle initially chosen for the role this variant played was the *Sd.Kfz. 250/5*. The *Sd.Kfz. 250/9* was found in company headquarters and line platoons of a Type "C" Armored Scout Company (*KStN 1162c*).

Several *Cäsar* vehicles move down the dusty roads of a Soviet town. The turrets have been covered to protect the weaponry. The vehicles have a spray-painted three-tone camouflage scheme. Behind the reconnaissance halftracks are several *Sd.Kfz. 251/9* close-support weapons carriers armed with short 7.5cm cannon.

A track commander of an *Sd.Kfz. 250/9* prepares to fire over the rear deck. This image comes from a series of photographs taken during training conducted by members of the *SS "Nordland" Division's* reconnaissance battalion in Croatia in late 1943. More images are featured in Chapter 5.

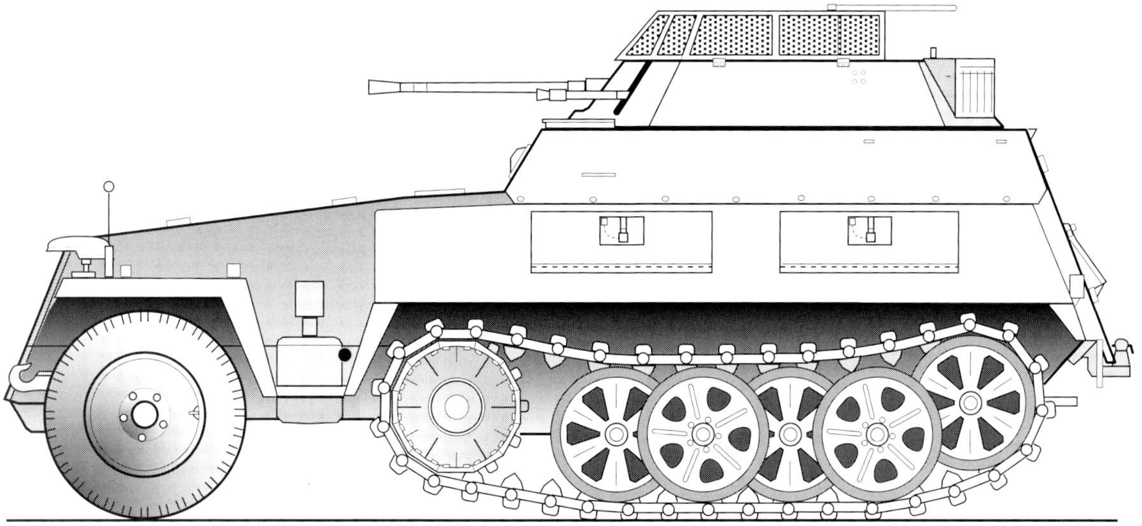

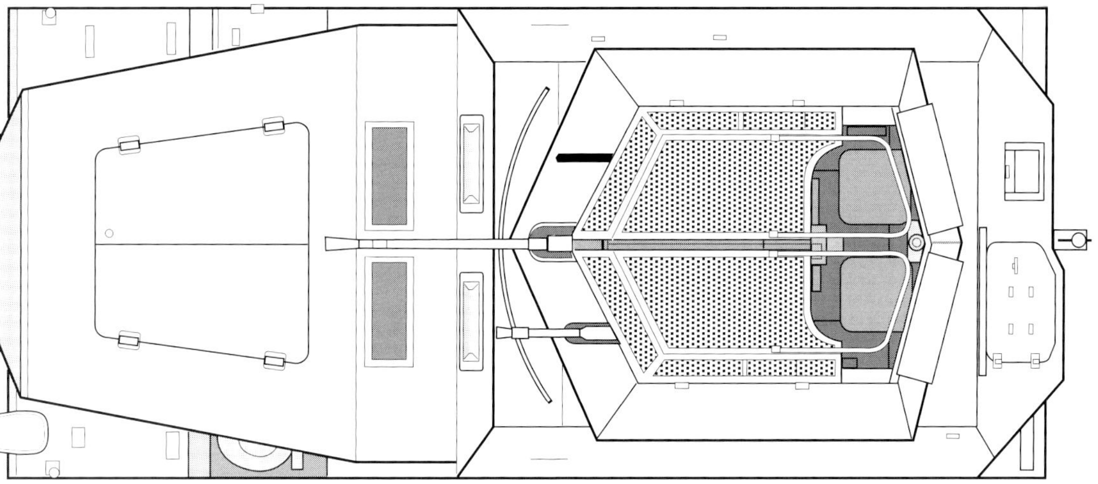

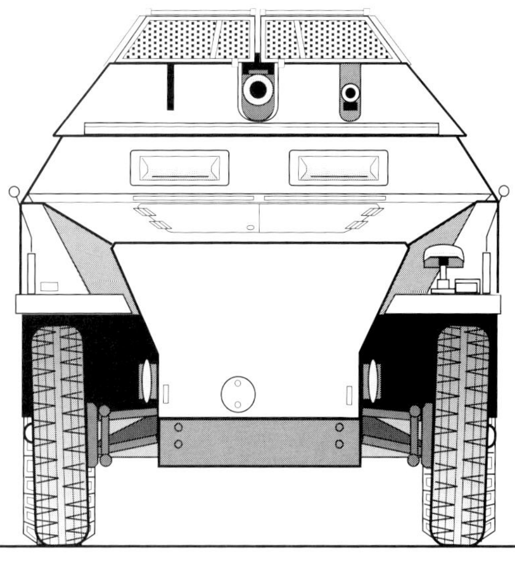

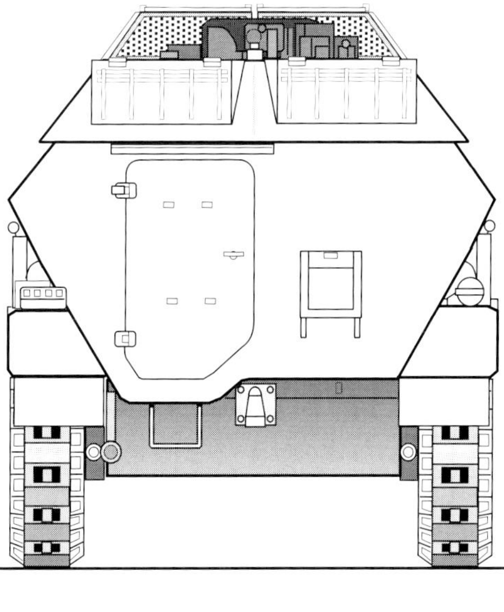

Sd.Kfz 250/10	
Crew:	4 (platoon leader/commander, driver, and two scouts)
Armament:	1x 7.92mm MG34 and 1x 3.7cm *PaK 35* or *36*
Speed:	See entry for *Sd.Kfz. 250/1*
Range:	See entry for *Sd.Kfz. 250/1*
Communications equipment:	See entry for *Sd.Kfz. 250/1*
Production Run:	See entry for *Sd.Kfz. 250/1*
Notes:	Found in the platoon headquarters section of light rifle companies (light reconnaissance companies).

Sd.Kfz. 250/11	
Crew:	6 (platoon leader/commander, gunner, driver, and three scouts)
Armament:	1x 7.92mm MG34 and 1x *2.8cm schwere Panzerbüchse 41*
Speed:	See entry for *Sd.Kfz. 250/1*
Range:	See entry for *Sd.Kfz. 250/1*
Communications equipment:	See entry for *Sd.Kfz. 250/1*
Production Run:	See entry for *Sd.Kfz. 250/1*
Notes:	Found in armored antitank gun sections of heavy companies. Main gun could be dismounted.

Sd.Kfz. 251/1	
Crew:	3+ (commander, driver, and varying numbers of scouts)
Armament:	1x 7.92mm MG34/42
Speed:	Approximately 31–33 mph
Range:	Approximately 112–186 miles
Communications equipment:	*FuG Spr Ger f* for intervehicular communications with a range of about six-tenths of a mile.
Production Run:	More than 15,000 produced of all variants, with 4,650 of *Ausführungen A, B,* and *C* manufactured (multi-angled superstructure) and 10,602 of *Ausführung D* (simplified superstructure) (with the majority being produced in 1944—7,800).
Notes:	Base model of the series.

Sd.Kfz. 251/3	
Crew:	7 (commander, driver, and five radio operators/scouts)
Armament:	2x 7.92mm MG34/42
Speed:	See *Sd.Kfz. 251/1*
Range:	See *Sd.Kfz. 251/1*
Communications equipment:	Varied, dependent upon command needs. Range of radio options: *FuG 4, 5, 8, 11*, and *12*.
Production Run:	See *Sd.Kfz. 251/1*
Notes:	Medium half-track command-and-control and communications vehicle. Found in headquarters sections.

Sd.Kfz. 251/7 (Armored Engineer Assault Vehicle)	
Crew:	7–8 (commander, driver, and six or seven combat engineers)
Armament:	2x 7.92mm MG34/42 and 1x 7.92mm antitank rifle
Speed:	See *Sd.Kfz. 251/1*
Range:	See *Sd.Kfz. 251/1*
Communications equipment:	Varied, based on command needs. Normally a *FuG 5*, with other configurations for command vehicles
Production run:	See *Sd.Kfz. 251/1*
Notes:	Combat engineer version with storage for mines, demolitions, and combat-engineer tools. Found in combat engineer platoons in heavy companies.

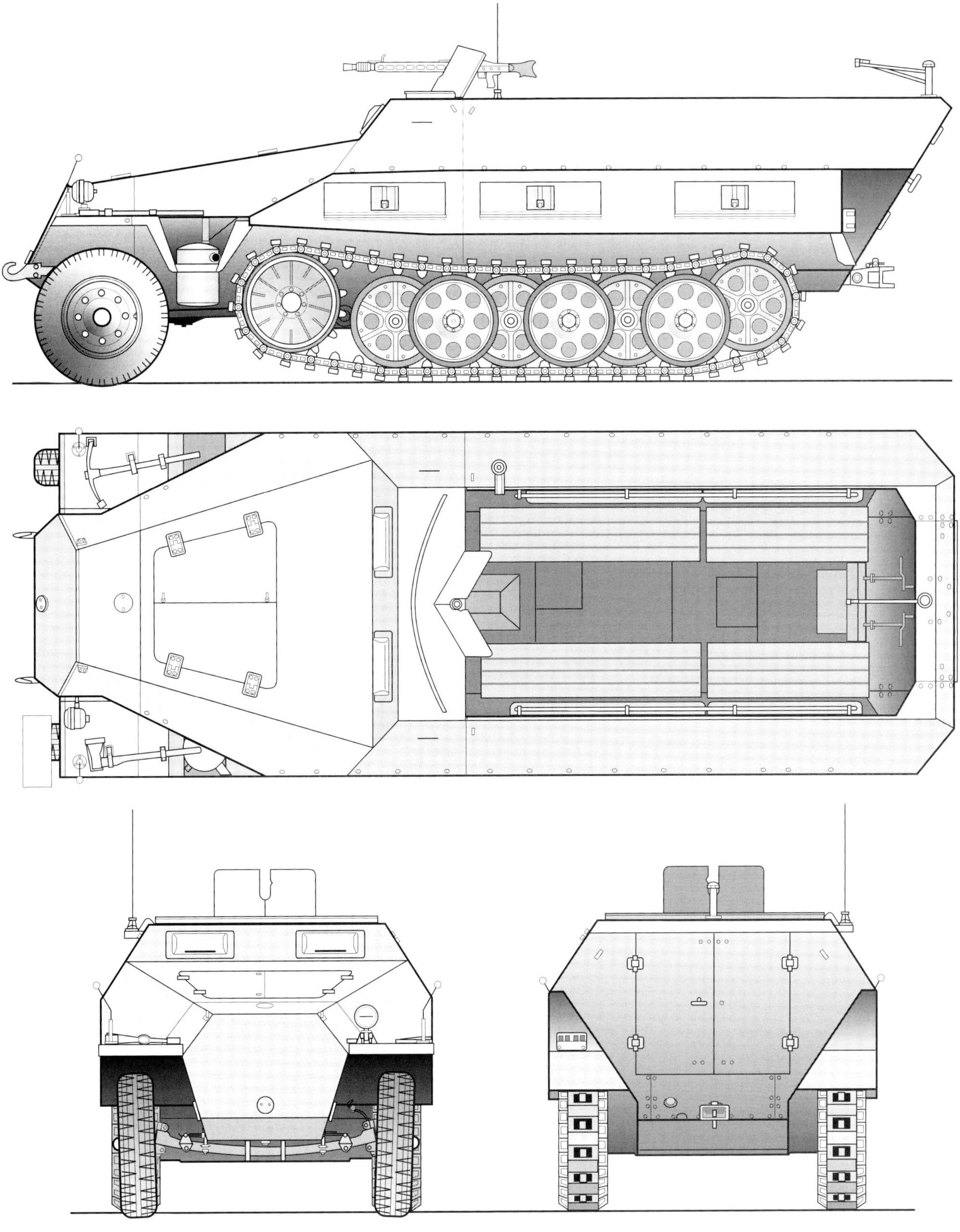

A division commander and senior armor officer receive a report from another officer. They are operating out of an *Sd.Kfz. 251/3* command-and-control half-track, identical to those found in armored reconnaissance battalions.

Sd.Kfz. 251/8

Crew:	2 (commander and driver, with capacity for four stretcher patients or ten sitting wounded)
Armament:	None
Speed:	See *Sd.Kfz. 251/1*
Range:	See *Sd.Kfz. 251/1*
Communications equipment:	One radio set *FuG 5 SE10u*, with a voice range of 1.6 miles and a Morse range of approximately 5 miles.
Production Run:	See *Sd.Kfz. 251/1*
Notes:	Medium half-track armored ambulance. Found in headquarters sections.

Sd.Kfz. 251/9

Crew:	3 (commander, gunner, and driver)
Armament:	1x 7.92mm *MG34/42* and 1x 7.5cm *StuK 37 L/24* main gun
Speed:	See *Sd.Kfz. 251/1*
Range:	See *Sd.Kfz. 251/1*
Communications equipment:	See *Sd.Kfz. 251/1*
Production Run:	See *Sd.Kfz. 251/1*
Notes:	Two versions produced, with the early one featuring the main gun offset to the side of the upper superstructure and the other with the main gun centrally mounted higher on the superstructure.

Sd.Kfz. 251/11

Crew:	5 (commander, driver, and three signaleers)
Armament:	1x 7.92mm MG34/42
Speed:	See *Sd.Kfz. 251/1*
Range:	See *Sd.Kfz. 251/1*
Communications equipment:	See *Sd.Kfz. 251/1*
Production Run:	See *Sd.Kfz. 251/1*
Notes:	Medium half-track communications vehicle for landline communications. Found in early-war *KStN's*.

Sd.Kfz. 251/21

Crew:	4–6 (commander, driver, gunner, and 1–3 assistant gunners
Armament:	3x 1.5cm MG151/15 or 3x 2cm MG151/20 mounted coaxially (with 2,000 rounds of ammunition and a maximum rate of fire of 700 rounds a minute)
Speed:	See *Sd.Kfz. 251/1*
Range:	See *Sd.Kfz. 251/1*
Communications equipment:	See *Sd.Kfz. 251/1*
Production Run:	See *Sd.Kfz. 251/1*
Notes:	Medium half-track antiaircraft vehicle. Found only in *KStN 1162e* of 1 February 1945 and *KStN f* of 1 April 1945 as an obvious response to Allied air supremacy.

Sd.Kfz 251/22

Crew:	4 (commander, gunner, loader, driver)
Armament:	1x 7.5cm *PaK 40 L/46* (with twenty-two rounds stowed on board)
Speed:	See *Sd.Kfz. 251/1*
Range:	See *Sd.Kfz. 251/1*
Communications equipment:	See *Sd.Kfz. 251/1*
Production Run:	Produced on direct orders of Hitler, starting in 1944. Unknown total production run.
Notes:	Found only in *KStN f* of 1 April 1945. The entire gun was mounted on the vehicle, except for the wheels.

TRACKED RECONNAISSANCE VEHICLES

Panzerkampfwagen 2, Ausführung L (2cm) (Sd.Kfz. 123)

Crew:	3 (commander, gunner, and driver)
Armament:	1 x 7.92 mm MG34/42; 1 x 2cm *KwK 38 L55* automatic cannon[15]
Speed:	32 mph
Range:	100 miles
Communications equipment:	One set *Fu 12 SE80*, with a range of around 40 miles with a 2-meter rod antenna
Production Run:	100 produced between September 1942 and January 1944, with some sources stating 131 were manufactured in all.
Notes:	Original order for 800 vehicles reduced to 100. Popularly known as the *Luchs*. Found in the company headquarters and platoons of a Type "B" armored scout company (*KStN 1162b*), with a total of 29 *Luchs* in the company (1 in the headquarters and 7 each of four line platoons). Fielded to the *2./Panzer-Aufklärungs-Abteilung 9* in April 1943 (later reconstituted as the 1st Company) and the *2./Panzer-Aufklärungs-Abteilung 4*.[16]

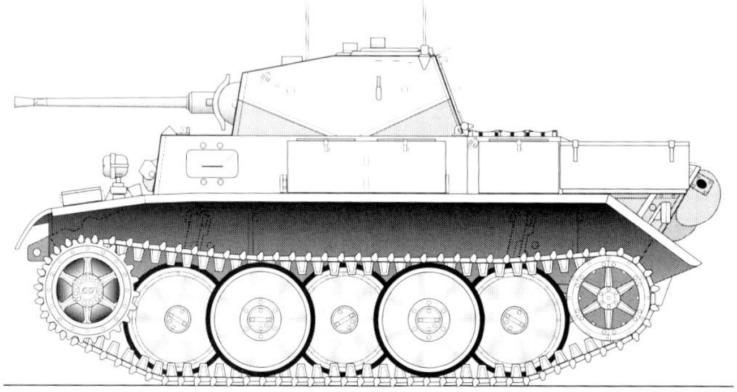

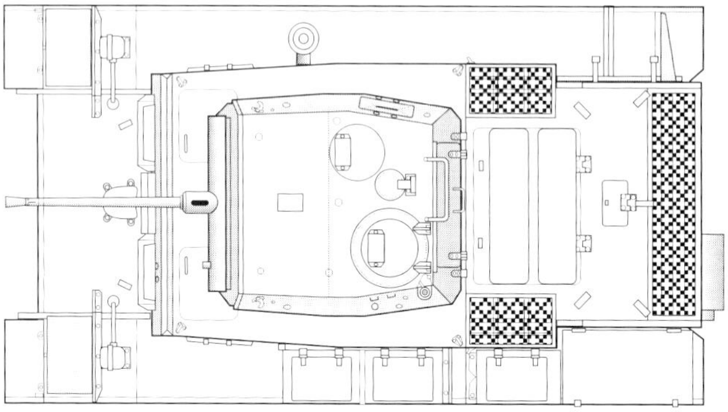

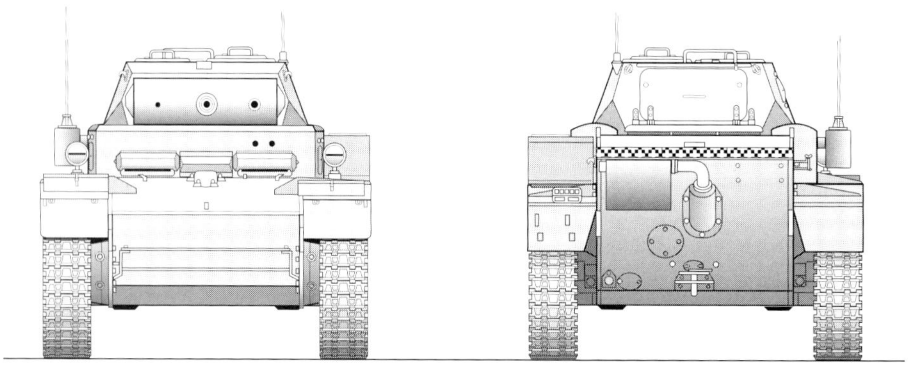

Aufklärungspanzerwagen 38 (2cm) (Sd.Kfz. 140/1)

Crew:	3
Armament:	1 x 7.92 mm MG34/42; 1 x 2cm *KwK 38 L55* automatic cannon
Speed:	Approximately 25 mph
Range:	Approximately 150 miles[17]
Communications equipment:	One set *Fu 12 SE80*, with a range of around 40 miles with a 2-meter rod antenna
Production Run:	70 (37 in February 1944 and 30 the following month)
Notes:	Found in the company headquarters and platoons of a Type "B" armored scout company (*KStN 1162b*). Two companies issued the vehicle: the *2./Panzer-Aufklärungs-Abteilung "Großdeutschland"* and the *1./Panzer-Aufklärungs-Abteilung 3*. In addition to initial issue of 25 vehicles each, both companies also eventually received 7 replacements vehicles. One vehicle was also sent to the replacement detachment for *"Großdeutschland."*

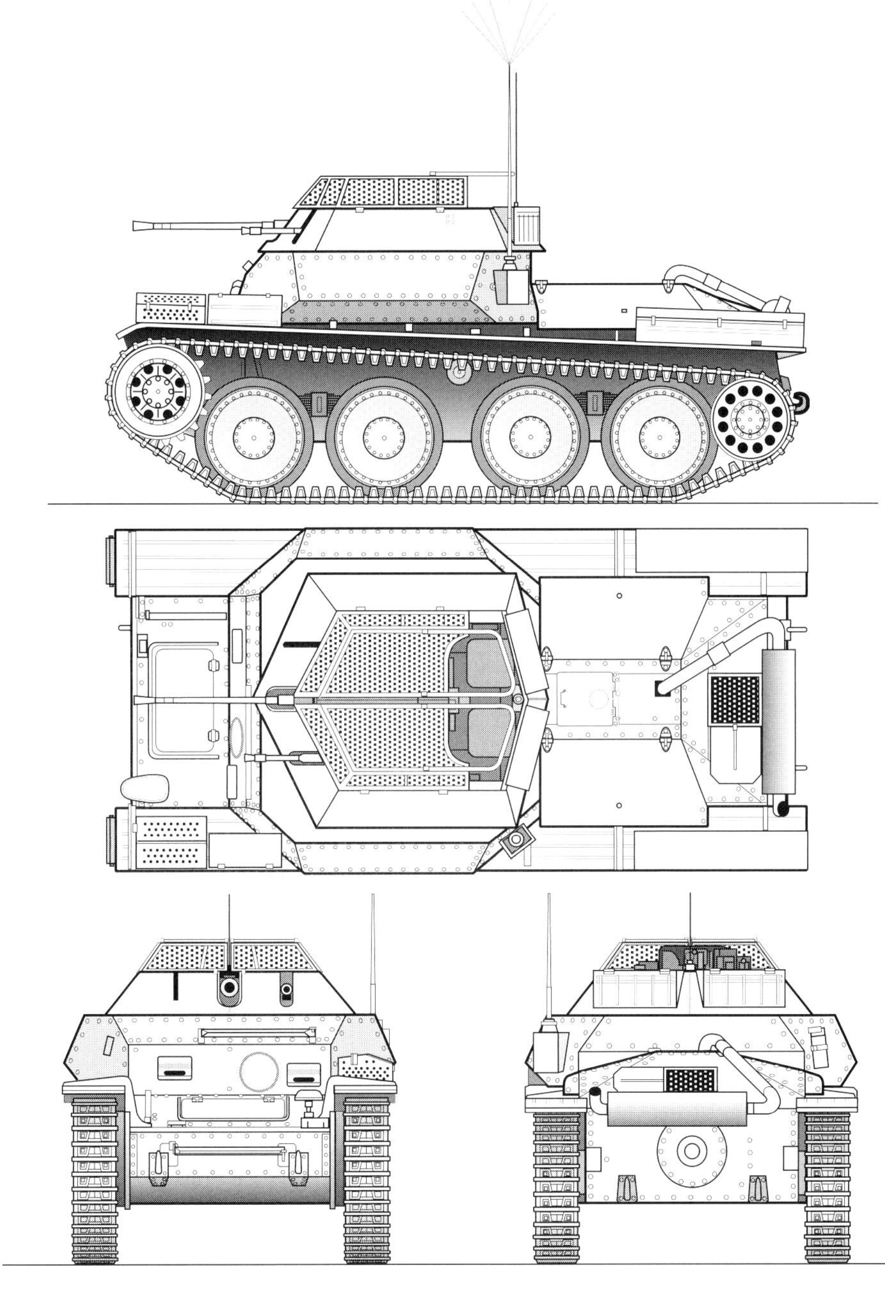

UNARMORED RECONNAISSANCE VEHICLES

Sidecar Motorcycle

Crew:	3 (driver and two passengers)
Armament:	None built in; 1x MG34/42 could be mounted on the sidecar for squad machine guns and heavy machine-gun sections.
Speed:	58 mph
Range:	215 miles
Communications equipment:	None
Production Run:	16,510 by war's end (BMW version)
Notes:	Various manufacturers, especially Zündapp, with the data for the BMW version cited here. Used for messenger duties and in motorcycle infantry companies to carry squad members, light machine guns, and light mortars.

A typical scene involving motorcycle infantry in the Soviet Union: a constant mad dash from one point to another, followed by the inevitable halt. These *Kradschützen* belong to either *Kradschützen-Bataillon 61* or *Aufklärungs-Abteilung 231* of the *11. Panzer-Division.*

Right: The sidecar motorcycle continued to be used until the war's end, albeit only in a messenger role. By 1943, when this type of headgear was introduced, almost all of the *Kradschützen* had traded in their motorcycles for wheeled vehicles or half-tracks.

Kfz. 1

Crew:	4 (driver and three other personnel)
Armament:	None
Speed:	62 mph
Range:	375 miles
Communications equipment:	None
Production Run:	Approximately 55,000 by war's end.
Notes:	Found in headquarters sections for command-and-control purposes. Also used for transporting armored reconnaissance personnel in later-war *KStN's* (intended as an interim measure until enough *Sd.Kfz. 250's* were available for fielding. There were numerous subvariants, including the Type 62 (initial prototype), Type 82 (main production version), Type 86 (featured a widened chassis), Type 92 (hardtop), and a tropical version (*tropenfest*). The Type 166, an amphibious version, was also issued to some reconnaissance battalions, especially in the SS.

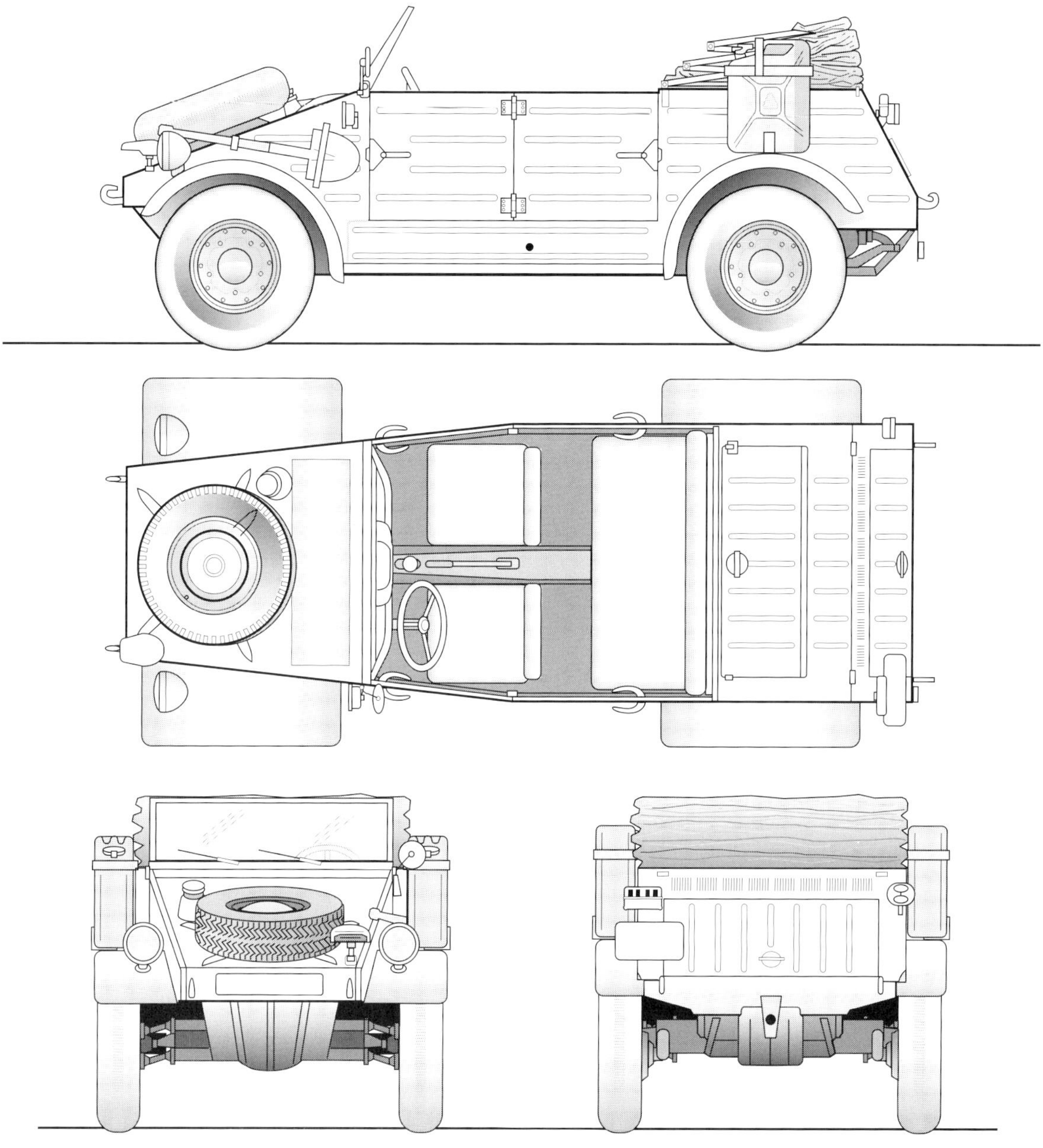

Kfz. 1 (Type 166: *Schwimmwagen*)	
Crew:	4 (driver and three other personnel)
Armament:	None
Speed:	50 mph (land), 7 mph (water)
Range:	250–290 miles
Communications equipment:	None
Production Run:	14,625 by war's end.
Notes:	The amphibious version was issued to some reconnaissance battalions, especially in the SS, although it is not found in any reconnaissance *KStN's*.

Sd.Kfz. 2	
Crew:	3 (driver and two scouts)
Armament:	None
Speed:	Approximately 48 mph
Range:	Approximately 62 miles
Communications equipment:	None
Production Run:	8,345 between 1941 and 1944.
Notes:	Originally designed for airborne use. Used in armored reconnaissance companies for the transport of scouts and equipment in certain *KStN's*. Payload limited to three or four soldiers. Great cross-country ability; limited personnel protection.

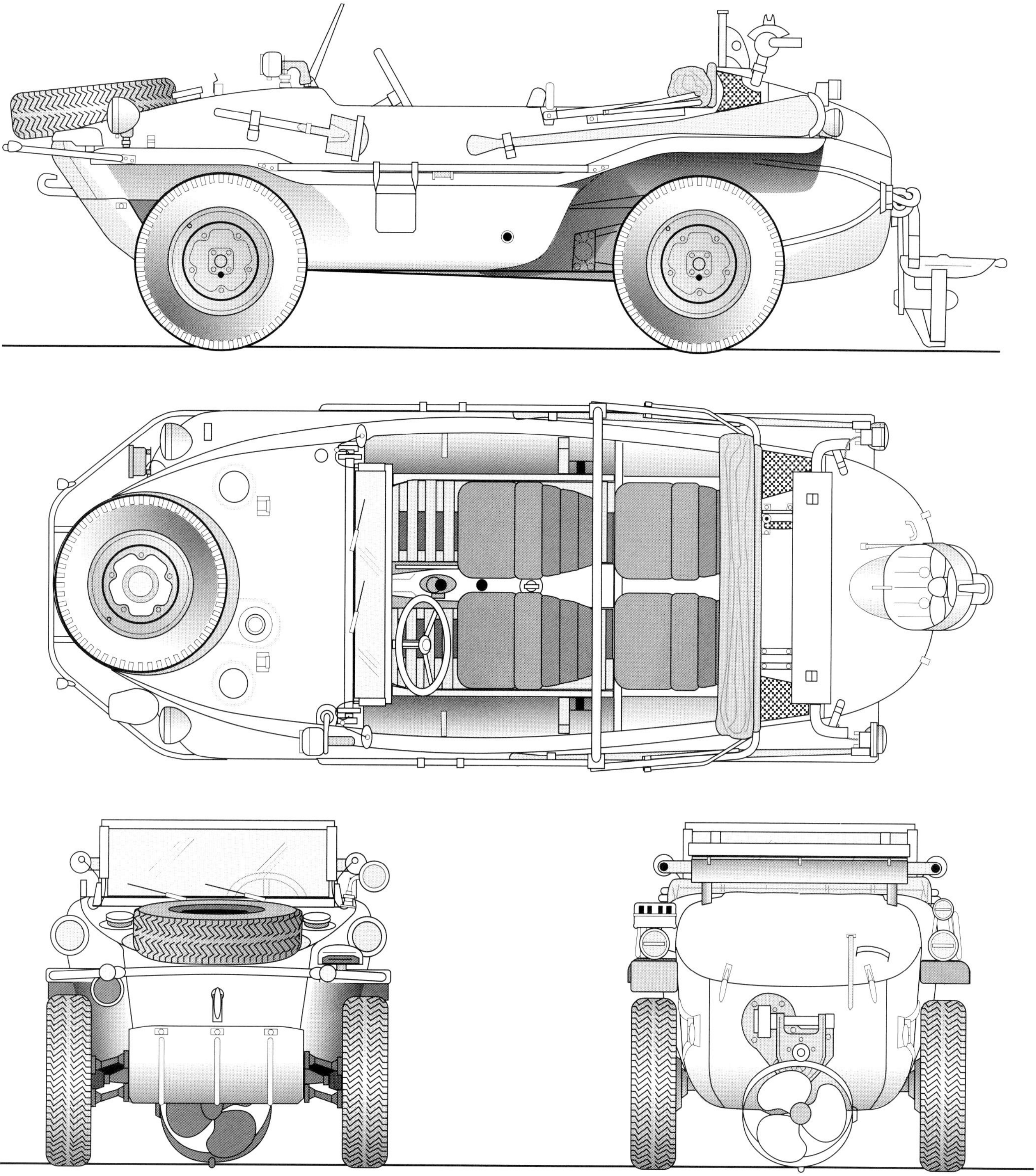

The Type 166 *Schwimmwagen* was often used in lieu of the *Volkswagen Kübelwagen* by reconnaissance forces, particularly the *Waffen-SS*, as seen here.

Numerous foreign vehicles were impressed into service in the German Army over the war years, and the reconnaissance forces were no exception. Some 200 French Panhards equipped several armored reconnaissance battalion scout companies, often being modified to meet German specifications and requirements. When used by the Germans, the official nomenclature was *P(anzerspähwagen) 204(f)*.

Minor allies of the Germans, the Hungarians were trained by them and employed their tactics on the battlefield. Although the numbers were limited, the Hungarians produced around 100 of the excellent Csaba armored cars, seen here lined up on a city street. The Hungarian insignia was painted in its national colors, with a red circle background, a green center cross, and a white outer cross.

CHAPTER 4

Uniforms, Insignia, and Ephemera

SETTING THE STAGE

As with the vehicles of the armored reconnaissance force, the subject of uniforms, insignia and ephemera has been covered in great detail elsewhere.[1] The purpose of this chapter is to show items that were unique to the force and to explain the somewhat confusing and frequently misunderstood nature of the various branch-of-service colors—*Waffenfarben*—that were employed at various times within the force: rose pink, golden yellow, meadow green, copper brown, and even white.

UNIFORMS

In general, the uniforms of the armored reconnaissance force were no different from those of other branches of service and mirrored the usage found in the *schnelle Truppen* and *Panzertruppe* as a whole—i.e., the black, field-gray, and special-purpose *Panzer* uniforms were intended for the crewmembers of armored vehicles, while the remaining uniforms, both field and dress, were intended for all personnel, including armored vehicle crewmembers when not actively on an armored vehicle. Over time, the lines began to blur about who was authorized to wear the distinctive *Panzer*-style uniform items since they were considered to be both stylish and iconic of an elite force.[2] By war's end, the popular style was worn by any number of personnel who had no relationship to armored vehicles.

The only known instance of a cap with a badge unique to a reconnaissance element is this stylized armored car worn on the cap of *Unteroffizier* Otto Henning, who, after serving in Africa, was reassigned to the *Panzer-Aufklärungs-Lehr-Abteilung* of the *Panzer-Lehr-Division*. Henning may have been "testing the waters" of his commander's forbearance with this device, since his is the only image of this cap badge that has surfaced. The badge is in the form of a stylized heavy armored reconnaissance car. GARY BEADLE

When wearing standard dress and field uniforms, there was no way of determining whether someone was from an armored reconnaissance unit, except through insignia and, to a limited degree, the types of combat badges awarded. There was some confusion about the types of badges armored reconnaissance personnel were authorized, and in the case of officers, frequent reassignments to differing types of armored formations—reconnaissance, tanks, or mechanized infantry—often resulted in the award of combat badges peculiar to those branches of the *schnelle Truppen*, which were allowed to be worn on all uniforms.

Even with the wear of strictly *Panzer*-related uniforms, it was sometimes difficult to determine the soldier's association with a certain branch, since distinctive unit insignia were phased out for operational security reasons early in the war and only reinstated again toward war's end. In addition, the sharing of branch colors—generally rose pink by tankers and armored reconnaissance personnel in armored divisions, but also the famous example of the *24. Panzer-Division*, where all personnel in line units wore golden yellow—make identification from period photographs difficult. Even where the *Waffenfarbe* would provide an obvious clue, the almost universal black-and-white photography of the era makes it almost impossible to discern the difference between rose pink and golden yellow.

Army *Panzer* uniforms were different in cut and appearance from their counterparts in the SS and, to a certain extent, the armored reconnaissance formations of the *Luftwaffe*. The most obvious differences follow:

Army

Jacket and trousers. Introduced in 1935,[3] the first-pattern jacket had small collars and a non-functioning lapel (for closing in cases of inclement weather). The second pattern, introduced in 1937, had larger collars and a functional lapel. After 1940, collar piping in the appropriate *Waffenfarbe* was discontinued and ordered removed on previously produced jackets, although the latter requirement was rarely observed. In 1944, a subvariant of the second pattern was introduced, whereby the *Waffenfarbe* was sewn directly to the lapels, replacing separately applied insignia (the stylized death's head was still pinned through the lapel, however). All versions had a slanted front outer closure and two interior pockets. A vertical seam on the back is a hallmark.

The field-gray version of the jacket, originally intended for crewmembers of assault guns and then tank destroyers, was later also worn by armored reconnaissance personnel, especially those in armored reconnaissance companies (vis-a-vis scout companies). There was a prototype with a dark-green collar, with very limited usage in the field.[4] The jackets were identical to the black second pattern described above, to include the sub-variant introduced in 1944.

The reed-green denim and mouse-gray cotton duck *Panzer* uniforms, with the former being introduced in 1941, were generally similar in appearance to second-pattern *Panzer* uniforms, although there were subvariants among these, with earlier first-pattern jackets generally most resembling the *Panzer* jacket and a second-pattern version distinguishable by a large exterior breast pocket.[5] There were numerous minor differences between these uniform items and standard wool *Panzer* uniforms, but those are left for the references cited in the end notes and bibliography.

Some camouflage was also worn, but these were universally field-made pieces and generally in army camouflage patterns, although use was made of Italian camouflage.

Black, field-gray, denim, and cotton duck *Panzer* trousers were all virtually identical in outward appearance and featured two front pockets slightly pointed in the middle with a single button. The denim and cotton duck trousers also came in two versions, with some having a large pocket on the upper left front thigh.

Headgear. Black overseas caps were officially introduced after the campaign in the West in 1940, although some tailor-made versions in black, were worn previous to that, especially by officers.[6] The beret/crash helmet combination, never popular with crews and phased out in the same time period, was produced in both field-gray and black versions, although only the black version is seen in wear by armored reconnaissance personnel.[7]

All other headgear introduced for the German Army—the M42 and the M43—was also produced in black for the *Panzertruppe*.

Waffen-SS

Jacket and trousers. The armored car crews of the *SS-Verfügungstruppe* started out wearing army first-pattern *Panzer* uniforms with SS insignia applied. The SS then introduced its own version of the black and field-gray *Panzer* uniforms—shorter in length than their army counterparts and featuring a vertical front closure and no back seam.[8] The tips of the collars were generally also more rounded. There is great variety in the collar patterns, especially in jackets privately tailored for officers and senior NCOs. Reed-green versions were also produced for the SS and worn in a manner analogous to their army counterparts.[9] There is no known cotton duck (mouse gray) version of the jacket or trousers for the SS. As with the army, there were also camouflage versions of the uniform worn, albeit officially authorized and issued to the force, with the most commonly encountered version being the so-called "pea" pattern introduced in 1944.[10] Earlier camouflage patterns are also encountered, some officially produced and others tailor-made. In addition, camouflage coveralls were also issued to crews, but only in earlier camouflage patterns, reminiscent of smocks.[11] There was a reversible winter coverall (green/white) also introduced, although it was generally only issued to tank crews.

On black and field-gray *Panzer*-type trousers, SS ones are generally recognizable by the pointed ends on the exterior pocket flaps and the use of two buttons, located on the outer edges of the flaps. Denim and camouflage trousers have only a centrally located button, however. There is no known version of SS denim trousers with a thigh pocket (see army trousers above).

Headgear. SS *Panzer* headgear was distinct from army styles, with black *Allgemeine SS* caps frequently being worn in the early years to complement the black *Panzer* uniform. Until 1940, the SS version of the beret/crash helmet was worn in both black and field gray, although it is not believed that SS armored reconnaissance personnel wore the field-gray beret/crash helmet. In 1940, a distinctive black overseas cap was introduced for both officers and enlisted personnel that was generally worn through war's end.[12] SS officers frequently wore modified army M38 officer caps with SS insignia applied as well. The SS also had its own version of the ubiquitous M43, with numerous variants being fielded and worn: single- and double-button fronts; single trapezoid insignia; and individual insignia ("skull" and national insignia, both front and sides).[13] Billed field caps in camouflage material were produced, although in limited quantities.

Luftwaffe

Jacket and trousers. Externally, *Luftwaffe Panzer* uniforms mimicked their army counterparts, with no known officially produced denim or cotton duck uniforms.[14] *Luftwaffe*-produced uniform items had *Luftwaffe* markings on the interior, and the lining was in typical bluish gray. There is a contentious argument in the collecting community concerning whether the *Luftwaffe* produced any assault-gun style uniforms in a bluish gray material (as opposed to the standard field gray). Regardless of whether it did, the item would have been extraordinarily rare. Occasionally, SS camouflage was also worn, particularly smocks. The uniform situation regarding *Luftwaffe Panzer* uniforms is made even more difficult by the fact that many personnel were transferred into the force from the army and wore their original uniforms, sometimes modified with *Luftwaffe* insignia and sometimes retaining the original insignia.

Headgear. Overseas caps and billed field caps in black with *Luftwaffe* insignia were produced. As with the uniforms, images of army headgear being worn are not uncommon.

INSIGNIA

Army

It is sometimes difficult to ascertain the proper *Waffenfarbe* for a particular formation or unit, because of the commingling of some branches—mostly cavalry and *schnelle Truppe/Panzertruppe*, but also the infantry—over the formative and war years when it came to responsibility for the armored reconnaissance forces. In theory, the armored reconnaissance battalions assigned to the armored divisions and the motorized rifle divisions in the prewar years wore rose pink (*rosa*) *Waffenfarbe*, while those associated with the cavalry branch, specifically the light divisions, wore golden yellow (*goldgelb*). Upon mobilization, the reconnaissance battalions of the infantry divisions were also a responsibility of the cavalry branch, including the scout sections and platoons of those limited number of battalions that had those assets. Motorcycle infantry battalions, which only existed in prewar armored divisions, wore rose pink as a rule. Since the infantry branch was responsible for training motorcycle infantry forces initially, some motorcycle elements initially wore the white (*weiß*) of infantry,[15] followed by the meadow green (*wiesengrün*) of the motorized infantry, especially when constituted within the framework of a motorized rifle division.[16]

The waters become muddied in November 1938, when all reconnaissance elements were transferred to the oversight of the cavalry.[17] With that transfer, the standard *Waffenfarbe* was supposed to be golden yellow, irrespective of the original branch color. Those orders were rescinded in 1939, thus restoring the original *Waffenfarben* for the forementioned entities. In 1939, a new *Waffenfarbe*—copper brown (*Kupferbraun*)—was introduced for reconnaissance forces, although the unpopular color was soon discontinued and the original colors restored.[18] The only theater where the copper brown color was actually used by most reconnaissance elements appears to have been in North Africa. Thus it is possible to see perfectly legitimate shoulder boards and straps with the same ciphers and numerals with differing *Waffenfarben*.

In addition to the generally confusing and often seemingly contradictory orders for the branch colors that were officially promulgated, there were a number of reasons why military personnel wore branch colors that were at odds with regulations of the time:

- Officers and senior noncommissioned officers often had an allegiance to a branch, particularly if they had been pre-war career soldiers. This was particularly true among cavalry personnel, who often remained "true" to their colors, regardless of what the uniform regulations called for with regard to *Waffenfarbe*. In some cases, they also dictated that their preferred *Waffenfarbe* be worn by all members of their unit or formation.
- Enlisted personnel were often issued whatever the required *Waffenfarbe* was whenever they entered basic training or attended professional development courses, which meant that they did not always have the *Waffenfarbe* that was being worn by their assigned units in the field when they arrived there.
- Supply shortages often forced the issue of shoulder straps (or the purchase of shoulder boards by officers) that did not necessarily match the Waffenfarben being worn by the unit or formation.

Prior to the start of the war, the unit of assignment of personnel could be identified by a combination of ciphers and numerals on their shoulder straps and boards. The Gothic-style A identified a reconnaissance element, while the K indicated a motorcycle infantry formation. In addition, the L would identify instructor personnel for a particular formation, based on its *Waffenfarbe*. Once the war started, operational security dictated the removal of any insignia that would reveal the designation of a formation.[19] These orders, which were generally, but not completely followed, were rescinded in 1944 by "order of the *Führer*," which again allowed the open display of unit-identifying insignia, although later-war shoulder straps and boards with identifying devices are rarely encountered.[20]

WAFFEN-SS

SS reconnaissance insignia is generally analogous to that of the army, although golden yellow was the standard *Waffenfarbe* for reconnaissance elements. Army-style ciphers—A, K, and L, for instance—were generally not worn, although formation distinctive ciphers, such as "LAH" or "DF," were also present on shoulder boards and straps piped in golden-yellow *Waffenfarbe* during the periods such devices were worn. A Latin-style "A" has also been seen on some shoulder straps and boards attributed to reconnaissance elements. Copper-brown *Waffenfarbe* was prescribed for wear at the same time as army regulations, although its usage was probably as inconsistent as that in the army.

LUFTWAFFE

Luftwaffe armored reconnaissance elements—for all intents and purposes, the *Hermann Göring* formations until the fielding of the corps armored reconnaissance battalions for the airborne corps toward the end of the war—wore rose-pink *Waffenfarbe* until 2 April 1943, when orders were issued changing the *Waffenfarbe* to golden yellow.[21]

EPHEMERA

While armored reconnaissance personnel wore the unauthorized but command-sanctioned cap badges that were increasingly encountered in the latter war years, the prewar traditions badges of the cavalry regiments, such as the *Preußischer Totenkopf* (Prussian Death's Head), the *Dragoner-bzw. Schwedter Adler* (Dragoon or Schwedt Eagle), and the *Braunscheiger-Totenkopf* (Braunschweig Death's Head) were generally only carried over to the cavalry force as it reinvented itself towards the end of the war. As such, personnel assigned to the armored reconnaissance elements of those regiments or brigades (divisions) were also authorized to wear those badges.[22] The only known reconnaissance element authorized the wear of the *Schwedter Adler* was *Kradschützen-Bataillon 3* of the *3. Panzer-Division*, where the golden-yellow *Waffenfarbe* was also worn, at least until 1939. In addition, *Aufklärungs-Abteilungen 33*, which traced its lineage back to *Kavallerie-Regiment 6*, also persisted in wearing the cap badge, as did a later formation, *Panzeraufklärungs-Abteilung 115*.

The only known cap badge worn exclusively within a unit was a stylized design of an 8-wheel armored car that was worn by some personnel of the *Panzer-Aufklärungs-Lehr-Abteilung* of the *Panzer-Lehr-Division*. Indeed, the only known photographs to exist of this are of only one individual, so it may have been a purely personal whim.

This motorcycle infantryman from *Kradschützen-Bataillon 1* of the *1. Panzer-Division* wears a *geschmückte Feldbluse* (ornamented field blouse), with embroidered K/1's.

This scout from either *Aufklärungs-Abteilung 7* of the *4. Panzer-Division* (rose-pink *Waffenfarbe*) or *Aufklärungs-Regiment 7* of the *2. leichte Division* (golden-yellow *Waffenfarbe*) has probably had his shoulder straps with the A/7's added by the photographer at the studio, since they are so small in comparison to the *geschmückte Feldbluse* he is wearing.

Top left: This reconnaissance soldier wears an M40 field blouse with unusual shoulder straps—the ciphers and numerals are metal, as opposed to embroidered, as one would expect for enlisted personnel. His battalion—*Aufklärungs-Abteilung 32*—was part of the *32. Infanterie-Division*, which, as a first-wave division, had an armored car section in its heavy company. GLEN HENDRICKS **Top right:** This serious-looking scout was assigned to *Aufklärungs-Abteilung 3* of the *3. Panzer Division*. Examples of both rose-pink and golden-yellow *Waffenfarben* have been encountered because of the history of the formation, which traced back to 1934 (*Kraftfahrabteilung Wünsdorf*).

A scout from *Aufklärungs-Abteilung 1 (mot)* of the *3. Panzer-Division* poses atop a knocked-out BT series light tank while an *Sd.Kfz. 223* passes around the obstacle in the Soviet Union, 1941.

A long column of prisoners is escorted to the rear by motorcycle infantry of *Aufklärungs-Abteilung 3*, a sight that was relatively common in the first summer of the campaign in the Soviet Union.

Knocked-out Soviet supply vehicles line the route of advance.

Top left: This scout wears a second-pattern *Panzer* tunic, easily distinguishable from the first-pattern tunic by its wider collar. All of the early tunics were collar-piped in the appropriate *Waffenfarbe* for the formation. **Top right:** This scout, also wearing a second-pattern *Panzer* tunic is believed to be from *Panzer Aufklärungs-Abteilung 10* of the *10. Panzer-Division* as evidenced by what appears to be embroidered A/10's on his shoulder straps.

This senior NCO wears the unpopular beret/crash helmet combination, probably around 1935–36, as no national insignia is seen above the cockade. At the time *Aufklärungs-Abteilung 6 (mot)*, to which this photograph is attributed, was a separate battalion, thus making it most likely the soldier had rose-pink *Waffenfarbe*. When the battalion became part of the *1. leichte Division* in 1938, it switched its *Waffenfarbe* to golden yellow.

Top left: This scout from *Aufklärungs-Abteilung 2 (mot)* of the *12. Panzer-Division* wears a first-pattern *Panzer* tunic, which must be considered somewhat unusual since the battalion was not formed until 1941 and the first-pattern jackets were phased out of service in the mid-1930s. **Top right:** This scout most likely was assigned to *Aufklärungs-Regiment 7* of the *2. leichte Division*, given the lightness to the color of his embroidered A/7's and the other piping seen.

These men in front of the *Sd.Kfz. 232 (Fu) (8 Rad)* appear to have donned denim work uniform trousers, which would have been considerably cooler than the black wool ones. JIM HALEY

The crew of an *Sd.Kfz. 263 (Fu) (8 Rad)* taking a smoke break in front of its vehicle. JIM HALEY

This scout poses with the popular turtleneck sweater, which helped to combat the cold in the open and unheated vehicles.

A crew poses with its *Sd.Kfz. 223*, with the frame antenna both lowered and raised. Of interest is the *Panzer* jacket seen on the left front of the vehicle. It appears to have a radio operator's badge on the upper left sleeve above the rank chevron. Normally, these were placed on the lower portion of the sleeve, about 13 centimeters from the cuff. JIM HALEY

This *SS-Panzeraufklärer* wears an army second-pattern jacket without collar piping and insignia distinctive to the reconnaissance elements of the *Leibstandarte*. The *Waffenfarbe* would have been golden yellow, including the *LAH* cipher on the shoulder strap. The scout also wears an early *Allgemeine SS* cap, to which a *soutache* has been applied as well as a more standard *Totenkopf* used by the *SS-Verfügungstruppe*.

Below: This SS soldier training on an *Sd.Kfz. 222* appears to be wearing an army-style *Panzer* uniform.

These scouts from *SS-Standarte "Deutschland"* enjoy a breather while on an exercise or at a gunnery range. In addition to the distinctive *Deutschland* cuff titles, the men also have a large stylized "D" on their shoulder straps and what appears to be twisted silver and black piping on their shoulder straps and, in some cases, the collars as well. The beret/crash helmets are standard army issue; distinctive SS insignia have been applied. JIM HALEY

Waterways crisscrossed the landmass of the Soviet Union and presented an obstacle about every 25 kilometers, on average. These scouts are lucky since they do not have to participate in a forced river crossing, which is one of the more difficult military operations to execute.

A *Panzer III* precedes an *Sd.Kfz. 231 (8 Rad)* and *Sd.Kfz. 232 (Fu) (8 Rad)* across an engineer bridge.

Below: These scouts from an unidentified *Aufklärungs-Abteilung (mot)* wear the first-pattern *Panzer* tunic and the crash helmet/beret.

This scout celebrates his wedding by wearing his second-pattern *Panzer* uniform without collar piping but with a distinctive "A" on the shoulder straps. (*Unteroffizier* was the highest rank authorized to still have embroidered ciphers and numerals.)

The vastness of the Soviet Union and its seemingly unending steppes came as both a surprise and a shock to many German soldiers. Here the crew of a Horch prime mover performs maintenance on its vehicle as armored car crews look on.

Uniforms, Insignia, and Ephemera

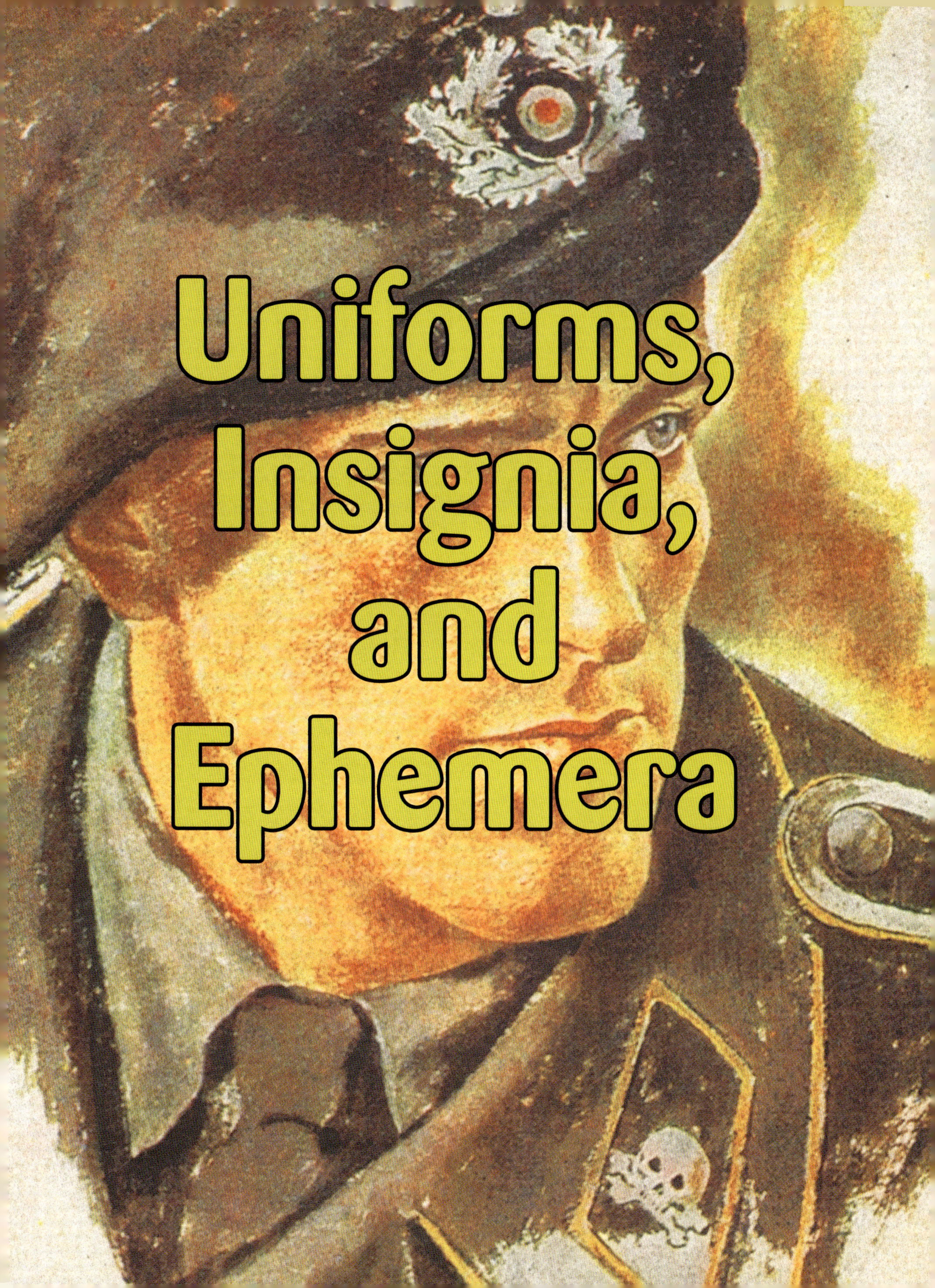

WH-66049

Prewar notions of the motorized reconnaissance forces are captured on the opposite page and above. With the exception of the scout signaling from the *Sd.Kfz. 231 (6 Rad)* on the far left, all are postcards that were sold in soldier canteens all across Germany. The remaining illustration is from a cigarette card collecting set. CIGARETTE CARD AND POSTCARD COURTESY OF MICHAEL H. PRUETT Seen to the right is a video capture of relatively rare color footage of reconnaissance forces. The officer wears an old-style "crusher" cap and golden yellow piping on his first-pattern *Panzer* jacket. The grayscale insert shows how difficult it can be to try to pinpoint the *Waffenfarbe* seen in black and white images, since the main colors used—rose pink (*rosa*), golden yellow (*goldgelb*), and copper brown (*kupferbraun*)—all look about the same when not rendered in full color.

More color video captures with comparison grayscale inserts. Of particular interest is the image above of the scout riding on the Panhard armored car. His black cap appears to be piped in copper brown, thus making it among the rarest pieces of headgear produced. While it cannot be verified with certainty, it appears that the *Kradschütze* on the left is also wearing copper-brown-piped shoulder straps. The next four full-color images are of *Aufklärungs-Abteilung 29 (mot)* of the *29. Infanterie-Division (mot)* in 1942 prior to and during its participation in the summer offensive of Field Army Group South, culminating in the disaster at Stalingrad. In the top image, a senior NCO sizes up a formation, while an officer pays final respects at the gravesite of a fallen comrade in the bottom image. All of the scouts and personnel in field-gray uniforms in these images have golden-yellow *Waffenfarbe*. **Overleaf**: Armored cars of the battalion, led by an *Sd.Kfz. 232 (Fu) (8 Rad)* and followed by an *Sd.Kfz.* 222, cross one of the innumerable waterways of the Soviet Union on an engineer bridge. IMAGES OF AUFKLÄRUNGS-ABTEILUNG 29 (MOT) COURTESY OF JASON MARK, LEAPING HORSEMAN BOOKS

Above: In this final image from *Aufklärungs-Abteilung 29 (mot)*, an officer bestows medals on deserving personnel, in this case an *Oberfeldwebel* wearing a second-pattern *Panzer* jacket without collar piping. The *Oberfeldwebel* was also a qualified radio operator, as indicated by the signals *Blitz* in golden yellow on his left upper sleeve. COURTESY OF JASON MARK, LEAPING HORSEMAN BOOKS **Below and opposite page**: Prewar and training footage of scouts most likely assigned to *Aufklärungs-Abteilung 92 (mot)* of the *20. Panzer-Division*. Both *Aufklärungs-Abteilung 37 (mot)* and this battalion were issued captured French Panhard armored cars after the fall of France. The tactical symbol seen on the Panhards looks like the horizontal "E" used by the *3. Panzer-Division* during the campaign in the West, but that division changed its insignia shortly afterwards. It was at that point that *Generalmajor* Stumpff, the former commander of the *3. Panzer-Division*, who was assuming command of the *20. Panzer-Division*, decided to use the tactical insignia of his former division. The *20. Panzer-Division* continued using this insignia in the early stages of the campaign in the East. In the earliest images, German armored cars are seen maneuvering, while Panhards predominate after the fall of France. The members of this battalion all wear golden-yellow *Waffenfarbe*.

The final sequence of video captures shows the battalion in the early days of *Operation Barbarossa*.

This sequence comes from the *Panzer-Aufklärungs-Lehr-Abteilung* of the *Panzer-Lehr-Division* while it prepares to rail back to Germany from its training time in Hungary in the early part of 1944. The personnel seen in the rest of the footage all wear golden-yellow *Waffenfarbe*. VIDEO COURTESY OF GARY BEADLE

Above: Examples of 𝔄 and 𝔎 ciphers in the four main *Waffenfarben* associated with reconnaissance and motorcycle infantry elements: rose pink (*rosa*), golden yellow (*goldgelb*), meadow green (also referred to as lime green) (*wiesengrün*), and copper brown (*kupferbraun*). INSIGNIA TOP LEFT, TOP RIGHT, BOTTOM LEFT, AND BOTTOM RIGHT COURTESY OF CHRIS VARRICHIO; THIRD FROM LEFT ON BOTTOM ROW, GLEN HENDRICKS

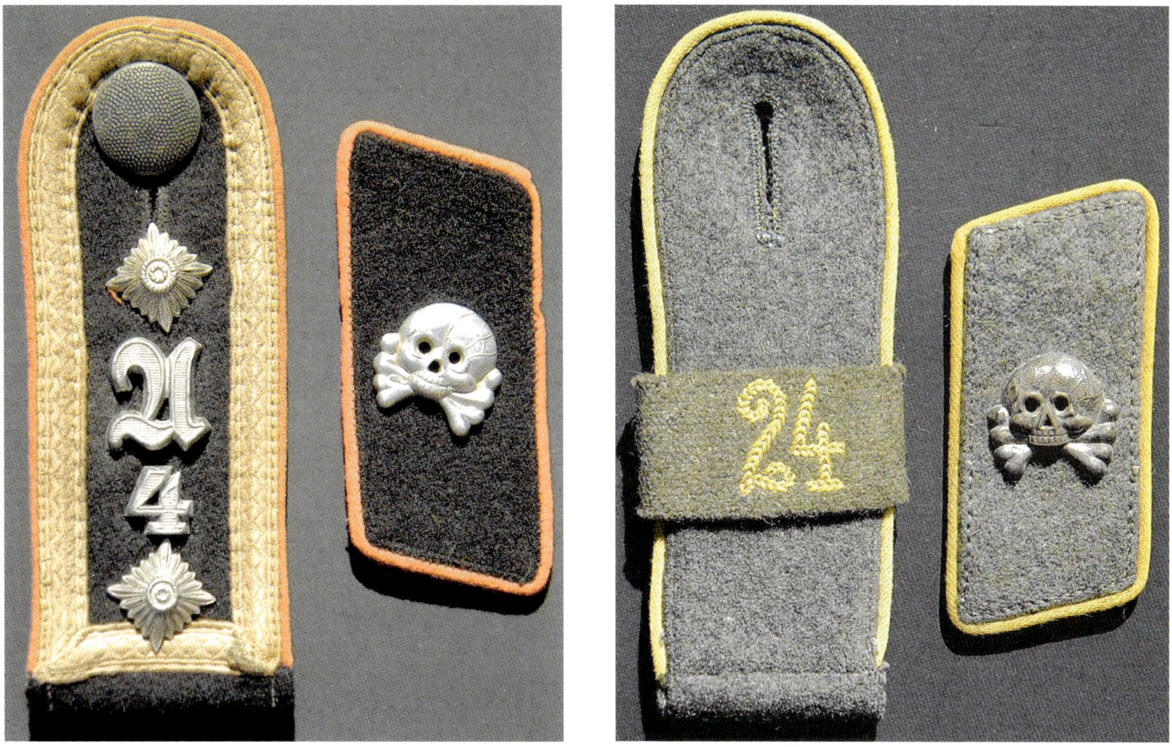

Below: Sample pairings of armored vehicle crewmen insignia in rose pink and golden yellow. The pink set is for *Aufklärungs-Abteilung 4 (mot)* of the *1. Panzer-Division* and the golden-yellow set is for *Panzer-Aufklärungs-Abteilung 24* of the reconstituted (post-1943) *24. Panzer-Division*. BOTH SETS COURTESY OF CHRIS VARRICHIO

The matched pairings continue above with enlisted slip-on straps in meadow green *Waffenfarbe* for an unknown *Kradschützen* formation and in copper brown for *Aufklärungs-Abteilung 7 (mot)* of the *4. Panzer-Division.* SET ON THE LEFT COURTESY OF SCOTT PRITCHETT AND, ON THE RIGHT, CHRIS VARRICHIO **Above**: Although copper brown assumed to be a rare *Waffenfarbe*, the color has been encountered on a variety of insignia, as evidenced here. Care must be taken not to confuse it with the early army signals brown of the mid 1930's or the later brown of construction engineers. Both tend to be passed off by militaria dealers as reconnaissance insignia, when they are not. The situation is not helped by the fact that the shades of copper brown vary considerably from one manufacturer and dye lot to the next, although the "preferred" shade is somewhat akin to a deeper shade of the rose pink of armored forces. INSIGNIA COURTESY OF CHRIS VARRICHIO

In the top row, the wide variety of *Waffenfarben* used for the same branch can be seen in these examples from motorcycle infantry elements. The same applies to the shoulder straps from reconnaissance elements shown in the bottom row.

EXAMPLES PROVIDED BY CHRIS VARRICHIO

More examples from the motorcycle infantry are seen above, including a very early one that was worn in the early 1930's, before *Waffenfarben* were worn on shoulder straps. **Below**: Individual examples of shoulder boards and straps from reconnaissance battalions. Here: *Aufklärungs-Abteilungen 2–4 (mot)*, representing the *12. Panzer-Division*, the *3. Panzer-Division*, and the *1. Panzer-Division*. The 𝔄/2 and the 𝔄/3 (next to last in the row) straps are both on black badge cloth, designed for wear on the *Panzer* uniform. The 𝔄/4 for the *Leutnant* could have been worn on either the black *Panzer* tunic or field-gray uniforms. The remaining straps are either sew-in for dress uniforms or slip-on for field uniforms. FROM LEFT TO RIGHT, INSIGNIA COURTESY OF GLEN HENDRICKS, SCOTT PRITCHETT, CHRIS VARRICHIO, GLEN HENDRICKS [2X], AND CHRIS VARRICHIO

Top Row: This row sees the addition of *Aufklärungs-Abteilung 5* of the *2. Panzer-Division* (rose-pink set for an *Unteroffizier*) and, most likely, *Aufklärungs-Abteilung 5* of the *5. Infanterie-Division* (golden-yellow set). The 𝔄/4 set for an *Oberfeldwebel* is on black badge cloth for the *Panzer* uniform. All of the remaining examples are of the sew-in, field-gray variety, indicating they were intended for dress uniforms. FROM LEFT TO RIGHT: CHRIS VARRICHIO, GLEN HENDRICKS, GARY BEADLE, AND GLEN HENDRICKS [2X] **Middle Row**: This row sees the addition of *Aufklärungs-Abteilung 6* of the *1. leichte Division* and then the *6. Panzer-Division*. The straps from this battalion with the pink *Waffenfarbe* are probably from the period it was initially formed and before it joined the light division, when the *Waffenfarbe* turned to golden yellow. The *Oberfeldwebel* straps in golden yellow are on black badge cloth. These could have been for an NCO assigned to the armored car section of the *5. Infanterie-Division*, but it is also possible that they belonged to an armored car crewman in *Reiter-Regiment 5* of the *4. Kavallerie-Brigade*, although all recorded instances of armored cars in the brigade were in the brigade's armored reconnaissance battalion, or to an NCO of *Panzer-Aufklärungs-Abteilung 5* of the *5. Panzer-Division*. FROM LEFT TO RIGHT: TOM SUTER, GLEN HENDRICKS [2X], CHRIS VARRICHIO, AND GLEN HENDRICKS **Bottom Row**: The confusing state of *Waffenfarben* is well represented by these early *Feldbluse* shoulder straps that started out in rose pink and ended up golden yellow. It is not known whether this was an austerity measure on the part of the soldier or unit or was done at the factory, when excess stock of rose-pink 𝔄/6 straps were no longer needed.

Top Row: Examples of shoulder straps and boards from either *Aufklärungs-Regiment 7* of the *2. leichte Division* or *Aufklärungs-Abteilung 7 (mot)* of the *4. Panzer-Division* and *Aufklärungs-Regiment 8* of the *3. leichte Division* or *Aufklärungs-Abteilung 8 (mot)* of the *5. Panzer-Division*. The early straps in rosa *Waffenfarbe* are probably from the early activation period of the formations (as battalions), whereas the golden-yellow straps and boards are most likely from *Aufklärungs-Regiment 7*. If so, then the board for an *Oberst*, could only have belonged to Walter Neumann-Silkow, the only commander of that brigade and a later recipient of the Knight's Cross to the Iron Cross. The enlisted straps to the same regiment are both on black badge cloth, indicating they were in the 2nd Battalion, which was the regiment's armored car battalion. FROM LEFT TO RIGHT: GLEN HENDRICKS, ROBERT J. EDWARDS, GLEN HENDRICKS, AND CHRIS VARRICHIO [2X] **Middle Row**: *Aufklärungs-Regiment 9* of the *4. leichte Division* and *Aufklärungs-Abteilung 9* of the *9. Panzer-Division* join the line-up in this row. The set of insignia on the far right is for the *Panzer* uniform, thus most likely from the reconnaissance battalion assigned to the *9. Panzer-Division*. FROM LEFT TO RIGHT: GLEN HENDRICKS, GLEN HENDRICKS, AND CHRIS VARRICHIO Insignia set for an unidentified officer (pictured) of *Panzer-Aufklärungs-Abteilung 14* of the *14. Panzer-Division*. COURTESY OF GLEN HENDRICKS

Top Row: Four more battalions join the line-up. First, a set of insignia on black cloth for an *Unteroffizier* and officer candidate of *Panzer-Aufklärungs-Abteilung 16* of the *16. Panzer-Division*. Some may argue that the light yellow on the shoulder straps is actually the lemon yellow (*zitronengelb*) of signals, but the wear and tear on the straps suggest the wearer was exposed to the elements in the field a great deal. *Aufklärungs-Abteilung 17* and *19* belonged to the armored divisions with the same numerical designator. Both of these straps are also on black, indicating wear by armored scout crews. The final straps pictured in this row are from either *Aufklärungs-Abteilung 20* of the *20. Infanterie-Division (mot)* (in the first instance) or *Panzer-Aufklärungs-Abteilung 20* of the *20. Panzer-Division* (in the second instance). FROM LEFT TO RIGHT: ROBERT J. EDWARDS, GLEN HENDRICKS [3X], AND GARY BEADLE **Middle Row**: Three more reconnaissance battalions are introduced in this row, with the 𝔄/24 straps coming from *Panzer-Aufklärungs-Abteilung 24* of the *24. Panzer-Division*, the 𝔄/27 straps from *Panzer-Aufklärungs-Abteilung 17* the *17. Panzer-Division*, and the 𝔄/29 straps from the *29. Infanterie-Division (mot)*. FROM LEFT TO RIGHT: GLEN HENDRICKS, EX ROBERT J. EDWARDS, CHRIS VARRICHIO [2X], AND GARY BEADLE **Bottom Row**: *Aufklärungs-Abteilung 33* was part of the *33. Infanterie-Division* before the division was reorganized and redesignated as the *15. Panzer-Division*. It was one of the few battalions to actually use copper brown for a while as its *Waffenfarbe*. The *A/34* straps are most likely from the *34. Infanterie-Division*, although it would not have had an armored reconnaissance component organic to it by the time these straps were introduced. FROM LEFT TO RIGHT: GLEN HENDRICKS [2X] AND GARY BEADLE [2X]

Top Row: Two more numbered formations are illustrated before moving to named formations. *Aufklärungs-Abteilung 37 (mot)* was the reconnaissance battalion of the *7. Panzer-Division. Aufklärungs-Abteilung 246* was part of the *246. Infanterie-Division.* It had no known armored reconnaissance assets. The reconnaissance assets of the *Großdeutschland* formations consistently wore golden-yellow *Waffenfarbe* through the years. All three enlisted sets seen here and in the next row were intended for wear with the black or field-gray *Panzer*-style uniforms. FROM LEFT TO RIGHT: GLEN HENDRICKS, GARY BEADLE, SCOTT PRITCHETT, EX ROBERT J. EDWARDS, AND CHRIS VARRICHIO **Middle Row**: *Großdeutschland* is joined by the *Aufklärungs-Lehr-Abteilung* in this row. FROM LEFT TO RIGHT: CHRIS VARRICHIO, SCOTT PRITCHETT [2X], CHRIS VARRICHIO [2X] **Bottom Row**: Another set of insignia intended for wear on the field-gray version of the *Panzer* uniform, followed by examples of shoulder straps and boards intended for or worn in tropical areas. The middle three sets of insignia are piped in copper brown, each displaying a slightly different shade of the color. The last strap is truly rare, a tropical strap with golden-yellow piping, one of only several in collections. FROM LEFT TO RIGHT: CHRIS VARRICHIO, SCOTT PRITCHETT, CHRIS VARRICHIO, EX ROBERT J. EDWARDS, AND GARY BEADLE

Insignia related to motorized infantry formations are presented on this page. **Top Row**: A “generic” motorcycle infantry *Hauptmann* board is followed by samples of straps and boards from *Kradschützen-Bataillone 1* and *2* of the first two armored divisions. Almost all straps and boards in collections from these battalions have rose-pink *Waffenfarbe*, but there is always an exception, as illustrated by the board for the *Leutnant* in *Kradschützen-Bataillon 2*. FROM LEFT TO RIGHT: SCOTT PRITCHETT, GLEN HENDRICKS, TOM SUTER, GLEN HENDRICKS [2X], CHRIS VARRICHIO [3X] **Middle Row**: *Kradschützen-Bataillon 3* belonged to the *3. Panzer-Division*, while *Kradschützen-Bataillon 4* was part of the *24. Panzer-Division*. In the case of the K/6 insignia, they were either *Kradschützen-Abteilung 6* of *Kavallerie-Schützen-Regiment 4* of the *1. leichte Division* (most likely in the first instance) or *Kradschützen-Bataillon 6* of the *6. Panzer-Division* (most likely in the latter instance). The *Oberst* boards are a bit of a mystery, inasmuch as the highest rank to command a motorcycle infantry battalion was usually *Oberstleutnant*. FROM LEFT TO RIGHT: GLEN HENDRICKS [2X], CHRIS VARRICHIO, EX ROBERT J. EDWARDS [2X], CHRIS VARRICHIO, AND GLEN HENDRICKS **Bottom Row**: K/16 was part of the *16. Panzer-Division*, while K/55 was assigned to the *5. Panzer-Division* and K/64 to the *14. Panzer-Division*. The latter strap is the only one shown here that is piped in copper brown. FROM LEFT TO RIGHT: GLEN HENDRICKS, CHRIS VARRICHIO, EX ROBERT J. EDWARDS, GLEN HENDRICKS, AND TOM SUTER

Several examples of unique insignia worn by reconnaissance and motorcycle infantry personnel are shown on this page. On the upper left are two officer boards with "home-made" camouflage bands. The first example for a *Hauptmann* is Army hard-edged "water" pattern camouflage; the *Leutnant* board is made out of tropical material and still has an 𝔄 underneath. EX ROBERT J. EDWARDS The 𝔎/23 board is unique in a number of respects. The 𝔎 has been removed although a "ghost" image remains. The officer who owned these must have been especially frugal—or could not find a set of boards in the appropriate *Waffenfarbe*—so he added copper-brown piping over the original rose-pink piping. This was not totally unique, however, inasmuch as some other officer boards have been seen over the years where this had been done. COURTESY OF CHRIS VARRICHIO The *Totenkopf* collar tab for an armored scout has also a *Braunschweiger*-style death's head mounted on it. This has been seen on pink-piped collar tabs before, but never in golden yellow. The soldier who wore them is also pictured. COURTESY OF SCOTT PRITCHETT

Above is an example of *SS* collar tabs piped in golden yellow. This has been seen in rose pink before, but never in golden yellow. The tabs are attributed to a member of the *"Das Reich"* reconnaissance battalion. The authors have also seen this same practice being done in a period image of members of the *Totenkopf* reconnaissance battalion—albeit with vertical skulls—but they were unable to obtain permission to publish the photograph. COURTESY OF MARTIN STILES OF HANNAH'S REICH Finally, a collar tab in the shape of one designed for wear on the *Panzer* uniform, but made out of tropical material and featuring golden-yellow wool piping. These were worn on the lapels of the tropical four-pocket field blouses of some members of the reconnaissance battalion of the *10. Panzer-Division*, when it was dispatched to North Africa late in 1942. This particular example was captured and catalogued by a U.S. Army intelligence officer, as evidenced by the writing on the back. COURTESY OF GARY BEADLE

FW

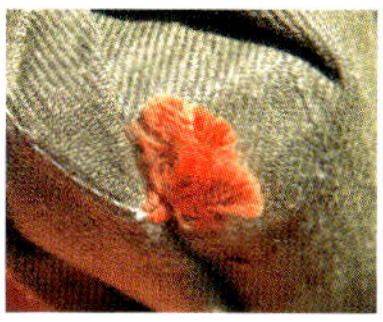

Opposite Page: Example of a privately purchased black officer's overseas cap with golden-yellow *soutache* with the owner's initials sewn into the lining of the cap. **This page**: A tropical enlisted overseas cap with copper-brown *Waffenfarbe*. Most of these caps in collections were never issued, although completely authentic. Note that the copper-brown color is substantially at variance from the sun-bleached copper brown seen on the tropical enlisted shoulder straps.

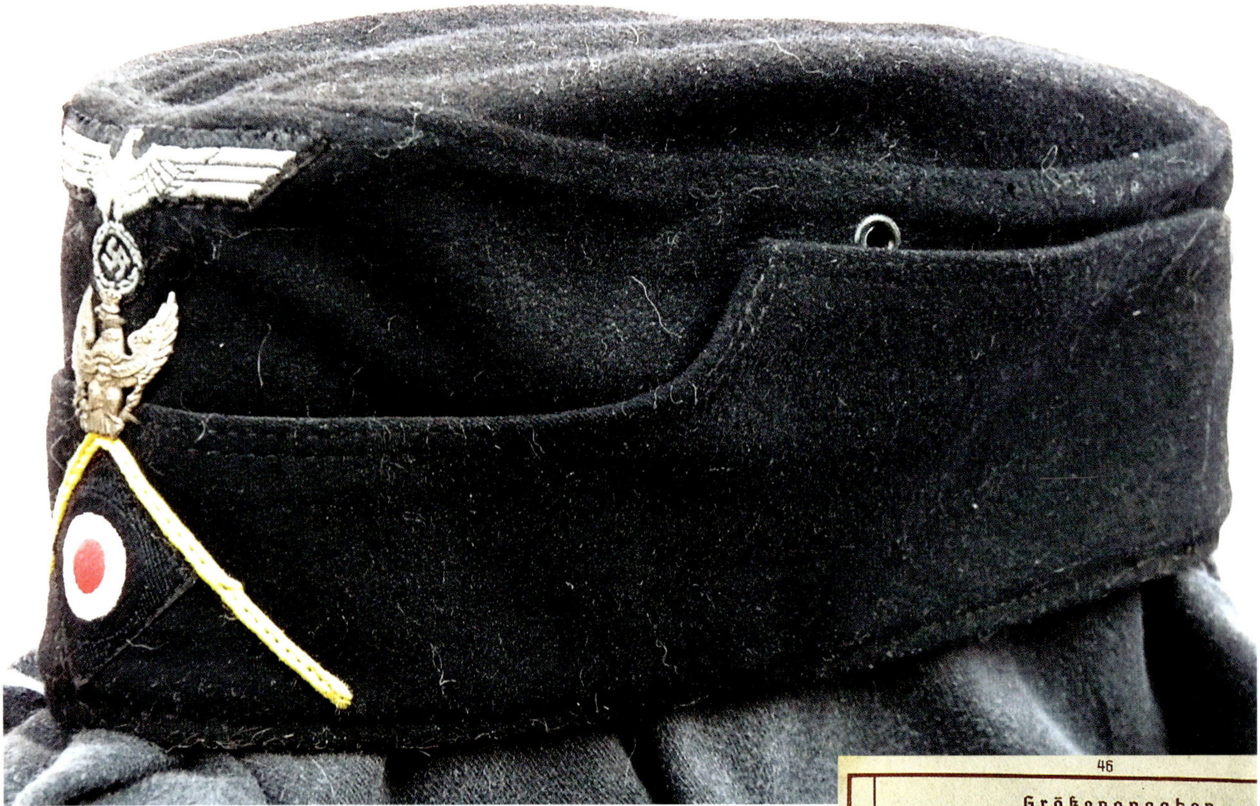

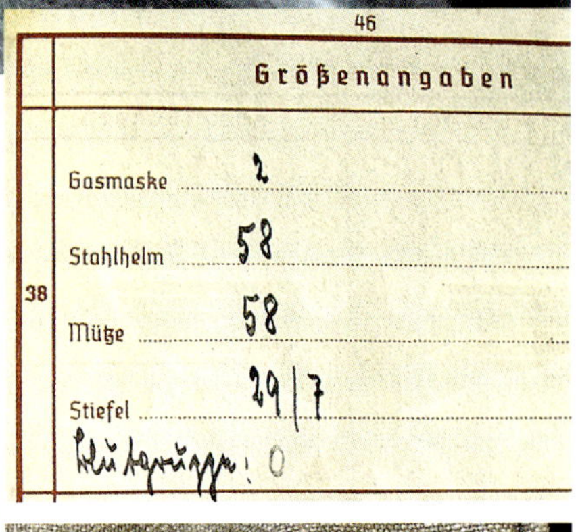

46

Größenangaben

38

Gasmaske 2

Stahlhelm 58

Mütze 58

Stiefel 29/7

Blutgruppe: 0

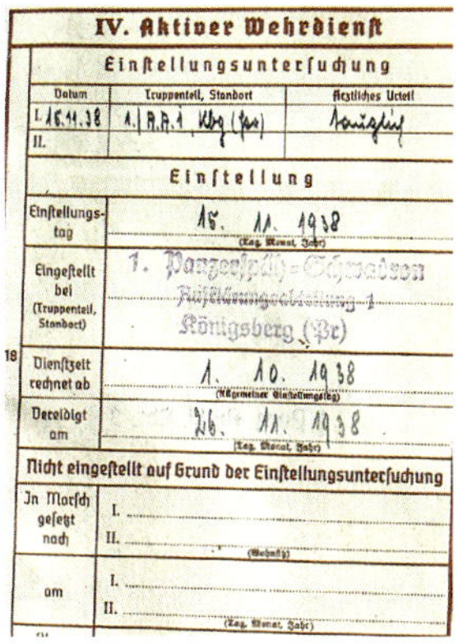

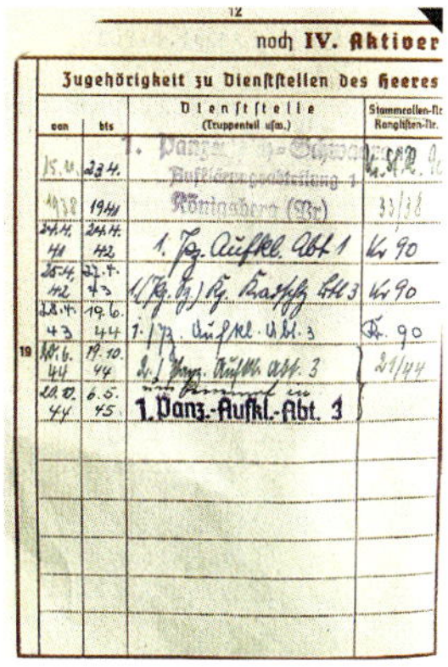

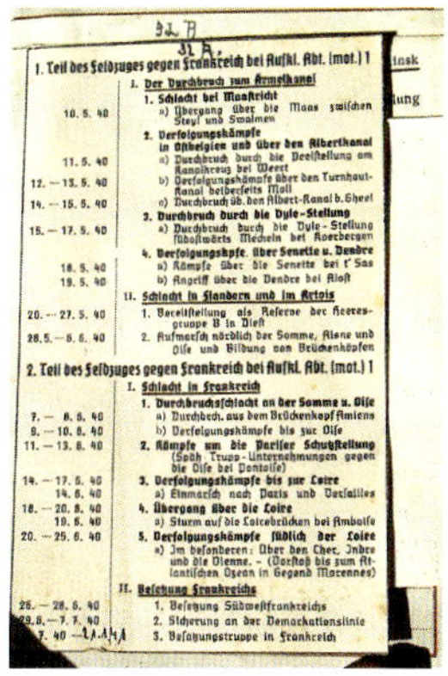

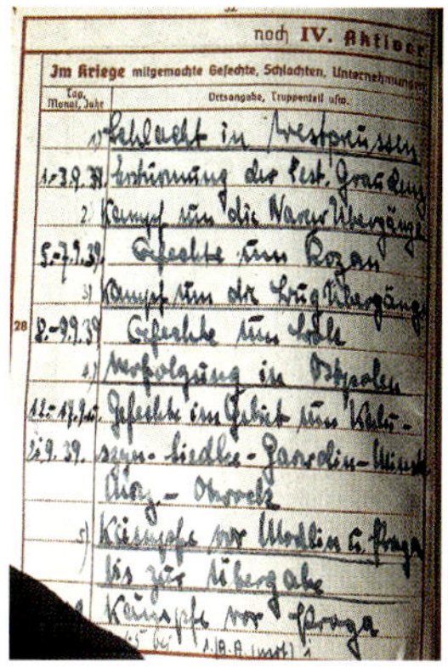

Artifacts that belonged to belonged to armored scout Gerhard Holzweiß, who was originally assigned to *Aufklärungs-Abteilung 1 (mot)* and then reassigned to *Panzer-Aufklärungs-Abteilung 3* of the *3. Panzer-Division*. While in the latter assignment, Holzweiß was authorized to wear the cavalry *Schwedter* eagle, as evidenced in the period images of him. The pages from his *Wehrpaß*—literally, a "military passport"—show his units of assignment, participation in operations, and, on the last page, his cap size, which corresponds to the size in the cap pictured. In the image on the right, we see Holzweiß as a recruit assigned to *Aufklärungs-Abteilung 1 (mot)*. The images of Holzweiß on the next page show him in his original battalion and then after reassignment to *Panzer-Aufklärungs-Abteilung 3*. In one of the images, he also wears a *Panzer* tunic with the numerals *33* on the straps. There is no way to explain this except that they may have been a prop lent him at the photography studio, where portraits with all sorts of odd uniform combinations can often be seen. Note also the wear of the *Schwedter* eagle *above* the national insignia on his visor cap, certainly a violation of regulations! CAP COURTESY OF JOHN SUPRIN, REMAINDER ROBERT J. EDWARDS

Opposite Page: Not all scouts and reconnaissance personnel wore the black *Panzer* uniform. In fact, most did not. To that end, field-gray caps can also be attributed to reconnaissance and motorcycle infantry formations in some instances. On the far left is a nice example of an officer's *M38* field cap withy golden yellow *soutache* and a *Schwedter* eagle. EX ROBERT J. EDWARDS On the right is an example of an enlisted overseas cap that has copper-brown *Waffenfarbe* and light infantry—*Jäger*—badge on the left side. Since light infantry formations were not authorized any motorized reconnaissance elements, it is hard to explain how the badge and the *Waffenfarbe* came together on one cap. COURTESY OF GARY BEADLE On this page are two caps from one individual, Hans-Joachim von Sell, a Knight's Cross recipient and successful postwar German author. Sell was awarded the Knight's Cross on 14 April 1945, while assigned duties as the commander of *Panzer-Aufklärungs-Abteilung 8* of the *8. Panzer-Division*. Like many reconnaissance officers, he probably had a background in the cavalry, and the "crusher" may have been worn by him earlier in his career. COURTESY OF GLEN MCINNIS

47
96
57
61
B 36

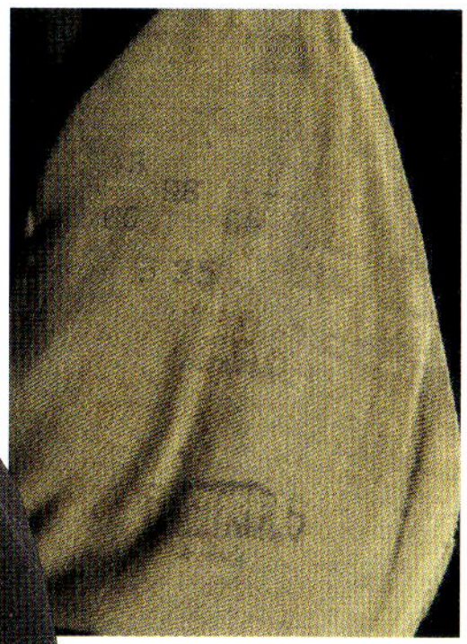

Two views of the first-pattern *Panzer* tunic. On the **opposite page** is a uniform worn by a scout assigned to the reconnaissance schoolhouse at Krampnitz. The interior stampings indicated the jacket was issued from the supply room of the armored car troop of the testing and training battalion. COURTESY OF JOHN SUPRIN On this page is a jacket from a scout assigned to two different reconnaissance formations, as indicated by the unit markings in his jacket from *Aufklärungs-Regiment 6* and *Aufklärungs-Abteilung 8*, both formations that wore golden yellow. The jacket, which was produced and issued in 1935, originally had rose-pink piping, which was probably removed when the scout had to change his *Waffenfarbe*. Several features indicate this jacket was worn in combat operations and the field: first, there is a snap fastener at the top of the front panel to facilitate access to the interior pocket; second, the lining has been extensively repaired, evidence of years of hard use.

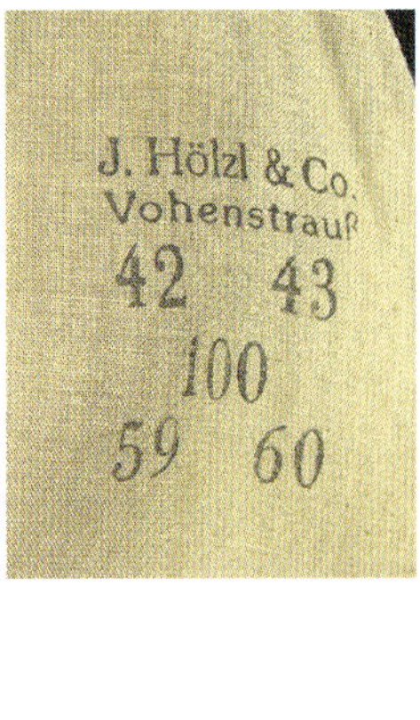
J. Hölzl & Co.
Vohenstrauß
42 43
100
59 60

9

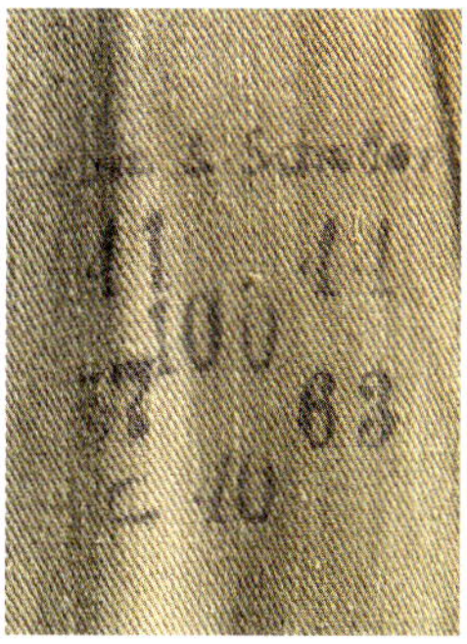

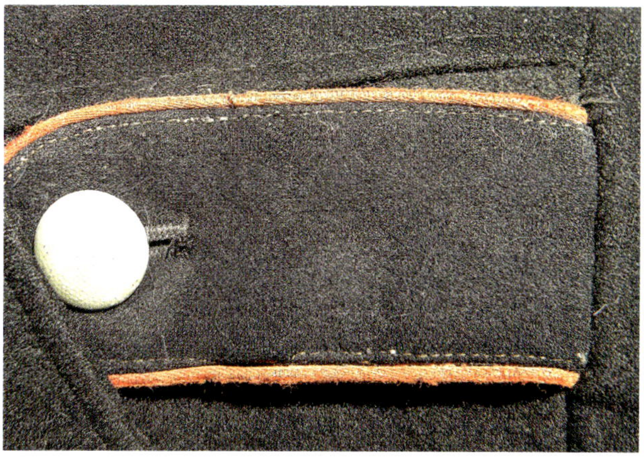

On the **opposite page** is a second-pattern *Panzer* tunic that was privately purchased by an officer in the headquarters of *Aufklärungs-Regiment 9* of the *4. leichte Division* or its 2nd Battalion, which was the armored car battalion. When the jacket was originally purchased, there was still a ticket stub for the movies in a town in the *Sudetenland* that the regiment was garrisoned in in 1939. **This page**: Another second-pattern jacket, this time without collar piping but having copper brown insignia. The *Waffenfarbe* was hand-applied after replacing the original rose-pink piping on the insignia. There is also a shadow on the lower left sleeve, which is the location where an *Afrika* campaign sleeve band would have been worn, leading one to the supposition that this scout may have been assigned to either *Aufklärungs-Abteilung 3* or *33* in North Africa.

KORPS

The *M41* first-pattern tropical four-pocket tunic on the **opposite page** has straps with copper brown *Waffenfarbe*. North Africa was the only theater where reconnaissance assets widely used the *kupferbraune Waffenfarbe.* EX ROBERT J. EDWARDS On **this page**, we see an example of the widely worn blue work uniform for crews of armored vehicles. It was widely assumed that these were phased out at the beginning of the war, but unissued stock was recently found with Munich depot stamps dating from 1943.

The reed-green and mouse-gray special-purpose uniforms were originally intended solely for armored car personnel, but the lighter-weight jackets and trousers caught on with crews of armored vehicles in general and thus found in a variety of units. The first-pattern tunics are shown on these two pages, while the second-pattern jackets and trousers with the distinctive outer patch pocket are shown **overleaf**. The reed-green version came in herringbone twill, while the mouse gray version was manufactured out of a cotton duck material. The jackets are similar in appearance to the second-pattern *Panzer* jacket, but have a number of different design details. No insignia other than the national insignia and sleeve rank insignia were supposed to be worn on these jackets, but many soldiers added shoulder boards or straps in the field and, sometimes, collar tabs, as seen here. BOTH JACKETS EX ROBERT J. EDWARDS

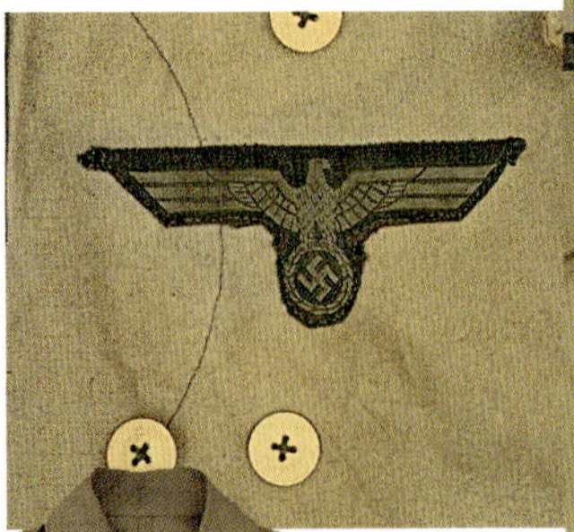

The *SS* also had its own unique style for its *Panzer* uniform articles. Because unit-unique insignia was not worn on their uniforms, except in the case of very early uniforms or the *Leibstandarte*, it is difficult to trace uniforms to particular types of formations, unless there is some provenance with the item. Shown here are two enlisted *SS Panzer*-style tunics that were worn by crewmembers of armored reconnaissance units. BOTH EX ROBERT J. EDWARDS

An example of the field-gray assault-gun or *Panzer*-style tunic, as worn by crews of scout or reconnaissance vehicles. EX ROBERT J. EDWARDS

A nice example of a second-pattern *Panzer* jacket as worn by an officer-candidate scout assigned to *Panzer-Aufklärungs-Abteilung "Großdeutschland."* COURTESY OF SCOTT PRITCHETT

Panzer tunic and ephemera related to Rolf Kaestel, who was assigned to *Panzer-Aufklärungs-Abteilung 7*. He served in *Aufklärungs-Abteilung 7 (mot)* as a reservist before the war and latter was commissioned a *Leutnant* in the same battalion after the war started. His officer's *Panzer* tunic is made out of gabardine, as are the collar tabs, a feature often identified with this particular manufacturer (*DEKAWE* in Frankfurt am Main). Additional photographs from his albums are to be found in Chapter 5.

1941 1942

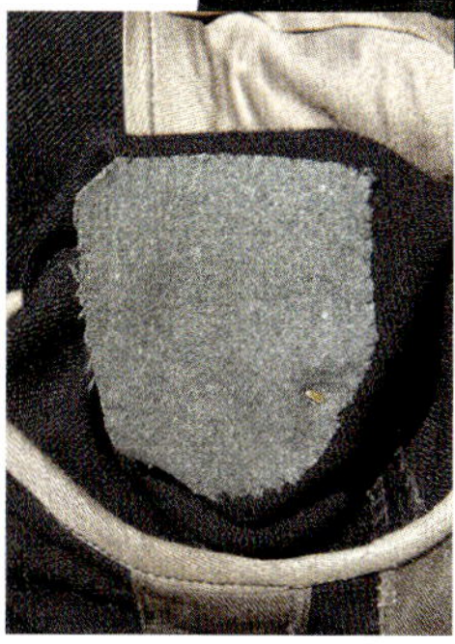

Wehrdienst-
Ehrendienst
Erinnerungen an meine Dienstzeit

DEKAWE
41 96
61
F.41

This collar-piped second-pattern *Panzer* belonged to Gustav Kraenkel, who had been assigned to *Kradschützen-Bataillon* and *Panzer-Aufklärungs-Abteilung 23* of the *23. Panzer-Division*. He ended the war in Berlin, where he commanded the security detachment for the *OKW*. He was given orders to hold off the advancing Soviet armored forces in the woods near Zossen in late April 1945. No match for the heavy Soviet armor with his reconnaissance elements, his force was decimated. COURTESY OF JOHN SUPRIN

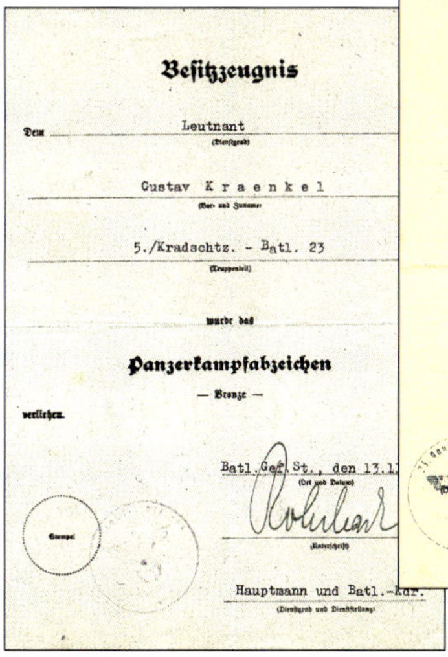

Besitzzeugnis

Dem Leutnant (Dienstgrad)

Gustav Kraenkel (Vor- und Zuname)

5./Kradschtz. - Batl. 23 (Truppenteil)

wurde das

Panzerkampfabzeichen

— Bronze —

verliehen.

Batl.Gef.St., den 13.1 (Ort und Datum)

(Unterschrift)

Hauptmann und Batl.-Kdr. (Dienstgrad und Dienststellung)

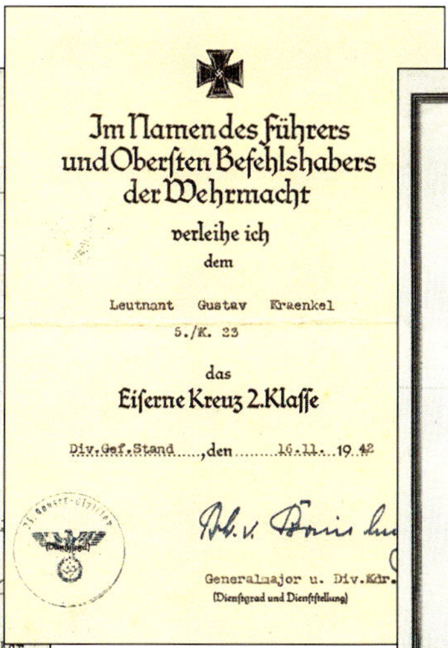

Im Namen des Führers und Obersten Befehlshabers der Wehrmacht

verleihe ich

dem

Leutnant Gustav Kraenkel

5./K. 23

das

Eiserne Kreuz 2. Klasse

Div.Gef.Stand ....., den ....16.11.. 19 42

Generalmajor u. Div.Kdr.

(Dienstgrad und Dienststellung)

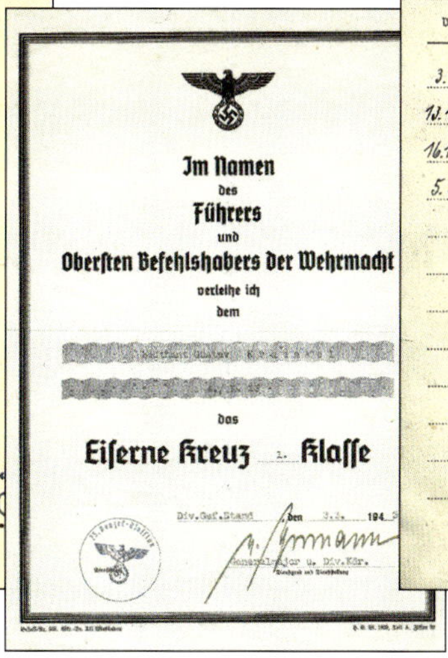

Im Namen

des

Führers

und

Obersten Befehlshabers der Wehrmacht

verleihe ich

dem

das

Eiserne Kreuz 1. Klasse

Div.Gef.Stand den 5.3. 194

Generalmajor u. Div.Kdr.

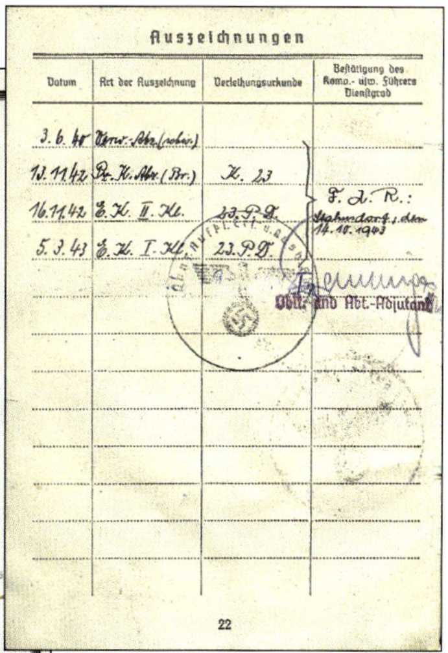

Auszeichnungen

Datum	Art der Auszeichnung	Verleihungsurkunde	Bestätigung des Komp.- usw. Führers Dienstgrad
3.6.40			
13.11.42	Pz. K. Abz. (Br.)	K. 23	
16.11.42	E.K. II. Kl.	23.P.D.	
5.3.43	E.K. I. Kl.	23.P.D.	

Obltn. und Abt.-Adjutant

22

A tailor-made black leather jacket that was worn by some personnel assigned to *Panzer-Aufklärungs-Abteilung 23* of the *23. Panzer-Division*. This particular jacket was owned by Horst Hain, the commander of the battalion's 3rd Company and a Knight's Cross recipient. The jacket and additional uniform items, medals, badges and ephemera were obtained directly from Hain at a veteran's meeting, with the grouping subsequently broken up. On these two pages are several views of the jacket along with an image of Hain talking to another battalion officer. The men had a stroke of great fortune at the end of the war, since the division surrendered to the Western Allies and was not turned over to the Soviets. It spent several months in the High Alps and the personnel were released for the most part to go back home at the end of the summer of 1945.

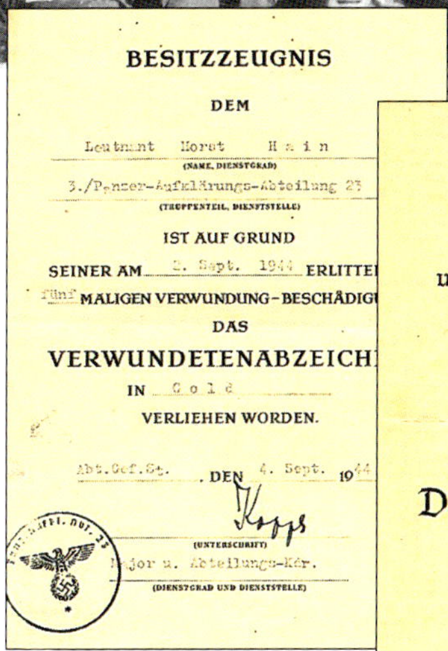

BESITZZEUGNIS

DEM

Leutnant Horst Hain
(NAME, DIENSTGRAD)

3./Panzer-Aufklärungs-Abteilung 23
(TRUPPENTEIL, DIENSTSTELLE)

IST AUF GRUND

SEINER AM 2. Sept. 1944 ERLITTE…

fünf MALIGEN VERWUNDUNG–BESCHÄDIG…

DAS

VERWUNDETENABZEICH…

IN Gold

VERLIEHEN WORDEN.

Abt.Gef.St., DEN 4. Sept. 1944

Kopps
(UNTERSCHRIFT)

Major u. Abteilungs-Kdr.
(DIENSTGRAD UND DIENSTSTELLE)

Vorläufiges Besitzzeugnis

Im Namen des Führers
und Obersten Befehlshabers
der Wehrmacht
verleihe ich
dem

Oberfeldwebel Hain
4./Kradschtz.Btl. 23

das

Deutsche Kreuz in Gold

HQu OKH, den 5. April 1943

Oberkommando des Heeres

Generalfeldmarschall

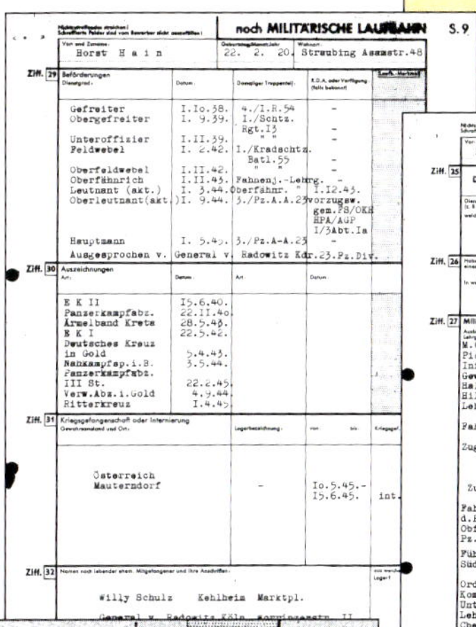

noch MILITÄRISCHE LAUFBAHN S.9

Nichtzutreffendes streichen! Schraffierte Felder sind vom Bewerber nicht auszufüllen!

Vor- und Zuname: Horst Hain | Geburtstag/Monat/Jahr: 22. 2. 20. | Wohnort: Straubing Asamstr.48

Ziff. 29 Beförderungen

Dienstgrad	Datum	Damaliger Truppenteil	R.D.A. oder Verfügung (falls bekannt)
Gefreiter	I.Io.38.	4./I.R.54	-
Obergefreiter	I. 9.39.	I./Schtz. Rgt.I3	-
Unteroffizier	I.II.39.	" "	-
Feldwebel	I. 2.42.	I./Kradschtz. Batl.55	-
Oberfeldwebel	I.II.42.	" "	-
Oberfähnrich	I.II.43.	Fahnenj.-Lehrg.	-
Leutnant (akt.)	I. 3.44.	Oberfähnr. "	I.I2.43.
Oberleutnant(akt.)	I. 9.44.	3./Pz.A.A.23	vorzugsw. gem.FS/OKH HPA/AGP I/3Abt.Ia
Hauptmann	I. 5.45.	3./Pz.A-A.23	-

Ausgesprochen v. General v. Radowitz Kdr.23.Pz.Div.

Ziff. 30 Auszeichnungen

Art	Datum
E K II	I5.6.40.
Panzerkampfabz.	22.II.4o.
Ärmelband Kreta	28.5.48.
E K I	22.5.42.
Deutsches Kreuz in Gold	5.4.43.
Nahkampfsp.i.B.	3.5.44.
Panzerkampfabz. III St.	22.2.45.
Verw.Abz.i.Gold	4.9.44.
Ritterkreuz	I.4.45.

Ziff. 31 Kriegsgefangenschaft oder Internierung

Gewahrsamsland und Ort	Lagerbezeichnung	von bis	Kriegsgef.
Österreich Mauterndorf	-	Io.5.45.- I5.6.45.	int.

Ziff. 32 Namen noch lebender ehem. Mitgefangener und ihre Anschriften:

Willy Schulz Kehlheim Marktpl.

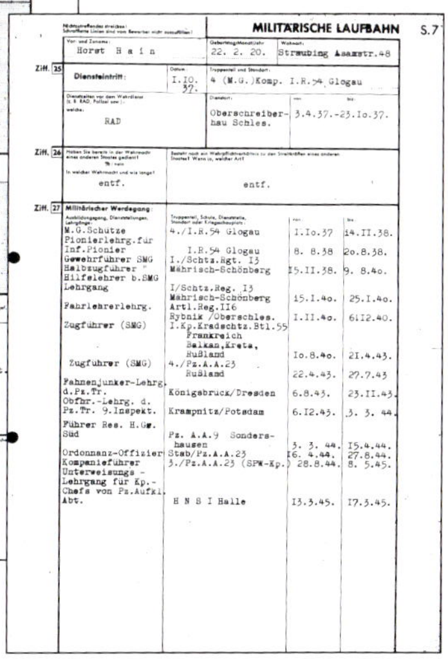

MILITÄRISCHE LAUFBAHN S.7

Nichtzutreffendes streichen! Schraffierte Linien sind vom Bewerber nicht auszufüllen!

Vor- und Zuname: Horst Hain | Geburtstag/Monat/Jahr: 22. 2. 20. | Wohnort: Straubing Asamstr.48

Ziff. 25 Diensteintritt: Datum: I.IO.37. | Truppenteil und Standort: 4 (M.G.)Komp. I.R.54 Glogau

Dienstzeiten vor dem Wehrdienst (z. B. RAD, Polizei usw.): welche: RAD | Dienstort: Oberschreiberhau Schles. | von – bis: 3.4.37.-23.Io.37.

Ziff. 26 Haben Sie bereits in der Wehrmacht eines anderen Staates gedient? In welcher Wehrmacht und wie lange? entf. | Besteht noch ein Wehrpflichtverhältnis zu den Streitkräften eines anderen Staates? Wenn ja, welcher Art? entf.

Ziff. 27 Militärischer Werdegang:

Ausbildungsgang, Dienststellungen, Lehrgänge	Truppenteil, Schule, Dienststelle, Standort oder Kriegsschauplatz	von	bis
M.G.Schütze	4./I.R.54 Glogau	I.Io.37	14.II.38.
Pionierlehrg.für Inf.Pionier	I.R.54 Glogau	8. 8.38	2o.8.38.
Gewehrführer SMG Halbzugführer "	I./Schtz.Rgt. I3 Mährisch-Schönberg	I5.II.38.	9. 8.4o.
Hilfslehrer b.SMG Lehrgang	I/Schtz.Reg. I3 Mährisch-Schönberg	15.I.4o.	25.I.4o.
Fahrlehrerlehrg.	Artl.Reg.II6 Rybnik /Oberschles.	I.II.4o.	6.I2.40.
Zugführer (SMG)	I.Kp.Kradschtz.Btl.55 Frankreich Balkan,Kreta, Rußland	Io.8.4o.	2I.4.43.
Zugführer (SMG)	4./Pz.A.A.23 Rußland	22.4.43.	27.7.43
Fahnenjunker-Lehrg. d.Pz.Tr.	Königsbrück/Dresden	6.8.43.	23.II.43.
Obfhr.-Lehrg. d. Pz.Tr. 9.Inspekt.	Krampnitz/Potsdam	6.I2.43.	3. 3. 44.
Führer Res. H.Gr. Süd	Pz. A.A.9 Sondershausen	3. 3. 44.	I5.4.44.
Ordonnanz-Offizier	Stab/Pz.A.A.23	I6. 4.44.	27.8.44.
Kompanieführer	3./Pz.A.A.23 (SPW-Kp.)	28.8.44.	8. 5.45.
Unterweisungs - Lehrgang für Kp.-Chefs von Pz.Aufkl. Abt.	H N S I Halle	I3.3.45.	I7.3.45.

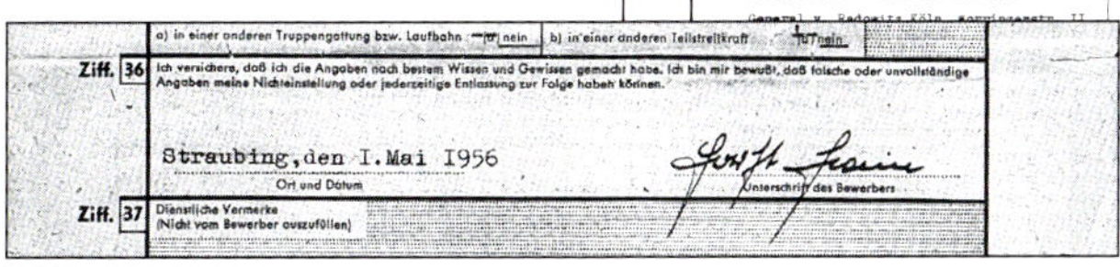

a) in einer anderen Truppengattung bzw. Laufbahn: ~~ja~~ nein b) in einer anderen Teilstreitkraft ~~ja~~ nein

Ziff. 36 Ich versichere, daß ich die Angaben nach bestem Wissen und Gewissen gemacht habe. Ich bin mir bewußt, daß falsche oder unvollständige Angaben meine Nichteinstellung oder jederzeitige Entlassung zur Folge haben können.

Straubing, den I. Mai 1956
Ort und Datum

Horst Hain
Unterschrift des Bewerbers

Ziff. 37 Dienstliche Vermerke (Nicht vom Bewerber auszufüllen)

An additional view of the jacket and some details of the insignia. Hain was one of the few personnel in the *Panzertruppe* who were also entitled to wear the *Kreta* cuff title, since he was in *Kradschützen-Battalion*, which participated in the invasion in 1941. Some of Hain's other high awards and assignments can be gleaned from the job application seen here that he prepared in order to work for the Allies after the war. The last image of the jacket on a mannequin shows how Hain might have looked with some of the awards seen in period images.

Two beer steins from reconnaissance battalions from the 1936 timeframe. These were usually ordered for units around Christmas (*Weihnachten*) and served as a memento for the personnel. They were often personalized, as seen below right, and sometimes featured engravings on the lids. Not many survived the war, regardless of what branch of service they came from.

Scouts relax next to an *Sd.Kfz. 221*. Soldiers increasingly had to rely on the local populace for billeting and some of the comforts of home.

As Operation Barbarossa continued throughout the summer and into the fall of 1941, casualties mounted. Here a knocked-out *Sd.Kfz. 231 (6 Rad)* is inspected by a mountain officer (as evidenced by his short-brimmed billed field cap).

Top left: A *Leutnant* of the *II./Aufklärungs-Regiment 9* of the *4. leichte Division* in his first-pattern *Panzer* jacket. It cannot be determined whether he wears the national insignia on his right breast, but the beret/crash helmet does not have any. SCOTT PRITCHETT

Top right: A scout from *Aufklärungs-Abteilung 5 (mot)* of the *2. Panzer-Division* in his first-pattern *Panzer* jacket. SCOTT PRITCHETT

A *Panzer III* helps recover a stuck *Sd.Kfz. 222*.

Top left: A scout in a second-pattern jacket. Both the jacket and the cap appear to have golden-yellow *Waffenfarbe*. It also appears that the unit number has been removed from the shoulder straps in accordance with regulation, since the "A" seems to be placed a bit high on the straps. SCOTT PRITCHETT **Top right:** A unit first sergeant, commonly referred to the soldiers as a *Spieß*, poses in his second-pattern *Panzer* jacket without collar piping. The "piston rings" (*Kolbenringe*) associated with that position are located on the sleeves of both arms. SCOTT PRITCHETT

Scouts pose in front of an *Sd.Kfz. 231 (8 Rad)* in a muddy field. This image is probably from the second winter in the Soviet Union, judging by the camouflage reversible parkas being worn. JIM HALEY

The capture of modern bridges was especially important in sustaining the advance, since detours and fords took time to discover and prepare for crossing. It was in those situations that the scouts and armored reconnaissance personnel earned their pay. Here an *Sd.Kfz. 222* makes its way along bottom ground near a destroyed bridge.

The first winter in the Soviet Union was filled with unimaginable hardships for most of the soldiers, especially in the northern and central sectors. It was no different for the armored reconnaissance forces, who were frequently employed in economy-of-force missions and delaying actions, something new for the force. Here a makeshift structure has been constructed for the *Sd.Kfz. 222* in the background.

As the weather turned colder, fixed structures became increasingly important, as well as the occupation of villages, towns, and cities critical for sustaining the force.
JIM HALEY

An NCO has mounted all possible insignia on his coveralls, including collar patches designed for the black *Panzer* uniform. This image comes from the photo albums of Knight's Cross recipient *Leutnant* Ulrich Kreß, a platoon leader in the *1./Aufklärungs-Abteilung 20 (mot)*, who was killed in action in September 1941. JIM HALEY

Until the introduction of the reed-green denim work outfits, many scouts preferred to wear coveralls. These were procured from a variety of sources, including Czechoslovakia, and were worn both with and without insignia. In this photo taken before the war, the soldiers around the *Sd.Kfz. 232 (Fu) (6 Rad)* have shoulder straps but no national insignia.

Despite the hardships, the young soldiers tried to maintain morale. Of interest here is the application of rudimentary whitewash over the dark *Panzer* gray original finish on this *Sd. Kfz. 222*.

These photos were probably taken during the winter of 1943–44, as evidenced by the wear of the M43 standardized field cap, which was officially introduced in the middle of 1943. The scouts wear a variety of clothing and uniform articles, all designed to keep themselves warm as best they could. JIM HALEY

The scout with the impish grin on his face has donned a captured Soviet early-war *budenovka*.

This scout from *Panzer Aufklärungs-Abteilung 24* of the *24. Panzer-Division* wears a black M42 with what appears to be a field-made M40-style cotton field blouse. The M42 was very unpopular with personnel and was quickly replaced with the ubiquitous M43 billed field cap. JIM HALEY

Members of this scout section seem to have all adopted pencil-thin moustaches and white scarves as their signature.

Although the field-gray version of the black *Panzer* uniform was introduced in 1940, it took some time to trickle down to armored car crews, where the black uniform or the reed-green work uniform seems to have been preferred. Later in the war, however, more examples of the field-gray uniform can be seen being worn, particularly among armored reconnaissance personnel in halftrack companies.

Oberwachtmeister Krüger from *Panzer-Aufklärungs-Abteilung 24* of the *24. Panzer Division* wears a custom-tailored water-pattern set of camouflage trousers. JIM HALEY

Once the worst of the winter was over, it was time to start digging out and preparing for mobile operations again. Spirits improved, as evidenced by these group photos of scouts behind and on their *Sd.Kfz. 232 (Fu) (8 Rad)* in a prepared position. JIM HALEY

In the southern part of the Soviet Union, German forces marched deep into the Caucasus, where scenes such as this one between the crew of an *Sd.Kfz. 222* and an Asiatic horseman were not uncommon. JIM HALEY

This scout, possibly from *SS-Panzer-Aufklärungs-Abteilung 1* around the time of the fighting in Normandy in 1944, wears the SS version of the reed-green uniform for armored car personnel. Keeping true to the SS style, the jacket is cut vertically, although the trousers have only a single-button flap.

An *Sd.Kfz. 232 (Fu) (8 Rad)* of *SS-Aufklärungs-Abteilung (mot) "Totenkopf"* leads a column of supply vehicles through the mud along the northern part of the Eastern Front.

Another view of the same scout seen on the previous page. This time the vehicle appears to be an *Sd.Kfz. 233*.

Several knocked-out KV-85 tanks along the *Totenkopf* reconnaissance battalion's trench line are seen.

The dark-blue *Panzer* denim work uniform, introduced before the war and produced until the end, is not an item of *Panzer* uniforms that most collectors are familiar with. Nonetheless, it was practical and frequently encountered in armor and armored reconnaissance formations, as see here in these pre-war recruit training images of future scouts.

An *Sd.Kfz. 221* of *Aufklärungs-Abteilung 29 (mot)* of the *29. Infanterie Division (mot)* during the summer offensive of 1942, which culminated in the drive on Stalingrad. Note the divisional insignia (left-rear engine-access panel), with the battalion insignia above it and a creeping white fox on the left front of the vehicle, an emblem found only on armored cars of the battalion. JASON MARK / LEAPING HORSEMAN BOOKS

The commander of the *29.Infanterie-Division (mot)*, *Generalleutnant* Max Fremerey, visits *Aufklärungs-Abteilung 29 (mot)'s* command post, which places the image sometime before 25 September 1942, when Fremerey relinquished command to *Generalmajor* Hans-Georg Leyser. JASON MARK / LEAPING HORSEMAN BOOKS

A long column of vehicles moves out along a road in the steppes, where the *Sd.Kfz. 223* in the foreground displays the divisional and battalion insignia previously seen, as well as a large "G," a holdover from the previous year when the *29. Infanterie-Division* operated under *Generaloberst* Guderian. JASON MARK / LEAPING HORSEMAN BOOKS

The officer checking his map board in the previous image is seen here again in a staff car. JASON MARK / LEAPING HORSEMAN BOOKS

Finally, several vehicles of the battalion are seen parked along the main "street" of an impoverished Soviet village. To the viewer's right, an early tank destroyer, a *Panzerjäger I*, moves down the road. JASON MARK / LEAPING HORSEMAN BOOKS

After 1943, the face of the German Army in the field became even less homogenous. These scouts of *Panzer-Aufklärungs-Abteilung 24* wear a mixture of regulation and non-regulation uniform articles. Two of the scouts have custom-tailored camouflage trousers. The scout in the middle wears an SS *Panzer* tunic with army insignia applied to it. Two men wear M43 field caps, while two other wear outmoded overseas caps that started to be phased out in 1942. The men stand in front of the *König*, *Oberwachtmeister* Krüger's *Sd.Kfz. 231 (8 Rad)*. JIM HALEY

This reconnaissance officer from *Panzer-Aufklärungs-Abteilung 16* of the *16. Panzer-Division* also wears a number of non-regulation items. His overseas cap has been upgraded from an enlisted version by the addition of crown piping in either white or silver-colored cord. He has the divisional cap badge on the side of his cap, which was authorized for wear by members of the division by an entry in each individual's *Soldbuch.* To top this off, he also wears a custom-made tunic in *Panzer* style that is constructed out of SS camouflage. STEVE ANDROSKO

The same officer talks to men from his unit, one of whom wears the first-pattern army-style reed green denim special-purpose uniform for armored car personnel. STEVE ANDROSKO

This photo from *Panzer-Aufklärungs-Abteilung 24*, which also graces the front cover, shows *Oberwachtmeister* Erwin Krüger outfitted in a complete camouflage uniform, while his comrade on the viewer's right wears a field-gray *Panzer*-style tunic with what appears to be golden-yellow collar piping! JIM HALEY

Left and below: These reconnaissance officers continue to wear the old-style M37 "crusher" cap well into the war, even though it was supposed to be replaced by the M38 officer overseas cap. JIM HALEY

This scout, originally from *Aufklärungs-Regiment 7*, was listed as missing-in-action at Stalingrad in the postwar Red Cross inquiry.

This *Panzeraufklärer* from *Aufklärungs-Abteilung 5 (mot)* of the *2. Panzer-Division* wear a first-pattern *Panzer* jacket and early beret/crash helmet with embroidered/metal cockade without national insignia, thus placing the image in the mid-1930s.

Left: One of the few known instances where cavalry-related traditions badges were officially worn by members of armored reconnaissance forces occurred in *Kradschützen-Bataillon 3* of the *3. Panzer-Division.* Since this scout also wears the ribbon for the Italo-German Campaign Medal, it is possible that he was assigned to *Aufklärungs-Abteilung 33 (mot)* of the *15. Panzer-Division* or its successor formation, *Panzer-Aufklärungs-Abteilung 115* of the *15. Panzergrenadier-Division*, where the badge was also known to have been worn. This badge is also presented in the color section, along with the cap and ephemera of the scout who wore it. SCOTT PRITCHETT

Photographs of reconnaissance forces after 1943 become increasingly harder to find due to the shortage of film for private purposes and the increasingly desperate situation. Despite those burdens, the occasional memento snapshot was taken, as seen here. Here scouts fide time to test the amphibious capabilities of their *Schwimmwagen* at a bivouac site. MICHAEL H. PRUETT

By far the rarest regulation *Panzer* tunic ever seen by the authors of this book is the one pictured here: A scout assigned to an unidentified *Kradschützen-Bataillon*, who has a chain-stitched embroidered "K" on the shoulder straps of his piped second-pattern *Panzer* tunic. Although almost impossible to tell in grayscale photography, the *Waffenfarbe* appears to be rose pink. SCOTT PRITCHETT

A scout finds time to smile in this blurry image of either an *Sd.Kfz. 250/9* or an *Sd.Kfz. 222.* MICHAEL H. PRUETT

A relatively rarely photographed *Sd.Kfz. 234/2* takes position behind staff cars on a road somewhere in Upper Silesia in the final desperate fighting for the homeland in 1945. MICHAEL H. PRUETT

CHAPTER 5

Major Reconnaissance Formations

This chapter provides an overview of the major reconnaissance formations assigned to brigades and divisions of the German Army, the *Waffen-SS*, and the *Luftwaffe*. It is broken down numerically by major formation. Needless to say, the earliest and longest-serving divisions and brigades will receive the most treatment since documentary materials concerning the formations tends to become less detailed as the war progressed—partly because of lack of time or personnel to prepare the records that were so meticulously maintained in the early war years, partly because many daily logs for echelons below field army were partially or completely lost for the years 1943–45. As a result, data are sometimes needed from first-hand accounts or published unit histories, which frequently also suffer from the lack of solid documentary background material.

The capsule histories will attempt to capture, where possible, the designations and organizations of the major reconnaissance formations of the superior commands, the commanders,[1] the recipients of high decorations (while in the formation), any anomalies in structure, and specific notes for information that is not related elsewhere.

These armored cars belong to *SS-Standarte "Deutschland"* (stylized D on shoulder straps). Of interest here is the large tactical symbol for a heavy armored car painted on the turret of the *Sd.Kfz. 232 (Fu) (8 Rad)*. JIM HALEY

ARMY

1. LEICHTE DIVISION

Campaigns: Poland

Reconnaissance Formations:

- ***Aufklärungs-Abteilung 6 (mot)***

Activated: 15 October 1935

Antecedent Formation: *Kraftfahr-Abteilung Münster* (activated on 1 October 1934)

Replacement Detachment: *Ersatz-Abteilung für motorisierte Einheiten 6*

Redesignated: Later reassigned to *6. Panzer-Division*, where it was eventually redesignated as *Panzer-Aufklärungs-Abteilung 57* (1 April 1940)

Organization: 1939—Headquarters, 1st Armored Scout Troop, 2nd Armored Scout Troop, 3rd Motorcycle Infantry Troop, 4th Troop (heavy)

Commanders: *Major Freiherr* von Eckhardtstein (1 September 1939–1 April 1940)

Notes: For a short time, the battalion was *I./Aufklärungs-Regiment 6*, before being designated a separate battalion again in 1938 and assigned to *1. leichte Division*.

- ***Kradschützen-Bataillon 6***

Activated: 1 April 1939

Antecedent Formation: *IV./Kavallerie-Schützen-Regiment 4*

Replacement Detachment: *Schützen-Ersatz-Bataillon 4*

Redesignated: Later reassigned to *6. Panzer-Division*, retaining its organization and designation

Organization: 1939—Headquarters, 1st Motorcycle Infantry Troop, 2nd Motorcycle Infantry Troop, 3rd Motorcycle Infantry Machine Gun Troop, and 4th Troop (Heavy)

Studio portrait of a scout assigned to *Aufklärungs-Abteilung 6 (mot)* wearing a second-pattern *Panzer* jacket and the beret/crash helmet combination. SCOTT PRITCHETT

The *Waffenrock* of a first sergeant assigned to *Kradschützen-Bataillon 6*.

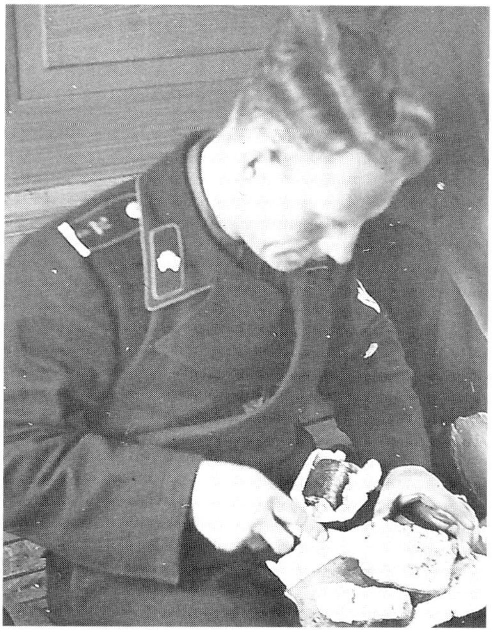

Early images of members of *Aufklärungs-Abteilung 6 (mot)*, with the first four of them probably around 1935 or 1936 before the battalion was assigned to *1. leichte Division*, in which case the *Waffenfarbe* would have still been rose pink. In the last two images, the solid white national cross on the *Sd.Kfz. 232 (Fu) (6 Rad)* probably places the images shortly before the war or just after the campaign in Poland. By then, the battalion should have switched to a golden-yellow *Waffenfarbe*, although it is impossible to tell in these images.

1. KAVALLERIE-DIVISION

Campaigns: France (1940), Soviet Union

Notes: The division had no organic motorized reconnaissance assets; however, it was augmented by *Aufklärungs-Lehr-Abteilung* during Operation Barbarossa. In November 1941, it was sent to Germany for reorganization and redesignation as *24. Panzer-Division.*

1. PANZER-DIVISION

Campaigns: Poland, France (1940), Soviet Union

Reconnaissance Formations:

- ***Aufklärungs-Abteilung 4 (mot)***

Activated: 15 October 1935

Antecedent Formation: *Kraftfahr-Abteilung Leipzig* (1 October 1934)

Replacement Detachment: *Ersatz-Abteilung für motorisierte Einheiten*

Redesignated: 1 April 1940 (see *Panzer-Aufklärungs-Abteilung 4*)

Organization: 1939—Headquarters, 1st Armored Scout Company, 3rd Motorcycle Infantry Company, and 4th Company (heavy)

Commanders: *Oberstleutnant Dr.* Ehlermann (15 October 1935–1 October 1936), *Oberstleutnant* Koelitz (1 October 1936–1 November 1939), *Oberstleutnant Dr.* von Scheele (1 November 1939–1 April 1940)

- ***Kradschützen-Bataillon 1***

Activated: 15 October 1935

Antecedent Formation: *Reiter-Regiment 16*

Replacement Detachment: *Schützen-Ersatz-Bataillon 1*, followed by *Kradschützen-Ersatz-Bataillon 1* in December 1940

Redesignated: 1 March 1943 (consolidated with *Panzer-Aufklärungs-Abteilung 4* and reorganized on 1 June 1942)

Organization: 1940–41—Headquarters, 1st Motorcycle Infantry Company, 2nd Motorcycle Infantry Company, 3rd Motorcycle Infantry Machine Gun Company, and 4th Company (heavy); Headquarters, 1st Motorcycle Infantry Company, 2nd Motorcycle Infantry Company, 3rd Motorcycle Infantry

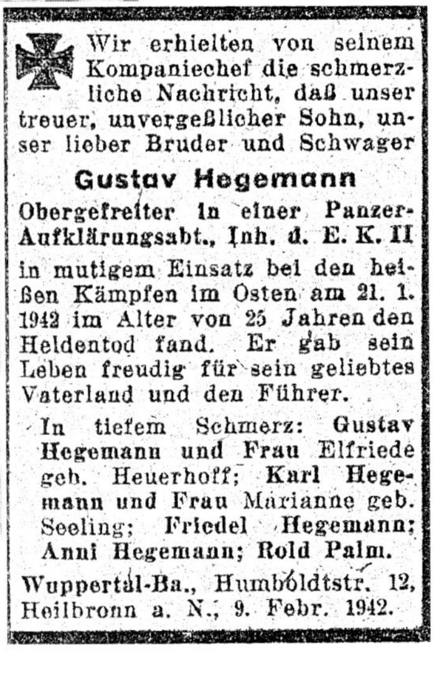

Wir erhielten von seinem Kompaniechef die schmerzliche Nachricht, daß unser treuer, unvergeßlicher Sohn, unser lieber Bruder und Schwager

Gustav Hegemann

Obergefreiter in einer Panzer-Aufklärungsabt., Inh. d. E. K. II

in mutigem Einsatz bei den heißen Kämpfen im Osten am 21. 1. 1942 im Alter von 25 Jahren den Heldentod fand. Er gab sein Leben freudig für sein geliebtes Vaterland und den Führer.

In tiefem Schmerz: Gustav Hegemann und Frau Elfriede geb. Heuerhoff; Karl Hegemann und Frau Marianne geb. Seeling; Friedel Hegemann; Anni Hegemann; Rold Palm.

Wuppertal-Ba., Humboldtstr. 12, Heilbronn a. N., 9. Febr. 1942.

An *Erkennungsmarke*, the equivalent of the "dog tag" in the U.S. Army, belonging to a scout from *Aufklärungs-Abteilung 4 (mot).*

Left: Gravesite and death notice of Gustav Hegemann, a scout in *Panzer-Aufklärungs-Abteilung 4.* He was killed by shrapnel on 21 January 1941. JIM HALEY

Panzer-Aufklärungs-Abteilung 4 in the Battle for France in May 1940

Panzer-Aufklärungs-Abteilung 4 was advancing via Aibre toward Héricourt in the meantime. The battalion commander, *Major* von Scheele, ordered *Graf* von Bellegarde and the battalion adjutant, *Oberleutnant* Seidel, to move on ahead with a small radio section to Belfort and demand that the fortress there surrender, since the reconnaissance battalion had reached Aibre with its main body and had encountered no resistance there.

When the two vehicles passed the outskirts of Héricourt, they were challenged by the enemy, but were soon past the outposts. *Hauptmann* Bellegrade moved along French columns with his radio section without anyone noticing him. French antitank guns were in position in Héricourt, and there was a throng of soldiers at one bridge. Bellegarde jumped down to the road, cursing in his best French, and regulated the traffic. Nonplussed, the French made way.

The radio vehicle approached the guard at the bridge. The guard asked, curious: "Have you heard where the Germans are?" *Obergefreiter* Hütter, who spoke fluent French, replied: "No, I haven't heard anything." He pointed to his headset and added: "But we don't have time to talk . . . we need to move on." At the same moment, the vehicle moved out. The path was clear. In front of them, they soon saw the shadows of a large military facility with casemates jutting out in the nighttime sky. They climbed a small rise and found themselves in front of the walls of Belfort.

It was only then that the Germans were recognized and had to stop.[2]

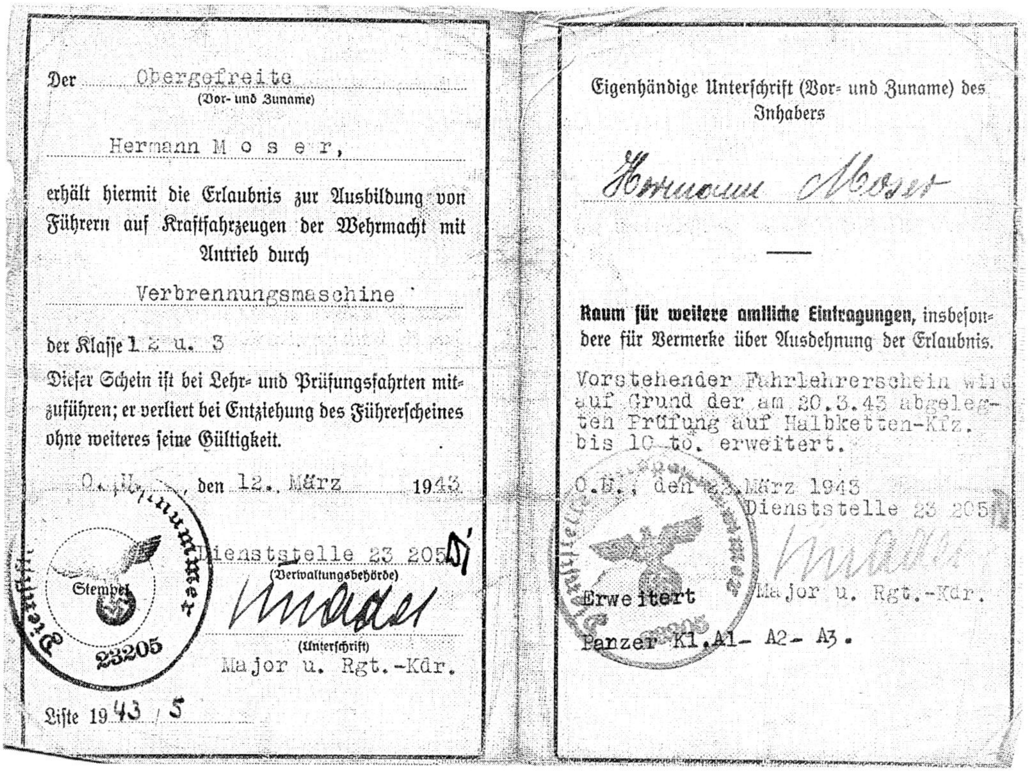

Der Obergefreite
(Vor- und Zuname)
Hermann M o s e r,
erhält hiermit die Erlaubnis zur Ausbildung von Führern auf Kraftfahrzeugen der Wehrmacht mit Antrieb durch
Verbrennungsmaschine
der Klasse 1 2 u. 3
Dieser Schein ist bei Lehr- und Prüfungsfahrten mitzuführen; er verliert bei Entziehung des Führerscheines ohne weiteres seine Gültigkeit.
O.U., den 12. März 1943
Dienststelle 23 205
(Verwaltungsbehörde)
Stempel
23205
(Unterschrift)
Major u. Rgt.-Kdr.
Liste 1943 / 5

Eigenhändige Unterschrift (Vor- und Zuname) des Inhabers
Hermann Moser

Raum für weitere amtliche Eintragungen, insbesondere für Vermerke über Ausdehnung der Erlaubnis.
Vorstehender Fahrlehrerschein wird auf Grund der am 20.3.43 abgelegten Prüfung auf Halbketten-Kfz. bis 10 to. erweitert.
O.U., den 23. März 1943
Dienststelle 23 205
Major u. Rgt.-Kdr.
Erweitert
Panzer Kl. A1- A2- A3.

The driver's license issued to Hermann Moser, who was assigned to both *Kradschützen-Bataillon 1* and *Panzer-Aufklärungs-Abteilung 1*.

Company, 4th Motorcycle Infantry Machine Gun Company, and 5th Company (heavy). June 1942—Headquarters, 1st Armored Scout Company, 2nd Motorcycle Infantry Company, 3rd Motorcycle Infantry Company, 4th Motorcycle Infantry Company, and 5th Company (heavy)

Commanders: *Major* Ulrich Kleemann (15 October 1937–31 December 1937); *Major (Oberstleutnant) Graf* von der Schulenburg (1 January 1938–March 1940); *Oberstleutnant* von Wietersheim (March 1940–5 July 1941); *Hauptmann* von der Chevallerie (acting) (5–11 July 1941); *Major Freiherr* von Wolff (12 July 1941–January 1942); *Hauptmann Freiherr* von Frydag (January–early July 1942); *Hauptmann* Paetzold (acting?) (early July–15 July 1942); *Hauptmann Freiherr* von Frydag (15 July–29 November 1942); *Hauptmann* Schönfeld (commander?) (December 1942–January 1943); *Major* Bradel (23 January–1 March 1943)

- ***Panzer-Aufklärungs-Abteilung 4***

Activated: 1 April 1940

Antecedent Formation: *Aufklärungs-Abteilung 4 (mot)*

Replacement Detachment: *Ersatz-Abteilung für motorisierte Einheiten* and later, in December 1941, *Kradschützen-Ersatz-Bataillon 9*

Redesignated: 1 June 1942 (see *Kradschützen-Bataillon 1*)

Organization: Fall 1940—Headquarters, 1st Armored Scout Company, 2nd Armored Scout Company, 3rd Motorcycle Infantry Company, and 4th Company (heavy). May 1941—Headquarters, 1st Armored Scout Company, 3rd Motorcycle Infantry Company, and 4th Company (heavy)

Commanders: *Oberstleutnant Dr.* von Scheele (1 April 1940–December 1941; Unknown (December 1941–1 June 1942)

Several views of the *Sd.Kfz. 231 (8 Rad)* armored car, as issued to *Aufklärungs-Abteilung 4 (mot).*

Above: An *Sd.Kfz. 232 (Fu) (8 Rad)* as seen from the rear deck. **Top right:** A unit commander takes time to play with a puppy, while soldiers of the unit look on. **Right:** An NCO takes time for a smoke break, the signs of combat etched on his face.

Notes: In the fall of 1940, the 2nd Armored Scout Company was reassigned to *Panzer-Aufklärungs-Abteilung 19*.

- ***Panzer-Aufklärungs-Abteilung 91***

Activated: 1 March 1943

Antecedent Formation: *Kradschützen-Bataillon 1*

Replacement Detachment: *Panzer-Aufklärungs-Ersatz-Abteilung 1*

Redesignated: 15 April 1943 (see *Panzer-Aufklärungs-Abteilung 4*)

Organization: Exact organization unknown (May 1941)

Commanders and Acting Commanders: *Major* Bradel (1 March–15 April 1943)

Notes: Formed from *Kradschützen-Bataillon 1* and initially reconstituted in France as *Panzer-Aufklärungs-Regiment 91* with two battalions of three reconnaissance companies each and a 7th Armored Scout Company. Reassigned to *1. Panzer-Division* as *Panzer-Aufklärungs-Abteilung 91*.

Ju 52 transporters have landed in an open field to provide logistical support to the battalion. During far-ranging operations in the early years of the war, *Luftwaffe* support was often the only way to receive supplies in order to continue operations.

Below: The battalion prepares to move by rail. Motorized formations were usually moved by rail when speed was of the essence and it was necessary to cut down on wear and tear on the tactical vehicles.

Another knocked-out Soviet tank.

Panzer-Aufklärungs-Abteilung 1 in the Fighting along the Vistula in Hungary in August 1944

The mounted patrols of *Panzer-Aufklärungs-Abteilung 1* were constantly in contact with the enemy during the period, which was marked by constant changing of the areas of operations and the combat situation, in an effort to provide the division with as clear and comprehensive picture of the situation as possible, to determine the situation of the friendly elements to the flanks or perform screening missions along a broad front in the open flanks of attacking formations. It was in those trying times that the newly created supply company of the reconnaissance battalion under the command of *Hauptmann* Huppert proved itself through tireless support and adoptability . . .

After a number of operations, a mobile group under *Hauptmann* Huppert was formed on 26 August for the attack on Lagow. Reporting directly to the *III. Panzer-Korps*, the group consisted of the reconnaissance battalion, reporting to the battalion headquarters and its adjutant, *Oberleutnant* Streitz; *Panzer-Aufklärungs-Abteilung 23*; the *I./Panzer-Artillerie-Regiment 27*; and, later on, *Panzer-Aufklärungs-Abteilung 17*. *Major* Huppert, who had been awarded the Knight's Cross to the Iron Cross on 25 August 1944, took Plucki, about five kilometers north of Lagow, with the *2./Panzer-Aufklärungs-Abteilung 1* (*Leutnant* Dosser) and Zamkoqa-Wola with the *3./Panzer-Aufklärungs-Abteilung 1* (*Leutnant* Stark). There he was able to establish a flank guard for the corps . . .[4]

• ***Panzer-Aufklärungs-Abteilung 1***

Activated: 15 April 1943

Antecedent Formation: *Panzer-Aufklärungs-Abteilung 91*

Replacement Detachment: *Panzer-Aufklärungs-Ersatz-Abteilung 1*

Deactivated: 8 May 1945

Organization: 1943–44—Headquarters with armored scout platoon, 1st Armored Scout Company (Armored Car), 2nd Armored Scout Company (half-track), 3rd Armored Reconnaissance Company (*SPW*), 4th Armored Reconnaissance Company (*SPW*), 5th Heavy Armored Reconnaissance Company (*SPW*).[3] January 1945—Headquarters, 1st Armored Scout Company (armored Car), 2nd Armored Scout Company (half-track), 3rd Armored Reconnaissance Company (*Maultier*), 4th Heavy Armored Reconnaissance Company (*SPW*), and Supply Company

Commanders: *Major* Bradel (15 April–July 1943); *Major* Huppert (July–20 November 1943); *Hauptmann* Bärwinkel (acting) (20 November 1943); *Major* Huppert (November 1943–14 March 1944); *Hauptmann* Bärwinkel (acting) (14 March 1944–?); *Hauptmann* Schütt (acting) (early September–5 September 1944); *Hauptmann Dr.* Koehler (9–21 September 1944); *Hauptmann* Ritz (acting) (21–24 September 1944); *Hauptmann Dr.* Koehler (24 September 1944–13 May 1945)

Notes: On 13 April 1945, the battalion was detached from the division and allocated to *6. (SS-) Panzer-Armee*, where it fought in lower Austria until the end of the war.

Awards: Knight's Cross—*Hauptmann* Bellgarde, *3./Panzer-Aufklärungs-Abteilung 1* (28 November 1940); *Major* Huppert, *Panzer-Aufklärungs-Abteilung 1* (23 August 1944); *Hauptmann Dr.* Koehler, *Panzer-Aufklärungs-Abteilung 1* (3 November 1944). **Honor Roll (Clasp)**—*Oberleutnant* Eilhauer, *4./Panzer-Aufklärungs-Abteilung 1* (1945); *Hauptmann Freiherr* von Frydag, *Kradschützen-Bataillon 1* (8 February 1943); *Major* Huppert, *Panzer-Aufklärungs-Abteilung 1* (7 March 1944); *Leutnant* Heinz-Peter Huppert, *1./Kradschützen-Bataillon 1* (1 March 1942). **German Cross in Gold**—*Oberleutnant* Bärwinkel, *3./Kradschützen-Bataillon 1* (23 June 1942); *Hauptmann* von Berckefeldt, *2./Kradschützen-Bataillon 1* (16 February 1942); *Oberfeldwebel* Dölling, *1./Kradschützen-Bataillon 1* (14 February 1943); *Oberfeldwebel* Eilhauer, *3./Kradschützen-Bataillon 1*

This sequence of images were taken from the photo album of a scout assigned to *Panzer-Aufklärungs-Abteilung 4* and starts with the battalion being stationed in East Prussia after the fall of France. The photo album used is interesting in that it was "appropriated" while in the Soviet Union and filled with the soldier's own photos. It finishes up in March 1943. This group of photos shows the battalion in training and befriending the local populace in East Prussia, late in 1941.

WH

The training continues, with road marches and bivouacs and the tapping of a keg. The scout was most likely assigned to a *Sd.Kfz. 223 (Fu)*.

Whenever there was a break in the action, the soldiers of the unit gathered together to share experiences and camaraderie. In some of the photos, scouts have received medals, an important factor in maintaining unit morale—certainly necessary when encountering some of the Soviet behemoths of the period, such as the KV-II pictured.

(28 November 1942); *Oberleutnant Freiherr* von Frydag, *Kradschützen-Bataillon 1* (13 May 1942); *Oberfeldwebel* Häfner, Headquarters, *Kradschützen-Bataillon 1* (21 December 1942); *Oberfeldwebel* Herzog, *3./Kradschützen-Bataillon 1* (23 June 1942); *Oberleutnant Dr.* Koehler, *5./Kradschützen-Bataillon 1* (23 June 1942); *Hauptmann* Pätzol, *Kradschützen-Bataillon 1* (9 October 1942); *Feldwebel* Schemmel, *2./Panzer-Aufklärungs-Abteilung 1* (11 February 1945); *Leutnant* Stark, *4./Kradschützen-Bataillon 1* (14 February 1943); *Oberleutnant* von Wietersheim, *Kradschützen-Bataillon 1* (24 December 1941)

2. INFANTERIE-DIVISION (MOT)

Campaigns: Poland, France

Reconnaissance Formations:

- ***Aufklärungs-Abteilung 2 (mot)***

Activated: 10 November 1938

Antecedent Formation: None

Replacement Detachment: *Ersatz-Abteilung für motorisierte Aufklärungs-Einheiten 3*

Redesignated: When *2. Infanterie-Division (mot)* transitioned to become *12. Panzer-Division* on 10 January 1941, the battalion stayed with the division and retained its designation.

Organization: 1939—Headquarters, 1st Motorcycle Infantry Troop, 2nd Armored Scout Troop. June 1940—Headquarters, 1st Motorcycle Infantry Troop, 2nd Armored Scout Troop, 3rd Troop (heavy)

Commanders: *Major* (later *Oberstleutnant*) Kelpe (1 September 1939–August 1940); *Major* Wolf (August 1940–10 January 1941)

- ***Kradschützen-Bataillon 22***

Activated: 20 August 1940

Antecedent Formation: Formed from personnel levies against the rifle regiments of the division.

Replacement Detachment: *Schützen-Ersatz-Bataillon 3*

Redesignated: When *2. Infanterie-Division (mot)* transitioned to become *12. Panzer-Division* on 10 January 1941, the battalion stayed with the division and retained its designation.

Organization: 1940—Headquarters, 1st Motorcycle Infantry Company, 2nd Motorcycle Infantry Company, 3rd Motorcycle Infantry Company, 4th Motorcycle Infantry Machine Gun Company and 5th Company (heavy)

Commanders: *Oberstleutnant* Bayer (20 August 1940–10 January 1941)

2. LEICHTE DIVISION

Campaigns: Poland

Reconnaissance Formations:

- ***Aufklärungs-Regiment 7 (mot)***

Activated: 10 November 1938

Antecedent Formations: Personnel received from *Aufklärungs-Abteilung 6 (mot)*, *Kradschützen-Bataillon 1*, *Kradschützen-Bataillon 3*, and *Reiter-Regiment 17* to form the regiment.

Replacement Detachment: *Ersatz-Abteilung für motorisierte Einheiten 4*

Deactivation: Transferred to *7. Panzer-Division* on 18 October 1939, initially retaining its organization and designation. Deactivated on 1 November 1939.

Commander: *Oberst* Neumann-Silkow (10 November 1938–1 November 1939)

The regiment consisted of a motorcycle infantry battalion and an armored scout battalion:

- ***I./Aufklärungs-Regiment 7 (mot)***

Replacement Detachment: *Schützen-Ersatz-Bataillon 4*

Redesignation: After transfer to *7. Panzer-Division* and deactivation of the regiment, the battalion was redesignated as *Kradschützen-Battalion 7* and reassigned to the division.

Organization: 1939—Headquarters, 1st Motorcycle Infantry Troop, 2nd Motorcycle Infantry Troop, 3rd Motorcycle Infantry Troop, and 4th Troop (heavy)

- ***II./Aufklärungs-Regiment 7 (mot)***

Replacement Detachment: *Ersatz-Abteilung für motorisierte Einheiten 4*

Redesignation: After transfer to *7. Panzer-Division* and deactivation of the regiment, the battalion was redesignated as *Aufklärungs-Abteilung 37 (mot)* and reassigned to the division.[5]

Organization: 1939—Headquarters, 5th Armored Scout Troop, 6th Armored Scout Troop, and 7th Armored Scout Troop

2. PANZER-DIVISION

Campaigns: Poland, France (1940), Balkans, Soviet Union, France (1944), Ardennes, Germany

Reconnaissance Formations:

- ***Aufklärungs-Abteilung 5 (mot)***

Activated: 15 October 1935

Antecedent Formation: *Kraftfahr-Abteilung Cannstadt* (1 October 1934)

Replacement Detachment: *Ersatz-Abteilung für motorisierte Aufklärungs-Einheiten 9*, replaced by *Ersatz-Abteilung für motorisierte Aufklärungs-Einheiten 7* at the end of November 1939.

Redesignated: 1 March 1940 as *Panzer-Aufklärungs-Abteilung 5*

Organization: 1939—Headquarters, 1st Armored Scout Troop, 2nd Armored Scout Troop, 3rd Motorcycle Infantry Troop, 4th Troop (Heavy)

Commanders: *Major Freiherr* von Lüttwitz (6 October 1936–26 April 1938); *Oberstleutnant* Kitschmann (26 April 1938–28 February 1940)

- ***Panzer-Aufklärungs-Abteilung 5***

Activated: 1 March 1940

Antecedent Formation: *Aufklärungs-Abteilung 5 (mot)*

Replacement Detachment: *Ersatz-Abteilung für motorisierte Aufklärungs-Einheiten 7*

Deactivated: 11 August 1941 and personnel used to form *Kradschützen-Bataillon 24* of *22. Panzer-Division*

Organization: 1940—Headquarters, 1st Armored Scout Company, 2nd Armored Scout Company, 3rd Motorcycle Infantry Company, 4th Company (heavy); August 1940—1st Armored Scout Company, 3rd Motorcycle Infantry Company, 4th Company (heavy)

Commanders: *Oberstleutnant* Kitschmann (1 March–October 1940); *Major/Oberstleutnant* Schmidmann (October 1940–11 August 1941

Notes: In August 1940, the 2nd Armored Scout Company was reassigned to *Aufklärungs-Abteilung 231 (mot)* of *11. Panzer-Division*. On 21 May 1941, the 1st Armored Scout Company was sunk while being transported off the Greek mainland. The reconstituted 1st Armored Scout Company remained with the division, however, and was attached and then assigned to *Kradschützen-Bataillon 2*.

- ***Panzer-Aufklärungs-Abteilung 2***

Activated: 16 March 1943

Antecedent Formation: *Kradschützen-Bataillon 2*

Replacement Detachment: *Kradschützen-Ersatz-Bataillon 2*, followed by *Panzer-Aufklärungs-Ersatz- und Ausbildungs-Abteilung 2*

Deactivated: 8 May 1945

Organization: 1943—Headquarters, 1st Armored Scout Company, 2nd Motorcycle Infantry Company, 3rd Motorcycle Infantry Company, 4th Motorcycle Infantry Company, and 5th Company (heavy). March 1944—Headquarters with Armored Scout Platoon (*Sd.Kfz. 233*), 1st Armored Scout Company (armored car), 2nd Armored Scout Company (half-track), 3rd Armored Reconnaissance Company (half-track), 4th Armored Reconnaissance Company (half-track) and 5th Heavy Armored Reconnaissance Company.[6] October 1944—1st Armored Scout Company (half-track), 2nd Light Armored Reconnaissance Company (half-track), 3rd Armored Reconnaissance Company (half-track) and 4th Heavy Armored Reconnaissance Company. January 1945—Headquarters and 4th Heavy Armored Reconnaissance Company. April 1945—Headquarters, 1st Mixed Armored Scout and Reconnaissance Company, 2nd Armored Reconnaissance Company, 3rd Bicycle Company,[7] 4th Heavy Armored Reconnaissance Company

Commanders: *Major* Petri (16 March–10 October 1943); *Hauptmann/Major* Kuntz (October 1943–February 1944); *Hauptmann* Riedel (acting) (February–May 1944); *Hauptmann* Schulz (acting) (May–June 1944); *Major* von Schkopp (June–December 1944); *Major* von Laer (acting) (December 1944–April 1945); *Hauptmann* Dürkes (acting) (April–8 May 1945)

Notes: In December 1943, the division was withdrawn from the Eastern Front for reconstitution in France. *Panzer-Aufklärungs-Abteilung 2* was the last element to leave the front. It was attached from 16 to 27 December to *4. Panzer-Division*, before departing for France in January 1944. Battalion strength reduced by almost 70 during the fighting in Normandy. Reconstituted in October and November 1944. Elements of the battalion's 1st Company—perhaps even the entire company—were tasked to provide personnel for the formation of an armored scout company for *Panzer-Brigade 150* (Skorzeny's

Top left: This scout of the battalion has attempted to make his cumbersome beret/crash helmet look "jaunty" for a studio portrait. SCOTT PRITCHETT **Top right:** Otto Damm, a scout initially assigned to *Aufklärungs-Abteilung 5 (mot)* and subsequently reassigned to *11. Panzer-Division* after the fall of France. JIM HALEY

Left: An *Erkennungsmarke* for a scout assigned to *Aufklärungs-Abteilung 5 (mot).*

"brigade" for the Ardennes offensive) on 4 November 1944. The 1st Company was never reformed. The battalion was reconstituted after the Ardennes offensive (Milowitz Training Area in Czechoslovakia). It rejoined the division in April 1945.

- ***Kradschützen-Bataillon 2***

Activated: 15 October 1935[8]

Antecedent Formation: *Reiter-Regiment 16*

Replacement Detachment: *Schützen-Ersatz-Bataillon 2*

Redesignated: *Panzer-Aufklärungs-Abteilung 2* on 16 March 1943.

Organization: 1939–40—Headquarters, 1st Motorcycle Infantry Company, 2nd Motorcycle Infantry Company, 3rd Motorcycle Infantry Company, 4th Motorcycle Infantry Machine Gun Company and 5th Company (heavy). 1941–42—*1. (PzSpäh)/Aufklärungs-Abteilung 5 (mot)* attached to preceding; armored scout company designated as *6./Kradschützen-Bataillon 2*. March 1942—Headquarters, 1st Armored Scout Company, 2nd Motorcycle Infantry Company, 3rd Motorcycle Infantry Company, 4th Motorcycle Infantry Company and 5th Company (heavy)

Commanders: *Major* von der Decken (?–?); *Oberstleutnant* Stollbrock (February 1939–May 1941); *Major* Creuznacher (May 1941–9 August 1942); *Hauptmann* Forster (acting) (August–September 1942); *Major* Petri (September 1942–15 March 1943)

Awards: Knight's Cross—*Oberfeldwebel* Anders *3./Panzer-Aufklärungs-Abteilung 2* (14 August 1943); *Stabsfeldwebel* Gath, *2./Panzer-Aufklärungs-Abteilung 2* (11 October 1943); *Hauptmann* Kuntz, *Panzer-Aufklärungs-Abteilung 2* (6 February 1944); *Unteroffizier* Reittinger, *4./Panzer-Aufklärungs-*

Simulated vision ports have been painted on the sides of this *Sd.Kfz. 221* in an effort to confuse the enemy about the location of the real vision ports.

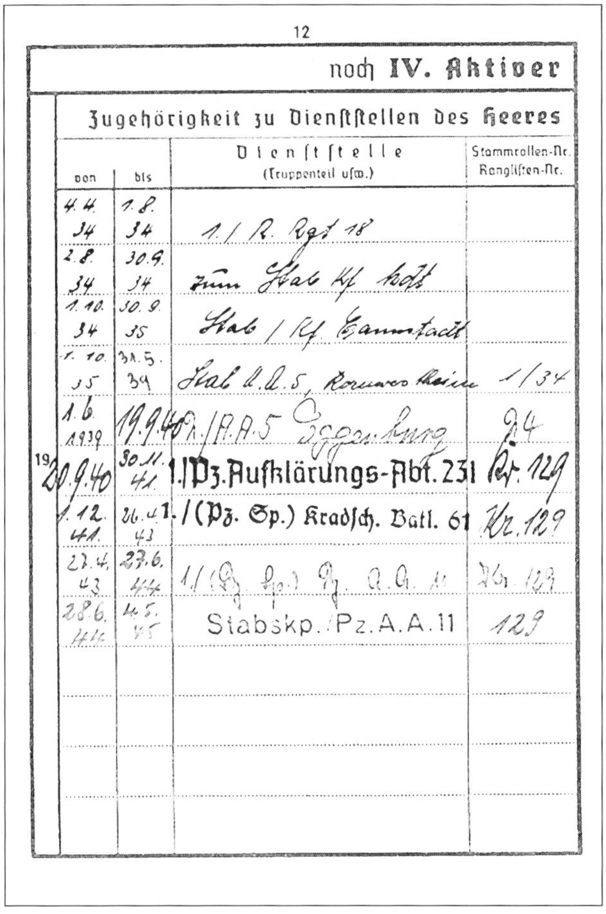

12

noch IV. Aktiver

Zugehörigkeit zu Dienststellen des Heeres

von	bis	Dienststelle (Truppenteil usw.)	Stammrollen-Nr. Ranglisten-Nr.
4.4. 34	1.8. 34	1./R. Rgt 18	
2.8. 34	30.9. 34	zum Stab Kf. Abt	
1.10. 34	30.9. 35	Stab / Kf. Cannstadt	
1.10. 35	31.5. 39	Stab A.A.5, [illegible]	1/34
1.6. 1939	19.9.40	1./A.A.5 [illegible]	94
19 20.9.40	30.11. 41	1./Pz.Aufklärungs-Abt.231	Kr. 129
1.12. 41	26.4. 43	1./(Pz. Sp.) Kradsch. Batl. 61	Kr. 129
27.4. 43	27.6. 44	1/(Pz. Sp.) Pz. A.A. 11	Kr. 129
28.6. 44	4.5. 45	Stabskp./Pz.A.A.11	129

Left: A page from Damm's *Wehrpaß* indicating units of assignment. JIM HALEY

Abteilung 2 (23 October 1944). **German Cross in Gold**—*Oberfeldwebel* Aeckerle, *2./Panzer-Aufklärungs-Abteilung 2* (12 March 1944); *Major* Creuznacher, *Kradschützen-Bataillon 2* (14 February 1942); *Oberleutnant* Dürkes, *Kradschützen-Bataillon 2* (5 April 1943); *Hauptmann* Forster, *Kradschützen-Bataillon 2* (29 March 1943); *Oberleutnant* Hild, *Panzer-Aufklärungs-Abteilung 2* (3 October 1944); *Oberleutnant* Kröcher, *Kradschützen-Bataillon 2* (14 February 1942); *Leutnant* Mirow, *Panzer-Aufklärungs-Abteilung 2* (12 October 1944); *Hauptmann* Roland, *4./Panzer-Aufklärungs-Abteilung 2* (3 November 1943); *Unteroffizier* Scheuering, *3./Kradschützen-Bataillon 2* (14 February 1942); *Major* von Schkopp, *Panzer-Aufklärungs-Abteilung 2* (21 October 1944); *Feldwebel* Schmidt, *5./Panzer-Aufklärungs-Abteilung 2* (21 October 1943)

Damm started his career as an armored scout in the *Adler Kfz. 13*. As with any career soldier of the time, he participated in numerous training exercises and took the opportunity to take a number of photographs, which are of interest to vehicle enthusiasts. On these two pages, we see the *Sd.Kfz. 221* armored car as well as a *PaK 36* 3.7cm antitank gun (below).

The *Sd.Kfz. 223* armored car.

Early models of the *Sd.Kfz. 231 (6 Rad)*.

The *Sd.Kfz. 232 (Fu) (6 Rad)*. Note the prewar three-tone camouflage scheme.

Of particular interest on this *Sd.Kfz. 223* is the stylized unit marking, commonly seen on armored cars of various *Aufklärungs-Abteilungen* in the mid-1930s.

Vehicles line up to continue a road march. Note the rear driver in the *Sd.Kfz. 231 (6 Rad)* in the foreground.

This *Sd.Kfz. 263 (Fu) (8 Rad)* is camouflaged in a patch of woods during the campaign in Poland.

Early models of the *Sd.Kfz. 231 (8 Rad)*. The initial issuance of the heavy armored car sparked a great deal of interest among the curious crews of the battalion.

The crew of an *Sd.Kfz. 223 (Fu)* takes a breather.

This unidentified officer is one of the early recipients of the Iron Cross, Second Class, a highly admired award at the time.

A casualty of war, this burnt-out *Sd.Kfz. 231 (6 Rad)* is transported back to Germany, most likely for salvage.

A long line of vehicles, typical of the early days of the campaign in France. The reconnaissance elements had to wait for the deliberate breach of the French lines.

The *Sd.Kfz. 222* must have been issued to the battalion relatively late, since this is the first time it surfaces in images from Damm.

Sd.Kfz. 221's, *Sd.Kfz. 222's*, and *Sd.Kfz. 223's* move through the streets of built-up areas in France.

As the campaign wound down, crews had a bit more time to relax on occasion, although the march south against the rapidly retreating French Army often looked more like competitive racing in tactical vehicles than a traditional pursuit.

Taking a breather after hard operations and heavy road marching, as indicated by the dusty faces.

The scouts used available infrastructure to cross water obstacles.

Casualties of war: knocked-out *Sd.Kfz. 232 (Fu) (6 Rad)'s*, an *Sd.Kfz. 222*, and an *Sd.Kfz. 231 (8 Rad)*.

WH-134344

The *Sd.Kfz. 263 (Fu) (8 Rad)* provided a vital communications link to higher headquarters during wide-ranging operations.

An *Sd.Kfz 232 (Fu) (6 Rad)* burns out after being hit.

A unit officer takes time to bond with a puppy.

Officers plan the next moves.

After the victory, it was back to Paris and Versailles for a victory parade and occupation duty.

Damm has received his Iron Cross, Second Class.

Above left: This *Sd.Kfz. 221* is being used to transport prisoners to the rear. **Above right:** Fritz Henke, a veteran scout, joined *Panzer-Aufklärungs-Abteilung 2* relatively late, after serving in North Africa. This prewar image shows an *Sd.Kfz. 231 (6 Rad)* that was in Henke's unit at the time.

Soldbuch

zugleich Personalausweis

Nr. 5837

für

den Soldat

(Dienstgrad)

ab .... (Datum) .... (neuer Dienstgrad)

ab

ab

Josef Wimmer

(Vor- und Zuname)

Beschriftung und Nummer der Erkennungsmarke Schtz. Ers. Kp. 3/10 5837

Blutgruppe 0

Gasmaskengröße 3

Wehrnummer

1

Im Namen des Führers und Obersten Befehlshabers der Wehrmacht

verleihe ich

dem

Unteroffizier

Fritz Henke,

Panzerarmee-Nachschubfuehrer Afrika,

das

Eiserne Kreuz 2. Klasse

Armee-Gef.St., den 8. 7. 1942

(Dienstsiegel)

Generalfeldmarschall und Oberbefehlshaber der Panzerarmee Afrika

(Dienstgrad und Dienststellung)

Soldbuch belonging to Josef Wimmer, who joined *Panzer-Aufklärungs-Abteilung 2* in 1943.

Left: Henke's award certificate for the Iron Cross, Second Class, has a facsimile Rommel signature.

3. INFANTERIE-DIVISION (MOT)

Campaigns: Poland and France (as *3. Infanterie-Division*), Soviet Union

Reconnaissance Formations:

- ***Aufklärungs-Abteilung 53 (mot)***

Activated: 27 October 1940

Antecedent Formation: Formed from personnel levies against *2./Aufklärungs-Abteilung 3* and *2./Panzer-Aufklärungs-Abteilung 37*

Replacement Detachment: Not certain, presumably *Ersatz-Abteilung für motorisierte Aufklärungs-Einheiten 3*

Redesignated: Consolidated with *Kradschützen-Bataillon 53* in March 1942, with its 1st and 2nd Companies becoming the 1st and 4th Companies of the motorcycle infantry battalion

Organization: 1940–42—Headquarters, 1st Armored Scout Company, 2nd Motorcycle Infantry Company, 3rd Company (heavy)

Commanders: *Hauptmann* Stephan (27 October 1940–July 1941); *Oberleutnant* Eisel (acting) (July 1941); *Hauptmann* Ball (acting) (July–9 October 1941); *Oberleutnant* Sauvant-Siegert (acting) (9 October 1941–15 March 1942)

- ***Kradschützen-Bataillon 53***

Activated: 27 October 1940

Antecedent Formation: Formed from personnel levies against *II./Infanterie-Regiment 50*, *leichter Infanterie-Geschütz-Zug* of the same regiment, *PaK-Zug* of *Infanterie-Regiment 8*, and a platoon from *3./Pionier-Bataillon 3*

Replacement Detachment: *Schützen-Ersatz-Bataillon 3*

Deactivation: Surrendered at Stalingrad in January 1943

Organization: 1940–42—Headquarters, 1st Motorcycle Infantry Company, 2nd Motorcycle Infantry Company, 3rd Motorcycle Infantry Company, 4th Motorcycle Infantry Machine Gun Company, and 5th Company (heavy). March 1942—Headquarters, 1st Armored Scout Company, 2nd Motorcycle Infantry Company, 3rd Motorcycle Infantry Company, 4th Motorcycle Infantry Company, and 5th Company (heavy)

Commanders: *Oberstleutnant* Erdmann (27 October 1940–20 August 1941); *Hauptmann* von Kessel (acting) (20–25 August 1941); *Oberstleutnant* Erdmann (25 August–October 1941); *Major* von Stein (October–7 November 1941); *Oberleutnant* Bolle (acting) (7 November–31 December 1941); *Major* Fau (31 December 1941–September 1942); *Oberleutnant* Schroeck (acting) (September 1942–January 1943)

Awards: Knight's Cross—Hauptmann Ball, *Aufklärungs-Abteilung 53 (mot)* (23 November 1943); *Oberstleutnant* Erdmann, *Kradschützen-Bataillon 53* (12 September 1941); *Oberleutnant* Stracke, *2./Kradschützen-Bataillon 53* (21 November 1942). Honor Roll (Clasp)—*Unteroffizier* Weise, *5./Kradschützen-Bataillon 53* (5 September 1942). German Cross in Gold—*Oberleutnant* Behne, *4./Kradschützen-Bataillon 53* (27 October 1942); *Major* Fau, *Kradschützen-Bataillon 53* (3 October 1942); *Leutnant* Froitzheim, *1./Aufklärungs-Abteilung 53 (mot)* (29 November 1941); *Leutnant* Hohmann, *1./Kradschützen-Bataillon 53* (18 June 1943); *Oberleutnant* Schroeck, *1./Kradschützen-Bataillon 53* (12 November 1942); *Leutnant* Stracke, *1./Kradschützen-Bataillon 53* (29 November 1942); *Stabsfeldwebel* Tiedemann, *1./Kradschützen-Bataillon 53* (29 November 1942).

3. PANZERGRENADIER-DIVISION

Campaigns: Soviet Union, Italy, France, Germany, Ardennes, Germany

Reconnaissance Formations:

- ***Panzer-Aufklärungs-Abteilung 53***

Activated: 1 March 1943

Antecedent Formation: Redesignated *Kradschützen-Bataillon 386*

Replacement Detachment: *Panzer-Aufklärungs-Ersatz-Abteilung 3*

Redesignated: *Panzer-Aufklärungs-Abteilung 103* on 19 April 1943

Organization: 1943—Headquarters, 1st Armored Scout Company (armored car), 2nd Armored Scout Company (half-track), 3rd Armored Reconnaissance Company (half-track), 4th Armored Reconnaissance Company (half-track), and 5th Company (heavy)

Commanders: *Hauptmann* Scharf (1 March–19 April 1943)

- ***Panzer-Aufklärungs-Abteilung 103***

Activated: 20 April 1943

Antecedent Formation: Formed from personnel levies against *2./Aufklärungs-Abteilung 3* and *2./Panzer-Aufklärungs-Abteilung 37*

Replacement Detachment: *Panzer-Aufklärungs-Ersatz-Abteilung 3*

Deactivation: Surrendered on 14 April 1945 (Ruhr Pocket)

Organization: 1943–44—Headquarters, 1st Armored Scout Company (armored car), 2nd Armored Scout Company (half-track), 3rd Armored Reconnaissance Company (half-track), 4th Armored Reconnaissance Company (half-track), and 5th Company (heavy). December 1944—1st Armored Scout Company (half-track), 3rd Armored Reconnaissance Company (light half-track), 4th Armored Reconnaissance Company (light half-track), and 5th Company (heavy half-track)

Commanders: *Hauptmann* von Zieten (20 April–4 November 1943); *Hauptmann* Abraham (commander) (4 November 1943); *Rittmeister* Kottmann (November 1943–November 1944); *Major* Feldhoff (November 1944–16 April 1945)

Awards: Honor Roll (Clasp)—*Hauptmann* Zimmermann, *3./Panzer-Aufklärungs-Abteilung 103* (21 October 1944). **German Cross in Gold**—*Oberleutnant* Braun, *5./Panzer-Aufklärungs-Abteilung 103* (10 January 1944); *Oberfeldwebel* Lingner, *2./Panzer-Aufklärungs-Abteilung 103* (8 November 1944); *Hauptmann* von Zieten, *Headquarters, Panzer-Aufklärungs-Abteilung 103* (12 March 1944)

3. LEICHTE DIVISION

Campaigns: Poland

Reconnaissance Formations:

- ***Aufklärungs-Regiment 8 (mot)***

Activated: 10 November 1938

Replacement Detachment: *Ersatz-Abteilung für motorisierte Einheiten 8*

Deactivation: Transferred to *8. Panzer-Division* on 16 October 1939, with battalions redesignated and regiment deactivated by November 1939

Commander: *Oberstleutnant* von Kessel (10 November 1938–16 October 1939)[9]

The regiment consisted of a motorcycle infantry battalion and an armored scout battalion:

- ***I./Aufklärungs-Regiment 8 (mot)***

Antecedent Formations: Battalion formed by redesignation of *Aufklärungs-Abteilung 2 (mot)*

Replacement Detachment: *Ersatz-Abteilung für motorisierte Einheiten 8*

Redesignation: Following attachment to *10. Panzer-Division* and fighting with it in Poland, the battalion was reassigned to that division and redesignated as *Panzer-Aufklärungs-Abteilung 90* on 1 April 1940.

Organization: 1939—Headquarters, 1st Armored Scout Troop, 2nd Armored Scout Troop, 3rd Motorcycle Infantry Troop, and 4th Troop (Heavy)

Commanders: Battalion commander—*Major Freiherr* von Lützow. 1st Troop—*Oberleutnant* Neubeck. 2nd Troop—*Rittmeister* von Görne. 3rd Troop—*Oberleutnant* von Plehwe. 4th Troop—*Rittmeister* Rudolf

- ***II./Aufklärungs-Regiment 8 (mot)***

Replacement Detachment: *Ersatz-Abteilung für motorisierte Einheiten 8*

Redesignation: After transfer to *8. Panzer-Division* and deactivation of the regiment, the battal-

Major Freiherr von Lützow was the commander of *I./Aufklärungs-Regiment 8 (mot)*. He came from a long line of cavalry officers, including the *General* Lützow of the Napoleonic Wars.

ion was redesignated as *Aufklärungs-Abteilung 59 (mot)* and reassigned to the division.[10]

Organization: 1939—Headquarters, 5th Armored Scout Troop, 6th Armored Scout Troop, 7th Motorcycle Infantry Troop, 8th Troop (heavy), 7th Armored Scout Troop

Commanders: Battalion commander—*Major* von Seidlitz. 5th Troop—*Oberleutnant Freiherr* von Thielmann. 6th Troop—*Rittmeister* von Witzleben. 7th Troop—*Oberleutnant* von dem Knesebeck. 8th Troop—*Oberleutnant* Richter

3. PANZER-DIVISION

Campaigns: Poland, France, Soviet Union

Reconnaissance Formations:

- ***Kradschützen-Bataillon 3***

Activated: 15 October 1935

Antecedent Formation: Personnel levies against *Reiter-Regiment 16*

Replacement Detachment: *Kradschützen-Ersatz-Abteilung 3*

Deactivation: 27 April 1943

Organization: 1939–40—Headquarters, 1st Motorcycle Infantry Company, 2nd Motorcycle Infantry Company, 3rd Motorcycle Infantry Company, 4th Motorcycle Infantry Machine Gun Company, and 5th Company (heavy). April 1942—Headquarters, 1st Armored Scout Company (armored car), 2nd Motorcycle Infantry Company, 3rd Motorcycle Infantry Company, 4th Armored Reconnaissance Company (light half-track), and 5th Company (heavy). September 1942—Headquarters, 1st Armored Scout Company (armored car), 2nd Armored Scout Company (half-track), 3rd Motorcycle Infantry Company, 4th Motorcycle Infantry Company and 5th Company (heavy)

Commanders: *Major/Oberstleutnant* von Manteuffel (15 October 1935–30 November 1939); *Oberstleutnant* Tröger (1 December 1939–June 1940); *Oberstleutnant/Oberst* von Manteuffel (June 1940–January 1941); *Oberstleutnant* Corvin-Wiersbitzki (January–August 1941); *Major* Pape (1 September 1941–May 1942); *Hauptmann* Knoblauch (acting) (May 1942–?); *Major* Pape

(?–7 August 1942); *Major* von Cochenhausen (7 August–October 1942)

- ***Aufklärungs-Abteilung 3 (mot)***

Activated: 15 October 1935

Antecedent Formations: Formed from personnel levies against *1./Kraftfahr-Abteilung 3*

Replacement Detachment: *Ersatz-Abteilung für motorisierte Aufklärungseinheiten 3*

Reassignment: In January 1941, the battalion was transferred to *5. leichte Division*

Organization: 1939—Headquarters, 1st Armored Scout Troop, 2nd Armored Scout Troop, 3rd Motorcycle Infantry Troop, 4th Troop (heavy). September 1940—Headquarters, 2nd Armored Scout Troop, 3rd Motorcycle Infantry Troop, 4th Troop (heavy)

Commanders: *Major Freiherr* von Wechmar (1 September 1939–14 January 1941

Notes: On 16 September 1940, the 1st Company was reassigned to *60. Infanterie-Division (mot)* and redesignated as *1.(Pz.Späh)/Aufklärungs-Abteilung 160 (mot)*.

- ***Aufklärungs-Abteilung 1 (mot)***

Activated: 10 October 1935

Antecedent Formations: Formed from personnel levies against *1./Kraftfahr-Abteilung 1*

Replacement Detachment: *Ersatz-Abteilung für motorisierte Aufklärungseinheiten 1*

Redesignation: Redesignated as *Panzer-Aufklärungs-Abteilung 1* on 23 April 1941

Organization: 1941—Headquarters, 1st Armored Scout Company, 3rd Motorcycle Infantry Company, 4th Company (heavy)

Commanders: *Major* Ziervogel (15 January–23 April 1941)

Notes: Replaced *Aufklärungs-Abteilung 3 (mot)*, which was reassigned to *5. leichte Division*, which was being activated for deployment to North Africa. Prior to being assigned to *3. Panzer-Division*, it had been a separate motorized reconnaissance battalion. Its 1st Company was reassigned to *18. Panzer-Division* and redesignated as *1.(Pz.Späh)/Aufklärungs-Abteilung 18 (mot)*.

- ***Panzer-Aufklärungs-Abteilung 1***

Activated: 24 April 1941

Antecedent Formations: *Aufklärungs-Abteilung 1 (mot)*

Replacement Detachment: Initially *Ersatz-Abteilung für motorisierte Aufklärungseinheiten 3*, then *Kradschützen-Ersatz-Bataillon 4* (effective 1 October 1941)

Deactivation/Redesignation: Consolidated with *Kradschützen-Bataillon 3* on 25 April 1942

Organization: 1941–42—Headquarters, 1st Armored Scout Company, 3rd Motorcycle Infantry Company, 4th Company (heavy)

Commanders: *Major* Ziervogel (24 April 1941–25 April 1942)

- ***Panzer-Aufklärungs-Abteilung 3***

Activated: 28 April 1943

Replacement Detachment: Initially *Panzer-Aufklärungs-Ersatz- und Ausbildungs-Abteilung 3*, then *Panzer-Aufklärungs-Ersatz-Abteilung 3*

Surrendered: 8 May 1945

Organization: 1943—Headquarters, 1st Armored Scout Company, 2nd Armored Reconnaissance Company (possibly half-track but listed as *Krad*), 3rd Armored Reconnaissance Company (*Krad*, later half-track), 4th Armored Reconnaissance Company (light half-track), and 5th Company (heavy). November 1944—Headquarters Company (with light armored cars), 1st Armored Scout Company, 2nd Armored Reconnaissance Company (half-track), 3rd Armored Reconnaissance Company (half-track), and 4th Company (heavy). 1945 (theoretical)—Headquarters, 1st Armored Scout and Reconnaissance Company (mixed), 3rd Armored Reconnaissance Company (half-track), 4th Armored Reconnaissance Company (half-track), and 4th Company (heavy)

Commanders: *Hauptmann* Deichen (July 1943–September 1944); *Hauptmann* Golze (September 1944–8 May 1945)

Notes: *3./Panzer-Aufklärungs-Abteilung 3* was disbanded after taking heavy losses in the fall of 1943 and did not rejoin the battalion until June of the following year.[11] The company was sent to Germany for reconstitution, and the battalion itself basically ceased as a fighting unit after taking heavy losses in the spring of 1944, with the 1st and 5th Companies ordered to Germany for reconstitution on 6 July and the 2nd Company on 18 July. On 21 July, the latter received instructions to reorganize as a Type "B" armored scout company (*Aufklärungspanzer 38[t]*).[12] For most of the summer of 1944, the reconnaissance only had an effective field strength of the equivalent of two companies. By December, the battalion was back to full strength. Around 10 April 1945, the battalion was detached from the division and never rejoined it.

Awards: Knight's Cross—*Hauptmann* Deichen, *Panzer-Aufklärungs-Abteilung 3* (10 September 1943); *Oberleutnant* Kleffel, *4./Panzer-Aufklärungs-Abteilung 3* (14 May 1944); *Major* Pape, *Kradschützen-Bataillon 3* (10 February 1942). **Honor Roll (Clasp)**—*Hauptmann* von Cochenhausen, *1./Kradschützen-Bataillon 3* (18 March 1942); *Oberfeldwebel* Friedrich, Headquarters, *Panzer-Aufklärungs-Abteilung 3* (1945); *Leutnant* Hess, *4./Kradschützen-Bataillon 3* (19 November 1942); *Stabsgefreiter* Nöske, *3./Panzer-Aufklärungs-Abteilung 3* (17 October 1944); *Unteroffizier* Paul, *2./Panzer-Aufklärungs-Abteilung 3* (1945); *Unteroffizier* Pollack, *3./Panzer-Aufklärungs-Abteilung 3* (27 November 1944); *Leutnant* Romeike, *1./Panzer-Aufklärungs-Abteilung 3* (17 November 1943). **German Cross in Gold**—*Unteroffizier* Blass, *3./Kradschützen-Bataillon 3* (8 May 1943); *Leutnant* Brandes, *Kradschützen-Bataillon 3* (18 October 1941); *Hauptmann* von Cochenhausen, *1./Kradschützen-Bataillon 3* (23

A nice portrait of a scout from *Aufklärungs-Abteilung 3 (mot)*, the first reconnaissance battalion of the *3. Panzer-Division*.

January 1942); *Hauptmann* Deichen, *2./Kradschützen-Bataillon 3* (8 May 1943); *Obergefreiter* Dickfoss, *3./Panzer-Aufklärungs-Abteilung 3* (22 March 1945); *Oberfeldwebel* Ehrat, *2./Kradschützen-Bataillon 3* (23 January 1942); *Oberleutnant* Erdmann, *2./Kradschützen-Bataillon 3* (23 January 1942); *Hauptmann* Golze, *1./Panzer-Aufklärungs-Abteilung 3* (4 February 1944); *Feldwebel* Haase, *2./Panzer-Aufklärungs-Abteilung 3* (8 September 1943); *Leutnant* Harbeck, *Kradschützen-Bataillon 3* (31 October 1942); *Unteroffizier* Hinz, *4./Panzer-Aufklärungs-Abteilung 3* (8 July 1944); *Feldwebel* Hoppe, *4./Panzer-Aufklärungs-Abteilung 3* (14 May 1944); *Oberfeldwebel* Kerstan, *4./Panzer-Aufklärungs-Abteilung 3* (12 October 1944); *Oberleutnant* Kleffel, *4./Panzer-Aufklärungs-Abteilung 3* (16 November 1943); *Unteroffizier* Lindemann, *4./Kradschützen-Bataillon 3* (14 March 1943); *Unteroffizier* Lüchtefeld, *4./Panzer-Aufklärungs-Abteilung 3* (21 October 1944); *Leutnant* von dem Osten, *4./Panzer-Aufklärungs-Abteilung 3* (14 November 1944); *Unteroffizier* Otte, *2./Panzer-Aufklärungs-Abteilung 3* (24 April 1944); *Major* Pape, *Kradschützen-Bataillon 3* (23 January 1942); *Feldwebel* Potthoff, Headquarters, *Panzer-Aufklärungs-Abteilung 3* (15 April 1945);

A prewar training breaching exercise conducted by *Aufklärungs-Abteilung 1 (mot)*, which would later replace *Aufklärungs-Abteilung 3 (mot)* in *3. Panzer-Division* when the latter was transferred to the *5. leichte Division*.

Right: Grave sites of the battalion's fallen from the campaign in Poland.

Oberfeldwebel Rüdenburg, *1./Kradschützen-Bataillon 3* (8 May 1943); *Obergefreiter* Schenk, *3./Panzer-Aufklärungs-Abteilung 3* (27 October 1944); *Leutnant* Schröder, Headquarters, *Panzer-Aufklärungs-Abteilung 3* (27 October 1944); *Leutnant* Schulz, *Panzer-Aufklärungs-Abteilung 1* (23 January 1942); *Oberleutnant* Voutta, *Kradschützen-Bataillon 3* (8 May 1943); *Hauptmann* Zeise, *2./Panzer-Aufklärungs-Abteilung 3* (21 February 1944); *Major* Ziervogel, *Panzer-Aufklärungs-Abteilung 1* (25 March 1942). **German Cross in Silver**—*Hauptfeldwebel* Altrock, Headquarters, *Panzer-Aufklärungs-Abteilung 3* (15 March 1945).

4. LEICHTE DIVISION

Campaigns: Poland

Reconnaissance Formations:

- ***Aufklärungs-Regiment 9***

Activated: 1 April 1938

Replacement Detachment: Initially *Ersatz-Abteilung für motorisierte Aufklärungseinheiten 9*, followed by *Ersatz-Abteilung für motorisierte Aufklärungseinheiten 7* in December 1939

Reorganization: On 3 January 1940, the division was reorganized and redesignated as *9. Panzer-Division*, with the regiment remaining intact through the campaign in the West.

Commanders: *Oberstleutnant/Oberst Ritter* von Hauenschild (1 April 1938–16 October 1939); *Oberstleutnant* Vichytil (16 October 1939–3 January 1940)

The regiment consisted of two battalions:

- ***I./Aufklärungs-Regiment 9***

Antecedent Formations: Formed from *Kraftfahr-Jäger-Bataillon 4* (4th Motorized Light Infantry Battalion) of the former Austrian *Bundesheer*

Organization: 1939—Headquarters, 1st Motorcycle Infantry Troop, 2nd Motorcycle Infantry Troop, 3rd Motorcycle Infantry Troop, and 4th Troop (heavy)

Commanders (as of 3 January 1939): Commander—*Oberstleutnant* Vichytil. Troop Commanders—1st Troop, *Rittmeister* Pfisterer; 2nd Troop, *Oberleutnant* Sartorius; 3rd Troop, *Oberleutnant* Soldan; 4th Troop, *Rittmeister* Schulz

- ***II./Aufklärungs-Regiment 9***

Antecedent Formations: Formed by personnel levies against *Aufklärungs-Abteilungen 5,7*, and *9*

Organization: 1939—Headquarters, 5th Armored Scout Troop, 6th Armored Scout Troop, and 7th Armored Scout Troop

Commanders: Commander—*Rittmeister Dr. Freiherr* von Ohlen und Adlerscron. Troop Commanders—5th Troop, *Oberleutnant* Poessel; 6th Troop, *Oberleutnant* Mayer; 7th Troop, *Rittmeister* Bentele

4. PANZER-DIVISION

Campaigns: Poland, France, Soviet Union

Reconnaissance Formations:

- ***Aufklärungs-Abteilung 7 (mot)***

Activated: 15 October 1935

Antecedent Formations: *Kraftfahr-Abteilung München*

Replacement Detachment: *Ersatz-Abteilung für motorisierte Aufklärungseinheiten 7*

Redesignation: 1 February 1940 as *Panzer-Aufklärungs-Abteilung 7*

Organization: 1939—Headquarters, 1st Armored Scout Company, 2nd Armored Scout Company, 3rd Motorcycle Infantry Company, and 4th Company (heavy)

Commanders: *Major* Marzahn (1939–31 January 1940)

- ***Panzer-Aufklärungs-Abteilung 7***

Activated: 1 February 1940

Antecedent Formations: *Aufklärungs-Abteilung 7 (mot)*

Replacement Detachment: *Ersatz-Abteilung für motorisierte Aufklärungseinheiten 7*, later replaced by *Kradschützen-Ersatz-Bataillon 7* (1 October 1941)

Deactivation/Redesignation: Consolidated with *Kradschützen-Bataillon 34* on 19 October 1941; deactivated on 12 December 1941 (unofficially) and 5 May 1942 (officially)

Organization: 1940–41—Headquarters, 1st Armored Scout Company, 2nd Motorcycle Infantry Company, and 3rd Company (heavy)

Commanders: *Major* Marzahn (1 February–November 1940); *Hauptmann* Nierle (November 1940–19 October 1941)

4. leichte Division

During the war, a book was published by Ferdinand Bentele with the title of *Im Panzer durch Polen* (*Through Poland in a Tank*), from which this excerpt was taken. The book portrayed the exploits of the *II./Aufklärungs-Regiment 9*, in which *Rittmeister* Bentele was a armored scout troop commander. It is one of the few records of fighting, albeit romanticized, concerning the short-lived formation. He describes the morning of 1 September 1939:

> My watch said 0435 hours. I got up and issued orders to be prepared to move out. I then stared up to the high ground, where the battalion command post was located. The minutes lasted forever. Then, all of a sudden, there were two flashes. Two dull reports of artillery firing were heard. At that point, two lines of light streamed skyward, only to fall back to earth as brilliant white balls. At almost the same time, there was an ear-deafening blast off to the left, and the first shell hissed its way toward enemy territory.
>
> Our engine thundered alive and propelled our vehicle at full throttle towards the border. With a loud crash, the border barriers cracked and splintered and flew off to the side. "Firing halt!" My gunner received directions from me for firing. Our weapons starting singing their song right away. The dull bum-bum-bum of the main gun was accentuated by the tack-tack-tack of our machine gun. The Polish machine-gun nests were under the concentrated fires of three heavy scout vehicles. The artillery successfully engaged the quarters of the Polish soldiers. That must have been a surprise for them! I could observe fleeing Polacks through my binoculars. Hladovka was burning. The livestock that had been released from its stalls was wandering aimlessly through the fields. In order to prevent senseless suffering by the civilian populace, I ordered the firing to cease.
>
> The artillery also stopped firing at the same time, and it was shifted forward two kilometers. We had to continuously observe the road, since there was the danger of mines. My vehicle was the first one to slowly descend the slope. After the first bend, I observed that the road was not trafficable, because it had been torn up. I was able to move forward in the field off the side of the road.
>
> Right in front of the bridge was a large abatis on the road. With the help of the ethnic Slovakians, who lives along the border, the obstacle was cut apart in short order. Once it was determined that the bridge was safe, we moved at high speed though a small village and in the direction of Sucha Hora . . .[13]

Later, Bentele describes an encounter with an anti-tank gun:

> I was moving in the lead vehicle. The armored car carefully felt its way forward into the curve. My face pressed tightly against optics, I was looking for enemy riflemen AT guns. But I couldn't find even a mouse.
>
> Krakowiec was all quiet ahead of us, as if it were peacetime. The morning sun was smiling on us and, despite that, we knew: Danger was lurking for us everywhere. Perhaps it would be riflemen or a well-camouflaged AT gun. That meant: Keep your eyes peeled!
>
> "Move out!" I ordered the vehicle driver. The speed increased as we approached the entrance to the village. An abandoned truck was off to the left of the road. It had already concealed us from quite a distance. Just before we got to it, we turned off to the right. Then there was a buzzing. I searched for the cause, but didn't see anything. Only the whistling of enemy machine guns and rifles could be heard off to the right, the left and in between.
>
> "AT?" I asked myself. That had to have been an AT gun!
>
> I traversed and searched with the turret. I was only able to discern a small cloud of smoke far off to the right. I knew what I had to do. "Back up!" I pulled the triggers. The main gun thundered dully.—It had a calming effect.
>
> Then I quickly reported: Enemy AT guns at the outskirts of the village. For the moment,

nothing stirred, however. Minutes of waiting passed. Only the sound of rifle rounds could be heard.

I thought to myself: Who dares, wins! I decided to advance for the second time. We slowly rolled forward. There it was—in the middle of the road—hardly recognizable. I took up a sight picture.

Once again, there was a buzz. But this time, it was drowned out by the sound of our main gun and from the high-pitched pinging of the machine gun.

I observed intently. I must have hit it. Or was it too late?

At that moment, we received a tremendous blow. Our vehicle pitched to the left. It had been hit.

We immediately attempted to find out whether it was still capable of functioning. Yes . . . it started to move.

We hobbled back to the rear. At the same time, burst after burst was being fired from our weapons. Finally, we were safe. We quickly took a look outside to see what the matter was and saw that the left front tire had been hit. Red earth pressed through the shredded tire. We looked at one another. One meter higher and—it would have been us. But things weren't intended to be that way. We were permitted to experience our victory.

Half an hour later, we took a closer look at our enemy. The gun was turned over in a roadside ditch. The main gun had done its job after all!

Shrugging our shoulders, we turned back to the shredded wheel. It was small change when you considered what we had achieved for it.[14]

Notes: In November 1940, the *2. (PzSpäh)/ Panzer-Aufklärungs-Abteilung 7* was reassigned to *17. Panzer-Division*, being redesignated there as *1./Panzer-Aufklärungs-Abteilung 27*. Internally, the armored scout company was not replaced, and the remaining companies of the battalion were renumbered.

- ***Kradschützen-Bataillon 34***

Activated: 7 January 1941

Antecedent Formations: Headquarters of *III./ Infanterie-Regiment 5* and personnel levies against *Schützen-Regimenter 12* and *33*

Replacement Detachment: *Kradschützen-Ersatz-Bataillon 1*, changing to *Kradschützen-Ersatz-Bataillon 7* on 11 May 1942

Redesignation: Redesignated *Panzer-Aufklärungs-Abteilung 4* on 30 April 1943

Organization: 1941—Headquarters, 1st Motorcycle Infantry Company, 2nd Motorcycle Infantry Company, 3rd Motorcycle Infantry Company, 4th Motorcycle Infantry Machine Gun Company, and 5th Company (heavy). October 1941 (unofficial consolidation with *Panzer-Aufklärungs-Abteilung 7*)—Headquarters, 1st Company (remnants of *1.* and *3./Kradschützen-Bataillon 34*), 2nd Company (*2./Kradschützen-Bataillon 34*), 3rd Company (*3./Panzer-Aufklärungs-Abteilung 7*), 4th Company (*4./Kradschützen-Bataillon 34*), and 5th Company (*5./Kradschützen-Bataillon 34* and *4./Panzer-Aufklärungs-Abteilung 7*). 1942—Headquarters, 1st Company (rifle), 2nd Company (bicycle), 3rd Company (rifle), 4th Company (armored car), 5th Company (heavy). 1943—Headquarters, 1st Company (partially horsedrawn), 2nd Company (partially horsedrawn), 3rd Company (Motorized with a motorcycle infantry platoon), 4th Company (armored car), and 5th Company (heavy)

Commanders: *Oberstleutnant Freiherr* von Korff (7 January–12 July 1941); *Major* Stegmann (July–23 August 1941); *Rittmeister* Bradel (23 August–19 October 1941); *Hauptmann* Nierle (14 December–December 1941); *Hauptmann* Anton (December 1941–8 January 1942); *Rittmeister* Bradel (9 Janu-

Armored cars of the battalion during a break in a road march or at the end of an exercise. Many German units held close ties to the communities they were stationed near and frequently held dances or other social events.

ary–1 July 1942); *Major* Kahler (1 July 1942–27 April 1943)

Notes: Unofficially consolidated with *Panzer-Aufklärungs-Abteilung 7* from 20 October to 13 December 1941 due to decimation of both formations. Officially consolidated on 13 December 1941.

- ***Panzer-Aufklärungs-Abteilung 4***

Activated: 30 April 1943

Antecedent Formations: *Kradschützen-Bataillon 34*

Replacement Detachment: *Panzer-Aufklärungs-Ersatz-Abteilung 7*

Deactivation: Surrendered on 8 May 1945

Organization: July 1943—Headquarters, 1st Armored Reconnaissance Company (half-track), 2nd Armored Reconnaissance Company (motorized), 3rd Heavy Armored Reconnaissance Company (half-track), 4th Armored Scout Company, and 5th Armored Reconnaissance Company (motorized and later—24 August 1943—light armored reconnaissance). October 1943—Headquarters, 1st Armored Reconnaissance Company (half-track), 2nd Armored Reconnaissance Company (motorized), 3rd Heavy Armored Reconnaissance Company (motorized), and 4th Armored Scout Company. November 1943—Headquarters, 1st Armored Scout Company with additional heavy armored scout platoon (*Sd.Kfz. 233*), 2nd Armored Scout Company (*Luchs*), 3rd Light Armored Reconnaissance Company (armored), and 4th Light Armored Reconnaissance Company (heavy). January 1945— Headquarters, 1st Armored Scout Company (armored car), 2nd Armored Scout Company (*Luchs*), 3rd Armored Reconnaissance Company (half-track), 4th Armored Reconnaissance Company (half-track), and 5th Heavy Armored Reconnaissance Company (motorized, receiving half-tracks in January 1944)

Commanders: *Major* Kahler (27 April–7 May 1943); *Hauptmann* Schmidt (acting) (7 May–10 July 1943); *Hauptmann* Westermann (17 August 1943–1944); *Hauptmann* Kendler (acting) (August 1944); *Hauptmann* Kelsch (October 1944–6 April 1945); *Major* von Gaupp-Berghausen (6 April–May 1945)

Notes: In July 1943, orders received to send the 2nd Company to Krampnitz to reorganize and reconstitute as a *Luchs* company. Intended completion of training was 15 September 1943. Around the same time, the battalion, augmented with artillery and

Ernst Rampl was a long-serving scout assigned to *2./Aufklärungs-Abteilung 7*. Like most soldiers of the period, he had a professional studio portrait done and kept a photo album of mementos from his service time. JIM HALEY

Candid poses of an officer and several enlisted personnel of the battalion. As with all prewar uniforms, the distinctive unit insignia can be seen—in this case, the A/7 cipher and numeral—linking the soldier to the formation.

Unteroffiziere des Heeres mit dem Ritterkreuz

Sammelbilder

(35)

Oberfeldwebel Hans Limmer,

geb. am 7. 10. 1914 in Pilsting (Gau Bayreuth), erhielt das Ritterkreuz am 27. 10. 1941 als Spähtruppführer in einer Panzer-Aufklärungs-Abteilung. Nachdem er sich bereits im Westfeldzug durch die Gefangennahme eines feindlichen Divisionskommandeurs mit seinem Stabe ausgezeichnet hatte, sprengte er am 8. 9. 1941 trotz des von den Sowjets eingesetzten Bahnschutzes die wichtige Bahnlinie Kiew—Kursk.

Foto: Brunner

Ein Sammelalbum zum Einkleben der Bilder ist bei der Annahmestelle für Unteroffizierbewerber des Heeres erhältlich

Hans Limmer was a scout assigned to *1./Panzer-Aufklärungs-Abteilung 7*, with which he was awarded the Knight's Cross on 27 October 1941. For operational security reasons, his exact unit is not mentioned on the collector card that featured him. According to the card, he took a French general officer prisoner during the campaign in the West and was part of a patrol that interdicted the Kursk to Kiev railway line, thus preventing reinforcement to the Kiev Pocket and the escape of encircled units; this action earend him the Knight's Cross. He was the only NCO in a reconnaissance element of *4. Panzer-Division* to be so honored.

A nice prewar image of early reconnaissance vehicles: the *Sd.Kfz. 223*, the *Sd.Kfz. 222*, and the *Kfz. 13*.

Kaestel elaborately mounted most of the images in his album and wrote rudimentary captions.

Right: Rolf Kaestel was a reservist assigned to *Aufklärungs-Abteilung 7 (mot)*. He participated in exercises in 1938 and rejoined the battalion when the war started. It is not certain whether he fought all the way through the war with *Aufklärungs-Abteilung 7 (mot)* and its successor formations, since only two pages of his *Wehrpaß* are available. His uniform and other artifacts are displayed in the color section of the book.

Übung macht den Meister—practice makes perfect. Essential training for scouts: map reading, tactical marching, gunnery, and water-crossing operations. For the gunnery exercise, the scouts are apparently at the ranges at Putlos, which faced out into the open Baltic.

WH
WH
72685

The scouts of the battalion find some time for a little public relations.

Some SA functionaries are given a cross-country ride on an *Sd.Kfz. 231 (8 Rad)*.

Scenes from a road march in the mountains.

The march continues through hill country.

Motorcycle messengers take a breather. Note the stylized armored car insignia present on the front fender.

These scouts in the *Sd.Kfz. 222* look serious as they pass what might be a unit commander in a *Kfz. 13*.

Perhaps more public relations work for members of the battalion? These look to be the same vehicles seen earlier.

This last series of images is purportedly of Kaestel in the war years, but this cannot be verified since they were acquired separately from the original grouping. The same source did provide the image of the pages from the *Wehrpaß*, however, so it is likely that they also come from his estate.

Right: A column of motorcyclists passes destroyed or abandoned French Army trucks;

Rail-loading operations, possibly somewhere in the Soviet Union.

The soldier in the black *Panzer* uniform might be Kaestel.

Final respects to a fallen comrade.

Unit officers smile for the camera. The one on the viewer's left wears an enlisted M40 tunic with *Oberleutnant* shoulder boards.

Time for a quick drink. (The NCO in the back seat resembles Kaestel.)

Unit soldiers peel potatoes along with local peasants, somewhere in the Soviet Union;

The potatoes are loaded into a large container, undoubtedly for the daily meal.

A soldier wearing the distinctive second-pattern reed-green trousers for armored car personnel emerges from a peasant's house.

engineers, was detached from the division and sent to Orel because of the critical situation. It formed *Kampfgruppe Schmall* with *Panzer-Aufklärungs-Abteilung 9* of *9. Panzer-Division*, fighting first with that division and then *Panzergrenadier-Division "Großdeutschland."* The battalion returned to the division in August. Late in August, the 5th Company was sent to the Senne Training Area for reconstitution. In February 1944, the 4th Company was sent to Senne Training Area, to be reorganized and reconstituted as an armored reconnaissance company. It returned to the division in June 1944. On 11 March 1945, the battalion was ordered to consolidate with *Panzer-Aufklärungs-Abteilung München*, which had been attached to the division since February.

Awards: Knight's Cross—*Leutnant* Feßmann, *1./Panzer-Aufklärungs-Abteilung 7* (27 October 1941); *Oberleutnant* Ißbrücker, *3./Panzer-Aufklärungs-Abteilung 7* (12 September 1941); *Major* Kahler, *Kradschützen-Bataillon 34* (14 April 1943); *Hauptmann* Kendler, *Panzer-Aufklärungs-Abteilung 4* (2 September 1944); *Oberfeldwebel* Limmer, *1./Panzer-Aufklärungs-Abteilung 7* (27 October 1941); *Oberleutnant* Rode, *2./Kradschützen-Bataillon 34* (17 September 1941). **Honor Roll (Clasp)**—*Oberleutnant* Bergmann, *Panzer-Aufklärungs-Abteilung 4* (19 September 1943); *Oberleutnant* von Gaupp-Berghausen, *1./Kradschützen-Bataillon 34* (20 September 1941); *Hauptmann* Kelsch, *Panzer-Aufklärungs-Abteilung 4* (15 December 1944); *Unteroffizier* Mayr, *3./Kradschützen-Bataillon 34* (28 April 1943); *Oberleutnant* Rode, *2./Kradschützen-Bataillon 34* (28 July 1941). **German Cross in Gold**—*Leutnant* Bergmann, *Kradschützen-Bataillon 34* (24 April 1943); *Leutnant* Deppisch, *1./Panzer-Aufklärungs-Abteilung 7* (2 January 1942); *Oberfeldwebel* Elling, *3./Panzer-Aufklärungs-Abteilung 4* (20 September 1943); *Obergefreiter* Frank, *2./Kradschützen-Bataillon 34* (24 April 1943); *Oberleutnant* von Gaupp-Berghausen, *1./Kradschützen-Bataillon 34* (2 January 1942); *Oberfeldwebel* Garner, *2./Panzer-Aufklärungs-Abteilung 4* (14 September 1943); *Feldwebel* Heller, *5./Panzer-Aufklärungs-Abteilung 4* (17 September 1944); *Unteroffizier* Lorenz, *1./Kradschützen-Bataillon 34* (11 March 1943); *Oberfeldwebel* Lützow, *2./Kradschützen-Bataillon 34* (2 April 1942); *Oberleutnant* Möller, *Kradschützen-Bataillon 34* (11 March 1943); *Hauptmann* Nierle, *Panzer-Aufklärungs-Abteilung 7* (2 January 1942); *Oberfeldwebel* Obermeier, *1./Panzer-Aufklärungs-Abteilung 4* (2 August 1944); *Oberleutnant* Schmidt, *Kradschützen-Bataillon 34* (29 March 1943); *Leutnant* Steinbeißer, *Panzer-Aufklärungs-Abteilung 4* (10 March 1944); *Oberfeldwebel* Then, *3./Panzer-Aufklärungs-Abteilung 4* (15 December 1944); *Oberfeldwebel* Wadenstorfer, *1./Panzer-Aufklärungs-Abteilung 4* (2 August 1944); *Hauptmann* Westermann, *Panzer-Aufklärungs-Abteilung 4* (28 April 1944).

5. PANZER-DIVISION

Campaigns: Poland, France, Balkans, Crete (elements), Soviet Union

Reconnaissance Formations:

- ***Aufklärungs-Abteilung 8 (mot)***

Activated: 15 October 1935

Antecedent Formations: *Kraftfahr-Abteilung Potsdam* (1 October 1934)

Replacement Detachment: *Ersatz-Abteilung für motorisierte Aufklärungseinheiten 3*

Redesignation: *Panzer-Aufklärungs-Abteilung 8* on 31 March 1940

Organization: 1939—Headquarters, 1st Armored Scout Troop, 2nd Armored Scout Troop, 3rd Motorcycle Infantry Troop, and 4th Troop (heavy)

Commanders: *Oberstleutnant* Grolig (1 September–15 December 1939); *Major* Büsing (15 December 1939–31 March 1940)

Notes: Originally a separate battalion, it was redesignated and a subordinate battalion of the short-lived in 1938, only to be redesignated as *Aufklärungs-Abteilung 8 (mot)* in late 1938 and assigned to *5. Panzer-Division*.

- ***Panzer-Aufklärungs-Abteilung 8 (mot)***

Activated: 1 April 1940

Antecedent Formations: *Aufklärungs-Abteilung 8 (mot)*

Replacement Detachment: Ersatz-Abteilung für motorisierte Aufklärungseinheiten 3

Deactivation/Redesignation: Reorganized and redesignated as *Kradschützen-Bataillon 23* of *23. Panzer-Division* on 4 September 1941

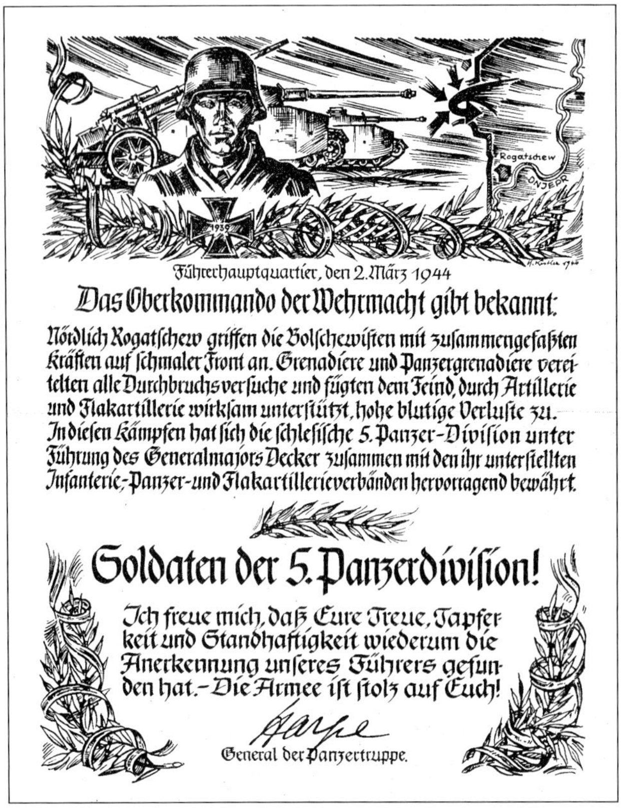

Führerhauptquartier, den 2. März 1944

Das Oberkommando der Wehrmacht gibt bekannt:

Nördlich Rogatschew griffen die Bolschewisten mit zusammengefaßten Kräften auf schmaler Front an. Grenadiere und Panzergrenadiere vereitelten alle Durchbruchsversuche und fügten dem Feind, durch Artillerie und Flakartillerie wirksam unterstützt, hohe blutige Verluste zu. In diesen Kämpfen hat sich die schlesische 5. Panzer-Division unter Führung des Generalmajors Decker zusammen mit den ihr unterstellten Infanterie-, Panzer- und Flakartillerieverbänden hervorragend bewährt.

Soldaten der 5. Panzerdivision!

Ich freue mich, daß Eure Treue, Tapferkeit und Standhaftigkeit wiederum die Anerkennung unseres Führers gefunden hat. – Die Armee ist stolz auf Euch!

Harpe

General der Panzertruppe.

In March 1944, the division received special praise in a *Wehrmacht* Daily Report, and the field army commander, *General der Panzertruppe* Harpe, used the occasion to have certificates printed for distribution to the soldiers as a morale booster.

Organization: 1940—Headquarters, 1st Armored Scout Troop, 2nd Armored Scout Troop, 3rd Motorcycle Infantry Troop, and 4th Troop (heavy)

Commanders: *Major* Büsing (1 April–1 October 1940); *Oberstleutnant* von Scheven (October 1940–1941)

Notes: Provided *Kradschützen-Bataillon 55* with an armored scout company (2nd) on 4 September 1941. The 2nd Armored Scout likewise reassigned on the same date to form *1./Panzer-Aufklärungs-Abteilung 40* of *14. Panzer-Division*. Remainder of battalion reassigned, reorganized and redesignated on 4 September 1941 as *Kradschützen-Bataillon 23* of *23. Panzer-Division*.

- ***Kradschützen-Bataillon 55***

Activated: 9 August 1940

Antecedent Formations: Formed from personnel levies against the headquarters of *Schützen-Regiment 14* and *1.* and *5./Schützen-Regiment 13*.

Replacement Detachment: *Kradschützen-Ersatz-Bataillon 55*

Redesignation: *Panzer-Aufklärungs-Abteilung 5* on 24 March 1943

Organization: 1939—Headquarters, 1st Motorcycle Infantry Company, 2nd Motorcycle Infantry Company, 3rd Motorcycle Infantry Company, 4th Motorcycle Infantry Machine Gun Company, and 5th Company (heavy). September 1941—1st Armored Scout Company, 2nd Motorcycle Infantry Company, 3rd Motorcycle Infantry Company, 4th Motorcycle Infantry Company, and 5th Company (heavy)

Commanders: *Oberstleutnant* Schacke (August 1940–October 1942); *Hauptmann* Hauptmann (October 1942–24 March 1943)

Notes: The battalion received *2.(Pz.Späh)/Panzer-Aufklärungs-Abteilung 8* in 4 September 1941, with the company being redesignated as the 1st Company. The battalion, separate from the division, participated in the fighting on Crete and remained there for three months on occupation duty, returning to the division in July 1941.

- ***Panzer-Aufklärungs-Abteilung 5***

Activated: 24 March 1943

Antecedent Formations: *Kradschützen-Bataillon 55*

Replacement Detachment: *Panzer-Aufklärungs-Ersatz-Abteilung 55*

Deactivation: 8 May 1945

Organization: 1943—Headquarters, 1st Armored Scout Company, 2nd Armored Reconnaissance Company (*Krad*), 3rd Armored Reconnaissance Company (*Krad*), 4th Armored Reconnaissance Company (*Krad*), and 5th Heavy Armored Reconnaissance Company (motorized). End of 1944—Headquarters, 1st Armored Scout Company (half-track), 2nd Light Armored Reconnaissance Company (half-track), and 3rd Armored Reconnaissance Company (half-track)

Commanders: *Hauptmann* Hauptmann (24 March–July 1943); *Major* Stephan (acting))1 August–7 September 1943); *Major* Besler (August 1943–1944); *Hauptmann* Kuczkowski (February–June 1944); *Hauptmann* Feßmann (30 June–11 October 1944); *Rittmeister* Eyrund (1 March 1945)

Notes: Orders were received on 24 August 1943 sending the 4th Company to the Senne Training Area for reconstitution intended to last six weeks. On 29

January 1944, orders were received sending the 2nd Armored Reconnaissance Company to the Senne Training Area for reconstitution. On the same day, *Heeresgruppe Mitte* was directed to conduct a battlefield reconstitution of the 5th Armored Reconnaissance Company. The orders were amended on 6 March 1944, sending the company to Military District VIII for reconstitution, with an intended completion of the process by 25 March. Orders were issued on 19 February for establishing a new 4th Company for the battalion; it was to be an armored reconnaissance company with half-tracks. Originally sent to the Senne Training Area, the company was transferred to the Wildflecken Training Area on 10 March 1944. By June, the reconstituted 2nd and 4th Companies were ordered to rejoin the division. In August 1944, *Panzer-Aufklärungs-Abteilung 20* of *20. Panzer-Division* was attached to the division, until *Panzer-Aufklärungs-Abteilung 5* could rejoin it (25 September 1944).

Awards: Knight's Cross—*Hauptmann* Feßmann, *Panzer-Aufklärungs-Abteilung 5* (23 October 1944) (Oak Leaves); *Hauptmann* Henrici, *Kradschützen-Bataillon 55* (15 March 1943); *Obergefreiter* Hoffmann, *4./Kradschützen-Bataillon 55* (3 April 1943); *Oberfeldwebel* Schreckenbach, *4./Panzer-Aufklärungs-Abteilung 5* (5 September 1944). Honor Roll **(Clasp)**—*Oberleutnant* Schacke, *Kradschützen-Bataillon 55* (16 October 1942); *Rittmeister* von Schimony-Schimonsky, *4./Panzer-Aufklärungs-Abteilung 5* (7 October 1944). **German Cross in Gold**—*Hauptmann* Böttger, *2./Panzer-Aufklärungs-Abteilung 5* (1 September 1944); *Leutnant* Burg, *5./Panzer-Aufklärungs-Abteilung 5* (11 November 1943); *Oberleutnant* von Ditfurth, *2./Panzer-Aufklärungs-Abteilung 5* (9 March 1945); *Oberfeldwebel* John, *4./Kradschützen-Bataillon 55* (13 May 1943); *Feldwebel* Kalinsky, *2./Panzer-Aufklärungs-Abteilung 5* (3 November 1943); *Oberleutnant* Könning, *1./Panzer-Aufklärungs-Abteilung 5* (26 September 1943); *Feldwebel* Miensok, *2./Panzer-Aufklärungs-Abteilung 5* (12 September 1944); *Oberstleutnant* Schacke, *Kradschützen-Bataillon 55* (25 March 1942); *Oberleutnant* von Schimony-Schimonsky, *3./Panzer-Aufklärungs-Abteilung 5* (22 May 1943); *Hauptmann* Stephan, *Panzer-Aufklärungs-Abteilung 5* (23 March 1944); *Unteroffizier* Weber, *2./Kradschützen-Bataillon 55* (15 March 1942).

5. LEICHTE DIVISION

Campaigns: North Africa

Reconnaissance Formations:

- ***Aufklärungs-Abteilung 3 (mot)***

Activated: 15 October 1935

Antecedent Formations: *Kraftfahr-Abteilung Wünsdorf*

Replacement Detachment: *Ersatz-Abteilung für motorisierte Aufklärungseinheiten 3*

Deactivation/Redesignation: Reassigned to *21. Panzer-Division* on 1 August 1941

Organization: 1941—Headquarters, 2nd Armored Scout Company, 3rd Motorcycle infantry Company, and 4th Company (heavy)

Commanders: *Oberstleutnant Freiherr* von Wechmar (18 February–31 July 1941)

Notes: Battalion previously assigned to *3. Panzer-Division.*

Awards: Knight's Cross—*Oberleutnant* Behr, *3./Aufklärungs-Abteilung 3 (mot)* (15 May 1941); *Oberstleutnant Freiherr* von Wechmar, *Aufklärungs-Abteilung 3 (mot)* (13 April 1941)

6. PANZER-DIVISION

Campaigns: France, Soviet Union

Reconnaissance Formations:

- ***Aufklärungs-Abteilung 6 (mot)***

Activated: 10 October 1935

Antecedent Formations: *Kraftfahr-Abteilung Münster*

Replacement Detachment: Initially *Ersatz-Abteilung für motorisierte Aufklärungseinheiten 7*, followed by *Schützen-Ersatz-Bataillon 7* on 20 November 1939

Redesignation: *Panzer-Aufklärungs-Abteilung 57* on 1 April 1940

Organization: 1940—Headquarters, 1st Armored Scout Troop, 2nd Armored Scout Troop, 3rd Motorcycle Infantry Troop, 4th Troop (heavy)

Commanders: *Major Freiherr* von Eckhardstein (10 October 1939–1 April 1940)

- ***Kradschützen-Bataillon 6***

Activated: 1 April 1939

Antecedent Formations: Formed from the redesignation and reorganization of *IV./Kavallerie-Schützen-Regiment 4*

Replacement Detachment: *Schützen-Ersatz-Bataillon 4*

Deactivation/Redesignation: 1 April 1943

Organization: 1939—Headquarters, 1st Motorcycle Infantry Company, 2nd Motorcycle Infantry Company, 3rd Motorcycle Infantry Company, and 4th Motorcycle Infantry Machine Gun Company with one antitank platoon. August 1940—Headquarters, Headquarters, 1st Motorcycle Infantry Company, 2nd Motorcycle Infantry Company, 3rd Motorcycle Infantry Company, 4th Motorcycle Infantry Machine Gun Company, and 5th Company (heavy). August 1942—1st Armored Scout Company, 2nd Armored Reconnaissance Company (half-track), 3rd Motorcycle Infantry Company, 4th Motorcycle Infantry Company, and 5th Company (heavy)

Commanders: *Oberstleutnant Freiherr* von Seckendorff (18 October 1939–25 July 1940); *Major* Schlieckmann (July 1940–23 June 1941); *Oberstleutnant* Unrein (June 1941–1 April 1942); *Hauptmann/Major* Quentin (July 1942–23 January 1943); *Oberleutnant* Querengässer (23 January–1 April 1943)

Notes: Battalion reassigned to the division from *1. leichte Division* on 17 October 1939.

- ***Panzer-Aufklärungs-Abteilung 57 (mot)***

Activated: 1 April 1940

Antecedent Formations: *Aufklärungs-Abteilung 6 (mot)*

Replacement Detachment: *Schützen-Ersatz-Bataillon 7*

Deactivation: Consolidated with *Kradschützen-Bataillon 6* on 1 February 1942

Organization: April 1940—Headquarters, 1st Armored Scout Troop, 2nd Armored Scout Troop, 3rd Motorcycle Infantry Troop, 4th Troop (heavy). August 1940—Headquarters, 1st Armored Scout Troop, 2nd Motorcycle Infantry Troop, 3rd Troop (heavy)

Commanders: *Major Freiherr* von Eckhardstein (1 April 1940–1941); *Oberstleutnant* Linbrunn (1941–1 January 1942); Unknown (acting) (1 January–1 February 1942)

Notes: 2nd Armored Scout Troop reassigned to *Panzer-Aufklärungs-Abteilung 16* of *16. Panzer-Division* in August 1940.

- ***Panzer-Aufklärungs-Abteilung 6***

Activated: 1 April 1943

Antecedent Formation: *Kradschützen-Bataillon 6*

Replacement Detachment: *Panzer-Aufklärungs-Ersatz-Abteilung 6* (*Panzer-Aufklärungs-Ersatz- und Ausbildungs-Abteilung 6*)

Deactivation: 8 May 1945

Organization: July 1943—Headquarters, 1st Armored Scout Company with an additional heavy armored scout platoon, 2nd Light Armored Reconnaissance Company (half-track), 3rd Armored Reconnaissance Company (*Krad*), 4th Armored Reconnaissance Company (*Krad*), 5th Heavy Armored Reconnaissance Company (motorized). July 1944—Headquarters (apparently with armored car section), 1st Armored Scout Company (half-track), 2nd Light Armored Reconnaissance Company (half-track), 3rd Armored Reconnaissance Company (half-track), and 4th Heavy Armored Reconnaissance Company (motorized)

Commanders: *Oberleutnant* Querengässer (1 April–1 June 1943); *Major* Quentin (1 June–November 1943); *Hauptmann/Major* Glatzel (1944–November 1944); *Hauptmann* Bock (January 1945)

Notes: The 3rd Company received orders on 10 October 1943 to report to the Senne Training Area for reconstitution and reorganization as a Type "C" armored scout company. It was given six weeks to make the transition. In the process, it was redesignated as the battalion's 2nd Company, with the former 2nd Company becoming the 3rd. At the beginning of January 1944, the 2nd Company was ordered to report back to the division. By the end of January 1944, the battalion was reduced to one operational company. The rest was in Germany for reconstitution or temporarily deactivated. On 19 February orders were issued to form a new 4th Company for the battalion at the Senne Training Area; on 10 March, the 4th Company moved to the Wildflecken Training Area. Only the 2nd Armored Scout Company at the front in July 1944; remainder of the battalion being reconstituted. Many scouts employed as infantry and sustained heavy losses. The 3rd Company, when reconstituted, only had light halftracks as opposed to medium halftracks. The 1st Armored Scout Company returned in August, while the 4th Company did not return until February 1945. Battalion detached from the division in the latter part of December and did not return until the second half of January. It was heavily engaged, but helped in stemming a Soviet offensive.

Awards: Knight's Cross—*Oberleutnant* Biermann, *3./Panzer-Aufklärungs-Abteilung 6* (31 August 1943); *Oberleutnant* Hasenbeck, *4./Panzer-Aufklärungs-Abteilung 6* (26 August 1943); *Oberfeldwebel* Krüger, Headquarters, *Panzer-Aufklärungs-Abteilung 6* (9 December 1944); *Major* Quentin, *Kradschützen-Bataillon 6* (8 February 1943); *Oberstleutnant Freiherr* von Seckendorff, *Kradschützen-Bataillon 6* (4 September 1940); *Leutnant* Wagner, *Kradschützen-Bataillon 6* (24 January 1943); *Hauptmann* Wissemann, *2./Kradschützen-Bataillon 6* (8 February 1943). **Honor Roll (Clasp)**—*Leutnant* Biermann, *Kradschützen-Bataillon 6* (8 March 1942); *Obergefreiter* Hutter, *Kradschützen-Bataillon 6* (27 May 1943); *Leutnant* Wissemann, *Kradschützen-Bataillon 6* (28 November 1941). **German Cross in Gold**—*Oberleutnant* Biermann, *Kradschützen-Bataillon 6* (17 April 1943); *Oberleutnant* Bockhoff, *Panzer-Aufklärungs-Abteilung 57* (26 December 1941); *Oberfeldwebel* Bußmann, *3./Panzer-Aufklärungs-Abteilung 6* (21 November 1943); *Oberleutnant* Fricke, *Kradschützen-Bataillon 6* (17 April 1943); *Leutnant* Hammer, *3./Panzer-Aufklärungs-Abteilung 6* (16 June 1944); *Oberleutnant* Hasenbeck, *Kradschützen-Bataillon 6* (13 May 1943); *Feldwebel* Haßlach, *2./Panzer-Aufklärungs-Abteilung 6* (2 March 1944); *Oberfeldwebel* Hilker, *Kradschützen-Bataillon 6* (17 April 1943); *Oberleutnant* Kreis, *1./Kradschützen-Bataillon 6* (26 December 1941); *Oberfeldwebel* Krömer, *Panzer-Aufklärungs-Abteilung 57* (28 February 1942); *Oberfeldwebel* Krüger, *Kradschützen-Bataillon 6* (5 May 1943); *Hauptmann* Kueper, *Kradschützen-Bataillon 6* (2 April 1942); *Oberstleutnant* Linbrunn, *Panzer-Aufklärungs-Abteilung 57* (26 December 1942); *Feldwebel* von den Linden, *Panzer-Aufklärungs-Abteilung 6* (10 January 1944); *Oberfeldwebel* Schleef, *Panzer-Aufklärungs-Abteilung 6* (11 November 1943); *Leutnant* Schneider, *Panzer-Aufklärungs-Abteilung 57* (26 December 1941); *Oberleutnant* Schrödelsecker, *2./Panzer-Aufklärungs-Abteilung 6* (27 April 1945); *Oberstleutnant* Unrein, *Kradschützen-Bataillon 6* (28 February 1942); *Leutnant* Wehlend, *2./Panzer-Aufklärungs-Abteilung 6* (14 September 1943); *Leutnant* Wissemann, *Kradschützen-Bataillon 6* (14 February 1942)

7. PANZER-DIVISION

Campaigns: France, Soviet Union

Reconnaissance Formations:

- ***Aufklärungs-Abteilung 37 (mot)***

Activated: 1 November 1939

Antecedent Formations: *II./Aufklärungs-Regiment 7*

Replacement Detachment: *Ersatz-Abteilung für motorisierte Aufklärungseinheiten 4*

Redesignation: *Panzer-Aufklärungs-Abteilung 37*

Organization: 1939—Headquarters, 1st Armored Scout Troop, 2nd Armored Scout Troop, 3rd Motorcycle Infantry Troop, and 4th Troop (heavy)

Commanders: *Major/Oberstleutnant* von Wagner (1 November 1939–April 1940)

- ***Kradschützen-Bataillon 7***

Activated: 25 October 1939

Antecedent Formation: *I./Aufklärungs-Regiment 7*

Replacement Detachment: *Kradschützen-Ersatz-Bataillon 1*

Redesignation: *Panzer-Aufklärungs-Abteilung 7* on 31 March 1943

Organization: 1939–40—Headquarters, 1st Motorcycle Infantry Company, 2nd Motorcycle Infantry Company, 3rd Company (heavy). May 1941—Headquarters, 1st Motorcycle Infantry Company, 2nd Motorcycle Infantry Company, 3rd Motorcycle Infantry Company, 4th Motorcycle Infantry Machine Gun Company, and 5th Company (heavy). July 1942—Headquarters, 1st Armored Scout Company, 2nd Armored Reconnaissance Company (halftrack), 3rd Motorcycle Infantry Company, 4th Motorcycle Infantry Company, and 5th Company (heavy)

Commanders: *Major* von Steinkeller (25 October 1939–13 May 1940); *Hauptmann* von Hagen (acting) (13 May–June 1940); *Major* von Steinkeller (June 1940–22 July 1941); *Hauptmann* von Luck (acting) (22 July–24 December 1941); *Oberstleutnant* von Steinkeller (24 December 1941–15 May 1942); *Major* Heilbronn (May 1942–February 1943); *Hauptmann* von Schütz (February–March 1943)

- ***Panzer-Aufklärungs-Abteilung 37***

Activated: 1 April 1940

Antecedent Formations: *Aufklärungs-Abteilung 37 (mot)*

Replacement Detachment: *Ersatz-Abteilung für motorisierte Aufklärungseinheiten 4*. Later: *Kradschützen-Ersatz-Bataillon 1* (1 October 1941)

Redesignation: *Kradschützen-Bataillon 7* on 23 May 1942 (unofficially already done in the fall of 1941)

Organization: 1940–41—Headquarters, 1st Armored Scout Troop, 2nd Armored Scout Troop, 3rd Motorcycle Infantry Troop, and 4th Troop (heavy)

Commanders: *Major* Erdmann (April–28 May 1940); *Hauptmann* von Luck (acting) (28 May–July 1940); *Major Freiherr* von Riederer (August 1940–5 December 1941)

Notes: In the fall of 1940, the 1st Troop was transferred to *Panzer-Aufklärungs-Abteilung 92* of *20. Panzer-Division*. The 2nd Troop was exchanged with the 1st Troop of *Aufklärungs-Abteilung 53 (mot)* of *3. Infanterie-Division (mot)*. In the spring of 1941, the battalion had two armored scout troops, both equipped with captured French armored cars.

- ***Panzer-Aufklärungs-Abteilung 7***

Activated: 1 April 1943

Replacement Detachment: Initially *Kradschützen-Ersatz-Bataillon 1*; later *Panzer-Aufklärungs-Ersatz-Abteilung 1*

Deactivation: 8 May 1945

Organization: May 1943—Headquarters, Heavy Armored Scout Platoon, 1st Armored Scout Company, 2nd Armored Reconnaissance Company (half-track), 3rd Armored Reconnaissance Company (*Krad*), 4th Armored Reconnaissance Company (*Krad*), and 5th Heavy Armored Reconnaissance Company. July 1944—Headquarters (with armored car sections), 1st Armored Scout Company, 2nd Light Armored Reconnaissance Company (half-track), 3rd Armored Reconnaissance Company (half-track), 4th Heavy Armored Reconnaissance Company (half-track). April 1945—Headquarters and four line companies (2nd equipped with VW's)

Commanders: *Hauptmann* Güthling (April 1943–1943); *Hauptmann* Girgensohn (acting) (6 August–15 September 1943); *Oberleutnant* Knauf (acting) (15–28 September 1943); *Major* Güthling (28 September 1943–1944); *Rittmeister* Kolczyk (3 February–December 1944); *Major* Schütz (March–1 April 1945); Unknown (acting) (1 April–3 May 1945)

Notes: On 18 October 1943, the 2nd Company was ordered to the Senne Training Area for reconstitution and reorganization as a Type "C" armored scout company. It received orders on 11 January 1944 directing it to complete its training by 1 February. In December 1943, the battalion had only the 1st Company operational. The 2nd and 5th Companies were being reconstituted and reorganized. In May 1944, the battalion was detached from the division to form an *ad hoc* brigade-size element. It did not return to the division until July and was committed primarily as infantry. On 23 April 1945, *3./Panzer-Aufklärungs-Abteilung 12* was moved from the Milowitz Training Area and absorbed into the division.

Awards: Knight's Cross—*Unteroffizier* Geißler, *5./Panzer-Aufklärungs-Abteilung 7* (14 May 1944); *Oberleutnant* Grünert, *3./Kradschützen-Bataillon 7* (14 October 1941); *Rittmeister* Kolczyk, *Panzer-Aufklärungs-Abteilung 7* (6 April 1944); *Leutnant* Neubrandt, *Panzer-Aufklärungs-Abteilung 37* (29 September 1940); *Major* Schütz, *Panzer-Aufklärungs-Abteilung 7* (5 April 1945). **Honor Roll (Clasp)**—*Oberfeldwebel* Pieper, *1./Panzer-Aufklärungs-Abteilung 7* (15 March 1945). **Close Combat Clasp in Gold**—*Obergefreiter* Carl, *3./Panzer-Aufklärungs-Abteilung 7* (8 September 1944); *Unteroffizier* Heinemann, *2./Panzer-Aufklärungs-Abteilung 7* (9 November 1944). **German Cross in Gold**—*Oberfeldwebel* Arndt, *3./Kradschützen-Bataillon 7* (11 April 1942); *Oberfeldwebel* Cudok, *5./Panzer-Aufklärungs-Abteilung 7* (17 August 1944); *Oberfeldwebel* Eisele, *1./Panzer-Aufklärungs-Abteilung 7* (23 June 1943); *Feldwebel* Förster, *1./Panzer-Aufklärungs-Abteilung 7* (3 August 1943); *Oberleutnant Freiherr* von Fürstenberg, *Panzer-Aufklärungs-Abteilung 7* (17 August 1942); *Oberleutnant* Girgensohn, *1./Panzer-Aufklärungs-Abteilung 7* (3 August 1943); *Oberleutnant* Grafe, *2./Panzer-Aufklärungs-Abteilung 7* (8 May 1945); *Leutnant* Hartenfeller, *Panzer-Aufklärungs-Abteilung 7* (9 March 1945); *Unteroffizier* Heinemann, *2./Panzer-Aufklärungs-Abteilung 7* (30 December 1944); *Oberfeldwebel* Hintz, *5./Panzer-Aufklärungs-Abteilung 7*

Images of *II./Aufklärungs-Regiment 7* of *2. leichte Division*. This was the antecedent formation for *Aufklärungs-Abteilung 37*, which became the reconnaissance battalion for *7. Panzer-Division*.

(16 November 1943); *Hauptmann* von Luck, *Kradschützen-Bataillon 7* (2 January 1942); *Oberfeldwebel* Pieper, *2./Panzer-Aufklärungs-Abteilung 7* (12 October 1944); *Oberfeldwebel* Sagorske, *Panzer-Aufklärungs-Abteilung 7* (21 July 1944); *Unteroffizier* Schlepphorst, *2./Panzer-Aufklärungs-Abteilung 7* (7 August 1943); *Oberfeldwebel* Schmauch, *5./Panzer-Aufklärungs-Abteilung 7* (9 June 1943); *Hauptmann* von Schütz, *Panzer-Aufklärungs-Abteilung 7* (10 July 1943); *Oberleutnant* Stassdt, *4./Kradschützen-Bataillon 7* (3 June 1943); *Oberstleutnant* von Steinkeller, *Kradschützen-Bataillon 7* (25 May 1942); *Oberfeldwebel* Wellnitz, *3./Panzer-Aufklärungs-Abteilung 37* (2 April 1942). **Certificate of Recognition by the Commander in Chief of the Army**—*Unteroffizier* Hackl, *3./Panzer-Aufklärungs-Abteilung 37* (10 September 1941); *Major* Kolczyk, *Panzer-Aufklärungs-Abteilung 7* (1945); *Major Freiherr* von Paar zu Schoenau Riederer, *Panzer-Aufklärungs-Abteilung 37* (10 August 1941); *Major* von Steinkeller, *Kradschützen-Bataillon 7* (7 July 1941). **Mention in the Wehrmacht Daily Report**—*Rittmeister* Kolczyk, *Panzer-Aufklärungs-Abteilung 7* (1 March 1944)

8. PANZER-DIVISION

Campaigns: France, Soviet Union

Reconnaissance Formations:

- ***Aufklärungs-Regiment 8 (mot)***

Activated: 10 November 1938

Replacement Detachment: *Ersatz-Abteilung für motorisierte Einheiten 8*

Deactivation: Transferred to *8. Panzer-Division* on 16 October 1939. *I./Aufklärungs-Regiment 8* had already been detached and pending reassignment to *10. Panzer-Division*. When the regiment transferred to *8. Panzer-Division*, it brought only its 2nd Battalion with it, which became *Panzer-Aufklärungs-Abteilung 59*.

By 1940, the *II.Aufklärungs-Regiment 7* was assigned to *7. Panzer-Division*, as evidenced by the divisional markings on this *Sd.Kfz. 231 (8 Rad)*, most likely shortly before the campaign in the West.

Major Riederer, the commander of *Panzer-Aufklärungs-Abteilung 7* was wounded in action during the withdrawals conducted in December 1941 and died at the military hospital in Gshatsk on 28 December 1941.

A grave marker for an *Unteroffizier* of the headquarters of *Kradschützen-Bataillon 7*. By the end of the month, the battalion would cease to exist.

By the time this image was taken in the Soviet Union, the battalion had been redesignated as *Panzer-Aufklärungs-Abteilung 37* and probably unofficially already had been consolidated with *Kradschützen-Bataillon 7*. Little would prepare the Germans for the shock of the first winter in the Soviet Union.

The winter conditions do not seem as harsh for this *Sd.Kfz. 223*, perhaps the same one seen in the previous photograph. After the consolidation, the resulting formation remained *Kradschützen-Bataillon 7*, as was the case with all of the reconnaissance and motorcycle infantry battalions in 1942. Less than a year later, the battalions would re-emerge as *Panzer-Aufklärungs-Abteilungen*, and the *Kradschützen-Bataillone* would be a thing of the past.

Commander: *Oberstleutnant* von Kessel (10 November 1938–16 October 1939)[15]

- ***Kradschützen-Bataillon 8***

Activated: 1 April 1940

Antecedent Formations: *II./Kavallerie-Schützen-Regiment 9*

Replacement Detachment: Initially *Schützen-Ersatz-Bataillon 8*; replaced in 1941 by *Kradschützen-Ersatz-Bataillon 3*

Redesignation: Redesignated *Panzer-Aufklärungs-Abteilung 8* effective 1 April 1943

Organization: 1940—Headquarters, 1st Motorcycle Infantry Company, 2nd Motorcycle Infantry Company, 3rd Motorcycle Infantry Company, and 4th Company (heavy). April 1941—Headquarters, 1st Motorcycle Infantry Company, 2nd Motorcycle Infantry Company, 3rd Motorcycle Infantry Company, 4th Motorcycle Infantry Machine Gun Company, and 5th Company (heavy). April 1942—Headquarters, 1st Armored Scout Company, 2nd Motorcycle Infantry Company, 3rd Motorcycle Infantry Company, 4th Motorcycle Infantry Company, and 5th Company (heavy)

Commanders: *Oberstleutnant* Soergel (1 April–December 1940); *Oberstleutnant* Kütt (1 January–September 1941); *Hauptmann* Neise (acting) (September–17 October 1941); *Oberstleutnant/Oberst* Kütt (17 November 1941–?); *Hauptmann* Neise (acting) (November 1941–16 January 1942); *Oberstleutnant* Wolff (16 January–March 1942); *Major* Neise (March 1942–February 1943); *Hauptmann* Brandt (acting) (26 February–1 April 1943)

- ***Panzer-Aufklärungs-Abteilung 59***

Activated: 1 April 1940

Antecedent Formations: *II./Aufklärungs-Regiment 8*

Replacement Detachment: *motorisierte Aufklärungs-Ersatz-Abteilung 3*

Redesignation: Consolidated with *Kradschützen-Bataillon 8* on 25 January 1942

Organization: April 1940—Headquarters, 1st Armored Scout Troop, 2nd Armored Scout Troop, 3rd Motorcycle Infantry Troop, and 4th Troop (heavy). November 1940: Headquarters, 1st Armored Scout Troop, 2nd Motorcycle Infantry Troop, and 3rd Troop (heavy).

Commanders: *Oberstleutnant* Erdmann (1 April 1940–?); *Hauptmann* von Eicke und Polwitz (acting) (?–December 1940); *Major* von Bandemer (January–December 1941)

Notes: On 15 November 1940, the 2nd Armored Scout Troop was transferred to *Aufklärungs-Abteilung 25 (mot)* of *25. Infanterie-Division (mot)*, where it became the 3rd Troop. Effective 27 October 1941, the battalion headquarters and the 1st Company were employed in traffic control, while the remaining companies were attached to *Kradschützen-Bataillon 8*. The battalion officially consolidated with *Kradschützen-Bataillon 8* on 25 January 1942.

- ***Panzer-Aufklärungs-Abteilung 8***

Activated: 1 April 1943

Antecedent Formation: *Kradschützen-Bataillon 8*

Replacement Detachment: Unknown

Deactivation: 8 May 1945

Organization: 1943—Headquarters, 1st Armored Scout Company, 2nd Armored Reconnaissance Company (*Krad*), 3rd Armored Reconnaissance Company (*Krad*), 4th Armored Reconnaissance Company (*Krad*), and 5th Heavy Armored Reconnaissance Company (motorized). October 1943—1st Armored Scout Company, 2nd Light Armored Reconnaissance Company (half-track), 3rd Armored Reconnaissance Company (half-track), 4th Motorcycle Infantry Company, and 5th Company (heavy). October 1944–45—Headquarters with armored car sections, 1st Armored Scout Company (half-track), 2nd Light Armored Reconnaissance Company (half-track), 3rd Armored Reconnaissance Company (half-track), 4th Heavy Armored Reconnaissance Company (half-track)

Commanders: *Hauptmann* Brandt (acting) (1–20 April 1943); *Major* von Mitzlaff (20 April–13 August 1943); *Hauptmann* Machwirth (acting) (13 August–September 1943); *Major* von Mitzlaff (September–16 November 1943); *Hauptmann* Machwirth (acting) (16 November–December 1943); *Major* von Mitzlaff (to June 1944); *Hauptmann* Sell (June 1944–March 1945); *Hauptmann* Finckenstein (March–8 May 1945)

Notes: Orders were issued on 15 July 1943 to transfer the battalion headquarters and the 3rd Company to the Senne Training Area for reconstitution. The intent was to complete the reconstitution efforts by 5 September. At the beginning of September,

Kradschützen-Bataillon 8

A description of the pursuit against broken French forces during the second phase of the campaign in the West in 1940 by *Oberstleutnant* Kütt, the commander of *Kradschützen-Bataillon 8*:

> Escles reached at 0850 hours. No enemy resistance at all. At first individually, but then in small groups and then large, ill-disciplined batches they voluntarily approach us to surrender . . . Negros, Moroccans, Bushmen are among them. All of them scattered forces of the French 6th Colonial Division. Dompaire was reached at 0950 hours. The French forces located there were still intact, but our sudden appearance surprised them. After a short firefight, several hundred French and Begors were taken prisoner.
>
> At 1015 hours, we continued via Mazeley in the direction of Nomexy . . .
>
> At 1100 hours, I had everyone halt just east of Frizon. I gave the order in shotgun style to deploy and ococcupy the bridgehead on the far side of Model, if we succeeded in taking the bridge at Chatal intact. . . . In front of us was the attached armored reconnaissance section from the reconnaissance battalion under the brave leadership of a *Feldwebel*. Behind it was a engineer section from our battalion under the command of *Feldwebel* Rosenthal. . . . I followed closely behind with my battle staff and right behind the 1st Company of *Oberleutnant* Kühls . . .
>
> Nomexy was reached at 1115 hours. The place was swarming with French, who imagined that they were in the rear area . . .
>
> Armored scouts and the engineer section thrust through the throng to the canal bridge on this side of the Mosel . . . in a flash, 1,500 prisoners were taken . . . among the spoils of war were six limbered antiaircraft guns, a truck company with ammunition and rations and a mountain machine-gun company with 10 horse-drawn machine-gun carriages . . . [16]

orders were received for both elements to rejoin the division. In January 1944, division reduced to battle groups and virtually combat ineffective. Battalion attached to *19. Panzer-Division*, along with other combat-capable elements and did not return to division until beginning of February. In July, the battalion was attached to *1. Panzer-Division* for an extended period. That same month, orders were received directing the 3rd Company to the Wildflecken Training Area, where it was to be reorganized, reconstituted and ready for deployment by 20 September. It was to become a Light Armored Reconnaissance Company (half-track). Orders dated 13 August directed the rest of the battalion to Wildflecken as well for reconstitution. It was be ready for redeployment by 20 September. On 1 October, orders were received directing the battalion to report to *8. Armee* near Kielce. It spent nearly a month there before reporting back to the division in November. In December, the battalion was dispatched as a fire brigade again, when it was attached to the Hungarian 2nd Armored Division.

Awards: Knight's Cross— *Oberfeldwebel* Böhm, *1./Panzer-Aufklärungs-Abteilung 8* (17 March 1945); *Oberleutnant* Etzold, *Kradschützen-Bataillon 8* (3 June 1940); *Unteroffizier* Greck, *4./Panzer-Aufklärungs-Abteilung 8* (5 February 1945); *Hauptmann* Kloos, *3./Panzer-Aufklärungs-Abteilung 8* (13 December 1943); *Major* von Mitzlaff, *Panzer-Aufklärungs-Abteilung 8* (20 December 1943); *Hauptmann* Sell, *Panzer-Aufklärungs-Abteilung 8* (14 April 1945). **Honor Roll (Clasp)**— *Hauptmann* Meschkat, *Panzer-Aufklärungs-Abteilung 8* (27 October 1944); *Oberleutnant* Scharffetter, *1./Panzer-Aufklärungs-Abteilung 8* (27 February 1944); *Leutnant* Schlepple, *5./Kradschützen-Bataillon 8* (9 September 1941); *Hauptmann* Sell, *Panzer-Aufklärungs-Abteilung 8* (15 February 1945); *Oberleutnant* Teltz, *Panzer-Aufklärungs-Abteilung 8* (1945); *Oberleutnant Dr.* Wiswedel, *Panzer-Aufklärungs-Abteilung 8* (5 March

Panzer-Aufklärungs-Abteilung 8

By the end of 1943, the division had been largely decimated and was in the laborious process of both defending a sector and attempting to reconstitute itself. The commander of *Panzer-Aufklärungs-Abteilung 8*, *Major* Mitzlaff, described one attack by his *Kampfgruppe* in an effort to regain lost ground:

> In the meantime, we heard the sounds of fighting from the intermediate piece of high ground. That meant that *Hauptmann* Kloos had already encountered the enemy; the unmistakable sound of *MG42's* could be heard. Ivan only replied hesitantly. . . . I then issued orders to advance north. . . . The terrain was no longer so broken up. In front of us was a hill that looked like a dune. That meant that Janowka had to be behind it . . .
>
> The armored vehicles crossed the dune. Ivan had woken up and was greeting us with heavy antitank-gun fire. . . . By then, we had disappeared into the far side of the depression between the dunes. One armored vehicle was firing toward the east and a few *SPW's* were up close to it. . . . It turned out that everything up to that point had succeeded beyond all expectations. The Russians had been completely surprised and started fleeing after a short defense. The *SPW's* raced on to Janowka in an aggressive assault. They caught the Russians in the rear there. His artillery and antitank guns were overrun. As it turned out later, there was also an entire regimental headquarters. . . . The *SPW's*, driven forward by the young *Leutnant* Corsepius, pursued the Russians fleeing from Janowka as far as the Pripet [River] . . .
>
> *Hauptmann* Kloos and I cobbled together everything we had in the way of vehicles in the area for an assault on the high ground. . . . The hill was still occupied by the enemy. Nonetheless, they were surprised that we had approached from the rear. . . . We churned our way through deep sandy soil up the hill and, at that point, the brave *Panzergrenadiere* appeared. Who had moved out from Chernobyl. It was *Oberleutnant* von Bredow's company![17]

With the help of the mechanized infantry and a few *Panzer IV's*, the Soviets were driven off the hill, thus ending von Mitzlaff 's mission successfully.

1945). German Cross in Gold— *Oberfeldwebel* Fischer, *3./Panzer-Aufklärungs-Abteilung 8* (3 January 1944); *Oberfeldwebel* Kaudel, Headquarters, *Panzer-Aufklärungs-Abteilung 8* (27 April 1945); *Feldwebel* Ksyk, *2./Kradschützen-Bataillon 8* (26 December 1941); *Oberfeldwebel* Löhnert, *Panzer-Aufklärungs-Abteilung 8* (11 September 1944); *Hauptmann* Mahr, *2./Panzer-Aufklärungs-Abteilung 8* (28 May 1944); *Major* von Mitzlaff, *Panzer-Aufklärungs-Abteilung 8* (25 October 1943); *Hauptmann* Neise, *Kradschützen-Bataillon 8* (31 January 1942); *Oberleutnant* Scharffetter, Headquarters, *Panzer-Aufklärungs-Abteilung 8* (17 September 1944); *Oberleutnant* von Scheliha, *Panzer-Aufklärungs-Abteilung 59* (3 March 1942); *Feldwebel* Schicketanz, *4./Panzer-Aufklärungs-Abteilung 8* (27 April 1945); *Leutnant* Schlepple, *5./Kradschützen-Bataillon 8* (5 November 1941); *Oberfeldwebel* Schmerbauch, *1./Kradschützen-Bataillon 8* (26 December 1941); *Oberleutnant* Seehaus, *2./Panzer-Aufklärungs-Abteilung 8* (17 September 1944); *Hauptmann* Vogt, *2./Kradschützen-Bataillon 8* (19 May 1942); *Oberleutnant Dr.* Wiswedel, *2./Panzer-Aufklärungs-Abteilung 8* (3 January 1944). **Certificate of Recognition by the Commander in Chief of the Army**—*Leutnant* Hundt, *Panzer-Aufklärungs-Abteilung 59* (18 March 1942); *Leutnant* Kress, *3./Panzer-Aufklärungs-Abteilung 8* (5 February 1945)

9. PANZER-DIVISION

Campaigns: France, Balkans, Soviet Union, Western Europe

Reconnaissance Formations:

- ***Aufklärungs-Regiment 9***

Activated: 1 April 1938, joining *9. Panzer-Division* on 3 January 1940 (see also *4. leichte Division*)

Replacement Detachment: *Ersatz-Abteilung für motorisierte Aufklärungseinheiten 7*

Reorganization/Deactivation: 1 August 1940, with the 1st Battalion becoming *Kradschützen-Bataillon 59* and the 2nd Battalion *Aufklärungs-Abteilung 9 (mot)*

Commanders: *Oberstleutnant* Vichytil (1 April–31 July 1940)

The regiment consisted of two battalions:

- ***I./Aufklärungs-Regiment 9***

Antecedent Formations: Formed from *Kraftfahr-Jäger-Bataillon 4* (4th Motorized Light Infantry Battalion) of the former Austrian *Bundesheer*

Organization: 1940—Headquarters, 1st Motorcycle Infantry Troop, 2nd Motorcycle Infantry Troop, 3rd Motorcycle Infantry Troop, and 4th Troop (heavy)

Commanders (as of 3 January 1939): Commander—*Oberstleutnant* Vichytil. Troop Commanders—1st Troop, *Rittmeister* Pfisterer; 2nd Troop, *Oberleutnant* Sartorius; 3rd Troop, *Oberleutnant* Soldan; 4th Troop, *Rittmeister* Schulz

- ***II./Aufklärungs-Regiment 9***

Antecedent Formations: Formed by personnel levies against *Aufklärungs-Abteilungen 5, 7,* and *9*

Organization: 1940—Headquarters, 4th Armored Scout Troop, and 5th Armored Scout Troop

Commanders (as of 3 January 1939): Commander—*Rittmeister Dr. Freiherr* von Ohlen und Adlerskron. Troop Commanders—5th Troop, *Oberleutnant* Poessel; 6th Troop, *Oberleutnant* Mayer; 7th Troop, *Rittmeister* Bentele

Notes: It is not known why there were two 4th Troops in the regiment.

- ***Kradschützen-Bataillon 59***

Activated: 1 August 1940

Antecedent Formations: *I./Aufklärungs-Regiment 9*[18]

Replacement Detachment: *Kradschützen-Ersatz-Bataillon 55*

Redesignation: 13 April 1943 as *Panzer-Aufklärungs-Abteilung 8*

Organization: 1940—Headquarters, 1st Motorcycle Infantry Company, 2nd Motorcycle Infantry Company, 3rd Motorcycle Infantry Company, 4th Motorcycle Infantry Machine Gun Company, and 5th Company (heavy). July 1942—Headquarters, 1st Armored Scout Company, 2nd Armored Reconnaissance Company (half-track), 3rd Motorcycle Infantry Company, 4th Motorcycle Infantry Company, and 5th Company (heavy)

Commanders: *Major Freiherr* von Lüttwitz (1 August–6 September 1940); *Major* Schmalz (7 September 1940–26 January 1942); *Major/Oberstleutnant* Gorn (26 January–5 October 1942); *Major* Heraucourt (October 1942–13 April 1943)

- ***Aufklärungs-Abteilung 9 (mot)***

Activated: 1 August 1940

Antecedent Formations: *II./Aufklärungs-Regiment 9*[19]

Redesignation: 14 March 1942, consolidated with *Kradschützen-Bataillon 59*

Organization: August 1940—Headquarters, 1st Armored Scout Troop, 2nd Armored Scout Troop, 3rd Motorcycle Infantry Troop, and 4th Troop (heavy). June 1941—Headquarters, 1st Armored Scout Troop, 3rd Bicycle Troop, and 4th Troop (heavy)

Commanders: *Major Freiherr* von Ohlen und Adlerscron (1 August–18 November 1940); *Hauptmann* Gutmann (acting) (18 November–21 December 1940); *Major/Oberstleutnant Freiherr* von Ohlen und Adlerscron (21 December 1940–14 March 1942)

Notes: The 2nd Armored Scout Troop was reassigned to *16. Infanterie-Division (mot)* and redesignated as *I./Aufklärungs-Abteilung 341* in the fall of 1940.

- ***Panzer-Aufklärungs-Abteilung 9***

Activated: 13 April 1943[20]

Antecedent Formations: *Kradschützen-Bataillon 59*

Replacement Detachment: *Panzer-Aufklärungs-Ersatz-Abteilung 2*

Deactivation: 26 April 1945

Organization: 1943—Headquarters, 1st Armored Scout Company (armored car) with armored scout platoon (*Sd.Kfz. 233*), 2nd Armored Scout Company (*Luchs*), 3rd Armored Reconnaissance Company (half-track), 4th Armored Reconnaissance Company (half-track). April 1944—Headquarters, 1st Armored Scout Company (*Luchs*), 2nd Light Armored Reconnaissance Company (half-track), 3rd Armored Reconnaissance Company (half-track), 4th Heavy Armored Reconnaissance Company (half-track)

Commanders: *Hauptmann* von Bünau (10 June–15 August 1943); *Hauptmann* Leichs (acting) (August 1943); *Hauptmann* Bockhoff (August 1943–26 October 1944); *Hauptmann* Zimmermann (acting) (October–November 1944); *Hauptmann* Voutta (November 1944–1 April 1945); *Oberleutnant* Wiedmann (acting) (April 1945)

Notes: Orders issued 4 May 1943 to reconstitute virtually the entire battalion at Bruck an der Leitha Training Area. Two light armored reconnaissance companies (half-track) and one heavy armored reconnaissance company (partly armored) were to be formed. On 19 April, additional orders were received for the attachment of a Type "B" armored scout company, with the *Luchs*. (The company had been intended for *9. SS-Panzer-Division "Hohenstaufen"* originally.) That company moved from France to Germany on 26 April to join the battalion. Battalion detached from division as part of *Kampfgruppe Schmall* for much of fighting at Kursk, only returning to the division in August 1943. In September 1943, the 3rd Light Armored Reconnaissance Company was formed. In October 1943, the 2nd Company was sent to Krampnitz for reconstitution and reorganization, where it was to be outfitted with the *Luchs*. Due to the depleted state of the division, many combat elements attached out in January 1944; the reconnaissance battalion served briefly with *97. Jäger-Division*. In April 1944, the *Luchs* company was rejoined the battalion, where it was redesignated as the 1st Company. By the fall of 1944, after the fighting in Normandy, the battalion was down to an effective strength of one armored scout company (half-tracks and one platoon of armored cars) and one light armored reconnaissance company. In February 1945, the 1st Company was disbanded.

Awards: Knight's Cross—*Hauptmann* Bockhoff, *Panzer-Aufklärungs-Abteilung 9* (8 August 1943); *Oberfeldwebel* Ernst, *2./Panzer-Aufklärungs-Abteilung 9* (23 March 1945); *Feldwebel* Most, *2./Panzer-Aufklärungs-Abteilung 9* (23 October 1944); *Leutnant* Pültz, *5./Panzer-Aufklärungs-Abteilung 9* (10 August 1943); *Hauptmann* Voutta, *Panzer-Aufklärungs-Abteilung 9* (23 March 1945). **Honor Roll (Clasp)**—*Obergefreiter* Auer, *4./Panzer-Aufklärungs-Abteilung 9* (25 October 1943); *Hauptmann* Bockhoff, *Panzer-Aufklärungs-Abteilung 9* (27 October 1943); *Oberleutnant* Erdl, *2./Kradschützen-Bataillon 59* (22 July 1941); *Leutnant* Kroitzsch, *5./Panzer-Aufklärungs-Abteilung 9* (25 May 1944); *Feldwebel* Liersch, *1./Panzer-Aufklärungs-Abteilung 9* (27 May 1944); *Feldwebel* Messer, Headquarters, *Panzer-Aufklärungs-Abteilung 9* (7 December 1944); *Leutnant* Metelka, *4./Panzer-Aufklärungs-Abteilung 9* (7 September 1943); *Oberleutnant* Naegele, *1./Panzer-Aufklärungs-Abteilung 9* (7 August 1943). **German Cross in Gold**—*Oberfeldwebel* Arndt, *3./Kradschützen-Bataillon 59* (4 September 1942); *Oberleutnant* Blank, *Panzer-Aufklärungs-Abteilung 9* (27 November 1944); *Leutnant* Degenhart, *5./Panzer-Aufklärungs-Abteilung 9* (17 November 1943); *Oberleutnant* Ellfeldt, *3./Kradschützen-Bataillon 59* (19 September 1942); *Unteroffizier* Fraissl, *4./Panzer-Aufklärungs-Abteilung 9* (17 October 1943); *Unteroffizier* Hackl, *2./Panzer-Aufklärungs-Abteilung 9* (30 March 1945); *Oberleutnant* Hormann, *5./Panzer-Aufklärungs-Abteilung 9* (10 August 1943); *Oberleutnant* Hübner, *2./Kradschützen-Bataillon 59* (23 August 1942); *Leutnant* Maier, *3./Panzer-Aufklärungs-Abteilung 9* (5 December 1943); *Oberleutnant* Mayer, *1./Kradschützen-Bataillon 59* (12 September 1942); *Major* Schmaltz, *Kradschützen-Bataillon 59* (8 February 1942); *Oberleutnant* Schröfl, *1./Kradschützen-Bataillon 59* (24 December 1941); *Oberfeldwebel* Vorac, *3./Panzer-Aufklärungs-Abteilung 9* (10 August 1943); *Leutnant* Vouk, *Panzer-Aufklärungs-Abteilung 9* (12 October 1943); *Oberleutnant* Weiller, *Panzer-Aufklärungs-Abteilung 9* (12 October 1943). **Certificate of Recognition by the Commander in Chief of the Army**—*Unteroffizier* Haas, Headquarters, *Panzer-Aufklärungs-Abteilung 9* (7 September 1943); *Major* Heraucourt, *Kradschützen-Bataillon 59* (8 February 1943); *Oberleutnant* Zangen, *3./Kradschützen-Bataillon 59* (5 October 1942).

10. INFANTERIE-DIVISION (MOT)

Campaigns: Poland and France (as *10. Infanterie-Division*), Soviet Union

Reconnaissance Formations:

- ***Aufklärungs-Abteilung 10 (mot)***

Activated: 15 November 1940

Antecedent Formations: *Aufklärungs-Abteilung 10* (originally formed from personnel levies against *Kavallerie-Regiment 17*) and the armored car platoon of *Panzer-Aufklärungs-Lehr-Abteilung*

Replacement Detachment: Unknown

Redesignation: Consolidated with *Kradschützen-Bataillon 40* on 13 July 1940

Organization: 1941—Headquarters, 1st Armored Scout Company, 2nd Motorcycle Infantry Company, and 3rd Company (heavy)

Commanders: *Hauptmann* Martini (June 1941); *Hauptmann* Winter (acting) (March 1942); *Major* Mayer (May–13 July 1942)

- ***Kradschützen-Bataillon 40***

Activated: 15 November 1940

Antecedent Formations: *MG-Bataillon 6*

Replacement Detachment: *Kradschützen-Ersatz-Bataillon 7*

Deactivation/Redesignation: *Panzer-Aufklärungs-Abteilung 110* on 1 April 1943

Organization: 1941—Headquarters, 1st Motorcycle Infantry Company, 2nd Motorcycle Infantry Company, 3rd Motorcycle Infantry Company, 4th Motorcycle Infantry Machine Gun Company, and 5th Company (heavy). July 1942—Headquarters, 1st Armored Scout Company, 2nd Motorcycle Infantry Company, 3rd Bicycle Company, 4th Bicycle Company, 5th Company (heavy). End of 1942—Headquarters with one armored car platoon, 2nd Motorcycle Infantry Company, 3rd Motorcycle Infantry Company, 4th Motorcycle Infantry Company, and 5th Company (heavy)

Commanders: *Major/Oberstleutnant* Plagemann (15 November 1940–16 June 1942); *Major* Mayer (13 July 1942–31 March 1943)

Notes: In the fall of 1942, the personnel of the 1st Company were reassigned to form *Panzer-Späh-Kompanie 700*, a field-army asset.

- ***Panzer-Aufklärungs-Abteilung 110***

Activated: 1 April 1943

Antecedent Formations: *Kradschützen-Bataillon 40*

Replacement Detachment: Unknown

Deactivation: 8 May 1945

Organization: 1943—Headquarters, 1st Armored Scout Company, 2nd Motorcycle Infantry Company, 3rd Motorcycle Infantry Company, 4th Motorcycle Infantry Company, and 5th Company (heavy)

Commanders: *Major* Mayer (1 April–13 June 1943)

Awards: Honor Roll (Clasp)—None. **German Cross in Gold**—*Leutnant* Dietel, *4./Kradschützen-Bataillon 40* (10 June 1942); *Hauptmann* Gabler, *2./Kradschützen-Bataillon 40* (18 May 1942); *Leutnant Freiherr* von Könitz, *Aufklärungs-Abteilung 10 (mot)* (6 January 1942); *Oberleutnant* Wagner, *1./Kradschützen-Bataillon 40* (6 January 1942); *Hauptmann* Winter, *Aufklärungs-Abteilung 10* (14 March 1942)

10. PANZERGRENADIER-DIVISION

Campaigns: Soviet Union

Reconnaissance Formations:

- ***Panzer-Aufklärungs-Abteilung 110***

Activated: 1 April 1943

Antecedent Formation: *Kradschützen-Bataillon 40*

Replacement Detachment: Unknown

Deactivation: 8 May 1945

Organization: 1943–44—Headquarters, 1st Armored Scout Company, 2nd Motorcycle Infantry Company, 3rd Motorcycle Infantry Company, 4th Motorcycle Infantry Company, and 5th Company (heavy). December 1944—Headquarters, 1st Armored Reconnaissance Company (VW), 2nd Armored Reconnaissance Company (VW), 3rd Armored Reconnaissance Company (VW), and 4th Company (heavy) (motorized). March 1945—Headquarters, Armored Car Platoon, 1st Light Armored Reconnaissance Company (VW), 7.5cm Cannon Platoon (half-track), 2nd Antitank Company (towed)

Commanders: *Major* Mayer (14 June–29 September 1943); *Oberleutnant* Naser (acting) (29 September–9 October 1943); *Hauptmann/Major* von Massow (9 October 1943–5 January 1944); *Hauptmann* Naser (acting) (5 January–May 1944); *Major* von Massow (July–August 1944); *Hauptmann* Stephan (acting) (August 1944); *Oberleutnant* Heppner (acting) (September–November 1944); *Rittmeister* Konrad (November 1944–May 1945)

Notes: On 16 January 1944, 3rd and 5th Companies temporarily disbanded, with 3rd Company being reformed on 16 March 1944. Battalion decimated in August 1944, undergoing battlefield reconstitution in October 1944. Effectively wiped out again in January 1945. Consolidated with *Panzer-Aufklärungs-Abteilung Steinberg*, which had previously been attached to *Panzer-Brigade 103*. In March, the armored car company the division had established in the meantime was reassigned to *Panzer-Division Müncheberg* as its armored car company.

Awards: Knight's Cross—*Oberfeldwebel* Pollner, *3./Panzer-Aufklärungs-Abteilung 110* (3 November 1944). **Honor Roll (Clasp)**—*Feldwebel* Deiler, *2./Panzer-Aufklärungs-Abteilung 110* (15 February 1945). **German Cross in Gold**—*Hauptmann* Bütterich, *3./Panzer-Aufklärungs-Abteilung 110* (24 April 1944); *Feldwebel* Deiler, *2./Panzer-Aufklärungs-Abteilung 110* (8 June 1944); *Major* Mayer, *Panzer-Aufklärungs-Abteilung 110* (7 October 1943); *Hauptmann* Naser, *2./Panzer-Aufklärungs-Abteilung 110* (2 July 1944); *Oberfeldwebel* Rainer, *4./Panzer-Aufklärungs-Abteilung 110* (24 August 1943); *Leutnant* Schulze, *1./Panzer-Aufklärungs-Abteilung 110* (1 December 1943); *Feldwebel* Triltsch, *4./Panzer-Aufklärungs-Abteilung 110* (1 December 1943)

10. PANZER-DIVISION

Campaigns: Poland, France, Soviet Union, North Africa

Reconnaissance Formations:

- ***I./Aufklärungs-Regiment 8***

Activated: 10 November 1938

Antecedent Formations: Battalion formed by redesignation of *Aufklärungs-Abteilung 2 (mot)*. Technically still a part of *3. leichte Division* until 1 April 1940, when assigned to *10. Panzer-Division* and redesignated as *Panzer-Aufklärungs-Abteilung 90*.

Replacement Detachment: *Ersatz-Abteilung für motorisierte Einheiten 8*

Deactivation/Redesignation: *Panzer-Aufklärungs-Abteilung 90* on 1 April 1940

Organization: 1940—Headquarters, 1st Armored Scout Troop, 2nd Armored Scout Troop, 3rd Motorcycle Infantry Troop, and 4th Troop (heavy)

Commanders: *Major Freiherr* von Lützow (1 September 1939–1 April 1940)

- ***Panzer-Aufklärungs-Abteilung 90***

Activated: 1 April 1940

Antecedent Formations: *I./Aufklärungs-Regiment 8*

Replacement Detachment: *Ersatz-Abteilung für motorisierte Einheiten 4*

Deactivation/Redesignation: Consolidated with *Kradschützen-Bataillon 10* in February 1942

Organization: 1940—Headquarters, 1st Armored Scout Troop, 2nd Armored Scout Troop, 3rd Motorcycle Infantry Troop, and 4th Troop (heavy). 1941—Headquarters, 2nd Armored Scout Troop, 3rd Motorcycle Infantry Troop, 4th Troop (heavy). February 1942—2nd Armored Scout Troop (*Panzer-Späh-Kompanie Heldt*)

Commanders: *Major/Oberstleutnant Freiherr* von Lützow (1 April–August 1940); *Major* Klitzing (August 1940–30 June 1941); *Hauptmann* Siebel (acting) (30 June–8 August 1941); *Major* von Hagen (9 August–4 September 1941); *Major* Schmelzer (4 September–29 November 1941); *Oberleutnant* Helm (acting) (29 November–December 1941); *Major* Schmelzer (December 1941–20 January 1942); Unknown (February 1942–?)

Notes: 1st Armored Scout Troop reassigned to *15. Panzer-Division* on 19 December 1940 and redesignated as *1./Aufklärungs-Abteilung 33 (mot)*. Battalion disbanded with the exception of the 2nd Armored Scout Troop. On 1 April 1942, it was redesignated and reassigned as *1./Kradschützen-Bataillon 10*.

- ***Kradschützen-Bataillon 10***

Activated: 1 March 1941

Antecedent Formations: Formed from personnel levies against the Headquarters of *I./Infanterie-Regiment 86*, *7./Infanterie-Regiment 86*, *5/Infanterie-Regiment 69*, and other elements

Replacement Detachment: *Kradschützen-Ersatz-Bataillon 10*

Panzer-Aufklärungs-Abteilung 90

After breaking through French lines during the second phase of the fighting in France in June 1940, *Panzer-Aufklärungs-Abteilung 90* was ordered south to exploit the situation and find weakness in the enemy front. On 8 June, the situation developed unexpectedly:

> A special adventure was to await *Panzer-Aufklärungs-Abteilung 90* in St. Just. The battalion, which had wanted to continued on to Verberie, another forty kilometers distant, at 1800 hours—confident of victory and its abilities—wound up in an increasingly difficult situation in the middle of two withdrawing but still thoroughly combat capable that were also willing to fight. In the course of the evening, the battalion was ordered to hold St. Just and cover all entrances. But by 2100 hours, the ammunition was running out. A call for help from the battalion reached the division command post. It especially needed ammunition for its light infantry, antitank and machine guns. Soon afterwards, the battalion reported that a French column breaking out to the south had cut off the rearward lines of communication.. The battalion had been cut off and was being pushed out of St. Just. It was being forced to occupy to occupy the dominant high ground at La Folie, where it was setting up an all-round defense. With its weak forces, the battalion was unable to interdict the French columns moving through St. Just. It had to be content with being able to save itself. Although the division sent a company form the *II./Schützen-Regiment 69* to help, it was unable to break through in the rapid onset of darkness.
>
> At first light, the situation became even more critical for the battalion, which had been completely surrounded. Enemy tanks were attacking in small groups from all sides. Fortunately, they did not have unity of command. The lack of ammunition became ever more noticeable. The division was only capable of telling it to hold out and inform the battalion that help was on the way in the form of *Panzer-Regiment 7*. The intent was for the tanks to give the battalion 3.7cm ammunition.
>
> But it was not until 1000 hours on 9 June that the armor brigade reached the cut-off reconnaissance battalion. The ammunition drop off was a flop. The 3.7cm ammunition of the tank main guns did not fit the 3.7cm antitank guns of the battalion. Nevertheless, the battalion had been relieved.[21]

Deactivation/Redesignation: *Panzer-Aufklärungs-Abteilung 10* on 24 March 1943

Organization: June 1941—Headquarters, 1st Motorcycle Infantry Company, 2nd Motorcycle Infantry Company, 3rd Motorcycle Infantry Company, 4th Motorcycle Infantry Machine Gun Company, and 5th Company (heavy) (motorized). June 1942—1st Armored Scout Company, 2nd Light Armored Reconnaissance Company (half-track), 3rd Motorcycle Infantry Company, 4th Motorcycle Infantry Company, and 5th Company (heavy) (motorized)

Commanders: *Oberstleutnant* Görger (15 March–21 July 1941); *Hauptmann* Lotz (acting) (21 July 1941–?); *Major* von Hagen (4 September–17 October 1941); *Hauptmann* Lotz (acting) (17 October–12 November 1941); *Hauptmann/Major Dr.* Drewes (12 November 1941–24 March 1943)

Notes: In February and March 1942, the battalion was temporarily disbanded. It was reformed starting with the assignment of *Panzer-Späh-Kompanie Heldt* (see *Panzer-Aufklärungs-Abteilung 90*).

- ***Panzer-Aufklärungs-Abteilung 10***

Activated: 24 March 1943

Antecedent Formation: *Kradschützen-Bataillon 10*

Replacement Detachment: Initially *Kradschützen-Ersatz- und Ausbildungs-Abteilung 2*, later redesignated as *Panzer-Aufklärungs-Ersatz-Abteilung 2*

Deactivation: May 1943 (surrender in North Africa)

Organization: April 1943—Headquarters, 1st Armored Scout Company, 2nd Light Armored Reconnaissance Company (half-track), 3rd Motorcycle Infantry Company, 4th Motorcycle Infantry Company, 5th Company (heavy) (motorized)

Commanders: *Major Dr.* Drewes (24 March–May 1943)

Awards: Knight's Cross—*Major Dr.* Drewes, *Kradschützen-Bataillon 10* (24 April 1943). **German Cross in Gold**—*Oberleutnant* Baumgardt, *1./Kradschützen-Bataillon 10* (14 January 1942); *Oberleutnant* Felder, *2./Kradschützen-Bataillon 10* (24 April 1943); *Oberleutnant* Pschorr, *3./Kradschützen-Bataillon 10* (25 January 1943). **Mention in the Wehrmacht Daily Report**—*Major Dr.* Drewes, *Kradschützen-Bataillon 10* (28 April 1943)

11. PANZER-DIVISION

Campaigns: Soviet Union, West

Reconnaissance Formations

- ***Kradschützen-Bataillon 61***

Activated: 6 August 1940

Antecedent Formations: Formed from personnel levies against *11./Schützen-Regimenter 110* and *111* (motorcycle companies), *14./Infanterie-Regimenter 302* and *342* of *231. Infanterie-Division* (antitank companies)

Replacement Detachment: Initially *Kradschützen-Ersatz-Bataillon 1*, then *Kradschützen-Ersatz-Bataillon 55* (1 December 1941)

Deactivation/Redesignation: *Panzer-Aufklärungs-Abteilung 11* on 27 April 1943

Organization: 1940—Headquarters, 1st Motorcycle Infantry Company, 2nd Motorcycle Infantry Company, 3rd Motorcycle Infantry Company, 4th Motorcycle Infantry Machine Gun Company, and 5th Company (heavy). December 1941—Headquarters, 1st Armored Scout Company, 2nd Motorcycle Infantry Company, 3rd Motorcycle Infantry Company, 4th Motorcycle Infantry Company, and 5th Company (heavy). July 1942—Headquarters with Light Armored Scout Section, 1st Armored Scout Company, 2nd Armored Reconnaissance Company (half-track), 3rd Motorcycle Infantry Company, 4th Motorcycle Infantry Company, and 5th Company (heavy)

Commanders: Unknown (August 1940–May 1941); *Major* von Usedom (May 1941–April 1942); *Hauptmann Freiherr* von Hauser (April 1942–23 January 1943); *Hauptmann* Ladewig (acting) (February–April 1943)

- ***Panzer-Aufklärungs-Abteilung 231***

Activated: 5 September 1940

Antecedent Formations: *Aufklärungs-Abteilung 231* (reassigned from *231. Infanterie-Division*) and *2.(PzSpäh)/Panzer-Aufklärungs-Abteilung 5* of *2. Panzer-Division*

Replacement Detachment: *Ersatz-Abteilung für motorisierte Aufklärungseinheiten 4*, followed by *Ersatz-Abteilung für motorisierte Aufklärungseinheiten 7* and then *Kradschützen-Ersatz-Bataillon 7*

Deactivation/Redesignation: Consolidated with *Kradschützen-Bataillon 61* on 1 December 1941

Organization: September 1940—Headquarters, 1st Armored Scout Troop, 2nd Bicycle Troop, and 3rd Troop (heavy)

Commanders: *Major Freiherr* von Gebsattel (1 August–October 1940)

- ***Panzer-Aufklärungs-Abteilung 11***

Activated: 27 April 1943

Antecedent Formations: *Kradschützen-Bataillon 61*

Replacement Detachment: *Panzer-Aufklärungs-Ersatz-Abteilung 55*

Deactivation: 4 May 1945

Organization: 1943–44—Headquarters, 1st Armored Scout Company, 2nd Light Armored Reconnaissance Company (half-track) (later 2nd Armored Scout Company [light half-track]), 3rd Armored Reconnaissance Company (half-track), and 4th Armored Reconnaissance Company (half-track). May 1944—Headquarters with armored car sections, 1st Armored Scout Company (light half-track), 2nd Light Armored Reconnaissance Company (light half-track), 3rd Armored Reconnaissance Company (half-track), and 4th Heavy Armored Reconnaissance Company (half-track)

Commanders: *Oberstleutnant* Lindner (May–July 1943); *Hauptmann* Pirch (acting) (August 1943–?); *Major Freiherr* von Ruepprecht (January–June 1944); *Major* Thieme (acting) (mid-1944–

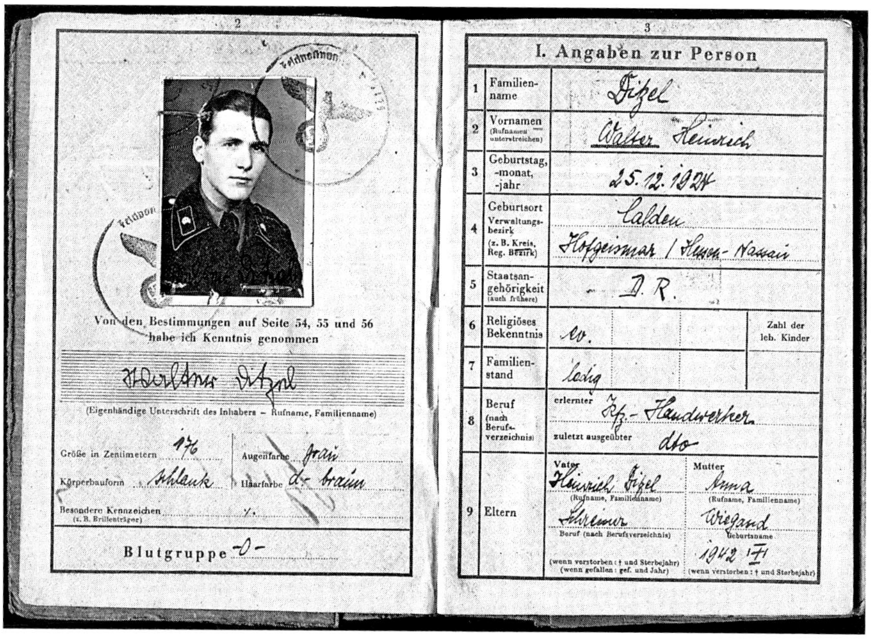

Pages from the *Wehrpaß* of Walter Ditzel, a scout assigned to *1.(Pz.Späh)/Kradschützen-Bataillon 55* until wounds sidelined him for the rest of the war. (His last *Wehrpaß* entry shows him being released from service in late May 1945 by order of *11. Panzer-Division* and U.S. Third Army!)

August 1944); *Major* Bode (September–November 1944); Unknown (November 1944–February 1945); *Hauptmann* Riedinger (February 1945–?)

Notes: On 5 September 1943, orders issued for the transfer of the 2nd Company to the Senne Training Area for reconstitution and reorganization as a Type "C" armored scout company. It was further ordered to complete its training by the end of December. On 31 October 1943, orders were received directing a battlefield reconstitution, reorganization and redesignation of the 5th Company (Heavy) as the 5th Armored Reconnaissance Company (heavy) (half-track). On 2 January 1944, the 2nd Armored Scout Company (half-track) began rail movement to rejoin the division. *Panzer-Aufklärungs-Abteilung 11* among the last combat elements of the division to leave the Eastern Front, when the division was ordered reconstituted in the spring of 1944. One armored reconnaissance company (VW) was added by command action in June 1944, only to be disbanded in November 1944.

Awards: Knight's Cross—*Oberfeldwebel* Harthan, *5./Panzer-Aufklärungs-Abteilung 11* (12 June 1944); *Hauptmann Freiherr* von Hauser, *Kradschützen-Bataillon 61* (25 January 1943); *Hauptmann* Pirch, *Panzer-Aufklärungs-Abteilung 11* (13 September 1943); *Unteroffizier* Rothardt, *2./Panzer-Aufklärungs-Abteilung 11* (30 September 1943); *Major* von Usedom, *Kradschützen-Bataillon 61* (31 December 1941). **Honor Roll (Clasp)**—*Hauptmann Freiherr* von Hauser, *Kradschützen-Bataillon 61* (5 October 1942). **Close Combat Clasp in Gold**—*Oberfeldwebel* Harthan, *5./Panzer-Aufklärungs-Abteilung 11* (1944);[22] *Unteroffizier* Kretzschmar, *4./Panzer-Aufklärungs-Abteilung 11* (4 December 1944); *Obergefreiter* Zakel, *Panzer-Aufklärungs-Abteilung 11* (30 October 1943). **German Cross in Gold**—Leutnant Garbe, *4./Kradschützen-Bataillon 61* (11 February 1943); *Oberfeldwebel* Gerstner, *2./Panzer-Aufklärungs-Abteilung 11*; *Feldwebel* Harthan, *Kradschützen-Bataillon 61* (20 September 1942); *Oberleutnant* Pirch, *2./Kradschützen-Bataillon 61* (26 September 1942). **German Cross in Silver**—*Hauptwerkmeister* Bickel, *Panzer-Aufklärungs-Abteilung 11* (31 January 1945); *Oberfeldwebel* Klaus, *2./Panzer-Aufklärungs-Abteilung 11* (29 April 1945). **Certificate of Recognition from the Commander in Chief of the Army**—*Oberfeldwebel* Gerstner, *Panzer-Aufklärungs-Abteilung 11* (17 September 1943)

Images of Otto Damm, his *Sd.Kfz. 222*, and an *Sd.Kfz. 231 (8 Rad)*, most likely somewhere in the Soviet Union in 1941 or 1942. Entries for Otto Damm were last seen in the section on the 2. Panzer-Division.

ZÜNDAPP

12. PANZER-DIVISION

Campaigns: Soviet Union

Reconnaissance Formations:

• ***Aufklärungs-Abteilung 2 (mot)***

Activated: 10 November 1938

Antecedent Formations: None

Replacement Detachment: *Ersatz-Abteilung für motorisierte Aufklärungs-Einheiten 3*

Deactivation/Redesignation: *Panzer-Aufklärungs- und Voraus-Abteilung 2* on 27 November 1941

Organization: 1941—Headquarters, 1st Motorcycle Infantry Troop, 2nd Armored Scout Troop, and 3rd Troop (heavy)

Commanders: *Oberstleutnant* Wolf (10 January–13 August 1941)

• ***Panzer-Aufklärungs- und Voraus-Abteilung 2***

Activated: 13 August 1941

Antecedent Formations: *Aufklärungs-Abteilung 2 (mot)* and *Kradschützen-Bataillon 22*

Replacement Detachment: Initially *Ersatz-Abteilung für motorisierte Aufklärungseinheiten 3* and, on 1 October 1941, *Kradschützen-Ersatz-Bataillon 4*

Deactivation/Redesignation: *Kradschützen-Bataillon 22* on 27 November 1941

Organization: 1941—Headquarters, 1st Motorcycle Infantry Company, 2nd Motorcycle Infantry Company, 3rd Motorcycle Infantry Company, 4th Motorcycle Infantry Machine Gun Company, 5th Company (heavy), and 6th Armored Scout Company

Notes: The battalion was the result of a consolidation and reorganization of the armored reconnaissance and motorcycle infantry battalions and the redesignation given above. The 6th Armored Scout Company was the former *2.(Pz.Späh)/Aufklärungs-Abteilung 2 (mot).*

• ***Kradschützen-Bataillon 22***

Activated: 20 August 1940

Antecedent Formations: Formed from personnel levies against the headquarters of *I./Infanterie-Regiment 25 (mot)*, as well as the battalion's 3rd Company, and *3.*, *6.*, and *12./Infanterie-Regiment 5*

Replacement Detachment: Initially *Kradschützen-Bataillon 3*, followed by *Kradschützen-Bataillon 4* on 19 February 1942 and, finally, *Kradschützen-Bataillon 24* on 14 May 1942

Deactivation/Redesignation: 20 April 1943 (aside from interim redesignation as *Panzer-Aufklärungs- und Voraus-Abteilung 2*)

Organization: 1941—Headquarters, 1st Motorcycle Infantry Company, 2nd Motorcycle Infantry Company, 3rd Motorcycle Infantry Company, 4th Motorcycle Infantry Machine Gun Company, and 5th Company (heavy). November 1941—Headquarters, 1st Motorcycle Infantry Company, 2nd Motorcycle Infantry Company, 3rd Motorcycle Infantry Company, 4th Motorcycle Infantry Machine Gun Company, 5th Company (heavy), and 6th Armored Scout Company. July 1942—Headquarters, 1st Armored Scout Company, 2nd Motorcycle Infantry Company, 3rd Motorcycle Infantry Company, 4th Motorcycle Infantry Company, and 5th Company (heavy)

Commanders: *Oberstleutnant* Bayer (10 January–13 August 1941, 30 November 1941–1 March 1942); *Oberstleutnant* Renner (1–27 March 1942); *Major* Kahler (27 March–July 1942); *Hauptmann* Blaese (acting) (mid-1942–September 1942); *Major Graf* von Brockdorff-Ahlefeldt (September–5 December 1942); *Hauptmann* Noeske (5 December 1942–20 April 1943).

Notes: *Oberstleutnant* Bayer also commanded *Panzer-Aufklärungs- und Voraus-Abteilung 2*, which explains the break in his command dates.

• ***Panzer-Aufklärungs-Abteilung 12***

Activated: 20 April 1943

Antecedent Formations: *Kradschützen-Bataillon 22*

Replacement Detachment: Initially *Panzer-Aufklärungs-Ersatz- und Ausbildungs-Abteilung 24*, followed by *Panzer-Aufklärungs-Ersatz- und Ausbildungs-Abteilung 4* on 1 April 1944

Deactivation/Redesignation: 8 May 1945

Organization: 1943—Headquarters, 1st Armored Scout Company, 2nd Motorcycle Infantry Company, 3rd Motorcycle Infantry Company, 4th Motorcycle Infantry Company, and 5th Company (heavy). July 1944—Headquarters with armored scout sections (wheeled), 1st Armored Scout Company (half-track), 2nd Light Armored Reconnaissance Company (half-track), 3rd Armored Reconnaissance Company (half-track), and 4th Heavy Armored Reconnaissance Company (half-track). January 1945—Headquarters, 1st Armored Scout Company, 2nd Light Armored

Kradschützen-Bataillon 22

The following is a firsthand account of fighting north of Orscha in the summer of 1941. It was written after the war by Gerhard Möws, a Knight's Cross recipient of the *3./Kradschützen-Bataillon 22* (1 November 1942), who was a platoon leader at the time of this account. Later on, he would also serve as the acting commander of *Panzer-Aufklärungs-Abteilung 12*:

> My platoon was moving at the end of the company. We were held up at a temporary crossing point over a creek. The company had disappeared. I assembled my men and formed a new lead element, since the woods in front of us weren't too beckoning. Armored cars from the reconnaissance battalion came back: "Watch out! Russians in front . . . two kilometers along the route of advance . . . they have AT with them." Well, well. Following me at some distance were the motorcycle infantry of the 2nd Company. There was a smoky smell in the air; the woods were on fire. On top of that was artificial smoke, which was growing thicker, which the armored cars had fired. The lead squad started to be fired upon. The squad leader had a jam in his submachine gun and was badly wounded. We closed up, spread out and attacked. Hand grenades were in the air. My mortar spat into the woods. In the haze, you couldn't see your hand in front of your face. I crawled along the path. I intended to dress the *Unteroffizier* and fetch him back to cover. He had been hit bad.
>
> We were all riled up, but we were unable to advance. We also had to watch out so that we did not get enveloped. The 2nd Company approached. *Oberleutnant* Jung, a tall man, jumped towards me. I briefed him and his riflemen started moving forward in into the woods to the right. That took some pressure off. Even the Russian AT guns were under pressure. Our battalion commander, *Oberstleutnant* Bayer, had seen that we had not caught up and he sent some tanks back. We formed up again and linked up with the battalion at the crossroads that we were acquainted with to the northwest of Orscha. While moving there, hand grenades flew through the air into the column, but they didn't cause any damage That meant that the Russians were everywhere in the woods, however.
>
> Tanks moved out to the south along the road towards Orscha. My company followed. To the right and left were thick woods, some of which was on fire. The lead elements of the tanks crossed over the ridge of a hill, where they encountered numerous heavy Russian tanks. The tanks had to pull back. Two 10cm cannon of our heavy artillery battalion went into position at the crossroads behind us. Along the edge of the road were some 3.7cm *Flak*. We were on the ground off to the side in the vegetation. Up front, on the crest of the high ground along the road, the first Russian tanks appeared.
>
> At that point, the fireworks began. Up front, there was the barking of the main guns. Behind us were the hard cracks of the cannon and the *Flak*. Toward the enemy, smoke mushrooms were rising. My driver came running over to me; our vehicle was gone. Food items we had carefully stored for emergencies . . . our clothes . . . reserves of hand grenades for the platoon . . . everything was hanging up in the trees. Shit!
>
> The Russian tanks were burning. It was quiet for a moment. Then new ones arrived. With infantry this time. Our machine guns were put to work. The Russians continued on, obstinately. A main gun round hit our commander, *Oberleutnant* Lange, a good man. He was buried at the crossroads, along with my squad leader. The men of the company were very depressed. All of us had liked him.
>
> During one of the longer breaks in the firing, I went with one of the men to the knocked-out tanks on the high ground. Once there, we saw to our disbelief a long column of Russian infantry, approaching us on the road as if on peacetime maneuvers. The commander was high atop a horse. We made out way back

Kradschützen-Bataillon 22 continued

stealthfully. We briefed the machine guns. We would let them come closer until we were certain to get them. They were shot to pieces . . . a merciless war.

Far to the rear, it turned lively. On the road to the north, there was a crossing point over a small waterway. Engineers were preparing it for our continued march, since we were unable to advance any further to the south. The Russians attacked the bridge hard. We were encircled. During the day, unbearable heat . . . at night, an unimaginable plague of mosquitos. Thirst. And only a small well was available for all of the forces there. The woods were burning in places. We had to wait there for a few days until tired infantry relieved us. They were to hold up for a while and then follow us. We advanced north.

The next day, we passed elements of the 5th Regiment [*Schützen-Regiment 5* of the division]. They had engaged in intense close combat with Russian infantry which had broken out of the woods with fixed bayonets. At the crossing point over a creek, there were burnt-out vehicles from the division trains. Nighttime artillery fire had sent them up in flames. We heard that among the many prisoners had also been Stalin's son. During the night, we reached the major road from Vitebsk to Smolensk. There were no enemy forces in front of us. We had advanced right through the middle of a pocket being formed.[23]

Reconnaissance Company (half-track), and 4th Heavy Armored Reconnaissance Company (half-track)

Commanders: *Hauptmann* Noeske (20 April–June 1943); *Hauptmann* Möws (acting) (to 16 July 1943); *Hauptmann* Noeske (16 July–2 August 1943); *Major* Bock (8 August–October 1943); *Major* Langenfaß (to February 1944); *Hauptmann/Major* Ellfeldt (February–July 1944); *Major* Engelien (acting) (July 1944); *Major* Noeske (acting) (July 1944); *Hauptmann* Ibach (23 July–September 1944); *Hauptmann* Ellfeldt (September 1944–February 1945)

Notes: Later in 1943, the three motorcycle infantry companies were reorganized as armored reconnaissance companies, equipped with *Kettenkräder*. On 24 August 1943, the headquarters and the 3rd Company were ordered to Senne Training Area for reconstitution, with the process to last six weeks. At the beginning of 1944, the 2nd through 4th Companies were temporarily equipped with trucks. From April to June 1944, the battalion was at the Wildflecken Training Area for reorganization and reconstitution. In July 1944, the battalion was ordered to rejoin the division, minus its 1st Company. In January 1945, the 3rd Company sent to the Milowitz Training Area for reconstitution, never returning to the division and its personnel eventually being assigned to *7. Panzer-Division*. In February 1945, the battalion was detached from the division to help form *Panzer-Brigade "Kurland,"* never returning to the division fold.

Awards: Knight's Cross—*Oberstleutnant* Bayer, *Kradschützen-Bataillon 22* (17 July 1941); *Rittmeister Graf* von Brockdorff-Ahlefeldt, *Kradschützen-Bataillon 22* (16 December 1942); *Major* Engelien, *Panzer-Aufklärungs-Abteilung 12* (12 August 1944); *Leutnant* Meyer, *3./Panzer-Aufklärungs-Abteilung 12* (5 March 1945); *Oberleutnant* Möws, *3./Kradschützen-Bataillon 22* (1 November 1942); *Oberfeldwebel* Unruhe, *2./Panzer-Aufklärungs-Abteilung 12* (28 March 1945). **Honor Roll (Clasp)**—*Hauptmann* Ellfeldt, *Panzer-Aufklärungs-Abteilung 12* (5 April 1945); *Oberleutnant* Wilimzig, *Kradschützen-Bataillon 22* (27 May 1943). **German Cross in Gold**—*Oberleutnant* Fehler, *1./Panzer-Aufklärungs- und Voraus-Abteilung 2* (19 January 1942); *Unteroffizier* Heller, *3./Panzer-Aufklärungs-Abteilung 12* (28 November 1944); *Hauptmann* von Metnitz, *Panzer-Aufklärungs-Abteilung 12* (20 January 1945); *Hauptmann* Noeske, *Panzer-Aufklärungs-Abteilung 12* (20 July 1943); *Oberfeldwebel* Nolte, *Panzer-Aufklärungs-Abteilung*

12 (13 December 1944); *Hauptmann* Schulz, *Panzer-Aufklärungs-Abteilung 12* (27 January 1945); *Oberleutnant* Springorum, *6./Panzer-Aufklärungs- und Voraus-Abteilung 2* (19 January 1942); *Stabsfeldwebel* Timmreck, *1./Panzer-Aufklärungs-Abteilung 12* (17 March 1944); *Fahnenjunker-Oberfeldwebel* Trebesch, *2./Panzer-Aufklärungs-Abteilung 12* (22 November 1943); *Oberfeldwebel* Unruhe, *Panzer-Aufklärungs-Abteilung 12* (15 May 1943); *Oberleutnant* Wilimzig, *Panzer-Aufklärungs-Abteilung 12* (4 February 1944); *Oberfeldwebel* Ziemer, *1./Panzer-Aufklärungs-Abteilung 12* (21 October 1943)

13. INFANTERIE-DIVISION (MOT)

Campaigns: Poland, France

Reconnaissance Formations:

- ***Aufklärungs-Abteilung 13 (mot)***

Activated: 12 October 1937

Deactivation/Redesignation: *Lehr-Aufklärungs-Abteilung "R"*

Organization: 1939—Headquarters, 1st Armored Scout Company, and 2nd Motorcycle Infantry Company. 1940—Headquarters, 1st Armored Scout Company, 2nd Motorcycle Infantry Company, and 3rd Company (heavy)

Commanders: *Major* von Scheele (1 September–October 1939); *Major* von Hake (October 1939–11 October 1940)

Notes: The battalion did not receive its heavy company until after the fall of France. It went with the division in November 1940 to serve as an instructor battalion for Romanian forces, returning to Germany in May 1941.

- ***Kradschützen-Bataillon 43***

Activated: 2 August 1940

Antecedent Formations: Formed thorough personnel levies against *Infanterie-Regiment 66* and *93* (divisional regiments)

Replacement Detachment: Unknown

Deactivation/Redesignation: *Lehr-Kradschützen-Bataillon 43*

Organization: 1941—Headquarters, 1st Motorcycle Infantry Company, 2nd Motorcycle Infantry Company, 3rd Motorcycle Infantry Company, 4th Motorcycle Infantry Machine Gun Company, and 5th Company (heavy)

Commanders: *Major* Stolz (6 August–11 October 1940)

Notes: Like the reconnaissance battalion, the motorcycle infantrymen were dispatched to Romania as instructional troops in November 1940, receiving the designation of *Lehr-Kradschützen-Bataillon 43*.

13. PANZER-DIVISION

Campaigns: Soviet Union

Reconnaissance Formations

- ***Aufklärungs-Abteilung 13 (mot)***

Activated: 12 October 1937

Antecedent Formations: Unknown

Replacement Detachment: Unknown

Deactivation/Redesignation: *Panzer-Aufklärungs-Abteilung 13* on 28 May 1941

Organization: 1940—Headquarters, 1st Armored Scout Company, 2nd Motorcycle Infantry Company, and 3rd Company (heavy)

Commanders: *Major* von Hake (11 October 1940–28 May 1941)

Notes: Designated *Lehr-Aufklärungs-Abteilung "R"* during its time in Romania as instructional forces (9 November 1940–21 May 1941).

- ***Kradschützen-Bataillon 43***

Activated: 2 August 1940

Antecedent Formations: Formed thorough personnel levies against *Infanterie-Regimenter 66* and *93* (divisional regiments)

Replacement Detachment: Unknown

Deactivation/Redesignation: *Panzer-Aufklärungs-Abteilung 13* on 1 April 1943

Organization: 1940—Headquarters, 1st Motorcycle Infantry Company, 2nd Motorcycle Infantry Company, 3rd Motorcycle Infantry Company, 4th Motorcycle Infantry Machine Gun Company, and 5th Company (heavy). July 1942—Headquarters, 1st Armored Scout Company, 2ndLight Armored Reconnaissance Company (half-track), 3rd Motorcycle Infantry Company, 4th Motorcycle Infantry Company, and 5th Company (heavy)

Commanders: *Oberstleutnant* Stolz (11 October 1940–September 1942); *Major* Creutznacher (20 September–13 November 1942); *Hauptmann* Schütz (acting) (26 October–13 November 1942); *Major* Brux (13–24 November 1942); *Hauptmann* Froemel (acting) (24 November 1942–?); *Major* Brux (to 12 January 1943); *Hauptmann* Werdermann (to 1 April 1943)

Notes: Designated *Lehr-Kradschützen-Bataillon "R"* during its time in Romania as instructional forces (27 October 1940–28 May 1941).

- ***Panzer-Aufklärungs-Abteilung 13 (first iteration)***

Activated: 28 May 1941

Antecedent Formations: *Aufklärungs-Abteilung 13 (mot)*

Replacement Detachment: Unknown

Deactivation/Redesignation: Consolidated with *Kradschützen-Bataillon 43* on 10 April 1942

Organization: June 1941–42—Headquarters, 1st Armored Scout Company, 2nd Motorcycle Infantry Company, and 3rd Company (heavy)

Commanders: *Major* von Hake (28 May 1941–10 April 1942)

- ***Panzer-Aufklärungs-Abteilung 13 (second iteration)***

Activated: 1 April 1943[24]

Antecedent Formations: *Kradschützen-Bataillon 43*

Replacement Detachment: Unknown

Deactivation/Redesignation: *Panzer-Aufklärungs-Abteilung "Feldherrnhalle 2"* in April 1945

Organization: July 1943—Headquarters, 1st Armored Scout Company, 2nd Armored Reconnaissance Company (half-track), 3rd Armored Reconnaissance Company (motorized), 4th Armored Reconnaissance Company (*Krad*), and 5th Heavy Armored Reconnaissance Company (motorized). February 1944—Headquarters, 1st Armored Scout Company, 2nd Armored Scout Company (half-track), 3rd Armored Reconnaissance Company (half-track), 4th Armored Reconnaissance Company (motorized), and 5th Heavy Armored Reconnaissance Company (half-track). September–November 1944—Headquarters, 1st Armored Scout Company, and 3rd Armored Reconnaissance Company (half-track). December 1944—Headquarters, 1st Armored Scout Company, 2nd Armored Reconnaissance Company (half-track), and 3rd Company (motorized). March 1945 (planned)—Headquarters, 1st Armored Scout Company, and 2nd Armored Reconnaissance Company (VW)

Commanders: *Hauptmann* Schütz (acting) (1 April 1943–?); *Hauptmann* Sassenberg (acting) (to 25 October 1943); *Hauptmann/Major* Schütz (February–November 1944); *Rittmeister* Papst (to 14 February 1945); Unknown (March–April 1945)

Notes: In September 1943, orders were issued directed the battalion's 2nd and 5th Companies to move west of the Dnjepr to reorganize and reconstitute. The 2nd was to be converted to a Type "C" armored scout company, while the 5th was to become a heavy armored reconnaissance company with medium half-tracks. The companies completed the process in December and returned to the division then. On October 24 1943, orders were issued to Military District VI to activate a heavy armored scout platoon, with the platoon being ready for deployment by November 1943. On 10 November 1943, movement orders were issued for the platoon to join *Panzer-Aufklärungs-Abteilung 13* in Ukraine; the platoon had six *Sd.Kfz. 233's*. On 27 July 1944, the battalion's 3rd Company was sent to the Wildflecken Training Area for reorganization and reconstitution as a light armored reconnaissance company (half-track). On 4 August, it was given until 20 September to complete the process. The company received orders on 21 September to rejoin the division with its thirty light half-tracks. The battalion was badly battered in August 1944, with the 2nd and 5th Companies essentially written off. It was reconstituted in September. It was basically destroyed in the fighting around Budapest in the winter of 1944–45 and an attempt was made to reconstitute it in March 1945 as *Aufklärungsgruppe 13* (basically a reinforced VW company).[25] It reported to *Panzer-Division "Feldherrnhalle 2,"* the new designation for what was left of *13. Panzer-Division*, in April 1945.

Awards: Knight's Cross—*Rittmeister* Papst, *Panzer-Aufklärungs-Abteilung 13* (15 January 1945); *Leutnant* Reverchon, *1./Kradschützen-Bataillon 43* (16 September 1942); *Leutnant* Sassenberg, *2./Panzer-Aufklärungs-Abteilung 13* (23 October 1941); *Oberstleutnant* Stolz, *Kradschützen-Bataillon 43* (28 August 1942). **Honor Roll (Clasp)**—*Leutnant* Borg, *1./Panzer-Aufklärungs-Abteilung 13* (19 August 1941). **Close Combat Clasp in Gold**—*Unteroffizier* Liebl, *3./Panzer-Aufklärungs-Abteilung 13* (9 August 1944); *Obergefreiter* Rusdorf, *4./Panzer-Aufklärungs-*

Abteilung 13 (27 September 1943); *Unteroffizier* Schöntaube, *3./Panzer-Aufklärungs-Abteilung 13*. **German Cross in Gold**—*Major* Brux, *Kradschützen-Bataillon 43* (23 January 1943); *Oberleutnant* Eick, *1./Kradschützen-Bataillon 43* (14 October 1942); *Major* von Hake, *Panzer-Aufklärungs-Abteilung 13* (22 November 1941); *Unteroffizier* Heller, *3./Panzer-Aufklärungs-Abteilung 13* (28 January 1945); *Oberfeldwebel* Hilski, *3./Kradschützen-Bataillon 43* (14 February 1942); *Oberleutnant Graf* Kalckreuth, *2./Panzer-Aufklärungs-Abteilung 13* (2 July 1944); *Leutnant* Kretzig, *3./Panzer-Aufklärungs-Abteilung 13* (4 February 1945); *Oberfeldwebel* Lehmann, *1./Panzer-Aufklärungs-Abteilung 13* (1 December 1941); *Oberleutnant* Mielke, *4./Kradschützen-Bataillon 43* (30 April 1943); *Feldwebel* Möhring, *4./Kradschützen-Bataillon 43* (18 March 1943); *Leutnant* Müller, Headquarters, *Kradschützen-Bataillon 43* (18 March 1943); *Oberfeldwebel* Oertel, *1./Kradschützen-Bataillon 43* (19 September 1942); *Oberleutnant* Rahn, *3./Kradschützen-Bataillon 43* (26 August 1942); *Leutnant* Roock, *4./Kradschützen-Bataillon 43* (21 January 1943); *Feldwebel* Simon, *1./Kradschützen-Bataillon 43* (2 October 1942); *Hauptmann* Taschner, *Panzer-Aufklärungs-Abteilung 13* (2 July 1944); *Oberleutnant* Wolff von der Sahl, *4./Kradschützen-Bataillon 43* (19 September 1942)

14. INFANTERIE-DIVISION (MOT)

Campaigns: Soviet Union

Reconnaissance Formations:

- ***Kradschützen-Bataillon 54***

Activated: 15 October 1940

Antecedent Formations: Formed through personnel levies against *I./Infanterie-Regiment 101* of *4. Infanterie-Division*

Replacement Detachment: *Kradschützen-Ersatz-Bataillon 55*

Deactivation/Redesignation: *Füsilier-Bataillon 14* in March 1943

Organization: 1941—Headquarters, 1st Motorcycle Infantry Company, 2nd Motorcycle Infantry Company, 3rd Motorcycle Infantry Company, 4th Motorcycle Infantry Machine Gun Company, and 5th Company (heavy). 1942–43—Headquarters, 1st Armored Scout Company, 2nd Motorcycle Infantry Company, 3rd Motorcycle Infantry Company, 4th Motorcycle Infantry Company, and 5th Company (heavy)

Commanders: *Oberstleutnant* Dietlen (October 1940–November 1941); *Major* Schulze (acting) (17 November 1941–14 January 1942); *Oberleutnant* Baar (acting) (14 January 1942); *Major/Oberstleutnant* Moeller (14 January–3 December 1942); *Oberleutnant* Seidel (acting) (3–30 December 1942); *Hauptmann* Schleipen (30 December 1942–March 1943)

Notes: The division was demotorized in March 1943 and reverted to a standard infantry division.

- ***Aufklärungs-Abteilung 14 (mot)***

Activated: 15 October 1940

Antecedent Formations: Formed by the reorganization of *2.(Radfahr)/Aufklärungs-Abteilung 14*, the reassignment of *1. (Pz.Späh)/Aufklärungs-Abteilung 88* of *18. Panzer-Division*, and the activation of a heavy company

Replacement Detachment: Unknown

Deactivation/Redesignation: *Kradschützen-Bataillon 54*

Organization: 1941—Headquarters, 1st Armored Scout Company, 2nd Motorcycle Infantry Company, and 3rd Company (heavy)

Commanders: *Oberstleutnant/Oberst* von Wagner (December 1940–March 1942)

Notes: The division was demotorized in March 1943 and reverted to a standard infantry division.

Awards: Knight's Cross—*Oberstleutnant* Dietlen, *Kradschützen-Bataillon 54*. **German Cross in Gold**—*Feldwebel* Auert, *4./Kradschützen-Bataillon 54* (26 May 1943); *Oberleutnant* Baar, *Aufklärungs-Abteilung 14 (mot)* (25 May 1942); *Oberfeldwebel* Gläser, *2./Kradschützen-Bataillon 54* (2 April 1943); *Oberfeldwebel* Haake, *2./Kradschützen-Bataillon 54* (2 April 1943); *Oberleutnant* Hoy, *3./Kradschützen-Bataillon 54* (14 February 1943); *Leutnant* Käther, *2./Kradschützen-Bataillon 54* (8 June 1942); Feldwebel Martin, *4./Kradschützen-Bataillon 54* (26 May 1943); *Oberleutnant* von Oehmichen, *4./Kradschützen-Bataillon 54* (30 July 1942); *Oberleutnant* Seidel, *Kradschützen-Bataillon 54* (20 November 1942); *Oberst* von Wagner, *Aufklärungs-Abteilung 14 (mot)* (19 April 1942)

14. PANZER-DIVISION

Campaigns: Balkans, Soviet Union

Reconnaissance Formations:

- ***Kradschützen-Bataillon 64***

Activated: 16 August 1940

Antecedent Formations: Formed from personnel levies against *1.* and *2./MB-Bataillon 7*, *3./Infanterie-Regiment 10*, *3./Infanterie-Regiment 5*, and *5.* and *9./Infanterie-Regiment 103*

Replacement Detachment: *Kradschützen-Ersatz-Bataillon 55*

Deactivation/Redesignation: *Panzer-Aufklärungs-Abteilung 43* in February 1943

Organization: 1940–41—Headquarters, 1st Motorcycle Infantry Company, 2nd Motorcycle Infantry Company, 3rd Motorcycle Infantry Company, 4th Motorcycle Infantry Machine Gun Company, and 5th Company (heavy). April 1942—Headquarters, 1st Armored Scout Company, 2nd Motorcycle Infantry Company, 3rd Motorcycle Infantry Company, 4th Motorcycle Infantry Company, and 5th Company (heavy)

Commanders: *Oberstleutnant* Tröger (October 1940–17 July 1941); *Hauptmann* Berndt (acting) (17–27 July 1941); *Oberstleutnant* Tröger (27 July–20 December 1941); *Hauptmann* Berndt (acting) (20 December 1941–?); *Major* Grams (April–10 December 1942); *Hauptmann* Weller (acting) (10 December 1942–10 January 1943)

Notes: Apparently, the 2nd Company was equipped with half-tracks in the summer of 1942.

- ***Panzer-Aufklärungs-Abteilung 40***

Activated: 15 August 1940

Antecedent Formations: Formed through the reorganization and redesignation of *Divisions-Aufklärungs-Abteilung 4*, the reassignment of *1.(PzSpäh)/Aufklärungs-Abteilung 8*,[26] and personnel levies against *Aufklärungs-Abteilung 7*

Replacement Detachment: Unknown

Deactivation/Redesignation: Consolidated with *Kradschützen-Bataillon 40* on 15 April 1942

Organization: 1940–41—Headquarters, 1st Armored Scout Company, 2nd Motorcycle Infantry Company, and 3rd Company (heavy)

Commanders: *Major* Uber (15 August 1940–6 November 1941); *Rittmeister* Grams (7 November 1941–22 January 1942); *Hauptmann* Strathmann (acting) (22 January–20 February 1942); *Major* Grams (20 February–15 April 1942)

- ***Panzer-Aufklärungs-Abteilung 64***

Activated: 3 March 1943

Antecedent Formations: *Kradschützen-Bataillon 64*

Replacement Detachment: Unknown

Deactivation/Redesignation: *Panzer-Aufklärungs-Abteilung 14* on 21 May 1943

Organization: 1943—Headquarters, 1st Armored Scout Company, 2nd Light Armored Reconnaissance Company, 3rd Armored Reconnaissance Company, 4th Armored Reconnaissance Company, and 5th Heavy Armored Reconnaissance Company

Commanders: *Major* Rehm (April–21 May 1943)

- ***Panzer-Aufklärungs-Abteilung 14***

Activated: 21 May 1943

Antecedent Formations: *Panzer-Aufklärungs-Abteilung 64*

Replacement Detachment: Unknown

Deactivation: 8 May 1945

Organization: 1943—Headquarters, 1st Armored Scout Company with heavy armored scout platoon (*Sd.Kfz. 233*), 2nd Armored Scout Company (half-track), 3rd Light Armored Reconnaissance Company (half-track), 4th Light Armored Reconnaissance Company (half-track), and 5th Heavy Armored Reconnaissance Company (half-track). 1944–45—Headquarters with armored scout sections, 1st Armored Scout Company (half-track), 2nd Armored Light Reconnaissance Company (half-track), 3rd Light Armored Reconnaissance Company (half-track), and 4th Heavy Armored Reconnaissance Company (half-track)

Commanders: *Major* Rehm (21 May–December 1943); *Oberstleutnant* Hansen (acting) (December 1944); *Major* Rehm (February–May 1944); *Hauptmann* Schammler (September 1944–January 1945); *Hauptmann/Major Graf* von Rittberg (February–March 1945)

Notes: In December 1943, *Oberstleutnant* Hansen was the commander of *Panzergrenadier-Regiment 103* at the same time as his acting command of the battalion while the wounded *Major* Rehm was convalescing. When reorganized in

August 1944, the headquarters company had a mix of light and heavy armored car sections. In March 1945, the battalion was detached from the division in order to become part of *Panzer-Brigade "Kurland."*

Awards: Knight's Cross—*Oberleutnant* Feßmann, *1./Kradschützen-Bataillon 64* (4 January 1943) (Oak Leaves); *Oberfeldwebel* Lutze, *1./Kradschützen-Bataillon 64* (2 October 1942); *Oberfeldwebel* Petermann, *4./Kradschützen-Bataillon 64* (17 August 1942); *Oberfeldwebel* Przyklenk, *1./Panzer-Aufklärungs-Abteilung 40* (1 August 1940); *Major* Rehm, *Panzer-Aufklärungs-Abteilung 14* (16 November 1943); *Hauptmann* Stoewaß, *2./Panzer-Aufklärungs-Abteilung 14* (14 April 1945); *Leutnant* Velten, *3./Panzer-Aufklärungs-Abteilung 14* (4 October 1944). **Honor Roll (Clasp)**—*Leutnant* Engel, *3./Panzer-Aufklärungs-Abteilung 14* (17 July 1944); *Leutnant* Flister, *Panzer-Aufklärungs-Abteilung 14* (7 February 1944); *Oberleutnant* Hollenweger, *4./Kradschützen-Bataillon 64* (14 December 1942); *Leutnant* Jasmund, *5./Panzer-Aufklärungs-Abteilung 14* (15 May 1944); *Oberleutnant* Krause, Headquarters, *Panzer-Aufklärungs-Abteilung 14* (15 May 1944); *Oberstleutnant* Uber, *Panzer-Aufklärungs-Abteilung 40* (8 January 1942); *Leutnant* von Zeddelmann, *2./Panzer-Aufklärungs-Abteilung 14* (7 November 1944). **Close Combat Clasp in Gold**—*Fahnenjunker-Unteroffizier* Hofmeier, *4./Panzer-Aufklärungs-Abteilung 14* (30 April 1944). **German Cross in Gold**—*Unteroffizier* Esser, *3./Kradschützen-Bataillon 64* (18 June 1943); *Feldwebel* Fritzsche, *3./Panzer-Aufklärungs-Abteilung 14* (11 February 1945); *Oberleutnant* Gersch, *2./Kradschützen-Bataillon 64* (21 August 1942); *Major* Grams, *Kradschützen-Bataillon 64* (24 November 1942); *Oberleutnant* Hackenschmidt, *1./Kradschützen-Bataillon 64* (5 November 1942); *Oberleutnant* Hötzel, *2./Kradschützen-Bataillon 64* (9 October 1942); *Oberfähnrich* Kloes, *4./Panzer-Aufklärungs-Abteilung 14* (27 January 1945); *Oberleutnant* Kretschmer, *4./Kradschützen-Bataillon 64* (18 June 1943); *Oberfeldwebel* Lutze, *1./Panzer-Aufklärungs-Abteilung 40* (28 February 1942); *Oberleutnant* Reimann, *3./Panzer-Aufklärungs-Abteilung 14* (14 May 1944); *Oberleutnant* Schammler, *3./Kradschützen-Bataillon 64* (6 November 1942); *Oberleutnant* Silbermann, *3./Kradschützen-Bataillon 64* (23 February 1943); *Feldwebel* Stelzmann, *3./Panzer-Aufklärungs-Abteilung 14* (29 October 1944); *Leutnant* Stoewaß, *2./Panzer-Aufklärungs-Abteilung 14* (24 April 1944); *Oberstleutnant* Tröger, *Kradschützen-Bataillon 64* (15 November 1941); *Oberfeldwebel* Volpers, *1./Panzer-Aufklärungs-Abteilung 14* (24 April 1944); *Oberleutnant* Wündrich, *3./Kradschützen-Bataillon 64* (28 February 1942). **German Cross in Silver**—*Hauptwerkmeister* Weißbach, *5./Panzer-Aufklärungs-Abteilung 14* (8 February 1945). **Certificate of Recognition from the Commander in Chief of the Army**—*Schütze* Anuisius, *Kradschützen-Bataillon 64* (3 July 1941); *Oberleutnant* Hackenschmitt, *Kradschützen-Bataillon 64* (3 July 1941); *Oberfeldwebel* Petermann, *Kradschützen-Bataillon 64* (3 July 1941); *Oberstleutnant* Tröger, *Kradschützen-Bataillon 64* (20 August 1941); *Oberleutnant* Wündrich, *5./Kradschützen-Bataillon 64* (5 May 1941). **Announcement in the Wehrmacht Daily Report**—*Oberleutnant* Hackenschmitt, *Oberfeldwebel* Petermann, and *Schütze Anuisius (4 July 1941)*

15. PANZER-DIVISION

Campaigns: North Africa

Reconnaissance Formations:

• ***Kradschützen-Bataillon 15***

Activated: 11 November 1940

Antecedent Formations: Formed from reorganization and redesignation of *III./Infanterie-Regiment 93* of *13. Infanterie-Division*

Replacement Detachment: Initially *Kradschützen-Ersatz-Bataillon 3*, followed by *Kradschützen-Ersatz-Bataillon 6* on 1 December 1940

Deactivation/Redesignation: Reassigned to *21. Panzer-Division* in April 1942 and reorganized and redesignated as *III./Panzergrenadier-Regiment 104*

Organization: April 1941—Headquarters, 1st Motorcycle Infantry Company, 2nd Motorcycle Infantry Company, 3rd Motorcycle Infantry Company, 4th Motorcycle Infantry Machine Gun Company, and 5th Company (heavy)

Commanders: *Oberstleutnant* Knaabe (1 November 1940–July 1941); *Major* Ehle (7 July 1941–November 1942)

Funeral services are held for fallen members of *Panzer-Aufklärungs-Abteilung 33* sometime in March 1943. JIM HALEY

4.Pz.A.A.33
Gefr.
Matthias Rodermann
Oberarzt
Dr. Hellmut Hirsch
Pz.A.A.33
*15.3.15.
†9.3.43.
4.Pz.A.A.33
LEUTNANT
JÜRG v. TREUENFELD
4.Pz.A.A.33
GEFREITER
REINHOLD PREUSCHL

Panzer-Aufklärungs-Abteilung 33

The desert landscape and weather caused their share of problems for the forces that arrived in Africa, as described in this excerpt from the battalion history of *Panzer-Aufklärungs-Abteilung 33*, which leads up to the initial fighting around Halfaya Pass in May 1941:

> At 0700 hours on 7 May, the battalion moved out from its rest area in the vicinity of the fork in the Tobruk–Acroma road and headed south. We reached the desert fort of Acroma moving along a trail that was completely worn out, covered with dust and large gravel and filled with numerous potholes. Following that, we continued south-southeast. Keeping a distance of ten kilometers from the outer defensive belt around Tobruk, we moved in the direction of the crossroads of trails at El Adem. There, we turned to the east, with a march objective of the airfield at Gambut. After passing the orientation point of Sidi Rezegh, the battalion ran into difficulties. We got lost in the trackless and—at least to us—completely foreign desert landscape. We were forced to halt again and again. The *ghibli* [sandstorm] from the previous day had completely covered up the tracks from vehicles. There were no trees or vegetation, let alone any directional signs of even the most primitive type. There was only sand, rock, and the occasional hardwood dried-out camel thorn bush. The heat juggled objects and sections of terrain through a *fata morgana*, which made it even more difficult for us—inexperienced in desert warfare—to get oriented . . . [27]

The book also describes a trap set by the English in July 1941:

> Outside of Sidi Suleiman, there was a German *VW* moving back and forth through the area. We were certain that he had gotten lost. He was getting closer and closer to the English outposts. Then we saw an English armored car slowly approach the *VW*. He couldn't just sit by idly; we had to keep the men on the *VW* safe from the palpably close grasp of the enemy. Our patrol moved in the direction of the *VW*, which kept on moving closer to the English outposts, for some unaccountable reason. We saw it moving in the direction of its own misfortune. At that point, a vehicle form our patrol broke off and moved towards the *VW* at high speed. But not for long. A hit from an enemy antitank gun stopped his movement. An English gun, which was positioned behind a slope, had waited for him. A well-laid trap by the British had snapped shut . . . [28]

- ***Panzer-Aufklärungs-Abteilung 33***

Activated: 10 November 1940

Antecedent Formations: *Aufklärungs-Abteilung 33*

Replacement Detachment: Unknown

Deactivation/Redesignation: Redesignated as *Panzer-Aufklärungs-Abteilung 15* on 29 April 1943; capitulated on 9 May 1943

Organization: 1941—Headquarters, 1st Motorcycle Infantry Troop, 2nd Troop (heavy) (motorized), and 3rd Armored Scout Troop.
1942–43—Headquarters, 1st Armored Scout Troop with cannon platoon, 2nd Troop (armored) (captured), 3rd Troop (heavy) (motorized), and 4th Battery (8.76cm) (captured)

Commanders: Unknown (10 November 1940–12 June 1942); *Hauptmann* Hößlin (12 June 1942 to ?); *Hauptmann* Lienau (August 1942–9 May 1943)

Notes: In December 1940, *1.(Panzer-Späh)/Panzer-Aufklärungs-Abteilung 90* of *10. Panzer-Division* joined the battalion, where it was redesignated as the 3rd Troop. In the spring of 1942, the battalion reorganized as seen above, with troops changing numerical designations. The cannon platoon consisted of the *Sd. Kfz. 233*. The 2nd Motorcycle Infantry Troop reorganized with captured armored vehicles. The 4th Battery was established through command channels, although the battery was later approved by the *Organizations-Abteilung*.

Awards: Knight's Cross—*Hauptmann* Ehle, *1./Kradschützen-Bataillon 15* (27 July 1941); *Hauptmann* von Hößlin, *Panzer-Aufklärungs-Abteilung 33* (23 July 1942); *Oberstleutnant* Knabe, *Kradschützen-Bataillon 15* (1 June 1941); *Hauptmann* Lienau, *Panzer-Aufklärungs-Abteilung 33* (9 May 1943). **Honor Roll (Clasp)**—*Feldwebel* Apsel, *Panzer-Aufklärungs-Abteilung 33* (4 May 1942). **German Cross in Gold**—*Feldwebel* Apsel, *Panzer-Aufklärungs-Abteilung 33* (1 May 1942); *Oberleutnant* Bentlage, *Panzer-Aufklärungs-Abteilung 33* (9 October 1942); *Oberleutnant Freiherr* von Gienanth, *3./Panzer-Aufklärungs-Abteilung 33* (9 October 1942); *Hauptmann* Heraucourt, *Panzer-Aufklärungs-Abteilung 33* (2 April 1942); *Feldwebel* Klein, *3./Panzer-Aufklärungs-Abteilung 33* (26 November 1943); *Hauptmann* Lienau, *Panzer-Aufklärungs-Abteilung 33 9* (October 1942); *Oberleutnant* von Mutius, *Panzer-Aufklärungs-Abteilung 15* (9 May 1943); *Feldwebel* Servas, *Kradschützen-Bataillon 15* (21 February 1942)

15. PANZERGRENADIER-DIVISION

Campaigns: Italy, Western Europe; Eastern Front (*Panzer-Aufklärungs-Abteilung 115*)

Reconnaissance Formations:

- ***schnelle Abteilung/15. Panzergrenadier-Division***

Activated: 29 June 1943

Antecedent Formations: *schnelle Abteilung Sizilien*

Replacement Detachment: Unknown

Deactivation/Redesignation: *Panzer-Aufklärungs-Abteilung 115* in October 1943

Organization: 1943—Headquarters, one mechanized infantry company (partly armored), one light howitzer section (towed), one antitank company (towed), and armored scout platoon (*Panzerspähzug 15*)

- ***Panzer-Aufklärungs-Abteilung 115***

Activated: October 1943

Antecedent Formations: *schnelle Abteilung/15. Panzergrenadier-Division*, remnants of *Panzer-Aufklärungs-Abteilung 33*, and personnel from the disbanded *Panzergrenadier-Regiment Reggio*

Replacement Detachment: *Panzer-Aufklärungs-Ersatz- und Ausbildungs-Abteilung 4*

Deactivation/Redesignation: May 1945

Organization: 1944—Headquarters, 1st Armored Scout Company, 2nd Armored Reconnaissance Company (motorized), 3rd Armored Reconnaissance Company (motorized), 4th Armored Reconnaissance Company (motorized), and 5th Company (heavy)

Commanders: *Rittmeister Freiherr* von der Borch (January–March 1944); *Oberleutnant Freiherr* von Glienanth (acting) (March 1944–?); *Rittmeister Freiherr* von der Borch (20 June 1944–?)

Notes: Battalion personnel assembled in December 1943. In December 1944, the battalion was sent to the Milowitz Training Area for reconstitution. The battalion never returned to the division and fought under *Heeresgruppe Weichsel* in the vicinity of Frankfurt an der Oder.

Awards: Knight's Cross—*Rittmeister Freiherr* von der Borch, *Panzer-Aufklärungs-Abteilung 115* (19 August 1944). **Honor Roll (Clasp)**—*Leutnant* Mann, *3./Panzer-Aufklärungs-Abteilung 115* (7 June 1944). **German Cross in Gold**—*Oberfeldwebel* Kraus, *4./Panzer-Aufklärungs-Abteilung 115* (12 March 1944); *Leutnant* Mann, *3./Panzer-Aufklärungs-Abteilung 115* (5 March 1944); *Hauptmann* Möcker, *3./Panzer-Aufklärungs-Abteilung 115* (27 October 1944); *Fahnenjunker-Feldwebel* Schröer, *2./Panzer-Aufklärungs-Abteilung 115* (8 July 1944); *Oberleutnant* Wolff, *2./Panzer-Aufklärungs-Abteilung 115* (27 October 1944)

16. INFANTERIE-DIVISION (MOT)

Campaigns: Soviet Union

Reconnaissance Formations:

- ***Aufklärungs-Abteilung 341 (mot)***

Activated: 1 August 1941

Antecedent Formations: *1./Aufklärungs-Abteilung 341* of *311. Infanterie-Division*, *1./Aufklärungs-Abteilung 228* of *228. Infanterie-Division*, and *6./Aufklärungs-Regiment 9* of *9. Panzer-Division*

Replacement Detachment: Initially *Ersatz-Abteilung für motorisierte Aufklärungseinheiten 7*

Hans-Jörg Fein was inducted into the army in 1937 and trained as a machine gunner. After transfer to *Kradschützen-Bataillon 165* in 1940, he was assigned to the 2nd Motorcycle Infantry Company. He was killed in action on 14 April 1941 during the Balkan campaign.

Deactivation/Redesignation: Consolidated with *Kradschützen-Bataillon 165* on 28 December 1941

Organization: 1940–41—Headquarters, 1st Armored Scout Troop, 2nd Bicycle Troop, and 3rd Troop (heavy)

Commanders: *Major* Neumeister (September 1940–June 1941); *Hauptmann* Kleinschmitt (June 1941–?)

- ***Kradschützen-Bataillon 165***

Activated: 6 August 1940

Antecedent Formations: *MG-Bataillon 6*

Replacement Detachment: *Kradschützen-Ersatz-Bataillon 6*

Deactivation/Redesignation: *Panzer-Aufklärungs-Abteilung 116* on 1 May 1943

Organization: 1940–41—Headquarters, 1st Motorcycle Infantry Company, 2nd Motorcycle Infantry Company, 3rd Motorcycle Infantry Company, 4th Motorcycle Infantry Machine Gun Company, and 5th Company (heavy). November 1941—Headquarters, 1st Motorcycle Infantry Company, 2nd Company (sniper), 3rd Motorcycle Infantry Company, 5th Company (mixed) (motorized). January 1942—Headquarters, Armored Scout Element, 1st Motorcycle Infantry Company, 2nd Company (sniper), 3rd Motorcycle Infantry Company, 4th Motorcycle Infantry Company, and 5th Company (heavy). June 1942–43—Headquarters, 1st Armored Scout Company, 2nd Motorcycle Infantry Company, 3rd Motorcycle Infantry Company, 4th Motorcycle Infantry Company, and 5th Company (heavy) (motorized)

Commanders: *Major/Oberstleutnant* Eisermann (6 August 1940–1 May 1942); *Hauptmann/Major* Brede (1 May–12 August 1942); *Oberstleutnant* La Roche (12 August 1942–?); *Hauptmann* Wenzel (acting) (to January 1943); *Hauptmann* Ganter (to 4 February 1943); *Oberleutnant* Zehner (acting) (4–7 February 1943); *Hauptmann* Ganter (7 February 1943–?)

- ***Panzer-Aufklärungs-Abteilung 116***

Activated: 1 May 1943

Antecedent Formations: *Kradschützen-Bataillon 165*

Replacement Detachment: Unknown

Deactivation/Redesignation: Reassigned to *16. Panzergrenadier-Division* with the same designation on 23 June 1943

Organization: 1943—Headquarters, 1st Armored Scout Company, 2nd Motorcycle Infantry Company, 3rd Motorcycle Infantry Company, 4th Motorcycle Infantry Company, and 5th Company (heavy)

Awards: Knight's Cross—*Hauptmann* Borchardt, *1./Aufklärungs-Abteilung 341 (mot)* (23 August 1941); *Hauptmann* Kleinschmitt, *Aufklärungs-Abteilung 341 (mot)* (14 December 1941); *Oberfeldwebel* Kunze, *2./Aufklärungs-Abteilung 341 (mot)* (22 February 1942). **Honor Roll (Clasp)**—*Hauptmann* Borchardt, *1./Aufklärungs-Abteilung 341 (mot)* (22 July 1941); *Leutnant* Gottlieb, *2./Kradschützen-Bataillon 165* (14 August 1942). **German Cross in Gold**—*Hauptmann* Brede,

3./Kradschützen-Bataillon 165 (27 November 1941); *Oberstleutnant* Eisermann, *Kradschützen-Bataillon 165* (27 November 1941); *Oberleutnant* Euler, *5./Kradschützen-Bataillon 165* (29 March 1943); *Oberfeldwebel* Fromm, *3./Kradschützen-Bataillon 165* (14 February 1942); *Unteroffizier* Giloy, *4./Kradschützen-Bataillon 165* (16 April 1943); *Oberleutnant* Gottlieb, *4./Kradschützen-Bataillon 165* (17 July 1943); *Oberfeldwebel* Hohnstein, *2./Kradschützen-Bataillon 165* (13 September 1942); *Oberleutnant* Kendler, *4./Kradschützen-Bataillon 165* (29 May 1943); *Oberleutnant* Meier, *2./Kradschützen-Bataillon 165* (9 October 1942); *Unteroffizier* Prottung, *1./Aufklärungs-Abteilung 341 (mot)* (11 April 1942); *Oberleutnant* Querengässer, *2./Aufklärungs-Abteilung 341 (mot)* (27 November 1941); *Oberleutnant* Runge, *Aufklärungs-Abteilung 341 (mot)* (14 January 1942); *Oberleutnant* Schleicher, *1./Kradschützen-Bataillon 165* (10 January 1943); *Oberfeldwebel* Tertel, *3./Kradschützen-Bataillon 165* (29 May 1943); *Oberleutnant* Voigtmann, *2./Kradschützen-Bataillon 165* (14 February 1942); *Hauptmann* Wenzel, *3./Kradschützen-Bataillon 165* (9 April 1943).

16. PANZERGRENADIER-DIVISION

Campaigns: Soviet Union

Reconnaissance Formations:

- ***Panzer-Aufklärungs-Abteilung 116***

Activated: 1 May 1943

Antecedent Formations: *Kradschützen-Bataillon 165*

Replacement Detachment: Unknown

Deactivation/Redesignation: Reassigned to *116. Panzer-Division* with the same designation on 23 June 1944

Organization: 1943–44—Headquarters, 1st Armored Scout Company, 2nd Motorcycle Infantry Company, 3rd Motorcycle Infantry Company, 4th Motorcycle Infantry Company, and 5th Company (heavy) (motorized)

Commanders: *Major* Schmid (23 June–19 July 1943); *Oberleutnant* Zehnder (acting) (20 July 1943); *Hauptmann* Schleicher (acting) (20 July–28 September 1943; *Major* Wolff (acting) (28 September–24 November 1943); *Hauptmann* Niedergesäß (acting) (25 November 1943–February 1944); *Hauptmann* Winter (February–March 1944); *Hauptmann* Zehnder (13 April–1 May 1944)

Notes: Available organization charts through the end of 1943 indicate that the battalion only had motorcycle infantry companies, but it is assumed that it may have already started the switch to armored reconnaissance companies prior to the division being reorganized and redesignated as *116. Panzer-Division* on 30 March 1944

Awards: Honor Roll (Clasp)—*Hauptmann* Schleicher, *Panzer-Aufklärungs-Abteilung 116* (7 December 1943); *Oberleutnant* Zinke, *2./Panzer-Aufklärungs-Abteilung 116* (15 November 1943). **Close Combat Clasp in Gold**—*Stabsgefreiter* Dornhoff, *2./Panzer-Aufklärungs-Abteilung 116* (12 January 1944); *Unteroffizier* Roth, *4./Panzer-Aufklärungs-Abteilung 116* (12 January 1944); *Unteroffizier* Weckmann, *2./Panzer-Aufklärungs-Abteilung 116* (2 March 1944). **German Cross in Gold**—*Unteroffizier* Moser, *1./Panzer-Aufklärungs-Abteilung 116* (23 March 1944); *Oberfeldwebel* Weismayer, *1./Panzer-Aufklärungs-Abteilung 116* (4 February 1944); *Leutnant* Weißflog, *2./Panzer-Aufklärungs-Abteilung 116* (28 April 1944). **Certificate of Recognition from the Commander in Chief of the Army**—*Oberleutnant* Fischer, *3./Panzer-Aufklärungs-Abteilung 116* (5 November 1943)

16. PANZER-DIVISION

Campaigns: Soviet Union, Italy, Soviet Union

Reconnaissance Formations:

- ***Panzer-Aufklärungs-Abteilung 16 (first iteration)***

Activated: 2 August 1940

Antecedent Formations: *Aufklärungs-Abteilung 16* with assignment of *2.(Pz.Späh)/Panzer-Aufklärungs-Abteilung 57* of *6. Panzer-Division* as the 1st Company

Replacement Detachment: *Ersatz-Abteilung für motorisierte Aufklärungseinheiten 7*

Deactivation/Redesignation: Consolidated with *Kradschützen-Bataillon 16* on 1 May 1942

Organization: 1940–42—Headquarters, 1st Armored Scout Troop, 2nd Bicycle Troop, 3rd Troop (heavy) (motorized)

Commanders: *Major* von Witzleben (2 August 1940–1 May 1942)

• ***Kradschützen-Bataillon 16***

Activated: 2 August 1940

Antecedent Formations: Formed through redesignation and reorganization of *MG-Bataillon 1*

Replacement Detachment: *Kradschützen-Ersatz-Bataillon 6*

Deactivation/Redesignation: Effectively destroyed in Stalingrad; reconstituted on 1 March 1943; redesignated as *Panzer-Aufklärungs-Abteilung 16* on 31 March 1943

Organization: 1940–41—Headquarters, 1st Motorcycle Infantry Company, 2nd Motorcycle Infantry Company, 3rd Motorcycle Infantry Company, 4th Motorcycle Infantry Machine Gun Company, and 5th Company (heavy). June 1942—Headquarters, 1st Armored Scout Company, 2nd Armored Reconnaissance Company (half-track), 3rd Motorcycle Infantry Company, 4th Motorcycle Infantry Company, and 5th Company (heavy)

Commanders: *Oberstleutnant* Reimann (August 1940–July 1941); *Major* von Witzleben (1 May–July 1942); *Hauptmann* Dörnemann (July 1942–18 January 1943); *Oberleutnant* Schluth (acting) (18 January 1943–?); *Hauptmann* Fischer (acting) (1 March 1943–30 March 1943)

• ***Panzer-Aufklärungs-Abteilung 16 (second iteration)***

Activated: 1 April 1943

Antecedent Formations: *Kradschützen-Bataillon 16*

Replacement Detachment: *Panzer-Aufklärungs-Ersatz-Abteilung 6*

Deactivation/Redesignation: Effectively wiped out in January 1945; at the beginning of March 1945, a mixed armored reconnaissance company formed out of the battalion's remnants and *Panzer-Aufklärungs-Kompanie Jüterbog*

Organization: May 1944—Headquarters, 1st Armored Scout Company with heavy armored scout platoon (*Sd.Kfz. 233*), 2nd Armored Scout Company (half-track), 3rd Armored Reconnaissance Company (light half-track), 4th Armored Reconnaissance Company (light half-track), and 5th Heavy Armored Reconnaissance Company. January 1945—Headquarters with armored car sections, 1st Armored Scout Company (half-track), 2nd Armored Reconnaissance Company (light half-track?), 3rd Armored Reconnaissance Company (light half-track), and 4th Heavy Armored Reconnaissance Company (half-track). March 1945—Headquarters, one armored scout company (half-track), one armored scout company (wheeled), and one armored reconnaissance company (half-track)

Commanders: *Major* Dörnemann (April–September 1943); *Hauptmann* Schiller (March 1944); *Hauptmann* Kunz (acting) (September 1944); *Hauptmann* Vetter (1944–May 1945)

Notes: Much of the battalion badly battered in the spring of 1944, with some companies without motorized transport for considerable periods (e.g., 3rd Company until August 1944). In June 1944, the battalion incorporated the armored car company into its headquarters company with a subsequent renumbering of the line companies. In December 1944, the 3rd Company was ordered to the Wildflecken Training Area for reconstitution; it did not rejoin the battalion until April 1945.

Awards: Knight's Cross—Major Dörnemann, *Panzer-Aufklärungs-Abteilung 16* (28 November 1943); *Hauptmann* Schiller, *Panzer-Aufklärungs-Abteilung 16* (6 April 1944); *Major* von Witzleben, *Panzer-Aufklärungs-Abteilung 16* (6 February 1942). **Honor Roll (Clasp)**—*Feldwebel* Deutscher, *2./Panzer-Aufklärungs-Abteilung 16* (17 November 1944); *Leutnant* Völker, *4./Kradschützen-Bataillon 16* (8 February 1943). **German Cross in Gold**—*Hauptmann* Dörnemann, *Kradschützen-Bataillon 16* (25 January 1943); *Hauptmann* Dormann, *3./Panzer-Aufklärungs-Abteilung 16* (16 March 1942); *Leutnant* Hoube, *3./Panzer-Aufklärungs-Abteilung 16* (20 May 1944); *Oberfeldwebel* Jansen, *2./Kradschützen-Bataillon 16* (6 November 1942); *Feldwebel* Müller, *2./Panzer-Aufklärungs-Abteilung 16* (28 February 1942); *Oberleutnant* von Neumann-Cosel, *4./Kradschützen-Bataillon 16* (26 September 1942); *Oberfeldwebel* Pressman, *3./Panzer-Aufklärungs-Abteilung 16* (8 November 1943); *Stabsfeldwebel* Schmelzer, *5./Panzer-Aufklärungs-Abteilung 16* (12 October 1943); *Leutnant* Schnippenkötter, *5./Kradschützen-Bataillon 16* (26 September 1942); *Unteroffizier* Suetterlin, *3./Panzer-Aufklärungs-Abteilung 16* (17 September 1944);

Leutnant Thywissen, *Panzer-Aufklärungs-Abteilung 16* (26 June 1942); *Oberfeldwebel* Tönshoff, *2./Panzer-Aufklärungs-Abteilung 16* (17 September 1944); *Oberleutnant* Vetter, *Panzer-Aufklärungs-Abteilung 16* (28 May 1944); *Feldwebel* Wiedmann, *4./Kradschützen-Bataillon 16* (6 September 1942). **Certificate of Recognition from the Commander in Chief of the Army for the Shooting Down of Aircraft with Infantry Weapons**—*Oberfeldwebel* Kremer, Headquarters, *Panzer-Aufklärungs-Abteilung 16* (15 October 1941); *Obergefreiter* Schambony, *2./Panzer-Aufklärungs-Abteilung 16* (8 February 1942); also awarded to *2./Kradschützen-Bataillon 16* (18 May 1942). **Announcement in the Wehrmacht Daily Report**—*Panzer-Aufklärungs-Abteilung 16*, under *Hauptmann* Schiller (20 March 1944)

17. PANZER-DIVISION

Campaigns: Soviet Union

Reconnaissance Formations:

- ***Panzer-Aufklärungs-Abteilung 27***

Activated: 21 November 1941

Antecedent Formations: *Aufklärungs-Abteilung 17* of *17. Infanterie-Division* with reassignment and redesignation of *2.(Pz.Späh)/Aufklärungs-Abteilung 7* as the 1st Company

Replacement Detachment: Unknown

Deactivation/Redesignation: *Kradschützen-Bataillon 17* on 1 April 1942

Organization: 1941–42—Headquarters, 1st Armored Scout Troop, 2nd Motorcycle Infantry Troop, and 3rd Troop (heavy)

Commanders: *Major Freiherr* von Lerchenfeld (1 November 1940–January 1942)

- ***Kradschützen-Bataillon 17***

Activated: 11 October 1940

Antecedent Formations: Formed by the reassignment, redesignation, and reorganization of *II./Infanterie-Regiment 63*

Replacement Detachment: Unknown

Deactivation/Redesignation: *Panzer-Aufklärungs-Abteilung 17* on 1 May 1943

Organization: 1941—Headquarters, 1st Motorcycle Infantry Company, 2nd Motorcycle Infantry Company, 3rd Motorcycle Infantry Company, 4th Motorcycle Infantry Machine Gun Company, and 5th Company (heavy). May 1942—Headquarters, 1st Armored Scout Company, 2nd Motorcycle Infantry Company, 3rd Motorcycle Infantry Company, 4th Motorcycle Infantry Company, and 5th Company (heavy)

Commanders: *Major* Fritz (September 1941); *Hauptmann* Prugger (to 7 July 1942); Unknown (7 July–September 1942); *Hauptmann* Naumann (September–December 1942); *Hauptmann/Major* Prugger (December 1942–March 1943); *Hauptmann* Rieger (acting) (March–5 April 1943); *Hauptmann* Vocke (5 April–1 May 1943)

Notes: Battalion temporarily disbanded in the winter of 1941–42. In February 1943, the battalion was temporarily organized like a mechanized infantry battalion.

- ***Panzer-Aufklärungs-Abteilung 17***

Activated: 1 May 1943

Antecedent Formations: *Kradschützen-Bataillon 17*

Replacement Detachment: Unknown

Deactivation/Redesignation: May 1945

Organization: July 1943—Headquarters, 1st Armored Scout Company, 2nd Armored Reconnaissance Company (*Krad*), 3rd Armored Reconnaissance Company (*Krad*; half-track in July 1943), 4th Light Armored Reconnaissance Company (half-track), and 5th Heavy Armored Reconnaissance Company (motorized). May 1944—Headquarters, 1st Armored Scout Company, 2nd Armored Scout Company (half-track), 3rd Armored Reconnaissance Company (half-track), 4th Armored Reconnaissance Company (half-track), and 5th Heavy Armored Reconnaissance Company (half-track). July 1944—Headquarters, 1st Armored Scout Company (half-track), 2nd Armored Reconnaissance Company (half-track), 3rd Armored Reconnaissance Company (half-track), and 4th Heavy Armored Reconnaissance Company (half-track). February 1945—Reconnaissance company (VW). March 1945—Headquarters, 1st Armored Scout Company (half-track), 2nd Armored Scout Company (half-track), 3rd Reconnaissance Company (VW), 4th Armored Reconnaissance Company (motorized), and 5th Heavy Armored Reconnaissance Company (half-track)

Commanders: *Hauptmann/Major* Vocke (1 May–October 1943); *Major* Schoenfeld (October 1943–September 1944); *Rittmeister* von Loeben (Acting) (September–6 December 1944); *Hauptmann* Meier (December 1944–?)

Notes: On 15 July 1943, orders were received directing the 3rd Company to the Senne Training Area for reorganization; it was to complete the process by 5 September. Orders were issued on 16 September directing the company to rejoin the battalion. The company had been issued thirty-one light half-tracks. By the end of November 1943, the 5th Company had been essentially wiped out. Orders were received on 5 December for the company to undergo a battlefield reconstitution in the rear area of *Heeresgruppe Süd* and reorganize as a heavy armored reconnaissance company (half-track). It was probably issued twenty-seven medium halftracks at the time. On 16 April 1944, the 2nd Company was ordered from the Wildflecken Training Area to the Mielau Training Area, where it was to move together with other elements of the division to rejoin it. On 11 September, the 2nd Company was ordered to reorganize as a light armored reconnaissance company; in the process, it received thirty light half-tracks. Reorganization in March 1945 brought about by the consolidation with *Panzer-Aufklärungs-Abteilung Hirschberg* (formerly a part of *Panzer-Brigade 103*).

Awards: Honor Roll (Clasp)—*Unteroffizier* Graml, *2./Panzer-Aufklärungs-Abteilung 27* (9 September 1941); *Oberleutnant* Hopp, *Kradschützen-Bataillon 17* (27 May 1943); *Oberarzt Dr.* Joachim, Headquarters, *Kradschützen-Bataillon 17* (7 June 1943); *Oberfeldwebel* Roß, *3./Panzer-Aufklärungs-Abteilung 17* (25 December 1944); *Leutnant Freiherr* von Schnurbein, *2./Kradschützen-Bataillon 17* (16 October 1942). **Close Combat Clasp in Gold**—*Obergefreiter* Hermann, *3./Panzer-Aufklärungs-Abteilung 17* (22 May 1944); *Feldwebel* Hofner, *4./Panzer-Aufklärungs-Abteilung 17* (22 May 1944); *Unteroffizier* Luksch, *3./Panzer-Aufklärungs-Abteilung 17* (22 May 1944); *Feldwebel* Paffrath, *1./Panzer-Aufklärungs-Abteilung 17* (22 May 1944); *Feldwebel* Rennert, *2./Panzer-Aufklärungs-Abteilung 17* (24 November 1943); *Oberfeldwebel* Schäfer, *3./Panzer-Aufklärungs-Abteilung 17* (11 November 1944). **German Cross in Gold**—*Leutnant* Anzenhofer, *3./Panzer-Aufklärungs-Abteilung 17* (30 March 1945); *Hauptmann* Bapst, *4./Kradschützen-Bataillon 17* (20 November 1942); *Feldwebel* Bossler, *2./Panzer-Aufklärungs-Abteilung 17* (14 November 1944); *Hauptmann* Daeschler, *Kradschützen-Bataillon 17* (7 October 1942); *Feldwebel* Daffner, *Panzerspäh-Kompanie/Panzer-Aufklärungs-Abteilung 17* (6 January 1942); *Feldwebel* Graml, *2./Kradschützen-Bataillon 17* (31 October 1942); *Oberleutnant* Hardt, *2./Panzer-Aufklärungs-Abteilung 17* (22 December 1944); *Obergefreiter* Hauser, *Kradschützen-Bataillon 17* (11 March 1943); *Oberfeldwebel* Heiß, *Panzer-Aufklärungs-Abteilung 27* (20 March 1942); *Major Freiherr* von Lerchenfeld, *Panzer-Aufklärungs-Abteilung 27* (6 January 1942); *Hauptmann* Naumann, *Kradschützen-Bataillon 17* (13 November 1942); *Feldwebel* Neuhaus, *1./Panzer-Aufklärungs-Abteilung 17* (20 January 1944); *Oberfeldwebel* Paffrath, *1./Panzer-Aufklärungs-Abteilung 17* (21 October 1944); *Hauptmann* Perzl, *4./Panzer-Aufklärungs-Abteilung 17* (13 January 1944); *Oberfeldwebel* Pfaff, *4./Kradschützen-Bataillon 17* (20 November 1942); *Hauptmann* Prugger, *Kradschützen-Bataillon 17* (14 March 1943); *Feldwebel* Rennert, *Panzer-Aufklärungs-Abteilung 17* (4 October 1944); *Oberleutnant* Rinklef, *Kradschützen-Bataillon 17* (11 Match 1943); *Oberleutnant Freiherr* von Rotenhan, *2./Panzer-Aufklärungs-Abteilung 27* (21 October 1941); *Oberfeldwebel* Schäfer, *3./Panzer-Aufklärungs-Abteilung 17* (30 December 1944); *Oberleutnant* Scheer, *Kradschützen-Bataillon 17* (14 March 1943); *Hauptmann* Schönfeld, *Panzer-Aufklärungs-Abteilung 17* (5 March 1944); *Feldwebel* Schreyer, *4./Panzer-Aufklärungs-Abteilung 17* (9 June 1943). **Certificate of Recognition from the Commander in Chief of the Army**—*Oberleutnant Freiherr* von Rotenhan, *Panzer-Aufklärungs-Abteilung 27* (22 September 1941)

18. INFANTERIE-DIVISION (MOT)

Campaigns: Soviet Union

Reconnaissance Formations:

- ***Aufklärungs-Abteilung 18 (mot)***

Activated: 15 November 1940

Antecedent Formations: Redesignation and reorganization of *Aufklärungs-Abteilung 18* of *18.*

Infanterie-Division and reassignment and redesignation of *2.(Pz.Späh)/Aufklärungs-Abteilung 1 (mot)* as the 1st Company.

Replacement Detachment: Unknown

Deactivation/Redesignation: Consolidated with *Kradschützen-Bataillon 38* on 1 November 1942

Organization: 1940–42—Headquarters, 2st Armored Scout Company, 2nd Motorcycle Infantry Company, and 3rd Company (heavy)

Commanders: *Major* Gerloff (acting?) (1 November 1940–January 1941); *Major* Sperling (January 1941–April 1942); *Oberleutnant* Proske (acting) (May–1 November 1942)

- ***Kradschützen-Bataillon 38***

Activated: 18 November 1940

Antecedent Formations: Reorganization and redesignation of *III./Infanterie-Regiment 51*

Organization: 1940–41—Headquarters, 1st Motorcycle Infantry Company, 2nd Motorcycle Infantry Company, 3rd Motorcycle Infantry Company, 4th Motorcycle Infantry Machine Gun Company, and 5th Company (heavy). October 1942—Headquarters, 1st Armored Scout Company, 2nd Motorcycle Infantry Company, 3rd Motorcycle Infantry Company, 4th Motorcycle Infantry Company, and 5th Company (heavy).

Commanders: *Major/Oberstleutnant* Kuhnert (18 November 1940–10 July 1942); *Major* Reichel (July 1942–30 March 1943)

Notes: The battalion established a heavy mortar company on 1 December 1942, designating it as its 6th Company.

- ***Panzer-Aufklärungs-Abteilung 118***

Activated: 1 April 1943

Antecedent Formations: *Kradschützen-Bataillon 38*

Replacement Detachment: Unknown

Deactivation/Redesignation: Stayed with the division under the same designation when the division was reorganized and redesignated as *18. Panzergrenadier-Division*

Organization: 1943—Headquarters, 1st Armored Scout Company, 2nd Motorcycle Infantry Company, 3rd Motorcycle Infantry Company, 4th Motorcycle Infantry Company, 5th Company (heavy), 6th Company (heavy mortar) (motorized?)

Commanders: *Major* Reichel (1 April–22 June 1943)

Awards: Knight's Cross—*Oberleutnant* Bernack, *1./Kradschützen-Bataillon 38* (13 August 1941). **German Cross in Gold**—*Hauptmann* Fischer, *5./Kradschützen-Bataillon 38* (14 April 1942); *Oberleutnant* Jeschek, *1./Kradschützen-Bataillon 38* (17 April 1943); *Oberleutnant* Köppen, *Kradschützen-Bataillon 38* (14 February 1942); *Feldwebel* Krause, *5./Kradschützen-Bataillon 38* (11 April 1942); *Leutnant* Meschkat, *1./Aufklärungs-Abteilung 18 (mot)* (1 May 1942); *Oberleutnant* Mielsch, *2./Kradschützen-Bataillon 38* (11 March 1943); *Oberleutnant* Proske, *2./Aufklärungs-Abteilung 18 (mot)* (24 May 1942); *Major* Sperling, *Aufklärungs-Abteilung 18 (mot)* (14 April 1942); *Oberleutnant* Voigt, *3./Kradschützen-Bataillon 38* (11 March 1943). **Certificate of Recognition from the Commander in Chief of the Army**—*Oberleutnant* Bernack, *1./Kradschützen-Bataillon 38* (3 July 1941); *Major* Kuhnert, *Kradschützen-Bataillon 38* (3 July 1941)

18. PANZERGRENADIER-DIVISION

Campaigns: Soviet Union

Reconnaissance Formations:

- ***Panzer-Aufklärungs-Abteilung 118 (first iteration)***

Activated: 1 April 1943

Antecedent Formations: *Kradschützen-Bataillon 38*

Replacement Detachment: Unknown

Deactivation/Redesignation: July 1944 (destroyed in the vicinity of Volma as a result of the Soviet Operation Bagration)

Organization: June 1943–44—Headquarters, 1st Armored Scout Company, 2nd Motorcycle Infantry Company, 3rd Motorcycle Infantry Company, 4th Motorcycle Infantry Company, 5th Heavy (motorized), and 6th (heavy mortar) (motorized?)

Commanders: *Major* Reichel (23 June–5 October 1943); *Hauptmann* Neugebauer (acting) (5–24 October 1943); *Hauptmann* von Dippe (24 October 1943–January 1944); *Hauptmann* Sauvant-Siegert (January–February 1944); *Rittmeister* von Lyncker

These images come from a grouping for an officer who was probably assigned to *Aufklärungs-Abteilung 18 (mot)* at some point in his career. Images for reconnaissance elements of the division are somewhat rare because of its relatively short existence and the severe mauling it took at the Eastern Front. The unidentified officer in question gets steadily promoted and decorated, culminating with the award of the German Cross in Gold. He seems to get along well with his men. One of the scouts in the group image wears his Iron Cross, Second Class, in an unusual fashion (low and across the lapel of his jacket). The officer seems to be a bit of a dandy, as evidenced by the home-leave image and the scene in the trenches with a fellow officer. JIM HALEY

(to 4 July 1944); *Oberleutnant* Kolek (acting) (4 July 1944)

- ***Panzer-Aufklärungs-Abteilung 118 (second iteration)***

Activated: 31 August 1944

Antecedent Formations: *Panzer-Aufklärungs-Abteilung 118*

Replacement Detachment: Unknown

Deactivation/Redesignation: 23 February 1945 (division disbanded)

Organization: September 1944—*Panzerspähzug 118*

Commanders: *Hauptmann* Jescheck (acting) (to February 1945)

Notes: When reconstituted, it was initially only as a platoon (*Panzerspähzug 118*). It was later expanded to two companies before being disbanded.

- ***Panzer-Aufklärungs-Abteilung 18***

Activated: 21 March 1945

Antecedent Formations: Formed from the disbanded *Panzer-Aufklärungs-Abteilung 44* of *Panzer-Division Holstein*

Replacement Detachment: Unknown

Deactivation/Redesignation: 2 May 1945

Organization: 1945 (theoretical)—Headquarters, 1st Armored Scout Company (mixed), 2nd Armored Reconnaissance Company (VW), and 3rd Armored Reconnaissance Company (VW)

Notes: The organization chart dated for September 1944 shows the division headquarters as having a platoon of armored cars.

Awards: Knight's Cross—*Hauptmann* Jescheck, *Panzer-Aufklärungs-Abteilung 118* (5 March 1945); *Leutnant* Löring, *Panzer-Aufklärungs-Abteilung 118* (7 April 1944). **Honor Roll (Clasp)**—*Leutnant* Bruß, *3./Panzer-Aufklärungs-Abteilung 118* (7 June 1944); *Hauptmann* Sauvant-Siegert, *Panzer-Aufklärungs-Abteilung 118* (27 March 1944); *Oberfeldwebel* Wagner, *1./Panzer-Aufklärungs-Abteilung 118* (17 April 1944); *Leutnant* Werner, *2./Panzer-Aufklärungs-Abteilung 118* (1945). **German Cross in Gold**— *Oberfeldwebel* Behrens, *1./Panzer-Aufklärungs-Abteilung 118* (3 January 1944); *Oberfeldwebel* Grestrich, *5./Panzer-Aufklärungs-Abteilung 118* (30 November 1944); *Hauptmann* von Dippe, *Panzer-Aufklärungs-Abteilung 118* (23 April 1944); *Oberleutnant* Kolek, *5./Panzer-Aufklärungs-Abteilung 118* (1 November 1943); *Oberleutnant* Olearius, *2./Panzer-Aufklärungs-Abteilung 118* (15 April 1945); *Feldwebel* Titze, *4./Panzer-Aufklärungs-Abteilung 118* (15 April 1944). **Certificate of Recognition from the Commander in Chief of the Army**—*Leutnant* Etzold, *5./Panzer-Aufklärungs-Abteilung 118* (25 or 27 March 1944); *Oberleutnant* Grundmann, *4./Panzer-Aufklärungs-Abteilung 118* (7 September 1943). **Certificate of Recognition from the Commander in Chief of the Army for the Shooting Down of Aircraft with Infantry Weapons**—*Obergefreiter* Kunz, *1./Panzer-Aufklärungs-Abteilung 118* (1 May 1944)

18. PANZER-DIVISION

Campaigns: Soviet Union

Reconnaissance Formations:

- ***Panzer-Aufklärungs-Abteilung 88***

Activated: 15 October 1940

Antecedent Formations: Formed by the reorganization and redesignation of *Panzer-Aufklärungs-Abteilung "Werder,"* which had originally been formed out of four troops from *Kavallerie-Lehr- und Ersatz-Abteilung der Kavallerie-Schule Potsdam-Krampnitz*

Replacement Detachment: *Ersatz-Abteilung für motorisierte Aufklärungseinheiten 3*

Deactivation/Redesignation: Temporarily consolidated with *Kradschützen-Bataillon 18* on 7 November 1941 and retaining its designation, it was redesignated as *Kradschützen-Bataillon 18* on 24 January 1942

Organization: 1940–41—Headquarters, 1st Armored Scout Company, 2nd Motorcycle Infantry Company, and 3rd Company (heavy). November 1941—Headquarters, 1st Motorcycle Infantry Company, 2nd Motorcycle Infantry Company, 3rd Motorcycle Infantry Company, 4th Company (heavy) (motorized), and 5th Company (heavy infantry gun)

Commanders: *Major/Oberstleutnant* von Seidlitz (June 1941–24 January 1942)

- ***Kradschützen-Bataillon 18***

Activated: 15 October 1940

Antecedent Formations: Formed by the reorganization and redesignation of *I./Infanterie-Regiment 52* of *14. Panzer-Division*

Replacement Detachment: *Kradschützen-Ersatz-Bataillon 55*

Deactivation/Redesignation: *Panzer-Aufklärungs-Abteilung 18* on 31 March 1943

Organization: 1940–41—Headquarters, 1st Motorcycle Infantry Company, 2nd Motorcycle Infantry Company, 3rd Motorcycle Infantry Company, 4th Motorcycle Infantry Machine Gun Company, and 5th Company (heavy). January 1942—Headquarters, 1st Motorcycle Infantry Company, 2nd Motorcycle Infantry Company, 3rd Motorcycle Infantry Company, 4th Machine Gun Company (motorized), and 5th Company (heavy). June 1942—2nd Motorcycle Infantry Company, 3rd Motorcycle Infantry Company, 4th Motorcycle Infantry Company, and 5th Company (heavy)

Commanders: *Oberstleutnant* Mielke (October 1940–March 1941); *Major* Sperling (March–July 1941); *Oberstleutnant* Mielke (29 July–October 1941); *Major* Sperling (October–7 November 1941); *Oberstleutnant* von Seidlitz (24 January–6 March 1942); *Hauptmann Freiherr* von Wolff (acting) (8 March–1 September 1942); *Oberleutnant* Hartwig (acting) (1 September–14 February 1942); *Major* Friedrichs (14 February–31 March 1943)

Notes: At the end of July 1941, the 3rd Company was temporarily disbanded. Battalion was temporarily consolidated with *Panzer-Aufklärungs-Abteilung 88* on 7 November 1941,with the reconnaissance battalion retaining the designation, only to be redesignated on 24 January 1942 in accordance with the standard procedure at the time, which was for the motorcycle infantry battalion to retain its designation. It was attempted to reconstitute the 1st Armored Scout Company in 1942, but the effort was never realized

- ***Panzer-Aufklärungs-Abteilung 18***

Activated: 1 April 1943

Antecedent Formation: *Kradschützen-Bataillon 18*

Replacement Detachment: Initially *Kradschützen-Ersatz-Bataillon 55*, followed by *Panzer-Aufklärungs-Ersatz- und Ausbildungs-Abteilung 55* (date of redesignation unknown)

Deactivation/Redesignation: *Schützen-Bataillon 88* of *18. Artillerie-Division* in October 1943

Organization: Summer 1943—Headquarters, 2nd Armored Reconnaissance Company (*Maultier* and half-track), 3rd Armored Reconnaissance Company (*Maultier* and half-track), 4th Armored Reconnaissance Company (*Maultier* and half-track), and 5th Company (heavy) (motorized)

Commanders: *Major* Friedrichs (1 April–15 July 1943); *Hauptmann* Paulussen (acting) (15 July–27 July 1943); *Major* Klehmet (27 July–9 August 1943); *Rittmeister* von Lyncker (August–3 September 1943); *Hauptmann* Paulussen (acting) (3–7 September 1943); *Rittmeister* von Lyncker (9 September 1943–October 1943)

Awards: Knight's Cross—*Hauptmann* Paullusen, *Panzer-Aufklärungs-Abteilung 18* (18 September 1943). **Honor Roll (Clasp)**—*Oberleutnant Freiherr* von Wolff, *1./Kradschützen-Bataillon 18*. **German Cross in Gold**—*Oberleutnant* Böhm, *1./Kradschützen-Bataillon 18*; *Oberleutnant* Hedrich, *4./Panzer-Aufklärungs-Abteilung 18* (3 November 1943); *Stabsarzt Dr.* Hoffmeister, *Panzer-Aufklärungs-Abteilung 18* (16 November 1943); *Oberstleutnant* von Seidlitz, *Panzer-Aufklärungs-Abteilung 88* (27 November 1941); *Major* Sperling, *Kradschützen-Bataillon 18* (27 November 1941); *Oberleutnant Freiherr* von Wolff, *1./Kradschützen-Bataillon 18* (18 October 1941). **Certificate of Recognition from the Commander in Chief of the Army**— *Oberleutnant* Wecke, *3./Kradschützen-Bataillon 18* (28 March 1942). **Certificate of Recognition from the Commander in Chief of the Army for the Shooting Down of Aircraft with Infantry Weapons**—*2./Kradschützen-Bataillon 18* for actions performed on 6 July 1942

19. PANZER-DIVISION

Campaigns: Soviet Union

Reconnaissance Formations:

- ***Panzer-Aufklärungs-Abteilung 19 (first iteration)***

Activated: 11 November 1940

Antecedent Formations: Formed through redesignation and reorganization of *Aufklärungs-Abteilung 19* of *19. Infanterie-Division* and the reassignment and redesignation of *2./Panzer-Aufklärungs-*

Abteilung 4 of *1. Panzer-Division* as the 1st Company

Replacement Detachment: *Ersatz-Abteilung für motorisierte Aufklärungseinheiten 4*

Deactivation/Redesignation: Consolidated with *Kradschützen-Bataillon 19* on 30 April 1942

Organization: 1941—Headquarters, 1st Armored Scout Company, 2nd Motorcycle Infantry Company, and 3rd Company (heavy). September 1941–42—Headquarters, 1st Armored Scout Company, 2nd Motorcycle Infantry Company, 3rd Motorcycle Infantry Company, 4th Motorcycle Infantry Company, and 5th Company (heavy)

Commanders: *Rittmeister* von Engel (1 November 1940–27 June 1941); *Major* Booth (27 June–29 December 1941); *Hauptmann* Wilmsen (January–30 April 1942)

Notes: For a short period in the fall of 1941, *Kradschützen-Bataillon 18* was consolidated with the battalion, with *Panzer-Aufklärungs-Abteilung 18* retaining the designation.

- ***Kradschützen-Bataillon 19***

Activated: 1 November 1940

Antecedent Formations: Formed by the reorganization and redesignation of *I./Infanterie-Regiment 73*

Replacement Detachment: *Kradschützen-Ersatz-Bataillon 3*

Deactivation/Redesignation: Consolidated with *Panzer-Aufklärungs-Abteilung 19* on 14 August 1941; redesignated as *Kradschützen-Bataillon 19* on 1 May 1942; redesignated as *Panzer-Aufklärungs-Abteilung 19* on 23 March 1943

Organization: 1941—Headquarters, 1st Motorcycle Infantry Company, 2nd Motorcycle Infantry Company, 3rd Motorcycle Infantry Company, 4th Motorcycle Infantry Machine Gun Company, and 5th Company (heavy). May 1942–43—Headquarters, 1st Armored Scout Company, 2nd Motorcycle Infantry Company, 3rd Motorcycle Infantry Company, 4th Motorcycle Infantry Company, and 5th Company (heavy) (motorized)

Commanders: *Hauptmann* Stegmann (1 November 1940–?); *Major* Bruns (24 May–14 August 1941); *Hauptmann* Wilmsen (1 May 1942–24 March 1943)

- ***Panzer-Aufklärungs-Abteilung 19 (second iteration)***

Activated: 25 March 1943

Antecedent Formations: *Kradschützen-Bataillon 19*

Replacement Detachment: *Ersatz-Abteilung für motorisierte Aufklärungseinheiten 4*

Deactivation/Redesignation: 8 May 1945

Organization: September 1943—Headquarters, 1st Armored Scout Company, 2nd Armored Scout Company (*Krad*), 3rd Armored Reconnaissance Company (*Krad*), 4th Motorcycle Infantry Company (*Krad*), and 5th Company (heavy) (half-track). August 1944–45—Headquarters with light armored scout sections, 1st Armored Scout Company (half-track), 2nd Light Armored Reconnaissance Company (half-track), 3rd Armored Reconnaissance Company (half-track), and 4th Heavy Armored Reconnaissance Company (half-track)

Commanders: *Hauptmann* Wilmsen (25 March–July 1943); *Major i.G. Freiherr* von Rotberg (acting) (July 1943); *Rittmeister* von Moltke (acting) (July–August 1943); *Major* Fleck (September 1943–?); *Oberstleutnant* Fanelsa (to February 1944); *Hauptmann/Major* Meister (to December 1944); *Hauptmann* Guderian (January–March 1945); *Hauptmann* Brandes (April–May 1945)

Notes: By April 1944, the division had been heavily attrited. The 1st, 4th, and 5th Companies of *Panzer-Aufklärungs-Abteilung 19* were essentially wiped out. By January 1945, the division again in desperate straits, with the battalion reporting no reconnaissance vehicles on hand.

Awards: Knight's Cross—*Oberleutnant* Kreuzinger, *4./Panzer-Aufklärungs-Abteilung 19* (18 October 1944) (Oak Leaves); *Oberfähnrich* Krei, *5./Panzer-Aufklärungs-Abteilung 19* (10 February 1944); *Oberleutnant* Kreuzinger, *4./Panzer-Aufklärungs-Abteilung 19* (14 May 1944); *Rittmeister* von Moltke, *Panzer-Aufklärungs-Abteilung 19* (22 September 1943). **Honor Roll (Clasp)**—*Gefreiter* Rothenstein, *Kradschützen-Bataillon 19* (22 July 1941); *Feldwebel* Schade, *3./PzA19* (25 November 1944); *Oberleutnant* Schubert, *3./Kradschützen-Bataillon 19* (20 September 1941). **German Cross in Gold**—*Major* Booth, *Panzer-Aufklärungs-Abteilung 19* (29 November 1941); *Leutnant* König,

1./Panzer-Aufklärungs-Abteilung 19 (8 June 1942); *Feldwebel* Kudritzki, *3./Panzer-Aufklärungs-Abteilung 19* (27 April 1945); *Oberleutnant* Kühl, *2./Kradschützen-Bataillon 19* (7 October 1942); *Hauptmann* Meister, *Panzer-Aufklärungs-Abteilung 19* (13 December 1944); *Oberleutnant* Wenzel, *Panzer-Aufklärungs-Abteilung 19* (27 April 1945); *Oberfeldwebel* Willeges, *1./Panzer-Aufklärungs-Abteilung 19* (25 October 1943). **German Cross in Silver**—*Stabsfeldwebel* Hermann, *2./Panzer-Aufklärungs-Abteilung 19* (27 October 1944). **Certificate of Recognition from the Commander in Chief of the Army**—*Gefreiter* Kaldewey, *3./Panzer-Aufklärungs-Abteilung 19* (4 October 1941); *Feldwebel* Wedekin, *4./Panzer-Aufklärungs-Abteilung 19* (4 October 1941)

20. INFANTERIE-DIVISION (MOT)

Campaigns: Poland, France, Soviet Union

Reconnaissance Formations:

- ***Aufklärungs-Abteilung 20 (mot)***

Activated: 10 November 1938

Antecedent Formations: None identified

Replacement Detachment: *Ersatz-Abteilung für motorisierte Aufklärungseinheiten 4*

Deactivation/Redesignation: Consolidated with *Kradschützen-Bataillon 30* in April 1942

Organization: 1939–40—Headquarters, 1st Armored Scout Troop, and 2nd Motorcycle Infantry Troop. August 1940–41—Headquarters, 1st Armored Scout Troop, 2nd Motorcycle Infantry Troop, and 3rd Troop (heavy)

Commanders: *Major/Oberstleutnant* Schönfeld (1 September 1939–August 1940); *Major/Oberstleutnant* Seitz (1941–April 1942)

- ***Kradschützen-Bataillon 30***

Activated: 23 December 1940

Antecedent Formation: Formed from the redesignation and reorganization of *III./Infanterie-Regiment 25*

Replacement Detachment: Unknown

Deactivation/Redesignation: *Panzer-Aufklärungs-Abteilung 120* on 24 March 1943

Organization: 1941—Headquarters, 1st Motorcycle Infantry Company, 2nd Motorcycle Infantry Company, 3rd Motorcycle Infantry Company, 4th Motorcycle Infantry Machine Gun Company, and 5th Company (heavy). April 1942–43—Headquarters, 1st Armored Scout Company, 2nd Motorcycle Infantry Company, 3rd Motorcycle Infantry Company, 4th Motorcycle Infantry Company, and 5th Company (heavy)

Commanders: *Hauptmann* Gusmann (1941)

- ***Panzer-Aufklärungs-Abteilung 120***

Activated: 24 March 1943

Antecedent Formation: *Kradschützen-Bataillon 30*

Replacement Detachment: Unknown

Deactivation/Redesignation: Battalion designation remained the same when the division transitioned to *20. Panzergrenadier-Division*

Organization: 1943—Headquarters, 1st Armored Scout Company, 2nd Motorcycle Infantry Company, 3rd Motorcycle Infantry Company, 4th Motorcycle Infantry Company, and 5th Company (heavy) (motorized)

Commanders: *Major* Hantelmann (1943–23 July 1943)

Awards: Knight's Cross—*Feldwebel* Huber, *Aufklärungs-Abteilung 20 (mot)* (4 December 1941); *Leutnant* Kreß, *1./Aufklärungs-Abteilung 20 (mot)* (22 September 1941); *Oberstleutnant* Schönfeld, *Aufklärungs-Abteilung 20 (mot)* (15 August 1940); *Oberstleutnant* Seitz, *Aufklärungs-Abteilung 20 (mot)* (12 April 1942). **German Cross in Gold**—*Hauptmann* Gusmann, *Kradschützen-Bataillon 30* (19 January 1942); *Oberleutnant* Hagen, *Aufklärungs-Abteilung 20 (mot)* (25 March 1942); *Leutnant* Meissner, *1./Kradschützen-Bataillon 30* (13 March 1942); *Oberleutnant* Peters, *1./Kradschützen-Bataillon 30* (25 March 1942); *Major* Seitz, *Aufklärungs-Abteilung 20 (mot)* (11 December 1941). **Certificate of Recognition from the Commander in Chief of the Army**—*Major* Seitz, *Aufklärungs-Abteilung 20 (mot)* (20 August 1941)

Ulrich Kreß started his career in the army before the war, becoming a scout in *Aufklärungs-Abteilung 5 (mot)*. He was assigned to the 2nd Troop of that battalion before he was eventually reassigned to *1./Aufklärungs-Abteilung 20 (mot)* of *20. Infanterie-Division (mot)*. He worked his way up the ranks and became a scout platoon leader and, eventually, a company commander. Kreß was awarded the Knight's Cross to the Iron Cross on 22 September 1941 after conducting a number of highly successful patrols. He was killed in action a little more than a year later on 15 January 1943 during the seesaw fighting conducted by the division in the Wilikije Luki area. Kreß was an avid photographer with a keen eye for framing images, and his parents kept his albums as a memorial to him. He liked taking pictures of his comrades and also depicted a variety of light and heavy armored cars, most of them very early models in these prewar images. JIM HALEY

WH-50637
WH-50590

Prewar training included not only road marches but frequent movements by rail to distant training areas or gunnery ranges. Here *Sd.Kfz. 231* and *232 (6 Rad)* armored cars have been loaded on the train and are prepared for travel. The wheels of the vehicles had had chock blocks placed in front of, in back of, and to the sides of the tires to prevent slippage during rail movement.

Training also involved the occasional mishap, such as getting a vehicle stuck. As the crews soon learned, even 8-wheel all-wheel drive vehicles such as this *Sd.Kfz. 231 (8 Rad)* could be hindered by manmade or natural obstacles.

This armored car will require assistance to get unstuck.

An *Sd.Kfz. 231 (8 Rad)* lends a hand in recovering a stuck *Sd.Kfz. 221*. Although the scene looks relatively benign, a farmer's muddy fields were often treacherous to negotiate.

These *Sd.Kfz. 232 (Fu) (8 Rad)* armored cars appear to be testing the limits of the climbing ability of the vehicle as they attempt to negotiate a steep grade in a large ditch between a rail embankment and a road.

An armored car troop is putting the finishing touches on a bivouac site for the night, perhaps during maneuvers. Shelter halves have been assembled and tarps placed over many of the vehicles. Two mess trucks stand by in the foreground.

An armored reconnaissance battalion provides an interesting diversion for interested citizenry during a halt in a town square. Almost the entire inventory of prewar German armored cars can be seen assembled here.

In the period leading up to the war, the training became more prolonged and intense, with the scouts learning battle drills and skill craft. As can be seen overleaf, the training in the mountainous regions of southern Germany could provide a breathtaking backdrop.

Kreß participated in the campaign in Poland, as evidenced by these images of an *Sd.Kfz. 221* making its way down a road past refugees.

Once the forces returned home, there were the inevitable victory parades, like the one seen here. It is not known whether this one was staged after Poland or France, but the barren trees would suggest the former. If that was the case, then Kreß was already in *Aufklärungs-Abteilung 20 (mot)* at the start of the war (see unit markings on the Horch staff car).

An imposing view of the heavy armored cars of the battalion lined up in a motor pool.

The campaign against the Soviet Union brought heretofore unheard of challenges for all branches of the military. For the men on the ground, it meant weeks of constant, almost uninterrupted operations. In the summer of 1941, spirits were still high, and the exertions and hardships were taken in stride. Here crews of an *Sd.Kfz. 223* and *Sd.Kfz. 231 (8 Rad)* put on a happy face for the photographer. Apparently, the gray coveralls were a unit issue, since almost all crewmembers seem to be wearing them in these earlier shots of the campaign in 1941.

Grave markers for entire crews and individual soldiers dotted the routes of advance. It would take some time before the Germans would have enough of an operational pause to establish military cemeteries for their dead.

Sometimes a bit of military sightseeing was in order, since soldiers of all armies enjoy looking at military equipment, even that on display from World War I.

The most common complaint of a soldier in the field was that there was never enough time for sleep. This was especially true for scouts, since they often operated in small teams for several days without any breaks. Consequently, soldiers took their rest whenever and however they could.

This *Sd.Kfz. 231 (8 Rad)* is awaiting repairs after sustaining battle damage, most likely from a mine.

The strain of combat and constant operations can be seen on Kreß's and an officer comrade's exhausted faces after returning from a particularly harrowing patrol.

In addition to national insignia, rank, and the occasional set of *Totenkopf* collar tabs, the men of the unit seemed to uniformly wear their awards on their coveralls—including a ribbon bar in Kreß's case—a practice that must be considered fairly unusual.

This sequence of photographs was probably taken on the day Kreß was formally presented with his Knight's Cross. If the situation allowed, the personnel attempted to make themselves "presentable," and the formal presentation in front of the unit or even the entire battalion was usually followed by a great deal of celebration and drinking.

Atmospheric images of winter operations along the Eastern Front. On the opposite page, the armored cars make their way along a railway embankment, oftentimes the only manmade feature that could be recognized and negotiated through the high snowdrifts.

Knüppelweg!
erbaut v. 1 A.A. 20
November 1941

For the winter, living quarters and dug-outs had to be established if the unit was to remain anywhere for an extended period of time. Once established, the men attempted to make things as "cozy" as possible.

On 15 January 1943, Ulrich Kreß was killed in action. By then, he had been promoted to *Oberleutnant* and was serving as the company commander of *1./Kradschützen-Bataillon 30*, the armored car company of the motorcycle infantry battalion.

20. PANZERGRENADIER-DIVISION

Campaigns: Soviet Union

Reconnaissance Formations:

- ***Panzer-Aufklärungs-Abteilung 120***

Activated: 24 March 1943

Antecedent Formation: *Kradschützen-Bataillon 30*

Replacement Detachment: Unknown

Deactivation/Redesignation: 2 May 1945

Organization: 1943—Headquarters, 1st Armored Scout Company, 2nd Motorcycle Infantry Company, 3rd Motorcycle Infantry Company, 4th Motorcycle Infantry Company, and 5th Company (heavy) (motorized). September 1944—1st Light Armored Reconnaissance Company (VW), 2nd Light Armored Reconnaissance Company (VW), 3rd Light Armored Reconnaissance Company (VW), and 4th Heavy Armored Reconnaissance Company (motorized). April 1945—Headquarters, 1st Armored Reconnaissance Company (mixed), 2nd Light Armored Reconnaissance Company (VW), and 3rd Light Armored Reconnaissance Company (VW)

Commanders: *Major* Hantelmann (23 July–August 1943); *Hauptmann* Karst (acting) (December 1943); *Hauptmann* Boldenkamp (October 1944–January 1945); Unknown (January–May 1945)

Awards: Knight's Cross—*Oberleutnant* Hoyer, *4./Panzer-Aufklärungs-Abteilung 120* (8 October 1943). **German Cross in Gold**—*Oberleutnant* Bredenkamp, *5./Panzer-Aufklärungs-Abteilung 120* (28 April 1944); *Oberfeldwebel* Halder, *1./Panzer-Aufklärungs-Abteilung 120* (22 November 1943); *Oberfeldwebel* Paulsen, *5./Panzer-Aufklärungs-Abteilung 120* (5 March 1944); *Leutnant* Sander, *3./Panzer-Aufklärungs-Abteilung 120* (30 September 1944); *Oberleutnant* Sautter, *1./Panzer-Aufklärungs-Abteilung 120* (29 February 1944); *Oberfeldwebel* Schenk, *2./Panzer-Aufklärungs-Abteilung 120* (22 March 1945); *Oberleutnant* Werdin, *2./Panzer-Aufklärungs-Abteilung 120* (14 July 1944); *Unteroffizier* Winter, *4./Panzer-Aufklärungs-Abteilung 120* (6 November 1943)

20. PANZER-DIVISION

Campaigns: Soviet Union

Reconnaissance Formations:

- ***Panzer-Aufklärungs-Abteilung 92***

Activated: 23 October 1940

Antecedent Formations: Formed by *Ersatz-Abteilung 4 für motorisierte Aufklärungs-Einheiten 4*, with *1./Panzer-Aufklärungs-Abteilung 37* of *7.Panzer-Division* being reassigned and redesignated as the 1st Company

Replacement Detachment: *Ersatz-Abteilung 4 für motorisierte Aufklärungs-Einheiten 4*

Deactivation/Redesignation: Consolidated with *Kradschützen-Bataillon 20* in January 1942

Organization: 1941—Headquarters, 1st Armored Scout Company, 2nd Motorcycle Infantry Company, and 3rd Company (heavy) (motorized)

Commanders: *Hauptmann* Bentele (November 1940–3 August 1941); Unknown (4 August–8 September 1941)

Notes: In January 1941, the 1st Company was reassigned and redesignated as *1./Aufklärungs-Abteilung 36 (mot)* of *36. Infanterie-Division (mot)*, with *1./Aufklärungs-Abteilung 36 (mot)* taking its place.

- ***Kradschützen-Bataillon 20***

Activated: 4 November 1940

Antecedent Formations: Formed by redesignation and reorganization of *III./Infanterie-Regiment 115* of *33. Infanterie-Division*

Replacement Detachment: *Kradschützen-Ersatz-Bataillon 1*

Deactivation/Redesignation: *Panzer-Aufklärungs-Abteilung 20* on 31 March 1943

Organization: 1941—Headquarters, 1st Motorcycle Infantry Company, 2nd Motorcycle Infantry Company, 3rd Motorcycle Infantry Company, 4th Motorcycle Infantry Machine Gun Company, and 5th Company (heavy). July 1942–43—Headquarters, 1st Armored Scout Company, 2nd Motorcycle Infantry Company, 3rd Motorcycle Infantry Company, 4th Motorcycle Infantry Company, and 5th Company (heavy)

Commanders: *Major* Mowitz (4 November 1940–March 1941); *Major* van Hettinga (March–26 July 1941); *Major* Wolf (16 August 1941–21 February 1942; *Hauptmann* Romey (acting) (21 February–March 1942); *Oberstleutnant* Kempchen (March–21 May 1942); *Major* Schönbeck (21 May–November 1942); Unknown (November 1942–March 1943)

Notes: Temporarily disbanded except for cadre elements in September 1941. In 1942 and 1943, the armored scout company existed only on paper.

- ***Panzer-Aufklärungs-Abteilung 20***

Activated: 1 April 1943

Antecedent Formations: *Kradschützen-Bataillon 20*

Replacement Detachment: Initially *Panzer-Aufklärungs-Ersatz- und Ausbildungs-Abteilung 1*, then *Panzer-Aufklärungs-Ersatz-Abteilung 1*

Deactivation/Redesignation: May 1945

Organization: 1943—Headquarters, 1st Armored Scout Company, 2nd Armored Reconnaissance Company (*Krad*), 3rd Armored Reconnaissance Company (*Krad*), and 4th Heavy Armored Reconnaissance Company (motorized). October 1944–45—Headquarters with armored car sections, 1st Armored Scout Company (half-track), 2nd Light Armored Reconnaissance Company (half-track), 3rd Armored Reconnaissance Company (half-track), and 4th Heavy Armored Reconnaissance Company (half-track)

Commanders: *Major* Schönbeck (April–July 1943); *Hauptmann* Gabler (August 1943–February 1944); *Hauptmann* Ilse (March 1944); *Hauptmann* von Hannecken (April–July 1944); *Hauptmann* Lehner (August 1944–?); *Hauptmann* Petersmann (to 1945)

Notes: On 24 August 1943, orders were issued sending the headquarters and the 3rd Company to Senne Training Area for reconstitution and reorganization; the process was to last six weeks. In March 1944, orders were issued for the entire battalion to be reorganized. It was to be withdrawn from the front by 20 April and moved to the Wildflecken Training Area, where the headquarters qompany received the *Sd.Kfz. 234/2 Puma*. On 15 July, the battalion moved to Warsaw from Wildflecken, where it was attached to *5. Panzer-Division* and fought with it until September. Orders were again issued in October to reconstitute the battalion. The process was to last two weeks at the Arys Training Area in East Prussia.

Awards: Honor Roll (Clasp)—*Oberleutnant* Becker, *2./Panzer-Aufklärungs-Abteilung 20* (25 October 1944); *Leutnant Freiherr* von Lüttwitz, *Panzer-Aufklärungs-Abteilung 20* (17 October 1944). **German Cross in Gold**—*Leutnant* Becker, *2./Panzer-Aufklärungs-Abteilung 20* (10 August 1943); *Stabsarzt Dr.* Popp, Headquarters, *Kradschützen-Bataillon 20* (26 September 1943); *Leutnant* Röhrig, *1./Panzer-Aufklärungs-Abteilung 20* (15 December 1944); *Oberfeldwebel* Schäfer, *3./Panzer-Aufklärungs-Abteilung 20* (8 November 1943); *Major* Schönbeck, *Panzer-Aufklärungs-Abteilung 20* (13 August 1943); *Oberleutnant* Stamm, *1./Kradschützen-Bataillon 20* (11 February 1943); *Leutnant* Unger, *Kradschützen-Bataillon 20* (3 February 1943). **German Cross in Silver**—*Stabsfeldwebel* Mathes, Headquarters, *Panzer-Aufklärungs-Abteilung 20* (19 December 1944). **Certificate of Recognition from the Commander in Chief of the Army**—*Feldwebel* Rudi Schmuker, *Panzer-Aufklärungs-Abteilung 20* (5 March 1945)

21. PANZER-DIVISION (AFRIKA)

Campaigns: North Africa

Reconnaissance Formations:

- ***Aufklärungs-Abteilung 3 (mot)***

Activated: 15 October 1935 (originally assigned to *3. Panzer- Division*; transferred to *5. leichte Division* in January 1941; reassigned to *21. Panzer-Division* on 31 July 1941, when *5. leichte Division* was reorganized and redesignated as the former division)

Antecedent Formations: *Kraftfahr-Abteilung Wünsdorf*

Replacement Detachment: *Ersatz Abteilung für motorisierte Aufklärungseinheiteu 3*

Deactivation/Redesignation: Reassigned to *90. leichte Division* in February 1943 and redesignated as *Panzer-Aufklärungs-Abteilung 90*

Organization: August 1941—Headquarters, 2nd Armored Scout Company, 3rd Motorcycle Infantry Company, and 4th Company (heavy). April 1942—Headquarters, 2nd Armored Scout Company, 3rd Motorcycle Infantry Company, 4th Company (heavy), and unofficial battery of captured British 6-pounders. July 1942—Headquarters, 1st Armored Scout Company with Heavy Armored Car Platoon (*Sd.Kfz. 233*), 2nd Armored Company (half-track), 3rd Company (heavy), and 4th Battery (captured English 8.62cm artillery)

Commanders: *Oberstleutnant Freiherr* von Wechmar (1 August 1941–15 January 1942); *Haupt-*

Panzer-Aufklärungs-Abteilung 20

Excerpts from the reminiscences of Rudi Zwiener, a longtime radio operator in *Panzer-Aufklärungs-Abteilung 20*, are collected below.[29] Zwiener served as the radio operator and rear driver on the *Puma* of *Hauptmann* Petersmann, the last commander of the battalion, but he rode with most of the other *Puma* crews of the Headquarters Company as well.

> In April 1944, *Panzer-Aufklärungs-Abteilung 20* was loaded on trains that were headed in the direction of the homeland. The goal was the reconstitution of [the battalion] at Wildflecken [Training Area] in the Rhön Mountains. We stayed at Wildflecken until 15 July 1944, being trained on the latest eight-wheeled armored car [*Puma*] and where I was brought up to speed on the latest developments in radio communications.

The *Puma* armored cars of the Headquarters Company were all given names, with Zwiener being able to remember almost all of the them. The vehicles were numbered and named as follows: 001—*Tiger*; 021—*Falke* (Falcon); 022—?; 023—*Hornisse* (Hornet); 024—*Wespe* (Wasp); 025*Leopard*; 026—*Panther*; 031—*Hummel* (Bumble Bee); 032—*Biene* (Bee); 033—*Greif* (Griffon); 034—?; 035—?; 036—?; 041—*Hai* (Shark); 042—*Marder* (Marten); and 043—*Iltis* (Polecat). The company commander was in *Tiger*, while two company officers were in *Falke* (*Leutnant* von Lüttwitz) and *Hummel* (*Oberfähnrich* Reichenbächer).

Hauptmann Petersmann, the last commander of *Panzer-Aufklärungs-Abteilung 20*, whose headquarters company had the *Sd.Kfz. 234/2 Puma* in 1944 and 1945. PETERSMANN ESTATE VIA MICHAEL H. PRUETT

In July, the company returned to the front and its parent division:

> **Friday, 21 July 1944**: Wake-up was at 0345 hours, with departure at 0430 hours (the battalion had already taken off at 0300 hours!). We moved back through Grajewo in the direction of Grodno (sixty kilometers). After changing a tire, we reached the battalion at 1315 hours. We continued on at 1345 hours, about ten kilometers. In the vicinity of Dabrowna. We took up quarters there, camouflaged the vehicles with vegetation, repaired the tire, and washed up. At 2000 hours, we continued east and then to the north into a salient in the front between Grodnow and Lipsk. We were surrounded on three sides by the enemy! At 2200 hours, we took off to pull security and camouflage with [*Feldwebel*] Heuer's vehicle [023—*Hornisse*] . . .
>
> **Sunday, 23 July 1944**: . . . Enemy breakthrough in the sector of the 2nd Company (only one platoon as security for a section of front four kilometers long). Main breaththough in the direction of Rakowicze. Moved back to the old location. The 2nd vehicle remained 800 meters in front of the village and screened. The company commander came on a motorcycle: Put on the tire chains. A scout vehicle had gotten stuck in the rain-softened terrain. I went back into the village with Peter Kiefer and put all eight sets of chains on. An *SPW* from the 2nd Company came back: The enemy was pursuing with strong forces! Half an hour later, the 2nd Company came back.

Friday, 28 July 1944: Off early to the grain field and observing. Slept in the shadow of the vehicle until 1230 hours. The sun was hot! Muller was with me pulling radio watch. Henrich came over the radio: We were supposed to go to the road. *Leutnant* Hermann was there! New orders from the commander: Went with *Leutnant* Hermann about two kilometers to the crossroads at Podcisowek. Stopped there for half an hour. The second vehicle remained there. We moved on as far as Zissow (orphanage). Moved another 800 meters and ran into the park. At 1345 hours, we ate lunch outside the vehicle. Sat in the grass and monitored the radio traffic with headphones. At 1610 hours, I received a message: Are the fuel and ammo trucks at your location? At 1700 hours, there was an inquiry from the supply vehicles: Where is the distribution point? I wound up being the middle man between the tanks that had been ordered there because they urgently need fuel and ammunition. At 2030 hours, we moved the 800 meters to the second vehicle, which was waiting to move out along the edge of the road at the entrance to a trail into the woods. We took up position ten meters behind it. The requested fuel and ammunition section was also at the edge of the road. *Feldwebel* Bliemeister was talking to the convoy leaders from his turret.

A short while later, the sounds of engines and tracks could be heard coming from the woods. That could only be the tank unit that was coming to be resupplied. Nevertheless, a whip-like shot destroyed the quiet mood. I was right in the middle of sending a location report, when *Feldwebel* Bliemeister's sharp voice reverberated in the vehicle's interior: Kiefer, move out! We took off, passed the cut in the woods and the burning second vehicle when we heard the second round. Our camouflage flew off the rear deck and I suddenly had a clear view through the opened hatch. While I radioed . . . an immediate *fga* [*Feind greift an* = "enemy attacking"], I saw a blazing figure climb out of the rearward hatch and run over to the waiting truck. I could see it was Müller 2, a radio operator. A truck driver threw a blanket over the burning body that was racing around crazily and threw it into a ditch. It couldn't be ruled out that he might have gotten too close to the cargo area with the fuel containers.

Bliemeister had us halt after about a kilometer . . . [the crew receives new orders and has to move back past the scene of what turned out to be a friendly-fire incident] . . .

At the fuel point, there was hectic activity. Thirty meters away from the blazing second vehicle, we halted and looked at the inferno helplessly. It turned out that the gunner who had delivered the deathblow was an acting company commander, a combat-experienced *Oberleutnant* who had fired from 200 meters, when he saw the turret of the second vehicle traversing toward him. It was Heinz Justus, who had committed that fateful error. He had said: "I just want to see what it looks like to have a tank in my sights." He had said that to *Schütze* Heinrich, who was sitting on the fender. At that point, the *Oberleutnant* had issued the fire command. The antitank round had slammed into the front of the vehicle, killing the front driver (Kurt Hoffmann, who had just been proxy-married two weeks previously) Heinz Justus was also hit and the round also took off the leg of the vehicle commander (*Unteroffizier* Velechowski, who hailed from Vienna), who was sitting outside but had a leg dangling inside the hatch of the turret. Fritz Müller, who was sitting to the left rear, was not hit, but the round—glowing hot—continued on through both of the fuel tanks in front of him and exited out of the engine compartment. *Schütze* Henrich had instinctively taken a leap into the ditch and was still standing there in shock, when we reached the accident site. The same for the unfortunate tank officer, who explained what had happened with tears in his eyes. He and his company had been in combat for several hours with the enemy forces that had broken through and he himself had already knocked out six enemy tanks (T-34's). The strain had been too much for him . . .

Images of a rail-loaded *Sd.Kfz. 231 (8 Rad)* and the *Sd.Kfz. 234/2 Puma* of the company. Petersmann wears a tailor-made *Panzer* jacket made out of an army hard-edge water-pattern camouflage. (These photographs were scanned from images printed on rag paper—hence the poor quality. Because field shots of the *Puma* are relatively rare, they have been included nevertheless.) PETERSMANN ESTATE VIA MICHAEL H. PRUETT

Hauptmann Petersmann's golden-yellow piped collar tabs and shoulder boards. MICHAEL H. PRUETT

A *Puma* from the headquarters company of *Panzer-Aufklärungs-Abteilung 20* in a U.S. Army vehicle collection point at the end of the war. The unit insignia can be seen on the left rear fender. In addition to this *Sd.Kfz. 234/2*, apparently about four others from the unit surrendered to U.S. forces in Czechoslovakia, as well as an *Sd.Kfz. 234/3* and an *Sd.Kfz. 234* with a *Schwebelafette*.

mann/Major von Luck (15 January–27 May 1942); *Hauptmann* Everth (29 May 1942–February 1943)

Notes: Reorganized in 1942, with the 2nd Company becoming the 1st and the 3rd Company the 2nd. The new 2nd Company was outfitted with half-tracks, although the official organization chart shows wheeled vehicles. The 4th Company was consolidated into the newly formed 3rd Company. The 4th Battery consisted of captured English 6-pounder guns. It was initially formed through command channels, but it eventually was administratively approved and budgeted and officially became part of the battalion.

- ***Aufklärungs-Abteilung 580 (mot)***

Activated: 1 August 1941 (company); Summer 1942 (battalion)

Antecedent Formations: *Aufklärungs-Kompanie 580*

Replacement Detachment: *Panzer-Aufklärungs-Ersatz- und Ausbildungs-Abteilung 4*

Deactivation/Redesignation: *Panzer-Aufklärungs-Abteilung 21* on 28 April 1943

Organization: 1942–43—Headquarters, 1st Armored Scout Company, 2nd Armored Reconnaissance Company (half-track), 3rd Company (heavy), and 4th Battery (captured English 8.62cm artillery)

Commanders: *Rittmeister* von Homeyer (1 August 1941–3 July 1942) (KIA); *Hauptmann/Major* Voss (January–28 April 1943)

Notes: Began serving with *21. Panzer-Division* as early as January 1943.

- ***Panzer-Aufklärungs-Abteilung 21***

Activated: 28 April 1943

Antecedent Formations: *Aufklärungs-Abteilung 580 (mot)*

Replacement Detachment: *Panzer-Aufklärungs-Ersatz- und Ausbildungs-Abteilung 4*

Deactivation/Redesignation: 12 May 1943 (capitulation in North Africa)

Organization: 1943—Headquarters, 1st Armored Scout Company, 2nd Armored Reconnaissance Company (half-track), 3rd Company (heavy), and 4th Battery (captured English 8.62cm artillery)

Commanders: *Major* Voss (28 April–12 May 1943)

Awards: Knight's Cross—*Hauptmann* Everth, *Aufklärungs-Abteilung 3 (mot)* (6 July 1942). **German Cross in Gold**—*Oberleutnant* Kettler, *Aufklärungs-Abteilung 580 (mot)* (10 May1943); *Oberleutnant* Kiehl, *4./Aufklärungs-Abteilung 3 (mot)* (29 January 1942); *Oberstleutnant Freiherr* von Wechmar, *Aufklärungs-Abteilung 3 (mot)* (16 January 1942)

21. PANZER-DIVISION (NEW)

Campaigns: Western Europe, Eastern Front

Reconnaissance Formations:

- ***Panzer-Aufklärungs-Abteilung 21***

Activated: 4 July 1943

Antecedent Formations: Initially formed from *Panzer-Aufklärungs-Kompanie 931* (two companies), then from reassigned and redesignated elements of *Panzer-Aufklärungs-Lehr-Abteilung*

Replacement Detachment: *Panzer-Aufklärungs-Ersatz- und Ausbildungs-Abteilung 4*

Deactivation/Redesignation: 29 April 1945

Organization: July 1943—Headquarters, 1st Motorcycle Infantry Company, and 2nd Motorcycle Infantry Company. October 1943—Headquarters, 1st Armored Scout Company with heavy armored scout platoon (*Sd.Kfz. 233*), 2nd Light Armored Reconnaissance Company, 3rd Light Armored Reconnaissance Company (half-track), 4th Armored Reconnaissance Company (half-track), 5th Heavy Armored Reconnaissance Company (half-track). December 1944–45—Headquarters with armored car sections, 1st Armored Scout Company (half-track), 2nd Light Armored Reconnaissance Company (half-track), 3rd Armored Reconnaissance Company (half-track) and 4th Heavy Armored Reconnaissance Company (half-track)

Commanders: *Hauptmann Graf* von Hahn (July 1943–?); *Hauptmann* Waldow (to June 1944); *Hauptmann/Major* Brandt (July 1944–1945)

Notes: In February 1945, the 3rd Company received orders to transition from medium to light half-tracks.

Awards: German Cross in Gold—*Oberfeldwebel* Sonnenschein, *1./Panzer-Aufklärungs-Abteilung 21* (15 April 1945)

22. PANZER-DIVISION

Campaigns: Soviet Union

Reconnaissance Formations:

- ***Kradschützen-Bataillon 24***

Activated: 10 September 1941

Antecedent Formations: Formed from personnel levies against the headquarters, *3.* and *4./Panzer-Aufklärungs-Abteilung 5* of *2. Panzer-Division*, a newly formed armored scout company from *Kradschützen-Ersatz-Bataillon 7* and *5./Infanterie-Regiment 586* of *320. Infanterie-Division*

Replacement Detachment: Initially *Kradschützen-Ersatz-Bataillon 7*, followed by *Kradschützen-Ersatz-Bataillon 6* effective 6 June 1942

Deactivation: 3 March 1943 (elements continued to fight with *Kampfgruppe 22* when the division ceased to exist as an effective fighting force)

Organization: 1941–43—Headquarters, 1st Armored Scout Company, 2nd Motorcycle Infantry Company, 3rd Light Armored Reconnaissance Company (half-track), 4th Motorcycle Infantry Company, and 5th Company (heavy) (motorized)

Commanders: *Oberstleutnant* Schmidmann (September 1941–June 1942); *Major* Sander (June–July 1942); *Hauptmann* von Leistner (acting) (July 1942); *Hauptmann* von Cochenhausen (acting) (July–October 1942); *Hauptmann* Ebeling (October 1942–29 January 1943); *Hauptmann* Kratochwilla (to 15 February 1943); *Major Ritter* von Poschinger (15 February 1943–?)

Notes: When the division was disbanded and *Kampfgruppe 22* was formed, the elements of the battalion reporting to the latter organization were assembled as *Kradschützen-Kompanie 24*. On 7 April 1943, the battle group was attached to *23. Panzer-Division*. On the next day, it was disbanded and its forces integrated into the formations of *23. Panzer-Division*, with *Kradschützen-Kompanie 24* being reassigned and redesignated as *2./Kradschützen-Bataillon 23* of *23. Panzer-Division.*

- ***Panzerspäh-Kompanie 140***

Activated: May 1942 (through command channels)

Antecedent Formations: Elements received from *Aufklärungs-Abteilung 22* of *22. Infanterie-Division*

Replacement Detachment: None

Deactivation/Redesignation: Apparently on hand through the end of November 1942

Organization: 1942—two light armored scout platoons, one heavy armored scout platoon, two motorcycle infantry platoons, one heavy motorcycle infantry platoon

Commanders: *Major* von Cochenhausen (May 1942–?)

Notes: Unit reported directly to the operations officer of the division

Awards: Knight's Cross—*Oberleutnant* Schreiber, *4./Kradschützen-Bataillon 24* (3 January 1943). **Honor Roll (Clasp)**—*Leutnant* Luippold, *2./Kradschützen-Bataillon 24* (17 March 1943). **German Cross in Gold**—*Hauptfeldwebel* Schipfer, *3./Kradschützen-Bataillon 24* (14 February 1943)

23. PANZER-DIVISION

Campaigns: Soviet Union

Reconnaissance Formations:

- ***Kradschützen-Bataillon 23***

Activated: 13 September 1941

Antecedent Formations: Formed from the Headquarters of *Panzer-Aufklärungs-Abteilung 8*, elements of *Kradschützen-Ersatz-Bataillon 6* (1st Company), elements of *3./Panzer-Aufklärungs-Abteilung 8* (2nd and 4th Companies), *4./Kradschützen-Bataillon 55* (3rd and 4th Companies), and *4./Panzer-Aufklärungs-Abteilung 8* (5th Company)

Replacement Detachment: Initially *Kradschützen-Ersatz-Bataillon 22*, followed by *Kradschützen-Ersatz-Bataillon 9* in September 1942

Deactivation/Redesignation: *Panzer-Aufklärungs-Abteilung 23* on 22 April 1943

Organization: 1942—Headquarters, 1st Armored Scout Company, 2nd Light Armored Reconnaissance Company (half-track), 3rd Motorcycle Infantry Company, 4th Motorcycle Infantry Company, and 5th Company (heavy). November 1942—Headquarters only (see notes below). January 1943—Headquarters, 1st Armored Scout Company, one motorcycle infantry company

Commanders: *Hauptmann* von Kunow (acting) (September–October 1941); *Hauptmann* von Goerne (October 1941–October 1942); *Major* von Haagen (October 1942–?); *Major* Richter (to January 1943);

Hauptmann Rohrbach (January 1943–?); *Hauptmann/Major* von Kunow

Notes: The battalion was temporarily disbanded in November 1942. The headquarters remained intact, but the 1st Armored Scout Company was attached to the divisional signals battalion, the 3rd and 4th Companies were combined to a single motorcycle infantry company and attached to *Panzergrenadier-Regiment 128* and the remaining personnel reassigned to *Panzergrenadier-Regimenter 128* and *126*. Reformed at the beginning of February 1943, with an armored scout company, a motorcycle infantry company, and the battalion headquarters. An additional motorcycle infantry company was formed by the incorporation of *Kradschützen-Kompanie 24* (see *22. Panzer-Division* above).

- ***Panzer-Aufklärungs-Abteilung 23***

Activated: 22 April 1943

Antecedent Formations: *Kradschützen-Bataillon 23*

Replacement Detachment: *Panzer-Aufklärungs-Ersatz-Abteilung 9*

Deactivation/Redesignation: 8 May 1945

Organization: May 1943—Headquarters, 1st Armored Scout Company, 2nd Light Armored Reconnaissance Company (half-track), 3rd Armored Reconnaissance Company (*Krad*), 4th Armored Reconnaissance Company (*Krad*), and 5th Company (heavy). April 1944–45—Headquarters Company with armored car sections, 1st Armored Scout Company (half-track), 2nd Light Armored Reconnaissance Company (half-track), 3rd Armored Reconnaissance Company (half-track), and 4th Heavy Armored Reconnaissance Company (half-track)

Commanders: *Oberleutnant* von Süßkind (acting) (April 1943–?); Rittmeister Weißbach (to July 1943); *Major* Schägger (21 July–September 1943); *Major* von Einem (acting) (September–October 1943); *Hauptmann* Hoffmann (acting) (October 1943); *Hauptmann* Koppe (October 1943–26 February 1944); *Oberleutnant* Abel (acting) (26 February–March 1944); *Hauptmann/Major* Koppe (March–November 1944); *Hauptmann* Schulz (February–8 May 1945)

Notes: In October 1943, orders were received to transfer the 2nd Company to the Senne training Area for reorganization and reconstitution as a Type "C" armored scout company. That same October, orders were issued to Military District VI to form a heavy armored scout platoon for the battalion and the battalion's 5th Company was ordered to conduct a battlefield reconstitution and reorganization as a heavy armored reconnaissance company (half-track) in the rear area of *Heeresgruppe Süd*. In November, the recently formed heavy armored scout platoon with six *Sd.Kfz. 233's* was ordered to join the battalion. On 8 February 1944, the 2nd Company was ordered to rejoin the battalion at the front. That same February, the 4th Company was ordered to the Senne Training Area for reconstitution and reorganization as an armored reconnaissance company (half-track); in March, it was transferred to the Wildflecken Training Area to complete the process. In June, the company was ordered to rejoin the battalion in the field. In the summer of 1944, the reconnaissance battalion was one of the few formations in the division to be at essentially full strength. By the end of the war, the armored car sections in the headquarters company were equipped only with light armored cars.

Awards: Knight's Cross—*Unteroffizier* Bade, *4./Panzer-Aufklärungs-Abteilung 23* (26 August 1943); *Oberleutnant* Bergerhoff, *3./Panzer-Aufklärungs-Abteilung 23* (27 August 1944); *Feldwebel* Eisermann, *1./Panzer-Aufklärungs-Abteilung 23* (9 December 1944); *Oberleutnant* Horst Hain, *3./Panzer-Aufklärungs-Abteilung 23* (28 March 1945); *Leutnant* Keck, *2./Panzer-Aufklärungs-Abteilung 23* (18 February 1945); *Hauptmann* Koppe, *Panzer-Aufklärungs-Abteilung 23* (18 November 1944); *Major* Schägger, *Panzer-Aufklärungs-Abteilung 23* (16 September 1943). **Honor Roll (Clasp)**—*Hauptmann* Koppe, *Panzer-Aufklärungs-Abteilung 23* (15 May 1944); *Oberfeldwebel* Ruhl, *Panzer-Aufklärungs-Abteilung 23* (19 September 1943); *Oberleutnant* Wenzel, *4./Panzer-Aufklärungs-Abteilung 23* (27 August 1943). **German Cross in Gold**—*Oberleutnant* Abel, *4./Panzer-Aufklärungs-Abteilung 23* (4 September 1944); *Leutnant* Borbonus, *1./Kradschützen-Bataillon 23* (12 February 1943); *Feldwebel* Donner, *4./Panzer-Aufklärungs-Abteilung 23* (30 March 1945); *Major* von Einem, *Panzer-Aufklärungs-Abteilung 23* (11 December 1943); *Oberleutnant Dr.* Güthling, *Kradschützen-Bataillon 23* (28 November 1942); *Oberfeldwebel*

Härtig, *1./Panzer-Aufklärungs-Abteilung 23* (14 September 1943); *Oberleutnant* Hagelloch, *2./Panzer-Aufklärungs-Abteilung 23* (7 December 1944); *Oberfeldwebel* Hain, *4./Kradschützen-Bataillon 23* (5 April 1943); *Leutnant* Havenstein, *4./Panzer-Aufklärungs-Abteilung 23* (20 June 1944); *Oberfeldwebel* Hey, *1./Panzer-Aufklärungs-Abteilung 23* (28 February 1945); *Oberfeldwebel* Höll, *3./Panzer-Aufklärungs-Abteilung 23* (11 December 1943); *Oberleutnant* Kappauf, *2./Kradschützen-Bataillon 23* (29 March 1943); *Oberleutnant* Koppe, *2./Kradschützen-Bataillon 23* (28 November 1942); *Leutnant* Mischke, *1./Panzer-Aufklärungs-Abteilung 23* (7 January 1945); *Feldwebel* Moldaschl, *1./Panzer-Aufklärungs-Abteilung 23* (9 March 1945); *Oberfeldwebel* Nagel, *2./Panzer-Aufklärungs-Abteilung 23* (25 October 1943); *Oberfeldwebel* Nettel, *2./Panzer-Aufklärungs-Abteilung 23* (15 April 1945); *Unteroffizier* Reinwald, *3./Panzer-Aufklärungs-Abteilung 23* (30 March 1945); *Oberfeldwebel* Röhsler, *4./Kradschützen-Bataillon 23* (5 April 1943); *Oberfeldwebel* Ruhl, *1./Panzer-Aufklärungs-Abteilung 23* (11 April 1944); *Oberfeldwebel* Schmauder, *Panzer-Aufklärungs-Abteilung 23* (6 January 1945); *Hauptmann* Schulz, *Panzer-Aufklärungs-Abteilung 23* (15 April 1945); *Leutnant Freiherr* von Thielmann, *2./Panzer-Aufklärungs-Abteilung 23* (1 December 1943). **Certificate of Recognition from the Commander in Chief of the Army for the Shooting Down of Aircraft with Infantry Weapons**—*Gefreiter* Dimars, *2./Panzer-Aufklärungs-Abteilung 23* (1 February 1944); *Gefreiter* Herbrich, *2./Panzer-Aufklärungs-Abteilung 23* (30 May 1944); *Gefreiter* Hirsch, *2./Panzer-Aufklärungs-Abteilung 23* (1 June 1944); *Obergefreiter* Hoffmann, *2./Panzer-Aufklärungs-Abteilung 23* (31 May 1944); *Gefreiter* Müller, *1./Panzer-Aufklärungs-Abteilung 23* (31 May 1944); *Gefreiter* Reichert, *1./Panzer-Aufklärungs-Abteilung 23* (31 May 1944); awarded to *2./Panzer-Aufklärungs-Abteilung 23* (24 August 1944)

24. PANZER-DIVISION

Campaigns: Soviet Union

Reconnaissance Formations:

- ***Kradschützen-Bataillon 4***

Activated: 1 December 1941

Antecedent Formations: Formed through the reorganization and redesignation of *Radfahr-Abteilung 1*. The 1st Armored Scout Troop was formed from unidentified sources.

Replacement Detachment: *Kradschützen-Ersatz-Bataillon 24*

Deactivation/Redesignation: Effectively destroyed in January 1943 (Stalingrad)

Organization: January 1942—Headquarters, 1st Armored Scout Troop, 2nd Armored Reconnaissance Troop (light half-track), 3rd Motorcycle Infantry Troop, 4th Motorcycle Infantry Troop, 5th Troop (heavy) (motorized), and 6th Troop (field replacement). March 1942-Headquarters, 1st Armored Scout Troop, 2nd Armored Reconnaissance Troop (light half-track), 3rd Motorcycle Infantry Troop, 4th Motorcycle Infantry Troop, and 5th Troop (heavy) (motorized)

Commanders: *Oberstleutnant* Baade (1 December 1941–6 March 1942); *Oberstleutnant* von Hellermann (6 March–1 September 1942); *Rittmeister* von Götz (to 2 February 1943)

Notes: Early on in the organization, there was also an escort battery attached to the battalion, but it was reassigned in March 1942, as was the field replacement troop. It is also known that a battery of 10.5-cm *Leichtgeschütz 40* (recoilless cannon) towed by *Kettenkräder* was attached to *Kradschützen-Bataillon 4* at some point prior to Stalingrad.

- ***Panzer-Aufklärungs-Abteilung 4***

Activated: March 1943

Antecedent Formation: *Kradschützen-Bataillon 4*

Replacement Detachment: *Kradschützen-Ersatz-Bataillon 24*

Deactivation/Redesignation: *Panzer-Aufklärungs-Abteilung 24* on 7 April 1943

Organization: 1943—Headquarters, 1st Armored Scout Troop, 2nd Light Armored Reconnaissance Troop (half-track), 3rd Armored Reconnaissance Troop (half-track), 4th Armored Reconnaissance Troop (half-track), and 5th Heavy Armored Reconnaissance Troop (half-track)

- ***Panzer-Aufklärungs-Abteilung 24***

Activated: 7 April 1943

Antecedent Formations: *Panzer-Aufklärungs-Abteilung 4 (Kradschützen-Bataillon 4)*

This series of photographs of *Kradschützen-Bataillon 4* and *Panzer-Aufklärungs-Abteilung 24/Panzerspäh Schwadron 24* are believed to come from a soldier who was ultimately assigned to the crew of future Knight's Cross recipient *Oberwachtmeister* Krüger. These photos are most likely from the time that *1.Kavallerie-Division* was redesignated and reconstituted as *24. Panzer-Division* in late 1941 and 1942. After suffering horrendous losses in its prior incarnation, *24. Panzer-Division* participated in the ill-fated German summer offensive of 1942, where it fought at Stalingrad and was effectively destroyed in February 1943.

The division was reconstituted in Normandy in the spring of 1943 and was shipped to Italy in the summer to complete the process. It participated in the disarming of the Italian forces in September 1943 and was returned to the Eastern Front in October of that year, but not before the soldiers of the battalion were able to spend some pleasant times in the sunny clime. Note the interesting camouflage pattern on the *Sd.Kfz. 232 (Fu) (8 Rad)*.

These images must have been taken after the winter of 1943–44, when shirtsleeve order was again permissible and endurable. The *Sd.Kfz. 232 (Fu) (8 Rad)* seems to have survived the winter well.

This crew has taken pains to camouflage its vehicle with natural foliage in the barren landscape. The wooden box seen on the ground appears to contain a speaker. Crews often hooked up their tactical radios to receive military entertainment radio stations when the situation allowed.

After a while, the scout came to regard his binoculars as an extension of his eyes. When the terrain was broken up, standing on top of the vehicle was sometimes necessary to get a better field of observation.

Scouts perform their daily routines, interrupted by the occasional taking of a set of portraits and shots of comrades for future memories. Once again, note the large variety of uniforms. Since the scouts considered themselves elites and the unit in question here was probably *Panzerspäh-Schwadron 24*—which meant the troop reported directly to the division, where it would have had little supervision—there was a great deal of latitude in making the equivalent of a military "fashion statement."

Future Knight's Cross recipient *Oberwachtmeister* Erwin Krüger is seen here pointing out some information in a document. In divisional histories, he is referred to as *der blaue Krüger*, which indicates he may have had a fondness for alcohol, since *blau* in colloquial German means "tipsy" or "drunk."

It appears the water-pattern tailor-made field trousers were quite popular among the crews.

Replacement Detachment: *Kradschützen-Ersatz-Bataillon 24?*

Deactivation/Redesignation: 6 April 1945

Organization: 1943—Headquarters, 1st Armored Scout Troop with heavy armored scout platoon, 2nd Armored Scout Troop (half-track), 3rd Armored Reconnaissance Troop (half-track), 4th Armored Reconnaissance Troop (half-track), and 5th Heavy Armored Reconnaissance Troop (half-track). 1944—*Panzerspäh-Schwadron 24*. January 1945—Headquarters with armored scout sections, 1st Armored Scout Troop (half-track), 2nd Light Armored Reconnaissance Troop (half-track), 3rd Armored Reconnaissance Troop (half-track), and 4th Heavy Armored Reconnaissance Troop (half-track)

Commanders: *Major/Oberstleutnant* von Heyden (April 1943–?); *Rittmeister* Overbeck (acting) (September 1943); *Oberstleutnant* von Heyden (to 12 November 1943); *Rittmeister* Dannebaum (acting) (12–22 November 1943); *Oberstleutnant* von Heyden (22 November 1943–?); *Rittmeister* von Langenn-Steinkeller (February–27 March 1944); *Oberstleutnant* Blume (acting) (May 1944); *Oberleutnant* Dittmar (acting) (to 30 May 1944); *Rittmeister* Danneberg (acting) (August 1944); *Major* Blume (January–March 1945)

Notes: In 1943–44, the 2nd Troop was disbanded and remnants apparently consolidated with the 1st Troop. From 15 January to December 1943, the battalion (minus the 1st Armored Scout Troop) was attached to *Panzergrenadier-Regiment 26*. The 1st Armored Scout Troop reported directly to the division headquarters during that period. The term "troop" was used throughout the war in lieu of company. The ground combat elements of the division all wore golden-yellow for their *Waffenfarbe*, with the exception of the artillery and engineers.

Awards: Knight's Cross—*Rittmeister* Blume, *Panzer-Aufklärungs-Abteilung 24* (11 March 1945); *Rittmeister* Danneberg, *Panzer-Aufklärungs-Abteilung 24* (17 September 1944); *Oberfähnrich* Krüger, *Panzerspäh-Schwadron 24* (17 September 1944); *Rittmeister* von Lagenn-Steinkeller, *Panzer-Aufklärungs-Abteilung 24* (9 June 1944); *Oberfeldwebel* Neufeld, *2./Kradschützen-Bataillon 4* (3 January 1943). **Honor Roll (Clasp)**—*Wachtmeister* Magdsack, *3./Panzer-Aufklärungs-Abteilung 24* (7 August 1944); *Oberwachtmeister* Neumann, *3./Panzer-Aufklärungs-Abteilung 24* (15 February 1945); *Oberleutnant* Roßberg, *3./Panzer-Aufklärungs-Abteilung 24* (5 November 1944); *Rittmeister* Schlaefereit, *3./Panzer-Aufklärungs-Abteilung 24* (15 March 1945); *Oberwachtmeister* Wilke, *4./Panzer-Aufklärungs-Abteilung 24* (27 July 1944). **German Cross in Gold**—*Unteroffizier* Grefer, *4./Panzer-Aufklärungs-Abteilung 24* (28 April 1944); *Oberstleutnant* von Hellermann, *Kradschützen-Bataillon 4* (20 September 1942); *Rittmeister* Karkowski, *4./Panzer-Aufklärungs-Abteilung 24* (8 May 1945); *Rittmeister* Kolczyk, *2./Kradschützen-Bataillon 4* (5 November 1942); *Oberwachtmeister* Neubacher, *3./Panzer-Aufklärungs-Abteilung 24* (23 May 1944); *Oberleutnant* Schaefereit, *4./Panzer-Aufklärungs-Abteilung 24* (6 January 1945); *Fahnenjunker-Oberwachtmeister* Schlemmer, *Panzer-Aufklärungs-Abteilung 24* (14 May 1944); *Oberleutnant* von Senger und Etterlin, *3./Panzer-Aufklärungs-Abteilung 24* (4 September 1944); *Wachtmeister* Voosen, *5./Panzer-Aufklärungs-Abteilung 24* (9 March 1945); *Leutnant* Vormeier, *3./Panzer-Aufklärungs-Abteilung 24* (14 July 1944). **Certificate of Recognition from the Commander in Chief of the Army**—*Stabswachtmeister* Heß, *Panzerspäh-Schwadron 24* (5 February 1945)

25. INFANTERIE-DIVISION (MOT)

Campaigns: Soviet Union

Reconnaissance Formations:

- ***Aufklärungs-Abteilung 25 (mot)***

Activated: 15 November 1940

Antecedent Formations: Formed from *Aufklärungs-Abteilung 25* of *25. Infanterie-Division*, with *2.(Pz.Späh)/Panzer-Aufklärungs-Abteilung 59* being reassigned and redesignated as the 1st Armored Scout Company

Replacement Detachment: Unknown

Deactivation/Redesignation: Consolidated with *Kradschützen-Bataillon 25* on 1 May 1942.

Organization: 1941–42—Headquarters, 1st Armored Scout Troop, 2nd Motorcycle Infantry Troop, and 3rd Troop (heavy) (motorized)

Commanders: *Rittmeister* Menke (15 November 1940–5 February 1941); *Hauptmann* Eicke (5 February–20 July 1941); *Oberleutnant* Uebelhoer (acting)

(20 July–7 August 1941); *Hauptmann Graf* von Bellegarde (7 August–19 December 1941); *Oberleutnant/Hauptmann* Uebelhoer (acting) (19 December 1941–1 May 1942)

- ***Kradschützen-Bataillon 25***

  Activated: 15 November 1940

  Antecedent Formations: Formed by the reassignment, reorganization, and redesignation of *III./Infanterie-Regiment 40* of *27. Infanterie-Division*

  Replacement Detachment: *Kradschützen-Ersatz-Bataillon 25*

  Deactivation/Redesignation: *Panzer-Aufklärungs-Abteilung 125* on 1 April 1943

  Organization: 1941—Headquarters, 1st Motorcycle Infantry Company, 2nd Motorcycle Infantry Company, 3rd Motorcycle Infantry Company, 4th Motorcycle Infantry Machine Gun Company, and 5th Company (heavy) (motorized). May 1942–43—Headquarters, 1st Motorcycle Infantry Company, 2nd Motorcycle Infantry Company, 3rd Motorcycle Infantry Company, 4th Armored Scout Company, and 5th Company (heavy) (motorized)

  Commanders: *Oberstleutnant* Blecher (25 November 1940–1 May 1941); *Oberstleutnant* Schulte-Heuthaus (1 May 1941–1 March 1942); *Hauptmann* Ruisinger (1 March–July 1942); *Hauptmann* von Schenk zu Schweinsberg (July 1942–February 1943); *Hauptmann* Wiedemann (February 1942–1 April 1943)

Above left: This scout from *Panzer-Aufklärungs-Abteilung 24* appears to be enlisted yet wears an officer-quality "eagle" on his tunic. He also wears what seems to be collar piping on his field-gray tunic. The piping was not authorized for the field-gray version of the *Panzer* jacket, so this must have been yet another modification made within the unit. He wears an officer-style embroidered breast eagle on his uniform jacket. **Above right:** Wilhelm Rüger was awarded the German Cross in Gold on 11 March 1943 while serving in *Kradschützen-Bataillon 25*. Here he is wearing the black *Panzer* uniform while still on convalescent leave in April 1945.

Trench fighting. Note the use of a Soviet submachine gun.

Rüger is prepared to go on a dismounted patrol in 1942.

Left: Rüger proudly shows off his recently awarded German Cross in Gold while pointing something out to a comrade.

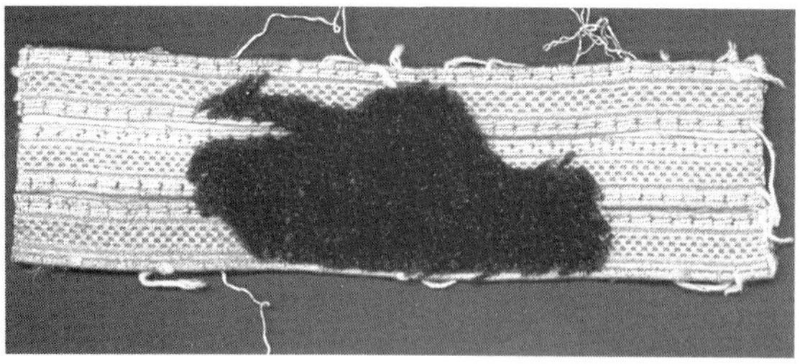

Rüger's field-made awards—two versions of the Tank Destruction Badge and the German Cross in Gold—were made for him in the Soviet Union by a peasant woman in exchange for food. He stated after the war that he was unable to obtain the authorized versions of the badges and had these made in their stead. Evidently, he liked them since he continued to wear them through war's end. FRODE STEINE

- ***Panzer-Aufklärungs-Abteilung 125***

Activated: 1 April 1943

Antecedent Formations: *Kradschützen-Bataillon 25*

Replacement Detachment: *Panzergrenadier-Ersatz- und Ausbildungs-Bataillon 2*

Deactivation/Redesignation: Became part of *25. Panzergrenadier-Division* when the division reorganized and was redesignated on 23 June 1943

Organization: 1943—Headquarters, 1st Motorcycle Infantry Company, 2nd Motorcycle Infantry Company, 3rd Motorcycle Infantry Company, 4th Armored Scout Company, and 5th Company (heavy) (motorized)

Commanders: *Hauptmann* Wiedemann (1 April–23 June 1943)

Awards: Knight's Cross—*Oberstleutnant* Schulte-Heuthaus, *Kradschützen-Bataillon 25* (23 January 1942). **Close Combat Clasp in Gold**—*Oberleutnant* Gerloff, *3./Kradschützen-Bataillon 25* (25 March 1942); *Oberfeldwebel* Häberle, *2./Kradschützen-Bataillon 25* (22 November 1942); *Oberleutnant* Jedermann, *2./Aufklärungs-Abteilung 25 (mot)* (29 January 1942); *Feldwebel* Rüger, *Kradschützen-Bataillon 25* (11 March 1943); *Leutnant* Weis, *Kradschützen-Bataillon 25* (11 March 1943)

25. PANZERGRENADIER-DIVISION

Campaigns: Soviet Union, Western Europe, Eastern Front

Reconnaissance Formations:

- ***Panzer-Aufklärungs-Abteilung 125 (first iteration)***

Activated: 1 April 1944

Antecedent Formation: *Kradschützen-Bataillon 25*

Replacement Detachment: *Panzergrenadier-Ersatz- und Ausbildungs-Bataillon 2*

Deactivation/Redesignation: Effectively destroyed in July 1944 (Soviet Operation Bagration)

Organization: 1943—Headquarters, 1st Motorcycle Infantry Company, 2nd Motorcycle Infantry Company, 3rd Motorcycle Infantry Company, 4th Armored Scout Company, and 5th Company (heavy) (motorized). November 1944—Headquarters, 1st Light Armored Reconnaissance Company (VW), and 2nd Light Armored Reconnaissance Company (VW)

Commanders: *Hauptmann* Wiedemann (23 June–6 September 1943); *Hauptmann/Major* Harneit (September 1943–23 June 1944); Unknown (acting) (23 June–July 1944)

- ***Panzer-Aufklärungs-Abteilung 125 (second iteration)***

Activated: October 1944

Antecedent Formations: Initially formed as an armored scout platoon. In November 1944, an armored reconnaissance company (VW) was received from *78. Sturm-Division*, which was reorganized and redesignated as the 2nd Company of the battalion. The 3rd and 4th Companies, raised by Military District IV did not arrive until January 1945.

Replacement Detachment: Unknown

Deactivation/Redesignation: May 1945

Organization: November 1944—Headquarters, 1st Light Armored Reconnaissance Company (VW) and 2nd Light Armored Reconnaissance Company (VW). February 1945—Headquarters with armored scout sections, 1st Light Armored Reconnaissance Company (VW), 2nd Light Armored Reconnaissance Company (VW), 3rd Light Armored Reconnaissance Company (VW), 4th Heavy Armored Reconnaissance Company (motorized)

Commanders: Unknown (November 1944–January 1945); *Hauptmann* Pickenhahn (January–April 1945)

Awards: Knight's Cross—*Unteroffizier* Münst, *1./Panzer-Aufklärungs-Abteilung 125* (14 April 1945); *Hauptmann* Wiedemann, *Panzer-Aufklärungs-Abteilung 125* (25 January 1945). **Honor Roll (Clasp)**—*Feldwebel* Berning, *3./Panzer-Aufklärungs-Abteilung 125* (1945); *Oberleutnant* Dierlamm, *5./Panzer-Aufklärungs-Abteilung 125* (18 August 1943); *Leutnant* Weis, *Panzer-Aufklärungs-Abteilung 125* (15 October 1943); *Hauptmann* Wiedemann, *Panzer-Aufklärungs-Abteilung 125* (27 March 1943). **German Cross in Gold**—*Feldwebel* Bussinger, *1./Panzer-Aufklärungs-Abteilung 125* (23 April 1944); *Oberfeldwebel* Dorn, *2./Panzer-Aufklärungs-Abteilung 125* (3 August 1943); *Hauptmann* Harneit, *Panzer-Aufklärungs-Abteilung 125* (30 December 1943); *Obergefreiter* Herzog, *2./Panzer-Aufklärungs-Abteilung 125* (3 August 1943); *Hauptmann* Irion, *3./Panzer-Aufklärungs-Abteilung 125* (3 August 1943); *Oberleutnant* Steinkirchner, *1./Panzer-Aufklärungs-Abteilung 125* (3 August 1943); *Obergefreiter* Strohmayr, *Panzer-Aufklärungs-Abteilung 125* (7 October 1943); *Oberfeldwebel* Vogelsang, *3./Panzer-Aufklärungs-Abteilung 125* (4 July 1943)

25. PANZER-DIVISION

Campaigns: Soviet Union

Reconnaissance Formations:

- ***Kradschützen-Bataillon 87***

Activated: 11 October 1942

Antecedent Formations: Formed from *III./Panzergrenadier-Regiment 146* of the division.

Replacement Detachment: *Kradschützen-Ersatz-Bataillon 6*

Deactivation/Redesignation: *Panzer-Aufklärungs-Abteilung 25* on 7 April 1943

Organization: November 1942—Headquarters, 2nd Motorcycle Infantry Company, 3rd Motorcycle Infantry Company, 4th Motorcycle Infantry Company, and 5th Company (heavy) (motorized). February 1943—1st Armored Scout Company, 2nd Motorcycle Infantry Company, 3rd Motorcycle Infantry Company, 4th Motorcycle Infantry Company, and 5th Company (heavy) (motorized)

Commanders: *Oberstleutnant* Eschenbach (March–7 April 1943)

Notes: Referred to as *Kradschützen-Bataillon "Rheinsberg"* until 5 November 1942. In February a newly formed armored scout company, raised by Military District VI, was assigned to the battalion and designated as its 1st Company.

- ***Panzer-Aufklärungs-Abteilung 25 (first iteration)***

Activated: 7 April 1943

Antecedent Formation: *Kradschützen-Bataillon 87*

Replacement Detachment: *Panzer-Aufklärungs-Ersatz-Abteilung 6*

Deactivation/Redesignation: Effectively destroyed February 1944

Organization: April 1943—Headquarters, 1st Armored Scout Company, 2nd Armored Reconnaissance Company (*Krad*), 3rd Armored Reconnaissance Company (*Krad*), 4th Armored Reconnaissance Company (*Krad*), and 5th Company (heavy) (motorized). August 1943—Headquarters with heavy armored scout platoon, 1st Armored Scout Company, 2nd Armored Scout Company (*VW-Schwimmwagen*),[1] 3rd Light Armored Reconnaissance Company (half-track), 4th Armored Reconnaissance Company (*Krad*), and 5th Heavy Armored Reconnaissance Company (motorized)

Commanders: *Oberstleutnant* Eschenbach (7 April–25 December 1943); *SS-Obersturmführer* Prix (acting) (25–28 December 1943); *Hauptmann* Guderian (acting) (28 December 1943–?)

Notes: In August, orders were received to send the 2nd Company to the Senne Training Area for reorganization as a Type "C" Armored Scout Company. The process was directed to be completed by 20 October, along with the establishment of a heavy armored scout platoon for the battalion. In September, the 3rd Company was ordered to reorganize and redesignate as an armored reconnaissance company equipped with half-tracks, while the 4th Company was to be equipped with the *Volkswagen*. The organization chart for October 1943 shows some variance to what is listed for August. The battalion theoretically had two armored scout companies (one armored car and one half-track), two motorcycle infantry companies, and a heavy company (motorized). Training was hampered in late 1943 by the delay in receiving authorized equipment. The unusual situation of acting command of the battalion by an SS officer was probably prompted by the attachment of the battalion to *SS-Kampfgruppe "Weiß"* and the battalion's separation from its parent division at the time a new commander was needed.

- ***Panzer-Aufklärungs-Abteilung 25 (second iteration)***

Activated: August 1944

Antecedent Formations: *Panzer-Aufklärungs-Abteilung 25*

Replacement Detachment: *Panzer-Aufklärungs-Ersatz-Abteilung 6*

Deactivation/Redesignation: May 1945

Organization: November 1944—Headquarters with light armored scout sections, 2nd Light Armored Reconnaissance Company (half-track), 3rd Light Armored Reconnaissance Company (half-track), and 4th Heavy Armored Reconnaissance Company (half-track). March 1945—Headquarters, 1st Armored Reconnaissance Company (half-track and bicycle), 2nd Armored Reconnaissance Company (VW), 3rd Antiarmor Company (motorized)[30]

Commanders: *Major* Hoppe (August–September 1944); *Hauptmann* Aicher (October 1944–January 1945); *Hauptmann* Brezenthal (acting) (January–April 1945)

Notes: In some respects this is only a delayed reconstitution, since efforts were underway since early 1944 to rebuild the division after its disastrous debut on the Eastern Front. Every time the division was brought up to some semblance of its authorized organization, it was stripped of personnel and equipment to help build other formations. The battalion proper was ordered reconstituted in orders dated 25 July 1944 at the Wildflecken Training Area. There was to be no Type "C" armored scout company. The personnel were ordered to report there by the middle of August. At the end of August, the battalion was ordered to rejoin the divisional *Kampfgruppe* in the East. The battalion was used to help quell the Warsaw Uprising. By September, the battalion was at nearly full strength, minus a Type "C" armored scout company. Orders were issued for the 1st Company to be formed at Wildflecken, with a completion date set for 1 November 1944.

26. PANZER-DIVISION

Campaigns: Italy

Reconnaissance Formations:

- ***Kradschützen-Bataillon 26***

Activated: 15 September 1942

Antecedent Formations: Formed from reassignment, redesignation and reorganization of *Radfahr-Abteilung 23* of *23. Infanterie-Division*. The 1st and 2nd Companies were activated for the battalion, source unknown.

Replacement Detachment: *Kradschützen-Ersatz-Bataillon 3*

Deactivation/Redesignation: *Panzer-Aufklärungs-Abteilung 26* on1 April 1943

Organization: 1943—Headquarters, 1st Armored Scout Company, 2nd Light Armored Reconnaissance Company (half-track), 3rd Armored Reconnaissance Company (half-track), 4th Armored Reconnaissance Company (half-track), and 5th Heavy Armored Reconnaissance Company (half-track)

Commanders: *Major Freiherr* von Ruepprecht (15 September 1942–1 April 1943)

- ***Panzer-Aufklärungs-Abteilung 26***

Activated: 1 April 1943

Antecedent Formations: *Kradschützen-Bataillon 26*

Replacement Detachment: *Panzer-Aufklärungs-Ersatz-Abteilung 3*

Deactivation/Redesignation: May 1945

Organization: 1943–44—Headquarters, 1st Armored Scout Company, 2nd Light Armored Reconnaissance Company (half-track), 3rd Armored Reconnaissance Company (half-track), 4th Armored Reconnaissance Company (half-track), and 5th Heavy Armored Reconnaissance Company (half-track). 1945—Headquarters with armored scout sections, 1st Armored Scout Company (half-track), 2nd Light Armored Reconnaissance Company (half-track), 3rd Armored Reconnaissance Company (half-track), and 4th Heavy Armored Reconnaissance Company (half-track)

Commanders: *Major Freiherr* von Ruepprecht (1 April–11 September 1943); *Oberleutnant* Aberl (acting) (11 September–2 October 1943); *Rittmeister* Klemme (4 October–10 December 1943); *Oberleutnant* Aberl (acting) (10 December 1943–21 January 1944); *Major* Heraucourt (21 January–May 1944); *Oberleutnant* Beyer-Fehling (acting) (May–12 June 1944); *Oberleutnant* Schepple (acting) (12 June–17 July 1944); *Rittmeister/Major* Strauch (July 1944–March 1945); *Hauptmann* Stracke (March–2 May 1945)

Notes: Orders received on 26 December 1943 to send the 4th Company to the Senne Training Area for reorganization. In January, orders dictated a conversion to a Type "C" Armored Scout Company, with a completion of the process set for six weeks. For some reason, the company was not ordered to rejoin the battalion until September 1944.

Awards: Knight's Cross—*Oberleutnant* Schepple, *Panzer-Aufklärungs-Abteilung 26* (27 July 1944). **Honor Roll (Clasp)**—*Oberleutnant* Beyer-Fehling, *5./Panzer-Aufklärungs-Abteilung 26* (7 September 1944); *Hauptmann* Ettling, *Panzer-Aufklärungs-Abteilung 26* (15 February 1945); *Rittmeister* Klemme, *Panzer-Aufklärungs-Abteilung 26* (27 January 1944); *Leutnant* Wiersing, *3./Panzer-Aufklärungs-Abteilung 26* (5 September 1944). **German Cross in Gold**—*Rittmeister* Strauch, *Panzer-Aufklärungs-Abteilung 26* (27 January 1945); *Hauptmann* Wübbens, *Panzer-Aufklärungs-Abteilung 26* (24 April 1944)

27. PANZER-DIVISION

Campaigns: Soviet Union

Reconnaissance Formations:

- ***Panzer-Aufklärungs-Kompanie 127***

Activated: November 1942

Antecedent Formations: Formed by *Kradschützen-Ersatz-Bataillon 4*

Replacement Detachment: *Kradschützen-Ersatz-Bataillon 4*

Deactivation/Redesignation: February 1943

Organization: 1943—no details, presumably a light armored reconnaissance company

Commanders: *Hauptmann* Fürbringer (December 1942–15 February 1943)

Notes: Division was essentially an *ad hoc* formation formed out of *Kampfgruppe Michalik*, which was the remnant of *22. Panzer-Division*. It is uncertain where this armored reconnaissance company was reassigned upon the disbanding of the "division" in February 1943.

29. INFANTERIE-DIVISION (MOT)

Campaigns: Poland, France, Soviet Union

Reconnaissance Formations:

- ***Aufklärungs-Abteilung 29 (mot)***

Activated: 10 October 1937

Antecedent Formations: Unknown.

Replacement Detachment: Unknown

Deactivation/Redesignation: *Kradschützen-Bataillon 29* at the beginning of June 1942

Organization: 1939–40—Headquarters, 1st Armored Scout Troop, and 2nd Motorcycle Infantry Troop.

1941—Headquarters, 1st Armored Scout Troop, 2nd Motorcycle Infantry Troop, and 3rd Troop (Heavy)

Commanders: *Oberstleutnant* Pochat (1 September 1939–1 November 1940); *Major* von Blomberg (1 November 1940–June 1941); *Hauptmann* Schule-Ingenohl (June–July 1941); *Hauptmann* von Goerne-Plaue (July–September 1941); *Hauptmann* Gerecht (to 28 March 1942); *Hauptmann* von Mutius (28 March–June 1942)

Notes: Did not receive a heavy troop until after the campaign in the West

• ***Kradschützen-Bataillon 29***

Activated: 25 February 1941

Antecedent Formations: Formed from the reassignment, reorganization, and redesignation of *4.* and *7./Infanterie-Regiment 15 (mot)* and *2.* and *7./Infanterie-Regiment 71 (mot)*, both of the division

Replacement Detachment: Unknown

Deactivation/Redesignation: Effectively destroyed by 31 January 1943 (Stalingrad)

Organization: 1941—Headquarters, 1st Motorcycle Infantry Company, 2nd Motorcycle Infantry Company, 3rd Motorcycle Infantry Company, 4th Motorcycle Infantry Machine Gun Company, and 5th Company (heavy). June 1942—Headquarters, 1st Armored Scout Company, 2nd Motorcycle Infantry Company, 3rd Motorcycle Infantry Company, 4th Motorcycle Infantry Company, and 5th Company (heavy) (motorized)

Commanders: *Major* Grundmann (February–July 1941); *Major* Engel (July–August 1941); *Major* Einstmann (August–September 1941); *Hauptmann* Belzer (September 1941–June 1942); *Hauptmann* von Mutius (June 1942–15 January 1943)

Awards: Knight's Cross—*Hauptmann* von Goerne-Plaue, *Aufklärungs-Abteilung 29 (mot)* (20 October 1941); *Oberstleutnant* Pochat, *Aufklärungs-Abteilung 29 (mot)* (5 August 1940). **Honor Roll (Clasp)**—*Oberleutnant* Belzer, *Kradschützen-Bataillon 29* (6 November 1941). German Cross in Gold— *Leutnant* Arnz, *3./Kradschützen-Bataillon 29* (15 November 1942); *Hauptmann* Belzer, *Kradschützen-Bataillon 29* (29 November 1941); *Unteroffizier* Görbing, *2./Kradschützen-Bataillon 29* (14 January 1942); *Oberfeldwebel* Mellem, *4./Kradschützen-Bataillon 29* (5 November 1942); *Hauptmann* von Mutius, *Kradschützen-Bataillon 29* (21 January 1943); *Stabsfeldwebel* Richter, *1./Aufklärungs-Abteilung 29 (mot)* (29 November 1941); *Oberleutnant* Schleipen, *1./Kradschützen-Bataillon 29* (16 February 1942). **Certificate of Recognition from the Commander in Chief of the Army**—*Leutnant* Euler, *2,.K29* (8 March 1942); *Hauptmann* von Mutius, *Kradschützen-Bataillon 29* (5 October 1942).

29. PANZERGRENADIER-DIVISION

Campaigns: Italy

Reconnaissance Formations:

• ***Panzer-Aufklärungs-Abteilung 129***

Activated: 1 April 1943

Antecedent Formations: *Panzer-Aufklärungs-Abteilung 29*, which had been established on 1 March 1943. Formed from remnants of the original *Kradschützen-Bataillon 29* (from Stalingrad) and *Kradschützen-Bataillon 345* of *345. Infanterie-Division (mot)*

Replacement Detachment: Unknown

Deactivation/Redesignation: 2 May 1945

Organization: 1943—Headquarters, 1st Armored Scout Company, 2nd Armored Scout Company (armored cars and half-tracks), 3rd Armored Reconnaissance Company (half-track), 4th Armored Reconnaissance Company (half-track), and 5th Company (heavy) (half-track). October 1943—Headquarters (with armored car sections), 1st Armored Scout Company (half-track), 2nd Light Armored Reconnaissance Company (half-track), 3rd Light Armored Reconnaissance Company (half-track), and 4th Company (heavy) (half-track)

Commanders: *Hauptmann/Major* Ziegler (1 April 1943–September 1944); *Hauptmann* Schulz (to 2 May 1945)

Notes: Even after movement to Italy, the 1st Armored Scout Company did not have its heavy armored scout platoon and the 2nd Armored Scout Company only had half-tracks. In September 1944, the battalion was reduced to four companies. It is believed that the 1st Armored Scout Company was combined with elements of the division's tank battalion to form *Panzer-Sturm-Kompanie 29* from October 1944 to March 1945. Effective January 1945, the 3rd Armored Reconnaissance Company no longer had any half-tracks.

Awards: Knight's Cross—*Hauptmann* Drexler, *4./Panzer-Aufklärungs-Abteilung 129* (12 January 1945). **Honor Roll (Clasp)**—*Oberleutnant* Drexler, *5./Panzer-Aufklärungs-Abteilung 129* (15 August 1944). **German Cross in Gold**—*Leutnant* Hagedorn, *4./Panzer-Aufklärungs-Abteilung 129* (19 October 1944); *Oberfeldwebel* Kägelitz, *3./Panzer-Aufklärungs-Abteilung 129* (18 December 1944); *Oberfeldwebel* Täuber, *4./Panzer-Aufklärungs-*

Abteilung 129 (26 July 1944); *Major* Ziegler, *Panzer-Aufklärungs-Abteilung 129* (26 September 1944)

36. INFANTERIE-DIVISION (MOT)

Campaigns: Soviet Union

Reconnaissance Formations:

- ***Aufklärungs-Abteilung 36 (mot)***

Activated: 11 November 1940

Antecedent Formations: *Aufklärungs-Abteilung 36 (36. Infanterie-Division)* with *Panzer-Aufklärungs-Abteilung 92* being reassigned and redesignated as the 1st Troop of the battalion

Replacement Detachment: *Aufklärungs-Ersatz-Abteilung 7*

Deactivation/Redesignation: Consolidated with *Kradschützen-Bataillon 36* unofficially in October 1941 and redesignated as *Voraus-Abteilung 36* (36th Advance Guard Battalion) on 7 November 1941

Organization: 1941—Headquarters, 1st Armored Scout Troop, 2nd Motorcycle Infantry Troop, and 3rd Troop (heavy)

Commanders: *Rittmeister/Major* Bronsart von Schnellendorf (1 November 1940–7 November 1941)

- ***Kradschützen-Bataillon 36***

Activated: 9 November 1940

Antecedent Formations: Formed by the reassignment, redesignation, and reorganization of *MG-Bataillon 8*

Replacement Detachment: *Kradschützen-Ersatz-Bataillon 7*

Deactivation/Redesignation: Consolidated with *Aufklärungs-Abteilung 36 (mot)* unofficially and redesignated as *Voraus-Abteilung 36* (36th Advance Guard Battalion) on 7 November 1941. Officially redesignated on 7 November 1941. Redesignated as *Kradschützen-Bataillon 36* on 15 March 1942. Redesignated as *Aufklärungs-Abteilung 36* in April 1943 (conversation of the battalion back to standard infantry reconnaissance formation).

Organization: 1941—Headquarters, 1st Motorcycle Infantry Company, 2nd Motorcycle Infantry Company, 3rd Motorcycle Infantry Company, 4th Motorcycle Infantry Machine Gun Company, and 5th Company (heavy). Disbanded—see *Voraus-Abteilung 36*. 1942—Headquarters, 1st Armored Scout Company, 2nd Motorcycle Infantry Company, 3rd Motorcycle Infantry Company, 4th Motorcycle Infantry Company (?), and 5th Company (heavy). June 1942—Headquarters, 2nd Motorcycle Infantry Company, and 3rd Motorcycle Infantry Company. August 1942—Headquarters, 1st Armored Scout Company, 2nd Motorcycle Infantry Company, 3rd Motorcycle Infantry Company, 4th Motorcycle Infantry Company (?), and 5th Company (heavy)

Commanders: *Major* Freytag (9 November 1940–7 July 1941); Disbanded (7 November 1941–March 1942); *Rittmeister/Major* Bronsart von Schnellendorf (15 March–26 October 1942); *Major* Landerer (26 October 1942–30 April 1943)

Voraus-Abteilung 36

Activated: 7 November 1941

Antecedent Formations: *Kradschützen-Bataillon 36* and *Aufklärungs-Abteilung 36 (mot)*

Replacement Detachment: Unknown (*Kradschützen-Ersatz-Bataillon 7?*)

Deactivation/Redesignation: Redesignated as *Kradschützen-Bataillon 36* on 15 March 1942

Organization: 1941–42—Headquarters, 1st Armored Scout Company, 2nd Motorcycle Infantry Company, 3rd Motorcycle Infantry Company, 4th Motorcycle Infantry Company (?), and 5th Company (heavy)

Commanders: *Rittmeister/Major* Bronsart von Schnellendorf (7 November 1941–15 March 1942)

Awards: Honor Roll (Clasp)—*Hauptmann* Abs, *3./Kradschützen-Bataillon 36* (16 October 1942). **German Cross in Gold**—*Hauptmann* Abs, *3./Voraus-Abteilung 36* (14 February 1942); *Major* Bronsart von Schellendorff, *Kradschützen-Bataillon 36* (24 May 1942); *Unteroffizier* Goltz, *3./Kradschützen-Bataillon 36* (9 October 1942); *Oberleutnant* Lauer, *3./Kradschützen-Bataillon 36* (24 April 1943); *Oberleutnant* Rücker, Headquarters, *Kradschützen-Bataillon 36* (20 November 1942); *Feldwebel* Wirwahn, *3./Kradschützen-Bataillon 36* (24 April 1943)

60. INFANTERIE-DIVISION (MOT)

Campaigns: Balkans, Soviet Union

Reconnaissance Formations:

• ***Aufklärungs-Abteilung 160 (mot)***

Activated: 1 August 1940

Antecedent Formations: Formed from elements of *Aufklärungs-Abteilung 228*, unknown how the 1st Armored Scout Troop was formed.

Replacement Detachment: Military District II

Deactivation/Redesignation: Consolidated with *Kradschützen-Bataillon 160* on 1 April 1942

Organization: April 1940–April 1942—Headquarters, 1st Armored Scout Troop, 2nd Motorcycle Infantry Troop, and 3rd Troop (heavy)

Commanders: *Major* Fabeck (dates unknown)

Notes: The organization chart dated April 1940 already shows the battalion as being motorized and equipped with armored cars.

• ***Kradschützen-Bataillon 160***

Activated: 7 August 1940

Antecedent Formations: Formed by the reassignment, reorganization, and redesignation of *MG-Bataillon 15*, a separate corps-level asset

Replacement Detachment: Unknown

Deactivation/Redesignation: Effectively destroyed in January 1943 (Stalingrad)

Organization: 1940–April 1942—Headquarters, 1st Motorcycle Infantry Company, 2nd Motorcycle Infantry Company, 3rd Motorcycle Infantry Company, 4th Motorcycle Infantry Machine Gun Company, and 5th Company (heavy). April 1942–January 1943—1st Armored Scout Company, 2nd Motorcycle Infantry Company, 3rd Motorcycle Infantry Company, 4th Motorcycle Infantry Company, and 5th Company (heavy)

Commanders: *Oberstleutnant Dr.* Boelsen (July–December 1941)

Notes: Despite its elite status, it is difficult to find exact information on the formations of the division, even after it attained the honorific of *Feldherrnhalle*.[31]

Awards: Honor Roll (Clasp)—*Major* Fabeck, *Aufklärungs-Abteilung 160 (mot)* (28 November 1941); *Leutnant* Teichert, *2./Kradschützen-Bataillon 160* (4 May 1942). **German Cross in Gold**—*Oberleutnant* Behrend, *1./Kradschützen-Bataillon 160* (14 October 1942); *Oberstleutnant Dr.* Boelsen, *Kradschützen-Bataillon 160* (17 November 1941); *Rittmeister der Reserve* Coelle, *2./Aufklärungs-Abteilung 160 (mot)* (1 December 1941); *Oberfeldwebel* Friemelt, *2./Kradschützen-Bataillon 160* (27 October 1942); *Oberfeldwebel* Schöning, *1./Aufklärungs-Abteilung 160 (mot)* (26 December 1941); *Oberleutnant* Teichert, *Kradschützen-Bataillon 160*, 9 July 1942; *Oberfeldwebel* Wolfshausen, *3./Kradschützen-Bataillon 160* (6 November 1942)

90. LEICHTE DIVISION / 90. LEICHTE AFRIKA-DIVISION (MAY 1942)

Campaigns: North Africa

Reconnaissance Formations:: When initially formed as *Afrika-Division z.b.V.* in August 1941, the formation had no organic reconnaissance assets. They were proved on an alternating basis by other divisions in the theater at the time.

• ***gemischte Aufklärungs-Kompanie 580***

Activated: Summer 1941

Antecedent Formations: Formed in Military District III

Replacement Detachment: Uncertain, most likely *Schützen-Ersatz-Abteilung 3*

Deactivation/Redesignation: *Aufklärungs-Abteilung 580 (mot)* in summer 1942

Organization: 1941—Headquarters with half-track, armored scout platoon (light and heavy), light motorized rifle platoon (half-track), antitank platoon (5cm) (towed), and antiaircraft platoon (2cm *Flak 38*). 1942—Headquarters with half-track, armored scout platoon (light and heavy), light armored reconnaissance platoon (half-track), antitank platoon (5cm) (towed), antiaircraft platoon (2cm *Flak 38*), and artillery battery (captured English 8.7cm guns)

Commanders: *Rittmeister* von Homeister (to 23 May 1942)

Notes: It took until almost January 1942 before the final elements of the company arrived, which explains the images seen earlier in the book. They were probably among the last elements to ship out, sometime in the winter of 1941–42. The addition of the four-gun battery on 21 April 1942 was brought about by orders that directed *Artillerie-Abteilung 361* to provide the battery and personnel.[32]

- ***Aufklärungs-Abteilung 580 (Panzer-Aufklärungs-Abteilung 580)***

Activated: 23 May 1942

Antecedent Formations: *gemischte Aufklärungs-Abteilung 580*

Replacement Detachment: *Schützen-Ersatz-Abteilung 3*

Transfer: Reassigned to *21. Panzer-Division* on 26 February 1943

Organization: September 1942—Headquarters, 1st Armored Scout Company with heavy armored scout platoon, 2nd Company (half-track), 3rd Reconnaissance Company (mixed), 4th Battery (captured English 8.7cm guns). October 1942—Headquarters, 1st Armored Scout Company, 2nd Company (mixed—half-track infantry platoon, half-track combat engineer platoon, 3.7cm antitank platoon), 3rd Antitank Company (5cm antitank guns), 4th Battery (captured English 8.7cm guns), 5th Battery (captured English 8.7cm guns), and 6th Antiaircraft Company (2cm?)

Commanders: *Rittmeister* Homeister (23 May–3 July 1942); *Oberleutnant* Steffen (acting) (3–17 July 1942); *Hauptmann* Voß (July 1942–26 February 1943)

Notes: At some point, the battalion was redesignated as a *Panzer-Aufklärungs-Abteilung* while retaining the same organization. Initial (acting) battalion commander was the company commander of *gemischte Aufklärungs-Kompanie 580*. It is not sure when the battalion received the *Sd.Kfz. 233's* authorized for the heavy armored scout platoon by orders dated 15 October 1942 (probably January 1943). The October 1942 organization listed is the actual organization for combat by the battalion during the fighting around El Alamein. During the reconnaissance battalion swap in February 1943, *90. Leichte Afrika-Division* received *Panzer-Aufklärungs-Abteilung 3* of *21. Panzer-Division*.

- ***Panzer-Aufklärungs-Abteilung 3***

Activated: 15 October 1935 (originally assigned to *3. Panzer- Division*; transferred to *5. leichte Division* in January 1941; reassigned to *21. Panzer-Division* on 31 July 1941, when *5. leichte Division* was reorganized and redesignated as the former division)

Antecedent Formations: *Kraftfahr-Abteilung Wünsdorf*

Replacement Detachment: Unknown

Deactivation/Redesignation: Reassigned to *90. leichte Division* on 26 February 1943 and redesignated as *Panzer-Aufklärungs-Abteilung 90*

Organization: July 1942—Headquarters, 1st Armored Scout Company with Platoon (*Sd.Kfz. 233*), 2nd Armored Company (half-track), 3rd Company (heavy), and 4th Battery (captured English 8.7cm guns)

Commanders: *Hauptmann* Voß (February–May 1943)

Notes: It is not certain when the change of command occurred between Everth and Voß, but it most likely occurred when the battalion was transferred to the division.

116. PANZER-DIVISION

Campaigns: Western Europe

Reconnaissance Formations:

- ***Panzer-Aufklärungs-Abteilung 116***

Activated: March 1944

Antecedent Formation: Formed from remnants of *Panzer-Aufklärungs-Abteilung 116* of the decimated *16. Panzer-Grenadier-Division* and personnel levies against *Reserve-Panzer-Aufklärungs-Abteilung 1*

Replacement Detachment: *Reserve-Panzer-Aufklärungs-Abteilung 1*

Deactivation/Redesignation: April 1945 (Ruhr Pocket)

Organization: September 1944—Headquarters with armored scout sections, 1st Armored Scout Company (half-track), 2nd Light Armored Reconnaissance Company (half-track), 3rd Armored Reconnaissance Company (half-track), and 4th Heavy Armored Reconnaissance Company (half-track)

Commanders: *Hauptmann* Zehner (March 1944?–29 July 1944); *Major* Stephan (August 1944–April 1945); *Major* Tebbe (acting) (March 1945); *Hauptmann* Fischer (acting) (March–April 1945)

Awards: Knight's Cross—*Major* Stephan, *Panzer-Aufklärungs-Abteilung 116* (12 January 1945); *Untesoffizier* August Roth, *3./Panzer-Aufklärungs-Abteilung 116* (20 January 1945); *Leutnant* Auert, *2./Panzer-Aufklärungs-Abteilung 116* (28 March 1945); *Feldwebel* Muster, *Panzer-Auf-*

Panzer-Aufklärungs-Abteilung 116

At the beginning of September, the *116. Panzer-Division* received orders to relieve the Local Area Commander for Lüttich (Liège), who had reported being under siege and encircled. The *LXXXI. Armee-Korps* thereupon ordered the division to relieve the German forces entrapped there. As it turned out, the Local Area Commander was already negotiating with American forces for the surrender of the city, but this fact was not known to the German Command and *Panzer-Aufklärungs-Abteilung 116* under *Major* Stephan was sent to relieve the beleaguered city. His firsthand account:

> After a thorough briefing and directives from the division commander and the reorganization of the battle group, we moved out in the direction of Lüttich, advancing through Herve–Micheroux–Flèron–Beyne. The enemy had already occupied the built-up areas outside of Lüttich and was being celebrated as liberators by the Belgians. . . . It was already dark. The streets of the villages we were moving through were decorated with garlands. There were American combat vehicles on both sides of the street that were thoroughly covered with flowers. The soldiers had been briefed to open up with everything they had in case of enemy resistance. The battle group had reached Flèron when it started receiving rifle and machine-gun fire. The lead vehicle replied from its main gun. The firing of that round had such an effect in the victory frenzy that evening—just from the acoustics alone—that the streets and marketplace were swept clean. All of the windows were immediately closed and shuttered, and the flower-laden American vehicles stood there abandoned. Nothing stirred. Only the rattling of the tracks and the howling of the engines disrupted the eerie silence. The battle group was already moving beyond Flèron, when the commander of the reconnaissance battalion received the following radio traffic: "Call off the operation! Encircled German garrison has broken out!" [For the vehicles in the town] it was not possible to turn around in the narrow streets. In an open area outside of the town, the lead elements of the battle group turned around as if on parade. With the engines at full throttle, we reached our line of departure without encountering appreciable enemy resistance. The reconnaissance company brought back twelve flower-bedecked American jeeps as spoils of war.[33]

klärungs-Abteilung 116 (14 April 1945). **Honor Roll (Clasp)**—*Major* Stephan, *Panzer-Aufklärungs-Abteilung 116* (25 December 1944). **German Cross in Gold**—*Major* Stephan, *Panzer-Aufklärungs-Abteilung 116* (23 March 1943). **Close Combat Clasp in Gold**—*Stabsgefreiter* Alois Dornoff, *2./Panzer-Aufklärungs-Abteilung 116* (12 January 1944); *Unteroffizier* August Roth, *4./Panzer-Aufklärungs-Abteilung 116* (12 January 1944); *Unteroffizier* Erwin Weckmann, *2./Panzer-Aufklärungs-Abteilung 116* (2 March 1944)

164. LEICHTE DIVISION / 164. LEICHTE AFRIKA-DIVISION

Campaigns:

Reconnaissance Formations:

- ***Aufklärungs-Abteilung 220 (mot)***

Activated: 15 February 1942

Antecedent Formations: *Aufklärungs-Abteilung 220*

Replacement Detachment: Unknown

Deactivation/Redesignation: *Panzer-Aufklärungs-Abteilung 220* on 10 October 1942

Organization: 1942—Headquarters, 1st Armored Scout Company, 2nd Motorized Rifle Company (half-track), and 3rd Company (heavy). September 1942—Headquarters, 1st Armored Scout Company with heavy armored scout platoon, 2nd Light Rifle

Company (half-track), 3rd Mixed Company (combat engineers and heavy antitank guns), and 4th Artillery Battery (captured English 8.7cm guns)

Commanders: Rittmeyer?

- ***Panzer-Aufklärungs-Abteilung 220***

Activated: 10 October 1942

Antecedent Formations: *Aufklärungs-Abteilung 220 (mot)*

Replacement Detachment: Unknown

Deactivation/Redesignation: *Panzer-Aufklärungs-Abteilung 164* on 29 April 1943

Organization: 1942—Headquarters, 1st Armored Scout Company with heavy armored scout platoon, 2nd Light Rifle Company (half-track), 3rd Mixed Company (combat engineers and heavy antitank guns), and 4th Artillery Battery (captured English 8.7cm guns)

Commanders: Unknown

- ***Panzer-Aufklärungs-Abteilung 164***

Activated: 29 April 1943

Antecedent Formations: *Panzer-Aufklärungs-Abteilung 220*

Replacement Detachment: Unknown

Deactiviation/Redesignation: May 1943 (capitulation in Tunisia)

Organization: 1943—Headquarters, 1st Armored Scout Company with heavy armored scout Platoon, 2nd Light Rifle Company (half-track), 3rd Mixed Company (combat engineers and heavy antitank guns), and 4th Artillery Battery (captured English 8.7cm guns)

Commanders: Unknown

Notes: An organization chart from 1943 shows no 1st Company.

PANZER-LEHR-DIVISION

Campaigns: Western Front

Reconnaissance Formations:

- ***Panzer-Aufklärungs-Lehr-Abteilung 130***

Activated: 21 January 1944 (4 April 1944 for *Panzer-Aufklärungs-Lehr-Abteilung 130*)

Antecedent Formations: *Panzertruppenschule II Krampnitz* (schoolhouse instructional battalion)

Replacement Detachment: *Aufklärungs-Ersatz-Abteilung 4*

Deactivation/Redesignation: April 1945 (Ruhr Pocket)

Organization: June 1944—Headquarters, 1st Armored Scout Company, 2nd Armored Scout Company (half-track), 3rd Light Armored Reconnaissance Company (half-track), 4th Light Armored Reconnaissance Company (half-track), and 5th Heavy Armored Reconnaissance Company (half-track)

Commanders: *Hauptmann* Hübner (dates unknown); *Major* von Fallois (February 1944); *Oberleutnant* Werren (acting) (February 1944); *Major* von Fallois (February–24 December 1944)

Notes: In August 1944, after the fighting in Normandy, the battalion had been reduced to approximately 150 men and 8 armored cars. In September, the battalion was consolidated with *Panzer-Aufklärungs-Abteilung 520* as part of its reconstitution.[34] Part of the battalion escaped the pocket and withdrew to the east, where it became *Kampfgruppe von Fallois* and attached to *9. Panzer-Division.*

Awards: Knight's Cross—*Oberfeldwebel* Keichel, *1./Panzer-Aufklärungs-Lehr-Abteilung 130* (18 January 1945); *Major* von Fallois, *Panzer-Aufklärungs-Lehr-Abteilung 130* (29 January 1945)

An *Sd.Kfz. 221* with the distinctive *Lehr* insignia visible on the left front fender. Snow chains have been outfitted—perhaps this was a test of winter driving capabilities.

This appears to be a prototype for the reconnaissance version of the light armored personnel carrier, the *Sd.Kfz. 250/9*. This vehicle has a body style previously unseen but similar to what is usually called *alt* ("old") for the 250 series of vehicles. References indicate that testing on the *Sd.Kfz. 250/9* did not begin until 1942. Also obvious in these photographs is the failure of the front axle. This was a common design defect in the 250 series of half-tracks, which was never completely corrected.

The differences are clear in the *neu* (new) version seen here in service with *Panzer-Aufklärungs-Abteilung 2* of *2. Panzer-Division* in Normandy in 1944. The vehicles were also called *Cäsar* (Caesar) vehicles because they outfitted the Type "C" armored scout company. (*Cäsar* was the alphanumeric used to denote the letter "c.") MICHAEL H. PRUETT

The crews assigned to escort the *Führer* prior to the start of the war and into the campaign in Poland have gathered for a group portrait in front of their *Sd.Kfz. 222* armored cars. These men were detached from the *Aufklärungs-Lehr-Abteilung (mot)* for this duty and wore the distinctive *Führerhauptquartier* sleeve band (it was only supposed to be lightly tacked on to the sleeve of the uniform so it could be easily removed while not performing escort duties).

Another view of the *Karlsruhe* seen on the previous page.

MICHAEL H. PRUETT

This scout wears a cut-down field blouse with *Totenkopf* collar tabs applied, a style that seemed to come into favor in 1944.

MICHAEL H. PRUETT

This scout poses proudly atop his *Sd.Kfz. 222* in an unidentified German-speaking town. The temporary nature of the *Führerhauptquartier* sleeve band can clearly be seen, as well as Hitler's parked touring car in the background.

Even though Geller was awarded the *Afrika* campaign sleeve band, it was not present among his artifacts. Instead, his *Afrikakorps* service sleeve band, the one he would have worn while assigned duties in the field in North Africa, was present.

Left: Wilhlem Geller was a career NCO who started his service with *Aufklärungs-Abteilung 3 (mot)* in the late 1930s. He later served in Africa with *Panzer-Aufklärungs-Abteilung 3* and was evacuated from the theater long enough to miss the capitulation of his battalion there in May 1943. Like many of his comrades who did not surrender, he was reassigned to *Panzer-Aufklärungs-Lehr-Abteilung*, with many of those soldiers ultimately being transferred to *Panzer-Aufklärungs-Abteilung 21* of *21. Panzer-Division*, even though the "new" version of the division had little to do with the old, except for its designation.

PANZER-DIVISION BERGEN

PANZER-DIVISION CLAUSEWITZ

PANZER-DIVISION DOEBERITZ / HOLSTEIN / SCHLESIEN

PANZER-DIVISION JUETERBOG

PANZERGRENADIER-DIVISION KURMARK / PANZER-DIVISION KURMARK

PANZER-DIVISION MUENCHEBERG

PANZER-DIVISION TATRA / 232. PANZER-DIVISION

233. PANZER – DIVISION

All formed in late February 1945 or later, these formations, if they existed at all, were divisions in name only. None had any discernible reconnaissance assets, with the exception of *Panzer-Division Clausewitz* and *Panzer-Division Müncheberg*, which both had about a company's worth of reconnaissance assets.

GROSSDEUTSCHLAND FORMATIONS

WACH-BATAILLON BERLIN

INFANTERIE-REGIMENT "GROSSDEUTSCHLAND" (12 JUNE 1939)

INFANTERIE-REGIMENT "GROSSDEUTSCHLAND" (MOT) (1 OCTOBER 1939)

INFANTERIE-DIVISION "GROSSDEUTSCHLAND" (12 MARCH 1942)

PANZERGRENADIER-DIVISION GROSSDEUTSCHLAND (19 MAY 1943)

Campaigns: France, Balkans, Soviet Union

Reconnaissance Formations:

- ***Kradschützen-Bataillon "Großdeutschland"***

Activated: 1 March 1942

Antecedent Formations: Motorcycle infantry company and armored scout platoon from *V./Infanterie-Regiment "Großdeutschland" (mot)*, with the armored scout company coming from elements of both *1.* and *2./Aufklärungs-Abteilung 92* of *20. Panzer-Division*.

Replacement Detachment: *Ersatz-Brigade "Großdeutschland"*

Deactivation/Redesignation: *Panzer-Aufklärungs-Abteilung "Großdeutschland"* on 4 January 1943

Organization: September 1942—Headquarters, 1st Armored Scout Company, 2nd Light Armored Reconnaissance Company (half-track), 3rd Armored Reconnaissance Company (VW), 4th Armored Reconnaissance Company (VW), and 5th Company (heavy) (motorized)

Commanders:) *Major* von Usedom (1 April–29 July 1942); *Major* Wätjen (July 1942–4 January 1943)

Notes: In April 1940, the 5th Battalion of the regiment was structured as a heavy battalion and had a motorcycle infantry company and an armored scout platoon with seven armored cars (organization charts from November 1940 and February 1941 show the same organization).

- ***Panzer-Aufklärungs-Abteilung "Großdeutschland"***

Activated: 14 January 1943

Antecedent Formations: *Kradschützen-Bataillon "Großdeutschland"*

Replacement Detachment: *Panzergrenadier-Ersatz- und Ausbildungs-Brigade "Großdeutschland"*

Organization: February 1944—Headquarters, 1st Armored Scout Company, 2nd Armored Reconnaissance Company (half-track), 3rd Armored Reconnaissance Company (VW), 4th Armored Reconnaissance Company (VW), and 5th Heavy Armored Reconnaissance Company (motorized). June 1944—Headquarters with armored scout sections, 1st Armored Scout Company (Type "B"), 2nd Light Armored Reconnaissance Company (half-track), 3rd Armored Reconnaissance Company (half-track), and 4th Heavy Armored Reconnaissance Company (half-track)

Commanders: *Major* Wätjen (14 January–4 September 1943); *Rittmeister* Spaeter (acting commander) (4 September–18 October 1943); *Major* Wätjen (18 October 1943–12 November 1943); *Major* von Schkopp (20 November 1943–8 June 1944); *Rittmeister* von Plathen (acting) (7–13 June

The *Sd.Kfz. 140/1*—also known as the *Aufklärungspanzer 38(t)*—was produced in limited quantities and known to be issued to only two operational units: *Panzer-Aufklärungs-Abteilung "Großdeutschland"* and *Panzer-Aufklärungs-Abteilung 3* of *3. Panzer-Division*. These two images of the vehicle are from an enemy vehicle collection point near the end of the war or shortly thereafter. AKIRA TAKIGUCHI

1944); *Rittmeister* Schroedter (acting) (14–21 June 1944); *Rittmeister Freiherr* von Gienanth (acting) (21 June–16 August 1944); *Rittmeister* Schroedter (August 1944–mid-March 1945); *Rittmeister* Seele (acting) (March–10 April 1945); *Rittmeister* Düvel (acting) (17 April–May 1945)

Notes: On 9 February 1944, orders were received directing the establishment of a new 4th Company at the Senne Training Area. Orders were also received that same day directing that the battalion's heavy company undergo a battlefield reconstitution in the rear area of *Heeresgruppe Süd* to be reorganized as a heavy armored reconnaissance company (half-track). Later in the month, on 19 February, the 3rd Company was also directed to the Senne Training Area for reconstitution. It was to be structured as an armored reconnaissance company (half-track). It received orders on 10 March transferring it to the Wildflecken Training Area for the completion of the process. All of those companies had previously been equipped with soft-skinned vehicles. On 13 March, additional orders were received to restructure the 4th Company as a Type "B" armored scout company (*Aufklärungspanzer 38[t]*). By May, the entire battalion was directed to be reconstituted and reorganized under the *freie Gliederung* concept. It was given until 10 June to complete the process and, by the end of June, the 2nd, 3rd and 4th Companies were heading eastward to rejoin the division. From 7 June 1944 until the end of the war, the battalion went through five commanders or acting commanders, of which three were killed in action (von Plathen, von Gienanth, and Seele) and one had to relinquish command due to wounds (Schroedter). (Schroedter was in command twice, once as an acting commander and once as the official commander.)

Awards: Knight's Cross—*Oberwachtmeister* Kessel, *3./Panzer-Aufklärungs-Abteilung "Großdeutschland"* (23 February 1944); *Obergefreiter* Maaz, *3./Panzer-Aufklärungs-Abteilung "Großdeutschland"* (4 October 1944); *Rittmeister* Spaeter, *2./Panzer-Aufklärungs-Abteilung "Großdeutschland"* (28 July 1943); *Major* Wätjen, *Panzer-Aufklärungs-Abteilung "Großdeutschland"* (14 April 1943)

PANZERGRENADIER-DIVISION BRANDENBURG

Campaigns: Eastern Front

Reconnaissance Formations:

- ***Panzer-Aufklärungs-Abteilung "Brandenburg"***

Activated: 13 September 1944

Antecedent Formations: Formed from other *Brandenburg* elements.

Replacement Detachment: *Panzergrenadier-Ersatz- und Ausbildungs-Brigade "Großdeutschland"?*

Deactivation/Redesignation: May 1945

Organization: September 1944—Headquarters with armored scout platoons, 1st Armored Scout Company (half-track), 2nd Light Armored Reconnaissance Company (half-track), 3rd Armored Reconnaissance Company (half-track), and 5th Heavy Armored Reconnaissance Company (half-track)

Commanders: Unknown

Notes: Battalion forming at Wildflecken Training Area in October 1944. Not known whether it reached anything approaching the organizational model under which it was established. To be the second division of *Panzer-Korps "Großdeutschland."*

FÜHRER-BEGLEIT-DIVISION

Campaigns: Western Europe, Eastern Front

Reconnaissance Formations:

- ***Panzer-Späh-Kompanie 101***

Activated: 24 January 1945

Antecedent Formations: Armored Scout Company in the *Führer-Begleit-Brigade*

Replacement Detachment: *Panzergrenadier-Ersatz- und Ausbildungs-Brigade "Großdeutschland"?*

Deactivation/Redesignation: *Führer-Panzer-Späh-Kompanie* on 2 March 1945

Notes: The brigade was designated a division although it essentially retained its old structure.

FÜHRER-GRENADIER-DIVISION

Campaigns: Eastern Front

Reconnaissance Formations:

- ***Panzer-Späh-Kompanie 102***

Antecedent Formations: *17./Führer-Grenadier-Brigade*

Replacement Detachment: *Panzergrenadier-Ersatz- und Ausbildungs-Brigade "Großdeutschland"?*

Deactivation/Redesignation: *Führer-Panzer-Späh-Kompanie 2* on 2 March 1945

Organization: Probably a mixed armored reconnaissance company with armored cars and light half-tracks

Commanders: Unknown.

Notes: The brigade was designated a division although it essentially retained its old structure.

PANZERGRENADIER-DIVISION KURMARK

Campaigns: Eastern Front

Reconnaissance Formations:

- ***Panzer-Aufklärungs-Abteilung 151***

Activated: 31 January 1945?

Antecedent Formations: Formed from personnel levies against *Panzergrenadier-Ersatz- und Ausbildungs-Brigade "Großdeutschland"*

Replacement Detachment: Unknown, presumably *Panzergrenadier-Ersatz- und Ausbildungs-Brigade "Großdeutschland"*

Deactivation/Redesignation: May 1945

Organization: Probably a mixed armored reconnaissance company with armored cars and light half-tracks

Notes: Fought at Küstrin, then probably eliminated in the Halbe Pocket.

FELDHERRNHALLE FORMATIONS

PANZERGRENADIER-DIVISION "FELDHERRNHALLE"

Campaigns: Soviet Union

Reconnaissance Formations:

- ***Panzer-Aufklärungs-Abteilung "Feldherrnhalle"***

Activated: 20 June 1943

Antecedent Formations: *Panzer-Aufklärungs-Abteilung 160* of *60. Panzergrenadier-Division*, which was formed from remnants of *Kradschützen-Bataillon 160*

Replacement Detachment: *Panzer-Aufklärungs-Ausbildungs-Kompanie/Panzertruppen-Ersatz- und Ausbildungs-Abteilung "Feldherrnhalle"* (as of 1 September 1943)

Deactivation/Redesignation: Effectively destroyed in the summer of 1944 (Soviet Operation Bagration)

Organization: October 1943—Headquarters, 1st Armored Scout Company with heavy armored scout platoon, 2nd Armored Scout Company (half-track), 3rd Armored Reconnaissance Company (half-track), 4th Armored Reconnaissance Company (half-track), and 5th Heavy Armored Reconnaissance Company (half-track)

Commanders: *Major* Wallbaum (June–September 1944)

Awards: German Cross in Gold—*Oberfeldwebel* Dahlmeyer, *2./Panzer-Aufklärungs-Abteilung "Feldherrnhalle"* (15 May 1944); *Oberleutnant* Starostzi, *5./Panzer-Aufklärungs-Abteilung "Feldherrnhalle"* (4 February 1944); *Oberfeldwebel* Strunz, *5./Panzer-Aufklärungs-Abteilung "Feldherrnhalle"* (4 February 1944)

When *60. Panzergrenadier-Division* was reconstituted and redesignated as *Panzergrenadier-Division "Feldherrnhalle"* in France in 1943, it held a parade in Nîmes on 23 June. *Sd.Kfz. 222's* from the reconnaissance battalion were used as a backdrop for the reviewing tribune that included local dignitaries, senior officers, and *SA-Obergruppenführer* Jüttner.
JIM HALEY

PANZER-DIVISION "FELDHERRNHALLE"

PANZER-DIVISION "FELDHERRNHALLE 1"

Campaigns: Eastern Front

Reconnaissance Formations:

- ***Panzer-Aufklärungs-Abteilung "Feldherrnhalle"***

Activated: 27 November 1944

Antecedent Formations: *Panzer-Aufklärungs-Abteilung "Feldherrnhalle" of Panzergrenadier-Division "Feldherrnhalle"*

Replacement Detachment: *Panzer-Aufklärungs-Ausbildungs-Kompanie/Panzertruppen-Ersatz- und Ausbildungs-Abteilung "Feldherrnhalle"* (as of 1 September 1943)

Deactivation/Redesignation: Became part of *Panzer-Division "Feldherrnhalle 1"* when the division was redesignated and reorganized in March 1945 and redesignated as *Panzer-Aufklärungs-Abteilung "Feldherrnhalle 1"*

Organization: Uncertain, with probably only one company of the division operational by 1945.

Commanders: Unknown

Notes: The battalion was at the Wildflecken Training Area at the end of November 1944. It was ordered to reconstitute and be ready for deployment by 30 December. The 2nd Company became trapped in Budapest in the fighting there in December 1944. The division was effectively destroyed again in February 1945, when the encircled forces failed to break out and relief efforts failed. On 28 February, orders were issued to reconstitute the division, with the Replacement Army being held responsible for the reconstitution of the reconnaissance battalion. It proved impossible to reconstitute the battalion, so the original orders were rescinded and new orders issued on 16 March directing the formation of a *Panzer-Aufklärungs-Kompanie "Feldherrnhalle"* at the Milowitz Training Area. It was directed to complete the process and be equipped with VW's by 30 March. Orders did not arrive until 27 April, however, directing the company to rejoin the division in the area of operations of *Heeresgruppe Mitte*.

PANZER-DIVISION FELDHERRNHALLE 2

See *13. Panzer-Division*.

SS-VERFÜGUNGSTRUPPEN/ WAFFEN-SS

LEIBSTANDARTE SS ADOLF HITLER

INFANTERIE-REGIMENT (MOT) "LEIBSTANDARTE SS ADOLF HITLER"

VERSTÄRKTE "LEIBSTANDARTE SS ADOLF HITLER" (AUGUST 1940)

SS-DIVISION (MOT) "LEIBSTANDARTE SS ADOLF HITLER" (16 JULY 1942)

SS-PANZER-GRENADIER-DIVISION "LEIBSTANDARTE SS ADOLF HITLER" (9 NOVEMBER 1942)

1. SS-PANZER-DIVISION (22 OCTOBER 1943)

Campaigns: Poland, France, Balkans, Soviet Union, Western Front, Eastern Front

Reconnaissance Formations:

- ***15.(Kradschützen)/Infanterie-Regiment (mot) "Leibstandarte SS Adolf Hitler"***

Antecedent Formations: None

Deactivation/Redesignation: *Aufklärungs-Abteilung/verstärkte "Leibstandarte SS Adolf Hitler"* in August 1940

Organization: 1 September 1939–10 May 1940—one motorcycle infantry troop (three light mortars, two heavy machine guns, and nine light machine guns) and one armored scout platoon

Commanders: *SS-Hauptsturmführer* Hofmann (1 September 1939–?); *SS-Hauptsturmführer* Meyer (10 May 1940)

Notes: Organization chart for 15 January 1940 also indicates an armored car section of four medium and four light armored cars. An organization chart for 15 April indicates that the regiment was to have a reconnaissance battalion equivalent, inasmuch as there were two motorcycle infantry troops and one armored scout troop earmarked for a 6th Battalion. There was no heavy troop, however.

- ***Aufklärungs-Sturmbann/verstärkte "Leibstandarte SS Adolf Hitler"***

Activated: August 1940

Antecedent Formations: *15.(Kradschützen)/Infanterie-Regiment (mot) "Leibstandarte SS Adolf Hitler"*

Deactivation/Redesignation: *Aufklärungs-Abteilung/"Leibstandarte SS Adolf Hitler"* in July 1942[35]

Organization: 10 November 1940—1st Motorcycle Infantry Troop, 2nd Motorcycle Infantry Troop, and 3rd Armored Scout Troop. 10 February 1941—1st Motorcycle Infantry Troop, 2nd Motorcycle Infantry Troop, 3rd Armored Scout Troop, and 4th Troop (Heavy)[36]

Commanders: *SS-Sturmbannführer* Meyer (26 July 1940–July 1942)

Notes: The armored scout troop had eight medium and eight light armored cars.

- ***Aufklärungs-Abteilung/"Leibstandarte SS Adolf Hitler"***

Activated: July 1942

Antecedent Formations: *Aufklärungs-Abteilung/verstärkte "Leibstandarte SS Adolf Hitler"*

Deactivation/Redesignation: *SS-Panzer-Aufklärungs-Abteilung 1* on 22 October 1943

Organization: 1 September 1942—1st Armored Scout Company, 2nd Armored Reconnaissance Company (half-track), 3rd Motorcycle Infantry Company, 4th Motorcycle Infantry Company, and 5th Company (heavy) (motorized), with a separate light armored car section reporting to the battalion headquarters.[37] 4 July 1943—1st Armored Reconnaissance Company (VW), 2nd Armored Reconnaissance Company (VW), 3rd Light Armored Reconnaissance Company (half-track), 4th Armored Scout Company, and 5th Heavy Armored Reconnaissance Company (half-track)

Commanders: *SS-Sturmbannführer* Meyer (17 July 1942–13 May 1943); *SS-Sturmbannführer* Knittel (13 May–22 October 1943)

Notes: Retained the same designation and commander when the division was redesignated as *SS-Panzer-Grenadier-Division "Leibstandarte SS Adolf*

Scouts of the *Leibstandarte* undergoing training on the *Sd.Kfz. 222* and *Sd.Kfz. 231 (8 Rad)*, most likely at the Wildflecken Training Area. The scouts do not wear the "Adolf Hitler" cuff titles—typical for recruits and young soldiers who had not yet "paid their dues." The instructors wear the standard "A" of reconnaissance personnel, with one officer wearing a modified army cap with SS insignia applied.

70581

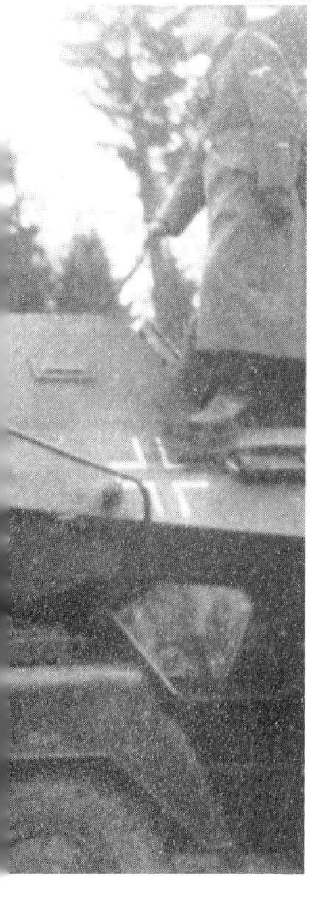

Walter Fielder was a scout who served in three different companies of the reconnaissance battalion of the *Leibstandarte*. BARRY SMITH

Hitler" on 9 November 1942. The organization chart from the *Organizations-Abteilung* dated 1 September 1942 refers to the formation as a *Kradschützen-Bataillon.*

- ***SS-Panzer-Aufklärungs-Abteilung 1***

Activated: 22 October 1943

Antecedent Formations: *Aufklärungs-Abteilung/ "Leibstandarte SS Adolf Hitler"*

Deactivation/Redesignation: May 1945

Organization: 1 May 1944—Headquarters with armored scout sections, 1st Armored Scout Company (half-track), 3rd Light Armored Reconnaissance Company (half-track), 4th Armored Reconnaissance Company (half-track), and 5th Heavy Armored Reconnaissance Company (half-track)

Commanders: *SS-Sturmbannführer* Knittel (22 October 1943–December 1944); *SS-Hauptsturmführer* Wawrzinek (December 1944–); *SS-Obersturmführer* Leidreiter (1 April 1945–); *SS-Hauptsturmführer* Löschnigg (8 May 1945)

Notes: 1st Armored Scout Company (half-track) was apparently still being reconstituted when division moved to Normandy in June 1944. The headquarters company was equipped with the *Sd.Kfz. 234/2* in May 1944.

Awards: Knight's Cross—*SS-Obersturmführer* Bremer, *1.(Kradschützen)/Aufklärungs-Abteilung/verstärkte "Leibstandarte SS Adolf Hitler"* (30 October 1941); *SS-Sturmbannführer* Knittel, *SS-Panzer-Aufklärungs-Abteilung 1* (4 June 1944); *SS-Sturmbannführer* Meyer, *Aufklärungs-Abteilung/verstärkte "Leibstandarte SS Adolf Hitler"* (18 May 1941); *SS-Sturmbannführer* Meyer, *Aufklärungs-Abteilung/"Leibstandarte SS Adolf Hitler"* (23 February 1943) (Oak Leaves); *SS-Obersturmführer* Weiser, *2.(Kradschützen)/Aufklärungs-Abteilung/"Leibstandarte SS Adolf Hitler"* (28 March 1943). **Close Combat Clasp in Gold**—*SS-Unterscharführer* Gilbert, *2./SS-Panzer-Aufklärungs-Abteilung 1* (28 February 1945); *SS-Sturmbannführer* Knittel, *SS-Panzer-Aufklärungs-Abteilung 1* (13 October 1944); *SS-Unterscharführer* Zander, *SS-Panzer-Aufklärungs-Abteilung 1* (28 February 1945). **German Cross in Gold**—*SS-Oberscharführer* Bügelsack, *3.(Panzer-Späh)/Aufklärungs-Abteilung/verstärkte "Leibstandarte SS Adolf Hitler"* (26 December 1941); *SS-Oberscharführer* Gernt, *Stabs-Kompanie/SS-Panzer-Aufklärungs-Abteilung 1* (30 December 1944); *SS-Sturmbannführer* Knittel, *SS-Panzer-Aufklärungs-Abteilung 1* (23 January 1944); *SS-Hauptsturmführer* Kraas, *2.(Kradschützen)/Aufklärungs-Abteilung/verstärkte "Leibstandarte SS Adolf Hitler"* (26 December 1941); *SS-Obersturmführer* Leidreiter, *2./SS-Panzer-Aufklärungs-Abteilung 1* (1 June 1944); *SS-Hauptscharführer* Lindenhahn, *1./Aufklärungs-Abteilung/"Leibstandarte SS Adolf Hitler"* (10 August 1943); *SS-Sturmbannführer* Meyer, *Aufklärungs-Abteilung/verstärkte "Leibstandarte SS Adolf Hitler"* (8 February 1942); *SS-Hauptsturmführer* Olboeter, *5.(schwere)/Aufklärungs-Abteilung/"Leibstandarte SS Adolf Hitler"* (21 March 1943); *SS-Obersturmführer* Reuss, *Stabs-Kompanie/SS-Panzer-Aufklärungs-Abteilung 1* (4 June 1944); *SS-Rottenführer* Sieronski, *1./Aufklärungs-Abteilung/"Leibstandarte SS Adolf Hitler"*; *SS-Obersturmführer* Wawrzikek, *3./Aufk-*

lärungs-Abteilung/"Leibstandarte SS Adolf Hitler" (21 March 1943); *SS-Oberscharführer* Windisch, *1./Aufklärungs-Abteilung/"Leibstandarte SS Adolf Hitler"* (21 March 1943)

DAS REICH

SS-STANDARTEN "DEUTSCHLAND," "GERMANIA," AND *"DER FUEHRER"*

SS-VERFÜGUNGSDIVISION (1 APRIL 1940)

SS-DIVISION "REICH" (21 DECEMBER 1940)

SS-DIVISION "DAS REICH"

SS-PANZER-GRENADIER-DIVISION "DAS REICH" (9 NOVEMBER 1942)

2. SS-PANZER-DIVISION "DAS REICH" (22 OCTOBER 1943)

Campaigns: France, Balkans, Soviet Union, Western Europe, Eastern Front

Reconnaissance Formations:

- ***Kradschützen-Kompanie/SS-Standarte "Deutschland," "Germania" and "Der Führer" and***
- ***Panzer-Späh-Zug/SS-Standarte "Deutschland," "Germania" and "Der Führer"M***

Activated: Late 1930s

Organization: Mid-1930s–1940—one motorcycle infantry troop (three light mortars, two heavy machine guns, and nine light machine guns) and one armored scout platoon

- ***SS-Aufklärungs-Abteilung***
- ***Aufklärungs-Abteilung SS-Division Reich***

Activated: June 1939

Antecedent Formations: *SS-Regiment z.b.V. Ellwangen (SS-Kradschützen-Bataillon I and SS-Kradschützen-Bataillon II)*

Organization: June 1938—Headquarters, 1st Motorcycle Infantry Troop, 2nd Motorcycle Infantry Troop, armored scout platoon, and antitank platoon. May 1940—1st Motorcycle Infantry Troop, 2nd Motorcycle Infantry Troop, 3rd Motorcycle Infantry Troop, 4th Armored Scout Troop, and 5th Troop (heavy). June 1941—1st Armored Scout Company, 2nd Motorcycle Infantry Company, 3rd Company (heavy) (motorized). July 1942—1st Armored Scout Company, 2nd Light Armored Reconnaissance Company (half-track), and 3rd Company (heavy) (motorized) with a light armored scout section reporting directly to the battalion headquarters. July 1943—Headquarters, 1st Armored Scout Company, 2nd Light Armored Reconnaissance Company (half-track), 3rd Armored Reconnaissance Company (VW), 4th Armored Reconnaissance Company (VW), and 5th Heavy Armored Reconnaissance Company (motorized)

Commanders: *SS-Sturmbannführer* von Wangenheim (1938–June 1939); *SS-Sturmbannführer Dr. Ing.* Brandt (June 1939); *SS-Hauptsturmführer* Kment (to February 1942); *SS-Hauptsturmführer* Weiß (dates unknown); *SS-Sturmbannführer* Weidinger (August–22 October 1943)

Notes: The individual *Standarten* retained their motorcycle infantry troops and armored scout platoons during the campaign in the West. By the start of Operation Barbarossa in 1941, the *Deutschland* and *Der Führer* regiments had consolidated their reconnaissance assets into a single company composed of two motorcycle infantry platoons and one armored scout section (two medium and two light armored cars). The *Germania* regiment had been reassigned to the activating *Wiking* division and was replaced by *SS-Infanterie-Regiment 11*, which had a motorcycle infantry company but no armored car assets.

- ***SS-Panzer-Aufklärungs-Abteilung 2***

Activated: 22 October 1943

Antecedent Formations: *Aufklärungs-Abteilung SS-Division Reich*

Deactivation/Redesignation: 9 May 1945

Organization: October 1943—Headquarters, 1st Armored Scout Company, 2nd Light Armored Reconnaissance Company (half-track), 3rd Armored Reconnaissance Company (VW), 4th Armored Reconnaissance Company (VW), and 5th Heavy Armored Reconnaissance Company (motorized). June 1944—Headquarters with armored scout sections, 1st Armored Scout Company (half-track), 2nd Light Armored Reconnaissance Company (half-track), 3rd Armored Reconnaissance Company (half-track), and 4th Heavy Armored Reconnaissance Company (half-track)

The armored car section of *SS-Standarte "Deutschland."* The *Sd.Kfz. 231 (8 Rad)* does well during a parade down a city street, but its counterpart, the *Sd.Kfz. 232 (Fu) (8 Rad)*, needs assistance in getting out of a muddy field. JIM HALEY

Commanders: *SS-Sturmbannführer* Weidinger (22 October 1943–June 1944); *SS-Sturmbannführer* Krag (June 1944–1945); *SS-Hauptsturmführer* Resch (dates unknown)

Notes: The 4th Armored Reconnaissance Company was disbanded in September 1943 and not reestablished until the spring of 1944. When division ordered to France in late 1943 for reconstitution, the divisional battle group initially left behind had one company from the reconnaissance battalion. Because of delays in reconstitution and the late arrival of the battle group from the Eastern Front (April 1944), most of the division did not become involved in the fighting in Normandy until the latter part of June. In July, the battalion headquarters company was dispatched to the Wildflecken Training Area for completion of its reconstitution, reorganization and redesignation (it was the former 1st Armored Scout Company). In January 1945, the headquarters was restructured as a motorized headquarters company, and the 3rd Armored Reconnaissance Company was reconstituted with *Volkswagen* in February 1945. During the fighting in Hungary in 1945, the battalion reported directly to the headquarters of *I. SS-Panzer-Korps* during *Operation Frühlingserwachen*.

- ***Kradschützen-Bataillon SS-Division Reich***

Activated: 20 February 1941

Antecedent Formations: *Kradschützen-Kompanie/SS-Standarte "Deutschland," "Germania" and "Der Führer"*

Deactivation/Redesignation: *I./SS-Regiment (mot) "Langemarck"* on 20 April 1942

Commanders: *SS-Sturmbannführer* Zehender (February 1941); *SS-Hauptsturmführer* Klingenberg (dates unknown); *SS-Hauptsturmführer* Tychsen (to February 1942); *SS-Sturmbannführer* Fick (dates unknown)

Notes: Reassigned and redesignated on 20 April 1942 as part of the relatively short-lived *schnelles Regiment* of the division. Correspondingly, employed more as mobile infantry than reconnaissance assets.

Awards: Knight's Cross—*SS-Sturmbannführer* Fick, *I./SS-Kradschützen-Regiment "Lange-*

This *Sd.Kfz. 231 (8 Rad)* appears to be broken down and has no shortage of "supervisors" willing to offer an opinion. JIM HALEY

The SS scouts in this image cannot be traced to one particular unit, although the time frame appears to be France 1940, thus most likely making them a part of *SS-Verfügungs-Division*. MICHAEL H. PRUETT

The next few images are prewar photographs of armored car assets of the *Standarten—Deutschland*, *Germania*, and *Der Führer*—of the *SS-Verfügungstruppe*. It is thought that because these regiments were initially separate formations not belonging to a division, they were given more combat-support assets than a standard motorized regiment, including a platoon of armored cars. The scouts seen standing in front of their *Sd.Kfz. 221* in this image cannot be linked to a specific unit. MICHAEL H. PRUETT

Scouts take a stretch break and engage in conversation during rest halts. JIM HALEY

Prewar maneuvers of *SS-Standarte "Deutschland."* JIM HALEY

A column of reconnaissance vehicles from *SS-Verfügungs-Division*, most likely in France in 1940. JIM HALEY

marck" (23 April 1943); *SS-Hauptsturmführer* Klingenberg, *2./Kradschützen-Bataillon 2 "Reich"* (14 May 1941); *SS-Sturmbannführer* Krag, *SS-Panzer-Aufklärungs-Abteilung 2 "Das Reich"* (23 October 1944); *SS-Sturmbannführer* Krag, *SS-Panzer-Aufklärungs-Abteilung 2 "Das Reich"* (28 February 1945) (Oak Leaves); *SS-Oberscharführer* Siegling, *1./SS-Panzer-Aufklärungs-Abteilung "Das Reich"* (2 December 1943); *SS-Obersturmführer* Vogt, *2./SS-Aufklärungs-Abteilung/SS-Verfügungs-Division* (4 September 1940); *SS-Sturmbannführer* Weidinger, *SS-Panzer-Aufklärungs-Abteilung 2 "Das Reich"* (21 April 1944); *SS-Hauptsturmführer* Weiß, *SS-Panzer-Aufklärungs-Abteilung 2 "Das Reich"* (6 April 1943). **Honor Roll (Clasp)**—*SS-Sturmmann* Buschner, *1./SS-Kradschützen-Bataillon "Reich"* (28 August 1941); *SS-Unterscharführer* Förster, *1./SS-Kradschützen-Bataillon "Reich"* (28 August 1941); *SS-Rottenführer* Klaiber, *1./SS-Kradschützen-Bataillon "Reich"* (28 August 1941); *SS-Sturmmann* Oldeboerhuis, *1./SS-Kradschützen-Bataillon "Reich"* (28 August 1941); *SS-Oberscharführer* Rambusek, *1./SS-Aufklärungs-Abteilung "Reich"* (18 April 1942); *SS-Sturmmann* Schwenk, *1./SS-Kradschützen-Bataillon "Reich"* (28 August 1941). **German Cross in Gold**—*SS-Hauptscharführer* Brandstätter, *2./SS-Kradschützen-Bataillon 2* (9 April 1943); *SS-Untersturmführer* Hansen, *3./SS-Kradschützen-Bataillon 2* (9 April 1943); *SS-Oberscharführer* Hoff, *4./SS-Panzer-Aufklärungs-Abteilung 2 "Das Reich"* (10 February 1945); *SS-Untersturmführer* Hofmann, *2./SS-Panzer-Aufklärungs-Abteilung 2* (22 March 1945); *SS-Hauptsturmführer* Kämpe, *2./SS-Aufklärungs-Abteilung 2* (11 March 1943); *SS-Hauptsturmführer* Kment, *1./Kradschützen-Bataillon/SS-Division "Reich"* (23 January 1942); *SS-Unterscharführer* Meier, *2./SS-Aufklärungs-Abteilung 2* (24 April 1943); *SS-Hauptsturmführer* Resch, *SS-Panzer-Aufklärungs-Abteilung 2 "Das Reich"* (8 February 1945); *SS-Obersturmführer* Scharfe, *1./Kradschützen-Bataillon 2* (14 April 1943); *SS-Oberscharführer* Scheibler, *1./Kradschützen-Bataillon 2* (9 April 1943); *SS-Untersturmführer* Scherg, *1./SS-Panzer-Aufklärungs-Abteilung 2 "Das Reich"* (8 November 1943); *SS-Untersturmführer* Thaler, *1./SS-Aufklärungs-Abteilung 2* (24 April 1943); *SS-Obersturmführer* Vogt, *2./SS-Aufklärungs-Abteilung "Reich"* (8 February 1942); *SS-Sturmbannführer* Weidinger, *SS-Panzer-Aufklärungs-Abteilung "Das Reich"* (16 November 1943).

TOTENKOPF

SS-TOTENKOPF-STANDARTE

SS-TOTENKOPF-DIVISION (MOT) (16 OCTOBER 1939)

SS-PANZERGRENADIER-DIVISION "TOTENKOPF" (9 NOVEMBER 1942)

SS-PANZER-DIVISION "TOTENKOPF" (21 OCTOBER 1943)

3. SS-PANZER-DIVISION "TOTENKOPF" (22 OCTOBER 1943)

Campaigns: France, Soviet Union

Reconnaissance Formations:

- ***SS-Totenkopf-Aufklärungs-Abteilung***

Activated: October 1939

Deactivation/Redesignation: *SS-Panzer-Aufklärungs-Abteilung 3 "Totenkopf"*

Organization: May 1940—Headquarters, 1st Motorcycle Infantry Troop, 2nd Motorcycle Infantry Troop, and 3rd Troop (heavy) (motorized). June 1941—Headquarters, 1st Motorcycle Infantry Company, 2nd Motorcycle Infantry Company, and 3rd Company (heavy) (motorized). June 1942—Headquarters, 1st Armored Scout Company, 2nd Motorcycle Infantry Company, and 3rd Company (heavy) (motorized). July 1943—Headquarters, 1st Armored Scout Company, 2nd Armored Reconnaissance Company (VW), 3rd Armored Reconnaissance Company (VW), 4th Armored Reconnaissance Company (halftrack), and 5th Heavy Armored Reconnaissance Company (motorized)

Commanders: *SS-Sturmbannführer* Hierthes, *SS-Hauptsturmführer* Grünewälder, *SS-Sturmbannführer* Bestmann (October 1939–spring 1941); *SS-Sturmbannführer* Bestmann, *SS-Hauptsturmführer* Knaack, *SS-Sturmbannführer* Deisenhofer, *SS-Sturmbannführer* Kurtz (summer 1941–autumn 1942); *SS-Hauptsturmführer* Maserie, *SS-Sturmbannführer* Kron, *SS-Hauptsturmführer* Maserie (acting), *SS-Hauptsturmführer* Lönholdt,

SS-Sturmbannführer Kraut, *SS-Obersturmführer* Fürter, *SS-Hauptsturmführer* Berg, *SS-Hauptsturmführer* Säumenicht, *SS-Sturmbannführer* Maserie (November 1942–April 1944)

Notes: The heavy company of the battalion had an armored scout section of four medium and three light armored cars in June 1941. In addition, the divisional regiments each had a motorcycle infantry company. According to some sources, the reconnaissance battalion formed *SS-Regiment (mot) "Thule"* together with the motorcycle infantry battalion sometime in 1943, however, most sources seem to indicate that it was solely the *Kradschützen-Bataillon* that was reorganized by expanding it into a regiment and redesignating it. The large number of commanders obviously includes acting commanders in addition to designated commanders.

- ***SS-Panzer-Aufklärungs-Abteilung 3 "Totenkopf"***

Activated: 22 October 1943

Antecedent Formations: *SS-Totenkopf-Aufklärungs-Abteilung*

Deactivation/Redesignation: May 1945

Organization: October 1943—Headquarters, 1st Armored Scout Company, 2nd Armored Reconnaissance Company (VW), 3rd Armored Reconnaissance Company (VW), 4th Armored Reconnaissance Company (half-track), and 5th Heavy Armored Reconnaissance Company (motorized). June 1944—Headquarters company with armored scout sections, 1st Armored Scout Company (half-track), 2nd Light Armored Reconnaissance Company (half-track), 3rd Armored Reconnaissance Company (half-track), and 4th Heavy Armored Reconnaissance Company (half-track)

Commanders: *SS-Hauptsturmführer* Maserie, *SS-Sturmbannführer* Kron, *SS-Hauptsturmführer* Maserie (acting), *SS-Hauptsturmführer* Lönholdt, *SS-Sturmbannführer* Kraut, *SS-Obersturmführer* Fürter, *SS-Hauptsturmführer* Berg, *SS-Hauptsturmführer* Säumenicht, *SS-Sturmbannführer* Maserie (November 1942–April 1944); *SS-Sturmbannführer* Maserie, *SS-Hauptsturmführer* Zech, *SS-Hauptsturmführer* Keidel, *SS-Sturmbannführer* Pellin, *SS-Hauptsturmführer* Frommhagen, *SS-Sturmbannführer* Pellin, *SS-Hauptsturmführer* Berg, *SS-Hauptsturmführer* Herrmann, *SS-Obersturmführer* Geiger (May 1944–May 1945)

- ***SS-Totenkopf-Kradschützen-Bataillon***

Activated: 6 March 1942

Deactivation/Redesignation: *I.* and *II./SS-Regiment (mot) "Thule"* on 1 August 1942

Organization: June 1942—Headquarters, 1st Motorcycle Infantry Company, 2nd Motorcycle Infantry Company, 3rd Motorcycle Infantry Company, 4th Motorcycle Infantry Machine Gun Company, and 5th Company (heavy) (motorized)

Commanders: *SS-Sturmbannführer* Kleffner, *SS-Hauptsturmführer* Häußler (?) (1942–43)

Notes: As with *SS-Regiment (mot) "Langemarck"* of *Das Reich*, the division's motorcycle infantry battalion was reassigned, redesignated, and reorganized as *I./SS-Regiment (mot) "Thule,"* where it was employed more as mobile infantry than reconnaissance assets. The regiment was also referred to as *SS-Kradschützen-Regiment "Thule"* as well. When disbanded in the spring of 1943, the remaining reconnaissance assets were reassigned to the reconnaissance battalion. The commander of the regiment was *SS-Obersturmbannführer* Lammerding. The commanders of the 1st Battalion are listed above. The commanders of the 2nd Battalion were *SS-Sturmbannführer* Bochmann, *SS-Hauptsturmführer* Deege, and *SS-Hauptsturmführer* Zech.

Awards: Knight's Cross—*SS-Sturmbannführer* Bestmann, *SS-Totenkopf-Aufklärungs-Abteilung* (28 September 1941); *SS-Sturmbannführer* Kleffner, *SS-Totenkopf-Kradschützen-Bataillon* (19 February 1942); *SS-Hauptsturmführer* Maserie, *SS-Panzer-Aufklärungs-Abteilung 3 "Totenkopf"* (3 April 1943); *SS-Unterscharführer* Titschkus, *3./SS-Panzer-Aufklärungs-Abteilung 3 "Totenkopf"* (11 December 1944). **Honor Roll (Clasp)**—*SS-Unterscharführer* Schneider, *5./SS-Totenkopf-Kradschützen-Bataillon* (18 April 1942); *SS-Untersturmführer* Wissebach, *1./SS-Totenkopf-Kradschützen-Bataillon* (18 April 1942). **Close Combat Clasp in Gold**—*SS-Untersturmführer* Schasche, *3./SS-Panzer-Aufklärungs-Abteilung 3 "Totenkopf"* (21 August 1944); *SS-Unterscharführer* Schmidt, *3./SS-Panzer-Aufklärungs-Abteilung 3 "Totenkopf"*. German Cross in Gold—*SS-Hauptsturmführer* Eichert, *2./SS-Totenkopf-Kradschützen-Regiment "Thule"* (14 April

The crew of this *Sd.Kfz. 232 (Fu) (8 Rad)* of *SS-Totenkopf-Aufklärungs-Abteilung* has used the area behind the deflection plate to stow personal items.

Scouts of the *SS-Totenkopf-Aufklärungs-Abteilung* prepare to move out by rail, perhaps to the Eastern Front.

Scouts of the battalion eat rations and take a break. It is interesting to note that in all of the images where armored car personnel can be seen, many of the men appear to be wearing the field-gray version of the special-purpose uniform, even though black would be expected around this time period (estimated 1941–42).

The *Totenkopf* applied to most vehicles of the division can be seen on the left rear portion of the engine compartment of this *Sd.Kfz. 232 (Fu) (8 Rad).*

These images are purported to be of *schnelles SS-Regiment "Thule,"* probably during its activation phase in France in late 1943. The SS was enamored of the *Schwimmwagen* for reconnaissance purposes, leading to the creating of the "fast regiments" in late 1942 in *SS-Panzergrenadier-Divisionen "Das Reich"* and *"Totenkopf."* The problem with large numbers of *Schwimmwagen* on the battlefield was essentially the same as with the motorcycle infantry companies: too much overhead for a small lift capacity per vehicle for a combat mission.

1943); *SS-Hauptsturmführer* Häußler, *I./SS-Totenkopf-Kradschützen-Regiment "Thule"* (9 April 1943); *SS-Obersturmführer* Hammer, *1./SS-Totenkopf-Kradschützen-Regiment "Thule"* (9 April 1943); *SS-Oberscharführer* Henschel, *3./SS-Panzer-Aufklärungs-Abteilung 3 "Totenkopf"* (16 June 1944); *SS-Sturmbannführer* Kurtz, *SS-Totenkopf-Aufklärungs-Abteilung* (20 July 1943); *SS-Standartenführer* Lammerding, *SS-Totenkopf-Kradschützen-Regiment "Thule"* (24 April 1943); *SS-Untersturmführer* Schasche, *3./SS-Panzer-Aufklärungs-Abteilung 3 "Totenkopf"* (19 October 1944); *SS-Unterscharführer* Schubert, *2./SS-Totenkopf-Kradschützen-Regiment "Thule"* (9 April 1943); *SS-Hauptsturmführer* Zech, *SS-Totenkopf-Kradschützen-Regiment "Thule"* (24 April 1943)

WIKING

SS-DIVISION "GERMANIA"

SS-DIVISION "WIKING" (21 DECEMBER 1940)

SS-PANZER-GRENADIER-DIVISION "WIKING" (9 NOVEMBER 1942)

5. SS-PANZER-DIVISION "WIKING" (22 OCTOBER 1943)

Campaigns: Soviet Union
Reconnaissance Formations:

- ***Aufklärungs-Abteilung "Germania"***
- ***Aufklärungs-Abteilung/SS-Division "Wiking" (fall 1942)***

Activated: 20 November 1940 (?)

Antecedent Formations: Unknown, presumably personnel levies against the three assigned regiments of the division (*Germania*, *Westland*, and *Nordland*)

Deactivation/Redesignation: *SS-Panzer-Aufklärungs-Abteilung 5 "Wiking"*

Organization: June 1941–July 1943—1st Armored Scout Company, 2nd Armored Reconnaissance Company (*Krad*), and 3rd Heavy Armored Reconnaissance Company (motorized)

Commanders: *SS-Sturmbannführer* von Reitzenstein (December 1940–April 1942); *SS-Sturmbannführer* Paetsch (April 1942–March 1943); *SS-Hauptsturmführer* Saalbach (March 1943)

- ***SS-Panzer-Aufklärungs-Abteilung 5 "Wiking"***

Activated: 22 October 1943

Antecedent Formations: *Aufklärungs-Abteilung/SS-Division "Wiking"*

Deactivation/Redesignation: May 1945

Organization: October 1943—Headquarters, 1st Armored Scout Company, 2nd Armored Reconnaissance Company (*Krad*), and 5th Heavy Armored Reconnaissance Company (motorized). June 1944—Headquarters Company, 1st Armored Scout Company (half-track), 2nd Light Armored Reconnaissance Company (half-track), 3rd Armored Reconnaissance Company (half-track), and 4th Heavy Armored Reconnaissance Company (half-track)

Commanders: *SS-Hauptsturmführer* Füting (dates unknown); *SS-Hauptsturmführer* Debus (December 1943); *SS-Obersturmbannführer* Hack (June 1944–August 1944); *SS-Sturmbannführer* Wagner (August 1944–March 1945); *SS-Sturmbannführer* Vogt (March–April 1945); *SS-Hauptsturmführer* Oeck (April–May 1945)

Notes: in the spring and early summer of 1944, the reconnaissance battalion was being reconstituted in the Bohemian Training Area. Although armored scout sections were authorized in the June organization charts, the headquarters did not have any armored cars. These were partly compensated by a scout section equipped with Volkswagen.

Awards: Knight's Cross—*SS-Obersturmbannführer* Debus, *SS-Panzer-Aufklärungs-Abteilung 5 "Wiking"* (4 May 1944). **Close Combat Clasp in Gold**—*SS-Obersturmführer* Jira, *3./SS-Panzer-Aufklärungs-Abteilung 5 "Wiking"* (4 December 1943). **German Cross in Gold**—*SS-Obersturmbannführer* Debus, *SS-Panzer-Aufklärungs-Abteilung 5 "Wiking"* (23 January 1944); *SS-Hauptscharführer* Heck, *2./Aufklärungs-Abteilung/SS-Division "Wiking"* (23 January 1942); *SS-Oberscharführer* Hess, *2./Aufklärungs-Abteilung/SS-Division "Wiking"* (3 August 1943); *SS-Obersturmführer* Jira, *3./Aufklärungs-Abteilung/SS-Division "Wiking"* (3 August 1943); *SS-Obersturmführer* Kaufmann, *1./SS-Panzer-Aufklärungs-Abteilung 5 "Wiking"* (10 March 1945); *SS-Hauptscharführer* Lebkücher, *1./SS-Panzer-Aufklärungs-Abteilung 5 "Wiking"* (6 January 1944); *SS-Obersturmführer* Niekamp, *2./SS-Panzer-Aufk-*

lärungs-Abteilung 5 "Wiking" (10 March 1944); *SS-Sturmbannführer* Paetsch, *SS-Panzer-Aufklärungs-Abteilung 5 "Wiking"* (24 April 1943); *SS-Obersturmführer* Schust, *2./SS-Panzer-Aufklärungs-Abteilung 5 "Wiking"* (24 April 1943); *SS-Obersturmführer* Stichnoth, *Stabs-Kompanie/SS-Panzer-Aufklärungs-Abteilung 5 "Wiking"* (10 March 1945)

HOHENSTAUFEN

SS-PANZERGRENADIER-DIVISION 9 (1 FEBRUARY 1943)

SS-PANZERGRENADIER-DIVISION 9 "HOHENSTAUFEN" (1 MARCH 1943)

SS-PANZER-DIVISION "HOHENSTAUFEN" (3 OCTOBER 1943)

9. SS-PANZER-DIVISION "HOHENSTAUFEN" *(22 OCTOBER 1943)*

Campaigns: Soviet Union, Western Europe, Eastern Front

Reconnaissance Formations:

- ***SS-Panzer-Aufklärungs-Abteilung 9 "Hohenstaufen"***

Activated: 22 October 1943

Antecedent Formations: *Kradschützen-Regiment/SS-Panzergrenadier-Division 9*

Deactivation/Redesignation: May 1945

Organization: October 1943—Headquarters Company, 1st Armored Scout Company, 2nd Armored Scout Company, 3rd Armored Reconnaissance Company (half-track), 4th Armored Reconnaissance Company (VW), and 5th Heavy Armored Reconnaissance Company (half-track). June 1944—Headquarters Company with armored scout sections, 1st Armored Scout Company (half-track), 2nd Light Armored Reconnaissance Company (half-track), 3rd Light Armored Reconnaissance Company (half-track), and 4th Heavy Armored Reconnaissance Company (half-track)

Commanders: *SS-Hauptsturmführer* Recke (1943–spring 1944); *SS-Hauptsturmführer* Gräbner (spring–September 1944); *SS-Hauptsturmführer/SS-Sturmbannführer* Recke (September 1944–May 1945)

Notes: In October 1943, orders were issued that the 4th Armored Reconnaissance Company was to be equipped with *Volkswagen*; by January 1944, the *Volkswagen* had been replaced with half-tracks. In February 1945, the 3rd Company was consolidated with the 2nd Company. In March 1945, the 1st Armored Scout Company was disbanded. For most of April 1945, the battalion was attached to *6. Panzer-Division* and engaged in operations with it.

Awards: Knight's Cross—*SS-Hauptsturmführer* Gräbner, *SS-Panzer-Aufklärungs-Abteilung 9 "Hohenstaufen"* (23 August 1944). Honor Roll (Clasp)— *SS-Unterscharführer* Kaiser, *3./SS-Panzer-Aufklärungs-Abteilung 9 "Hohenstaufen"* (25 December 1944). **German Cross in Gold**—*SS-Hauptsturmführer* Büdecker, *4./SS-Panzer-Aufklärungs-Abteilung 9 "Hohenstaufen"* (19 August 1944); *SS-Hauptscharführer* Göttfried, *3./SS-Panzer-Aufklärungs-Abteilung 9 "Hohenstaufen"* (17 September 1944)

FRUNDSBERG

SS-PANZERGRENADIER-DIVISION 10 (1 FEBRUARY 1943)

SS-PANZERGRENADIER-DIVISION "KARL DER GROSSE" (1 JUNE 1943)

SS-PANZER-DIVISION "FRUNDSBERG" *(3 OCTOBER 1943)*

10. SS-PANZER-DIVISION "FRUNDSBERG" *(22 OCTOBER 1943)*

Campaigns: Soviet Union, Western Europe, Eastern Front

Reconnaissance Formations:

- ***SS-Panzer-Aufklärungs-Abteilung 10 "Frundsberg"***

Activated: 22 October 1943

Antecedent Formations: *Kradschützen-Regiment/SS-Panzergrenadier-Division 10*

Deactivation/Redesignation: May 1945

Organization: October 1943—Headquarters, 1st Armored Scout Company, 2nd Armored Scout Company (half-track), 3rd Light Armored Reconnaissance Company (half-track), 4th Light Armored Reconnaissance Company (half-track), and 5th

Heavy Armored Reconnaissance Company (half-track). June 1944—Headquarters Company with armored scout sections, 1st Armored Scout Company (half-track), 2nd Armored Reconnaissance Company (half-track), 3rd Armored Reconnaissance Company (half-track), and 4th Heavy Armored Reconnaissance Company (half-track)

Commanders: *SS-Hauptsturmführer/SS-Sturmbannführer* Brinkmann (1943–45?)

Notes: By September 1944, battalion was only partially motorized and largely foot mobile. Reconstitution in Germany in December 1944, but 3rd Company only on paper as late as 1 January 1945 and 1st Company considered not ready for combat. By February 1945, the 3rd Company was partially ready for combat operations, but the 1st Company had been disbanded (consolidated with the Headquarters Company). In the last half of February, the battalion fought separately from the division. Remnants of the battalion broke out of the Halbe Pocket, crossing the Elbe to surrender to U.S. forces.

Awards: Knight's Cross—*SS-Oberscharführer* Rech, *2./SS-Panzer-Aufklärungs-Abteilung 10 "Frundsberg"* (23 August 1944). **Honor Roll (Clasp)**—*SS-Hauptscharführer* Küffner, *2./SS-Panzer-Aufklärungs-Abteilung 10 "Frundsberg"* (25 August 1944). **German Cross in Gold**—*SS-Obersturmführer* Harmsdorf, *2./SS-Panzer-Aufklärungs-Abteilung 10 "Frundsberg"* (27 October 1944); *SS-Obersturmführer* Hinze, *3./SS-Panzer-Aufklärungs-Abteilung 10 "Frundsberg"* (19 August 1944); *SS-Hauptscharführer* Thomas, *3./SS-Panzer-Aufklärungs-Abteilung 10 "Frundsberg"* (17 September 1944)

NORDLAND

SS-PANZERGRENADIER-DIVISION 11 (GERMANISCH) (10 APRIL 1943)

SS-PANZERGRENADIER-DIVISION "NORDLAND" (APRIL 1943)

11. SS-FREIWILLIGEN-PANZERGRENADIER-DIVISION (NORDLAND) (22 OCTOBER 1943)

Campaigns: Soviet Union, Eastern Front

Reconnaissance Formations:

- ***SS-Panzer-Aufklärungs-Abteilung 11 "Nordland"***

Activated: 22 October 1943

Antecedent Formations: *Kradschützen-Regiment/SS-Panzergrenadier-Division 11*

Deactivation/Redesignation: May 1945

Organization: October 1943—Headquarters, 1st Armored Scout Company, 2nd Armored Scout Company (half-track), 3rd Light Armored Reconnaissance Company (half-track), 4th Light Armored Reconnaissance Company (half-track), and 5th Heavy Armored Reconnaissance Company (half-track)

Commanders: *SS-Obersturmführer/SS-Hauptsturmführer* Saalbach (June 1943–?)

Notes: 1st Armored Scout Company was equipped with *Schwimmwagen* while finishing its activation process in Croatia in late 1943. It did not receive armored cars until employed on the Eastern front. The company only received approximately half of the authorized vehicles (six heavy and four medium armored cars).

Awards: Knight's Cross—*SS-Untersturmführer* Langendorf, *3.(schwere)/SS-Panzer-Aufklärungs-Abteilung 11 "Nordland"* (12 March 1944); *SS-Hauptsturmführer* Saalbach, *SS-Panzer-Aufklärungs-Abteilung 11 "Nordland"* (12 March 1944); *SS-Oberscharführer* Wild, *1./SS-Panzer-Aufklärungs-Abteilung 11 "Nordland"* (21 March 1944); *SS-Unterscharführer* Sprock, *5./SS-Freiwilligen-Panzer-Aufklärungs-Abteilung 11 "Nordland"* (23 October 1944). **Honor Roll (Clasp)**—*SS-Obersturmführer* Erichsen, *4./SS-Panzer-Aufklärungs-Abteilung 11 "Nordland"* (1945); *SS-Obersturmführer* Pehrsson, *3./SS-Panzer-Aufklärungs-Abteilung 11 "Nordland"* (25 December 1944). **German Cross in**

These photos were taken by Ernst Baumann, who is commonly considered an SS war correspondent, but who may not actually have been one. They represent the fielding of *SS-Panzer-Aufklärungs-Abteilung 11 "Nordland"* with the *Sd.Kfz. 250/9, Ausführung A* (the *Cäsar*) for the 2nd Company, which was a Type "C" armored scout company. These were issued to the unit in Croatia in late 1943, when the company was undergoing its final training prior to commitment in the northern part of the eastern front the following January. The field-grade officer seen here is *SS-Sturmbannführer* Hack, who was in Croatia at the same time supervising the train-up for the newly established *SS-Panzer-Regiment 5* headquarters and its 2nd Battalion, as well as *SS-Panzer-Regiment 11*, which eventually became *SS-Panzer-Abteilung 11* and *schwere SS-Panzer-Abteilung 103/503.* Hack apparently took an interest in the training of what would become the *2./SS-Panzer-Aufklärungs-Abteilung 11 "Nordland"* and used the opportunity to familiarize himself with the vehicle. This knowledge was most likely put to good use when Hack commanded *SS-Panzer-Aufklärungs-Abteilung 5 "Wiking"* from June through August 1944. HEINER DUSKE

Before departing, Hack is held up to be given some information by an unidentified SS soldier wearing the iconic SS camouflage in a four-pocket tunic and cap.

Several other vehicles of the company.

The rarely photographed *Panzer II, Ausführung J*, originally developed for scout duties with a production run of less than fifty vehicles, can be seen in the background. It is not known whether the company was issued any of these vehicles or it (and others?) was just lent to the company for training purposes.

More shots of Hack and his vehicle.

WH-1515501

The vehicle maneuvers a bit cross-country before it conducts some target practice in the open countryside.

515501

In addition to preparing for combat deployment, the company was also required to conduct show-of-force missions in an effort to reduce the number of partisan incidents and activities.

The old and the new. The motorized and armored SS vehicles pass a horsedrawn SS artillery battery.

Gold—*SS-Obersturmführer* Langendorf, *5./SS-Panzer-Aufklärungs-Abteilung 11 "Nordland"* (30 March 1945); *SS-Obersturmführer* Lorenz, *1./SS-Panzer-Aufklärungs-Abteilung 11 "Nordland"* (30 December 1944)

HITLERJUGEND

SS-PANZERGRENADIER-DIVISION "HITLERJUGEND" (APRIL 1943)

SS-PANZER-DIVISION "HITLERJUGEND"

12. SS-PANZER-DIVISION "HITLERJUGEND" (22 OCTOBER 1943)

Campaigns: Western Europe, Eastern Front

Reconnaissance Formations:

- ***SS-Panzer-Aufklärungs-Abteilung 12 "Hitlerjugend"***

Antecedent Formations: Cadre personnel drawn from the *Leibstandarte*, augmented by 450 Hitler Youth volunteers from Unna.

Deactivation/Redesignation: May 1945

Organization: October 1943—Headquarters Company, 1st Armored Scout Company, 2nd Armored Scout Company (half-track), 3rd Armored Reconnaissance Company (half-track), 4th Armored Reconnaissance Company (half-track), and 5th Heavy Armored Reconnaissance Company (half-track). June 1944—Headquarters Company with armored scout sections, 1st Armored Scout Company (half-track), 2nd Light Armored Reconnaissance Company (half-track), 3rd Armored Reconnaissance Company (half-track), and 4th Heavy Armored Reconnaissance Company (half-track)

Commanders: *SS-Sturmbannführer* Bremer (October 1943–May 1945)

Notes: In October 1944, the headquarters company was reorganized as a motorized company, and the 1st Armored Scout Company was a mix of both armored cars and halftracks. By November 1944, the battalion had no heavy wheeled armored cars left, although additional deliveries were received by the end of the year. In February 1945, the 1st Company became a pure Type "C" armored scout company again, while the 3rd Company was reorganized with Volkswagen.

Awards: Knight's Cross—*SS-Sturmbannführer* Bremer, *SS-Panzer-Aufklärungs-Abteilung 12 "Hitlerjugend"* (26 November 1944) (Oak Leaves). **German Cross in Gold**—*SS-Sturmbannführer* Bremer, *SS-Panzer-Aufklärungs-Abteilung 12 "Hitlerjugend"* (30 August 1944); *SS-Hauptscharführer* Mahl, *SS-Panzer-Aufklärungs-Abteilung 12 "Hitlerjugend"* (19 August 1944); *SS-Hauptscharführer* Sturm, *3./SS-Panzer-Aufklärungs-Abteilung 12 "Hitlerjugend"* (9 October 1944)

REICHSFÜHRER-SS

SS-PANZER-GRENADIER-DIVISION "REICHSFÜHRER-SS" (3 OCTOBER 1943)

16. SS-PANZERGRENADIER-DIVISION "REICHSFÜHRER-SS"

Campaigns: Italy

Reconnaissance Formations:

- ***SS-Panzer-Aufklärungs-Abteilung 16 "Reichsführer-SS"***

Activated: 22 October 1943

Antecedent Formations: Personnel levies against *Hohenstaufen* for the 2nd and 3rd Companies; 1st Company already formed?

Deactivation/Redesignation: May 1945

Organization: July 1944—Headquarters, 1st Armored Scout Company, 2nd Armored Reconnaissance Company (VW), 2nd Armored Reconnaissance Company (VW), 3rd Armored Reconnaissance Company (VW), and 5th Heavy Armored Reconnaissance Company (motorized)

Commanders: *SS-Sturmbannführer* Maier (November 1943–December 1944); *SS-Hauptsturmführer* Knobelspies (acting) (15–25 October 1944); *SS-Hauptsturmführer/SS-Sturmbannführer* Reder (December 1944–May 1945)

Notes: Apparently, reconnaissance companies initially formed with motorcycles. According to an organization chart for July 1944 (actual status), the 1st Armored Scout Company had no armored cars. The battalion apparently had only *Volkswagen* as reconnaissance vehicles through the end of the war. The Reder listed above is the one involved in the controversial Marzabotto war crimes tribunal after the war in Italy.

Awards: German Cross in Gold—*SS-Obersturmführer* Saalfrank, *5.(schwere)/SS-Panzer-Aufklärungs-Abteilung 16 "Reichsführer-SS"*

GÖTZ VON BERLICHINGEN

17. SS-PANZER-GRENADIER-DIVISION "GÖTZ VON BERLICHINGEN" (15 NOVEMBER 1943)

Campaigns: Western Europe

Reconnaissance Formations:

- ***SS-Panzer-Aufklärungs-Abteilung 17 "Götz von Berlichingen"***

Antecedent Formations: Formed from personnel levies against *Frundsberg*

Deactivation/Redesignation: May 1945

Organization: June 1944—Headquarters, 1st Armored Scout Company, 2nd Light Armored Reconnaissance Company (VW), 3rd Light Armored Reconnaissance Company (VW), 4th Light Armored Reconnaissance Company (VW), and 5th Heavy Armored Reconnaissance Company (motorized)

Commanders: *SS-Obersturmführer* Buck (acting) (24 November–16 December 1943); *SS-Sturmbannführer* Holzapfel (17 December 1943–11 July 1944); *SS-Hauptsturmführer* Mumm (12–14 July 1944); *SS-Hauptsturmführer* Grams (15 July–8 August 1944); *SS-Obersturmführer* von Sternenfels (acting) (9 August–28 September 1944); *SS-Sturmbannführer* Wahl (1 October–21 November 1944); *SS-Sturmbannführer* Linn (22 November–10 December 1944); *SS-Untersturmführer* Papas (acting) (11–24 December 1944); *SS-Sturmbannführer* Wahl (25 December 1944–10 January 1945); *SS-Obersturmführer* Grieger (acting commander) (11–29 January 1945); *SS-Sturmbannführer* Gwodz (30 January–31 March 1945); *SS-Sturmbannführer* Messner (1 April–9 May 1945)

Notes: Apparently no Type "C" armored scout company, with 1st Company having only armored cars (one heavy and three light sections). Remaining companies were outfitted with the *Schwimmwagen*.

Awards: Knight's Cross—*SS-Sturmbannführer* Wahl, *SS-Panzer-Aufklärungs-Abteilung 17 "Götz von Berlichingen"* (1 February 1945) (Oak Leaves); *SS-Untersturmführer* Kuske, *3./SS-Panzer-Aufklärungs-Abteilung 17 "Götz von Berlichingen"* (26 November 1944); *SS-Untersturmführer* Papas. **German Cross in Gold**—*SS-Obersturmführer Dr.* Berger, *SS-Panzer-Aufklärungs-Abteilung 17 "Götz von Berlichingen"* (30 March 1945); *SS-Oberscharführer* Lechner, *3./SS-Panzer-Aufklärungs-Abteilung 17 "Götz von Berlichingen"* (30 March 1945)

HORST WESSEL

18. SS-PANZER-GRENADIER-DIVISION "HORST WESSEL" (25 JANUARY 1944)

Campaigns: Eastern Front

Reconnaissance Formations:

- ***SS-Panzer-Aufklärungs-Abteilung 18 "Horst Wessel"***

Activated: 15 January 1944

Antecedent Formations: Formed from the reorganization and redesignation of *Kradschützen-Kompanie 51 "Reichsführer-SS,"* which had been attached to *1. SS-Infanterie-Brigade*

Deactivation/Redesignation: May 1945

Notes: Apparently no armored cars or half-tracks issued to the battalion

Commanders: *SS-Hauptsturmführer* Sonne (30 January–December 1944); *SS-Hauptsturmführer* von Fehrentheil (December 1944–?); *SS-Hauptsturmführer* Wagner (January 1945–?)

Awards: German Cross in Gold—*SS-Unterscharführer* Hammer, Headquarters, *SS-Panzer-Aufklärungs-Abteilung 18 "Horst Wessel"* (13 January 1945)

LUFTWAFFE

"HERMANN GOERING" FORMATIONS

BRIGADE "HERMANN GOERING" (15 JULY 1942)

DIVISION "HERMANN GOERING" (15 OCTOBER 1942)

PANZER-DIVISION "HERMANN GOERING" (21 MAY 1943)

FALLSCHIRM-PANZER-DIVISION "HERMANN GOERING" (FEBRUARY 1944)

FALLSCHIRM-PANZER-DIVISION "HERMANN GOERING" 1 (OCTOBER 1944)

Campaigns: North Africa, Italy, Eastern Front

Reconnaissance Formations:

- ***Panzer-Aufklärungs Abteilung "Hermann Göring" (15 October 1942)***
- ***Fallschirm-Panzer-Aufklärungs Abteilung "Hermann Göring" (6 January 1944)***
- ***Fallschirm-Panzer-Aufklärungs Abteilung "Hermann Göring" 1 (24 September 1944)***

Antecedent Formations: *10. (Kradschützen-)/Schützen-Regiment "Hermann Göring"* provided the nucleus for the 1st Motorcycle Infantry Company and the 2nd Armored Reconnaissance Company (VW); the 3rd Armored Scout Company was to be formed from the armored car platoon of *13. (Panzer-)/Schützen-Regiment "Hermann Göring"*; the 4th Antitank Company, presumably from *12. (Panzer-jäger-)/Schützen-Regiment "Hermann Göring"*; the 5th Heavy Armored Reconnaissance Company was formed from *8.(schwere)/Schützen-Regiment "Hermann Göring"*; the 6th Antiaircraft Company was formed from *10. (leichte)/Flak-Regiment "Hermann Göring"*

Organization: October 1942—Headquarters, 1st Armored Scout Company, 2nd Armored Scout Company (half-track), 3rd Armored Reconnaissance Company (VW), 4th Armored Reconnaissance Company (VW), 5th Heavy Armored Reconnaissance Company (half-track), and 6th Infantry Gun Company (heavy). November 1943—Headquarters, heavy armored scout platoon (*Sd.Kfz. 233*), 1st Armored Scout Company, 2nd Armored Scout Company (half-track), 3rd Armored Reconnaissance Company (half-track), 4th Armored Reconnaissance Company (VW), and 5th Heavy Armored Reconnaissance Company (motorized). September 1944—Headquarters company with armored scout sections, 1st Armored Scout Company (half-track), 2nd Light Self-Propelled Battery, 3rd Armored Reconnaissance Company (half-track), and 4th Heavy Armored Reconnaissance Company (half-track). February 1945 (unofficial)—Headquarters, 1st Armored Reconnaissance Company (half-track), 2nd Armored Reconnaissance Company (half-track), 3rd Armored Reconnaissance Company (half-track), 4th Heavy Armored Reconnaissance Company (half-track), and 5th Armored Scout Company

Commanders: *Major* Brandenburg (October 1942–May 1943); *Major* Preuss (15 July–August 1943); *Hauptmann* Rebholz (August 1943–February 1944); *Rittmeister* von Loeben (February–May 1944); *Oberstleutnant* Bach (May–1 July 1944); *Major* Roßmann (July 1944); *Hauptmann* Springorum (July–August 1944); *Rittmeister* Köther (August–24 September 1944); *Hauptmann* Fuchs (24 September–October 1944); *Hauptmann* Pautz (October–December 1944); *Hauptmann* Rebholz (December 1944–1945); *Hauptmann* Burchardt (to May 1945).

Notes: The 3rd Armored Scout Company was given until April 1943 to form. Sources differ on the exact organization of the reconnaissance battalion initially, especially because of the piecemeal commitment of the division to North Africa.[38] In March 1944, the 5th Company received half-tracks.

Awards: Knight's Cross—*Hauptmann* Kiefer, *2./Panzer-Aufklärungs-Abteilung "Hermann Göring"* (18 May 1943); *Hauptmann* Rebholz, *Panzer-Aufklärungs-Abteilung "Hermann Göring"* (2 August 1943)

FALLSCHIRM-PANZER-DIVISION "HERMANN GOERING" 2 (OCTOBER 1944)

Campaigns: Eastern Front

Reconnaissance Formations:

- ***Fallschirm-Panzer-Aufklärungs Abteilung "Hermann Göring" 2 (24 September 1944)***

Antecedent Formations: Formed from *II./Fallschirm-Panzergrenadier-Regiment "Hermann Göring" 3* (four companies)

Organization: September 1944 (theoretical)—Headquarters company with armored scout sections, 1st Armored Scout Company (half-track), 2nd Light Self-Propelled Battery, 3rd Armored Reconnaissance Company (half-track), and 4th Heavy Armored Reconnaissance Company (half-track)

Commanders: *Hauptmann* Springorum (September 1944–1945); *Hauptmann* Richter (to May 1945)

Notes: Actual organization is unknown; model above based on the organization of its counterpart battalion in *Fallschirm-Panzer-Division 'Hermann Göring" 1*

Appendix 1

Rank Table

U.S. Army	German Army	Waffen-SS	English Equivalent
Enlisted			
Private	*Schütze*	*SS-Schütze*[1]	Private
Private First Class	*Oberschütze*	*SS-Oberschütze*[2]	Private First Class
Corporal	*Gefreiter*	*SS-Sturmmann*	Acting Corporal
(Senior Corporal)	*Obergefreiter*	*SS-Rottenführer*	Corporal
(Staff Corporal)	*Stabsgefreiter*	*SS-Stabsrottenführer*[3]	
Noncommissioned Officers			
Sergeant	*Unteroffizier*	*SS-Unterscharführer*	Sergeant
(None)	*Unterfeldwebel*	*SS-Scharführer*	Staff Sergeant
Staff Sergeant	*Feldwebel*	*SS-Oberscharführer*	Technical Sergeant
Sergeant First Class	*Oberfeldwebel*	*SS-Hauptscharführer*	Master Sergeant
Master Sergeant	*Hauptfeldwebel*	*SS-Sturmscharführer*	Sergeant Major
Sergeant Major	*Stabsfeldwebel*		
Officers			
2nd Lieutenant	*Leutnant*	*SS-Untersturmführer*	2nd Lieutenant
1st Lieutenant	*Oberleutnant*	*SS-Obersturmführer*	1st Lieutenant
Captain	*Hauptmann*	*SS-Hauptsturmführer*	Captain
Major	*Major*	*SS-Sturmbannführer*	Major
Lieutenant Colonel	*Oberstleutnant*	*SS-Obersturmbannführer*	Lieutenant Colonel
Colonel	*Oberst*	*SS-Standartenführer*	Colonel
(None)	(None)	*SS-Oberführer*	(None)
Brigadier General	*Generalmajor*	*SS-Brigadeführer*	Brigadier General
Major General	*Generalleutnant*	*SS-Gruppenführer*	Major General
Lieutenant General	*General der Panzertruppen*, etc.	*SS-Obergruppenführer*	Lieutenant General
General	*Generaloberst*	*SS-Oberstgruppenführer*	General
General of the Army	*Feldmarschall*	*Reichsführer-SS*	Field Marshal

1. *SS-Mann* before 1942.
2. Not used before 1942.
3. Rank did not officially exist but has been seen in written records.

Notes

CHAPTER 1: THE DEVELOPMENT OF ARMORED RECONNAISSANCE

1. A detailed discussion follows, but the overarching theme of the necessity of intelligence gathering and reconnaissance can be found in the doctrinal manuals intended for the reconnaissance battalions of the German Army.
2. See Hasso Erb, *Kradschützen: Die Geschichte der schnellsten Truppe des Heeres* (Stuttgart: Motorbuch Verlag, 1981), 29, which argues that the cuirassiers were the logical antecedents of the *Panzertruppe*, the dragoons of the *Panzergrenadiere*, and the hussars and uhlans of the *Panzeraufklärungstruppe*. Erb considers the motorcycle infantry a unique force, more closely aligned with infantry, but it seems logical to associate them with the dragoons, at least in the sense of being mounted infantry, which dismounted when called upon to fight.
3. Wolfgang Fleischer and Richard Eiermann, *Die deutschen Panzeraufklärer: Technik, Gliederung und Einsätze der motorisierten und gepanzerten Aufklärungstruppe* (Wölfersheim, Germany: Podzun-Pallas-Verlag, 2005), 10–12. Fleischer and Eiermann also claim that the relatively unique German concept of two drivers, one facing forward and the other to the rear, was developed at the time. The vehicle was capable of moving forward and backward at the same speed, and the changeover from one driver to the other could be accomplished in a matter of seconds.
4. Oskar Munzel, *Die deutschen gepanzerten Truppen bis 1945* (Herford and Bonn, Germany: Maximilian Verlag, 1965), 84. Oskar Munzel was one of the leading lights in the development of German armor in the interwar years, one of its leading practitioners during the war, and one of the founding fathers of the postwar *Bundeswehr*, in which he eventually rose to the rank of *Generalmajor*. Munzel received the Knight's Cross to the Iron Cross on 16 October 1944 while serving as the acting commander of the *14. Panzer-Division*. Munzel's book is widely considered one of the best one-volume treatments on the *Panzertruppe*. It is interesting to note that Munzel started his career in the cavalry and, as an *Oberleutnant*, became the commander of the first troop (*3./Reiter-Regiment 4*) in that branch to experiment with motorization, in Potsdam in 1929. See Erb, *Kradschützen* , 27.
5. The first part of John J. McGraph, *Scouts Out!: The Development of Reconnaissance in Modern Armies* (Fort Leavenworth, KS: Combat Studies Institute Press, n.d.), provides an interesting discussion on the similar internecine friction that existed in the U.S. Army in the pre–World War II years and the subsequent development of reconnaissance theory, doctrine, and organization that was initially very similar to that of the German Army (and often influenced by it).
6. McGraph, *Scouts Out!*, 56.
7. Erb, *Kradschützen*, 25–26, identifies the commander of the *Kradschützen-Kompanie* as *Hauptmann* Walther K. Nehring, who was closely aligned with Guderian and served him in a number of capacities before serving as a commanding general of three different armored corps and ultimately being awarded the Oak Leaves to the Knight's Cross with Swords. *Lexikon der Wehrmacht* places Nehring's assumption of command on 1 August 1929 and lasting two and a half years (www.lexikon-der-wehrmacht.de/Personenregister/IndexN.htm, accessed 21 February 2013).
8. Fleischer and Eiermann, *Die deutschen Panzeraufklärer*, 30.
9. Fleischer and Eiermann, *Die deutschen Panzeraufklärer*, 37, list the six battalions and their garrisons as follows. On 1 October 1934, the first six reconnaissance battalions (motorized) were established and, as a deception measure, designated as *Kraftfahrabteilung Königsberg (Nr. 1), Wünsdorf (Nr. 3), Leipzig (Nr. 4), Cannstadt (Nr. 5), Münster (Nr. 6)*, and *München (Nr. 7)*. These are not to be confused with the later truck-transportation battalions that were established with the same numerical designations.
10. Part of this, no doubt, resulted from the continued influence of the cavalry, which maintained "oversight" of the reconnaissance divisions. In fact, the peacetime infantry divisions of the German Army had no organic reconnaissance assets. These were to be formed only in the case of mobilization, with the existing horse-mounted cavalry regiments being broken apart to form

a battalion within each division. Each battalion consisted of a horse-mounted troop, a bicycle troop (with a heavy machine-gun section on sidecar motorcycles), and a heavy troop, which had (theoretically) an armored car platoon, a cavalry gun platoon, an antitank platoon, and a signals platoon (horse mounted and motorized). See Munzel, *Die deutschen gepanzerten Truppen*, 84–85, for more information.

11. Munzel, *Die deutschen gepanzerten Truppen*, 90.
12. Although the schoolhouses at Döberitz and, later, Krampnitz would become the spiritual home for armored reconnaissance forces, it should be noted that the genesis of the instructional forces that would eventually become the *Kavallerie Lehr- und Versuchsabteilung* was also found in the initial schoolhouse at Wünsdorf, where the school's instruction detachment, the *Kraftfahrkampftruppen-Lehrabteilung*, had five companies, of which the 1st was the *Panzerspähkompanie*.
13. The modern reader may wonder about something that seems so commonplace today: the automobile was not so ubiquitous and much of the German Army was still supplied by horses. The motor industry in Germany was incapable of producing enough vehicles to meet the demands of the seemingly ever-expanding army. This was also true of most other armies of the world. While not true in the United States, budgetary constraints and the continued strong presence of the "horse" cavalry ensured that equines still served in the U.S. Army through its start in the war. In fact, the only completely "horseless" army prior to the outbreak of hostilities appears to have been the British.
14. Much of the information in this section comes from the excellent monograph written by Helmut Ritgen, *Die Schulen der Panzertruppen des Heeres, 1918 bis zum Aufbau der Bundeswehr* (Münster, Germany: Verein der Freunde und Förderer des Panzermuseums e.V., 1992).
15. See Hans Cramer, *Die Panzer-Aufklärungs-Lehrabteilung (Kavallerie Lehr- und Versuchsabteilung) von 1937–1940* (Minden, Germany: Albrecht Philler Verlag, n.d.). Cramer went on to some fame during the war while serving as the commander of *Panzer-Regiment 8* in North Africa. He was awarded the Knight's Cross to the Iron Cross on 27 June 1943 and eventually rose to the rank of *Oberst*. See Veit Scherzer, *Die Ritterkreuzträger, Die Inhaber des Ritterkreuzes des Eisernen Kreuzes, 1939–1945* (Ranis/Jena, Germany: Scherzers Militaer Verlag, 2005, 240. *Oberst* Bülow assumed command of the garrison when it moved to Krampnitz in 1938.
16. Cramer, *Die Panzer-Aufklärungs-Lehrabteilung*, 7.
17. Cramer notes that elements under *Oberleutnant* Kiehl guarded the *Führer* Headquarters when Hitler visited the occupied territories in Czechoslovakia. *Die Panzer-Aufklärungs-Lehrabteilung*, 7.
18. Gerd von Born-Fallois had been a part of *Aufklärungs-Abteilung 3 (mot.)* in North Africa. He eventually left with elements of the battalion that were transferred to the *Panzer-Lehr-Division*, for the formation of its reconnaissance battalion. He went on to earn the Knight's Cross to the Iron Cross as the commander of that formation on 2 January 1945, after previously being awarded the German Cross in Gold on 4 October 1944. He survived the war, entered the *Bundeswehr*, became an armored brigade commander as an *Oberst*, and passed away on 1 September 1998 in Arnsberg. Scherzer, *Die Ritterkreuzträger*, 213.
19. The troop had actually been released from attachment in September 1942, but it remained on the Eastern Front until 1943, where it had been redesignated as *Panzerspäh-Kompanie 700* as part of *Panzerverband 700*. The armored formation was composed of elements that had escaped encirclement at Stalingrad and were employed as a stopgap measure to curb the Soviet offensive. The formation was essentially wiped out, although specific information about the armored car troop is unknown, except that it was dispatched back to Krampnitz once the situation on the southern portion of the Eastern Front had stabilized somewhat.
20. *Lehrgruppe I* can roughly be translated as "Instructional Group I," which was the academic section responsible for classroom instruction. The *Aufklärungs-Lehr-Abteilung* is not to be confused with the *Panzer-Aufklärungs-Abteilung*. The former battalion also served with great distinction at the front, especially at the end of the war, when it was commanded by *Rittmeister* Günther Konopacki, arguably the most highly decorated company-grade officer of the German Army in World War II. In addition to becoming the 797th recipient of the Oak Leaves to the Knight's Cross of the Iron Cross (23 March 1945), he was also awarded the German Cross in Gold, the Honor Roll Clasp, and the Close Combat Clasp in Gold. He survived the war and served with distinction in the *Bundeswehr*.
21. Ritgen, *Die Schulen der Panzertruppen*,193–97.
22. Ritgen, *Die Schulen der Panzertruppen*, 209. One interesting aspect of this school was the fact that it was commanded by a *Major* Hößlin from March to August 1944, when he was arrested for complicity in the 20 July assassination attempt on Hitler. He was found guilty and executed on 13 October 1944.
23. Fleischer and Eiermann, *Die deutschen Panzeraufklärer*, 38.
24. Munzel, *Die deutschen gepanzerten Truppen*, 85.
25. These qualities were, more or less, demanded in the reconnaissance elements of the Allied forces as well. See, for instance, Richard Doherty, *Only the Enemy in Front (Every Other Bugger Behind . . .): The Recce Corps at War 1940–1946* (London: BCA, 1994); Harry Yeide, *Steeds of Steel: A History of American Mecha-*

nized Cavalry in World War II (Minneapolis: Zenith Press, 2008); and *The Cavalry Journal: Modern Reconnaissance: A Collection of Articles from the Cavalry Journal* (Harrisburg: The Military Services Publishing Company, 1944). (The Military Services Publishing Company was a forerunner of Stackpole Books.)

26. Five issues from 1944 with articles concerning the reconnaissance branch are on file at the National Archives (May, July, September, November, and December). They can be downloaded for free from www.sturmpanzer.com in PDF format.
27. Munzel, *Die deutschen gepanzerten Truppen*, 196–97. Munzel's comments should not be interpreted to denigrate the soldiers of the reconnaissance force. In fact, he and others are generally lavish with their praise in the ability of the force to adapt to changing circumstances and missions. By the end of the war, the reconnaissance elements had essentially become "rapid reaction" forces and often achieved results in that role that belied their actual strength in numbers and equipment. Munzel's comment that if "combat-capable reconnaissance assets are missing, armored vehicles from the [main] force must be temporarily used for *tactical reconnaissance*, especially during advances or during a mobile defense," is an argument that John McGraph uses in his monograph concerning the role of reconnaissance in the modern era, quoted below. He advances the interesting proposition in his summary that dedicated ground reconnaissance forces are not really needed, inasmuch as modern commanders task organize their forces any way, depending on what the mission calls for. He argues that specialized forces dedicated primarily to a reconnaissance or economy-of-force mission consume assets that could be better used in the main battle force, since brigade and division commanders are more than capable of determining the requirements for those missions with the assets at hand.
28. McGraph, *Scouts Out!*, 77.

CHAPTER 2: ORGANIZATION

1. For those interested in seeing microfiche copies of almost all of the records of the *Organizations-Abteilung*, they can be downloaded at www.sturmpanzer.com. Those interested in the German Army's order of battle can find invaluable information on Dr. Leo Niehorster's site at niehorster.orbat.com, as well as Christoph Awender's *World War II—Day-by-Day* site at www.wwiidaybyday.com.
2. While the *Luftwaffe* had its own force structure branch for its flying formations and ground-support organizations, it used army organizational documents as building blocks for its own ground combat formations. The same generally applies to the *Waffen-SS*.
3. Unit here is used in the way the U.S. Army and most other armies define it: a company, company-equivalent (e.g., battery or troop), or smaller element.
4. To cite but one example: In 1940, only 164 light and heavy armored cars were delivered to the field. In 1941, it was 384 vehicles. That hardly covered the eight formations being activated at the time. In February 1940, Army High Command announced that no further deliveries of armored radio cars could be expected in the near-term future. See Fleischer and Eiermann, *Die deutschen Panzeraufklärer*, 71.
5. Veit Scherzer, *Deutsche Truppen im Zweiten Weltkrieg, Band 1, Formationsgeschichte des Heeres und des Ersatzheeres 1919–1945, Gliederung—Stärke—Ausstattung—Bewaffnung, Teilband A* (Ranis/Jena, Germany: Scherzers Militaer Verlag, 2007), 51. Scherzer's multivolume series offers a wealth of knowledge for any student of German military organization during the period. Unfortunately, they will probably remain a source available only in German and only at a few universities.
6. As discussed in the first chapter, the German Army was "top heavy," with mounted cavalry assets, a direct result of the Treaty of Versailles. The infantry divisions had no organic reconnaissance elements, so the decision was made to basically disestablish most of the cavalry organizations to form the reconnaissance troops for the infantry divisions and use both horse-mounted and bicycle-mounted personnel to form the reconnaissance line companies.
7. Scherzer, *Deutsche Truppen im Zweiten Weltkrieg Ia*, 56.
8. By the end of the war, the infantry branch was overseeing light infantry, mountain infantry, ski, bicycle, security, fortress, and a host of other types of formations, in addition to numerous *ad hoc* ones.
9. Scherzer, *Deutsche Truppen im Zweiten Weltkrieg Ia*, 64.
10. Scherzer, *Deutsche Truppen im Zweiten Weltkrieg Ia*, 65. Scherzer relies heavily on Burkhart Mueller-Hillebrand, *Das Heer 1933–1945, Entwicklung des organisatorischen Aufbaus, Band III, Der Zweifrontenkrieg, Das Heer vom Beginn des Feldzuges gegen die Sowjetunion bis zum Kriegsende* (Frankfurt am Main, Germany: 1969), 42ff.
11. By the end of November 1941, some formations had only 11 percent of their authorized strengths in armored vehicles left. Within the reconnaissance force, it became increasingly difficult to conduct wide-ranging patrols. Due to losses, some reconnaissance and motorcycle infantry battalions combined as early as September 1941. See Scherzer, *Deutsche Truppen im Zweiten Weltkrieg Ia*, 79.
12. Some divisions did not even receive a full battalion. The *3. Infanterie-Division*, for instance, had only a single mounted troop. When the cavalry was given permission

to establish a division, the *1. Kavallerie-Division*, eight infantry divisions—3, 7, 8, 14, 17, 21, 28, and 30—had to give up their recently acquired reconnaissance battalions and troops. On the other hand, it appears that two infantry divisions (10 and 46) did have at least an armored car section, if not a heavy troop. See Scherzer, *Deutsche Truppen im Zweiten Weltkrieg Ia*, 97–104.

13. Apparently, *Aufklärungs-Abteilung 46* did retain its armored car section. In addition, the *22. Infanterie-Division (LL)*, an air-landed division, had a reconnaissance battalion similar to those of the armored force. See Scherzer, *Deutsche Truppen im Zweiten Weltkrieg Ia*, 105–6.
14. Once again, there were numerous deviations—e.g., the *78. Sturm-Division*, essentially an experimental construct in terms of its overall organization, had a bicycle troop in its division headquarters which, by May 1943, was redesignated and reorganized as a reconnaissance troop, which was equipped with VW's, thus allowing it at least partial status as an armored reconnaissance element. See Scherzer, *Deutsche Truppen im Zweiten Weltkrieg*, 120–23.
15. See Scherzer, *Deutsche Truppen im Zweiten Weltkrieg Ia*, 125. Once again, to make matters confusing, there were numerous exceptions.
16. For the exception that proves the rule this time, Scherzer cites the *314. Infanterie-Division*, which had an armored car platoon in its reconnaissance battalion. In addition, many third-wave divisions positioned along the border in the East had an armored car platoon (206, 209, 213, 218, 221, 228, 231, 239, and 341), but these were generally eliminated by May 1941, when the divisions were moved to the West for border-security duty. See Scherzer, *Deutsche Truppen im Zweiten Weltkrieg Ia*, 128.
17. The exception here is the *715. Infanterie-Division*, which apparently received a *Panzer-Aufklärungs-Kompanie*, equipped with motorcycles, in May 1944. See Scherzer, *Deutsche Truppen im Zweiten Weltkrieg*, 207.
18. The latter were the so-called *bodenständige Divisionen*, which possessed virtually no lift capability and relied entirely upon non-divisional assets for transportation.
19. Scherzer, *Deutsche Truppen im Zweiten Weltkrieg Ia*, 245.
20. Scherzer, *Deutsche Truppen im Zweiten Weltkrieg Ib*, 709. The authoritative web site, *Lexikon der Wehrmacht*, does not list this company in its entry concerning this regiment (www.lexikon-der-wehrmacht.de/Gliederungen/SichDiv/325SichDiv.htm, accessed 10 May 2013). In this matter, the author tends to lend Scherzer the benefit of the doubt, since he refers to primary sources, and it is not certain what sources were used for the *Lexikon* entry.
21. Scherzer, *Deutsche Truppen im Zweiten Weltkrieg Ia*, 431, states that each of the 1943-formed *Jäger-Divisionen* also had an armored reconnaissance platoon, although there are no details on composition. Since these were all occupation forces in Croatia, it may be assumed that they all received obsolescent or captured foreign stocks.
22. The training of a cavalry horse was a long process that lasted at least four years in the peacetime army. Like human losses, it could not be easily replaced. See Klaus Christian Richter, *Die Geschichte der deutschen Kavallerie 1919–1945* (Stuttgart, Germany: Motorbuch Verlag, 1982), 62–64, for an interesting discussion of this little understood fact.
23. See Scherzer, *Deutsche Truppen im Zweiten Weltkrieg Ib*, 670 ff.
24. See Scherzer, *Deutsche Truppen im Zweiten Weltkrieg Ia*, 673, for the former claim and George F. Nafziger, *The German Order of Battle: Panzers and Artillery in World War II* (Mechanicsburg, PA: Stackpole Books, 1999), 337, for the latter.
25. Nafziger, *German Order of Battle: Panzers and Artillery*, 554.
26. Scherzer, *Deutsche Truppen im Zweiten Weltkrieg Ia*, 377. *Kriemhilde* was a code word used to establish three operationally deployable divisions within three days. They were formed from assets maintained by the Replacement Army, which consisted of alert units stationed at training areas. The launching of *Kriemhilde* was obviously a response to what was happening in Stalingrad. *Kriemhild/Kriemhilde* was one of the main characters in the German epic of the Middle Ages, the *Nibelungenlied*, who is seen as a revenge figure and, in one version of the legend, eventually kills a figure based on Attila the Hun.
27. The *Kettenkrad*, a diminutive half-track/motorcycle combination, served in a variety of roles on the Eastern Front, due to its excellent cross-country mobility. The *Sd.Kfz. 2* thus saw limited use as a reconnaissance vehicle, even though its payload was relatively small (driver and two or three scouts). The *Kettenkrad* was one of the few vehicles that saw widespread use that continued to be produced after the war.
28. In addition, *Panzergrenadier-Division "Großdeutschland"* always had its own relatively unique organizational nuances.
29. Scherzer, *Deutsche Truppen im Zweiten Weltkrieg Ia*, 395–96. The orders from the *Generalinspekteur der Panzertruppen (GenStdH/Org.Abt.Nr.1/1600/45g .Kdos.)* dissolved the *Panzergrenadier-Divisionen* in their basic organization.
30. Niehorster 1/I, 13, 27 and 43. By contrast, Scherzer makes no mention of these platoons in either *Deutsche Truppen im Zweiten Weltkrieg Ib* or the individual division volumes. These may have been a theoretical construct and never fielded. Regardless, they disappear entirely from the organization charts of the divisions after the campaign in Poland.

31. See the cavalry section for a discussion of the organization of the light divisions. Although they played no major portion in the war, they were important in the sense that they often carried the traditions of the cavalry branch into the *schnelle Truppe*, especially when it came to uniforms.
32. Niehorster 3/I, 47, lists two exceptions: *Panzer-Aufklärungs-Abteilungen 37 (7. Panzer-Division)* and *92 (20. Panzer-Division)*, which were formed with two armored car companies. These two battalions used captured French stocks and Panhard armored cars, which had been redesignated as the *Panzerspähwagen 178(f)*.
33. See Scherzer, *Deutsche Truppen im Zweiten Weltkrieg Ib*, 581.
34. The entries concerning it on *Lexikon der Wehrmacht* indicate it was a penal formation and rank-and-file assigned to it had to perform well in the field and in combat in order to be exonerated from whatever offense landed them there. See www.lexikon-der-wehrmacht.de/Gliederungen/leichte%20Panzerdivisionen/999leDiv.htm (accessed 9 May 2013), especially the fourth section, which lists several sources indicating the formation may have also been a focal point for resistance to the National Socialist regime. By contrast, Scherzer states only that the units were made up of conditionally deployable soldiers (*bedingt wehrwürdig*). Scherzer, *Deutsche Truppen im Zweiten Weltkrieg Ib*, 584.
35. In January 1944, *Panzer-Aufklärungs-Abteilung 21* also received a half-tracked scout company equipped with twenty-five *Sd.Kfz. 250/9's*, thus making it a very potent combat force.
36. Order: *OKH/GenStdH/Org.Abt./Nr.1/4439/43 g.Kdos*. See Scherzer, *Deutsche Truppen im Zweiten Weltkrieg Ib*, 597).
37. In the *2. Panzer-Division* and *Panzer-Lehr-Division*, the battalion received a *Panzerspäh-Kompanie "A"* instead, which had twenty-five *Sd.Kfz. 234/2's* (one in the headquarters and six each in the four line platoons). Likewise, the *3.*, *4.*, and *9. Panzer-Divisionen* and *Panzergrenadier-Division "Großdeutschland"* had a *Panzerspäh-Kompanie "B"* instead, which authorized fully tracked reconnaissance vehicles. In the case of the *3. Panzer-Division* and *Panzergrenadier-Division "Großdeutschland,"* this was the *Aufklärungs-Panzer 38(t)*. In the other two divisions, it was the *Panzer II, Ausführung L*, commonly known as the *Luchs*. In all instances, the aggregate number of combat vehicles was one in the headquarters and six each in each of the four line platoons. See Kamen Nevenkin, *Fire Brigades: Panzer Divisions 1943–1945* (Winnipeg, Canada: J. J. Fedorowicz, 2007), 63ff.
38. See Nevenkin, *Fire Brigades*, 63ff.
39. Niehorster 3/II, 38, assigns *KStN 141*, dated 1 November 1939, to this organization.
40. Nevenkin, *Fire Brigades*, 70, indicates the number originally proposed was twelve. Timm Haasler, *Hold the Westwall or Perish With It: The History of Panzer-Brigade 105, September 1944* (Winnipeg, Canada: J. J. Fedorowicz Publishing, 2007), 5, likewise indicates twelve. Scherzer, *Deutsche Truppen im Zweiten Weltkrieg Ib*, 641, indicates only ten were directed initially, an assertion which is borne out by correspondence from the *Organizations-Abteilung*. The discrepancy may be the difference between what Hitler demanded and what that order eventually became to the *Organizations-Abteilung*. Regardless, the armored brigades were outfitted with the latest equipment, which might have been put to better use had it been issued to existing formations.
41. Nafziger, *German Order of Battle: Panzers and Artillery*, 204–5, provides a fairly detailed discussion of this headquarters, which was divorced from its original purpose of commanding *Panzer-Brigade 103*.
42. Nafziger, *German Order of Battle: Panzers and Artillery*, 312, mistakenly refers to this as *Panzergrenadier-Brigade "Rabenhügel."* In reality, *Rabenhügel* ("Raven Hill") was the name of the operation to solicit volunteers to form *Panzer-Brigade 150*. See Michael Schadewitz, *The Meuse First and Then Antwerp: Some Aspects of Hitler's Offensive in the Ardennes* (Winnipeg, Canada: J. J. Fedorowicz Publishing, 1999), for a detailed discussion of all aspects of the ill-fated mission.
43. See Roger James Bender and Richard D. Law, *Uniforms, Organization, and History of the Afrikakorps* (Mountain View, CA: R. James Bender Publishing, 1973), 33.
44. See *Lexikon*, www.lexikon-der-wehrmacht.de/Gliederungen/AufklAbt/Gliederung.htm (accessed 17 May 2013). According to the article entry, it is uncertain whether the redesignation ever took place with *21. Panzer-Division* in North Africa. It was used, however, with the reconstituted division in France and the remainder of the war.
45. *Sonderverband 287* was apparently intended to form the nucleus of a special-purpose corps (*Korps z.b.*V), which is indicated in *Organizations-Abteilung* organization chart dated 7 October 1942.
46. Note that the organization chart for the school at the Rembertow Training Area in occupied Poland also lists a training company for armored trains (from 1 September 1942 onward)!
47. An organization chart for field-army security assets dated 1 January 1944 shows one such detachment assigned to the senior local military command at Saloniki in Greece. It was equipped with thee captured Italian armored cars.
48. See organization chart dated 1 January 1944. This battalion was apparently eventually redesignated as *Sicherungs-Aufklärungs-Abteilung (mot.) 1000*, where

it was employed in antipartisan operations. According to the web site www.wehrmacht-awards.com/forums//showthread.php?t=96326 (accessed 17 May 2013), it was "formed February 1944 in France from *Sicherungs-Aufklärungs Abt. 100,* and under the command of the military commander France. Located in the area of Montargis, east of Orleans, it was later put under the command of the *189. Infanterie-Division* and was destroyed in February 1945 in Alsace."

49. See organization chart for 2 June 43 and others.
50. German Army, *Organizations-Abteilung, Frontnachweiser* (10th edition), 15 December 1944, sheets 234, 242. The *Frontnachweiser* ("Front Directory") was a detailed listing of all units and formations of the German Army and *Waffen-SS*, their military district of origination, and the locating service through which they could be contacted.
51. This is the corps headquarters that evolved out of *Generalleutnant* Felmy's *Sonderstab F*. It is not certain whether this armored car company was borne out of *Panzer-Späh-Kompanie 287* of *Sonderverband 287* (see above). See the organization chart for 1 September 1943.
52. German Army, *Organizations-Abteilung, Frontnachweiser*, 15 December 1944, sheets 234, 236, 242 and Nafziger, *German Order of Battle: Panzers and Artillery*, 200–201.
53. Nafziger, *German Order of Battle: Panzers and Artillery*, 200, and "OOB Panzerauffrischungsverband" at www.feldgrau.net/forum/viewtopic.php?f=24&t=11147#p67102 (accessed 18 May 2013). The second source is cited since Nafziger translates his German formation designations into English, thus making it sometimes difficult to pinpoint an element's exact designation.
54. For *Großdeutschland*, there were *KStN's* in the 6551 series.
55. Nafziger, *German Order of Battle: Panzers and Artillery*, 209, lists a *Reserve-Panzer-Aufklärungs-Abteilung 9* forming the reconnaissance asset of this reserve division.
56. Nafziger, *German Order of Battle: Panzers and Artillery*, 200, refers to this as *Panzer-Verband Stegemann*.
57. Ibid. Nafziger also lists *Panzer-Aufklärungs-Ausbildungs-Abteilung 3* as part of the formation.
58. Purists may take umbrage at the fact that the complete official designation may not always be used for the various SS formations, but as long as it is completely clear which formation is being discussed, a common denominator will be used, since the frequent and often convoluted redesignations can be easily researched if the exact designation is needed.
59. George F. Nafziger, *The German Order of Battle: Waffen-SS and Other Units in World War II* (Conshohocken, PA: Combined Publishing, 2001), 15–16.
60. Nafziger, *The German Order of Battle: Waffen-SS and Other Units*, 88.
61. Ibid, 65. This may be a typographical error on Nafziger's part, since both the light reconnaissance platoon and the company show the same outfitting of weaponry (two 8cm mortars, four heavy machine guns, and eighteen light machine guns).
62. *Lexikon*, www.lexikon-der-wehrmacht.de/Karte/TruppenubungsplatzeSS/TruppenubungsplatzeSSSeelager.htm (accessed 20 May 2013), contains a detailed discussion of the training area, which housed a number of other armor training elements, as well other facilities. By contrast, German Army, *Organizations-Abteilung, Frontnachweiser* (9th edition), not dated, sheet 1835, refers only to *SS-Panzer-Aufklärungs-Ausbildungs- und Ersatz-Abteilung 1* and gives its location as Wandern, which was its probable location in the west at the time of the report.
63. German Army, *Organizations-Abteilung, Frontnachweiser* (9th edition), sheet 1809. See also the corps organization chart dated 1 May 1944 and the entries for the SS corps in *Lexikon*.
64. Roger James Bender and George A. Petersen, *Hermann Göring from Regiment to Fallschirmpanzerkorps* (Atglen, PA: Schiffer Publishing, 1993), 9.
65. Ibid., 10. This was most likely the original three-vehicle armored-car section that had been established when the formation was still a police unit. The armored cars thus had little to do with reconnaissance and were instead intended for show-of-force missions in support of crowd control or other internal crisis situations.
66. Ibid., 21. Franz Kurowski, *The History of Fallschirm-Panzer-Korps "Hermann Göring"* (Winnipeg, Canada: J. J. Fedorowicz Publishing, 1995), 113–44, lists the organization differently, with the 3rd Company being an *SPW* company, the 4th Company the armored car company, the 5th Company a combat engineer company, and the 6th Company also the *Flak* company. Although Kurowski's book was written at a later date, he was notoriously inaccurate when it comes to orders of battle.
67. See organization chart in Kurowski, *History of Fallschirm-Panzer-Korps "Hermann Göring"*, 468–69, which appears to have come from the *Organizations-Abteilung* and is assigned a date of 1 January 1945. By contrast, Nafziger, *German Order of Battle: Panzers and Artillery*, 1780ff, indicates the divisions had the standard *Panzer-* and *Panzergrenadier-Division 44 KStN's* as their model for organization of the reconnaissance battalions.
68. German Army, *Organizations-Abteilung, Frontnachweiser*, 15 December 1944, sheet 238. Nafziger, *German Order of Battle: Panzers and Artillery*, 181, lists no such attachment.

CHAPTER 3: ARMORED RECONNAISSANCE VEHICLES

1. Fleischer and Eiermann, *Die deutschen Panzeraufklärer*, 12.
2. Ibid., 17.
3. As numerous monographs and book titles are devoted solely to these vehicles, what is presented here is intended to be a refresher for those already familiar with them and an introduction for those for whom this is new. The emphasis is on photographs of fielded vehicles that have not been published before or only published in obscure publications, wherever possible. In the case of later-war vehicles, there are generally few unpublished photographs of them so the authors have had to resort to whatever photographs were available. For those interested in more technical aspects of the vehicle, any of the Jentz and Doyle titles published under the header of *Panzer Tracts* are invaluable. For reference in this chapter, the following titles were used: Thomas L. Jentz and Hilary Louis Doyle, *Panzer Tracts No. 13: Panzerspähwagen, Armored Cars, Sd.Kfz. 3 to Sd.Kfz. 263* (Boyds, MD: Panzer Tracts, 2001), and *Panzer Tracts No. 11-2: Aufklärungspanzerwagen (Full- and Half-Tracked Armored vehicles), H8H to Vollkettenaufklärer 38* (Boyds, MD: Panzer Tracts, 2003). Several Internet sites also offer capsule information on the vehicles: *World War II Tanks* (www.wwiitanks.co.uk); Military Factory (www.militaryfactory.com); and World War II Vehicles (www.wwiivehicles.com/germany/default.asp). In each case, the landing pages are listed. As with all technical data, information from one source is often at variance with another source. This is especially obvious at World War II Vehicles, where all data are cited and often quite contradictory. Unless there is a great discrepancy, the generally accepted range is presented.
4. Jentz and Doyle, *Panzer Tracts No. 13*, 8, states that the numbers were actually 113 and 30, respectively.
5. Fleischer, *Die deutschen Panzeraufklärer*, 49, lists June 1943 as the last production month.
6. WW2Tanks, http://www.wwiitanks.co.uk/tankdata/1936-Germany-8WheelArmouredCar-SdKfz2318rad.php, lists the production run of the Sd.Kfz. 231 (8 Rad) as 507.
7. This is the commonly given figure, but Jentz and Doyle, *Panzer Tracts No. 13*, 36, state that the actual number is unknown.
8. Some sources cite 5, which would most likely entail the addition of a loader. This also applied to the *Sd.Kfz. 234/4*. See *WW2 Vehicles* (www.wwiivehicles.com/germany/armored-cars/sdKfz-234.asp).
9. Some sources give the *Sd.Kfz. 234/3* and *234/4* a maximum speed of 48 miles per hour and a range of 559 miles, which is slightly slower than the first two variants and yet with considerably more range. Correspondingly, the figures given are for the *Sd.Kfz. 234/1*, which seem more consistent. See *WW2 Vehicles* (www.wwiivehicles.com/germany/armored-cars/sdKfz-234.asp).
10. Some sources say ninety-eight. See *WW2 Vehicles* (www.wwiivehicles.com/germany/armored-cars/sdKfz-234.asp).
11. *WW2 Vehicles*, www.wwiivehicles.com/germany/armored-cars/sdkfz231-8-rad.asp, lists this as a *Satz Funkgerät für Panzer Funktrupp b*, which equates to a *FuG 11 SE 100*. See *Lexikon*, www.lexikon-der-wehrmacht.de/Waffen/Funkgeraete.htm.
12. *Lexikon*, www.lexikon-der-wehrmacht.de/Waffen/sonderkraftfahrzeuge-R.htm, breaks the production down as follows: 1940–41—1,030; 1942—1,337; 1943—2,895; 1944—1,701; 1945—269.
13. Ibid. for all 1 March 1945 entries, including the *Sd.Kfz. 250/8*, *Sd.Kfz. 250/9*, and *Sd.Kfz. 250/10* figures listed in the respective sections.
14. For those interested in more characteristics and details concerning German communications, *WWII Vehicles* (www.wwiivehicles.com/germany/radios.asp) is recommended.
15. *WWII Vehicles* (www.wwiivehicles.com/germany/tanks-light/pzkpfw-ii-luchs.asp) presents a wide variety of sources, which accounts for the fairly large discrepancy in numbers for a vehicle that was only produced in limited quantities. Some sources claim that the variant of the vehicle armed with a 5cm main gun was also produced—either thirty-one or thirty-five vehicles—but Jentz and Doyle, *Panzer Tracts No. 11-2*, make no mention of these other than they were envisioned, had there been a continued production run of the vehicles.
16. Jentz and Doyle, *Panzer Tracts No. 11-2*, 60, state that as of 30 December 1944, five *Luchs* were found within the *4. Kavallerie-Brigade* (only one operational) and one *Luchs* in the corps troops of *Fallschirm-Panzer-Korps "Hermann Göring"*. Three more *Luchs* were also in the training establishment as of 1 March 1945.
17. Speed and range are estimated, since not even Jentz and Doyle list performance characteristics for the vehicle.

CHAPTER 4: UNIFORMS, INSIGNIA, AND EPHEMERA

1. These include, but are not limited to Robert Edwards and Michael H. Pruett, *Field Uniforms of German Army Panzer Forces in World War 2* (1993) and *Field Uniforms of Germany's Panzer Elite* (1998), both published by J. J. Fedorowicz Publishing in Winnipeg, Canada; John R. Angolia and Adolf Schlicht's exhaustive *Uniforms and Traditions of the German Army, 1933–1945*, vol. 1 (San Jose, CA: R. James Bender Publishing, 1983); and Carsten Fries's excellent *Riding into the Twilight: Organization, Insignia, and Equipment of the German Army's Last Cavalrymen, 1920–1945* (Alpharetta, GA: Tiger III Books, 2010). For

those interested in the SS, there are no finer reference works than the late Michael Beaver's books: *Camouflage Uniforms of the Waffen-SS: A Photographic Reference—Patterns, Zeltbahns* [sic!], *Smocks, Headgear, Armored Personnel Clothing, Winter Clothing, Tropical, M-44 Camouflage Uniform, SS Paratroops, Modifications* (1995) and *Uniforms of the Waffen-SS: Armored Personnel, Camouflage, Concentration Camp Personnel, SD, SS Female Auxiliaries*, vol. 3 (2002), both published by Schiffer Publishing in Atglen, PA.

2. See *Heeresmitteilungen 40, Nr. 166* (Army Announcements 1940, No. 166), dated 7 February 1940, which reminded commanders that only personnel assigned to armored vehicles were allowed to wear the black special-purpose uniforms.
3. See *Heeresmitteilungen 1934, Nr. 85*, dated 15 November 1934 (introduction of special-purpose uniform items for personnel assigned to armored vehicles).
4. See *Heeresmitteilungen 40, Nr. 684*, dated 7 June 1940, which introduced the field-gray version of the *Panzer*-style uniform. Existing stocks of the field-gray prototype jackets with a dark-green collar were issued and worn in the field by *Sturmgeschütz-Batterie 742* assigned to *Armee Lappland* in Finland during 1943. See Kari Kuusela, *Wehrmachtin Panssarit Suomessa (Wehrmacht Panzers in Finland)* (Helsinki, Finland: Wiking-Divisioona Oy, 2000).
5. See *Heeresmitteilung 41, Nr. 473*, dated 5 May 1941, which introduced the reed-green two-piece protective suit for armored reconnaissance and scout crews. It was stated that the protective suits were to be worn as a work uniform, as a summer field dress and as a quasi camouflage uniform where the black Panzer uniform would have been too conspicuous.
6. See *Heeresmitteilung 40, Nr. 429*, dated 27 March 1940, which directed the issuance of black versions of the standard field-gray overseas caps worn by officers and enlisted personnel. It further stated that the beret/crash helmet was only to be worn while on an armored vehicle.
7. See *Heeresmitteilungen 41, Nr. 64*, dated 15 January 1941, which withdrew the black beret/crash helmet as authorized wear and replaced with the black version of the field-gray overseas caps worn by officers and enlisted personnel. The same directive also discontinued the field-gray version of the headgear as well. There were some exceptions to the ruling, and a further directive found in *Heeresmitteilungen 41, Nr. 277*, dated 7 March 1941, directed that drivers of *Sd.Kfz. 251's* (and presumably *Sd.Kfz. 250's*) were to continue to wear the beret/crash helmet. This latter order was largely disregarded.
8. According to Beaver, *Uniforms of the Waffen-SS*, 727 ff, there is no direct documentary evidence establishing the SS-style *Panzer* uniform in the *Verordnungsblatt der Waffen-SS*, which is the equivalent of the army documents cited here. He does state that *Verordnungsblatt der Waffen-SS, Nr. 16*, dated 16 August 1942 establishes the field-gray *Panzer*-style uniform in paragraph 283. See footnote 11 on page 809, also found in translation on page 764.
9. See *Verordnungsblatt der Waffen-SS, Nr. 16*, dated 1 September 1941, paragraph 434. This section found in translation in Beaver, *Uniforms of the Waffen-SS*, 784.
10. Beaver, *Camouflage Uniforms of the Waffen-SS*, 156, states that there was no formal notice of the introduction of the uniform in the *Verordnungsblatt der Waffen-SS*.
11. See *Verordnungsblatt der Waffen-SS, Nr. 5*, dated 15 January 1943, paragraph 26. This section found in translation in Beaver, *Uniforms of the Waffen-SS*, 864.
12. Andrew Mollo, *Uniforms of the SS*, vol. 6, *Waffen-SS Clothing and Equipment, 1939–1945* (London: Historical Research Unit, 1972), 16, cites the following *Verordnungsblätter der Waffen-SS* for this style of cap: *Nr. 21* (dated 1 November 1940, paragraph not listed), *Nr. 20* (dated 15 October 1940), and *Nr. 17* (dated 1 September 1942, paragraph 309). The first directive introduced the cap, the second dictated methods for attaching the soutache, and the third discontinued the use of soutache.
13. Mollo, *Uniforms of the SS*, vol. 6, 13, 16, cites *Verordnungsblatt der Waffen-SS, Nr. 19*, dated 1 October 1943, paragraph 355 for the introduction of the M43 cap.
14. *Luftwaffe* uniforms were regulated by *Luftwaffen-Verordnungsblätter*, but specific references governing special-purpose uniforms for armored vehicle crews could not be found by the authors.
15. Personnel permanently assigned to security elements of the *Führer* headquarters all wore white branch piping, irrespective of their parent branch. This most likely goes back to orders directing that all "Watch" battalions based in Berlin and, later, Vienna, wear white. It should also be noted the infantry branch technically "owned" all motorcycle infantry battalions until those assigned to armored divisions, which was nearly the entire force at the time, with the exception of those found in the light divisions, were reassigned to the *schnelle Truppen* by *Heeresmitteilung 1938, Nr. 495 "Änderungen der Befehlsbefugnisse,"* dated 31 July 1938 (transfer of branch responsibility). This accounts for the occasional "K" strap or board found with white piping.
16. See *Heeresverordnungsblatt 39A, Nr. 68*, dated 6 July 1939, which dictated that motorcycle infantry battalions were to wear the meadow green (*wiesengrün*) *Waffenfarbe*.
17. See *Heeresmitteilung 1938, Nr. 495 "Änderungen der Befehlsbefugnisse,"* dated 31 July 1938 (transfer of branch responsibility), *Heeresverordnungsblatt 1939A, Nr. 68, Waffengattung und Waffenfarbe für Panz-*

ertruppe und Kavallerie," dated 6 July 1939 (introduction of copper brown) and *Heeresverordnungsblatt 1939B, Nr. 429, "Waffenfarben,"* dated 25 September 1939 (deferral of wear of copper brown).

18. See previous footnote for the directives concerning the wear of copper brown. Additional directives concerning the wear of copper brown can be found in *Heeresmitteilungen 41, Nr. 1069*, dated 28 October 1941, which dictated that *Kupferbraun* was to be worn by motorcycle battalions of armored and motorized rifle divisions (without the "A" or "K" or the numerals).
19. See *Heeresmitteilungen 40, Nr. 159*, dated 15 January 1940, which ordered that all unit-identifying insignia was to be removed, covered or worn upside down in operational areas but allowed the open wearing of unit-identifying insignia in non-combat zones. It also introduced the use of "slides" for the shoulder boards and straps as a replacement for metal ciphers and numerals, dictating that future issuance of the straps and boards was to be without them.
20. See *Grundlegender Befehl Nr. 21*, dated 16 February 1944 for the restoration of permission to wear unit-identifying insignia. See orders from the Army High Command (*Chef des Generalstabs des Heeres, Organizations-Abteilung Nr. II/3118044 geheim*, for directives prescribing this was to be done in the form of shoulder strap/board slides.
21. Roger James Bender and George A. Petersen, *"Hermann Göring": From Regiment to Fallschirmpanzerkorps* (Atglen, PA: Schiffer Publishing, 1993, 111, although no specific *Luftwaffenverordnungsblatt* is cited.
22. Fries, *Riding into the Twilight*, 214ff.

CHAPTER 5: MAJOR RECONNAISSANCE FORMATIONS

1. Dates of wartime command stem from data provided in Scherzer's divisional history series (see bibliography), since his is the most thoroughly researched in this regard. Other command data from other sources, primarily *Lexikon*. If the date of assumption of command is listed as 1 September 1939, it is because no earlier command lists have been located.
2. Rolf Stoves, *Die 1. Panzer-Division* (Bad Nauheim, Germany: Verlag Hans-Henning Podzun, 1961), 157.
3. Nevenkin, *Fire Brigades*, 85, reports a slightly different organization undertaken in May 1944, with the 2nd Armored Scout Company (half-track) disappearing and its place taken by a light armored reconnaissance company. He also states that during the spring of 1944, the 1st, 2nd, and 4th Companies all had soft-skinned vehicles. By July, the 1st and 2nd Companies had received *SPW's*, and the 4th Company received a complement of *SPW's* in September 1944.
4. Stoves, *Die 1. Panzer-Division*, 643–44.
5. *Lexikon*, www.lexikon-der-wehrmacht.de/Gliederungen/schnelleTruppen.htm.
6. Nevenkin, *Fire Brigades*, 132–33, states that this organization was initiated earlier, in 1943. He also lists the two armored reconnaissance companies as being "light." He lists the 1st Armored Scout Company as being equipped with the *Sd.Kfz 234/2 Puma*.
7. Nevenkin, *Fire Brigades*, 126, states that the 3rd Company was equipped with bicycles as early December 1944—i.e., prior to the start of the Ardennes offensive.
8. *Lexikon*, www.lexikon-der-wehrmacht.de/Gliederungen/KradschBat/Gliederung.htm, lists the activation date as 1 October 1934.
9. *Lexikon*, www.lexikon-der-wehrmacht.de/Gliederungen/schnelleTruppen.htm, lists the final date of command as 1 November 1939.
10. *Lexikon*, www.lexikon-der-wehrmacht.de/Gliederungen/schnelleTruppen.htm.
11. Nevenkin, *Fire Brigades*, 165, 171.
12. Ibid., 169.
13. Ferdinand Bentele, *Im Panzer durch Polen* (Vienna, Austria: Ostmärkischer Landesverlag für Unterricht, Wissenschaft und Kunst, n.d.), 18–19.
14. Ibid., 54–55.
15. *Lexikon*, www.lexikon-der-wehrmacht.de/Gliederungen/schnelleTruppen.htm, lists the final date of command as 1 November 1939.
16. Werner Haupt, *Die 8. Panzer-Division im 2. Weltkrieg* (Friedberg, Germany: Podzun-Pallas-Verlag, 1987), 89.
17. Ibid., 308–9.
18. *Lexikon*, www.lexikon-der-wehrmacht.de/Gliederungen/KradschBat/Gliederung.htm, is quite at variance here, stating that the personnel for the battalion were drawn from the headquarters of *Schützen-Regiment 14, 1.* and *5./Schützen-Regiment 13, 1./Schützen-Regiment 14*, and *12./Infanterie-Regiment 243*.
19. *Lexikon*, www.lexikon-der-wehrmacht.de/Gliederungen/PanzerAufklAbt/Gliederung.htm, indicates that the motorcycle infantry company came from *4./Aufklärungs-Regiment 9* (i.e., the 1st Battalion).
20. Nevenkin, *Fire Brigades*, 266, lists the date as 29 April.
21. Albert Schick, *Die zehnte P.D., Die Geschichte der 10. Panzer-Division, 1939–1943* (Cologne, Germany: Self published by the Veterans' Association of the former 10th Armored Division, 1993), 205–6.
22. Harthan was one of only ninety-eight men who received both the Close Combat Clasp in Gold and the Knight's Cross to the Iron Cross. A biography of him can be found in Florian Berger, *The Face of Courage* (Winnipeg, Canada: J. J. Fedorowicz Publishing, 2007), 176ff.
23. *Die Panzer-Aufklärungs-Abteilung 12*, a collection of materials given as handouts at a meeting of veterans of the battalion, most likely in the 1950s.
24. Nevenkin, *Fire Brigades*, 332, states that the battalion was initially redesignated as *Panzer-Aufklärungs-*

Abteilung 43 on 1 April, only to be redesignated again on 29 April as *Panzer-Aufklärungs-Abteilung 13*.

25. Nevenkin, *Fire Brigades*, 346, refers to it as *Panzer-Aufklärungs-Kompanie 13*. The orders directing its formation at the Milowitz Training Area gave it a deadline of 30 March 1945 to complete the process.
26. *Lexikon*, www.lexikon-der-wehrmacht.de/Gliederungen/PanzerAufklAbt/Gliederung.htm, states the armored car company came from *1./Aufklärungs-Abteilung 5*.
27. Gerhard Fiebig and Johannes Keller, *Pz.A.A. 33 in Nordafrika* (Freiburg im Breisgau, Germany?: Self-published by the Veterans' Association, 1988?), 15.
28. Ibid., 33.
29. Rudi Zwiener, *Einsätze und Erlebnisse der Stabskompanie der Panzer-Aufklärungs-Abteilung 20 der 20. Panzer-Division* (unpublished manuscript dated January 1997).
30. Ibid., 559, states this was a standard heavy armored reconnaissance company.
31. One of the few titles in English gives an overview of all of the *Feldherrnhalle* formation, but even it does not have commander information or exact unit compositions. Nonetheless, Alfonso Escuadra Sanchez's *Feldherrnhalle: Forgotten Elite: The Panzerkorps Feldherrnhalle and Antecedent Formations, Eastern and Other Fronts, 1942–1943* (*sic!*) (Bradford, UK: Shelf Books, 1996), is recommended for those who cannot read German.
32. Much information on this section about *90. Leichte Afrika-Division* was gleaned form the excellent website about the *Deutsches Afrika-Korps*, www.afrika-korps.de. Specific information concerning *gemischte Aufklärungs-Kompanie 580 (mot)* is located at www.afrika-korps.de/einheiten/heer/90-leichte-afrika-division/gemischte-aufklaerungskompanie-mot-580.
33. Heinz Günther Guderian, *Das letzte Kriegsjahr im Westen, Die Geschichte der 116. Panzer-Division—Windhund-Division—1944–1945* (Sankt Augustin: Self-published, 1994), 138–39.
34. *Panzer-Aufklärungs-Abteilung 520* was formed in the summer of 1944 in an effort to combat insurgents in occupied France. It wound up as a combat line unit, took heavy losses and wound up being disbanded, with elements provided to *Panzer-Aufklärungs-Lehr Abteilung 130* and *Panzer-Aufklärungs-Abteilung 9* of *9. Panzer-Division*. The former received half-tracks from the 3rd Company, while the latter received the *Luchs* from the 1st Company. See the extensive discussion at the *Feldgrau* web site (www.feldgrau.net/forum/viewtopic.php?p=229119#p229119), led by the always informative Martin Block.
35. Some sources also refer to this as the *Kradschützen-Sturm* of the *Leibstandarte*, while others refer to it as the *Kradschützen-Aufklärungs-Abteilung*. See, for instance, Peter Schmitz et al., *Die deutschen Divisionen, 1939–1945: Heer/Landgestützte Kriegsmarine/Luftwaffe/Waffen-SS, Band 1, Die Divisionen 1–5* (Osnabrück, Germany: Biblio Verlag, 1993), 72, 75.
36. Niehorster 3-II, 49, indicates that the armored scout company was the 1st Company. Niehorster's information is based on the order of battle just prior to the start of Operation Barbarossa, so the battalion may have undergone the change just prior to the start of the campaign.
37. Niehorster 4/II, 75, shows the light armored reconnaissance company as being the 4th Company (date: 28 July 1942).
38. Bender and Law, *"Hermann Göring"*, 20-21, cites the following as the initial organization: Headquarters, 1st Motorcycle Infantry Company, 2nd Armored Reconnaissance Company (VW), 3rd Armored Scout Company, 4th Antitank Company, 5th Company (Heavy) and 6th Antiaircraft Company (based on the antecedent formations). This organization might have been theoretical. The organization listed here is based on information supplied by Nevenkin.

Bibliography

PRIMARY SOURCES

Die Panzer-Aufklärungs-Abteilung 12, a collection of writings and documentary materials used as handouts at a veterans' meeting in the 1950s.

Panzer-Aufklärungs-Abteilung "Großdeutschland," a collection of writings and documentary prepared for former members of the battalion. Undated.

Holdings in the U.S. National Archives, all in Record Group 242, Publication T78, with individual rolls listed (and available through www.sturmpanzer.com as PDF files):

- *Frontnachweiser*, 9th Edition (1943). Roll 402. Sturmpanzer file: T78R402_H1_082a.pdf.
- *Frontnachweiser*, 10th Edition (1944). Roll 400. Sturmpanzer file: T78R400_H1_067.pdf.
- *Gültigkeitslisten der Kriegsstärken- und Ausrüstungsnachweisungen*, files dated 15 July 1944. Roll 391. Sturmpanzer file: T78R391_H1_001.pdf
- *Gültigkeitslisten der Kriegsstärken- und Ausrüstungsnachweisungen*, files dated 1 April 1943. Roll 397. Sturmpanzer file: T78R397_H1_032.pdf
- *Kriegsstärkennachweisungen (Heer), Band 3, Aufklärungstruppen, schnelle Truppen, Kavallerie, 1943/1944*. Roll 392. Sturmpanzer file: T78R392_H1_006.pdf
- *Kriegsstärkennachweisungen (Heer), Band 8, Schnelle Truppen, Panzer-Einheiten, Panzer-Jäger-Einheiten, Panzer-Grenadier-Einheiten, 1943/1944*. Roll 393. Sturmpanzer file: T78R393_H1_012.pdf
- *Kriegsstärkennachweisungen (Heer), Band 8a, Schnelle Truppen, Panzer-Einheiten, Panzer-Jäger-Einheiten, Panzer-Grenadier-Einheiten, 1943/1944*. Roll 393. Sturmpanzer file: T78R393_H1_012.pdf
- *Kriegsstärkennachweisungen (Heer)*. A collection of assorted formations and commands. Roll 397. Sturmpanzer file: T78R397_H1_028a.pdf

SECONDARY SOURCES

Andoffer, Volker, Martin, et al. *Nuts and Bolts*. Volume 15: *Marder III (Sd.Kfz. 139) für 7,62cm PaK 36*.

———. *Nuts and Bolts*. Volume 18: *Marder III (Sd.Kfz. 138) für 7,5cm PaK 40/3 Ausf. H.*

Angolia, John R., and Adolf Schlicht. *Uniforms & Traditions of the German Army, 1933–1945*. Volume 1. San Jose, CA: R. James Bender Publishing, 1984.

Beaver, Michael D., with J. F. Borsarello. *Camouflage Uniforms of the Waffen-SS: A Photographic Reference—Patterns, Zeltbahns* [sic!], *Smocks, Headgear, Armored Personnel Clothing, Winter Clothing, Tropical, M-44 Camouflage Uniform, SS Paratroops, Modifications*. Atglen, PA: Schiffer Publishing, 1995.

Beaver, Michael D. *Uniforms of the Waffen-SS: Armored Personnel, Camouflage, Concentration Camp Personnel, SD, SS Female Auxiliaries. Volume 3*. Atglen, PA: Schiffer Publishing, 2002.

Bender, Roger James, and George A. Petersen. *"Hermann Göring from Regiment to Fallschirmpanzerkorps*. Atglen, PA: Schiffer Publishing, 1993.

Bender, Roger James, and Richard D. Law. *Uniforms, Organization and History of the Afrikakorps*. Mountain View, CA: R. James Bender Publishing, 1973.

Berger, Florian. *The Face of Courage*. Winnipeg, Canada: J. J. Fedorowicz Publishing, 2007.

Cramer, Hans. *Die Panzer-Aufklärungs-Lehrabteilung (Kavallerie Lehr- und Versuchsabteilung) von 1937–1940*. Minden, Germany: Albrecht Philler Verlag, n.d.

Doherty, Richard. *Only the Enemy in Front (Every Other Beggar Behind . . .): The Recce Corps at War, 1940–1946*. London: BCA, 1994.

Edwards, Robert J., and Michael H. Pruett. *Field Uniforms of German Army Panzer Forces in World War 2*. Winnipeg, Canada: J.J. Fedorowicz Publishing, 1993.

———. *Field Uniforms of Germany's Panzer Elite*. Winnipeg, Canada: J. J. Fedorowicz Publishing, 1998.

Erb, Hasso. *Kradschützen: Die Geschichte der schnellsten Truppe des Heeres*. Stuttgart, GErmany: Motorbuch Verlag, 1981.

Fries, Carsten. *Riding into the Twilight: Organization, Insignia, and Equipment of the German Army's Last Cavalrymen, 1920–1945*. Alpharetta, GA: Tiger III Books, 2010.

Fiebig, Gerhard, and Johannes Keller. *Pz.A.A. 33 in Nordafrika*. Freiburg im Breisgau (?): self-published by the veterans' association, 1988 (?).

Fleischer, Wolfgang, and Richard Eiermann. *Die deutschen Panzeraufklärer: Technik, Gliederung, und Einsätze der motorisierten und gepanzerten Aufklärungstruppe*. Wölfersheim, Germany: Podzun-Pallas-Verlag, 2005.

Guderian, Heinz Günther. *Das letzte Kriegsjahr im Westen: Die Geschichte der 116. Panzer-Division—Windhund-Division—1944–1945*. Sankt Augustin: Self-published, 1994.

Haasler, Timm. *Hold the Westwall or Perish with It: The History of Panzer-Brigade 105, September 1944*. Winnipeg, Canada: J. J. Fedorowicz Publishing, 2007.

Haupt, Werner. *Die 8. Panzer-Division im 2. Weltkrieg*. Friedberg, Germany: Podzun-Pallas-Verlag, 1987.

Henning, Otto. *Als Panzerschütze beim Deustchen Afrika Korps, 1941–1943*. Würzburg, Germany: Verlagshaus Würzburg (Flechsig), 2006.

———. *Als Panzer- und Spähtruppführer in der Panzer-Lehr-Division, 1943–1945*. Würzburg, Germany: Verlagshaus Würzburg (Flechsig), 2006.

Jentz, Thomas L., and Hilary Louis Doyle. *Panzer Tracts No. 11-2: Aufklärungspanzerwagen (Full- and Half-Tracked Armored vehicles), H8H to Vollkettenaufklärer 38*. Boyds, MD: Panzer Tracts, 2003.

———. *Panzer Tracts No. 13: Panzerspähwagen, Armored Cars, Sd.Kfz. 3 to Sd.Kfz. 263*. Boyds, MD: Panzer Tracts, 2001.

———. *Panzer Tracts No. 20-2-2: Paper Panzers, Aufklärungs-, Beobachtungs- and Flak-Panzer (Reconnaissance, Observation and Antiaircraft)*. Boyds, MD: Panzer Tracts, 2002.

Krag, Ernst August. *An der Spitze im Bild, Späher—Aufklärer—Kradschützen in den Divisionen der Waffen-SS*. Coburg, Germany: Nation Europa Verlag, 2005.

Kurowski, Franz. *The History of Fallschirm-Panzer-Korps "Hermann Göring."* Winnipeg, Canada: J. J. Fedorowicz Publishing, 1995.

Richter, Klaus Christian. *Die Geschichte der deutschen Kavallerie, 1919–1945*. 2nd edition. Stuttgart, Germany: Motorbuch Verlag, 1982.

McCoy, "Breaker." *German Army Recon, WW2 Reconnaissance Secrets*. No place: electronically published through www.quikmaneuvers.com, 2009.

McGraph, John J. *Scouts Out! The Development of Reconnaissance in Modern Armies*. Fort Leavenworth, KS: Combat Studies Institute Press, n.d.

Mollo, Andrew. *Uniforms of the SS*. Volume 6: *Waffen-SS Clothing and Equipment, 1939–1945*. London: Historical Research Unit, 1972.

Munzel, Oskar. *Die deutschen gepanzerten Truppen bis 1945*. Herford and Bonn, Germany: Maximilian Verlag, 1965.

Nafziger, George F. *The German Order of Battle: Panzers and Artillery in World War II*. Mechanicsburg, PA: Stackpole Books, 1999.

———. *The German Order of Battle: Waffen SS and Other Units in World War II*. Conshohocken, PA: Combined Publishing, 2001.

Nevenkin, Kamen. *Fire Brigades: Panzer Divisions, 1943–1945*. Winnipeg, Canada: J. J. Fedorowicz Publishing, 2007.

Niehorster, Dr. Leo G., *German World War II Organizational Series*. Volume 1/I: *Mechanized Army and Waffen-SS Units (1st September 1939)*. 2nd edition. Hannover, Germany: Self-Published, 1990.

———. *German World War II Organizational Series*. Volume 2/I: *Mechanized Army Divisions (10th May 1940)*. Hannover, Germany: Self-Published, 1990.

———. *German World War II Organizational Series*. Volume 2/II: *Mechanized GHQ Units and Waffen-SS Divisions (10th May 1940)*. Hannover, Germany: Self-published, 1990.

———. *German World War II Organizational Series*. Volume 3/I: *Mechanized Army Divisions (22nd June 1941)*. Hannover, Germany: Self-published, 1992.

———. *German World War II Organizational Series*. Volume 3/II: *Mechanized GHQ Units and Waffen-SS Divisions (22nd June 1941)*. Hannover, Germany: Self-published, 1992.

———. *German World War II Organizational Series*. Volume 4/II: *Mechanized GHQ Units and Waffen-SS Formations (28th June 1942)*. Hannover, Germany: Self-published, 2004.

———. *German World War II Organizational Series*. Volume 5/III: *Waffen-SS Higher Headquarters and Mechanized Formations (4th July 1943)*. Hannover, Germany: Self-published, 2005.

Ritgen, Helmut. *Die Schulen der Panzertruppen des Heeres, 1918 bis zum Aufbau der Bundesweghr*. Munster, Germany: Verein der Freunde und Förderer des Panzermuseums e.V., 1992.

Scheibert, Horst. *Panzergrenadiere, Kradschützen und Panzeraufklärer, 1935–1945, Entstehung, Gliederungen, Ausrüstung, Einsatz*. Hanau (?): Podzun-Pallas-Verlag, n.d.

Scherzer, Veit. *Deutsche Truppen im Zweiten Weltkrieg, Band 1, Formationsgeschichte des Heeres und des Ersatzheeres 1919–1945, Gliederung—Stärke—Ausstattung—Bewaffnung, Teilband A and Teilband B*. Ranis/Jena, Germany: Scherzers Militaer Verlag, 2007.

———. *Deutsche Truppen im Zweiten Weltkrieg, Band 2, Die Divisionen, Divisionen und Brigaden mit den Nummern 1 bis 3, Gliederung—Kommandeure—Einsatz—Inhaber höchster Auszeichnungen*. Ranis/Jena, Germany: Scherzers Militaer Verlag, 2007.

———. *Deutsche Truppen im Zweiten Weltkrieg, Band 3, Die Divisionen, Divisionen und Brigaden mit den Nummern 4 bis 8, Gliederung—Kommandeure—Einsatz—Inhaber höchster Auszeichnungen*. Ranis/Jena, Germany: Scherzers Militaer Verlag, 2008.

———. *Deutsche Truppen im Zweiten Weltkrieg, Band 4, Die Divisionen, Divisionen und Brigaden mit den Nummern 9 bis 14, Gliederung—Kommandeure—Einsatz—Inhaber höchster Auszeichnungen.* Ranis/Jena, Germany: Scherzers Militaer Verlag, 2008.

———. *Deutsche Truppen im Zweiten Weltkrieg, Band 5, Die Divisionen, Divisionen und Brigaden mit den Nummern 15 bis 20, Gliederung—Kommandeure—Einsatz—Inhaber höchster Auszeichnungen.* Ranis/Jena, Germany: Scherzers Militaer Verlag, 2009.

———. *Deutsche Truppen im Zweiten Weltkrieg, Band 6, Die Divisionen, Divisionen und Brigaden mit den Nummern 21 bis 28, Gliederung—Kommandeure—Einsatz—Inhaber höchster Auszeichnungen.* Ranis/Jena, Germany: Scherzers Militaer Verlag, 2010.

———. *Deutsche Truppen im Zweiten Weltkrieg, Band 7, Die Divisionen, Divisionen und Brigaden mit den Nummern 29 bis 50, Gliederung—Kommandeure—Einsatz—Inhaber höchster Auszeichnungen.* Ranis/Jena, Germany: Scherzers Militaer Verlag, 2011.

———. *Die Ritterkreuzträger: Die Inhaber des Ritterkreuzes des Eisernen Kreuzes, 1939–1945.* Ranis/Jena, Germany: Scherzers Militaer Verlag, 2005.

Schick, Albert. *Die zehnte P.D.: Die Geschichte der 10. Panzer-Division, 1939–1943. Cologne, Germany: Self-published by the Veterans' Association of the Former 10th Armored Division, 1993.*

Schmitz, Peter, et al. Die deutschen Divisionen, 1939–1945, Heer / Ladgestützte Kriegsmarine / Luftwaffe / Waffen-SS, Band 1, Die Divisionen 1–5. *Osnabrück, Germany: Biblio Verlag, 1993.*

———. Die deutschen Divisionen, 1939–1945: Heer / Ladgestützte Kriegsmarine / Luftwaffe / Waffen-SS, Band 2, Die Divisionen 6–10. *Osnabrück, Germany: Biblio Verlag, 1994.*

———. Die deutschen Divisionen, 1939–1945: *Heer / Ladgestützte Kriegsmarine / Luftwaffe / Waffen-SS, Band 3, Die Divisionen 11–16.* Osnabrück, Germany: Biblio Verlag, 1996.

———. *Die deutschen Divisionen, 1939–1945: Heer / Ladgestützte Kriegsmarine / Luftwaffe / Waffen-SS, Band 4, Die Divisionen 17–25.* Osnabrück, Germany: Biblio Verlag, 2000.

Stoves, Rolf. *Die 1. Panzer-Division.* Bad Nauheim, Germany: Verlag Hans-Henning Podzun, 1961.

Strauß, Franz Josef. *Geschichte der 2. (Wiener) Panzer-Division.* Friedberg, Germany: Podzun-Pallas-Verlag, 1987 (updated reprint).

Tolmein, Horst Günter. *Spähtrupp bleibt am Feind: Die Geschichte der deutschen Panzer-Aufklärungstruppe.* Stuttgart, Germany: Motorbuch Verlag, 1980.

Trojca, Waldemar, and Karlheinz Münch. *Panzerspähwagen at War.* Katowice, Poland, and Speyer, Germany: Model Hobby and Trojca, 2006.

Zwiener, Rudi. *Einsätze und Erlebnisse der Stabskompanie der Panzer-Aufklärungs-Abteilung 20 der 20. Panzer-Division.* Unpublished manuscript dated January 1997.

INTERNET SOURCES

Feldgrau. www.feldgrau.org. A general forum on all things related to the German military in World War II. Its threads often provide additional information not contained elsewhere.

Sturmpanzer. www.sturmpanzer.com. Although the focus is on the *Sturmpanzer IV*, there are invaluable links and downloads available at the site concerning the microfiched records of the German Army held at the U.S. National Archives (see above under primary sources).

niehorster.orbat.com. Dr. Leo Niehorster's excellent site devoted to researching the orders of battle of all of the combatants of World War II.

World War II–Day-by-Day. www.wwiidaybyday.com. Christoph Awender's site uses primary documents to discuss a number of topics concerning the Germany Army, among which are his excellent graphics for the *KStN's.*

www.afrika-korps.de. Highlights all aspects of the *Deutsches Afrika-Korps*—highly recommended.

Acknowledgments

Books such as this cannot be written without the help of a small army of friends, acquaintances, and kind-hearted souls who often spend a great deal of time and effort to provide input, advice, documents, photographs, and a set of well-trained eyes to assist in shaping the final product. Needless to say, the book is much richer for their effort and could not be done without them.

Two senior "staffers" in this army are my friends of many years, Michael Pruett and Michael Olive.

Mike Pruett and I met while I was still on active duty in the army and stationed in Wildflecken, where Mike had responded to a classified ad I had placed in a collector's magazine looking for *Panzer* "stuff." That was back in the 1980s, before the advent of the internet or even cheap international calling, so we communicated the old-fashioned way—through mailed correspondence. Over the years, an acquaintance turned into an abiding friendship and resulted in collaboration in writing two titles for J. J. Fedorowicz: *Field Uniforms of German Army Panzer Forces in World War 2* (1993) and *Field Uniforms of Germany's Panzer Elite* (1998). While a partner in J. J. Fedorowicz, I had the pleasure of editing and laying out Mike's solo effort, *Panzerkampfgruppe Strachwitz*, which had the distinction of being one of the fastest-selling titles J. J. Fedorowicz has ever produced. Mike graciously agreed to provide many photographs used in these volumes and also fact-checked the text. As always, he has a great eye for photographs that seem to capture a unique perspective. He has always helped to keep me honest whenever I have tried to cut corners and "shoot from the hip." He has a phenomenal memory for matters pertaining to this subject and has had to "set me straight" on a number of occasions when my conclusions were not supported by facts.

I met Mike Olive when I became a business partner with him and John Fedorowicz in 1999. Together we formed the "Three Fedamigos" and produced almost fifty titles before we parted company amicably with John in 2008. Since then, Mike and I have collaborated on a number of titles we have jointly prepared for Stackpole Books. Mike has always had a keen interest in the technical aspects of World War II–era vehicles and aircraft and has always been my "go-to" guy whenever I had questions concerning specifications of vehicles and their identification. It was natural, then, that I approached him to help write the chapter on the vehicles of the *Panzeraufklärungstruppe*, a task he willingly accepted.

To both of them, I owe a debt of gratitude.

Of course, they were not the only contributors to this book. Deserving special mention and thanks are

- Jim Haley, who gave me *carte blanche* to use any of several hundred high-quality photographs concerning the vehicles, equipment, and personnel of armored reconnaissance elements, many of which have never been published before. These include a number of extremely rare images of late-war vehicles as well as entire albums of Knight's Cross recipients of the *Panzeraufklärungstruppe*.
- Scott Pritchett, the well-known author of the three-volume treatment on the uniforms and insignia of the *Großdeutschland* formations, *Uniforms and Insignia of the Großdeutschland Division* (Atglen, PA: Schiffer Publishing, 2010), and the forthcoming four-volume opus, *Panzer Feldjacke: German Armored Crew Uniforms of the Second World War*. Scott graciously provided images of reconnaissance-related items from his personal collection, as well as some unique photographs that relate to them.

- Relatively late in the research process, I discovered the wonderful web site by Austrian World War II researcher Christoph Awender, whose *World War II–Day-by-Day* site at www.wwiiday-byday.com provides remarkably detailed and easy-to-understand organizational tables for myriad *KStN's* and other official documents of the former *Wehrmacht*. He is a true gentleman who gave me permission to use his tables and graphics as needed for this book. In the end, I designed my own tables, but he was the inspiration for the layout and design.
- George Bradford is no stranger to the armor enthusiast, and he was another pioneer in the study of armored vehicles. As a teenager, I always looked forward to getting his bimonthly *AFV News*, back when information and "experts" weren't so plentiful before the days of the internet. He has also graciously provided me with a number of scale drawings from his *World War II AFV Plans* series published by Stackpole Books.
- Jason Mark, another author, historian, and publisher of some renown (www.leapinghorseman-books.com) contributed many high-quality photographs, including several color photographs which have never been published before.
- Dr. Leo. G. Niehorster, whose *German World War II Organizational* series was started more than twenty years ago, still remains authoritative. The arrival of each of his separate volumes in the series was always eagerly anticipated by me. He has also branched out to the internet, where much of his work can be found at niehorster.orbat.com. He has graciously provided essentially *carte blanche* to use his graphics and the information in his books and web site.
- Chris Varrichio, Glen Hendricks, Tom Suter, Frode Steine, Gary Beadle, and John Suprin—collectors *par excellence* and good friends all—graciously provided access to their entire impressive collections for the purposes of providing examples of insignia, ephemera, and period images.
- Toward the end of the writing process, I gained the acquaintance of Heiner Duske, one of the senior armor "gurus" when it comes to World War II tactical vehicles. He was not only was able to provide some "fill-in-the-blanks" information, but he graciously provided access to the entire series of photographs of *Nordland* elements in Croatia training on their newly arrived and issued *Sd.Kfz. 250A9* reconnaissance half-tracks, a very difficult vehicle to find photos of. His *Nuts and Bolts* series of vehicle monographs are considered among the finest in the world (www.nuts-bolts.de).
- Also contributing material for the book, some of which could not be used due to final space considerations, were a worldwide network of collectors, militaria dealers, and historians, including Henner Lindlar, Barry Smith, Akira Takiguchi, Michael Xiberras, Marc Rikmenspoel, Steve Androsko, Martin Stiles, Rico Unger, Chris Derka, Kevin Huckfield, Henner Lindlar, and Carsten Fries.

Of course, I would be remiss not to mention the patience and forbearance shown to me by my wonderful and loving wife, Ramona, who had to put up with my mental absence for the past several months.

If I have left anyone out, please accept my apologies.

With any relatively complex undertaking such as this, mistakes are bound to have crept in despite the legion of help I have had. I hope they are minimal, and of course, I accept responsibility for them since I had final say in approving the book. For those who like to keep running tabs on such things, errata, additional photographs and text, and last-minute discoveries that could not make this edition of the book will be posted at my website, www.battlebornbooks.com. For those interested, a largely complete series of organizational charts for reconnaissance elements is available at this page on the site: http://battleborn books.com/?page_id=491.

Of course, all those willing to bequeath their "useless relics" from bygone days are welcome to inquire with the publisher to find out how to contact me directly.

Scouts out!